T0336684

Enhancing the Human Experience through Assistive Technologies and E–Accessibility

Christos Kouroupetroglou
Caretta–Net Technologies, Greece

A volume in the Advances in Medical Technolgies
and Clinical Practice (AMTCP) Book Series

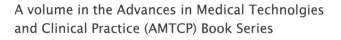

Medical Information Science
REFERENCE
An Imprint of IGI Global

Managing Director:	Lindsay Johnston
Production Editor:	Jennifer Yoder
Development Editor:	Austin DeMarco
Acquisitions Editor:	Kayla Wolfe
Typesetter:	James Knapp
Cover Design:	Jason Mull

Published in the United States of America by
Medical Information Science Reference (an imprint of IGI Global)
701 E. Chocolate Avenue
Hershey PA 17033
Tel: 717-533-8845
Fax: 717-533-8661
E-mail: cust@igi-global.com
Web site: http://www.igi-global.com

Library of Congress Cataloging-in-Publication Data

Kouroupetroglou, Christos, 1979-
 Enhancing the human experience through assistive technologies and e-accessibility / by Christos Kouroupetroglou.
    pages cm.
 Includes bibliographical references and index.
 Summary: "This book discusses trends in ICT in relation to assistive technologies and their impact on everyday tasks for those with disabilities"-- Provided by publisher.
 ISBN 978-1-4666-6130-1 (hardcover) -- ISBN 978-1-4666-6131-8 (ebook) -- ISBN 978-1-4666-6133-2 (print & perpetual access) 1. Assistive computer technology. 2. Computers and people with disabilities. 3. Computerized self-help devices for people with disabilities. 4. Self-help devices for people with disabilities. I. Title.
  HV1569.5.K676 2014
  362.4'0483--dc23
                             2014014036
This book is published in the IGI Global book series Advances in Medical Technologies and Clinical Practice (AMTCP) (ISSN: 2327-9354; eISSN: 2327-9370)

British Cataloguing in Publication Data
A Cataloguing in Publication record for this book is available from the British Library.

All work contributed to this book is new, previously-unpublished material. The views expressed in this book are those of the authors, but not necessarily of the publisher.

For electronic access to this publication, please contact: eresources@igi-global.com.

Advances in Medical Technologies and Clinical Practice (AMTCP) Book Series

Srikanta Patnaik
SOA University, India
Priti Das
S.C.B. Medical College, India

ISSN: 2327-9354
EISSN: 2327-9370

MISSION

Medical technological innovation continues to provide avenues of research for faster and safer diagnosis and treatments for patients. Practitioners must stay up to date with these latest advancements to provide the best care for nursing and clinical practices.

The **Advances in Medical Technologies and Clinical Practice (AMTCP) Book Series** brings together the most recent research on the latest technology used in areas of nursing informatics, clinical technology, biomedicine, diagnostic technologies, and more. Researchers, students, and practitioners in this field will benefit from this fundamental coverage on the use of technology in clinical practices.

COVERAGE

- Biomedical Applications
- Clinical Data Mining
- Clinical High-Performance Computing
- Clinical Studies
- Diagnostic Technologies
- E-Health
- Medical Imaging
- Neural Engineering
- Nursing Informatics
- Patient-Centered Care

IGI Global is currently accepting manuscripts for publication within this series. To submit a proposal for a volume in this series, please contact our Acquisition Editors at Acquisitions@igi-global.com or visit: http://www.igi-global.com/publish/.

Titles in this Series

For a list of additional titles in this series, please visit: www.igi-global.com

Enhancing the Human Experience through Assistive Technologies and E-Accessibility
Christos Kouroupetroglou (Caretta-Net Technologies, Greece)
Medical Information Science Reference • copyright 2014 • 345pp • H/C (ISBN: 9781466661301) • US $265.00
(our price)

Applications, Challenges, and Advancements in Electromyography Signal Processing
Ganesh R. Naik (University of Technology Sydney (UTS), Australia)
Medical Information Science Reference • copyright 2014 • 323pp • H/C (ISBN: 9781466660908) • US $235.00
(our price)

Innovative Technologies to Benefit Children on the Autism Spectrum
Nava R. Silton (Marymount Manhattan College, USA)
Medical Information Science Reference • copyright 2014 • 343pp • H/C (ISBN: 9781466657922) • US $195.00
(our price)

Assistive Technology Research, Practice, and Theory
Boaventura DaCosta (Solers Research Group, USA) and Soonhwa Seok (Korea University, South Korea)
Medical Information Science Reference • copyright 2014 • 342pp • H/C (ISBN: 9781466650152) • US $200.00
(our price)

Assistive Technologies and Computer Access for Motor Disabilities
Georgios Kouroupetroglou (University of Athens, Greece)
Medical Information Science Reference • copyright 2014 • 433pp • H/C (ISBN: 9781466644380) • US $200.00
(our price)

Disability Informatics and Web Accessibility for Motor Limitations
Georgios Kouroupetroglou (University of Athens, Greece)
Medical Information Science Reference • copyright 2014 • 443pp • H/C (ISBN: 9781466644427) • US $200.00
(our price)

Medical Advancements in Aging and Regenerative Technologies Clinical Tools and Applications
Andriani Daskalaki (Max Planck Institute for Molecular Genetics, Germany)
Medical Information Science Reference • copyright 2013 • 598pp • H/C (ISBN: 9781466625068) • US $245.00
(our price)

www.igi-global.com

701 E. Chocolate Ave., Hershey, PA 17033
Order online at www.igi-global.com or call 717-533-8845 x100
To place a standing order for titles released in this series, contact: cust@igi-global.com
Mon-Fri 8:00 am - 5:00 pm (est) or fax 24 hours a day 717-533-8661

Table of Contents

Section 1
Technological Game-Changers

Chapter 1

Chapter 2

Chapter 3

Chapter 4

Chapter 5

Section 2
Assisted and Independent Living Applications

Chapter 6

Chapter 7

Chapter 8

Chapter 9

Section 3
Common Issues

Chapter 15

Foreword

It is wrong for us to think of accessibility in relation to elderly or disabled people only. Making our world *accessible to all* people may be an ideal that we shall never be able to reach, but making our world, our daily lives, our infrastructures—both hard and soft ones—*accessible to more* is something we can comfortably plan to happen.

The current austerity we face in our economies should only increase our desire to make innovation part of our daily routine in the family, in the office, and in all other occurrences of collective, participatory, or cooperative acts such as businesses, government, schools, health services, and all other instances of public infrastructures. *An inclusive and accessible society can be regarded both as a means and as an end.*

However, there may still be some space for a dark side regarding accessibility: by 2020, we may suffer the consequences of austerity measures, spending cuts, high unemployment, and low growth for the next 10 years while compliance will remain very poor and more or less ignored as it is today. The elderly and the disabled may suffer though reduced services and neglect and so may the young. The kind of violence seen in many countries in the last years could become commonplace all over the world. What is the place of accessibility in such a worst-case scenario?

Charles Dickens (1859) opens his *Tale of Two Cities* by saying: "It was the best of times, it was the worst of times, it was the age of wisdom, it was the age of foolishness, it was the epoch of belief, it was the epoch of incredulity, it was the season of Light, it was the season of Darkness, it was the spring of hope, it was the winter of despair, we had everything before us, we had nothing before us, we were all going direct to heaven, we were all going direct the other way...."

It is thrilling how good Dickens describes our current situation: *so close* to make things accessible to more because the technologies, the tools, and the know-how are here; and *so far* as short-sighted attitudes and policies disable investments and make the prospects of accessibility even worse than 10 or even 20 years before.

In research, it is just as important to ask the right questions as to offer the right answers. Sometimes the right question matters more. Some questions that the book that Christos has written on *Enhancing the Human Experience through Assistive Technologies and E-Accessibility* is trying to shed light on are:

- Which are the trends that may affect the future of e-Accessibility (incorporating Web-accessibility, design for all, and assistive technology) in Europe and internationally?
- What may be the impact of those trends on the course of e-Accessibility?
- What visible interdependences exist between various trends affecting the future of e-Accessibility?
- What are the dynamics of e-Accessibility actors in Europe and globally? Where is the industry heading to?

- Are there different "schools of thought" among e-Accessibility stakeholders/experts? And if yes, do these schools follow the typical categorisation? (e.g. industry versus academy)
- What can be the alternative futures for e-Accessibility?
- How can the industry and other e-Accessibility stakeholders influence the future of e-Accessibility? (simply watching and doing nothing?)
- What relevant research priorities and policy measures are realistic and achievable by 2020?

Writing the foreword for this book that I have seen in all phases of its development, I would like to make four observations:

OBSERVATION #1

Many of the most significant accessibility advances of recent years have happened *outside* the domain of formal accessibility oriented research. Shouldn't we wonder why this happened in the past, if it is likely to happen in the future, and if so, how might future accessibility research and innovation programs harness this energy for the benefit of user and consumer communities?

OBSERVATION #2

In some ICT domains, most notably in the domain of smart-phone technology, the pace of innovation is accelerating and looks set to continue to do so for the near future. Shouldn't we ask ourselves what lessons this holds for the future of accessibility? And in particular, how it may be possible to accelerate innovation in other accessibility relevant domains leading to higher impact of research and innovation efforts and earlier benefits to users and consumers?

OBSERVATION #3

Compliance with accessibility guidelines has so far been very low. Shouldn't we ask ourselves again why this has happened in the past, if compliance will get easier or harder in the future, and what needs to be done to turn this around?

OBSERVATION #4

Design is a recurring theme at European conferences on accessibility, in particular the concept of universal design or design for all. It is widely considered essential for progress in terms of social justice, work insertion for people with disabilities, and quality of life for people of all ages. Nevertheless, the adoption of universal design principles either in ICT or by the wider design community remains very low. Shouldn't we ask ourselves why this is so, if this approach can ever be effective, and what would it take to bring about a sustainable change?

There is great concern regarding the cost(s) of accessibility. Living now in times where people live longer on less money and unemployed youth increasingly relies on older parents to support them in times of need, depleting the reserves they have set aside for medical emergencies, family crises, retirement, and old age, any accessibility solutions have to be affordable, even if there will always be a market for the odd Ferrari-like exoskeleton that enables a 120-year-old eccentric to potter about a 1000-hectare garden estate.

Trying to think outside the box, a 100,000-Euro exoskeleton may seem expensive as an impulse buy, but when offset against the total cost of care to the state of someone who cannot work due to their disability, it may seem like a very good price to pay if it enables them to return to work.

Enjoy the reading! And try making our world, your Apps, your offices, your services, and yourselves a little more accessible to other people! There is a cost in this, but believe me, it is seriously more fun!

Adamantios Koumpis
National University of Ireland, Galway

Adamantios Koumpis *has, since December 2012, been a Research Fellow at the Digital Enterprise Research Institute of the National University of Ireland, Galway, Republic of Ireland with responsibilities for fundraising, research strategy design, and development of synergies with European industry for new projects design. Before this, Adamantios headed the Research Programmes Division of ALTEC Software S.A., which he founded in 1996 (an independent division of Unisoft S.A.), where he was responsible for the design, planning, and implementation of research and development projects for funding by the European Commission. His first position was at the Institute of Computer Science, FORTH, Heraklio, Crete, where he worked in the Rehabilitation Tele-Informatics and Human-Computer Interaction Group upon several of the European Commission's RTD projects. He has successfully led more than 50 commercial and research projects for new technology development, technology adoption, and user uptake, both at the European and the national level in several areas such as E-Commerce, public sector, and business enterprise re-organisation and information logistics, involving the linking of data/information repositories with knowledge management and business engineering models. He lectured extensively for over 20 semesters in the subject areas of Management Information Systems, System Design, e-Commerce, Intellectual Capital and Knowledge Management, Intangible Assets, and Knowledge Accounting.*

REFERENCES

Dickens, C. (1859). *A tale of two cities*. London: Chapman & Hall.

Preface

I am a fan of technology and science fiction. Ever since I started my studies in Information Technology and even before that, I remember myself in numerous situations facing problems in everyday life and thinking: "How could I make this easier with use of technology?" Twenty years ago, I would go home and start coding a small program in my PC to make things easier. Then, about 10 years ago, my PhD research opened a whole new prospect to that question. I had the opportunity to work on a subject related with Web accessibility, and from the first moment I met the people in the school for blind children in Thessaloniki, I was fascinated. I found a whole new area of applications of new technologies, technologies that were not even known or thought by the rest of us, hidden in places like that and limited for people with disabilities. The same question was even stronger this time: "How can technology make things easier for people with disabilities?"

My research experience throughout my PhD brought me into contact with many people working on the eAccessiblity and Assistive Technologies domain. I had the opportunity to meet brilliant people in conferences and talks, and I started reading a lot about the whole area of accessibility. The area of eAccessibility and Assistive Technologies was feeding my passion for technology. Sometimes reading about new developments in the area, I was feeling like we were starting to touch aspects of the science fiction books of William Gibson that I was reading back in the beginning of my involvement with technology. However, there always seemed to be a line between my research and discoveries in eAccessibility and the rest of the world. Technologies in many cases were expensive and difficult to find and access because of their narrow targeting to people with disabilities. The market seemed to be quite limited, and my perception of technologies started to change.

It was at that time that I started noticing two basic patterns or trends:

1. Situations where I would like to have an assistive technology to make my life easier, and
2. Situations where mainstream technologies that we are using could probably be used by persons with disabilities to solve some of their (many) problems.

For example, the need to read my SMS or emails while driving my car or having a videoconference and realizing that such tools have probably made phone calls a reality for deaf people. The mobile revolution with smartphones has made such situations happen even more often. This made me realize that it was not a question about disabilities – it was all about needs! Needs that we all have under specific circumstances. Needs that were now even more common with everyday needs of persons with disabilities. We are all of us potentially disabled depending on the particular situation or the circumstances we are facing!

On the other side, new technologies are not always aiming towards the direction of facilitating accessibility. Many of them might build even more barriers to accessibility. Therefore, there was now a battle in myself: my passion for technology and new developments of any kind in the area on the one side, and on the other side, my involvement and new passion for accessibility. This battle led me to look into new technology developments through the prism of accessibility. How could some technology be repurposed to help people with disabilities? What problems could it pose? How can we face them in the first place? These are now the questions I ask myself every time I read about a new technology, and all these questions and thoughts led me to write this book.

Therefore, this book is not intended to be an exhaustive guide to Assistive Technologies and eAccessiblity technologies. It does not really aim to help people in the accessibility domain. It aims to connect accessibility with the rest of the world. What I would like to achieve with this book is to make people active in research in all technology domains see through the prism of accessibility that I am now looking at things. To offer these accessibility "glasses" to the reader. To change our perception of accessibility, Assistive Technologies, and eAccessibility, and bring it a step closer to rest of us. Therefore, by the end of this book, I hope that you will be able to see the world through a different perspective and try to make it a more accessible world for all!

OVERVIEW

The main goal of this book is to identify the range of technologies that will contribute to improving the lives of people with disabilities, enabling them to live fuller, more independent lives. Nowadays, the concept of disability includes a wide range of physical, cognitive, and behavioural conditions. In a few years, society and research communities will have completely internalized the idea that most people can benefit from the use of technologies originally intended for people with disabilities or to improve human performance. This will expand the market for e-access, e-assistive, e-inclusive, and enhancing performance technologies, boosting the economic viability of invention in this domain, and encouraging innovation and investment.

This book describes a wide range of relevant technologies available and emerging today, their maturity, possible future development, and the ways in which they may be of benefit to those interested or involved in the way technology affects people with disabilities, the elderly, or anyone trying to improve their performance in professional or other aspects of happy, healthy, and productive living.

The main guiding principles have been as follows, all of which are explained in more detail at various points in the chapters of this book:

- An economic model of disability that completes the well-established medical and social models and changes the basic driver from a rights and compliance issue to a market-demand driver; hence, the consumer-oriented model is, as expected, an integral part of a wider-scope economic model.
- A broad concept of disability that goes beyond permanent disabilities to include progressive and situational disabilities arising through work, injury, specific circumstances or old age.
- A focus on abilities rather than disabilities, in the interest of social justice, as well as with a view to expanding the market for assistive technologies by making it relevant to the greatest possible population of users.
- Recognition of the need to connect research with innovation, demonstration, and deployment to ensure the highest possible impact of investment in research in this domain.
- Awareness of the fact that there is a great degree of innovation in the way that research is carried out and these new methods may be very important for the future. Particularly strong trends include

the use of prizes and competitions, as well as the role of design, the need for research on business models, and the need to integrate end-users and lead-users into networks for open-innovation.

Apart from the above principles, the book is also based on a series of general observations:

- Specific different disabilities might affect the ability of someone to use the rapidly developing mainstream technologies that have become an essential part of all our lives. These include mobile telephony, the Internet, TV, ATMs, vending machines, etc.
- Some technologies originally developed for use by people with disabilities have proven very useful for mainstream users as well. Especially after the evolution of the mobile market that made needs of people with disabilities a common place for all under specific circumstances.
- Looking at the broad spectrum of disabilities, we can see a number of technologies are applied in each case that might have application in the future.
- Finally, new and emerging technologies that seemed to hold promise for the future were investigated. In particular, the book is focusing on new and emerging technologies that seem to be going through some kind of a transition due to a change in the dynamic or pace of change, a significant breakthrough, or a rapid growth in interest.

Thus, this book intends to help the reader understand how these technologies would serve as access technologies, as assistive technologies, or as a means to support inclusion of people with disabilities in all of the major activities of living including activities that require mobility and transport, shopping, the consumption of media or entertainment, the experience of citizenship, and work.

To help the reader in his reading experience, the book is divided into three main sections.

FIRST SECTION: TECHNOLOGICAL GAME-CHANGERS

The first section deals with new and emerging technologies that are potential game-changers, in the sense that they could one day surpass or replace many of the classical approaches to solving the problems of e-access, e-inclusion, and e-assistance. This section titled "Technological Game-Changers" deals with possible disruptions from advances in the following areas:

1. Sensors, Networks, and Cloud
2. Keyboards, Screens, and Mice
3. Robotic Exoskeletons and Social, Companion, and Service Robots
4. BCI (Brain Computer Interfaces), BNCI (Brain Neural Computer Interfaces), and BMI ((Brain Machine Interfaces)
5. Advanced Prosthetics, Neuroprosthetics, and Artificial Limbs

Each area is presented and discussed in a respective chapter. This section presents latest developments in these areas in order to give the reader an overview of what has been achieved lately, what is the pace of development in each area, and what are the problems and key challenges to be faced in the future. Therefore, this section of the book does not aim to provide an extensive and exhaustive guide to all available existing Assistive and eAccessibility Technologies. It focuses on specific technologies that are considered game-changing technologies due to their potential impact for accessibility.

This section also helps the reader get the bigger picture on a number of technologies in order to read easier and understand better the next section that focuses more on the applications of these technologies in aspects of real life.

SECOND SECTION: ASSISTED AND INDEPENDENT LIVING APPLICATIONS

The second section presents a series of technological advances and potential future developments in various technologies having as a main axis the user's point of view. It addresses basic user needs for every person in the following eight chapters:

6. Health and Human Services
7. Transport and Mobility
8. Training, Teaching, and Learning
9. Employment and Employability
10. Consumer and Lifestyle
11. Media and Entertainment
12. Democracy, Citizenship, and Activism

In each chapter user needs related to that area are analysed, accessibility issues for these needs are identified, and combined with the technological advances, they produce specific future cases describing instances of the future in a particular part of the general theme. Each chapter covers a variety of specific aspects related with the theme trying to cover it from all angles and throughout the life span of a person. This section aims to offer the reader with a number of key issues to be addressed and taken into account in the future research development of technologies while also there are suggestions for roadmaps or policies that could help achieving the future cases described.

THIRD SECTION: COMMON ISSUES

The third section contains three horizontal themes, which we believe are best discussed after exposure to the range and complexity of issues discussed above. These themes deal with human performance as a driver for developments and the organisation of research and innovation for greatest impact. They also deal with the need to address issues of a systemic nature. These three chapters are titled:

13. Human Performance
14. Systems and COMPLEXITY
15. Innovation

Christos Kouroupetroglou
Caretta-Net Technologies, Greece

Acknowledgment

During the journey of writing this book, a number of dear friends, colleagues, and relatives have stood by my side and supported me. First and most important of all, I would like to thank my dear friend and colleague Adamantios Koumpis. His continuous support through difficult times, his advice whenever needed, and his encouragement were invaluable. Without Adamantios, this book would never have happened. That is why he was rightfully selected to be the author of the foreword.

During the period of writing this book, there was also another dear and very close friend and colleague who helped with his support in that process. This is Dimitrios Tektonidis, who was always there for me. He believed in me and offered the right opportunities to help me evolve in my professional career all the time. His support and valuable advice was always there, provided with abundance when needed, and that is why I would like to thank him for everything he has done.

This book is all about accessibility and new and emerging technologies. During the last three years, I had the opportunity to be a member of a working group within W3C that is devoted to a similar cause. Having the opportunity to work within the Research and Development Working Group (RDWG) from Web Accessibility Initiative (WAI), to talk with people in that group, listen to their opinions, thoughts, and concerns, and discuss the future of accessibility was a great inspiration for many of the thoughts shared in this book. More particularly, I would like to thank the chair, Simon Harper, and staff contact, Shadi Abou-Zahra.

Another important source of inspiration for the book was my work as a chair of experts team in the European Commission-funded study "Study on Implications from Future ICT Trends on Assistive Technology and Accessibility." During that period, I had the opportunity to meet a number of experts in the area of accessibility and also work with a group of open-minded and talented persons such as Patrick Crehan and Ioannis Ignatiadis. Mentioning the whole group of accessibility experts would take almost another page, and I am afraid I might forget some people, so suffice it to say that I thank all of them for our conversations and exchange of ideas. Having such minds in the field will guarantee a better future for accessibility.

Last but not least, I would like to thank the closest of all, my family, in particular, my fiancé Margarita, for her help in proofreading parts of the book and my brother, Angelos, for being patient while hearing me explaining ideas and parts of the book. They both were two of my first test subjects in testing out (crazy or not) ideas and thoughts to include in the book, and they deserve acknowledgements for their patience. Moreover, I would also like to thank my parents, Nikolaos and Eleni, who have supported me in all possible ways. Without this support and their selfless love, I would not have succeeded in anything. Finally, I would also like to thank my grandmother, Anthoula, who has secretly been a source of inspiration for some parts of this book.

Christos Kouroupetroglou
Caretta-Net Technologies, Greece

Section 1
Technological Game-Changers

Chapter 1
Sensors, Networks, and Clouds

ABSTRACT

This chapter presents an overview of the latest developments in sensor technologies and discusses issues, challenges, and potentials that sensors present for eAccessibility technologies. Going a step further, it also presents the challenges and potential that network technologies bring in combination with sensors. Given the developments in sensors and networks, it then proceeds to present the developments in the level of cloud technologies and semantics and how all these connected together are now starting to form what we today call the Internet and Web of Things. Starting from the low level of sensors, this chapter aims to zoom out to the bigger picture of Web of Things, Big Data, and Semantic technologies in order to help the reader understand the interconnection in the technologies and the potentials that all of them together present for the future.

SENSORS

Begging our exploration to emerging and future technologies we will follow a bottom up approach starting from the lowest level of technologies that could enable a more accessible future. In that respect sensors can be considered the smallest and nearest to the real world technology. Sensors are actually the technology that can connect the real world with the digital world by sensing various environmental conditions and produce respective digital information.

Based on conclusions from the COST Foresight 2030 workshop series ("COST I COST Foresight 2030 - Living the Digital Revolution", 2009), it is predicted that in near future nanoprocessors and sensors that currently are at the size of a grain of

rice will decrease even further in size. This will make even easier their usage for a variety of applications and in a vast variety of products. Starting from our clothes and homes and continuing with work environments and public spaces, sensors will enable the monitoring and measuring of a series of variables and conditions related to our everyday lives. From personal weight, blood pressure and temperature to light conditions, location and proximity, sensors will be able to record and monitor our everyday lives without even being noticed. According to McKinsey Report, (McKinsey & Company, 2010) sensors could also be at the size of pills that will be swallowed and function within our bodies enabling the measurement of various other variables.

DOI: 10.4018/978-1-4666-6130-1.ch001

Such sensors, in combination with the ubiquitous internet connection will enable the development of even more user-centered products and applications aiming to help us improve our everyday lives. However, although the infrastructure for such sensors and connectivity seems to be very close there is still the problem of communication between all these sensors and their data in order for a network of products and people to be developed (Uckelmann, Harrison, & Michahelles, 2011).

In the following paragraphs we are going to present some of the opportunities and pitfalls that lie ahead in sensors technology.

Monitoring and Tracking Behavior

One of the first and most popular uses of sensors in the terms of improving everyday lives of persons with disabilities and elderly are applications that monitor and track behavior of such persons in order to predict or respond in time in case of an emergency. Fall detectors, smart pill dispensers, RFID tags on food packaging, medical equipment to test heart rate and blood pressure, GPS trackers and so on, can create a safer environment to live for people with sensory, cognitive or physical disabilities. Knowing what a person is doing, their vital functions, their location etc. can give such persons the freedom to live independently on environments that could take care of them in an emergency situation. It can give their relatives and career a piece of mind that they will be notified in case something happens.

One such example is the EU-funded project, eCAALYX (ECAALYX, 2009). The project is targeted to older people with multiple chronic conditions and has developed a smart phone app that receives input from a Body Area Network (BAN) which is actually a patient-wearable smart garment with wireless health sensors and the GPS (Global Positioning System) location sensor in their smartphone. The application is responsible for communicating over the Internet with a remote server accessible by healthcare professionals who are in charge of the remote monitoring and management of the older patient with multiple chronic conditions. This way, patients can live in their homes while receiving health care services distantly.

Currently one of the biggest barriers to this direction is the cost of such sensors including their installation, technical support and also the development of respective business models for such health care services. However, as mobile and smart home devices become cheaper these technologies will become even more everyday reality for all of us and even more for persons with disabilities and elderly and business will have to respond to that challenge.

Currently, according to Gartner research (Gartner, 2010), some 4000 apps were available within the Apple App Store aimed at patient end-users, and Gartner named mobile health as one of its top ten applications for 2012. Furthermore, the combination of sensors, RFID, NFC (near field communication), Bluetooth, ZigBee, 6LoWPAN, WirelessHART, ISA100 and of course WiFi will give significantly improved measurement and monitoring methods of vital functions (temperature, blood pressure, heart rate, cholesterol levels, blood glucose etc.). Such evidence is making even clearer the possibilities and challenges that lie ahead in the area of monitoring and health care solutions.

Awareness of Context

Sensors for monitoring and tracking behavior can be strengthened even more when their data are combined to present the broader picture of their data collection. Combining data from various sensors could give caretakers, relatives and applications a general context in within a person's situation. Detecting for example that an elderly person is still on his bed an hour after his usual wake up time could mean a lot of things. Combining that information with his temperature and could notify caretakers that there is a problem and the person needs help. However, if temperature measurements are normal such as other vital functions it could mean that the person just overslept. Going a step further and tying that information with wake up times and weather conditions the system could know that in rainy days the person just likes to wake up and lie on his bed starring and enjoying the view from his window.

Context awareness can make the difference between obtrusive and unobtrusive services and products for persons with disabilities and elderly. A person who is every now and then annoyed by doctors coming to his place only to realize that they were alerted falsely by a single sensor's data could easily get frustrated and drop out of such a service. It could also mean that his/her trust on such systems will be severely compromised making it even harder to accept future solutions and improvements.

Therefore, combining data from multiple sensors is paramount in providing services based on them. Context awareness could in some cases mean the measurement of a single variable but in most cases this one variable combined with a set of others can strengthen its functionality and give caretakers a general context. Systems that will take this general wider context under account could make respective services more acceptable and easier adoptable especially with persons that do not easily trust such solutions.

Continuous Sensor Data Streams

The evolution of sensors and their use on an increasing number of devices from wearable to smart home appliances together with ubiquitous internet connection enables them to create continuous data streams uploaded to the cloud. In terms of people with disabilities and elderly apart from the obvious usage in remote health monitoring systems that will be able to predict and alert in real time whoever is needed it is possible that such big data can lead to new horizons for many disabilities and especially on cognitive and behavioral disorders.

Being able to monitor and gather information of such persons big data analytics will be able in the future to predict, diagnose and even suggest therapies based on observations that today are not possible. Medicine is largely based on observations of the effects of a medicine and with such continuous data streams opportunities will probably arise in that area for better diagnosis and prescriptions especially in cases of chronic conditions, cognitive and behavioral disorders.

In general, sensors will enable the usage of much larger volumes of data about persons. Given the progress in cloud computing, processing power etc. it is highly possible the big data analytics will be used for an increasing number of purposes. eAccessibility and assistive technologies can definitely benefit from that evolution and should keep an eye for such technologies and how to exploit them.

Energy Issues

One of the most prominent issues sensors face is energy consumption. When sensors are part of a device then power source can be easily found from the device. However in cases where sensors are developed in pill size and are going to be injected, swallowed or wore by persons then energy consumption and power sources that last over time can be a critical factor in adopting or not such as sensor-based solution.

If wearable sensors need to be plugged in to get charged every two or three days this might mean problems for users. People are used to charge their mobile phones but how easy can they get used to charging their watch, glasses, or even t-shirt. Especially in cases of persons with disabilities and elderly being heavily dependent on frequent charging might mean a huge problem for a sensor-based application. This is why one of the most relevant areas of R&D is batteries and energy consumption. Given that sensor packed devices do not need charging frequently and that their dependency is low then we can expect them to invade our lives even more rapidly.

In addition to battery life issues, sensors will also need to respect several economic and environmental constraints. That is why researchers and R&D engineers are looking for new green and unlimited energy sources (Boisseau & Despesse, 2012) that will allow to remove batteries or wires and to develop autonomous wireless sensor networks with theoretical unlimited lifetimes. These new sources are based on ambient energy.

Four main ambient energy sources are present in our environment: mechanical energy (vibrations, deformations), thermal energy (temperature gradients or variations), radiant energy (sun, infrared, RF) and chemical energy (chemistry, biochemistry).

These sources are characterized by different power densities. Currently, solar energy harvesting seems to be the most powerful. However, solar energy harvesting is not possible in dark. Similarly, it is not possible to harvest energy from thermal gradients when there is no thermal gradient or to harvest vibrations when there is no vibration. This makes energy harvesting much more difficult because it heavily depends on the environment which a sensor or a sensor network is being used. This means that the source of ambient energy must be chosen according to context of usage and that there is no universal ambient energy source.

Even though many developments have taken place over the past 10 years, energy harvesting –except for Photovoltaic (PV) cells– is still an emerging technology that has not yet been adopted by industry.

Nevertheless, improvements of present technologies should enable to meet the needs expressed by industrialists. Each area has its own different problems to be tackled. For vibration energy harvesters for example, the most important area of research is probably the increase of the working frequency bandwidth. Tackling that challenge will enable that kind of technology to become a more viable and versatile supply source.

The energy harvesting market, estimated at US$700 Million in 2012 according to IDTechEx research published in the "Energy Harvesting and Storage for Electronic Devices 2012-2022" report (Zervos, 2012), will be more than doubling in the next 5 years, eventually reaching US$1.5 Billion by 2017. Other estimates are even more optimistic: According to the UK's National Physical Laboratory's (NPL) official Markys Cain, "the energy harvesting market was worth $605 million in 2010 but is predicted to reach $4.4 billion by the end of this decade ... for the market to reach its true potential we need to develop the products that can guarantee a greater energy yield and drive industrial adoption of energy harvesting products." (Knovel, 2012)

Energy harvesting can be – and probably will be – a viable solution to develop autonomous wireless sensor networks. The market for energy harvesting (including for sensor networks) is foreseen to grow substantially in the next years. Together with this growth however, come many technical uncertainties on how best to exploit the available power sources. The benefits from this technology can be multiple with negligible maintenance requirements and increased user mobility and independence being on top of the list. This makes energy harvesting one of the most important research areas related to sensors.

Standardization Issues

Apart from energy issues, sensor technologies face also another very crucial challenge. Sensors will enable much more applications and devices if they are able to work in networks and cooperate with each other. Given the proliferation in sensors and manufacturers the need for standards so that these sensors can cooperate with each other and with applications is evident.

Several standardization initiatives have already started working on the problem but most of them are still in early stage to be widely adopted. One of these attempts is the EPC Sensor Network which is an effort of the Auto-ID Lab Korea to incorporate Wireless Sensor Networks (WSN) and sensor data into the EPCglobal Network (GS1, n.d.) architecture and standards. Another example is the Open Geospatial Consortium (OGC) Sensor Web Enablement (SWE) (OGC, n.d.) initiatives which are trying to establish the interfaces and protocols that will enable a web of sensors. This sensor's web will enable applications and services to access sensors of all types over the Web and use their data. The OGC SWE defines standards for modeling, encoding, transporting, querying and discovering sensor data.

For more information on the subject one can look at the public deliverable from the BRIDGE project (Bowman, Ng, Harrison, Lopez, & Illic, 2009) which provides a detailed survey of standards relevant for integration of sensor information. In addition GRIFS (GRIFS, 2008) project tries to identify all relevant standards for the operating characteristics of physical things (readers, tags, and sensors), infrastructure standards for defining the communications and data exchange standards. Obviously the standardization of sensors interoperability and communication are quite fragmented and young to get wider adoption by manufacturers. However, as the number of sensors in everyday life devices is increasing, so should the efforts for standardization.

Apart from sensor integration and interoperability there is also another area which needs particular focus on standardization issues especially for persons with disabilities or elderly. Sensors gather and expose data that sometimes users would not want to be exposed widely. Privacy of these data, their storage and their transport is essential especially for persons with disabilities if they are to accept and adopt sensor based assistive technologies in their lives. Privacy is one of the biggest concerns of these user groups and needs to be tackled firmly before proceeding to applying sensor based assistive solutions to persons with disabilities.

To that direction CASAGRAS2 (CASAGRAS2, n.d.) looks at global standards, regulatory and other issues concerning RFID and PRIME project (PRIME, 2008) focuses on privacy and identity management for private consumers. Finally the European Research Cluster on the Internet of Things (IERC, 2010) is aiming to achieve a consensus on how to realize the vision of the Internet of Things in Europe. Part of this cluster's concerns is also standardizations around privacy issues of sensor technologies.

NETWORKS

The Power of Sensor Networks

Sensor networks and smart sensors are being used widely (PRWEB, 2012) in most of the industries, including the automotive, medical, entertainment, security, and defense sectors due to increased usage of process controls and sensing elements. Changing end-user requirements in these sectors are being met through advancements in sensor network and smart sensor technologies. While micromachining enhanced the scope of sensor fabrication applications, nanotechnology and micro-electromechanical technology led to improvements in sensor development, design, and the production of inexpensive compact sensors. The aforementioned developments led to the production of more compact implantable biosensors, biomedical sensors and electronic noses. Advanced models of such sensors possess the capability to normalize, digitize, learn, fuse, sense, understand, adapt, and initiate appropriate action.

As stated by the new market research report on Smart Sensors (Global Industry Analysts, Inc., 2012), Europe represents the largest market worldwide, followed by North America. Asia-Pacific is forecasted to emerge into the fastest growing regional market trailing a projected annual growth of 5.5%, between 2011 and 2017. Growth in this region will primarily stem from lower cost, which in turn is a factor of faster technology diffusion in the region.

Regarding wearable sensors, the market for wearable sports and fitness activity sensors is expected to explode over the next few years as a new generation of devices collect and automatically share data online. Nike, Adidas, and Motorola are just some of the companies to recently launch new wearable wireless products and there are plenty more to follow them. Mobile handset accessory vendors, consumer electronics companies, fitness management service offerings, and online services providers will all join a market that has long been the preserve of specialist, high-end vendors such as Polar and Garmin.

Strong growth will also take place within home monitoring applications for assisted living, remote patient care to help manage chronic conditions, and within hospitals and clinics. Over the next five years, the total market for wearable wireless devices in sports and healthcare will grow to 169.5 million devices in 2017 (ABI Research, 2012), up from 20.77 million in 2011, an annual growth rate of 41%. It is expected that at the heart of this growth will be ultra-low power wireless connectivity from wearable devices to mobile phones through support for Bluetooth Smart in handsets and devices.

At an even smaller scale, during the International Solid-State Circuits Conference in February 2012, before an audience of her peers, Ada Poon demonstrated a tiny, wirelessly powered, self-propelled medical device (Next Big Future, 2012) capable of controlled motion through a fluid – blood, to be exact. The era of swallow-the-surgeon medical care may no longer be the stuff of science fiction.

Poon, an assistant professor of electrical engineering, is developing a new class of medical devices that can be implanted or injected into the human body and powered wirelessly using electromagnetic radio waves. No batteries to wear out. No cables to provide power.

Researchers have also created a new thin flexible sensor (Chappell, 2011) that can be applied with water, like a temporary tattoo. Measuring activity in the brain, heart and muscles, the innovation could cut down on the number of wires and cables medical personnel use to monitor patients, among other applications. Electronics can be bent, stretched and squeezed along with human skin, and maintain contact by relying on natural stickiness credited for geckoes' ability to cling to surfaces.

In addition to being designed with a hardy serpentine pattern that resists tearing, the sensors are thinner than a human hair. The sensors could even be integrated into actual temporary tattoos, making patients feel comfortable — and even offering a chance for style points. However, the new electronic tattoos should not be confused with the Digital Tattoo Interface (Eaton, 2008), a 2x4-inch touch-screen implanted subcutaneously and powered by blood.

Examples of sensor functionalities for people with disabilities (Libelium, 2013) include measuring biometric parameters, capable of detecting heartbeats, breathing rates, movements, etc. and also environmental sensors to control the patient's surroundings (e.g. to ensure a room has the correct oxygen level. If an abnormal value is detected, the incident can be recorded on the internal network and/or an SMS can be sent to the doctor's PDA, reducing warning and therefore action times. This helps to monitor patients in a hospital or clinic as well as in their own homes while sleeping.

On more concrete terms, a company called Asthmapolis (http://asthmapolis.com/) provides tools to track, manage and control asthma. One of their products is an inhaler with a Wi-Fi-enabled built in GPS system. It allows an individual user to understand where and at what time the attacks occur. It allows their physician to remotely monitor the condition of the patient. At a collective level it allows pubic authorities or a service provider to identify trends and even find root causes of asthma attacks. This data can be displayed to someone with asthma using a map-based app on their iPhone. Inspired by a story (Aceves, Grimalt, Sunyer, Anto, & Reed, 1991) of how emergency room records for asthma attacks in the city of Barcelona enabled the identification of the cause of the attacks as the offloading and storage of soybeans, the hope is that a large community of users of the Asthmapolis device will enable smart management of the condition in future.

In addition, a Wi-Fi weighing scale costing $160 was released by Withings (Withings, n.d., b) in time for the 2011 Christmas gift market. When one steps on this with bare feet, it records and transmits both the weight and body-mass statistics to a password-protected website that can be consulted using an iPhone. This is aimed at sports people and families who want to monitor the weight, fat, muscle and body-mass index of the whole family with a view to managing diet and maintaining health and fitness. The same company produces baby-monitors and blood pressure monitors. An interesting phenomenon from an innovation perspective is the companies that are associated with this product using the data it generates as the basis for a wide range of value added health and lifestyle services (Withings, n.d., a).

The potential for the uses of sensors and sensor networks in the future is enormous. Sensors are getting smaller and smaller, come in a variety of forms, and possess even greater capabilities. With Europe being the largest market worldwide, this may also be an opportunity to increase the use of sensor (networks) for the benefit of people with disabilities.

Wireless Body Area Networks / Wireless Body Sensor Networks

The increasing use of wireless networks and the constant miniaturization of electrical devices have empowered the development of Wireless Body Area Networks (WBANs) and Wireless Body Sensor Networks (WBSN). In these networks various sensors are attached on clothing or on the body or even implanted under the skin. The wireless nature of the network and the wide variety of sensors offer numerous new, practical and innovative applications to improve health care and the Quality of Life. The sensors of a WBAN measure for example the heartbeat, the body temperature or record a prolonged electrocardiogram. Using a WBAN, the patient experiences a greater physical mobility and is no longer compelled to stay in the hospital (Latré, Braem, Moerman, Blondia, & Demeester, 2011).

The main cause of death in the world is Cardiovascular Disease (CVD), representing 30% of all global deaths. According to the World Health Organization, world-wide about 17.5 million people die of heart attacks or strokes each year; in 2015, almost 20 million people will die from CVD. These deaths can often be prevented with proper health care (WHO, 2013). Worldwide, more than 246 million people suffer from diabetes, a number that is expected to rise to 380 million by 2025. Frequent monitoring enables proper dosing and reduces the risk of fainting and in later life blindness, loss of circulation and other complications (IDF, n.d.). These two examples already illustrate the need for continuous monitoring and the significance of WBANs in the future. In the same way, numerous other examples of diseases would benefit from continuous or prolonged monitoring, such as hypertension, asthma, Alzheimer's disease, Parkinson's disease, renal failure, post-operative monitoring, stress-monitoring, prevention of sudden infant death syndrome etc.

A WBAN can also be used to offer assistance to the disabled (Latré, Braem, Moerman, Blondia, & Demeester, 2011). For example, a paraplegic can be equipped with sensors determining the position of the legs or with sensors attached to the nerves (Li, Takizawa, Zheri, & Kohno, 2007). In addition, actuators positioned on the legs can stimulate the muscles. Interaction between the data from the sensors and the actuators makes it possible to restore the ability to move. Another example is aid for the visually impaired. An artificial retina, consisting of a matrix of micro sensors, can be implanted into the eye beneath the surface of the retina. The artificial retina translates the electrical impulses into neurological signals. The input can be obtained locally from light sensitive sensors or by an external camera mounted on a pair of glasses (Theogarajan et al., 2006).

Wireless body sensor network (WBSN) is widely used in patient's monitoring, and risk prediction of e-health system. Wearable sensors are introduced that RFID tags embedded with sensor are allocated to each position where risk is predictable. Body sensors are very useful in patients' health monitoring and risk prediction systems. When they are used with RFID tags, e-health systems and communications are processed easily, accurately and quickly. Body sensors are implantable for long term diseases (Thayananthan & Alzahrani, 2012) such as cancer, diabetic etc. without major surgery. For example, diabetic patient may have a lot of other symptoms because it will easily damage most of the human organs very quickly. Risk prediction system will help to find all risks in a daily basis without pricking pain. In order to improve the risk prediction methodology in the e-health system, risk prediction and patient monitoring should be integrated with WBSN or RFID technologies.

Internet Connectivity and People with Disabilities

Internet users are currently growing rapidly all over the world. In December 1995 only a 0.4% (IDC, n.d.) of the world population was connected to Internet. In December 2011 this percentage has grown to 32.7% (Internet World Stats, 2012). Especially in Europe, numbers have grown rapidly in recent years with internet connectivity increasing almost 5% every year between 2008 and 2010 (Eurostat, 2013). However this doesn't mean that this progress is equally shared by all countries. Internet connectivity in Europe alone varies from 33% in Bulgaria to 91% in the Netherlands and

from 23% in Romania to 83% in Norway and Sweden for broadband access

For people with disabilities the internet can increase their independency (Speedmatters.org, n.d.) by empowering to complete tasks that otherwise would require help by other persons. High speed internet connectivity that allows voice and video data transfer can now enable people with disabilities to participate in many more everyday activities that relate to employment, education, civic responsibilities, social interaction etc. breaking the barriers of communication and social participation. More specifically some examples of how internet connectivity can benefit persons with disabilities include the following:

- Video calls and text messaging can be used by deaf and hard of hearing persons to replace standard phone calls.
- People with physical disabilities such as mobility impairments can participate in classes or job meetings remotely.
- Internet connectivity also enables remote working so that persons with disabilities can work from their own environment avoid the hassle of unnecessary or difficult commutes or trips.
- Internet connectivity allows medical consultation meetings with specialists around the world so that people with disabilities can enjoy better and more specialized health services.
- People with disabilities can search for and enjoy a wide variety of educational, recreational and vocational content through the web with the use of specialised software and hardware.
- They can complete civic responsibility tasks such as paying bills, applying for benefits, taking care life insurance policies, etc. without the need to move into unknown and sometimes inaccessible buildings, read paper printed bills or communicate with civic officers.

However, studies in US show that people with disabilities use the internet approximately half as much as those without disabilities and less than 24% of homes of people with disabilities have adopted broadband internet compared with 63% of all homes. Number like these should be alarming for policy makers so that they take appropriate measures to make internet connectivity possible and affordable especially for persons with disabilities and even more for unemployed or underemployed persons with disabilities.

Internet of Things

In 2007 Kevin Kelly, the co-founder of Wired magazine, gave a talk (Kelly, 2008) at the EG conference (EG, n.d.) with the subject of "The first 5,000 days of the web, and the next 5,000". In that talk Kevin Kelly talks about the web as the most amazing machine ever built. He says that despite that this machine in now 20 years old, it hasn't stopped working and instead of getting rustier and slower and more difficult to use it's getting better and more useful than ever. Back then he predicted that the web is going to evolve from a web of documents to a web that will allow almost everything in the real world to be connected with the digital leading to a new web of things. This is actually the idea of what was later named as the Internet of Things.

Given the availability and progress in sensor technologies things in the real world will start evolving to smarter connected and sensing things that will be able to identify measure and record data from their environment. These large amounts of data gathered (nowadays called Big Data) will on their turn enable applications to run on these devices in order to make then even more user friendly, useful and smart. Analyzing those big data will empower the creation of new devices and applications.

Among these devices and application assistive devices as we know them today will probably evolve to smarted, sensors packed and ubiquitous connected devices that will enable the design and development of really useful and even more assisting applications. People with disabilities can certainly expect large benefits from the Internet of Things and research and development in the area of assistive devices and applications should certainly exploit the opportunities arising from these developments.

SMART ENVIRONMENTS: FROM THE WEB TO THE CLOUDS

The Current State of the Web

When in March 1989 Tim Berners-Lee wrote his proposal at CERN he could not imagine the magnitude that his system for transferring hypertexts would take. Today the World Wide Web is primary source of all kind of information and a vital part of our lives. People all over the world are using it for education, recreation, work and almost any aspect of life. In its first 20 years the web transformed form a system for sharing and communicating information for academics to a system widely used to consume and produce content. In its first stages people that could create content in the web were experts and scientists that had the appropriate knowledge of writing HTML code.

With the evolution of HTML and web authoring tools content creation in the web became much easier for other people to know how to operate a computer and use these tools. From then on the pace of evolution was increasing rapidly and now almost anyone can produce content for the web. However in its initial form, the web had some shortcomings that the rapid evolution brought to front and today new web technologies are trying to deal with them.

The most important one is that the web is composed from a large number of unstructured documents, so there was a need for promoting common formats for data on the Web and converting the current web of unstructured documents into a "web of data" so as to encourage the inclusion of semantic content in web pages. This is the case of Semantic Web which aims primarily to describe web content in a machine understandable way.

Another opportunity that rose with the evolution of web was to use it as a platform for providing services. From the simple subscription service to a newsletter we have now passed to web applications offering word processing tools, social networking tools, content management systems, etc. All the above have led to the evolution of what we call today Web 2.0, a new web that combines the classic content delivery service with richer and more interactive services as well.

The new developments in the web together with its inherent shortcomings and its rapid evolutions also lead to a number of accessibility issues for persons with disabilities. Projects like Monitoring eAccessibility (Monitoring eAccessibility, n.d.) show very clearly the problems that web accessibility is facing right now and how the state of the play is expected to evolve in the next years to the horizon of 2020. A more analytical discussion on web accessibility problems is to follow on the chapter on Media and Entertainment, however it is essential to state that software developer communities and stakeholders have to learn from web accessibility problems up to day and not make the same mistakes in the current transitory phase that the web is making.

The Effects of the Mobile Web

A critical factor affecting the changes in the web is the explosion in mobile computing. In its 2010 Internet trends report, Morgan Stanley (Meeker, Devitt, & Wu, 2010) predicted that mobile web access is going to surpass desktop web access in about 5 years. However, this prediction is not to be seen alone. Mobile industry is in the forefront of the evolution of other industries as an "innovation enabler", sometimes bringing major disruptions

to those industries: we have seen major impacts of mobile technology in the digital media, such as music, movies, and the news industries while content delivery as well as the business models in digital media have gone through a major transition, thanks to mobile technology.

Mobile access to web content today is not happening only from mobile web browsers. It is largely happening through specific applications developed for providing that content through a specific interface. This is also one of the points that Roger McNamee makes in his TED talk (McNamee, 2011) about the future of the web. Deloitte's report (Deloitte, 2012) also pays specific attention to mobile devices and how these are going to affect the evolution of web.

With global mobile phone use at an all-time high, there has been a surge of interest in developing Web sites that are accessible from a mobile device. Similarly, making websites accessible for people with disabilities is an integral part of high quality websites, and in some cases a legal requirement. Most mobile web specialists have no skills or expertise in developing accessible applications, same way as most web accessibility specialists have not acquired know-how for mobile web design. Web sites can more efficiently meet both goals when developers understand the significant overlap between making a website accessible for a mobile device and for people with disabilities. The similarities are introduced below along with the corresponding benefits.

Mobile platform providers should include accessibility features in their platforms to facilitate development of accessible mobile apps by developer communities and the software industry at large. Moreover new innovation ecosystems enabled by these platforms should also pay specific attention to accessibility and help creating open standard APIs to enable the authoring and playback of rich media on a wide variety of mobile platforms and devices.

The Impact of Social Web

As people's activities on the Web increase, information about their social relationships become more available; social networking sites such as Facebook, as well as similar infrastructures that will appear in the following years, will pose increasing importance to emotional aspects of the human-to-human interaction as well as the offer of more substantial means of interaction amongst the users (deepen the communication channels, substantiate and supplement the existing communication modalities, etc.).

This will open individuals and communities to new, scale-free communication structures that, if used appropriately may increase the quality of life for many millions of citizens all over the globe: elderly people who shall be able to communicate with other elderly people from other countries with the help of natural language processing and instant translation services. Same holds also for people with other types of disabilities that would be difficult to find friends in their physical environment and who are currently lacking the means to interact with others. And, most importantly, will help intergenerational and intercultural relations and transmission. What is transmitted is intangible and may include beliefs, norms, values, attitudes, and behaviors specific to the persons involved in the interaction, as well as any other sociocultural, religious, and ethnically relevant practices and beliefs. In this respect, accessibility will affect the individual's value system, into the pragmatics of interaction with others. In this respect, beneficiaries may be the same as the audience addressed by the Global Public Inclusive Infrastructure (GPII) (Raising the Floor, 2011) which is focused "on anyone who has trouble using ICTs effectively including: (1) literacy (including those facing problems with a second language), (2) those with disabilities or functional limitations, (3) those with limited or no digital literacy (not familiar with the

new technologies being thrown at them) those who are aging and face these and other problems dealing with technologies they now want to or are forced to use in their environments."

The globality element mentioned before seems to be of utmost importance as recognized by the ICT SHOK Future Internet Research Agenda (ICT SHOCK Future Internet, 2007): "What looms ahead is an Internet that will merge with mobile communications and the "real world", for the first time opening the door of a truly global information network reachable by the whole population of the planet."

The web and cloud starts to know us: our habits, our interests, our activities, jobs, hobbies, family, friends etc. everything including our well-hidden secrets, dreams and aspirations. This will lead to highly personalized services apps and content. In addition, applications up to now wait the user to use them - in the future they will act on their own or proactively without the user having to control them so much. This will, again, pose increased needs for research in matters related to security and protection of individual's identity and personal data.

End User Computing

While the model-driven development paradigm forms a well-accepted approach for professional software development, such an approach is in its infancy in end-user software development. It still needs to be investigated and evaluated, whether end-users are willing to develop high-level, abstract models instead of directly dealing with low-level programs. In addition, it has to be investigated what kind of modeling languages are appropriate for end-users. This has to be accompanied by setting up and evaluating case studies within real scenarios. Furthermore, it has to be investigated whether and how standard model analysis techniques can be transferred to end user software development. In particular, appropriate explanation and help systems have to be designed which translate analysis results into a representation which is understandable by end users.

Early HCI methodologies aimed to match known work tasks with suitable interfaces; this human factors approach focused on the line between man and machine and the interfaces that afford interactions between the two. In the 1990s, when technology moved into the home and into more complex environments of use and practice, HCI methodologies began to take a broader view of interaction, supporting human actors who controlled the technologies used in their daily lives. Our current HCI methodologies and theories are largely oriented towards this "human actors" relationship between technology, users, and use.

However, recent technology trends (HTML5 and other Web 2.0 technologies making the web more interactive and more 'semantic', combined with new interfaces as these have been presented in the previous chapter) and new ways that people interact with each other and the web allow for complex and shifting contexts of use as well as empowered users to design their own technological environments.

Novel means of information and technology production (e.g. open source software development, mash-ups, commons-based peer production) have radically changed the technological landscape. Users are again behaving as crafters – controlling, designing, and developing not only their relationships with technology, but the very form and function of this technology. As a result, traditional HCI design time activities have become increasingly ill-suited to the unpredictability of real life use: as users become more empowered to design their own technology environments, HCI theory and methodology must shift as well to better support and shape these activities.

Rich Internet Applications (RIAs) denote a novel generation of online applications that merges a variety of technologies to provide an extremely sophisticated user experience on top of the open architectural standards of the Internet and the Web. Although the most noticeable innovation of RIAs for the end users lies in the powerful interaction mechanisms of the interface (like native multimedia support, transition effects, animations, widgets, drag & drop, etc.), these applications deeply renovate the way in which computation takes place on the Web, by reintroducing a more flexible partition of work between the client and the server which in our times are the mobile device and the cloud, comparable to that of pre-Web client-server applications.

Rich Internet Applications (RIAs) have introduced powerful novel functionalities into the Web architecture, borrowed from client-server and desktop applications. The resulting platforms allow designers to improve the user's experience, by exploiting client-side data and computation, bidirectional client-server communication, synchronous and asynchronous events, and rich interface widgets.

Research is required for modeling RIA accessibility requirements at a high-level using a platform-independent notation, and generate the client-side and server-side code automatically making use of all HCI interaction modalities including, amongst others, voice interaction, gesture interaction, BCI etc.. The results should be assessed in terms of expressive power, ease of use, and wide-scale adoption potential and implement ability.

More Semantics

The latest development in the web that may potentially bring great impact on it is HTML 5. The new version of HTML standard changes the way web documents are structured and the web content in two ways. First it makes easier to enhance in web pages elements that are more interactive. This means that not only creating a website but creating a web application becomes a lot easier for non-professional developers i.e. the 'end users'. This is expected to have a major impact in the future of web allowing people to form and customize easily their applications.

The second major change HTML 5 is that it introduces a variety of new tags intending purely to communicate semantics of web content. Thus, it makes easier for machines to understand web pages and it also pushes towards an already established practice that separated the content of a web page from its presentation. This means that the same content can now have multiple presentations according to the device showing it. It can appear differently in a smartphone, in a desktop computer screen and in a tablet. This practice is not new in the web community and a movement towards it is evident especially after the wide adoption of mobile devices. However, HTML5 makes even clearer this distinction and integrates it within the major standard of the web.

Accessibility can benefit significantly from the developments in HTML5. However, there is a fear that technological advances in scripting packages, interaction widgets and elements that constitute the basis for future web application development do not take accessibility into account. It is essential in this turning point of the web for the accessibility community to push forward and demonstrate the benefits from accessible web development in order to push and introduce accessibility features in the core of new emerging technologies and standards.

Moving To the Cloud

High-scale cloud services provide economies of scale of five to ten times over small-scale deployments, and are becoming a large part of both enterprise information processing and consumer services. Cloud computing will be a big part of the future of server-side systems. This is a lasting and fast growing economy with clear economic gains. These workloads are already substantial and growing incredibly fast. And it is a new frontier where there are many new tough problems to be solved. High-scale service workloads are very different from enterprise workloads. Enterprise

workloads typically have people as the number 1 cost. Cloud computing affords greater scale, a deeper investment in automation and, as a consequence, people costs are actually very low.

We expect to see more companies offering cloud based capabilities and services, not to mention cloud-based storage, backup, sharing, etc. This is one hot area and everyone is getting into the cloud. Mobile operators are expected to lead in some interesting cloud based services, especially targeting tablets and Smartphones. We will also see more hybrid cloud solutions, merging public and private clouds for enterprise networks. Finally, we expect more security challenges and solutions for the cloud during this period.

A central issue that will attract more interest in the years to come will be this of Cloud-based Mobile Device Management. While ubiquitous computing was introduced as a post-desktop model of human-computer interaction in which information processing is thoroughly integrated ('ubiquitous') into everyday objects and activities. The term later appears in the research bibliography as pervasive computing, ambient intelligence, and more recently named as the Internet of Things, the emergence of Cloud shall necessitate a repositioning of all previously mentioned terms with respect to the cloud, hence Cloud-based Mobile Device Management may be the term that will lead developments in the area for the years to come in the horizon of 2020:

Over the next decade, the cloud will alter the dynamics of the mobile market just as it has computing and IT infrastructure. Every aspect of the mobile environment – from devices to applications, services, and usage models – will be impacted by the use of the cloud to execute, communicate, and store information. While the cloud represents a new frontier in consumer electronics technology, it also comes with the challenge of balancing resources of all three types (human, technology and monetary) and managing change.

Processing power and capabilities for servers is increasing rapidly, and this reduces the processing power needed in devices and increases requirements in servers. Cloud technologies actually make this processing power available to all and changes also lead to a web dominated by cloud services. As costs for end-user devices are dropping, cloud services are provided for free or are extremely inexpensive because they address large audiences all over the globe, thus being able to produce economies of scale.

The implications for accessibility are immense as user groups and categories which would not have been otherwise as attractive or of any business interest (even for a niche market), will now concentrate the interest of several competitors globally.

Big Data for Everyone

The IBM Deep Blue ("Deep Blue (chess computer)", n.d.) project to build a world class chess playing computer, won its first great visitor in 1996 when it became the first ever machine to win a game against a reigning world champion, in this case Gary Kasparov. In 1997 it made history again, by winning a whole match game, once more against the reigning champion Gary Kasparov. The match was controversial in that Kasparov claimed that he sometimes saw "deep intelligence and creativity" in the machine's moves and suspected that human chess players had intervened on behalf of the machine. The machine was dismantled and since then both IBM and Kasparov have moved on to other things. Despite the controversy, these events mark an important milestone in our understanding of what can be achieved by machine intelligence.

IBM made the headlines again in February 2011 when a system called Watson (IBM, n.d.) developed by IBM competed against two human contestants in Jeopardy one of the most popular quiz shows in the US, and won convincingly. The IBM computer was competing against the two most powerful Jeopardy contestants ever, one who had a record number of consecutive wins and the other who had a record number of competition

earnings. The response of the contestants was less controversial than in the case of Deep Blue. One of them said at the end that *"I for one welcome our new computer overlords"*.

If Deep Blue showed an ability of a machine to deal with great complexity, Watson showed an ability to deal with great subtlety. The questions posed in Jeopardy are often highly ambiguous. They often employ, use world play or double meanings, ambiguous grammatical structure or are sensitive to context. The triumph of Watson was a convincing demonstration that human like machine intelligence able to cope with the complexity of natural language might indeed be possible.

The next major step forward came from Apple with the release of Siri (Apple, n.d.) in October 2011. Although it is formally only in betas phase, it is available on the iPhone 4S. Siri incorporates voice recognition allowing the user to place calls, send messages and schedule meetings using voice input alone. It is a smart-assistant and knowledge-navigator able to answer simple questions. Instead of struggling with keys or a touch pad, it is possible to talk to the phone in a natural way. Siri understands and answers back in the same way. It even understands humor, recognizing jokes and responding in kind. For example if you ask it "will you marry me?" it will reply "let's just be friends OK?" If you ask "what is the answer to the ultimate question" it will come up with some remark around the number 42.

Siri used to be an independent company. It was founded by Dag Kittlaus in 2007 and sold to Apple for $120M in 2010. Kittlaus has since left Apple to work on new entrepreneurial ideas. Siri was a spin-out from the SRI International Artificial Intelligence Centre. It was an offshoot of a DARPA-funded project called CALO ("CALO", n.d.) that SRI was involved in. CALO stands for Cognitive Assistant that Learns and Organizes and was originally intended to produce technologies for military and civilian use. Much of the technology developed in the CALO project is now available via the PAL project framework (PAL Framework, n.d.) managed by SRI.

The Siri system is far from perfect, but it is a significant step forward. To give an idea of the kind of problems that social computing may run into however, note that early complaints about the Siri system in the US included complaints about the fact that whereas Siri would suggest locations to buy illegal drugs, hire a prostitute, or dump a corpse, but not find birth control or abortion services! It seems that these glitches will be solved any time soon.

According to the iPhone hacks site, it is possible that a Siri API will be made available in future. This will enable Siri to act as an interface to any iPhone app that uses this API. This will save developers a lot of effort re-inventing the wheel in smart search or language engineering. It is possible that other phone makers out there have similar technologies in the pipeline. Certainly there is already a range of Siri look-alike products available to Android. It seems as though whether Apple releases a Siri API or not we may already be at the start of an age of mass market social computing.

Combining the functions of Siri smart assistant with search, cloud services, social networking and advances in computer generated speech, a whole new range of smart services will be created. Although the basic technologies will continue to advance, existing systems such as Siri are good enough to use as a platform for the developing next generation services. These will be also of use to people with disabilities.

REFERENCES

Aceves, M., Grimalt, J., Sunyer, J., Anto, J., & Reed, C. (1991). Identification of soybean dust as an epidemic asthma agent in urban areas by molecular marker and RAST analysis of aerosols. *The Journal of Allergy and Clinical Immunology, 88*(1), 124–134. doi:10.1016/0091-6749(91)90309-C PMID:2071776

Apple. (n.d.). *Apple - iOS 7 - Siri*. Retrieved February 7, 2014, from http://www.apple.com/ios/siri/

Boisseau, S., & Despesse, G. (2012, February 27). Energy harvesting, wireless sensor networks & opportunities for industrial applications. *Embedded*. Retrieved from http://www.embedded.com/design/smart-energy-design/4237022/Energy-harvesting--wireless-sensor-networks---opportunities-for-industrial-applications

Bowman, P., Ng, J., Harrison, M., Lopez, T. S., & Illic, A. (2009). *Sensor based condition monitoring*. Retrieved from http://www.bridge-project.eu/data/File/BRIDGE_WP03_sensor_based_condition_monitoring.pdf

CALO. (n.d.). *Wikipedia, the free encyclopedia*. Retrieved February 8, 2014, from http://en.wikipedia.org/wiki/CALO

CASAGRAS2. (n.d.). *CSA for Global RFID-related Activities and Standardisation (CASAGRAS2) | CASAGRAS2 - INTERNET OF THINGS*. Retrieved February 7, 2014, from http://www.iot-casagras.org/

Chappell, B. (2011, April 11). *New Electronic Sensors Stick To Skin As Temporary Tattoos: The Two-Way: NPR*. Retrieved January 7, 2014, from http://www.npr.org/blogs/thetwo-way/2011/08/11/139554014/new-electronic-sensors-stick-to-skin-as-temporary-tattoos

COST | COST Foresight 2030 - Living the Digital Revolution. (2009, October 9). Retrieved from http://www.cost.eu/events/foresight_2030_society

Deep Blue (Chess Computer). (n.d.). *Wikipedia, the free encyclopedia*. Retrieved February 8, 2014, from http://en.wikipedia.org/wiki/Deep_Blue_%28chess_computer%29

Deloitte. (2012). *Technology, Media & Telecommunications Predictions*. Retrieved from Deloitte website: https://www.deloitte.com/assets/Dcom-Global/Local%20Content/Articles/TMT/TMT%20Predictions%202012/16264A_TMT_Predict_sg6.pdf

Eaton, K. (2008, February 21). *Cellphone Display Concept Designed for Dracula Is Bloody, Ridiculous*. Retrieved February 7, 2014, from http://gizmodo.com/359018/cellphone-display-concept-designed-for-dracula-is-bloody-ridiculous

ECAALYX. (2009). *Welcome to eCAALYX!* Retrieved February 7, 2014, from http://ecaalyx.org/

EG. (n.d.). *Welcome | e.g. Conference*. Retrieved February 7, 2014, from http://www.the-eg.com/

Eurostat. (2013, December). *Information society statistics at regional level - Statistics Explained*. Retrieved February 7, 2014, from http://epp.eurostat.ec.europa.eu/statistics_explained/index.php/Information_society_statistics_at_regional_level

Framework, P. A. L. (n.d.). *Overview — PAL*. Retrieved February 7, 2014, from https://pal.sri.com/Plone/framework

GS1. (n.d.). *EPCglobal | Products & Solutions | GS1 - The global language of business*. Retrieved from http://www.gs1.org/epcglobal

Gartner. (2010, November 10). *Gartner Says Worldwide Mobile Phone Sales Grew 35 Percent in Third Quarter 2010, Smartphone Sales Increased 96 Percent*. Retrieved from http://www.gartner.com/newsroom/id/1466313

Global Industry Analysts, Inc. (2012, February). *Smart Sensors (MCP-1234) - Global Industry Analysts, Inc.* Retrieved February 7, 2014, from http://www.strategyr.com/Smart_Sensors_Market_Report.asp

GRIFS. (2008). *Home*. Retrieved February 7, 2014, from http://www.grifs-project.eu/

IBM. (n.d.). *IBM Watson*. Retrieved February 7, 2014, from http://www-03.ibm.com/innovation/us/watson/index.html

ICT SHOCK Future Internet. (2007). *Research agenda*. Retrieved from http://www.futureinternet.fi/publications/ICT_SHOK_FI_SRA_Research_Agenda.pdf

IDC. (n.d.). *IDC Home: The premier global market intelligence firm*. Retrieved February 7, 2014, from http://www.idc.com/

IDF. (n.d.). *International Diabetes Federation*. Retrieved February 7, 2014, from http://www.idf.org/

IERC. (2010). *IERC-European Research Cluster on the Internet of Things*. Retrieved February 7, 2014, from http://www.internet-of-things-research.eu/

Internet World Stats. (2012). *World Internet Users Statistics Usage and World PopulationStats*. Retrieved February 7, 2014, from http://www.internetworldstats.com/stats.htm

Kelly, K. (2008, July 29). *The first 5,000 days of the web, and the next 5,000: Kevin Kelly on TED.com | TED Blog*. Retrieved February 7, 2014, from http://blog.ted.com/2008/07/29/the_first_5000/

Knovel. (2012, March 5). *Engineers unveil new framework to enhance efficiency of energy harvesting devices*. Retrieved February 7, 2014, from http://why.knovel.com/all-engineering-news/1316-engineers-unveil-new-framework-to-enhance-efficiency-of-energy-harvesting-devices.html

Latré, B., Braem, B., Moerman, I., Blondia, C., & Demeester, P. (2011). A survey on wireless body area networks. *Wireless Networks*. doi:10.1007/s11276-010-0252-4

Li, H., Takizawa, K., Zheri, B., & Kohno, R. (2007). Body Area Network and Its Standardization at IEEE 802.15.MBAN. *Mobile and Wireless Communications Summit, 2007. 16th IST*, 1-5. doi:10.1109/ISTMWC.2007.4299334

Libelium. (2013, January). *Libelium - Redes Sensoriales Inalámbricas - ZigBee - Mesh Networks | Libelium*. Retrieved February 7, 2014, from http://www.libelium.com/130220224710

McKinsey & Company. (2010, March). *The Internet of Things | McKinsey & Company*. Retrieved February 7, 2014, from http://www.mckinsey.com/insights/high_tech_telecoms_internet/the_internet_of_things

McNamee, R. (2011, November). *Roger McNamee: 6 ways to save the internet | Video on TED.com*. Retrieved February 7, 2014, from http://www.ted.com/talks/roger_mcnamee_six_ways_to_save_the_internet.html

Meeker, M., Devitt, S., & Wu, L. (2010). *Internet Trends*. Retrieved from http://comunicaciondecrisis.wikispaces.com/file/view/Internet_Trends_041210+Morgan | Stanley.pdf/289548087/Internet_Trends_041210%20Morgan%20Stanley.pdf

Monitoring eAccessibility. (n.d.). *Monitoring eAccessibility*. Retrieved February 7, 2014, from http://www.eaccessibility-monitoring.eu/

Next Big Future. (2012, February 22). *Swimming through the blood stream: Stanford engineers create wireless, self-propelled medical device*. Retrieved February 7, 2014, from http://nextbigfuture.com/2012/02/swimming-through-blood-stream-stanford.html

OGC. (n.d.). *Sensor Web Enablement DWG | OGC(R)*. Retrieved February 7, 2014, from http://www.opengeospatial.org/projects/groups/sensorwebdwg

PRIME. (2008, September 29). *PRIME - Privacy and Identity Management for Europe — Portal for the PRIME Project*. Retrieved February 7, 2014, from https://www.prime-project.eu/

PRWEB. (2012, March 5). *Global Smart Sensors Market to Reach US$6.7 Billion by 2017, According to New Report by Global Industry Analysts, Inc*. Retrieved February 7, 2014, from http://www.prweb.com/releases/smart_sensors/flow_pressure_sensors/prweb9251955.htm

Raising the Floor. (2011). *Components of the GPII | gpii.net*. Retrieved February 7, 2014, from http://gpii.net/components

Research, A. B. I. (2012). *Body Area Networks for Sports and Healthcare | ABI Research*. Retrieved from https://www.abiresearch.com/research/product/1005246-body-area-networks-for-sports-and-healthca/

Speedmatters.org. (n.d.). *Enabling People With Disabilities | Speed Matters - Internet Speed Test*. Retrieved February 7, 2014, from http://www.speedmatters.org/benefits/archive/enabling_people_with_disabilities/

Thayananthan, V., & Alzahrani, A. (2012). RFID-based Body Sensors for e-Health Systems and Communications. *eTELEMED 2012, The Fourth International Conference on eHealth, Telemedicine, and Social Medicine*, (pp. 237-242). Retrieved from http://www.thinkmind.org/index.php?view=article&articleid=etelemed_2012_10_30_40172

Theogarajan, L., Wyatt, J., Rizzo, J., Drohan, B., Markova, M., Kelly, S., & Yomtov, B. (2006). Minimally Invasive Retinal Prosthesis. *Solid-State Circuits Conference, 2006. ISSCC 2006. Digest of Technical Papers. IEEE International*, 99-108. doi:10.1109/ISSCC.2006.1696038

Uckelmann, D., Harrison, M., & Michahelles, F. (2011). *An Architectural Approach Towards the Future Internet of Things*. Architecting the Internet of Things. doi:10.1007/978-3-642-19157-2_1

WHO. (2013, March). *WHO | Cardiovascular diseases (CVDs)*. Retrieved February 7, 2014, from http://www.who.int/mediacentre/factsheets/fs317/en/index.html

Withings. (n.d.a). *Withings - Partner apps.* Retrieved February 7, 2014, from http://www.withings.com/en/app/partners

Withings. (n.d.b). *Withings - Smart products and apps - Homepage.* Retrieved February 7, 2014, from http://www.withings.com/

Zervos, H. (2012). Positive Adoption Trends Expected to Double the Market Within 5 Years. *Energy Harvesting Journal.* Retrieved from http://www.energyharvestingjournal.com/articles/energy-harvesting-positive-adoption-trends-expected-to-double-00004265.asp?sessionid=1

KEY TERMS AND DEFINITIONS

Big Data: Big data is the term for a collection of data sets so large and complex that it becomes difficult to process using on-hand database management tools or traditional data processing applications.

Body Area Networks: A body area network (BAN), also referred to as a wireless body area network (WBAN) or a body sensor network(BSN), is a wireless network of wearable computing devices.

Internet of Things: The Internet of Things (IoT) is a computing concept that describes a future where everyday physical objects will be connected to the Internet and be able to identify themselves to other devices.

Networks: A network is a group of two or more computer systems linked together.

Semantics: Semantics is the study of meaning in language.

Sensor Network: A sensor network is a group of specialized transducers with a communications infrastructure intended to monitor and record conditions at diverse locations.

Sensor: A sensor is a device that detects and responds to some type of input from the physical environment.

Web of Things: The Web of Things (WoT) is a computing concept that describes a future where everyday objects are fully integrated with the Web.

Chapter 2
Keyboards, Screens, and Mice

ABSTRACT

This chapter deals generally with the developments in various interaction technologies. Interaction paradigms have shifted in the past from command line interfaces to graphical user interfaces exploiting heavily metaphors from the real to the digital world. Today, the traditional paradigm of interaction with a computer using a mouse, a keyboard, and a screen starts again to shift into new emerging paradigms employing a variety of technologies such as speech and gesture recognition. The functionality of a PC is now being transferred into devices such as mobile and wearable devices, exposing the need for new ways of interacting with devices. This chapter discusses how emerging interaction technologies can affect the eAccessibility domain by presenting opportunities, challenges, and dangers that lie ahead.

INTRODUCTION

For decades access devices such as special keyboards, switches, pointing devices, screen readers, TTS, Speech to Text apps, AAC devices have been developed and penetrated the market in order to facilitate the access in ICT for disabled people as well as to improve their quality of life. However, most of such devices are expensive to purchase, limited in capabilities with respect to functionalities supported, require special training and they are difficult to use especially for first time users. Therefore, such developments although they allowed disabled people to use ICT and in some cases actually to master the use of such access devices, the ICT penetration in the disability community is relatively low. In fact only 15% of those who need Assistive Tools and other devices, have these

tools (Milliken, 2011). The reason for this can be multifold, i.e. expensive tools and lack of affordability, limited offer of functionalities, difficult to use and hard to learn how to use them, lack of innovation, platform dependency and lack of interoperability. Therefore, our analysis on new HCI interfaces that can advance eAccessbility by 2020 should identify such tools, applications and products that fulfil or have the potential to fulfil the following criteria:

- *Affordability* and low cost/benefit ratio
- *User friendliness* i.e. Easy to learn how to use them as well as easy to operate them
- *Significance* i.e. to support functionalities that allow the disabled users implement as many tasks as possible that improve their quality of life and independent living

DOI: 10.4018/978-1-4666-6130-1.ch002

- *Reachability* i.e. easy for the disabled users to reach points of purchase (places virtual or brick and mortar that the disabled user can reach for purchasing them

Based on the above, it is not surprising that at the end of 2011, there were 6 billion mobile subscriptions (MobiThinking, 2013), (estimates The International Telecommunication Union -2011). That is equivalent to 87% of the world population. And this is a huge increase from 5.4 billion in 2010 and 4.7 billion mobile subscriptions in 2009. Current mobile devices (based on iOS, Android, Symbian, Blackberry, Bada, Windows phone, etc.) satisfy at some level all the above four selection criteria which indicates that eAccessbility by 2020 should be based heavily on mobile technologies and phones and the applications and services that support them. Their functionality through the installation of new software apps can be significantly increased from measuring temperature to using them as universal remote controls for domestic appliances.

Furthermore, according to latest NMC Horizon Report (The New Media Consortium, 2012), released by the New Media Consortium and Educause Learning Initiative, four technologies that will affect the future are Mobile Apps, Tablet Computing, Gesture based computing, Internet of Things. More specifically:

- **Mobile Apps:** Time to adoption: One year or less. According to a report from Ericsson, by 2015, 80% of people accessing the Internet worldwide will be doing so from a mobile device. Mobile applications are no longer considered cutting-edge technology

- **Tablet Computing:** Time to adoption: One year or less. More than simply being viewed as an add-on to mobile devices, tablets have become a branch in their own right — blending features of laptops and smartphones, applications and Internet access.

- **Gesture-Based Computing:** Time to adoption: Two to three years. It is now commonplace for those in the developed technologically countries, including younger generations, to own devices that function through the use of gestures rather than just via typing or moving a mouse. From smartphones such as the iPhone, to gaming devices such as the Nintendo Wii, taps, swipes and body movement are normal ways to interact with a device. The use of gesture-based control mechanisms allows a user to engage virtually, as well as manipulate digital information in a more intuitive fashion.

- **Internet of Things:** Time to adoption: Two to three years. Simply put, the 'Internet of Things' is a means to describe network-aware smart objects that connect the physical world with the world of digital information and communication. Such objects have four key attributes — a unique identifier, information storage capabilities, ease of connection and the capacity to communicate with an external device when required. Furthermore, while conveying data via TCP/IP, it is also assigned an address, and therefore findable online. Having been used in the past for tasks including equipment monitoring, point-of-sale purchase and tracking, 'smart objects' now have developed to be able to detect additional information — such as cost, age, colour and pressure — which can be passed along through its communication capabilities. The 'Internet of Things' would allow easy access, analysis and research concerning this kind of additional information.

There is a major shift coming in the following years in the interaction of people with ICT. The traditional devices such as keyboards and mice are going to be replaced by other input devices and technologies and the following analysis aims to pinpoint the major changes and their potential benefits and issues for accessibility.

KEYBOARDS AND POINTING DEVICES

Most of the developments in keyboards and pointing devices (the list is not exhaustive but indicative) are switches in combination with switch accessible software, braille keyboards and note takers, ergonomic keyboards, virtual keyboards, key guards, keyboards with stickers, larger keyboards, mini keyboards, overlay and concept keyboards, portable keyboards, joysticks, trackballs, head mounted pointers, touch pads, touch screens.

However these are devices and software already in use as assistive technology. In the following paragraphs we are going to present a number of software and hardware that will potentially replace large part of today's keyboards and mice. These are: Virtual Keyboards, Keyboards on Touch screens, Virtual Laser Keyboard, Eye/gaze Interaction through eye tracking that are integral part of either mobile apps or tablet computing or of gesture computing.

Virtual Keyboards

There are virtual keyboards that work in PCs and in fact they are integrated as accessibility features in the operating system such as in windows, OS X, and Linux or some can be downloaded and installed for free such Click-N-Type virtual keyboard or Dasher (Dasher Project, 2011) (A software solution for entering text by zooming through letters). However, they are operated mainly through a pointing device (such as mouse, mini-mouse, trackball, joystick/stylus/light pen) and consequently, they are difficult to use or require a lot of effort to master them.

However, virtual keyboards in order to become more user friendly, need to be customisable easy, i.e. the user to select specific key strokes for specific functions and if desire to display only specific keystrokes or group them according to their frequency of use. For example some people with learning disabilities may need to use just a limited set of keys for doing specific actions, or even be able to adjust the size of the keyboard and support other languages other than the ones based on the Latin alphabet. Such virtual keyboards have started to be developed such as Touch-It Virtual Keyboard (Chessware SA, 2013) from chess ware at affordable prices but still the customisation can be a tedious task for first time users.

Furthermore, they need to predict words according to the language (spelling and syntax and also support other languages than English) of the user but also according to the writing style (frequent/recent use) of each user. In fact, there are word prediction software programs such as Swiftkey (TouchType Ltd., n.d.) that can predict the next word without even writing its first letter by learning your writing style from following your text from your widely used applications such as Gmail, Facebook, Twitter or your blog posts.

Currently, word prediction software is available in touch screen enabled devices such as tablet PCs and smart mobile phones. This kind of software could boost productivity of non-disabled persons while at the same time boost productivity and interaction of persons with disability.

Virtual Laser Keyboards

The Virtual Laser Keyboard (ISL Trading, n.d.) (VKB - Magic Cube) is an accessory (The only keyboard that operates in total darkness) for iPhone, iPad, Smartphone, PDA, MAC & Tablet PC and any device that operates Bluetooth.

The Virtual Keyboard (VKB) by Celluon, uses state of the art infrared & laser technology to project a full-size keyboard onto any flat surface. For the first time mobile device users can actually type normally on this virtual keyboard (VKB), enabling them to work quickly and effectively, taking the pain and frustration out of existing minuscule keyboards and handwriting recognition software.

Such a development may be the basis in the near future not only for projecting and working with a virtual keyboard on any flat surface but also on possibly customizing easily the keys and projecting only those for the specific special needs of a person with disability. On the other hand, potential problems may rise for other groups of people with disabilities such as visually impaired.

Both touch screen keyboards and virtual keyboards are examples of how a specific input technology can provide solutions for specific types of users while at the same time become a barrier for another group. This demonstrates how difficult is to provide one interaction solution that can accommodate almost all people.

Eye/Gaze Interaction

Standard keyboards and pointing devices can currently be replaced also by eye tracking systems linked with virtual keyboards. Eye/gaze communication means that a person is using his or her eyes to communicate. Thus, eyes can be used to point at items. People who lack the control of muscle movement may still be able to move their eyes and interact by using their gaze. An eye tracking device tracks the person's eye movement and determines where on screen their gaze is targeted. Such "eye mouse" can then be used to control the mouse pointer on-screen (instead of hand mouse or head mouse). If the person is able to blink (wink) or press a separate button/switch, sip/puff or make a sound (voice command), then the target pointed by the "eye mouse" can be selected by using a separate switch. However, many people are not able to press a separate switch or cannot even blink, or such activity is very tiring for them. In such a case the selection of the pointed target can be done with a "dwell time", which means

the user keeps the gaze on the target for a certain duration of time (e.g. 1-2 seconds), thus "dwelling on it" to select the item (COGAIN, n.d.).

For some people, eye control is a necessity and the only option, for example, people who are totally paralyzed and who can only control their eye movements. For other people, eye control can be an option that is faster and less tiring than the other options such as switches. There are currently several different eye control systems (COGAIN, n.d.) available for purchase, that work satisfactorily but most of them are not cheap at all, since the technology is relatively new. However, prices are expected to go down and there are also low-cost and open source systems being developed but up to date, none of them are yet stable and user friendly for people with disabilities.

Keyboards on Touchscreens

Touch screens enable a user to control an ICT device by pointing or touching an area of the screen. A touch screen as access device has been developed many years ago but most touch screens for computers use clear plastic window placed in front of a standard monitor and may be used as a keyboard alternative. However, in this case, such screens can work with any mouse-driven software but they are designed for small cursors rather than large fingers, so some users may not be able to locate/touch the precise often small, areas required.

The popularity of smartphones, tablet computers, portable video game consoles and many types of information appliances has been supported by the advancement of common touchscreens, for portable devices. With a display of a simple smooth surface, and direct interaction with a finger or a light pen without any hardware (keyboard or mouse) between the user and content, fewer accessories are required.

In addition to Swiftkey indicated above, there is also other interesting apps form mobile devices (phones, tablets) such as Swype (Nuance, n.d.b) for a very effective input solution for all virtual keyboard applications. With one continuous finger or stylus motion across the screen keyboard, the patented technology of Swype enables users to input words faster and easier than other data input methods - at over 40 words per minute without any previous training. The application is designed to work across a variety of devices such as phones, tablets, game consoles, kiosks, televisions, virtual screens, and more.

Given the popularity and rapid penetration of smartphones, tablets and other touch-screen enabled devices, keyboards on touch screens could potentially evolve in one of the major input devices for the next years. However, as easy as it seems for persons with disabilities to use them they pose significant barriers for persons with visual impairments since most touch-screens (at least for the time being) cannot give tactile feedback that could help blind or visually impaired people to identify keys and use them. It is therefore necessary for alternatives to be provided when accessing such devices in order not to exclude these groups from using touch screen enabled devices.

SCREENS AND TOUCHSCREENS

From Single to Multiple Screens

Multiple Screen or Multi-Monitor, also called Multi-Display is the use of multiple physical display devices, such as monitors, televisions, and projectors, in order to increase the area available for computer programs running on a single computer system. Multi-Screen Computing (Multiple Monitors dot Org, n.d.) is a user-friendly, cost-effective way to increase productivity, enhance capabilities and significantly improve the quality of the user experience.

However, although there are assistive technology tools such as screen readers and zooming software that support multiple screens, their configuration by the user for doing this can be a bad experience. Therefore, future developments in eAccessibility should ensure easy set-up process for multi-screen support.

Multiple screen settings might not be very common in household systems; however the increase in productivity they offer makes them ideal solutions for work environments. As more and more work environments start to embrace this trend, it is obvious that whatever problems it poses for accessibility will be transferred as problems for employment of persons with disability. Thus, it is imperative that future R&D looks into that problems and provides solutions for them

Touchscreens

Touchscreens are becoming ubiquitous in mobile devices: tablets, smartphones, e-readers, etc. However, individuals who have either visual or dexterity disabilities (or both) may have difficulties using standard touchscreen technology. Traditional touchscreen use based on pointing device, requires good hand/eye coordination. If users cannot see the target, they cannot activate it. This affects opening applications, using the virtual keyboard, and most other touch screen functions. However, recent touchscreens have built-in solutions for this problem. Most of mobile devices have integrated screen readers (e.g. VoiceOver screen reader (Apple, n.d.a) in iOS products) that make it relatively easy for a person with sight loss to navigate and select items. Also most mobile devices have a "pinching gesture" as feature that allows users to easily enlarge or decrease items on the screen. Furthermore, people with dexterity disabilities may face problems with touch screens functions such as on the "pinching" function as described above or on pressing, since users may have difficulty on pressing hard or accurately enough to interact with virtual keyboards or with tapping functions (e.g. to open an app).

Most mobile devices can be operated via external physical keyboards and some mobile devices (e.g. iOS 5 enabled) include a full-featured speech recognition for control as well as dictation. It is encouraging that such developments are already integrated in the mobile devices and in the near future, it is expected such developments to work in many languages as well as to further improve the user experience.

Tactile Screens

A technology lately introduced in touch screen interfaces that could potentially increase even more accessibility of such devices is tactile touch screens. Tactile touch screens are literally "Feel Screens". Tactile touch screens (e.g. Senseg (Senseg, n.d.)), come alive with textures, contours and edges that users can feel. Using Tactile Screen technology, makers of tablet computers, smart phones, and any touch interface device can deliver revolutionary user experiences with high fidelity tactile sensations. When it comes to practicality, tixel (i.e. tactile pixel, tixels are the functional, durable surfaces that output tactile effects) technology could potentially make touchscreen keyboards as well as touch enabled/operated applications more intuitive for all users that want to feel the things they touch as well as for people with disabilities such as people with sight loss or people with learning difficulties that can use also the tactile sense for a better learning and user experience.

Samsung has presented Senseg, a product for tactile touch screens which as they say is quite expensive. Currently they are looking for partnerships with other device manufacturer such as Toshiba who already hopped on board to take advantage of the solution by embedding it to their products. Apple was recently granted a patent (Wong, 2011) for tactile touch screens and there is a lot speculation about its next product that will use this kind of technology. Microsoft has also filed a patent for tactile touch screens (Dillow, 2010) but the technology introduced is aiming large touch screen interfaces like Microsoft's Surface (Microsoft, n.d.d). Other solutions

available are introduced by smaller companies like PB Interfaces and Immersion (Immersion, 2013). The increased interest by major players in the area indicates that this might be a technology that can potentially go widely commercial in the next years. Nevertheless, the fact that it even exists seems like a good sign for eAccessibility in the near future.

Apparently, tactile touch screens when introduced in tablets, smartphones or even Surface-like devices will be able to provide a plethora of accessibility solutions (Rock, n.d.) for persons with disabilities. The most obvious ones have to do with persons who are blind but more research could reveal potential benefits for other groups too such cognitive impaired persons. In education the introduction of tablets with tactile screens in schools could potentially solve a lot of problems existing now in teaching in large auditoriums. The most important one could be the presentation of drawings, sketches and graphs used by educators either in traditional or in interactive whiteboards. The wired university auditorium of the future could possibly include technology that will transfer the drawings form the whiteboard on a tactile touch screen of a student who is blind.

FLEXIBLE SCREENS

3D Imaging

3-D imaging or stereoscopy refers to a technique for creating or enhancing the illusion of depth in an image by presenting two offset images separately to the left and right eye of the viewer. These two-dimensional images are then combined in the brain to give the perception of 3-D depth. Mainly, three strategies have been used to mechanically present different images to each eye: have the viewer wear eyeglasses to combine separate images from two offset sources, have the viewer wear eyeglasses to filter offset images from a single source separated to each eye, or have the light source split the images directionally into the viewer's eyes (no glasses required; known as Autostereoscopy) which is also the latest development. Many organizations have developed autostereoscopic 3D displays, ranging from experimental displays in university departments to commercial products, and using a range of different technologies. Although, these technologies are starting to appear now commercially for a 3D TV for home use that will not require glasses - it will probably take a few years as the technology is very costly currently, is usually limited in the number of 'viewpoints' it provides and the quality isn't so good.

Three-dimensional imaging is a technology that is quickly making its way into the classroom, allowing for virtual tours of museums or views from inside the human heart. Students focus on the content more and paid more attention in all the classrooms using 3D technology as it was reported by a recent study from the Boulder Valley School District (Boulder Valley School District, n.d.). But not everyone can see in 3D and some children experience problems. According to a study from Children's Vision Coalition (CVC) (Children's Vision Coalition, 2013) that 10% of survey respondents report their child experienced headaches; 7% indicated nausea and 6% said their kids felt dizzy after using 3D technology. Furthermore, the Children's Vision Coalition estimates anywhere from 1% of people have problems with binocular vision, prohibiting them from viewing 3D images.

Future research on 3-D imaging should also focus on the problems it causes to some users and provide solutions. In addition, future research and innovation should ensure that latest developments in 3D imaging:

- support eye comfort
- provide 3-D viewing of high quality
- are of low cost and easy to use without the need of external devices such as special glasses.

GESTURE RECOGNITION

Gesture recognition ("Gesture recognition", n.d.) is a topic in computer science and language technology with the goal of interpreting human gestures via mathematical algorithms. Gesture recognition enables humans to interface with the machine (HMI) and interact naturally without any mechanical devices. Using the concept of gesture recognition, it is possible to point a finger at the computer screen so that the cursor will move accordingly. This could potentially make conventional input devices such as mouse, keyboards and even touch-screens redundant.

Gesture recognition is useful for processing information from humans which is not conveyed through speech or other type. As well, there are various types of gestures which can be identified by computers. For example, just as speech recognition can transcribe speech to text, certain types of gesture recognition software can transcribe the symbols represented through sign language into text.

It is now commonplace for those in the technologically developed countries to own devices that function through the use of gestures rather than just via typing or moving a mouse — whether for business purposes, education or purely for entertainment. In this sense gesture recognition can be a very good alternative for people with disabilities in order to interact with ICT. Gesture recognition can be applied on touch screens or on air with external controllers or without.

Gestures on Touchscreens and Surfaces

Most mobile devices and tablets that are touch screen enabled, are gesture-based devices that receive signals in the form of physical movements – including tapping, swipes, touches that allow a user to control the device. However, the more gestures a touch screen can recognize the more opportunities it gives for developers to develop applications for persons with disabilities allowing to use the screen in a wider variety of ways. Multi-touch is also an important issue in that direction. Allowing and recognizing more than one touches at the same time allows also for wider spectrum of gestures.

Future research on gesture recognition for touch screens should exploit possibilities offered by multi touching and wider ranges of gestures to allow more users to interact with them. In addition there is also a critical aspect of intuitiveness behind new gestures implemented and recognised by touch screens. In order to learn easily and remember a wide range of gestures available and also remember their association with specific functions increases the cognitive overhead needed for operating such a device. If gestures are transferred as metaphors from everyday life gestures, this problem can be overcome. Finally, the more gestures recognizable by a device, the more are the opportunities for customization of each device according to user needs (e.g. in cases of persons with dexterity problems).

Gestures on Air

Nintendo Wii, Microsoft Xbox 360 Kinect technology and other gesture-based devices (Savitha, 2014) and software receive signals in the form of physical movements. This kind of technology does not necessarily require an external controller — in the way the Nintendo Wii does for example — and Microsoft's Kinect (Foley, 2012) technology is based on this idea. Instead of a peripheral device, your entire body acts as a control mechanism. Instead, a camera based device can recognize body movements, gestures and faces and provide an interaction with an Xbox (Microsoft, n.d.e) device through them. Microsoft also released an API for developers (Microsoft, n.d.c) in order to take advantage of Kinect's potentials by developing their own applications. From then on there's been a variety of applications coming from various developers allowing people to control and interact

with their computers through movements and gestures. In August, Apple has also filed a patent (Pachal, 2011) for a similar system allowing users to control their devices through movements showing that motion control of devices is a possible emerging trend of the future.

The same concept is applied as we have discussed before on Eye/gaze Interaction through eye tracking, that eye gestures are recognized as signals to control your computer. Future accessibility research should support/include the affordability of such systems, their expansion to recognize even further gestures and physical movements not only for controlling purposes but also for communication purposes in the area of disability.

One of the major areas of research related with accessibility and gesture recognition is sign language recognition. There are already significant research efforts made such as the ones in Aberdeen University in Scotland (Turner, 2012). Researchers at Georgia Tech College of Computing (Grant, 2010) have also recently produced a Kinect Hack to recognize American Sign Language (ASL). However, there is still need for including a larger vocabulary and also research on how such systems can be easily transferred and developed for other languages too. Although it might seem that sign language could be a universal one there are respective sign languages for different countries and even regions and this means that developments for ASL might need some time to become widely and universally available and usable.

Another critical issue that such gesture-based systems have to deal with is facial expression recognition which plays a significant role in sign language. Additionally, facial expression recognition, although it seems a bit different area than gesture recognition, can provide solutions in other areas of research too. Affective computing is one of them. Recognising a person's facial expression can lead to systems that respond to users feelings and emotions making them more user friendly.

Finally, some really innovative applications for gesture recognition such as the highly intuitive interface called SixthSense which was presented in a TED talk by Parnav Mistry (Mistry, 2009) and the device called DiVA (Wall Street Journal Live, 2012) developed by researchers at the University of British Columbia show the potentials of this technology in many other areas too such creative arts.

BODY POSTURE RECOGNITION

Speech Technologies

Speech Recognition

Speech recognition is the translation of spoken words into text and their transformation into a) commands (voice commands) or b) into text processing (speech to text processing). Voice commands can be voice dialling (e.g. call home) supported by most phones, domotic appliance control (e.g. open door), search (e.g. search for the term "iCloud" that is supported by search engines like Google), simple data entry (e.g. entering orally your personal details ("Speech synthesis", n.d.)), etc.

Speech-to-text processing for allowing writing text on email systems or word processors is currently supported by many vendors (e.g. dragon dictate). There are also solutions that allow both giving commands as well typing with your voice (e.g. Dragon Speech Recognition Software from Nuance (Nuance, n.d.a)). Such facilities can be very useful for people with physical impairments that cannot use the keyboard or the mouse for working with their computers or their ICT device (e.g. mobile phone).

However, still such products require some training in order to operate at a satisfactory level and they can still present some problems (I2osig. org, 2004) such as the peculiarities in the speech of some users, especially the ones with some speech impairments, or with different accent.

Future research is expected to advance developments that allow affordable and user friendly applications can be fully functional with voice especially by individuals with some peculiarities in their speech (e.g. impairment or accent) and also without the need of any user training. To that direction research is lately helped by crowdsourcing applications. Listening and analysing large number of persons while they speak, provides a really interesting and useful pool of data for such applications and mobile phone vendors can provide such data very easily if users accept to provide such recordings. Crowdsourcing could also provide the key to transferring easier speech recognition in many languages. Since significant amount of data is needed in ordered for speech recognition systems to be developed for a language, crowdsourcing applications could provide such data easier than ever before.

However, the "understanding" of the meaning of spoken words can be regarded as part of natural language understanding. NLP effectively requires human knowledge and experience, and would thus require advanced artificial intelligence technologies to be implemented on a computer. In particular, statistical language models are often employed for disambiguation and improvement of the recognition accuracies.

Text to Speech

Text-to-speech facility has long been a vital assistive technology tool and its application in this area is significant and widespread. It allows environmental barriers to be removed for people with a wide range of disabilities. The longest application has been in the use of screen readers for people with visual impairment, but text-to-speech systems are now commonly used by people with dyslexia and other reading difficulties. They are also frequently applied to support those with severe speech impairment. Text to speech is also finding new applications outside the disability market. Mobile devices such as tablets and mobile phones are already come with text-to-speech facilities via a variety of screen reader software such as VoiceOver (Apple, n.d.b) or Talkback (Warrior, 2011), allowing access to persons with disabilities.

The discussion about the cost of compliance should give an idea of the challenge faced by people developing software for tasks such as screen reading. The good news is that the uptake of screen reader technology has received a boost due to the popularity of smart-phones. The screen reader is a necessity for someone with poor eyesight, but can start out as a mere convenience and become a necessity too. for people who need to use the system without looking at it, either because their hands are busy while driving or doing something else, or because the screen is too small and too tiring to use for long periods of time. The popularity of advanced mobile devices such iPhones, android based ones or the Blackberry that have integrated screen readers sparked interest in screen readers from people who would normally never have considered them. This suggests that markets for such products may extend far beyond that for which it was originally intended. It is therefore interesting to imagine how the screen reader might evolve in the coming decade.

The eAccessibility domain should support the development of affordable and user friendly text-to-speech tools and screen readers with no significant training needed. This will allow any Braille display to work with any screen reader automatically, be able to read text on web pages and web applications that are much more complex and dynamic. Furthermore, since the role of computing has shifted significantly the last years, in a way that cloud computing is the current trend in the area of ICT, it is required that future technologies in text-to-speech and screen reading to be able to work under the cloud.

Natural Language Processing

Natural language processing requires human knowledge and experience, and would thus require advanced artificial intelligence technologies to be implemented on a computer. In particular, statistical language models are often employed for disambiguation and improvement of the recognition accuracies. Such developments currently can be found at *Siri* (Apple, n.d.a) on iPhone 4. Siri is the intelligent personal assistant that helps you get things done just by asking. It allows you to use your voice to send messages, schedule meetings, place phone calls, and more. But Siri isn't like traditional voice recognition software that requires you to remember keywords and speak specific commands. Siri understands your natural speech, and it asks you questions if it needs more information to complete a task. Siri works right out of the box, without any work or training from the user. And the more the user uses Siri, the better it will understand them. It does this by learning about their accent and other characteristics of their voice. Siri uses voice recognition algorithms to categorize the voice into one of the dialects or accents it understands. As more people use Siri and its exposed to more variations of a language, its overall recognition of dialects and accents will continue to improve, and Siri will work even better.

There have been some issues, mainly connection issues with the Siri intelligent personal assistant, but definitely, one of the best examples of applying natural language processing at widely used devices such as mobile phones and table computers in an affordable way, can be found at Siri.

Immersive Environments

There are already a bunch of libraries widely used such as OpenGL (OpenGL, n.d), Direct3D (Microsoft, n.d.a), Java3D (Oracle, 2013) and VRML (Bell, Parisi, & Pesce, 1996) for rendering 3D virtual reality scenes. For experiencing the 3D virtual environments, mainly head mounted displays are used as we will see next. However, a complete virtual reality system must also use some kind of input devices beyond the traditional keyboard and mouse. Advances in that area can be seen in combination with developments on gesture recognition (e.g. through Microsoft's Kinect) as we have seen before. Having seen the latest developments in virtual reality gear and related software libraries, one can see that the future might see a wider spread of virtual reality interfaces in various aspects of life, e.g. in shopping (see The Mall Plus, Trillenium (Trillenium, 2012) and Coex), learning (second life (Second Life Wiki, n.d.)) and collaboration (Bourke, 2008).

In addition, major companies in the ICT industry such as Sony are investing on virtual reality gear such as head mounted displays as we will below.

The devices presented earlier are mainly used for output of virtual reality scenes. However, a complete virtual reality system must also use some kind of input devices beyond the traditional keyboard and mouse. Advances in that area can be seen by Microsoft which presented Kinect (Microsoft, n.d.b), a camera based device which can recognize body movements, gestures and faces and provide interaction with their game console Xbox (Microsoft, n.d.e).

Online Virtual Worlds

According to Wikipedia, a virtual world ("Virtual world", n.d.) is an online community that takes the form of a computer-based simulated environment through which users can interact with one another and use and create objects. Users take the form of avatars visible to others. These avatars usually appear as textual, two-dimensional, or three-dimensional representations, although other forms are possible (auditory and touch sensations for example). An example of virtual worlds is Second Life and such virtual environment can be used in different areas such as for leisure/ social activities, for business, for education, for rehabilitation.

Virtual worlds enable people with disabilities to experience and act beyond the restrictions of their disability and help to relieve stress as well as self-esteem and improve in general their quality of life. For example, they can leave temporarily their disabilities behind and through their avatars, can do simple things that would have been impossible in real life such as walking, running, dancing, sailing, fishing, swimming, surfing, flying, skiing, gardening, socialising, etc.

Technical issues on virtual world environments such as unfamiliarity with such environments, requirement of specific system configurations, blurry avatars, poor sound or visual quality, performance issues (e.g. difficulty on teleporting, search not working, lag time), non-accessible environments mainly for people with sight loss (Wood, Morris, & Ussery, 2009) should be considered for future research and developments in the area.

Head Mounted Displays

A head-mounted display is a display device, worn on the head. Major companies in the ICT industry such as Sony are investing on virtual reality gear such as the new head mounted display by Sony (Sony, n.d.) introduced lately[1]. In addition to its normal use as display connected to a computer, the display has the ability to display images into the line of vision, integrating them with the natural world giving a stereoscopic view with many applications in simulation based training, or in medicine. A head mounted display can be connected to computers and mobile devices such as iPads and iPhones and it is very handy for people that that are bedridden.

Although prices of head mounted displays are starting getting down, they still need to get further decreased for becoming affordable and there are still incompatibility and connectivity issues with computers and mobile devices (tablets, mobile phones) that have to be addressed in the future.

3D Sound

The voice vision technology (Sharpio, 2011) for the totally blind offers the experience of live camera views through sophisticated image-to-sound renderings. In theory this use of digital senses could lead to synthetic vision with truly visual sensations ("qualia") through cross modal sensory integration, by exploiting the existing multisensory processing and neural plasticity of the human brain through training and education. The vOICe converts live camera views from a video camera into soundscapes., i.e. the system uses general video to audio mapping by associating height to pitch and brightness. When a person becomes blind they generally do not lose the ability to hear, they simply lose their ability to transmit the sensory signals from the periphery (retina) for visions to brain. Since the vision processing pathways are still intact, a person who has lost the ability to retrieve data from the retina can still see subjective images by using data gathered from other sensory modalities such as touch or audition.

The system of vOICe vision technology is still not at a commercial distribution and it is provided for free for personal use for educational uses. Additional research and development is required for its further improvements in order to be considered a medical device. As an educational tool, it requires quite extensive training by the user (i.e. it is similar to learn another language). However, such systems may form the basis for further developments in 3D sound environments supplementing a sensory modality such as vision and this can provide persons with visual impairments a whole different experience of virtual environments tailored to their needs.

Touch Gloves

In July 2011, Gallotti, Raposo, and Soares (2011) presented in a research paper a virtual reality glove (v-Glove) able to simulate touch through haptic feedback. The objective of this work is to develop a device that maps a touch interface in a virtual reality immersive environment. In order to interact in 3D virtual reality immersive environments a wireless glove (v-Glove) was created, which has two main functionalities: tracking the

position of the user's index finger and vibrate the fingertip when it reaches an area mapped in the interaction space to simulate a touch feeling. Other such gloves are the "Power Glove", the P5 Glove and the "Cyberglove" that have been developed for recreating the motions of a user wearing it on screen (mainly for computer gaming). Furthermore, Macquarie University in Sydney, Australia has developed a system that through "datagloves" that a quadriplegic person wears can control a car interface (Savitha, 2014).

However, developments in virtual reality gloves so far are either very expensive or imprecise on motion tracking) and further research and development is needed in order also to be considered in the eAccessibility 2020 features.

REFERENCES

I2osig.org. (2004). *Speech Recognition*. Retrieved February 10, 2014, from http://www.i2osig.org/speech.html

Apple. (n.d.a). *Apple - Accessibility - iOS*. Retrieved February 10, 2014, from http://www.apple.com/accessibility/ios/

Apple. (n.d.b). *Apple - Accessibility*. Retrieved February 10, 2014, from http://www.apple.com/accessibility/

Bell, G., Parisi, A., & Pesce, M. (1996, January 25). *VRML 1.0C Specification*. Retrieved February 10, 2014, from http://www.web3d.org/x3d/specifications/vrml/VRML1.0/index.html

Boulder Valley School District. (n.d.). *Boulder Valley School District*. Retrieved February 10, 2014, from http://www.bvsd.org/Pages/default.aspx

Bourke, P. D. (2008). Evaluating Second Life as a tool for collaborative scientific visualisation. *Computer Games and Allied Technology*. Retrieved from http://paulbourke.net/papers/cgat08/

Chessware, S. A. (2013). *Touch-It - Home*. Retrieved February 10, 2014, from http://www.chessware.ch/virtual-keyboard/

Children's Vision Coalition. (2013). *Children's Vision Coalition*. Retrieved February 10, 2014, from http://cvcny.org/

COGAIN. (n.d.). *Communication by Gaze Interaction | The COGAIN Association, evolved from the COGAIN Network of Excellence*. Retrieved February 10, 2014, from http://www.cogain.org/

Dasher Project. (2011, February 16). *Inference Group: Dasher Project: Home*. Retrieved February 10, 2014, from http://www.inference.phy.cam.ac.uk/dasher/

Dillow, C. (2010, January 12). Microsoft Building Shape-Shifting Touchscreen For True Tactile Touch Tech. *Popular Sicence*. Retrieved from http://www.popsci.com/technology/article/2010-12/patent-filing-reveals-microsofts-novel-attempt-true-tactile-touchscreen-tech

Foley, M. J. (2012, March 6). Microsoft showcases new Kinect-centric projects at its TechFest research fair. *ZDNet*. Retrieved from http://www.zdnet.com/blog/microsoft/microsoft-showcases-new-kinect-centric-projects-at-its-techfest-research-fair/12131

Gallotti, P., Raposo, A., & Soares, L. (2011). v-Glove: A 3D Virtual Touch Interface. *Virtual Reality (SVR), 2011 XIII Symposium on Virtual Reality*, (pp. 242-251). doi:10.1109/SVR.2011.21

Gesture Recognition. (n.d.). *Wikipedia, the free encyclopedia*. Retrieved February 10, 2014, from http://en.wikipedia.org/wiki/Gesture_recognition

Grant, C. (2010, December 20). Kinect Hacks: American Sign Language recognition. *Joystiq*. Retrieved from http://www.joystiq.com/2010/12/20/kinect-hacks-american-sign-language-recognition/

Immersion. (2013). *TouchSense Tactile Feedback Systems*. Retrieved February 10, 2014, from http://www.immersion.com/products/touchsense-tactile-feedback/

Kelly, G. (2011, September 21). *Vuzix Wrap 1200 Video Eyewear review - Peripheral - Trusted Reviews*. Retrieved February 10, 2014, from http://www.trustedreviews.com/vuzix-wrap-1200-video-eyewear_Peripheral_review

Microsoft. (n.d.a). *Download DirectX Software Development Kit from Official Microsoft Download Center*. Retrieved February 10, 2014, from http://www.microsoft.com/en-us/download/details.aspx?id=9977

Microsoft. (n.d.b). *Kinect - Xbox.com*. Retrieved February 10, 2014, from http://www.xbox.com/en-US/kinect

Microsoft. (n.d.c). *Kinect for Windows | Voice, Movement & Gesture Recognition Technology*. Retrieved February 10, 2014, from http://www.microsoft.com/en-us/kinectforwindows/

Microsoft. (n.d.d). *Microsoft Surface Tablets - The Windows Tablet That Does More*. Retrieved February 10, 2014, from http://www.microsoft.com/surface/en-US

Microsoft. (n.d.e). *Xbox Home Page | Games and Entertainment | Microsoft - Xbox.com*. Retrieved February 10, 2014, from http://www.xbox.com/

Milliken, N. (2011, August 14). *Inclusivity Requires A Paradigm Shift | atrophiedmind*. Retrieved February 10, 2014, from http://atrophiedmind.wordpress.com/2011/08/14/inclusivity-requires-a-paradigm-shift/

Mistry, P. (2009, November). *Pranav Mistry: The thrilling potential of SixthSense technology | Video on TED.com*. Retrieved February 10, 2014, from http://www.ted.com/talks/pranav_mistry_the_thrilling_potential_of_sixthsense_technology.html

MobiThinking. (2013, December). *Global mobile statistics 2013 Home: all the latest stats on mobile Web, apps, marketing, advertising, subscribers, and trends. | mobiThinking*. Retrieved February 10, 2014, from http://mobithinking.com/mobile-marketing-tools/latest-mobile-stats#subscribers

Multiplemonitors.org. (n.d.). *Multiple Monitors dot Org | Multi Monitor Video Wall Collective & Blog*. Retrieved February 10, 2014, from http://www.multiplemonitors.org/

New Media Consortium. (2012). *NMC Horizon Report > 2012 Higher Education Ed*. Retrieved from http://www.nmc.org/pdf/2012-horizon-report-HE.pdf

Nuance. (n.d.a). *Dragon - Dragon Naturally-Speaking - Nuance - Nuance*. Retrieved February 10, 2014, from http://www.nuance.com/dragon/index.htm

Nuance. (n.d.b). *Swype | Type Fast, Swype Faster*. Retrieved February 10, 2014, from http://www.swype.com/

Open, G. L. (n.d.). *OpenGL - The Industry Standard for High Performance Graphics*. Retrieved February 10, 2014, from http://www.opengl.org/

Oracle. (2013). *Java 3D Parent Project — Project Kenai*. Retrieved February 10, 2014, from https://java3d.java.net/

Pachal, P. (2011, December 9). Will Apple iTV Trade the Remote for Kinect-Like Control? *Mashable*. Retrieved from http://mashable.com/2011/12/09/apple-itv-gestures/

Rock, M. (n.d.). New Touch Screens Allow Blind to Read Braille. *Mobiledia*. Retrieved from http://www.mobiledia.com/news/97666.html

Savitha. (2014, December 20). Disabled Can Use Computers With Gesture Recognition System. *MedIndia*. Retrieved from http://www.medindia.net/news/Disabled-Can-Use-Computers-With-Gesture-Recognition-System-45409-1.htm

Second Life Wiki. (n.d.). *Second Life Education - Second Life Wiki*. Retrieved February 10, 2014, from http://wiki.secondlife.com/wiki/Second_Life_Education

Senseg. (n.d.). *Senseg*. Retrieved February 10, 2014, from http://senseg.com/

Sharpio, L. (2011, November 16). Sony's 3D Headset: Virtual Reality Goes Mainstream. *Sound and Vision*. Retrieved from http://www.soundandvision.com/content/sonys-3d-headset-virtual-reality-goes-mainstream

Silicon Micro Display. (2012). *ST1080 features, 1080p hmd features, hmd specs | SiliconMicroDisplay, Silicon Micro Display, SMD - Silicon Micro Display*. Retrieved February 10, 2014, from http://www.siliconmicrodisplay.com/st1080-features.html

Sony. (n.d.). *Head Mounted Display - Personal 3D HDTV Viewer - HMZ-T3W Review - Sony US*. Retrieved February 10, 2014, from http://store.sony.com/wearable-hdtv-2d-3d-virtual-7.1-surround-sound-zid27-HMZT3W/cat-27-catid-3D-Personal-Viewer,pgid=rHRaIrP3UbxSRpRBmHdDPVWB0000bbXsVyFV?_t=pfm%3Dsearch%26SearchTerm%3DHMZ

Speech Synthesis. (n.d.). *Wikipedia, the free encyclopedia*. Retrieved February 10, 2014, from http://en.wikipedia.org/wiki/Text-To-Speech

TouchType Ltd. (n.d.). *SwiftKey - smart prediction technology for easier mobile typing*. Retrieved February 10, 2014, from http://www.swiftkey.net/en/

Trading, I. S. L. (n.d.). *Celluon Virtual Keyboard - A laser projected full-sized virtual QWERTY keyboard*. Retrieved February 10, 2014, from http://www.virtual-laser-devices.com/?an=vlk-new

Trillenium. (2012). *Trillenium*. Retrieved February 10, 2014, from http://www.trillenium.com/home

Turner, L. (2012, March 13). Computer turns sign language into text, creating new world for deaf trainees. *The Sunday Morning Herald*. Retrieved from http://www.smh.com.au/technology/technology-news/computer-turns-sign-language-into-text-creating-new-world-for-deaf-trainees-20120312-1uwer.html

Virtual World. (n.d.). *Wikipedia, the free encyclopedia*. Retrieved February 10, 2014, from http://en.wikipedia.org/wiki/Virtual_world

Wall Street Journal Live. (2012, March 16). *Video - The DiVa Voice Synthesizer Translates Hand Gestures to Speech - WSJ.com*. Retrieved February 10, 2014, from http://live.wsj.com/video/new-voice-synthesizer-interprets-hand-gestures/316CC7FA-876C-4265-9913-0ABE4827191D.html#!316CC7FA-876C-4265-9913-0ABE4827191D

Warrior, P. (2011, May 24). *TalkBack for Android (reviewed)*. Retrieved February 10, 2014, from http://www.appszoom.com/android_applications/tools/talkback_eq.html

Wong, G. (2011, June 4). *Apple granted patent for bumpy tactile touchscreens | Ubergizmo*. Retrieved February 10, 2014, from http://www.ubergizmo.com/2011/04/apple-patent-tactile-touchscreens/

Wood, D., Morris, C., & Ussery, J. (2009). Accessibility Solutions for 3D Virtual Learning Environments. In *Proceedings of IEEE Accessing the Future Conference*. IEEE.

KEY TERMS AND DEFINITIONS

Gesture Recognition: Gesture recognition is the mathematical interpretation of a human motion by a computing device.

Human Computer Interaction: HCI (human-computer interaction) is the study of how people interact with computers and to what extent computers are or are not developed for successful interaction with human beings.

Immersive Environments: An artificial, interactive, computer-created scene or 'world' within which a user can immerse themselves.

Natural Language Processing: Natural language processing (NLP) is the ability of a computer program to understand human speech as it is spoken. NLP is a component of artificial intelligence.

Speech Recognition: Speech recognition is the ability of a machine or program to identify words and phrases in spoken language and convert them to a machine-readable format.

Tactile Interfaces: A haptics interface is a system that allows a human to interact with a computer through bodily sensations and movements.

Touchscreens: A touch screen is a computer display screen that is also an input device.

Virtual Reality: Virtual reality is an artificial environment that is created with software and presented to the user in such a way that the user suspends belief and accepts it as a real environment.

ENDNOTES

[1] HMZ-11 as it is called, costs $799.99 and is able to display 2D and 3D immersive scenes. The small screens in the device are equivalent of having your very own 150 inch movie screen only twelve feet away. It also a built-in virtual 5.1 surround sound headphones which can simulate a movie theatre's surround sound. Similar devices have also been presented by other manufacturers such as the WRAP1200 by Vuzix (Kelly, 2011) and the ST1080 by SiliconMicroDisplay (Silicon Micro Display, 2012).

Chapter 3
Robotic Exoskeletons and Social, Companion, and Service Robots

ABSTRACT

Robotics is an emerging technology presenting great opportunities for the future of eAccessbility and Assistive Technologies. This is why this chapter aims to present the current state of the art in the domain together with the potential that robotics holds for the future. More specifically, it presents recent efforts on social and companion robotics and the dangers and current challenges we are facing in that area, such as autonomy, security, the risk of seclusion for people being taken care of by robots, etc. Furthermore, this chapter is also discussing the developments in another area of robotics dealing with robotic exoskeletons. Exoskeletons are now being used in specific working environments and could in the future become a useful technology of people with disabilities. Some first examples are presented, and the chapter discusses issues such as the potential transfer of knowledge and expertise from other applications and the use of assistive technologies for helping caretakers instead of the actual persons in need.

SOCIAL, COMPANION, AND SERVICE ROBOTS

Industrial robots are designed to carry out limited numbers of complex tasks such as welding, placing and assembly with high speed and high precision. They operate expensive custom-build tools with great destructive force for welding, cutting and shredding metal. They are dangerous when operated close to humans and tend to operate in cages or in controlled areas. They require integration into assembly lines, complex tightly scheduled environments that operate 24-7. They must be physically very robust and almost never fail. They require highly trained and often highly paid engineers to manage tool changes or intervene when there is a breakdown. The cost of delays in the work of an industrial robot can often be measured in millions of dollars. They are made from hard metals, using fast-hydraulics and precision engineering with high speed real-time controls. They are very expensive and require special industrial environments in which to operate.

DOI: 10.4018/978-1-4666-6130-1.ch003

Social, companion and service robots are a very different matter. They are intended for non-industrial market. They are consumer oriented and must be safe near humans. They must be capable of learning. They must be able to operate in proximity to humans, especially children or small animals such as household pets. They have to interact with people on a one-to-one basis, in small groups and in unstructured domestic and public spaces. They must maintain themselves as much as possible, for example by re-charging themselves whenever it is necessary and managing their own range anxiety[1]. Eventually they will adapt to new task and new environments by learning. The technologies and systems that allow robots to act in this way have already become available.

Reporters writing about the first Innorobo summit ("INNOROBO 2011 - Video by TLM", 2011) held in Lyon on 23-25 March of this year, claim that the current market for service robots (L' express, 2011) that is robots used in the home, in games or for entertainment, in education or as personal assistants is already worth $3.3B per year and that it is expected to be worth $100B per year by 2020. Many see this sector as one of the biggest new or emerging categories of electronic consumer goods.

The first real service for non-industrial use was the Roomba made by iRobot ("iRobot", n.d.) founded in the USA in 1990. The Roomba was a sweeping or cleaning robot that did its work when no-one was around and re-charged itself by finding a power outlet automatically. Costing between $350 and $800, more than 100,000 of these have been sold in France alone. Since then progress in domestic robotics has been very rapid.

The Japanese have produced a range of high profile proof of concept robots. The first was Asimo by Honda, arguably the most advanced humanoid robot in the world, the result of secret research effort that started back in the 1980s. The latest version of Asimo (Honda, 2014) improves on many ways on the performance of the previous version, and is also capable of autonomous

behaviour. Asimo is not available commercially and it is not clear when Honda intends to release it into the market.

Sony has been active as well. Its first major robotic success was Aibo (AIBO-Life.org, 2012), a robotic dog intended for the toy and entertainment sector. Aibo was commercialised, but has since been discontinued. It used to sell in the US for about $1,600. It could recognise its master and would run to welcome him or her when they came home. It was able to play soccer with its other robotic doggy friends.

Sony also developed a humanoid robot called QRIO ("Sony Qrio", 2009) in 2003. Originally called the SDR or Sony Dream Robot, it was intended for the entertainment market and the original plan was to commercialise it by about 2010, but the project was discontinued in 2006. This project though technically successful … An interesting aspect of Aibo was the OPEN-R (SONY, 1998) architecture it developed for Aibo, enabling the dog to be build using interchangeable or replaceable modules. Aibo is now one of many electronic pets listed on electronic pets' website.

Toyota is also in the robot business (Kessler, 2011). It has followed a keep-it-simple philosophy and seems to have more of an eye on cost and early market entry. It recently revealed plans to develop a high-tech robot nurse that is able to lift disabled patients out of bed and can help them walk. It has already developed the "Independent Walk Assist" robot, which consists of a computer controlled leg brace initially designed for help with rehabilitation. Another e-assistance device is the "Patient Transfer Assist" which is intended to help transport someone who is bed-ridden to the toilet. These tools are all intended to ease the physical burden on nurses who may have to move or lift patients up to 40 times in a day. Toyota expects these three devices to be available commercially by 2013.

Japan is not the only country to make great strides in this area. A group at VUB in Brussels created Probo (Vrije Univeriteit Brussel, 2009) an elephant like emotive robot intended as a toy for entertainment or for use in cognitive therapy. A robotic seal from Japan called Paro (Mackenzie, 2010), produced by a company called Parorobots (PARO, 2014) has been in use as a therapeutic or healing robot in hospitals and clinics in both Europe and Japan since 2003. It is extremely life-like. It responds to touch in a very realistic animal-like way. It is mainly used for cognitive therapy in the care of older people with dementia. It is now in its 8th generation of development and is considered to be the most advanced robot of its kind.

KIST (KIST, n.d.) of South Korea has led the development of a humanoid teaching robot (Mangu-Ward, 2011) called Enki. This has been under trial for about a year now as an assistant primary-school teacher. South Korea imports many foreign teachers every year so at least until now there have been no protests from teachers who fear losing their jobs to androids. The main challenges have had to do with how to handle breakdowns. What is a teacher to do when the kids break or bully the robot or when it simply runs out of power? The idea is to use them with young children to teach them to play, develop social skills - how to greet for example, and practise using basic words in foreign languages such as English. Though intended for use by non-disabled users, Enki is therefore an assistive technology for teacher to use in classroom situations. The cost of Enki will be about $8,700. The South Korean government intends to roll out about 8,000 of these starting in 2012 once trials have finished.

These systems don't have to be complex to be effective. There is a thin line between a toy that can be used in cognitive therapy and a child's toy. Indeed there may be many opportunities for transfer of technology between these normally unconnected domains. One of the biggest marketing phenomena in the toy world in Japan is the emergence of a robot chick. At a cost of about €10 this presents an opportunity to explore cognitive therapy at low cost. One could buy 100 of these for just one Paro. There are not many reasons why the cost of Paro, Probo or other cognitive

therapy robots should not come down to about €100 by 2020.

For those who remember Tamagochi ("Tamagochi", n.d.) one of the world's first mass market virtual pets launched by Bandai in 1996, and the craze that it sparked almost overnight, you will enjoy reading about one of the newest toy crazes in Japan. This is a life-like robot chick called Yume Hiyoko ("Tiny Chick Robot", 2008). It does not do much. It simply chirps and flaps its wings when stroked. It is made by Sega Toys modelled on a real 3 day old chick and costs about €15. Over 18,000 were sold when they first went on sale.

This is 2 orders of magnitude cheaper than the seal-like Paro or elephant-like Probo. This may be a much cheaper option. If successful it highlights the value of good design in the provision of therapeutic ICT technologies. It seems highly desirable to involve psychologists and designers as well as robotics scientists in research on therapeutic ICT based products. The risk is otherwise to end up with over engineered systems, of great scientific interest, but overpriced and of little immediate utilities to the communities they are meant to assist.

A robotic dog developed by NSK of Japan is already capable of leading a blind person up and down a flight of stairs. The 'dog' travels on even ground using wheels, but climbs stairs and cross uneven ground using its legs and paws. It responds to the touch of the user and talk to the user using a synthetic female voice. Future versions will integrate GPS and more complex navigation options.

This is a low-tech variant on the Big Dog ("Boston Dynamics Big Dog (new video March 2008)", 2008) project developed by Boston Dynamics (Boston Dynamics, 2013) for the US military, intended to accompany soldiers across rough terrain, doing reconnaissance work or carry loads. Already in 2008 Big Dog was able to trot at about 4 miles per hour, climb a 35 degree slope, walk across rough terrain with even snow and ice, and carry a 340 lb. load.

Sarcos (Raytheon, 2003) of the US has developed a high powered exoskeleton ("High power militar robotic exoskeleton",2007) for military use. On its own it is essentially a humanoid robot and can move and walk and lift things on its own. When a human steps into it however, it moves in sympathy with the person multiplying their strength and enabling them to much more strenuous work and for much longer than they could without it.

Sarcos works in military and medical applications of robotics and AI. It also develops advanced humanoid robots. Sarcos also develops and sells dexterous telerobotic manipulators that provide telepresence and the ability to manipulate remote or hazardous environments. Applications include acquiring and disabling explosives, maintaining nuclear plants, maintaining high-voltage electrical transmission lines, processing bio-hazardous materials, and cleaning hazardous waste sites. One of its humanoid robots, featured on its website is even able to juggle balls.

DARPA of the US currently runs the M3 program (DARPA, n.d.) to develop new robotic technologies for maximum Mobility and Manipulation.

There is a lot of activity all over the world in robots. Lego Mindstorm (LEGO, n.d.) has played a role in this and Microsoft is also in the game (Microsoft, 2012) in 2008 it launched a robotics competition called Robochamps (Osborne, 2008) and in 2011 another called Robotics at Home (Heydarian, 2012). All of these feature humanoid robots in some way. The players in humanoid robotics are therefore not just major car companies such as Honda or entertainment companies such as Sony. The field is already quite rich with experts and enthusiasts at all levels.

But arguably the big success story in humanoid robots from the EU is Nao, pronounced "now". Nao retails at $16,000 in the US. It is provided to members of the NAO developer program for a mere €3,600. Nao was created by Aldebaran Robotics (Aldebaran Robotics, 2014), a five year old French company. The CEO claims that he would

like to see the basic price come down to the order of €1,000 to €2,000 within the next five years.

Nao recently appeared as an actor in the first Robot Film Festival ("Robot Film Festival", n.d.) held in New York City, appearing in its own short film Nao 1337 Audition ("Nao 1337 Audition on Vimeo", 2012). This idea of robots being used as actors in films is not entirely new. The Japanese have also experimented with robots used in theatre.

Already 20 universities around the world are using Nao for their research. YouTube videos of Nao show it acting like a child ("Surprised Nao (Original)", 2011) and finding its own charging station ("NAO Charging Station Prototype", 2011). It is being used by experts in machine ethics to understand how to model and implement ethics in robotics ("Chat About News (University of Connecticut - USA) human machine interaction / ethics",2011). A humanoid robot cannot simply obey orders from anyone it meets on the street. It must understand whose orders it should obey. How to resolve conflicts between its owner, the person it cares for, or even someone in authority. It must understand right from wrong. It must understand moods of people and how to respond appropriately to a person depending on their mood. It must do the same depending on the level of tiredness of the person or the importance of the situation. Eventually it must learn what is right and wrong by observation.

A further sub-sector of domestic robotics is remote telepresence robotics enabling a user to visit sites virtually using a robot proxy with a camera and a screen and able to rove around attend meetings, and go from room to room to be addressed in more detail in the section of transport and mobility further on.

In each of these cases there is a fine line between device intended to assist someone who is disabled and the person who is helping them.

Major competitions and fora such as these to do 'open innovation' around the theme of companion robotics may possibly leveraged towards e-Access applications. As far the user is concerned, the game-like approach in robotics can help to improve the acceptance of advanced robotics among elderly or disabled users, while not far in the future advanced versions of Lego's Mindstorm can become the daily 'crossword puzzle' for a high-tech older generation people, providing cognitive therapy and training at the same time. Furthermore, research in robot-theatre and robot-film could be useful with a view to encourage or accelerate development on the ability of humanoid and animaloid robots to emote and simulate human feeling and emotion.

Many of the technologies dealt with robotics (e.g. humanoid robots, exoskeletons and social, companion and service robots) apply not so much to people with (permanent) disabilities but to people with situational disabilities due to the difficulty of the working environment or the kind of clothing hey need to wear for protection. Although the extreme cases are people working in war zone, astronauts in the vacuum of space or near zero-gravity situations such as space walks or deep-sea diving, they also apply in principle to security, policing and peace-keeping and humanitarian aid situations, working in proximity to live power lines, fire-fighting and hazardous cleaning jobs. However, such situations might also lead to applications of robotics for helping persons with disabilities. This is one of the roads that eAccessibility has to look into for getting most out of robotics. In this context, EU-funded research should fully support the development of humanoid robotics, exoskeletons, and telepresence robots as key enabling technologies for e-Access applications.

The Importance of Robots

Social, companion and service robots are important for at least three reasons.

The first is that they can be considered a platform for a wide range of tasks that replace the need for as many stand-alone devices and systems. That is specialized devices and systems for folding clothes, reminding someone to take their medicine, providing cognitive therapy based on reminding, repeating and questioning. In principle they should replace stand-alone robotic spoons. They could also read the newspaper, provide directions, pick things up, monitor the status of the human companion for signs of distress and raise the alarm when a problem arises. They could read a newspaper, play music or just act silly and tell jokes to amuse. In the end they may be the best and most economical way to deliver the wide range of e-Access and e-Assistive technologies and services that future EU society will require.

It is clear that the current generation of humanoid robots is not capable of doing many or all of these tasks, but progress has been so rapid in recent years and the ambition of companies to create a totally new category of consumer electronics is so strong that most if not all of this vision will one day be achieved.

The presence of a wide range of devices that can be considered platforms for the development of applications changes the dynamics of research and innovation, as does the fact that a market for low cost useful humanoid robotic devices already seems to have emerged. According to one estimate, currently worth \$33.B with the possibility of growing to \$100B by 2020.

Another reason is that there may be too few human carers to take care of our needs as European society grows old. This is not so much a risk as a certainty. We seem to be up against a demographic wall that not even large waves of immigrants or radical re-training programs will fully address. This is one of the main reasons behind the push for humanoid service robots in Korea and Japan.

The third reason is that the area of applications that we refer to as e-Access technologies is a point more or less midway on the path to addressing bigger issues and other markets, that will generate further waves of employment and entrepreneurial activity many years in the future.

The Tipping Point is Close

In 2006 in an article in Scientific American titled "A robot in every home" (Gates, 2007), Bill Gates wrote "I can envision a future in which robotic devices will become a nearly ubiquitous part of our day-to-day lives. I believe that technologies such as distributed computing, voice and visual recognition, and wireless broadband connectivity will open the door to a new generation of autonomous devices that enable computers to perform tasks in the physical world on our behalf." He saw parallels between the robotics industry and the computer industry in the 70's when it started its first steps. Back then he cited data from International Federation of Robotics (IFR, n.d.) projecting the installation of 9 million personal-use robots by 2009. Updated information (IFR, 2013) from IFR reports that 8.7 million units were sold in 2011 alone and the projections for the period 2011-2014 are estimating that 14.4 million service robots for personal use will be sold.

In a more recent article (D'Costa, 2011) commenting on Bill Gates article in 2006 and presenting the latest developments form Microsoft-Robotics (Microsoft, 2012) Team there are two major arguments supporting this dynamic that robotics now have. The first one is that technology in robotics has now reached a level that is able to provide developers with API's to manage such devices and leave them free from the hassle to manage and process raw data from sensors of the robot and manipulate simultaneous functions that the robot should do. Microsoft for example released such a programming model to allow developers built applications in robots like EDDIE that is presented in the article.

A similar attempt is also made by Willow Garage (Willow Garage, 2008c) with PR2 (Willow Garage, 2008b), a robot that comes with an API for programming applications on it for research and innovation. The community (Willow Garage, 2008a) of developers doing research with PR2 and developing applications for it now includes institutes such as the Stanford University, MIT and the Freiburg University etc. and companies such as BOSCH.

The second point made in the article is that the innovation and progress in the area of robotics is going to be largely based in DIY applications based on the platforms provided. The key to success for this kind of innovation is to connect and encourage the community of developers. Competitions such as the Robotics @ Home Competition (Heydarian, 2012) by Microsoft, intent to do just that.

Another article referring to Bill Gates article (Gates, 2007) is also explaining why the tipping point for robotics has not yet reached but also presents a new programming language for robots called LabVIEW (National Instruments, 2014) which intends to give developers tools to develop applications on robots. It concludes that we are closing to that tipping point for robotics since solutions such as the LabVIEW are now emerging in the industry.

Articles on the future of robotics and the increasing sales figures are pointing that we are possibly in front of a trend break for robotics. The idea of robots as platforms will inevitably lower the cost for developers to get their hands on robots and develop applications. The applications will add extra value to the robots themselves making them more useful for larger audiences and this will lead to even lower prices and more affordable robots for everyone. The ability of robots to use particular applications according to their owners needs will make them a highly customized and personalized product for everyone and persons with disabilities can certainly benefit from such a personalization. It is thus evident that the use of robots as platforms for software development will position whoever provides these platforms in a strong competitive position for the future of robotics.

The Risk of Replacing Humans

Not everyone see this in a positive light. There are fears that the introduction of companion robots in institutional environments such as elderly care homes, may lead to poor treatment and neglect for those being cared for.

People with disabilities are generally more vulnerable than most to the risk of abuse. This comes in many forms. It may take the form of physical or emotional bullying, sexual abuse, or simple neglect. The risk is there whether in the family, at work or in an institutional context.

General laws exist to cover this, but such laws have teeth, only in so far as there are carers or concerned individuals that can recognize cases of abuse and bring them into light. Given our rapidly increasing ability to monitoring physical, physiological and even cognitive or emotional states of individuals, it is interesting to ask if technology can help in this regard. Can pervasive or ambient intelligence be used to monitor the state of individuals to detect abuse, in the moment when it happens, or via the symptoms as they emerge?

This is a step beyond basic systems for fall-detection in the elderly that have often featured in research projects in e-assistive technology in the past. The case of physical abuse and bullying is immediate and graphic, but other forms of abuse for example emotional abuse and neglect are more subtle and just as devastating but may be harder to detect. There is evidence that these forms may even increase with the anticipated widespread adoption of social robots as carers, companions or assistants.

A 2008 position paper (AGE Platform, 2008) on ethical aspects of technology and the elderly by Isabel Borges of the European Older Peoples Platform referred to a number of issues to bear in mind in the development of technologies intended to be of assistance to elderly people.

She points out that there is "a fine line between technology that promotes independence and technology that threatens individual freedom" and advocates not only discussion but research to ensure that basic human rights such as autonomy, informed consent, privacy, and personal data are protected.

She stresses the need for "consultation and real end user involvement in the process of develop-

ment of technological products and services". It is possible that the living labs model discussed elsewhere, where R+D is located in the place of use and integrates the eventual user of the technology, may provide an important mechanism to systematically address her concern.

On the issue of individual privacy she points out that the development of assistive technology for older people's independent living calls into question the balance of an individual's privacy. In this case she is referring to systems based on tele-monitoring, fall monitors, dementia tagging or the use of urine sensors.

She considers there is a need to address a variety of ethical questions asking:

- Can the need for privacy be overridden to ensure the health, safety and independence of that person, relative or friends?
- Can cost alone override an individual's privacy?

She worries that technology is not a substitute for care and human contact and technology should not reduce the quality of services. This raises many questions about the meaning of quality of services, or indeed concerning the concept of privacy, independence, quality of life itself, and the nature of trade-offs people might be prepared to make as a result.

In a Science Daily article (University of Sheffield, 2008) in 2008, Professor Noel Sharkey from the University of Sheffield points out that the introduction of social robots may lead to unintended forms of neglect, against which we should be vigilant. He fears that as the use of robots increases, most decisions as to how they are used will be left up to the military, industry or busy parents and care-givers. He goes so far as to call for the development of international guidelines on the ethical and safe application of robots.

His concerns are based on the observation based on research that humans, especially the young demonstrate close bonding and attachment to service robots. In most cases, young children prefer a robot to a teddy bear. Is fear is that whereas short-term exposure can be enjoyable and entertaining, there is a risk of emotional damage after long-term exposure.

He fears that because of the physical safety that a robot minder can provide for children, there is a risk they will be left without human contact for many hours a day or perhaps for several days. He claims that risk arise because so little is currently known the impact of social isolation on development. He claims that similar problems arise in the case of the elderly. The relative rise in number of elderly compared to young care-givers means that robots intended to help the elderly maintain a level of independent living could lead to their being left in the exclusive care of machines and without sufficient human contact.

Studies carried out in Japan have often concluded that the elderly prefer to be cared for by robots than by young people. Anecdotes abound of older people saying that they find young carers impolite, uncaring and unable to make any kind of conversation. The reality is that care-givers are often from emigrant minorities that have difficulties with local languages, and fail to communicate despite their best efforts. Older people are not immune to feelings of anxiety around foreigners and even outright feelings of xenophobia.

It appears that there is a need to systematically study the social dynamics of robots interacting with groups. Great attention and creativity goes into the design of robots that are emotive or affective.(e.g. robots that express emotion such as joy or sadness, that can talk loudly or softly as appropriate). There is great scope for learning about the culture and the rituals they need to express, so they can better perform their tasks. It would be interesting to know how users react to patterns that resemble different races, that speak different accents or that evoke different cultures in their behaviour. It is possible that the results will be highly controversial or politically incorrect. Knowing the truth could be just as revealing about humanity as it would be about technology.

Responsibility, Loyalty, and Ethics

One response to the problem of neglect could be based on what is often referred to as machine ethics, the ability of a machine to know right from wrong. Mobile phones and laptops generally do not distinguish between users. A number typed in, is a call placed, without regard to who owns the phone or who pays the bill. Companion robots cannot act in this way. They cannot obey arbitrary instructions given to it by anyone. The robot must therefore 'know' that it needs to obey some people, and ignore others. It must understand that some people are vulnerable and require special care, children and elderly people for example. In particular it needs to be vigilant about the person it is caring for. It should understand how to interact with strangers. A social robot needs not only to be 'sociable' but to be 'worldly' as well.

At any time it should understand its mission and show responsibility by achieving that mission, if necessary by being resourceful by solving problems as they arise perhaps by collaborating with other people, with animals such as pets and with other robots. It should be ethical and act with integrity in that it always does the right thing, not just for the companion in its care, but for their family and close ones, the institutions looking after him or her and society as a whole. It should be loyal in the sense that its first duty is to the person in its care. It should be caring in the sense that its actions are not triggered by physical or logical necessity but by the situation, the mood of the companion, and their overall need for reassurance and companionship. Maybe its actions might include discretely ringing a son or a daughter, to suggest that their parent is feeling down, it might be a good time to give them a rind or make a surprise visit. Maybe it could mean saying to the person in their charge "how is your friend from the floor below, you have not been in touch with them for a while, maybe you should ring them up to see how they are?"

These are issues that could easily be ignored if one sees the humanoid robot primarily as a tool or a toy for use by non-disabled people. However, such issues become of paramount importance in the interaction between a social robot and a person with a disability. In this sense, machine ethics and other qualities such as loyalty, responsibility and sociability be important differentiating factors in future markets for companion and social robots

Autonomy and Survivability

One of the attractive features of modern humanoid robots such as Aibo, Asimo and Qrio is their ability to recognize faces and people and respond in ways that trigger emotion in real people. Recognition is important for the performance of the social robot in a social setting. It can also be thought of as a security device. The familiar face or voice can be like a password. It is linked to the ethical nature of the robot in that it reassures the robot that he is responding to the command from the right person. The problem of recognition may be more difficult in a crowd, in different weather and lighting conditions, at a distance, or combined with movement.

The parameters of the problem may be different from a standard biometric test, for example the robot-dog may take many views of a person to recognize them, all taken from different angles, they may combine many cues smell for example height and weight as well as appearance and behavior. It is not like a mobile phone or an ATM where once you are in you are in, the companion may need to continuously check the identity of the person it is with, to avoid losing them in a crowd, or to avoid a security breach using a bait and switch tactic.

One day it will be possible to use the companion robot at home, walk out the door with it, get on a bus, get off at the right stop, get lost, have the companion robot find you again, have him guide you through the streets and escort you to your destination. To do this reliably and securely

in Europe and the rest of the world is a long way off. But it would make a big contribution to independent living. So what problems can we solve know that provide useful intermediate steps along the way to achieving this goal?

Several challenges lie on the performance of the robot, the systems it draws upon for resources, the environment in which it operates and the extent to which it will be is accepted as part of the furniture of our lives. Additional, social and institutional issues may arise such as: Will social and companion robots be allowed to travel on the subway, the bus and use other means of public transport?

SECURITY

Machine Learning

To be really social and human-like a robot will need to emulate human learning. It will need to learn about the person in its care. It will need to discover and learn what is their life history? Who are their friends and family? What are their needs and preferences? What are their moods and how is it best to deal with them? To care for someone with a progressive condition such as Alzheimer's, they will need to understand about the condition and its progression? They will need to recognize its progression, spot the symptoms, perhaps consult with doctors and decide with the consultant if the symptom is real or the temporary effect of anxiety tiredness or depression?

An intermediate solution might be a relevant application or an upgrade delivered daily. The best way might be to learn these things naturally using natural language, conversation at a natural rhythm that accumulates language in a human-like way over a reasonable period of time that enables bonding.

The person being cared or served by a robot will have to learn about the robot too. A well-mannered robot might take charge of this, building the skills of the companion progressively, using a phased approach that is familiar to the designers of complex games. There may be a need for rituals and formal introductions. There will be no place for questionnaires or check lists to fill out the parameters of a person's life.

IPhone apps already exist that simulate having friends and friendships. Lonely guys in Japan can subscribe to a girl-friend service that sends them SMS messages, phones them or leaves them voice mail. The service now even involves hotels. The guys go to the hotel for the weekend along with their virtual girl-friend. They book in as a couple to a double room, paying double price of course and late enjoy dinner for two. The staff at the hotel is all trained to play along with the 'game'. Users claim that while they know it is not real, it makes them feel good, especially if they are working too hard to have real girl-friends of their own.

Already machines 'tweet' and have their own Facebook pages. This is now common practice for giant engineering companies such as GE. The engines on the wings of planes have Facebook pages. The wall for the machine shows their service history, current status and recent incidents. If there is an incident or abnormal reading the engineer responsible for the engine receives a tweet. He or she can go the Facebook page of the engine to see what is up and from there patch through the pilot of the craft to understand what has been going on.

A robot traveling with its companion in a public place will have the option of talking to it directly and loudly so that everyone will hear, or in a whisper. It could even share information by linking it directly into a cochlear implant or hearing aid. It could leave a message on their mobile phone, send an email or update their Outlook agenda.

Social robots of the future will no longer simply be programmed. They will program themselves using machine learning algorithms. They will learn to do things by observing others, by experimenting or by sharing the knowledge gained by other robotics with similar experiences. It may be a good time to accelerate work on machine learning for social

and companion robots and e-Access technologies and eAssistive devices could be considered as an early market area such applications.

ROBOTIC EXOSKELETONS

Examples

Many of the exoskeleton projects especially in the US aim in resisting soldier in combat. For example the Berkley Lower Extremity Exoskeleton (BLEEX) (Berkeley Robotics & Human Engineering Laboratory, n.d.b) developed by UC Berkley Robotics (Berkeley Robotics & Human Engineering Laboratory, n.d.c) and Human Engineering Laboratory Homayoon Kazerooni. The aim was to "to create an exoskeleton that combines a human control system with robotic muscle". The project was funded by DARPA and in 2004 it was the most advanced exoskeleton.

UC Berkley is also behind of another newer military exoskeletons as well titled Human Universal Load Carrier (HULC) (Berkeley Robotics & Human Engineering Laboratory, n.d.f). HULC incorporates features from two other models of Berkley Robotics the ExoHiker (Berkeley Robotics & Human Engineering Laboratory, n.d.e) and ExoClimber (Berkeley Robotics & Human Engineering Laboratory, n.d.d) which were designed for carrying heavy loads during long missions and climbing stairs and steep slopes rapidly.

Another DARPA funded project was the Sarcos exoskeleton which recently was improved by Raytheon (Raytheon, 2003) to a newer stronger faster and better model titled XOS2 (Topolsky, 2007). This exoskeleton, much like the Berkeley suit, works much like a human nervous system. A complex set of sensors act as nerves and hydraulics act as muscle

The same lab has recently presented a new exoskeleton system called eLEGS aiming to help paraplegics and those with mobility disorder to stand and walk. eLEGS was selected as number

2 of the 10 Most significant Gadgets of 2010 by WIRED magazine (Gadget Lab Staff, 2010). In addition, a similar project called Austin (Berkeley Robotics & Human Engineering Laboratory, n.d.a) is also aiming to help individuals with mobility impairments to walk. However the project represents a series of technologies that lead to low cost and therefore accessible exoskeletons.

Argo Medical Technologies another US based company have recently established Bionics Research Inc. which presented an exoskeleton for persons with mobility impairments called ReWalk (Bionics Research, 2013). Its designers believe that the exoskeleton will be able to restore mobility to people with walking impairments and enhance their dignity, health, inclusion and self-esteem.

In Japan one of the most known examples of exoskeletons is HAL (Hybrid Assistive Limb). It is developed in the Tsukuba University and aims to assist people with mobility impairments to improve their capabilities. There are currently two prototypes: HAL 3, which has bulkier servo-motors and only has the leg function, and HAL 5, which is a full-body exoskeleton for the arms, legs, and torso. HAL 5 is currently capable of allowing the operator to lift and carry about five times as much weight as he or she could lift and carry unaided.

In Europe, the Italian Ministry for Defence has financed research for an exoskeleton meant to help soldiers or civil protection personnel engaged in rescue operations in unstructured environment. Designed by TECIP (Information Technology and Perception) of the Sant'Anna Institute in Pisa (Scuola Superiore Sant' Anna, 2014), the AVA-TAR exoskeleton is expected to be commercialized by 2016. It has four robotic limbs (arms and legs), a force correspondent to that of 20 men and 22 "degrees of freedom". Aside from civil protection, other field of operations might cover engineering in heavy manufacturing. In France, engineering company RB3D (RB3D, 2011) has developed Hercules, a battery powered robotic exoskeleton that can carry 100 kg at regular walking speed.

Dual Use

Dual-use is a term often used to refer to technology which can be used for both peaceful and military aims. More generally speaking, dual-use can also refer to any technology which can satisfy more than one goal at any given time. Thus, expensive technologies which would otherwise only serve military purposes can also be utilized to benefit civilian commercial interests - this is the case of the Global Positioning System (GPS).

HULC (Human Universal Load Carrier) which has already been presented earlier was developed to assist soldiers during combat. It could be used to help lift heavy loads while exerting minimal effort, with soldiers currently going into combat with up to 130 pounds of combat gear. Also, it could be used as a framework for body armour or sensor arrays that would allow for better situational awareness during combat. Lockheed Martin is also exploring exoskeleton designs to support industrial and medical applications.

In the given context, an exoskeleton originally conceived to help soldiers may not only help motor-impaired people to walk but also nurses lifting disabled patients out of bed or helping them walk such as the Toyota Patient Transfer Assist (Toyota, 2011) and the RIKEN RIBA II (Riken, 2011) robots, both developed in Japan. Exoskeletons are an area where dual-use could prove really beneficial for eAccessibility technologies. It is worth exploiting the potentials.

THE FASHION FACTOR

Assistive Devices not for Disabled

The exoskeleton as an assistive device is also interesting from another perspective. The obvious use in assistive technologies is that of helping paralyzed people to start walking (Whalen, 2012). However this is not the only case of using an exoskeleton. There are cases where their use might be beneficial to persons with disability in more indirect manner.

For example in the case of Toyota Patient Transfer Assist (Toyota, 2011) the system helps caretakers to lift patients off their beds. The example of HULC could also be used in such cases since it provides with a similar strength augmentation. Lifting a patient can be a strenuous task for nurses that might need to do this up to 40 times per day in Japan. Caretakers and nurses often suffer from extended exposure to back injuries (Ergonurse, n.d.). Giving them technology such as this that helps them respond to such tasks easier is certainly for the benefit of person with disability too.

A really interesting look at how exoskeletons and other similar suits can be used by care takers is presented in the case of AGNES (MIT AgeLab, 2013). The Age Gain Now Empathy System as the suit that MIT AgeLab has presented is a suit that simulates the experience that an elderly person with reduced capabilities has in real life. A similar approach has also been followed in the car industry by Nissan which use a similar suit (Worldcarfans, 2008) to find out the problems that elderly people have in driving in order to provide them with solutions. In any case these suits are not designed to augment a person's capabilities as normal exoskeletons do. One might consider them as a kind of virtual reality system. However the benefit for elderly people is that they take caretakers into the experience they live in. They help them better understand their problems and provide a different path for research and innovation.

Future professional caretakers might use specifically designed suits simulating the experience of persons with motor disabilities and advanced exoskeletons in their training. With this experience their behaviour to people with disabilities will be much more empathetic. It will also help to know how and what the person need exactly and what are the problems they are facing in each situation providing this way better help. It would be interesting to see if similar simulation tool come up for cognitive impairments, dementia, forgetfulness and similar conditions.

REFERENCES

AIBO-Life.org. (2012). *AIBO-Life Bot House: Forums Chat Shindig: Happy AIBOing*. Retrieved February 22, 2014, from http://www.aibo-life.org/

Aldebaran Robotics. (2014). *Aldebaran Robotics Aldebaran Community*. Retrieved February 22, 2014, from https://community.aldebaran-robotics.com/

Berkeley Robotics & Human Engineering Laboratory. (n.d.a). *Austin | Berkeley Robotics & Human Engineering Laboratory*. Retrieved February 22, 2014, from http://bleex.me.berkeley.edu/research/exoskeleton/medical-exoskeleton/

Berkeley Robotics & Human Engineering Laboratory. (n.d.b). *BLEEX | Berkeley Robotics & Human Engineering Laboratory*. Retrieved February 22, 2014, from http://bleex.me.berkeley.edu/research/exoskeleton/bleex/

Berkeley Robotics & Human Engineering Laboratory. (n.d.c). *Berkeley Robotics & Human Engineering Laboratory | | Berkeley Robotics & Human Engineering Laboratory*. Retrieved February 22, 2014, from http://bleex.me.berkeley.edu/

Berkeley Robotics & Human Engineering Laboratory. (n.d.d). *ExoClimber™ | Berkeley Robotics & Human Engineering Laboratory*. Retrieved February 22, 2014, from http://bleex.me.berkeley.edu/research/exoskeleton/exoclimber/

Berkeley Robotics & Human Engineering Laboratory. (n.d.e). *ExoHiker™ | Berkeley Robotics & Human Engineering Laboratory*. Retrieved February 22, 2014, from http://bleex.me.berkeley.edu/research/exoskeleton/exohiker/

Berkeley Robotics & Human Engineering Laboratory. (n.d.f). *HULC™ | Berkeley Robotics & Human Engineering Laboratory*. Retrieved February 22, 2014, from http://bleex.me.berkeley.edu/research/exoskeleton/hulc/

Bionics Research. (2013a). *Bionics Research ReWalk™ U.S. - the wearable bionic suit*. Retrieved February 22, 2014, from http://rewalk.us/

Boston Dynamics. (2013b). *Boston Dynamics: Dedicated to the Science and Art of How Things Move*. Retrieved February 21, 2014, from http://www.bostondynamics.com/

Boston Dynamics Big Dog. (2008, March 17). Retrieved from http://youtu.be/W1czBcnX1Ww

Chat About News. (2011, January 4). Retrieved from http://youtu.be/PbtaFPpiF08

D'Costa, K. (2011, September 19). *A Robot in Every Home? We're Getting Close | Anthropology in Practice, Scientific American Blog Network*. Retrieved February 22, 2014, from http://blogs.scientificamerican.com/anthropology-in-practice/2011/09/19/a-robot-in-every-home-were-getting-close/

DARPA. (n.d.). *Maximum Mobility and Manipulation (M3)*. Retrieved February 22, 2014, from http://www.darpa.mil/Our_Work/DSO/Programs/Maximum_Mobility_and_Manipulation_%28M3%29.aspx

Ergonurse. (n.d.). *Compression Force on the Back*. Retrieved February 22, 2014, from http://www.ergonurse.com/BackCompressionFlyer.pdf

Gadget Lab Staff. (2010, December 29). *The 10 Most Significant Gadgets of 2010 | Gadget Lab | Wired.com*. Retrieved March 14, 2014, from http://www.wired.com/gadgetlab/2010/12/top-tech-2010/?pid=928#slideid-928

Gates, B. (2007). A Robot in Every Home. *Scientific American*. doi:10.1038/scientificamerican0107-58 PMID:17186834

Heydarian, H. (2012, May 22). *Announcing the Winners of the Microsoft Robotics @ Home Competition - Microsoft Robotics Blog - Site Home - MSDN Blogs*. Retrieved March 14, 2014, from http://blogs.msdn.com/b/msroboticsstudio/archive/2012/05/22/announcing-the-winners-of-the-microsoft-robotics-home-competition.aspx

High power militar robotic exoskeleton. (2007, November 26). Retrieved from http://youtu.be/0hkCcoenLW4

Honda. (2014). *ASIMO by Honda | The World's Most Advanced Humanoid Robot*. Retrieved February 22, 2014, from http://asimo.honda.com/

IFR. (2013). *Statistics - IFR International Federation of Robotics*. Retrieved February 22, 2014, from http://www.ifr.org/service-robots/statistics/

IFR. (n.d.). *Home - IFR International Federation of Robotics*. Retrieved February 22, 2014, from http://www.ifr.org/

INNOROBO 2011 - Video by TLM. (2011, October 26). Retrieved from http://youtu.be/no2nUSkuqjw

iRobot. (n.d.). *Wikipedia, the free encyclopedia*. Retrieved March 4, 2014, from http://en.wikipedia.org/wiki/IRobot

Kessler, S. (2011, November 1). *Robot Invasion: Toyota Unveils Four Healthcare Assistants [PICS]*. Retrieved February 22, 2014, from http://mashable.com/2011/11/01/toyota-healthcare-robots/

KIST. (n.d.). *KIST Korea Institiute of Science and Technologhy*. Retrieved March 14, 2014, from http://eng.kist.re.kr/kist_eng/main/

L' express. (2011, March 26). *Ces robots qui vont devenir vos meilleurs amis - L'EXPRESS*. Retrieved February 22, 2014, from http://videos.lexpress.fr/economie/ces-robots-qui-vont-devenir-vos-meilleurs-amis_1240903.html

LEGO. (n.d.). *LEGO.com Mindstorms*. Retrieved February 22, 2014, from http://www.lego.com/en-us/mindstorms/?domainredir=mindstorms.lego.com

Mackenzie, A. (2010, October 2). *BBC News - Japan develops robotic seals to comfort sick and elderly*. Retrieved February 22, 2014, from http://www.bbc.co.uk/news/health-11459745

Mangu-Ward, K. (2011, August 10). *Robot Teachers Invade South Korea, Ruin Workers' Dance Party in Taiwan - Hit & Run: Reason.com*. Retrieved February 22, 2014, from http://reason.com/blog/2011/08/10/robot-teachers-invade-south-ko

Microsoft. (2012, June 3). *Download Microsoft Robotics Developer Studio 4 from Official Microsoft Download Center*. Retrieved February 22, 2014, from http://www.microsoft.com/en-us/download/details.aspx?id=29081

MIT AgeLab. (2013). *AGNES (Age Gain Now Empathy System) | MIT AgeLab*. Retrieved February 22, 2014, from http://agelab.mit.edu/agnes-age-gain-now-empathy-system

Nao 1337 Audition on Vimeo. (2012). Retrieved from http://vimeo.com/24947744

NAO Charging Station Prototype. (2011, March 8). Retrieved from http://youtu.be/0xHaxTM7KH8

National Instruments. (2014). *NI LabVIEW - Improving the Productivity of Engineers and Scientists - National Instruments*. Retrieved February 22, 2014, from http://www.ni.com/labview/

Osborne, B. (2008, April 25). *Microsoft issues RoboChamps challenge | Gadgets | Geek.com*. Retrieved March 14, 2014, from http://www.geek.com/gadgets/microsoft-issues-robochamps-challenge-574397/

PARO. (2014). *Paro Therapeutic Robot*. Retrieved February 22, 2014, from http://www.parorobots.com/

Platform, A. G. E. (2008). *Older people and Information and Communication Technologies: An Ethical approach*. Retrieved from http://www.age-platform.eu/images/stories/EN/pdf_AGE-ethic_A4-final.pdf

RB3D. (2011). *RB3D, solution mécatronique de prévention des TMS*. Retrieved February 22, 2014, from http://www.rb3d.com/

Raytheon. (2003). *Raytheon Company: Customer Success Is Our Mission*. Retrieved February 22, 2014, from http://www.raytheon.com/

Raytheon. (2014). *Raytheon Company: Businesses*. Retrieved February 22, 2014, from http://www.raytheon.com/ourcompany/businesses/

Riken. (2011, August 2). *RIBA-II, the next generation care-giving robot | RIKEN*. Retrieved February 22, 2014, from http://www.riken.jp/en/pr/press/2011/20110802_2/

Robot Film Festival. (n.d.). Retrieved February 22, 2014, from http://robotfilmfestival.com/

Scuola Superiore Sant' Anna. (2014, January 28). *Scuola Superiore Sant' Anna - Istituto TeCIP*. Retrieved February 22, 2014, from www.sssup.it/ist_home.jsp?ID_LINK=10509&area=199

SONY. (1998, June 10). *Sony Global - Press Release - Sony Develops OPEN-R Architecture for Entertainment Robots Demonstrates 4-legged robot prototypes based on the architecture*. Retrieved February 22, 2014, from http://www.sony.net/SonyInfo/News/Press_Archive/199806/98-052/

Sony Qrio. (2009, May 2). Retrieved from http://youtu.be/O8BFVLb-6IQ

Surprised Nao (Original). (2011, March 24). Retrieved from http://youtu.be/zJWFydDHJHw

Tamagotchi. (n.d.). *Wikipedia, the free encyclopedia*. Retrieved March 14, 2014, from http://en.wikipedia.org/wiki/Tamagotchi

Tiny Chick Robot. (2008, August 21). Retrieved from http://youtu.be/G5d3A-SV9Vo

Topolsky, J. (2007, November 25). *Sarcos' military exoskeleton becomes a frightening reality*. Retrieved February 22, 2014, from http://www.engadget.com/2007/11/25/sarcos-military-exoskeleton-becomes-a-frightening-reality/

Toyota. (2011, November 1). *TMC Shows New Nursing and Healthcare Robots in Tokyo | Toyota Motor Corporation Global Website*. Retrieved February 22, 2014, from http://www2.toyota.co.jp/en/news/11/11/1101.html

University of Sheffield. (2008, December 21). *British Scientist Warns We Must Protect The Vulnerable From Robots -- ScienceDaily*. Retrieved February 22, 2014, from http://www.sciencedaily.com/releases/2008/12/081218141724.htm

Vrije Univeriteit Brussel. (2009). Retrieved February 22, 2014, from http://probo.vub.ac.be/

Whalen, J. (2012, March 19). *Exoskeleton gets paralyzed man on his feet - News - Citizens' Voice*. Retrieved February 22, 2014, from http://citizensvoice.com/news/exoskeleton-gets-paralyzed-man-on-his-feet-1.1287452#axzz1qiQgrAVN

Willow Garage. (2008a). *Join the Community | Willow Garage*. Retrieved February 22, 2014, from http://www.willowgarage.com/pages/pr2/pr2-community

Willow Garage. (2008b). *Overview | Willow Garage*. Retrieved February 22, 2014, from http://www.willowgarage.com/pages/pr2/overview

Willow Garage. (2008c). *Willow Garage*. Retrieved February 22, 2014, from http://www.willowgarage.com/

Worldcarfans. (2008, February 25). *Nissan Engineers use Special Suit to Simulate the Elderly*. Retrieved February 22, 2014, from http://www.worldcarfans.com/10802252127/nissan-engineers-use-special-suit-to-simulate-the-elderly

KEY TERMS AND DEFINITIONS

Affective Computing: Affective computing is the study and development of systems and devices that can recognize, interpret, process, and simulate human affects.

Companion Robots: Robots used for keeping company to persons.

Dual Use: In politics and diplomacy, dual-use is technology that can be used for both peaceful and military aims.

Exoskeletons: An exoskeleton (from Greek ξω, éxō "outer" and σκελετός, skeletos "skeleton") is the external skeleton that supports and protects an animal's body, in contrast to the internal skeleton (endoskeleton) of, for example, a human.

Machine Learning: Machine learning, a branch of artificial intelligence, is about the construction and study of systems that can learn from data.

Robotics: The science or study of the technology associated with the design, fabrication, theory, and application of robots.

Robots: A mechanical device that sometimes resembles a human and is capable of performing a variety of often complex human tasks on command or by being programmed in advance.

Service Robots: Service robots assist human beings, typically by performing a job that is dirty, dull, distant, dangerous or repetitive, including household chores.

Social Robots: A social robot is an autonomous robot that interacts and communicates with humans or other autonomous physical agents by following social behaviors and rules attached to its role.

ENDNOTES

[1] A term used in conjunction with electric vehicles, relating to uncertainty while driving about the proximity of charging or battery swap stations.

Chapter 4
BCI, BNCI, and BMI

ABSTRACT

Brain Computer Interaction and Interfaces is another emerging technology that is presenting interesting potential for people with disabilities in their interaction with computers and machines in general. Combined with robotic arms, it can lead to prosthetic arms that can be handled though the brain like a natural hand. Apart from that, brain-computer interfaces can be used for a variety of other control operations over computers and machines in general and also for detecting the emotional state of a person. People with disabilities (and not only them) could use them to interact with a range of machines from traditional PCs to smart wheelchairs that will be able not only to accept commands but understand their emotions too. Therefore, this chapter is devoted to presenting recent efforts in the area and discussing issues and challenges that lie ahead in the domain of BCI so that the reader can get an overview of this new exciting technology.

INTRODUCTION

The dominant ICT user-interface paradigm is based on typing text into a keyboard and visualizing feedback on a screen. The keyboard may consist of physical keys or icons on a touch-screen. This principle holds not only for mobile phones and laptops but for essentially all consumer electronic goods such as video or DVD players and TVs, as well as for ATMs and vending machines. Some applications employ voice input or output. Others use physical manipulation of icons or physical objects such as buttons or joysticks. Although many inputs and outputs are no longer just text, they consist of graphics, photos, songs, videos or movies taken with cameras on mobile phones, but

again at some stage these depend on the use of keyboard and screen type interfaces.

Someone with even a minor disability, in terms of their sight, hearing, speech, physical movement or touch, will experience difficulties using ICT systems in this way. Direct brain-machine or brain-computer interfaces offer another way to interact with ICT systems and provide an alternative, and in principle universal solution to this category of e-access challenges. For some people this sounds like science fiction, but many proof-of-concept projects already demonstrating how this is feasible. Many companies already exist in this sector investing in research and innovation and extending the application domains of these technologies beyond those with the most conditions to new market segments.

DOI: 10.4018/978-1-4666-6130-1.ch004

BCI APPLICATIONS AND CHALLENGES

In a recent roadmap (Future BCNI, 2012) developed by the Future BNCI Project there is extensive reference on the part of BCI and BNCI applications for persons with disabilities. In particular according to Millan et. al. (Millan et al., 2010) the main areas of application of BCI for persons with disabilities are the following:

- Communication and control where persons with disabilities are using BCI to communicate with other or with an assistive device.
- Motor rehabilitation and recovery where persons with motor impairments and disabilities use BcI to recover their mobility.
- Moto substitution where persons with motor impairments can use BCI either to control an assistive device such as a wheelchair or to control other devices that can substitute their need for transport such as tele-presence robots.
- Mental state monitoring where BCI is used to monitor a person's state of mind and act accordingly.
- Entertainment and gaming
- Hybrid BCI (hBCI) where persons with disability are using BCI in combination with other assistive devices to improve their control.

BCI and Existing AT

An article entitled "Optimizing the P300 interface based Brain Computer Interface: Current status, limitations and future directions" (Mak et al., 2011), again in the Journal of Neural Engineering looks are closely at the most important class of headset-like non-invasive brain machine interfaces. These systems tend to be used mainly for people moderate to severe handicaps due to ALS, MS, stroke, cerebral palsy, traumatic brain injury. Nevertheless they can be sued by anyone. The main area of application is for people who have lost all voluntary muscle control but who remain cognitively unimpaired, people with so-called lock-in syndrome. Most results have been made available for people who are otherwise young and healthy. The focus of this book was to see how to make these systems more accessible to people with a wider range of disabilities. There is a need to make them more reliable, more easy to use and more affordable. One conclusion is that these systems are really used by a limited number of people, people who disability is adapted to the technology. The technology could be of benefit to a much wider group, but is generally not tried on a wider group when other approaches are available. The result is that until now the technology has been of benefit to a limited population, when potentially larger populations could benefit. The approaches taken tend to very specific cognitive tasks such as feature extraction, data classification and data pre-processing. So far very little has been done to exploit the interconnections between these tasks and the possibility of getting stronger signals using combinations of cues.

Many systems have been developed to help with writing for example by 'thinking' a letter or a word that is recognized by the BCI. The results have been promising for languages based on alphabets, but little has been done on other more visual languages such as Chinese.

Researchers recommend the development of standardized interfaces that allows people to connect BCI systems to other assistive technologies with a minimum of fuss and without customization. This is generally not the case today. They recommend research on alternative methods of use, moving away from the scenario of BCI as an alternative to a keyboard and mouse interface. Instead they focus on the use of BCIs for selecting objects or words from lists, movies or images. A new generation of interfaces for smart home is targeted, where objects light-up or are illuminated by projectors and can be selected by the user.

Preliminary results indicate that such interfaces have great promise and potentially high reliability.

A further article focuses on the possible use of passive BCI for healthy users (Zander & Kothe, 2011). Passive BCI refers to a BCI based on constant real-time monitoring of brain waves, not occasional monitoring as in the case of EEG headsets commonly used in hospitals. This approach is more about providing extra information about intentions, context and the emotional state of the user that can be processed by the system to complement the inputs. A good example of a possible use is in monitoring the attention of someone driving a car. Another is in the area of social robotics, where a "social" robot needs to develop an awareness of the emotional state of the person, so as to interact in a natural way.

The paper refers to possible users being people with a "temporary situational disability" such as an astronaut in a space-suit. Other examples are someone working in a virtual environment where the use lacks most of the usual intuitive channels for communication with the system.

The paper distinguishes between 3 kinds of BCI (active, reactive and passive) and points out that traditional BCI research considers only single brain inputs and not multiple brain inputs. These are commonly referred to as hybrid BCI systems to distinguish them from the default single input system. The main conclusion of the paper is to underline the usefulness of these 3 kinds of BCI as well as hybrid systems and they call for an expansion in the scope of research in the domain to reflect this.

In general experts seems to agree that the status of some AT is far more progressed than BCI; thus trying to substitute existing AT with BCI may lead research in the wrong direction. The path suggested by in the Future BNCI roadmap (Future BCNI, 2012) is this of BCI that is designed to cooperate with existing AT facilitating its control and use. This could be done either by BCI that helps in controlling already existing AT or by the development of systems working in combination with existing AT to augment the level of control. This model of BCI working complementary to already existing AT and in general other HCI technologies is often called Hybrid BCI (hBCI).

The Problems of BCI Illiteracy and Reliability

A recent article in IEEE Spectrum (Westly, 2011) refers to BCI as one of the most current areas for research in neuroscience. As a technology it has moved way beyond the demonstration phase and researchers are now focusing efforts on ways to improve it, and move application to new areas such as gaming and telecommunications, rather than the currently limited area of people with ALS or lock-in syndrome. Currently an important area for research aims at understanding differences in the abilities of people to use BCI systems.

It seems that somewhere between 20% and 30% of potential users are unable to use them. The reasons vary. Using them generally requires effort in learning and training to use them. External factors such as fatigue play a role. Scientists report cases where the simple act of observing the user causes accuracy to shoot from a range of 30% or 50% to 85% or 90%. Other physical factors make a difference such as facilitating co-adaptation of machine and brain. This is a question of more flexible SW systems that learn and adapt to the user, even as the users brain learns and adapts to the system.

Articles by Blanketz et al (2008) and Vidaurre & Blanketz (2010) discuss this issue which is often called "BCI illiteracy" or "BCI proficiency" and try to explain and solve it. In addition many experiments show that even persons that have good control of BCI devices demonstrate variable performance over time and days.

BCI applications and devices might seem a very attractive solution but there are still a number of issues to address in order to get them widely used. Addressing issues or BCI illiteracy and reliability is a cornerstone for further developments in the area. People buying a BCI device should be able to use it right of the box without experiencing problems that will discourage and frustrate them. Therefore issues of reliability and illiteracy should be high on the BCI research agenda.

BCI Usability and Device Design

Another challenge reported in the Future BNCI roadmap worth mentioning and discussing is the challenge of usability of such systems. Many of the systems until recently were requiring the use of gel in the head to apply electrodes. This doesn't seem an ideal solution if you intend to use a BCI device for controlling your TV or home entertainment systems. Not to mention that the cost and setup time of such systems was also discouraging and preventing for wide use and adoption.

Recent advances in the area include systems such as g.SAHARA (G.Tec, 2014b), Enobio (Starlab, 2011) and MindWave (Neurogadget, 2011) that do not require any gel to be used and claim that could be used right after unboxing them. In addition new electrodes were also recently developed that do not require washing up after use and their setup time is quite decent. However, some of the products in the market still seem to be quite difficult and uncomfortable to wear. Aesthetics is also playing a big role. People will not be inclined to use a system that makes them seem out of a sci-fi movie. On the other hand designs such as Mind Wave and Emotiv's EPOC (Emotiv, 2014) that look like headphones and pay attention to design might attract customers easier. There is however a compromise to make. Many of those systems not requiring gel and with appealing designs do not offer a good signal quality as gel based systems.

The role of aesthetics and setup time in BCI devices is going to be a decisive factor for adoption rates. Developers of such systems should have in mind these factors and try to solve problems of signal quality in devices that do not require gel to be used, look good and have minimum setup time. The goal is to have BCI devices working with the same effectiveness as gel based devices and in a "plug and play" style, so that people can use them with minimum effort and setup time. The future might see "plug 'n play" BCI devices in the form of headphones or caps being used for controlling all kinds of devices.

Where Europe Stands on BCI

European projects have already been funded in the area of BCI and there is already a cluster of 13 projects working on BCI technologies in Europe funded under the ICT Theme of the Seventh Framework Programme. The cluster is title H3 Research Cluster (European Commission, 2014) and includes 3 projects that started in 2008 (Brain (BRAIN, 2008), Tremor (European Commission, 2012b), and Tobi (TOBI: Tools for Brain-Computer Interaction, 2008)) with Tobi being the only one still running. 7 projects that started in 2010 (Asterics (ASTERICS, 2007), Brainable (Brainable, 2009), Decoder (DECODER, 2013), FBNCI (European Commission, 2012a), MindWalker (Mindwalker, 2009) and Mundus (MUNDUS, 2010)) and three that started just recently in 2011 (ABC (Instituto de Biomecánica, n.d.), BackHome (BackHome, n.d.), and Way).

Almost all of the projects are focusing on non-invasive BCI showing what is also presented in the book titled "'Brain Computer Interfaces: An international Assessment of Research and Development Trends" (Berger et. al., 2007) that Europe seems to be pioneering in non-invasive BCI. In particular it states that "*the WTEC panel found that the focus of BCI research throughout the world was decidedly uneven, with invasive BCIs almost exclusively cantered in North America, non-invasive BCI systems evolving primarily from European and Asian efforts, and the integration of BCIs and robotics systems championed by Asian research programs.*" Authors continue by saying "*Virtually all BCI research in Europe is non-invasive, attributable in large part to constraints and intimidations imposed by animal rights* organizations. BCI research in China appears to be almost exclusively non-invasive, though this reflects the relatively early stage of development of BCI research in that country."

The latter is also a conclusion in the Future BNCI roadmap (Future BCNI, 2012) where in the comparison between Europe and US research in the area of BCI the report states that

The European Union (EU) contains 27 member States. All of these member states of the European Union have different legal systems, regulations, procedures, traditions, infrastructures, per capita income, etc. The United States (US) contains 50 states. While the different states vary in many ways, the interstate differences in many factors are fairly minor. Many legal guidelines and regulations are established at a federal level, and there is a stronger tradition of interstate mobility and trade. Hence, in some ways, market analyses within the European Union must account for greater regional distinctions than analyses within the US. This is non-trivial and gives significant advantage to those launching medical devices in the US. However, if for the most part we are dealing with non-medical devices, the importance of this distinction will be reduced.

Europe seems to be involved primarily in research for non-invasive BCI. The main problem that poses a barrier for developing research in invasive BCI is the variety of legislation among member states regarding animal rights and the use of animals in medical research. Having said that we understand that unless significant legislative action is taken at a European level on issues of animal rights and medical research then Europe will still remain behind in invasive BCI research.

The Problem of Cost

A 2011 review of "Current trends in HW and SW for Brain-Computer Interfaces" (Brunner et. al., 2011) published in the Journal of Neural Engi-

neering describes the state of the art of research and commercial development in the field of BCI/BMI. The authors conclude that:

- The field of brain computer interface technology is in transition from isolated experiments and demonstrations to systematic research and commercial development.
- Barriers to progress include better integrated HW and SW systems, standardized interfaces, as well as procedures for certification, distribution and reimbursement.
- One of the biggest barriers for both further research and commercial development is the lack of low cost product grade HW and SW systems.

The cost issue in BCI is already being addressed. Some of the latest consumer BCI providers such as Emotiv provide non-invasive, no-gel-required, headset like EEG interfaces for use in gaming and research and general BCI applications. Their headset has 16 electrodes and retails for under $300 and there are already a number of developers working on developing applications for the device. However, this is just a first step and needs to be followed by other companies in the field while in parallel dealing with issues of reliability and usability already presented.

NON INVASIVE BCI: SUCCESS STORIES AND LESSONS FOR THE FUTURE

Consumer BCI by OCZ and Emotiv and the Idea of Platforms

OCZ Technology provides a single electrode EEG headband called NeuroSky that can distinguish two mental states and it sells for $50. This low cost gadget already enables disabled people to edit text (Neurogadget, 2011).

In December 2009 and to much acclaim Emotiv released its EPOC wireless headset. This retails for $299 and was developed with a variety of markets in mind, gaming, market research and clinical research on BCI systems.

The EPOC device has been described as a consumer EEG machine. It does not replace a full clinical EEG machine, but it totally changes the game. It is a cool looking easy to wear wireless headset with 16 sensors and no gel that retails at $299. Out of the box it can read 30 mental states divided into 3 rough categories - emotions, facial expressions and actions. It comes with 3 main software suites

- **Expressiv:** To recognize facial expressions
- **Affectiv:** To recognize emotions
- **Cognitiv:** Which can be trained to recognize thoughts

An application called "Neurokey" detects head and facial movements as well as thoughts and can be used to manipulate a virtual keyboard. The system can be used to interface not only a PC, but a wheelchair any other electronic device, games and toys such as toy helicopters, as well as smart-home devices to control household appliances, open and close curtains, use the remote controls of the TV.

Using the EPOC headset, it takes about out 8 seconds to train the system to recognize and respond to a single thought. Once a person's "thoughts" are trained, they can be mapped to any device, it is not necessary to retrain the system for every device. The system allows a measure of control over objects just by thinking about them. It also senses emotions and general cognitive states. A computer of machine can therefore respond not only to textual inputs from a user but from cognitive states such as anger, confusion or frustration.

The key to its success was based on directly tackling problems with EEG systems due to the fact that the surface of the brain is folded. This is important as the surface is where a lot of higher level brain events take place. The fact that no two brains are folded in the same way, not even those of identical twins, makes it hard to identify where specific neurological events originate within the brain. One of the early scientific accomplishments of Emotiv was to develop algorithms to "unfold" the brain allowing them to map more accurately where signals originate on the convoluted surface.

Founded in 2005, by 2007 Emotiv already had 5,000 pre-orders for its headset and rose $13.4M in a first round of venture capital in 2007. Tan Le the media friendly founder and President were profiled by Fast Company (Macsai, 2010). She has also spoken at TED. In a December 2008 profile in Inc. Magazine (Freedman, 2008), she explained that she wants "*to bring to computers and the Internet all the facial expressions and emotions that are so important in our interactions with each other.*" She has a strong and compelling vision of how she intends to "*create an industry that will revolutionize the whole framework of technology.*" She claims that "*we have an opportunity to revolutionize the way people interact with technology, … in 10 years or so, we will all go around in a world that will respond to our mental commands … fed by data wirelessly streaming in from a few freckle-size sensors in your scalp.*"

Emotiv is currently working with Boeing, IBM, Intel, Dell, MS, GM, Lockheed-Martin, and Siemens, France Telecom to develop real life applications of this type of BCI system. The system has been a boon for research and scientists are using it in clinical environments.

One new and burgeoning field of application is the field of neuromarketing. EmSense has developed an EEG headset aimed at the corporate market, which is used to understand the unconscious response of a consumer to an ad, a game or any other creative event. An early adopter of this technology was Coca-Cola who used it to fine tune its advertising for the super bowl in 2007.

Other companies in this space are Cyber Learning Technologies, OZT, Hitachi, Honda, ATR, Shimadzu, and Guger[1]. Intel is currently working on a "thought processor" microchip which when available will provide a competitive generally available computing platform for all kinds of BCI systems. Recent development projects include brain-to-mobile-phone and brain-to-twitter applications.

The success of the EPOC headset – a consumer EEG machine – and of its competitors lies not only on its low cost. The main reason is that they provide a platform where upon developers can develop applications for all kinds of needs. It might be applications for using a computer or a cell phone in case of users with a motor disability. It could also be an application for controlling and playing an already existing game or a game itself. In order to boost this kind of innovation, which is based on BCI devices working as platforms there might be a need for standardisation. Standards could be developed either for connecting and communicating with various ICT devices or also for developing API's so that applications could run on various devices.

Patient Ready BCI Systems by Guger Technologies

An Austrian biomedical device company called Guber Technologies (G.Tec, 2014a) or G.Tech launched its Intendix (Intendix, 2009) device at eBIT in 2010. They claim it is the first commercial, patient-ready BCI. It is intended for patients suffering from locked-in syndrome and other communication-impairing conditions. It allows users to input text by thought alone. It is based on standard EEG technology and retails at $12,000.

They describe it as an "EEG based personal spelling system" or as a "BCI speller". It recognizes "thought letters" so instead of typing words you think the letters that spell them. It requires some training, but the company claims that most subjects can use it reasonably well after only 10 minutes of training, and that a spelling rate of 5 to 10 characters per minute can be achieved by the majority of healthy users at their first trial.

It is intended for use by a care-giver of some-one with a severe handicap such as lock-in syndrome. For severely handicapped persons and patients close to the "locked-in state" the performance of such a BCI system depends on various factors such as training, visual faculty, concentration and cortical degeneration.

It can be used to control external devices. This is achieved using an extension tool called "extendiX" running on a separate computer that controls other devices/applications such as TV, music, assistive robots and games. The *extendiX* tool receives commands from *intendiX* via the UDP and starts or executes the corresponding application.

The user must wear a special EEG cap. The company claims it is comfortable to wear and easy to clean and that unlike many clinical EEG systems the electrodes do not require any special skin preparation. They have also developed a dry EEG electrode system called "Sahara". G.Tech offers an annual award (The Annual BCI Award, 2009) for progress in the area of BCI.

Typical examples of BCI devices intended for persons with disability have been recently launched in the market by pioneering European companies. An example of such a device requires minimum training and can be used to communicate with others. Usability, setup time and reliability are key issues to the success of non-invasive BCI. In this case the device is customized for patients and needs no special configuration apart from some minutes of training to be used.

The BCI as a UD Phenomenon

The brain computer interface is a form of UD or Universal Design solution that could ultimately provide an alternative to traditional interfaces, not only for disabled people, but for able bodied people and for those who have temporary situational disabilities such as dives and astronauts.

The potential market for these systems is huge. Typing is often a very inefficient way to input data into a machine. Why use a keyboard or a mouse when you can simply 'think' the text onto the screen?

The market for BCI devices is not limited to the replacement of the keyboard and the mouse. It is much larger than that. It is also the basis for social IT, or information technology that is sensitive to mood, expression, context or emotion. In this sense it has a key role to play in the development of social computing, more natural user-friendly, empathetic interfaces.

Commercial progress is also being made on BCI devices intended for mass consumer markets. These technologies are based on the same ones used in hospitals and clinical environments, but are much simpler and far less costly and free of the need for expert supervision by experts or care-givers. The initial drive was in the gaming industry. In traditional games, the game is blind to the user, their size and shape, their emotional state, the expression on their face.

BCI need not be limited to humans, they are already used in experimental research and may one day be applied to working animals in the military, police force or rescue services, as well as pets.

There is a tendency to dismiss claims by groups involved in the trans-humanist or the singularity movement as well as by those who pursue missions related to bionics and life-extension. This is understandable in the sense that their claims are too radical for most people, due to the consequences they have for religious feelings or a sense of what it is to be human. It is not necessary to get embroiled in this debate.

Considerable advances have already been achieved, while efforts continue in pursuit of ambitious BCI research agendas, which can have enormous impact in the field of e-access/e-assistive technologies. Relevant areas for examination include applications of new micro-electronics, computing, power sources and energy harvesting, sensors and electrodes (fractal antennae and patch clamps for ion channels) as well as brain modelling and simulation. Progress in all of these domains

is being made with only minimal concern for the field of e-access or e-assistive technologies. Therefore, it might be useful to encourage and motivate between teams working in these fields with teams and projects working in e-access and e-assistive technologies

The Future Of Non-Invasive Direct-Access Technologies

A number of low cost, easy to use EEG devices are available for prices such as $2999, $299 and $59. These can be used 'out of the box' and basic functions are available with only a few minutes of 'training'. In many cases developers' kits are also available. This means that a much larger population of researchers can now contribute to research in this domain. The barrier to entry is low. It is no longer confined to clinical environments. It no longer requires the use of expensive equipment or help from hospital technicians. This has opened up a whole range of new applications outside of clinical and hospital environments, in particular in the games industry and in market research. It is likely that most of the easy results have all been found. Now there is a need for new insights.

Non-Invasive Direct-Access Technologies: We can see a need for more mature systems based on standards and norms that enable information sharing and the systematic accumulation of knowledge created by a critical mass of activity. There are however various challenges that remain for the further development of non-invasive direct access technologies and there is a need to identify ways to support research in these domains. Possible suggestions could be:

- More RTD and innovation projects
- Community building and information sharing
- Hack-fests, competitions, prizes and tournaments
- A combination of all of the above

Invasive BCI, Implants, and Neuroscience

Braingate (BrainGate, 2013) has recently developed an implantable neural interface that enables "intuitive" or thought based control of computers, wheelchairs, advanced prosthetics including electro-stimulation systems that restore movement to muscles in the wake of injury or damage to the spinal cord. BrainGate is under development since 2002 and provides a combination of hardware and software that directly senses electrical signals in the brain that control movement. The device — a baby-aspirin-sized array of electrodes — is implanted in the cerebral cortex (the outer layer of the brain) and records its signals; computer algorithms then translate the signals into digital instructions that may allow people with paralysis to control external devices.

Progress by this company is significant in the sense that it has been relatively successful in supplying implants that remain in the body of the patient and retain their functionality for a long period of time. A recent article in the Journal of neural Engineering reported how a woman with lock-in syndrome was able to use it for more than 1,000 days.

One of the main applications for invasive BCI is the control of devices through it. However, given the evolution of smart environments and devices invasive BCI could give them an opportunity to person with lock-in syndrome, quadriplegia and similar severe motor impairments to control their environment effectively through their brains.

Since a lot of the applications of invasive BCI are going to be presented under the next chapter of neuroprosthetics in the following paragraphs we are going to focus on challenges related to BCI form and neuroscience in general.

The Virtual Brain

The EEG machine is the workhorse of neuroscience. It provides the basis for most non-invasive techniques. Emotiv, a leader in the development of commercial uses of EEG devices speculates that the headsets they sell today may one day be replaced by speck-like devices embedded in the scalp. Maybe one day we will all have electrodes implanted in the same way as some people get hair implants today.

Surgical implants are worth mentioning as they are used not only as an assistive device but as a diagnostic aid.

One of the big areas for progress is the area of real time fMRI. The machinery is very bulky but the spatial and temporal resolution of brain imagines is improving all the time enabling scientists to see what is happening in exactly what part of the brain as part of a given cognitive process.

In a talk at TED2008 Christopher de Charms (Christopher deCharms, 2008) explains that whereas brain imaging used to take days or months, and it can now be done in a few milliseconds, and that we are now in the era of real-time fMRI (functional Magnetic Resonance Imaging) scanning. In the same way that feedback enables babies to learn to control their own bodies, for example by moving their hands and observe where the hand moves, they learning how to control their movements. Chronic pain sufferers have been able to control their own pain, by controlling associated brain activities that they can visualize using real-time fMRI. This has been successful in 44% to 64% of chronic pain patients.

Perhaps the exciting new tool is that of simulation based research. Experimenting on the brain of either animals or humans is very difficult. Apart from regulatory issues and ethical concerns, there are practical problems of noise, working with small delicate tissues, dealing with noise, dealing with reproducibility of conditions. The latest approach is to build a complete, accurate working model of the brain and do virtual experiments on the model. Future BCI advances are expected to accelerate even more after successful modelling of the human brain. This is not the same as computational neuroinformatics, it is a new area called simulation based research.

Moore's Law and the Evolution in Studying the Brain

Jeff Hawkins in his 2003 TED talk (Jeff Hawkins, 2008) stressed that the 30 billion cells that make up the brains are highly structured, with oft repeated modules, much simpler than they appear at first sight. This view is born out by Henry Markum of the Blue Brain project who emphasizes how the same or some structures are repeated over and over again about a billion times in the neocortex of the brain. The upshot of this is that despite its complexity, the brain does have a lot of structure and the links between structure and function are becoming increasingly clear. Applying this understanding however requires building very complex models and is pushing the frontiers of computing.

The simulation of a single neuron requires running about 200 separate simulations. The human brain contains about 1 billion neurons connected through about 1 trillion synapses. Just storing this data would require 200 Petabytes. A Peta byte is 1 byte followed by 15 zeros. Put another way, Avatar the move used up about 1 Petabyte of data. According to Henry Markim this is about 200 times more storage than in all of Google's servers put together, and running a full bran simulation for a year would generate an electricity bill of a about $1 Billion. In 2008 Wired Magazine (Wired, 2008) explained a Petabyte as the amount of data processed by Google servers every 72 minutes.

Applying Moore's law however, Markum expects to be able to affordably simulate a full, bottom up model of the human brain by 2018. Ray Kurzweil disagrees and thinks that it will take until 2019. In any case, the best minds close to the project seem to think that a full human brain simulation will be achieved before 2020.

Just as in the case of the human genome project, robotics, automation, information science and modelling, all play a role in accelerating rates of progress. Already patch clamp ("Patch clamp", n.d.) robots automate the work of measuring real data from real neurons in real time. This enables scientists to parameterize and validate their models of individual neurons. Already 30 years of gathered data has been validated by 6 months' work using robots. These technologies are now used to validate models at single neuron, intra-neuron and neuronal system levels. It used to take a Ph.D. about 3 years to model a single neuron, but most of this work has now been automated and models for systems of up to 10,000 neurons can be routinely developed.

The Blue Brain Project and Potential Ethical Issues

So called because of the involvement of IBM and the use of the Blue Gene super-computer, the Blue-Brain (The Blue Brain Project - EFPL, 2014) project led by Henry Markram of the Brain-Mind Institute at Lausanne in Switzerland, intends to develop a bottom-up working model of the human brain. It started in 2005 and expects to achieve its goals by 2018.

This virtual brain will provide neuroscientists with a whole new tool for understanding the brain and neurological disease. So far the project has been a resounding success. Even if the project achieves all it sets out to achieve, many more things will need to be done. This is why Blue Brain recently joined with other 12 partners to propose the Human Brain Project (The Blue Brain Project - EPFL, 2013) a very large 10 year project that will pursue these other goals. The new consortium has just been awarded a € 1.4M EC grant to formulate a detailed proposal. The EU decision to launch the project is expected in 2012.

It may be of interest to see with this group how preliminary results or sub-models of the brain could help accelerate development of both invasive and non-invasive BCIs for example to help design and improve low cost, high performance EEG headsets.

As a first step, the project succeeded in simulating a rat cortical column. This neuronal network, the size of a pinhead, recurs repeatedly in the cortex. A rat's brain has about 100,000 columns of in the order of 10,000 neurons each. Humans of course have much more. A human cortex may have as many as two million columns, each with about 100,000 neurons each.

By 2011 the Blue Brain project had already succeeded in modelling a neo-cortical column in a 2 week old rat-brain. This 2mm long by 0.5 mm in diameter portion of brain tissue corresponds to a functional module that is repeated very many times in the neocortex of the rat-brain, so it is an important first step towards the modelling of the whole neocortex of the rat. Progress is happening fast and the team expects to complete a full simulation of the rat brain sometime in 2013.

The team is already in discussion with a Japanese company that wants to employ the final result in a mechanical toy rat. It does not really matter if the simulation can fit inside a toy, as most of it can be run in the cloud.

In an article entitled "Visions and Realities in Converging Technologies – exploring the technology base for convergence" (Beckert, Blumel, & Friedewald, 2007) the authors remark that "*plans to simulate and manipulate brain processes – if realized successfully – could directly affect our concept of human self and identity.*" This hints at a number of interesting ethical and philosophical issues that may interfere with the broader uptake of these technologies and may be worth addressing in the course of future research programmes. There are possible analogies with trends in the area of prosthetics as outlined in other sections of this book.

The Human Connectome Project and Imaging Technologies

The Human Connectome Project (Human Connectome Project, n.d.) of HCP is a major initiative to understand the complete details of neural connectivity. The first major goal is to construct a map of the complete structural and functional neural connections in vivo. A further goal is to understand the genetic basis for brain anatomy and variation across individuals. Progress is accelerating due to improvements in the imaging technologies. It is now possible to image the whole human brain in less than half a second

Given the progress in ambitious programs such as the Human Brain Project and the developments in virtual reality technologies it is possible to see these areas helping each other in the future. Researchers in neuroscience of the future might be using virtual reality systems and environments representing the simulating the human brain. Such a development will definitely boost even more neuroscience and related fields BCI included.

Problems and Progress in Neural Implants and their Material

Placing neural implants in the parts of the brain that are used for hearing, talking, seeing or for the control of different muscle groups, it is possible to identify the intention if the user to see certain images, says certain things or move certain groups of muscles.

These brain outputs can be used as inputs to neuroengineering systems intended to control computers, wheelchairs and prosthetic limbs and other machinery, as well as directly control muscles of the body based on implanted electrical stimulation devices.

There are many problems in the sense that a part of the brain containing millions of neurons is replaced by about 50 electrodes. When people move, their brain moves too, creating a tendency for a neural prosthesis to slip and for established contacts to change. Despite these difficulties and the very small number of people involved in these experiments, progress has been startling and many issues that seemed impossible or unlikely to solve, have proven to be not so bad at all.

There are many ways in which brain circuits can be improved. Researches have recently developed nanotechnology systems for isolating neurons. Others have created the first artificial neural network using DNA, while others have developed the elements of microcircuits based on blood that can be easily implanted in humans. These problems bring to the front a whole new area of research related with invasive BCI having to do with the materials used for implants. Future developments in the area could help significantly in the adoption and uptake of invasive BCI systems since they could provide safer and more reliable solutions.

REFERENCES

Annual, B. C. I. Award. (2009). *bci-award.com*. Retrieved March 8, 2014, from http://www.bci-award.com/

ASTERICS. (2007). *AsTeRICS: Homepage*. Retrieved from http://www.asterics.eu/index.php?id=2

BackHome. (n.d.). *BackHome | BackHome*. Retrieved March 8, 2014, from http://www.backhome-fp7.eu/

Beckert, B., Blumel, C., & Friedewald, M. (2007). Exploring the technology base for convergence. *Visions and Realities in Converging Technologies*, *20*(4), 375–394.

Berger, C. Gerhardt, McFarland, Principe, Soussou, … Tresco. (2007). *International Assessment of Research and Development in Brain-Computer Interfaces. WTEC Panel Report*. Retrieved from http://www.wtec.org/bci/BCI-finalreport-10Oct2007-lowres.pdf

Blankertz, B., Losch, F., Krauledat, M., Dornhege, G., Curio, G., & Muller, K. (2008). The Berlin Brain--Computer Interface: Accurate Performance From First-Session in BCI-Naïve Subjects. *IEEE Transactions on Biomedical Engineering*. doi:10.1109/TBME.2008.923152

Blue Brain Project (EFPL). (2014, February 27). *Bluebrain | EPFL*. Retrieved March 8, 2014, from http://bluebrain.epfl.ch/

Blue Brain Project (EPFL). (2013, February 6). *The Human Brain Project | EPFL*. Retrieved March 8, 2014, from http://jahia-prod.epfl.ch/site/bluebrain/op/edit/page-52741.html

BRAIN. (2008, September 1). *EU project BRAIN - Brain-project.org*. Retrieved March 8, 2014, from http://www.brain-project.org/

Brainable. (2009). *Home*. Retrieved March 8, 2014, from http://www.brainable.org/

BrainGate. (2013). *BrainGate - Home*. Retrieved March 8, 2014, from http://www.braingate2.org/

Brunner, P., Bianchi, L., Guger, C., Cincotti, F., & Schalk, G. (2011). Current trends in hardware and software for brain–computer interfaces (BCIs). *Journal of Neural Engineering*, *8*(2), 025001. doi:10.1088/1741-2560/8/2/025001 PMID:21436536

deCharms, C. (2008, February). *Christopher deCharms: A look inside the brain in real time | Talk Video | TED*. [Video file]. Retrieved from http://www.ted.com/talks/christopher_decharms_scans_the_brain_in_real_time

DECODER. (2013). *DECODER*. Retrieved March 8, 2014, from http://www.decoderproject.eu/

Emotiv. (2014). *Emotiv | EEG System | Electroencephalography*. Retrieved March 8, 2014, from http://www.emotiv.com/index.php

European Commission. (2012a). *European Commission : CORDIS : Projects : FUTURE BNCI*. Retrieved March 16, 2014, from http://cordis.europa.eu/projects/rcn/93832_en.html

European Commission. (2012b). *European Commission : CORDIS : Projects : TREMOR*. Retrieved March 16, 2014, from http://cordis.europa.eu/projects/rcn/87753_en.html

European Commission. (2014). *Digital Agenda for Europe - European Commission*. Retrieved March 16, 2014, from http://ec.europa.eu/digital-agenda/life-and-work

Freedman, D. (2008, December 1). *Reality Bites -- Emotiv -- Mind Reading Device | Inc.com*. Retrieved March 8, 2014, from http://www.inc.com/magazine/20081201/reality-bites.html

Future, B. C. N. I. (2012). *Future BCNI: A roadmanp for future directions in Brain / Neuronal Computer Interaction Research*. Retrieved from http://future-bnci.org/images/stories/Future_BNCI_Roadmap.pdf

Hawkins. (2008, February). *Jeff Hawkins: How brain science will change computing | Talk Video | TED*. [Video file]. Retrieved from http://www.ted.com/talks/jeff_hawkins_on_how_brain_science_will_change_computing

Human Connectome Project. (n.d.). *Human Connectome Project | Mapping the human brain connectivity*. Retrieved March 8, 2014, from http://www.humanconnectomeproject.org/

Instituto de Biomecánica. (n.d.). *Instituto de Biomecánica*. Retrieved March 8, 2014, from http://abcproject.ibv.org/

Intendix. (2009). *intendix.com*. Retrieved March 8, 2014, from http://www.intendix.com/

Macsai, D. (2010, March 30). *The Most Influential Women in Technology 2010 - Tan Le | Fast Company | Business + Innovation*. Retrieved March 8, 2014, from http://www.fastcompany.com/3017230/women-in-tech-2010/the-most-influential-women-in-technology-2010-tan-le

Mak, J. N., Arbel, Y., Minett, J. W., McCane, L. M., Yuksel, B., Ryan, D., & Erdogmus, D. (2011). Optimizing the P300-based brain-computer interface: current status, limitations and future directions. *Journal of Neural Engineering*. doi:10.1088/1741-2560/8/2/025003 PMID:21436525

Millan, J., Rupp, R., Muller-Putz, G. R., Murray-Smith, R., Giugliemma, C., Tengermann, M., & Vidaurre, C. (2010). Combining brain? computer interfaces and assistive technologies: state-of-the-art and challenges. *Frontiers in Neuroscience*. Retrieved from http://journal.frontiersin.org/Journal/10.3389/fnins.2010.00161/abstract

Mindwalker. (2009). *MINDWALKER Project Portal? mindwalker-project*. Retrieved March 8, 2014, from https://mindwalker-project.eu/

MUNDUS. (2010). *Home*. Retrieved March 8, 2014, from http://www.mundus-project.eu/

Neurogadget. (2011, April 22). *Video: Text Editor for Disabled People Using NeuroSky Mindset | Neurogadget.com*. Retrieved March 8, 2014, from http://neurogadget.com/2011/04/22/video-text-editor-for-disabled-people-using-neurosky-mindset/1939

Patch clamp. (n.d.). *Wikipedia, the free encyclopedia*. Retrieved March 8, 2014, from http://en.wikipedia.org/wiki/Patch_clamp

Starlab. (2011). *Starlab - Living Science*. Retrieved March 8, 2014, from http://starlab.es/products/enobio

Tec, G. (2014a). *Home - g.tec - Guger Technologies*. Retrieved March 8, 2014, from http://www.gtec.at/

Tec, G. (2014b). *g.SAHARA - active dry EEG electrode system: Perform recordings without gel*. Retrieved March 8, 2014, from http://www.gtec.at/Products/Electrodes-and-Sensors/g.SAHARA-Specs-Features

TOBI. Tools for Brain-Computer Interaction. (2008). *Welcome to TOBI | TOBI: Tools for Brain-Computer Interaction*. Retrieved March 8, 2014, from http://www.tobi-project.org/

Vidaurre, C., & Blankertz, B. (2010). Towards a Cure for BCI Illiteracy. *Brain Topography*. doi:10.1007/s10548-009-0121-6 PMID:19946737

Westly, E. (2011, June 17). *Fixing the Brain-Computer Interface - IEEE Spectrum*. Retrieved March 8, 2014, from http://spectrum.ieee.org/biomedical/bionics/fixing-the-brain-computer-interface

Wired. (2008, June 23). *The Petabyte Age: Because More Isn't Just More? More Is Different*. Retrieved March 8, 2014, from http://www.wired.com/science/discoveries/magazine/16-07/pb_intro

Zander, T. O., & Kothe, C. (2011). Towards passive brain-computer interfaces: applying brain-computer interface technology to human-machine systems in general. *Journal of Neural Engineering*. doi:10.1088/1741-2560/8/2/025005 PMID:21436512

KEY TERMS AND DEFINITIONS

Brain Computer Interface: A brain–computer interface (BCI), often called a mind-machine interface(MMI), or sometimes called a direct neural interface or a brain–machine interface (BMI), is a direct communication pathway between the brain and an external device.

Brain Machine Interface: A brain–computer interface (BCI), often called a mind-machine interface(MMI), or sometimes called a direct neural interface or a brain–machine interface (BMI), is a direct communication pathway between the brain and an external device.

EEG: Electroencephalography (EEG) is the recording of electrical activity along the scalp.

Implants: An implant is a medical device manufactured to replace a missing biological structure, support a damaged biological structure, or enhance an existing biological structure.

Invasive BCI: BCI that requires surgical placement of sensors in the brain.

Neural Implants: Brain implants, often referred to as neural implants, are technological devices that connect directly to a biological subject's brain - usually placed on the surface of the brain, or attached to the brain's cortex.

Neuroscience: Neuroscience is the scientific study of the nervous system.

Non-Invasive BCI: BCI that does not require surgical placement of sensors in the brain.

ENDNOTES

[1]   Provider of a system called "Intendix"

Chapter 5
Advanced Prosthetics, Neuroprosthetics, and Artificial Limbs

ABSTRACT

An area of research that is very close to invasive BCI presented earlier is the area of neuroprosthetics. This involves the use of invasive BCI systems aiming to control prosthetic devices (i.e. an artificial hand) or help in rehabilitation of human senses such as seeing and hearing. The most well-known advances in neuroprosthetics are in the area of seeing, the case of the artificial retina, the case of cochlear implants for hearing, and the use of thought-controlled artificial limbs. Building upon knowledge and developments presented in the previous chapters about BCI and robotics, this chapter combines these technologies and discusses advances and challenges to be met in the areas of advanced prosthetics, neuroprosthetics, and artificial limbs.

PROGRESS IN NEUROPROSTHETICS

Aside from the spectacular and media friendly cases of neuroprosthetics applied to hearing and sight, there is a vast array of treatments available for control of pain, incontinence, the restoration of movement and feeling to limbs, the restoration of smell, taste and speech. Progress has also been made in the area of controlling spasms and tremors due to conditions such as Parkinson's or epilepsy, as well as memory loss due to brain trauma or Alzheimer's.

Nearly 1 million people in the United States are affected by Parkinson's disease. It is expected that Alzheimer's disease will affect more than 107 million people worldwide by the year 2050. These two diseases alone indicate that there is already a large market for cognitive neural prosthetics. Other relevant markets correspond to traumatic brain injury. More than 1.4 million people in the United States suffer traumatic brain injury (Centers for Disease Control and Prevention, 2010). Another market is speech disorder. We have said very little about speech disorders in this book, but in the US alone approximately 7.5 million people in the United States have trouble speaking,

DOI: 10.4018/978-1-4666-6130-1.ch005

in many cases this can be attributed to aphasias ("Aphasia", n.d.) which are treatable in principle using advanced neural prosthetics. In many cases the cause of motor control or speech difficulties is stroke. This corresponds to a market of more than 6.5 million people (Rothwell, 2011) in the United States.

All off this will benefit in future from advances in the electrodes that interface with the brain, flexible and light biocompatible electronic circuits, as well as power sources, technologies for harvesting energy from the chemistry, natural movement or electricity of the boy, as well as the passage of air over specially designed surfaces, not to mention communications using wireless Body Area Networks.

A lot of progress in Neuroprosthetics in the past relied on experiments using monkeys. It may be more difficult to do this in future as many countries are considering banning the use of primates for this kind of work. Work is done using rats, cats and other animals. It may be useful to develop new experimental techniques to advance progress in this field.

Artificial Limbs

Dean Kamen is probably best known as the inventor of the Segway. Although the Segway was not as successful as many would have hoped it has provide a platform for mobile telepresence robotics. But that is not his first major venture and according to his own estimation not his greatest. Kamen's first venture was Autosyringe (Assistivetech.net, 2010) an automatic drug dispensing device that became the first real insulin pump. He created a sophisticated all-terrain wheelchair called iBot (Independence Technology, L.L.C, 2001) and has made important contributions in fields such as water purification and solar power. He also invented a compressed-air device that can shoot soldiers and security officers from the ground to the top of tall inaccessible buildings.

In 2005 Kamen was called upon by DARPA to get involved in their recently launched Revolutionizing Prosthetics (DARPA, n.d.) program. The goal of this program was to fund the development of two advanced prosthetic arms. One four year contract costing $30.4M, completed in 2009 developed a fully functioning neurally controlled prosthetic arm using experimental technology. The second contract was awarded to Deka Research and Development (DEKA, 2009) owned by Dean Kamen. The amount was $18.1M and it had two years in which to develop an advanced prosthesis for amputees that would be immediately available so they could just strap it on and go. A functioning prototype was demonstrated (Saenz, 2009) in 2007 and the arm is known generally known as the Luke arm in honour of life-like prosthetic worn by Luke Skywalker in Star wars.

It was featured at the D6 meeting of All Things Digital held in May 2008 and received a lot of publicity at technology meetings all around the world. By summer of 2009 it started clinical trials and will probably be commercially available soon.

Kamen once remarked that whereas in the 1600s soldiers had muskets and cannon for shooting at each other and when they lost a limb they were given a lump of wood with a hook on the end, nowadays they have F16s and billion dollar stealth planes but that when they lose a limb things are not much better for them today than it was back then.

Most prosthetic limbs have only 1 to 3 degrees of freedom. Most wearers of a prosthetic limb get over the shock of limb loss after one to two years and stop wearing the limb. The reason is that it gets hot and slippery it is not comfortable or convenient to wear. This is even worse for people who work out of doors in the sunshine for example. The limb may absorb so much heat that it becomes impossible to wear, the same for using it in the winter cold. In most cases the wearer just brings it back in a bag after one or two years of use, because the limited functionality it provides is not worth the trouble associated with wearing it. Such issues need to be addressed in future research for artificial limbs to be more successful.

A real human hand has 22 degrees of freedom. The Luke arm is revolutionary in the sense that it has 18 degrees of freedom. The wearer can grasp delicate objects, pour themselves a drink or eat soup with a spoon. The wearer controls the limb using pads placed under the feet and around the shoulder.

By comparison one of the most advanced commercially available prosthetic limbs is the iLimb (Touch Bionics, 2014) by Touch Bionics. It does not yet do arms, but it has a whole hand with 5 degrees of freedom. The publicity features someone wearing it and able to using a camera. It uses myoelectric sensors that pick up nerve signals in the muscles for control.

A prosthetic arm or limb with sufficient degrees of freedom provided to young persons injured in an accident can serve them for decades. This enables them to re-enter the work-force with little or no disadvantage. There is a need for a more detailed cost benefit analysis on the benefits of raising the bar on minimal levels of performance for modern prosthetic limbs intended to assist the users and re-include them in the normal tasks of living and working. There is also the need to identify which areas of progress in prosthetic limbs could achieve better benefits (22 degrees of freedom? touch and feeling? force feedback? life-like skin including temperature control? the ability to produce goose bumps?)

Direct Thought Control of Prosthetic Devices

One of the current frontiers of research on advanced prosthetics is on direct brain control of the prosthetic device. The ultimate goal is for the wearer to think a movement and for the movement to happen. This is still at an experimental stage, but progress is being made very rapidly.

In this sense advanced prosthetic devices lie at a point of convergence between technologies for robotic motion and control as well as neural interfaces and brain-machine or brain-computer interfaces.

Though controlled machinery will be discussed in more detail in the next section, we refer to some highlights in terms of recent achievement by researchers. Control is not a one way street. To achieve fine control of a prosthetic limb a user would benefit greatly from feedback in the form of feeling or a sense of touch.

In 2001 scientists at Duke University (Duke University, 2011) centre for neuroengineering demonstrated what they claim is the world's first BMBI of Brain Machine Brain Interface. The user was a monkey and it was able to manipulate virtual objects by thought alone. The interface was two way, not only could the virtual arm obey the monkey but provided feedback on the object being touched. The monkey was able to select the object with the desired texture. The usual method of feedback is visual in that the monkey or human user of BMI devices can usually see what it is doing. Feedback is essential to learning how to use the device to start with. I this case feedback was provided not only visually but through a sense of feeling provided by the artificial limb. The scientists in charge say that they expect to be able to use this as an e-access technology for quadriplegic and people who have lock-in syndrome in the next few years.

In 2006 a British woman was claimed to be the world's first person (Fleming, 2007) fitted with a brain controlled bionic arm after losing her arm in a motorcycle accident. In 2007 she scored another first when she received an upgrade as surgeons partially restored a sense of touch by virtue of a technique called TMR or Targeted Muscle Reinnervation.

Independently an Italian-Swedish group seems to have made similar claims that year. Things seem to be moving very fast as hardly a month goes by when some new advance is not announced in the area of sense of feeling and use of sensory feedback for motor control of prosthetic devices. One of the most recent announcements came from Sheffield University where a non-disabled professor gained controlled of a robotic arm by linking it up to the nerves of this arm, using a two way control and sensory feedback system,.

Many projects big and small are currently underway. In 2011 Trevor Prideaux from the UK commissioned his own prosthetic forearm with a built in mobile phone, in this case a Nokia C7. The arm was not a smart-arm but it is clear that some users are anxious to be actively involved in the development of the technology. One of the more ambitions or grand challenge project is the Walk Again Project to develop a fully mind-controlled exoskeleton for paralyzed patients led by Duke University of the US.

Now there are many advanced prosthetic hands, Fluidhand developed at the University of Karlsruhe, Pro-Digits, X-Finger and X-Thumbs by Touch bionics, in addition to the iLimb hand. There are the H2, C5M, C6M, ELU-2, DLR and EH1 hands. There is the Dexhand, the Ng hand, the Dart hand, the Lara hand, the Yokoi hand, the Harada hand, the Sheffield arm and hand, the Robonaut arm and hand, the Delft arm and hand. A regularly updated list of prosthetic or robotic arms and hands is provided here ("The best five anthropomorphic robotic hands/arms", n.d.).

More recently Touch Bionics has produced a prosthetic skin that is intended to restore a sense of feeling. Much more remains to be done. According to one report (Pappas, 2011) on advanced prosthetic limbs for every 10 people working on nerve control of motors only 1 is working on sensory feedback. The big area for innovation in the future is on the use of sensory feedback for motor control of prosthetic limbs.

One model for restoring movement is to make many 100s, 1000s, or millions of connections between the human nervous system and the object being controlled. Even with very few connections of the order of 10 or 100 it is possible to achieve good results. These are intermediate steps on the path to perfection are very useful for people with lock-in syndrome, quadriplegia or some other form of paralysis.

THE FUTURE OF PROSTHETICS

Given the evolution of prosthetics and the latest advancements in thought controlled prosthetic devices one might see the possibilities for the future of prosthetic devices

In the future, prosthetic devices will increasingly embed intelligence. They will match with those of the wearers other (usually natural) limb in terms of weight, strength and other physical properties. They will be controlled directly by the user's brain, rather than independently by the limb system itself. They will provide touch feedback as was demonstrated by Prof. Warwick in his work with Sheffield hospital in 2011.

Cochlear Implants

In December 2011 Helga Velroyen, an engineer living with hearing loss for nearly 4 years and author of a website called Hack and Hear (Hack and hear, 2012), gave a talk on bionic ears (Velroyen, 2011) at the 28C3 meeting of CCC (CCC-TV, 2014) – the Chaos Computer Club in Berlin. She described the state of the art of hearing aids and cochlear implants, her frustration at the slow progress of technology as well as the work of a small community of hearing aid hackers trying to improve things, as well as the efforts of a community of self-tuners. A recent overview of hearing fitting and tuning is provided on the website of the Hearing Review(Abrams, Edwards, Valentine, & Fitz, 2011), but the testimony of a Helga Velroyen is especially useful as she is herself has recently started using a hearing aid.

Hearing loss is a complex phenomenon in that when hearing declines it does so to a different extent for different frequency bands. In its simplest form the device amplifies different frequency components of the sound entering the ear, each in a different way, making it more audible. This is of course only possible with digital hearing aids. They incorporate tiny computers that carry out real time signal processing of natural sound reaching a person's ear. These computers not only amplify different frequency bands, but where a person has lost hearing in a band or range of frequencies, some systems are able to shift the frequency to an audible range or even compress the whole signal into the restrict range where the person is able to hear.

This is possible in principle but it seems that only one brand of hearing aid (phonak) (Phonak Hearing Systems, n.d.) actually provides this function. People wearing hearing aids experience many issues. They need to filter out foreground and background sounds, maybe focusing on one or the other, they need to eliminate or reduce unwanted sounds such as traffic, or sounds from the body created by simple acts of eating, breathing or the flow of blood. They need to eliminate feedback loops created in certain situations, such as when the ears are covered, when using a phone, when someone comes too close or tries to whisper in the ear. They need to tell the direction from which a sound is coming. This is helpful to avoid hazards as well as for picking out voices in a crowd. One of the issues is resistance to humidity, important to allow people to go swimming, engage in sports, or live in rainy countries, even places that are hot and humid.

Cochlear Implant as a Platform

Because everyone is different, the main process of fitting a hearing aid, the tuning of the aid to the specific nature of individual hearing loss, which may only affect one ear or may be different in each, is still very complex, far more complex than getting a pair of glasses for example. It generally involves a specialist who makes an initial guess at how the hearing aid should be parameterized. The wearer then uses it for a while and notes what bothers them. A new meeting is scheduled with the specialist who then makes another guess at what is a good set of parameters. The wearer then uses it for a while and the whole process repeats over several times. The process is long and frustrating. It may need to be repeated on a regular basis due to a gradual deterioration in the hearing ability of the user over time. For this reason some people have started to get interested in self-tuning, a DIY approach, where they do the tuning themselves and forgo the frustration and long-waits involved with a specialist.

In the UK an organization called self-programmer, already exists that markets and sells self-programmable hearing aids. An Australian company called Australia Hears has recently launched a new high performance, low cost hearing aid technology that users can tune themselves using their laptop or home PC. The technology was developed with help of the Bionic Ears Institute (Bionics Institute, n.d.) and prototyping was funded by a small company's grant of €40,000 Australian dollars. The company estimates that 1 in 6 Australians could benefit from the device and plan to sell it for between €800 and €1,200 per ear.

It might be useful to exploit the opportunities of a movement towards the hearing aid as a platform, served by a community of programmes and tuners that make available apps for use by those with hearing difficulty. Most people suffer from hearing loss at some stage in their life. Just as happens with eye-sight many people get by without feeling an urgent need for a hearing aid until their condition reaches a threshold of criticality. The market for such devices may be much larger than anyone imagines. Using the cochlear implants as a platform would encourage the development of communities using crowd-souring, open-standards, living labs or R+DIY models for the organization of research on this topic. Furthermore, the application of a combination of machine-learning and brain-reading techniques to enable continuous auto-adaptation of the hearing aid, remains a potential alternative.

The Variety in Hearing Devices Usage and Their Cost

The situation is actually more complex than that described above, because a good set of parameters are only good in a given situation. Hearing aids tend to have programmable settings allowing the user to switch between one program and another for optimal performance. The memory of hearing aids is limited however and so hearing aids typically only have about 5 programs available. In her talk to CCC Helga Velroyen expressed frustration at this and suggested that with the use of wireless or advanced mobile technology it should not be necessary to store programs on the hearing aid itself, but remotely.

To put this in perspective note that if hearing aids provided by Australia Hears cost between €800 and €1,200 per ear, high end ear plugs for use with devices such as the iPhone can cost up to almost $1,000. These are made for great comfort and include features such as ambient noise cancellation. In June 2011 Cool Hunting (Cool Hunting, n.d.) featured miniature moulded earplugs called Ultimate Ears (Ultimate Ears, n.d.) aimed at professional musicians. They need to hear their music in great detail, despite the sound on stage or the roar of the crowd. They also need to receive messages sent to them by their stage managers, security or sound engineers. The top of the line set of earplugs called UE18 sells for up to €1,350 and incorporate 6 separate speakers in each ear. The cost of high end ear-phones for use by gaming or music enthusiasts can go up to almost $10,000.

Costs in cochlear implants and more importantly on devices suitable for them today make this kind of technology very expensive. In addition the uses that have been demonstrated take the use of cochlear implants beyond people with disabilities. In the future there might be a need to distinguish between uses and persons using hearing devices if national healthcare budgets are going to pay for hearing devices.

Bridging Research in The Auditory Domain

A lot is already known about sound in terms of both the engineering of sound and its perception. High end conferencing facilities using an array of sound sources are able to "place" sounds anywhere in a room. They can create the effect of someone talking into a mike in one position, but the audience perceiving the speaker as being elsewhere.

Cinemas and home entertainment systems use "surround sound" to give the impression of movement. Cars use sophisticated sound engineering to cancel the noise of the road so s to make the interior close to the head of the driver and passengers as calm and peaceful as possible.

All of the available knowledge about sound engineering could be possibly used to address issues of high quality hearing aid. To achieve that there might be a need to bring together sound engineers working on problems in different domains such as music, cinema, automobiles, home entertainment etc.

Fitting the Cochlear Implant and 3D Printing

One of the biggest issues with ear phones is how well they fit. New ICT in the shape of 3D printing technology can help here as well. Austrian PhD student Klaus Stadlmann and his colleague Markus Hatzenbichler at the Technical University of Vienna recently created the smallest 3D printer in the world (Aigner, 2011). Stadlmann presented this at a recent TEDx (Stadlmann, 2011) event in Austria as well as at the October 2011 Start-Up Week in Austria (Startup Week 2011, n.d.). Their invention weighs only 1.5Kg, takes up as much space as a carton of milk, performs as well as commercially available printers costing €60,000. These two researchers built their prototype using components costing altogether about €1,200 and they are working on reducing the overall cost and lower the price even further.

3D printers like this can be used for a wide range of applications. In medicine for example they are used with biodegradable resins to create the scaffolds on which human tissue such as bone and other organs can form. Much of this work is still at an experimental or research phase. But the technology can already be used to create hearing aids customized to the ears of each user. Each hearing aid is customized to the user ear. The wearer goes to the clinic or shop and has the ear scanned. The shop sends this data by email to a service provider who uses their large in-house 3D printer to create the customized shell for the hearing aid. This is then returned to the clinic by ordinary post. They insert the electronics and invite the wearer back for a fitting. The process takes a total of about 5 days. Using the small desk top printer however there is no need to work with a service provider and the whole process can be done in a day or even less.

People who have poor hearing, but whose auditory hair cells are not badly damaged, use hearing aids. These essentially amplify the sounds going into to the ear. People who have damaged auditory hair cells cannot use hearing aids, they need cochlear implants. The cochlea of the inner ear is lined with hairs that pick sound of different frequencies. When these stop functioning correctly, the cochlear implant stimulates special cells known as auditory hair cells that under normal circumstances sense the movement of the hairs. In this way some of the hearing function is restored.

The fitting of a cochlear implant is an outpatient procedure that takes between 90 minutes and two hours done under general anaesthetic. The 'implant' however is not inside the body it is only placed inside the inner ear. Physically it lies on the outside of the body.

Both cochlear implants and hearing aids can fall out. This can be annoying when swimming, running or in the shower. The next step will be to have a real implantable device, one that is physical inside the body and cannot be lost. According to Deafness Research in the UK (Action on Hearing

Loss, n.d.) companies such as Otologics and Cochlear (Cochlear Ltd, 2014) are already working on fully implantable hearing aids that get around this problem. The technologies required to make this happen includes batteries that can be inserted under the skin and charged remotely, as well as microphones under the skin that pick up noises from the body such as the noise of ones eating and breathing, so that it can be cancelled from the outside world and only interesting sounds amplified or relayed to the hair cell stimulation.

Issues in Restoring Hearing

Because the cochlear implant sometimes involves surgery where a part of the system is embedded in a bone at the back of the ear it can be traumatic. Users of the system also have to devote time to learning how to hear with the device, especially if they have been deaf from a very young age or for a long period of time. People often require psychological evaluation prior to the operation and rehabilitation afterwards. This is an area where opportunities may exist to employ new ICT to assist those get the most benefit out of a new hearing device.

In a recent TED talk Charles Limb (2010), a cochlear implant specialist from the US explained that people fitted with today's top of the range cochlear implants have great difficulty hearing music. They can hear someone speaking and understand natural language, but only in the sense that they can tell what is being said. They do not hear words the same way as they did before their hearing started to decline. To be able to hear what is being said is great progress with respect to the past. In his TED talk, Charles Limb wanted to make the point that we should not stop at the restoration of basic functional hearing, but that we should go further to restore hearing to the point that full appreciation of music is possible.

People with a cochlear implant have difficulty with pitch perception. They can confuse tones that differ by as many as two octaves. They also have difficulties with timbre of tonal colour. For example many cannot tell the different between a trumpet and a violin. Brain images of people fitted with a cochlear implant show high levels of activity of the auditory cortex when someone speaks and low or almost no level of activity when listening to music. With training it is possible to overcome this to some extent. In his research Charles Limb described progress with a deaf cat and a boy from Singapore who became deaf when very young, yet managed to learn to play the piano. It would be interesting to see what can be done to improve the cochlear implant or to re-conceive the whole area of hearing restoration to enable people to enjoy music to the full.

Towards ABI and AMI

For people whose auditory hair cells have been damaged, the cochlear implant is of no assistance and so far their deafness cannot be cured or compensated for. The only option for these people lies in the future, with the development of bionic ears that rely on a direct interface with the auditory nerve, perhaps bypassing the ear and inner ear entirely.

This kind of interface is called an Auditory Brainstem Implant ("Auditory brainstem implant", n.d.) or ABI. It was first carried out in the US in 1979 and the interface consisted of two ball-electrodes placed close to the surface of the cochlear nucleus. In 1992 an 8 electrode system had been tried successfully. By 1999 a 12 electrode system was available from Med-EL (MED-EL, 2013), a 16 electrode system from Advanced Bionics (Advanced Bionics AG, 2013) and a 21 electrode system from Cochlear (Cochlear Ltd, 2014). The procedure is available in Europe as well as in the US. It is used in cases of neurofibromatosis, auditory nerve aplasia and cochlear ossification.

These procedures are rarely done because they require brain surgery. Whereas cochlear implants have been carried out many 100s of thousands of times, only about 1,000 ABI procedures have

been performed. The procedure does not restore haring. It enables the user to perceive the sensation of sound, making out beats and rhythm but not melody.

A variation on this is the AMI or Auditory Mid-brain Implant which by passes the auditory nerve going deeper into the brain to a place called the inferior colliculus where auditory signals are processed. This is used on people for whom little or no benefit can be derived from ABI. A review of AMI (Lim, Lenarz, & Lenarz, 2009) published in Trends in Amplification of the Journal of Neurophysiology in 2009, suggests that so far there are only a handful of procedures have been tried, and that the procedure is still in an experimental stage of development. Work published in the Journal of Neurophysiology in 2011 (Bulkin & Groh, 2011) indicated progress in understanding how sound is represented in the inferior colliculus of monkeys.

ABI and AMI are the new areas for research in hearing impairments and future research should focus in this direction while at the same time dealing with cochlear implant issues.

Artificial Retinas

The first artificial retina allowed the user to see 6 pixels. The claim made by the inventor was that this enabled the sufferer to read. In fact the six pixels were enough to represent Braille and the patient in effect read by seeing a visual representation of Braille. More recently 60 pixel implants have been approved for use and better versions are under development.

The 3 most important causes of failing eye-sight are RP (Retinitis Pigmentosa), AMD (Age related Macular Degeneration) and Usher Syndrome, with AMD being the main cause of blindness for people over 50. These conditions are quite widespread. In France alone, more than 1 million people suffer from some form of macular degeneration. Clearly the probability of suffering AMD increases with age. The incidence is likely to increase with the overall increase in age of the population. Other conditions such as diabetes are also associated with poor eyesight and even blindness.

Scientists consider that 75% of the information we receive, comes in through the eyes (Retina France, n.d.). Much of this is non-textual, being in the form of images or expressions. Even something as simple as the ability to recognize a smile is a very important boost to quality of life for someone who is not fully sighted.

The three conditions of RP, AMD and Usher syndrome are untreatable in the sense that they cannot be cured. The only recourse is a retinal implant.

It is one of the big challenges of ophthalmology to develop a therapy of congenital and degenerative retinal diseases. For decades, emphasis was placed on improving surgical procedures in cataract operations. There are many signs that the retina is moving centre-stage in ophthalmology. It is highly accelerate in this area, especially now that two commercial companies are available to provide solutions on a commercial (i.e. non experimental) basis.

The artificial retina technology is still in its early stages, but we can expect rapid progress in the coming years. The prospect of large scale adoption of retinal implants opens the door for new kinds of assistive technology. The issue is not just the restoration of sight, but the possibility of alternative strategies based on gesture recognition or on the use of the artificial retina as a platform for other service and systems for example based on useful forms of augmented reality.

A New Market

Until recently all work on the artificial retina or retinal implant was research. About 50 people have already benefited from some form of retinal implant and at least two companies have been approved by health authorities for the provision of retinal implants in Europe.

One is a German company founded in 2003 called Retina Implant AG (Retina Implant, n.d.).

It provides a sub-retinal implant that measures 3mm by 3mm and is 70 microns thick. The implant contains 1500 microelectrodes and it communicates with an external camera system and image processing unit.

The other company is California based Second Sight (Second Sight, 2013) and it provides a 60 electrode epi-retinal implant called the Argus II. This is the follow on to a previous experimental 16 electrode Argus I device.

When a patient receives the implant, the brain needs some time to adapt and "learn" how to see with the new device. This takes some time and some training. It relies on natural plasticity and self-organizing or self-learning properties of human neural systems.

The current generation of retinal implants can typically restores the sight of a blind person to about 10% of normal performance. They have limited resolution, of the order of 60 pixels, and they have limited angular range. They provide only monochrome images. Their application is confined to a limited number of conditions, conditions in which the retina remains intact and is not damaged. The cost is also prohibitive, being of the order of $115,000 per implant.

Those involved in artificial retina technology see this as a world market, and expect that the need for therapy will increase over the next century due to demographic trends i.e. ageing society. They note that:

- An increasing number of research groups worldwide are beginning to turn their attention to the area of retinal prosthesis. Groups exist in Germany, in the USA, in Japan, Korea and in Switzerland.
- Although pharmaceutical companies are developing drugs that aim at slowing down the course of the disease, the result is in many cases inevitable and sooner or later however a retinal prosthesis will be the only alternative to total blindness.

Market studies on ophthalmological products have begun dedicating entire chapters on prognoses concerning the future of the retina market and predict a growth of yearly sales in the range of $1B for retinal drugs and retinal prostheses by 2012.

The studies quoted are getting old, they date back to 2003. It is possible that progress was slower than expected, but it is promising none the less. One way of estimating growth is to look at how the now widely available cochlear implant has evolved. It looks likely that there will be a strong take-up of this technology by 2020.

It is the aim of Retinal Implant AG to have German medical insurance companies paying for the implant and the implantation surgery in analogy to the cochlear implant (hearing prosthesis). For the moment only a limited number of hospitals in Germany will be granted a license to charge for the costs.

The current resolution is retinal implants is about 64 pixels. The current level of connectivity between the implant and the brain is between 100 to 1000 connections.

Neural implants in general are hard and dense compared to the soft flexible tissue to which they are connected. There is an issue around the ability of the implant to maintain its connection to nerves over time and stay in place despite sudden or even violent movements. Other issues include the resolution of retina implants and how easy is to be increased and the life-time of such implants. In this directions it might be useful to exploit research in areas such as tissue engineering, flexible organic circuitry, body area networks and other aspects of micro-electronics for neuroengineering.

The Artificial Retina as a Platform

It seems as though there should be great scope for further developments based on wearable systems such as EYE2021. Why only use sounds to help the blind person to navigate? Why not use a human voice that provides more complex information

about the scene being observed or the terrain being navigated? One can imagine a person walking along and having the option of running dialogue describing the places being passed, a bit like a well design train that announces stations as they approach, a tour guide that flags important places, a helper that suggest the location of a restaurant, a virtual secretary that recognizes the faces of people in a room and suggests to the wearer "Your accountant is here, maybe you want to meet him?", or "your ex-wife is here, do you need to find an exit?" Many technologies already exist, that are available as APIs, for integration in interesting ways, to augment the function of wearable platforms such as EYE2021. One example is Google Goggles (Google, 2014), a system that allows the user to search using a picture as input.

Just as is already starting to happen with the hearing aid, it is reasonable to expect that by 2020, vision systems in general will consist of hardware platforms served by a complex industrial eco-system of application developers and service providers that compete to extent the functions of the basic product, targeting difference groups of users in new and creative ways, not only users with disabilities but non-disabled users as well, including those who experience situational disability as a part of their professional lives. This kind of competitive eco-system may be the best way to lower the price and raise the performance of even the most basic systems made available to users on the basis of the national health or disability care system.

The team that developed the system recently took part in the recent EC Innovation Union 2011 Conference in Brussels (European Commission, 2013). They spoke eloquently about the difficulty raising venture capital or seed funding to develop products and services for non-mass market applications such as vision systems for bind people. There seems to be a need to help companies like EYE2021 (EYE 2021, 2013) to raise initial capital needed to support clinical trials, prototyping, purchase of design services or anything else that will help it get past the proof of concept to product prototyping and testing.

A new area for attention, especially by ICT oriented innovation programs, may be the development of software innovation platforms based on successful prototypes and proof of concept projects. The purpose of these would be to move the product onto the next stage of deployment by crowd-sourcing creative and entrepreneurial energy of a diverse global eco-system of market specific application developers, or hardware innovation platforms based on open-source hardware or open source system architecture.

The Problem of Power

Fiona Macrae of the UK Daily Mail newspaper (Macrae, 2011) has written about progress in the development of "terminator style contact lenses" that will allow the wearer to see all kinds of information hands free. For example they will be able to see text messages, social network content, diagrams or map directions overlaid in their field of vision. Researchers estimate that fully functional contact lens like these will be available within the next 10 years. Similar problems are also faced in artificial retina and progress in the field will benefit a wider spectrum of technologies.

Prototypes of such systems have already been tested on rabbits without any observable adverse effects. One of the concerns with any kind of implant is that the energy required to make them work will generate heat that will eventually denature the tissue around it. This is a concern for those who wants to develop high density neural interface arrays to improve the resolution or retinal implant and other vision systems. This means that future progress will depend not only on improvements in the interface technologies but in the battery and power consumption of the processing technologies as well.

Next Generation Retinal Implants

In 2011 Sheila Nirenberg presented her work at TED (Nirenberg, 2011) on a new generation of prosthetic device that promises an improvement on existing retinal implant devices. She started out doing basic science to understand how the brain processes signals such as the image data it gets from the eye. She now claims to understand how the brain encodes image data that it receives from the retina and processes before sending it deep into the brain. She has recently developed a technology made up of two components an "encoder' that creates the code that the brain normally receives from the eye, as well as a transducer to distribute it to the right place in the brain. This technology has been prototyped and demonstrated on animals. She claims that her approach is much more effective than that which is currently available to blind people as a retinal implant.

Her approach is not to replace the damaged organ but to bypass it, interfacing directly with that part of the brain that normally processes the signal from the healthy organ. She claims that this approach can also be applied to restore other lost sense and capabilities such as hearing, or better control of limbs afflicted by a motor disorder. Certainly the results are impressive. She was featured in a 2010 issue of Wired Magazine (Sanders, 2010). This issue reported on the results she had achieved applying the technology to the case of blind mice. They found that the prosthetic allowed the animal to see the face of a baby with a high degree of definition. Not only to see that it is a baby but to recognize which baby it is. Others in the domain have described the results as a big step forward in the restoration of sight. So far it has not been tried in humans, but that day must not be very far off.

Given the way in which things have progressed in the case of retinal implants it may be reasonable to assume that this technique will be available by 2020.

Other Sensory Organ Prostheses

We are already in the age of the artificial retina and the neural prosthesis. Thus the market for sensory-organ-prostheses represents a strongly expanding branch of the medical technical sector. Problems with smell tend to go unreported by over 200,000 people every year visit doctors in the US to complain of problems with their sense of smell. Many of these are age-related deterioration that occur usually to people over 60 and is unpreventable. There are many other causes including neurodegenerative disorders such as Parkinson's, Alzheimer's and ALS.

Work is on-going to understand the function of the nose and how to engineering an artificial nose. A recent report (University of Pennsylvania, 2011) describes how researchers have grafted olfactory receptors onto carbon nano-tubes. This is a first step towards the development of an artificial nose or human nose-like sensors. There is potential for further development, not just within the area of sight but also in the area of smell and taste and feeling. Other possible applications are control of muscles related to incontinence, pain and phantom limb control as well as the restoration of large muscle control after spinal injury, paralysis or the re-attachment of limbs lost through violence or industrial accident.

Alternative Solutions Might Also be Promising

An entirely different approach from the one of the artificial retina has been developed by a group of Spanish researchers based at the Centro de Investigación en Tecnologías Gráficas of the Universitat Politècnica de València (Centro de Investigación en Tecnologías Gráficas, n.d.). The system called EYE2021 (EYE 2021, 2013) relies on the creative use of sound to compensate for poor sight. The basic prototype was developed as part of an EC FP6 project of the same name. It has now been spun off into a campus venture and development has continued on a self-funding basis in the intervening years. The system uses stereo cameras mounted in a pair of sunglasses to detect objects in the field of vision of the wearer. The system identifies significant objects and their position. It then transmits stereo sounds to the ears of the wearer. The wearer hears sounds in a headset or ear-piece that indicate various properties of the environment such as the direction and distance of the observed object, its size or texture or movement. The system is surprisingly easy to use. A user can learn to interpret distance and direction data almost immediately with no training. More complex functions can later be acquired. The system is of interest either as a stand-alone system or for use in combination with other approaches such as the retinal implant.

The earliest versions of the system involved hardware that was big, heavy and energy intensive. In the last few years it has become possible to reduce the system considerably in terms of size and complexity. The current model now looks more or less like a normal pair of sunglasses and a set of standard headphones.

Innovative systems using the sound to compensate for poor sight are also a reminder that many of the early attempts at vision for the blind relied on brain plasticity and the capacity of humans to learn to see in unexpected ways. An example is the use of electrical stimulation of image patterns on the skin of the arm, the belly or lower back. There may be many more good ideas out there worthy of pursuit due to the utility they provide at least in the short and medium term, while more ambitious technologies based on direct stimulation of the brain are being developed.

A US project called Brain Port is based on a camera worn by a blind person that captures images and transmits signals to electrodes slipped onto the tongue. This causes tingling sensations that the person can learn to decipher as the location and movement of objects.

REFERENCES

Abrams, H., Edwards, B., Valentine, S., & Fitz, A. (2011, March 2). *A Patient-adjusted Fine-tuning Approach for Optimizing the Hearing Aid Response | Hearing Review*. Retrieved March 8, 2014, from http://www.hearingreview.com/2011/03/a-patient-adjusted-fine-tuning-approach-for-optimizing-the-hearing-aid-response/

Action on Hearing Loss. (n.d.). *Deafness Research UK (DRUK) - Action On Hearing Loss: RNID*. Retrieved March 15, 2014, from http://www.actiononhearingloss.org.uk/about-us/druk.aspx

Advanced Bionics, A. G. (2013). *The Cochlear Implant Technology Innovation Leader | Advanced Bionics*. Retrieved March 8, 2014, from http://www.advancedbionics.com/

Aigner, F. (2011, May 17). *Technische Universität Wien: The World's Smallest 3D Printer*. Retrieved March 8, 2014, from http://www.tuwien.ac.at/news/news_detail/article/7009/EN/

Aphasia. (n.d.). *Wikipedia, the free encyclopedia*. Retrieved March 8, 2014, from http://en.wikipedia.org/wiki/Aphasia

Assistivetech.net. (2010, August 26). *AutoSyringe - ATWiki*. Retrieved March 8, 2014, from http://atwiki.assistivetech.net/index.php/AutoSyringe

Auditory Brainstem Implant. (n.d.). *Wikipedia, the free encyclopedia*. Retrieved March 8, 2014, from http://en.wikipedia.org/wiki/Auditory_brainstem_implant

Bionics Institute. (n.d.). *Home*. Retrieved March 8, 2014, from http://www.bionicsinstitute.org/Pages/default.aspx

Blamey & Saunders Hearing. (2014). *Hearing Aids | Blamey Saunders Buy Hearing Aids Online with IHearYou*. Retrieved March 8, 2014, from http://www.blameysaunders.com.au/

Bulkin, D. A., & Groh, J. M. (2011). Systematic mapping of the monkey inferior colliculus reveals enhanced low frequency sound representation. *Journal of Neurophysiology, 105*, 1785–1797. doi:10.1152/jn.00857.2010 PMID:21307328

CCC-TV. (2014, January 13). *CCC-TV*. Retrieved March 8, 2014, from http://media.ccc.de/index.html

Centers for Disease Control and Prevention. (2010, May 6). *CDC - Traumatic Brain Injury - Injury Center*. Retrieved March 15, 2014, from http://www.cdc.gov/TraumaticBrainInjury/index.html

Centro de Investigación en Tecnologías Gráficas. (n.d.). *Centro de Investigacion en Tecnologias-graficas - UPV*. Retrieved March 8, 2014, from http://www.citg.es/

Cochlear Ltd. (2014). *Home*. Retrieved March 8, 2014, from http://www.cochlear.com/wps/wcm/connect/intl/home

Cool Hunting. (n.d.). *Cool Hunting: Tech*. Retrieved March 8, 2014, from http://www.cool-hunting.com/tech

Coronado, V. G. (2011). *Surveillance for traumatic brain injury-related deaths: United States, 1997-2007*. Atlanta, GA: U.S. Department of Health and Human Services, Centers for Disease Control and Prevention.

DARPA. (n.d.). *Revolutionizing Prosthetics*. Retrieved March 8, 2014, from http://www.darpa.mil/Our_Work/DSO/Programs/Revolutionizing_Prosthetics.aspx

DEKA. (2009). *Welcome to DEKA Research and Development*. Retrieved March 8, 2014, from http://www.dekaresearch.com/index.shtml

Dow Jones & Company, Inc. (n.d.). *WSJ.D Conference 2014*. Retrieved March 8, 2014, from http://wsjdconference.wsj.com/

Duke University. (2011, July 10). *Monkeys 'Move and Feel' Virtual Objects Using Only Their Brains*. Retrieved March 8, 2014, from http://www.pddnet. com/news/2011/10/monkeys-move-and-feel-virtual-objects-using-only-their-brains

European Commission. (2013, March 27). *Home page - Innovation Union*. Retrieved March 8, 2014, from ec.europa.eu/research/innovation-union/ic2011/index_en.cfm

EYE 2021. (2013). *EYE21 is the first and only system in the world of mobility aids for the blind people which allows its use in any environment*. Retrieved March 8, 2014, from http://www.eye2021.com/

Fleming, N. (2007, February 2). *Woman with bionic arm regains sense of touch - Telegraph*. Retrieved March 8, 2014, from http://www.telegraph.co.uk/news/worldnews/1541406/Woman-with-bionic-arm-regains-sense-of-touch.html

Google. (2014). *Goggles overview and requirements - Search Help*. Retrieved March 8, 2014, from https://support.google.com/websearch/answer/166331

Hack and Hear. (2012). *hack and hear*. Retrieved March 8, 2014, from http://blog.hackandhear.com/

Independence Technology, L. L. C. (2001). *Independence Technology, L.L.C*. Retrieved March 8, 2014, from http://www.ibotnow.com/

Lim, H. H., Lenarz, M., & Lenarz, T. (2009). Auditory Midbrain Implant: A Review. *Trends in Amplification*. doi:10.1177/1084713809348372 PMID:19762428

Limb, C. (2010). *Your brain on improv*. Retrieved from http://www.ted.com/talks/charles_limb_your_brain_on_improv.html

Macrae, F. (2011, November 23). *Terminator-style contact lenses will keep you up to date with news | Mail Online*. Retrieved March 8, 2014, from http://www.dailymail.co.uk/sciencetech/article-2064543/Terminator-style-contact-lenses-date-news.html?ito=feeds-newsxml

MED-EL. (2013). *Cochlear Implants for Hearing Loss | MED-EL*. Retrieved March 8, 2014, from http://www.medel.com/

Nirenberg, S. (2011). *A prosthetic eye to treat blindness*. Retrieved from http://www.ted.com/talks/sheila_nirenberg_a_prosthetic_eye_to_treat_blindness.html

Pappas, S. (2011, May 10). *Machine that feels is key to 'Jedi' prosthetics - Technology & science - Science - LiveScience | NBC News*. Retrieved March 8, 2014, from http://www.nbcnews.com/id/44789955/ns/technology_and_science-science/t/machine-feels-called-key-jedi-prosthetics/#.UxtjcvmSzal

Phonak Hearing Systems. (n.d.). *Phonak Hearing Systems - life is on*. Retrieved March 8, 2014, from http://www.phonak.com/

Retina France. (n.d.). *Retina France - Accueil*. Retrieved March 8, 2014, from http://www.retina.fr/

Retina Implant. (n.d.). *Homepage - www.retina-implant.de*. Retrieved March 8, 2014, from http://retina-implant.de/default.aspx

Rothwell, C. (2011, January 20). *About NCHS - Homepage*. Retrieved March 8, 2014, from http://www.cdc.gov/nchs/about.htm

Saenz, A. (2009, January 12). *Deka's Luke Arm In Clinical Trials, Is it the Future of Prosthetics? (Video) | Singularity Hub*. Retrieved March 8, 2014, from http://singularityhub.com/2009/12/01/dekas-luke-arm-in-clinical-trials-is-it-the-future-of-prosthetics-video/

Sanders, L. (2010, November 15). *Retinal Implant Restores Vision in Blind Mice - Wired Science*. Retrieved March 8, 2014, from http://www.wired.com/wiredscience/2010/11/blind-vision-implant/

Second Sight. (2013). *Mission*. Retrieved March 8, 2014, from http://2-sight.eu/en/home-en

Stadlmann, K. (2011, November 11). *TEDxVienna - Klaus Stadlmann - The world's smallest 3D Printer*. [Video file]. Retrieved from http://youtu.be/D2IQkKE7h9I

Startup Week 2011. (n.d.). *Klaus Stadlmann (AUT) | Startup Week 2011 Vienna*. Retrieved March 8, 2014, from http://www.startupweek2011.com/speaker/klaus-stadlmann-aut/

The Best Five Anthropomorphic Robotic Hands/ Arms. (n.d.). Retrieved March 8, 2014, from mindtrans.narod.ru/hands/hands.htm

Touch Bionics. (2014). *The world's leading prosthetic hand Touch Bionics*. Retrieved March 8, 2014, from http://www.touchbionics.com/products/active-prostheses/i-limb-ultra/

Ultimate Ears. (n.d.). *Home | Ultimate Ears*. Retrieved March 8, 2014, from http://www.ultimateears.com/en-us/

University of Pennsylvania. (2011, July 26). *Researchers Help Graft Olfactory Receptors onto Nanotubes*. Retrieved March 8, 2014, from http://www.pddnet.com/news/2011/07/researchers-help-graft-olfactory-receptors-nanotubes

Velroyen, H. (2011, December 28). *Bionic Ears: Introduction into State-of-the-Art Hearing Aid Technology*. Retrieved March 8, 2014, from http://blog.hackandhear.com/wp-content/uploads/2011/12/2011_28c3_bionic_ears_v08_slides.pdf

KEY TERMS AND DEFINITIONS

Artificial Limbs: In medicine, an artificial limb is an artificial device that replaces a missing body part lost through trauma, disease, or congenital conditions.

Artificial Retina: A prosthetic device resembling the anterior surface of a normal eyeball.

Cochlear Implant: A cochlear implant (CI) is a surgically implanted electronic device that provides a sense of sound to a person who is profoundly deaf or severely hard of hearing.

Invasive BCI: BCI that requires surgical placement of sensors in the brain.

Neuroprosthetics: Neuroprosthetics (also called neural prosthetics) is a discipline related to neuroscience and biomedical engineering concerned with developing neural prostheses.

Prosthetics: In medicine, a prosthesis, is an artificial device that replaces a missing body part lost through trauma, disease, or congenital conditions.

Section 2
Assisted and Independent Living Applications

Chapter 6
Health and Human Services

ABSTRACT

Persons with disabilities and the elderly present an increased need for health and human services such as care taking, remote monitoring for hospital care, etc. Moreover, people's perceptions of the notion of disability and especially of cognitive impairments and disorders are beginning to change. The increase in people in need of health services because of ageing is another important factor making this aspect of life one of the most important aspects for independent and assisted living, which the second section discusses. This section focuses on issues that technologies and applications in the area have to face in the next years such as cost, human factors, privacy, the quality of services, etc. in order for people with disabilities and the elderly to benefit from them.

INTRODUCTION

Issues such as the future of retinal prosthetics, cochlear implants or advanced prosthetics and exoskeletons have been addressed elsewhere in this book, either under the heading of game-changing technologies or as part of another section on transport and mobility or human performance for example.

Suffice it to say that many more innovations are in the pipelines in terms of systems for dealing with pain, memory loss, incontinence or a wide variety of conditions that can be addressed using advances in neuroengineering and man-machine interfaces. Some of the most exciting advances will occur in relation to the restoration of sense not just hearing and sight, but motor-control,

touch or feeling, taste and even smell. These often require medical intervention of some form, or are funded by healthcare systems, but we do not consider them here.

Instead we focus on two areas that are linked in many ways. One is the area of ageing and care of the elderly. This has had a lot of attention in the last decade past, especially systems addressed to the needs of people with conditions such as Alzheimer's and Parkinson's. The kind of technologies considered under these headings had to do with smart homes, wearable computing as well as the monitoring and care in the home. In the following pages we will look at some of these and see what the next generation of solutions will look like.

DOI: 10.4018/978-1-4666-6130-1.ch006

The biggest innovation is arguable the rise in awareness of mental or cognitive disabilities. These are extremely widespread and chronic cases are associated with social stigma and difficulty in workplace insertion. Technologies that help people live with these conditions can be considered assistive technology, access technologies or inclusion technologies depending on the details of the condition.

The novel feature of these conditions is the role that ICT can play is not so much in curing or compensating for the condition, but as a medium for the provision of physical, cognitive and behavioral therapies.

An interesting feature of these systems is that they apply to common conditions of general that interest such as alcohol abuse, eating disorders like bulimia and anorexia, management of weight, blood-pressure, cholesterol, as well as shyness, anxiety, anger or depression. In other words general technologies of use for conditions such as ADHD[1] or Alzheimer's[2], which generally require specialist intervention, can also be applied to range of life-style disorders amenable to the overall management of lifestyle using advanced sensor technologies, knowledge gleaned from socially created big-data, as well as emerging disciplines from the cognitive sciences and neural engineering, as well as social and affective computing.

A related trend is the promise of being able to use big-data and communities doing forms of citizen science such as many of those involved in the QS movement. This has the potential to accelerate research and understanding of these conditions and how best to live with them.

The issue of ageing will continue to increase in importance. The reason is simple. Society is getting older, we are living longer after retirement and there is a shared interest in people living productive independent lives for as long as they possibly can. The potential for older people to benefit from e-assistive, e-access or e-inclusive technologies is clear when you consider that old age is inevitably accompanied by a deterioration of the faculties in ways that often resemble a disability. The problems older people may have to deal with are:

- Low strength
- Low stamina
- Low mobility
- Weak sight
- Poor hearing
- Poor coordination
- Difficulties making decisions
- Memory loss
- Dementia
- Diabetes
- Depression

Many of the challenges faced by elderly people resemble those faced by someone in mid-life who has had an operation, a serious illness, or obesity. They can al benefit from the use of ICT.

For the purpose of our research we consider three main categories of user needs that imply respective accessibility issues to be tackled with the appropriate use of ICT applications. These three user needs categories relate with monitoring, care and assistance:

People using monitoring services need to be able to:

  ○ Follow and monitor physiological data such as body weight, temperature, blood pressure etc.
  ○ Diagnose the slow progression of conditions such as Alzheimer's
  ○ Predict, understand and respond to physical hazards such as strange smells, naked flames, falls etc.
  ○ Diagnose and respond accordingly to loneliness, physical, emotional or sexual bullying and abuse etc.
  ○ Monitor and make sure that certain behavior such as diet, exercise, hydration, use of the toilet etc. is followed properly.

○ Understand and respond to moods, psychological well-being and social interactions etc.

People using care services need to be able to:
- ○ Effectively, smartly and effortlessly use reminders for appointments, medication, exercise routines etc.
- ○ Be reminded and prompted to consult and visit doctors, dentists and other specialists whenever necessary
- ○ Follow physical therapies such as to retain or regain strength, fitness, co-ordination etc.
- ○ Follow cognitive therapies such as to combat memory loss, maintain decision capability etc.
- ○ Follow behavioral therapies such as learn essential social skills, combat depression etc.
- ○ The performance of everyday tasks is not only a practical necessity but also a form of therapy. It is also important for one's sense of independence and identity. It is important for a person to be able to dress as they want, in the clothes that they like, but many people require assistance in doing this and many other everyday tasks as they get older or because of the specificity of their condition.

People using assistance services and devices (e.g. a robot, a smart home, etc.) need them to help them in:
- ○ Dressing
- ○ Using of the bathroom
- ○ Preparing food and feeding
- ○ Exercising
- ○ Socializing
- ○ Household maintenance and chores

These three clusters of user needs related to monitoring, care and assistance are all interlinked

issues in the sense that better knowledge of the progression of a condition or of a sudden change in mood or behavior should trigger changes in care or assistance.

It is likely that general purpose service, companion robots will in future be able to help to perform many of these tasks.

The potential for employing advanced robotics in this section is considerable. The 2009 Japanese Food Machinery and Technology expo (Diagonal View, 2009) featured a robotic chef making a Japanese style omelet called Okomiyaki, a robotic sushi chef, a mobile two-wheeled self-balancing dumb-waiter, as well as a kitchen robot cutting cucumbers at high speed. We don't go into this in detail here, but we do emphasize the potential importance of this field for the future. However it is hard to avoid the impression that Europe is very poorly placed to serve these markets in future.

Having said that much of the products and systems developed in the past will continue to be developed and the scope for such development is substantial.

We deal with some of these before turning to the new and emerging areas which we try to discuss in more detail.

In this chapter the following accessibility issues are raised that relate with the identified user needs:

Monitoring services for people with disabilities need to take under account the following issues:

- Privacy is of paramount importance in monitoring services in order these to be accepted easier and adopted by wider audiences. In the case of people with disabilities privacy is becoming one of the top priority problems to tackle.
- How to monitor a person's vital signs and behavior without the persons feeling stigmatized or under surveillance.
- How to keep interoperability of Quantified Self (QS) technologies with applications and services for monitoring, care and assistance.

- How to detect mood and adjust applications behavior using online content from social media, blogs, Twitter, etc.
- The measurement of the ease of use, the applicability and everyday lifestyle issues related to the adoption or not of new hardware, software and services by developers and manufacturers, while these are in the conceptualization and early design phases.
- Needs- and lifestyle based design of highly personalized smart environments with emphasis on the coverage of individual needs, preferences and capabilities of the individual user / customer. Interoperability with wearable body area networks and other ambient intelligence infrastructure and components should be supported.
- Compliance to common interoperability protocols and integration standards to facilitate DIY networks of service appliances.
- Support of end user computing paradigms to give users the necessary means to design their own environments according to their needs, preferences and their particular lifestyle.
- Recording of individual memories for later retrieval and / or study. Transfer of application and service concepts to broader applications of life logging, life-streaming and self-quantification, which have implications not only as an assistive technology to help older people dealing with memory loss, but as a technology to help in a much broader health and self-improvement programs of interest to the general population.

Care services for people with disabilities need to take under account the following issues:

- Most of the current reminder applications need users to configure them. however for people with disabilities this configuration poses problems and has to take place smartly by the applications themselves
- The later also implies that there is a need for task (semantics) translators to help people make sense out of incoming emails, messages or requests, as well as facilitate understanding and action taking for incoming information.
- Care services should also take under account different lifestyles of persons, habits, relatives, friends etc. in order not to become annoying and finally discarded by users.
- Design of the interface for care service related devices should be such that doesn't stigmatize persons and be able to used unobtrusively.
- There is a lack of tools and apps helping people dealing with pain, memory loss, incontinence, restoration of senses (hearing, sight, motor-control, touch or feeling, taste, smell), as well as with life-style disorders such as alcohol abuse, eating disorders like bulimia and anorexia, management of weight, blood-pressure, cholesterol, shyness, anxiety, anger, depression, etc.
- Social situation behavior management support applications should also be encouraged.

Assistance services and devices should take under account the following issues:

- They need to become more personalized for on-going training and support in learning everyday living skills such as banking, shopping, cooking, etc.
- Design of assistance services should support highly personalized solutions that address the entire gamut of life aspects components of the individual or his / her family or group he / she lives with.

- Design of the interaction dialogue and other interaction modalities for the communication between humans and companion / service robots should take under account emotional, cognitive and motor skills of both.

ISSUES WITH COGNITIVE, BEHAVIORAL, AND OTHER DISORDERS

Autism, ADHD and Other Cognitive Disabilities

ADHD or Attention Deficit Hyperactivity Disorder ("Attention deficit hyperactivity disorder predominantly inattentive", 2014), used to be called ADD or Attention Deficit Disorder. Someone with ADHD has difficulty paying attention for long periods of time, they have difficulty finishing projects or even completing tasks like reading email. It is one of many cognitive, psychological or neurophysiological conditions that can be considered a disability.

Other conditions include Asperger's syndrome[3] a milder form of autism often associated with 'geeks' or people who are good at mathematics but behave in strange oddly unsociable ways. This is a form of ASP or Autism Spectrum Disorder[4]. Other conditions are Bipolar Disorder[5] of type I, II and III as well as various forms of depression or anxiety. Tourette's syndrome[6] is one of the many physical or verbal tic disorders. It is often associated with spontaneous and uncontrollable use of obscene language. Face blindness known by the scientific term of Prosopagnosia[7] is an inability to recognize people's faces, even the face of members of one's immediate family. To this list we can add conditions such as Alzheimer's or Parkinson's disease, two progressive conditions associated with ageing that have received considerable attention in the last decade or so.

Someone living with one of these conditions faces many challenges, but these are mainly social in nature. Some with ADHD for example has difficulty paying attention, does not learn effectively and may be considered by both teachers and peers as being disruptive. As young adults they may have difficulty socializing, making friends and developing relationships. Later on in professional life they may have difficulty working in teams, retaining with clients or playing the many subtle social and political games that career development requires.

There are more than 200 diagnosable cognitive or psychological conditions that are disabling to some degree and increasingly recognized as formal disabilities. They present a problem in the sense that diagnosis, being subjective and based on behavior can be difficult. This is especially the case for milder forms of a condition. Many of these conditions are also poorly understood from an objective point of view based on our knowledge of domains such as brain chemistry or neurology. This seems to be changing however due to rapid progress in areas such as neuroscience, brain modeling, and techniques for high-speed high-resolution brain imaging.

Most of these conditions reflect a difference or divergence from the average or typical way in which the brain is organized and processes information. Their causes vary. They may be hereditary. They may occur as a result of trauma or injury to the brain, for example as a result of stroke. In some cases the condition is transient and rarely persists until old age. In other cases it is permanent. Many conditions represent a spectrum of similar conditions that vary greatly in their severity. All have some kind of an impact on the ability of the individual to learn, perform well in a professional environment so as to get and keep a well-paying job, to socialize, make friends and enjoy life to the full.

As we understand these conditions better, we realize that many more people have some form of cognitive disorder than previously thought. Of course most of these 'new' cases are located lower down on the range of severity. One name made familiar by the movies was John Nash, a mathematician who suffered from paranoid schizophrenia, but nevertheless won a Nobel Prize in economics for his work on game theory, and who was made famous in the movie "A Beautiful Mind" (Universal Studios Home Entertainment, 2010). Famous people, who have been diagnosed with Face Blindness or Prosopagnosia, include Duncan Bannatyne one of the stars of the BBC Dragons Den series on entrepreneurship, Paul Dirac the noble prize winning physicist who developed a relativistic quantum theory of the electron, as well as Jane Goodall the British primatologist who featured in the movie "Gorillas in the mist". According to notes in Wikipedia as many as 2.5% of the population may have an inheritable form of Prosopagnosia, whereas as many as 10% may have some other milder form. It is believed that up to 10% of the population has some form of a physical or verbal tic that is an uncontrollable involuntary movement of the face or the hands, verbalization or speech act.

These people were highly successful by many measures, but that does not mean they would not benefited from assistance in overcoming any challenges that they might pose.

If diagnosis relies on the observation of behavior, treatment will often rely on behavioral or cognitive therapy. In the case of Asperger's syndrome treatment often involves the drilling on how to behave in social situations, for example when answering a telephone, or when queuing to buy something in a shop. People with Asperger's have great difficulty noticing or tuning in to simple social cues and behaviors. They do not react to common social stimuli in the expected way and appear strange. They tend to understand things in a literal way and therefore respond in ways that are not appropriate or seem strange. They have to literally learn what people really mean, and how they are expected to react to social cues.

Nowadays these conditions are recognized for what they are and can be handled accordingly. As late as the 1970s however behaviors now associated with ADHD or autism were simply seen as bad behavior by disruptive children, who were often punished along with their parents who were often accused of bad parenting. Not everyone understands this however and even today these conditions are controversial in the sense that a part of the population of even developed countries, no doubt because they are unfamiliar with the condition and uninformed as to what can be done, tend to dismiss it and not take it seriously. In the 1990s parents of children with autism became increasingly worried about their exclusion from education, knowing full well that their best hope of living a normal life was to participate fully in education, learning both intellectual and emotional skills needed to function in society. Even today as few as one in 10 people with autism hold even a part-time job. Many live in state-supported group homes. Many who attend college often end up unemployed and isolated or remain all of their lives with their parents. One of the NYT articles cited below puts the average lifetime marginal cost of care of someone with Asperger's at about 1 Million USD.

The media is playing its part to remedy the situation. The New York Times for example recently featured articles about living with autism on topics such as Navigating Love and Autism (Harmon, 2011b) a story about a young autistic couple at college, dealing with the impact of autism on their relationship. Another story entitled Autistic and Seeking a Place in the Adult World (Harmon, 2011a) deals with the difficulties people with autism actually face when trying to enter the world of work. The NYT also has a blog on parenting and has published a series of articles on topics like adolescence and parenting the autism adult (Belkin, 2010) dealing with the transition from adolescence to adulthood.

Every time someone with autism encounters a new social situation, there is the risk that they will not have the skills needed to blend. Having left home they may need on-going training or support in learning everyday living skills such as banking, shopping or cooking. Of course a measure of patience and understanding is required on behalf of society, but many may not be familiar with the condition, and may not show the tolerance required. Educators are of the opinion that these transitions are best managed using community based instruction rather than classroom training or home-drilling. This is expensive however.

People with cognitive disabilities may benefit from advances in social and affective computing, the use of sensor technology combined with humanoid companion robots, smart avatars and virtual assistants. Such technologies may also reduce cost and increase effectiveness of services targeting people with cognitive disabilities. Another avenue to explore is the use of smart homes and smart environments adapted to the needs of people with cognitive disabilities.

It is possible that there are many overlaps with work already done for older people or for those with progressive conditions such as Alzheimer's and Parkinson's, but this is not known and needs to be verified. It is reasonable to expect that younger people with a cognitive disability trying to live an independent life away from their parents, will present a whole new set of needs and challenges that do not arise in the case of elderly people.

As part of its on-going coverage of autism, the NYT has published a recent survey of apps for autistic children (The New York Times, 2011). Already many hundreds of apps are available and many seem to provide good results. Another article (Joshi, 2011) warns that not all apps are equally effective.

Most are only available for English language users. As for the situation across Europe, our impression is that development is fragmented at best. Someone with Autism Spectrum Disorders (ASD) will have differing needs as they grow older and as a function of the specific nature and severity or their condition. It is possible that some

needs are well covered by that gaps remain. We suggest that this might be an area for more detailed investigation in future.

Many apps intended to help children with ASD can benefit people with other disorders. Children with autism often experience delays in language learning, and there is a need to boost their language skills so they don't fall behind other kids of the same age. But this can happen for a variety of reasons, not just because of ASD. Children with ASD often need to boost development of fine motor skills, another area where iPhone and Android apps seem to have been successful. But these are also needed by children suffering from cerebral palsy.

From an adult perspective Juriaan Persyn has published a paper on the design of websites for people with autism (Persyn, 2006). This is based on his experience working at Autisme Centraal (Autisme Centraal, n.d.) based in Gent. The needs of adults with autism go far beyond friendly website however.

It seems like now is the time to develop a comprehensive program for RTD and innovation that aims at addressing the specific needs of people with ASD. This effort should not stop at ASD. It may need to examine the full range of cognitive and developmental disorders to see where ICT based behavioral and cognitive aids and therapies can be developed and the kinds of breakthroughs required in ICT, cognitive, behavioral and medical sciences required to make them happen.

Autism Activism, Mad-Pride, and the Neurodiversity Movement

Consistent with the social model of disability, many who have been diagnosed with a cognitive disorder, stress that they are just different, that their brains are wired differently for example and make the inclusion of people with such a condition into society a social diversity issue. Some groups, in particular those with Asperger's have become advocates of a new way of looking at people, and talk in a humorous way about their condition.

In 2004 the New York Times picked up on this and writes about in an article entitled "Neurodiversity Forever: The Disability Movement Turns to Brains" (Harmon, 2004). One website, maintained by the fictional Institute for the Study of the Neurologically Typical (ISNT, 2002) otherwise known as ISNT, satirizes people who do not have a neurological disorder of some kind, referring to them as being Neurotypical or having a condition called NT.

ASAN the Autistic Self-Advocacy Network (Autistic Self Advocacy Network, 2014) is part of this emerging autism rights movement ("Autism rights movement", n.d.). It seeks to promote disability rights with respect to Autism. It was founded in 2005. It has chapters all over the US and affiliations with organizations in the UK, Canada and Israel. It stands by the principle of "Nothing about us, without us!" It promotes an "autism awareness day". It works with employers on the integration of people with Autism Spectrum Disorder into the work-force. It takes part in research on the ethical, legal and social implications of autism.

This autism rights movement seems to have something in common with the Mad Pride Movement ("Mad Pride", n.d.). Members are "glad to be mad", they work to banish prejudice and discrimination or misunderstanding and assert that their conditions do not preclude them from living productive lives.

The movement is made up of health workers and patients of psychiatric wards who want to overcome the social stigma associated with people who have been diagnosed with a psychiatric condition or spent time in a psychiatric ward. It started in 1993 in Toronto with the organization of the Psychiatric Survivors Pride Day and has since spread to other countries such as the UK and Ireland. The Irish mad pride organization wants to establish "the normality of madness". All of this is being done with considerable humor, but there is a serious issue here. Cognitive, psychological, de-

velopmental and neurological disorders challenge society in terms of inclusion and social justice, as well as in terms of the resources it has to help those with such conditions. It is in the interest of all concerned that the people represented by these groups achieve independent productive living to the fullest extent possible.

Advocacy groups have existed to promote the rights of individuals with disability for a very long time. The oldest ones tend to be work on behalf of people who are blind, hard of hearing or dependent on wheelchairs for mobility. Although the recent pioneers seem to be from the autism community, they are not limited to advocacy on behalf of people with this condition. The overall trend is for the emergence of a neurodiversity movement ("Neurodiversity", n.d.). The movement is slightly controversial due to the fact that these conditions are not well understood, but clarity will come with time.

As science clarifies the nature of autism-related conditions and facilitates better forms of diagnosis and treatment, the rights of those affected will be easier to define and defend. One can expect as a result of the work of these groups that the rights of people with cognitive and developmental disabilities will continue to grow in importance in the years to come.

Depression

Around 12%-17% of the population in Europe (Sobocki, Jonsson, Angst, & Rehnberg, 2006) will suffer at least one episode of depression in their lifetime and another 1% is affected by bipolar disorder. Every year around 6% (or 18 million people) and 1% (or 2,5 million people) of the European adult population is affected by depression and bipolar disorder respectively. Nearly half of them (Smith, 2011) experience multi-episodes and require closer and periodical monitoring and support. Episodes or symptoms – usually separate by a period of 'normal' mood - may range from mild up to severe involving, in this case, high risk for the life of patients.

Only for UK estimates (Mental Health Foundation, n.d.) show that:

- 1 in 4 people will experience some kind of mental health problem in the course of a year
- Mixed anxiety and depression is the most common mental disorder in Britain
- Women are more likely to have been treated for a mental health problem than men
- About 10% of children have a mental health problem at any one time
- Depression affects 1 in 5 older people
- Suicides rates show that British men are three times as likely to die by suicide than British women
- Self-harm statistics for the UK show one of the highest rates in Europe: 400 per 100,000 population
- Only 1 in 10 prisoners has no mental disorder

Depression is a common mental disorder, characterized by sadness, loss of interest or pleasure, feelings of guilt or low self-worth, disturbed sleep or appetite, low energy and poor concentration. These problems can become chronic or recurrent, substantially impairing an individual's ability to cope with daily life. At its most severe, depression can lead to suicide.

Bipolar affective disorder refers to patients with depressive illness along with episodes of mania characterized by elated mood, increased activity, over-confidence and impaired concentration. (Source: WHO)

Both disorders have significant impact on the economic, social even on the criminal and justice systems, while discrimination (stigma) of the mentally ill persons poses an additional challenge to European society (EC, DG Health & Consumer Protection, 2005). According to a 2004 WHO (Mathers, Fat, & Boerma, 2008) report depression ranks fourth among the ten leading causes of the global burden of diseases, while projections (if correct) show that depression will become the 2nd cause of the global disease burden by 2020. Data presented by WHO in the recently published Mental Health Atlas 2011 (World Health Organization, 2011) reassure the significance of the problem and situate it not only with the health system but also with what is called "informal human resources" namely the family and the user associations.

A recently published research within 2011 dealt with "Temporal patterns of happiness and information in a global social network" (Dodds, Harris, Kloumann, Bliss, & Danforth,2011). The authors called this "Hedonometrics" and research individual happiness as a fundamental societal metric. Normally measured through self-report, happiness has often been indirectly characterized and overshadowed by more readily quantifiable economic indicators such as gross domestic product. They examined expressions made on the online, global micro blog and social networking service Twitter, uncovering and explaining temporal variations in happiness and information levels over timescales ranging from hours to years. In measuring happiness, they used a real-time, remote-sensing, non-invasive, text-based approach — a kind of hedonometer. In building their metric, they conducted a survey to obtain happiness evaluations of over 10,000 individual words, representing a tenfold size improvement over similar existing word sets.

The researchers conclude that "... as we have seen in both the work of others and ours, Twitter and similar large-scale, online social networks have thus far provided good evidence that scientifically interesting and meaningful patterns can be extracted from these massive data sources of human behavior. The extent to which small-scale patterns can be elicited, e.g., for rare topics, also remains an open question, as does the true generalizability to the broader population. Whatever the case, Twitter is currently a substantial, growing element of the global media and is worth studying in its own right, just as a study of newspapers would seem entirely valid. And while current evidence suggests 'instant polls' created by remote-sensing text analysis methods are valid, and that these instruments complement and may in some cases improve upon traditional surveys, analysts will have to remain cognizant of the ever present problem of users gaming online expression systems to misinform.

Finally, the era of big data social sciences has undoubtedly begun. Rather than being transformed or revolutionized we feel the correct view is that the social sciences are expanding beyond a stable core to become data-abundant fields. In a data-abundant science, the challenge moves first to description and pattern finding, with explanation and experiments following. Instead of firs forming hypotheses, we are forced to spend considerable time and effort simply describing. The approaches applicable for a data-scarce science still remain of the same value but new, vast windows into social and psychological behavior are now open, and new tools are available and being developed to enable us to take in the view."

A number of state-of-the-art technologies / applications will be developed or adapted in this area. Below we list a representative set of what we consider as relevant state of the art (i.e. what has been done) and the research advances that are expected to take place (i.e. where does this need to go in the future).

State of the art applies mainly to the following:

- Scientific advances in mood disorders & mental health management, depression and bipolar disorder diagnosis and treatment (Cognitive Behavioral Treatment - CBT, self-treatment, etc.)
- Service Models & Web-based services / Personal health systems & e-Health / e-Psychiatry applications for depressive / bipolar out-patients
- Voice and Image analysis (facial expressions, etc.)
- Intelligent systems (expert systems, fuzzy logic)
- Virtual reality in user interfacing
- Wearable and portable devices & systems for patient monitoring (physiological, biological, etc. parameters)
- Interoperability issues in e-Psychiatry solutions

Solutions on depression may not build on entirely novel architectures but they could use various commercially-established technologies/applications e.g. web-services, data-security applications, natural language (speech) generation, etc. Such commercially available technologies can be utilized to build a technology platform and other parts of the solution, where research is not required.

Memory Loss

There are many causes for memory loss. They include depression and post-traumatic stress. They include diabetes, hypertension and traumatic brain-injury. They also include normal ageing as well as forms of dementia such as Alzheimer's or Parkinson's disease. Memory loss or forgetfulness on its own does mean the onset of dementia. This may simply be due to stress of other factors. It is easy to discount symptoms. Dementia is a progressive condition. The signs are very subtle at first and often over many years they gradually get worse. When it is diagnosed it is often quite established. Treatments are best when started early, but this is not so easy to ensure. There is evidence that self-diagnosis is very difficult. The important step is to schedule a meeting with ones doctors and undergo tests to check if the symptoms are significant or not. If they are significant then one must determine the cause.

There are a number of ways of dealing with this. Scientists have managed to restore memory to rats using neural prosthetics. This does not mean they restore memories of 'life as a young rat', but the ability to remember things lost due to trauma of injury to the brain. It is hoped, indeed expected by those who work in the domain that this approach will work as well on day in humans.

Memory loss associated with degenerative conditions such as Alzheimer's or Parkinson's is a progressive process taking many years. There are difficulties in diagnosis and monitoring the progress of the disease due to the slow progress and the fact that both the person suffering memory loss and even those close to them have difficulty monitoring progression and identifying when this might be accelerating or require medic intervention. The general approach is to slow down memory loss as much as possible and help the person to retain as much important memory as possible, memory about themselves and their close ones, essential to maintaining a sense of identity and the confidence required for independent living. The EC has funded projects in this area in the past, for example the FP7 CogKnow project.

The general approach towards memory loss involves recording memories of a person to play them back. This leads us to consider the broader applications of a series of technology trends including life logging, life-streaming and self-quantification, which have implications not only as an assistive technology to help older people dealing with memory loss, but as a technology to help in a much broader health and self-improvement programs of interest to the general population.

LIFE LOGGING, LIFE STREAMING, AND QS

Life logging, life casting, life caching, life streaming and quantifying are all technical activities that have had an impact on the evolution of media and which most likely will have an impact on areas

such as cognitive or behavioral therapy and the treatment of people with various forms dementia or various neurological conditions associated with ageing such as Alzheimer's and Parkinson's.

Life logging ("Lifelog", n.d.) also known as "flogging" is the capture of continuous data about one's everyday life. Professor Steven Mann currently at the University of Toronto, and founder of the wearable computing group at MIT, was one of the first people to experiment with the continuous recording of everyday life using wearable computers. In the early 1980s he developed a wearable wireless camera to support his experimental work. Since 1994 he has been continuously transmitting his life in video and pictures 24 hours a day 7 days a week. The continuous logging and publishing of details of one's life is a form of social networking. By 1998 Mann had a community of 20,000 people following his life log and involved in discussions about the future of this technology and its possible uses. Logging and publishing can be seen as a form blogging, also known as glogging, although glogging seems more associated with the continuous spontaneous broadcasting of news about one's life. The use of mobile telephones that integrated cameras gave boo to this and the trend of moblogging or mobile blogging was born. All of this resembles tweeting and reality TV in no small way. Early reality TV type experiments that relied on Life logging include "WeLiveInPublic" by internet artist Josh Harris, the JeniCam project ("Jennifer Ringley", n.d.) by conceptual artist Jennifer Ringley and the yearlong DotComGuy ("DotComGuy", n.d.) experiment. In 2007 Justin Kahn coined the term life casting to refer to his own Life logging adventures and since then many new people have become involved in this in of activity. One couple has tried to turn their joint life logging experience into a movie called FourEyedMonsters. Justin TV (Justin.tv Inc., 2014) provides a point of access for life loggers or life casters. Already there are more than 2300 life casts to choose from. Stickam (Stickam, n.d.) was a portal that allowed people not only to do live streaming but supports both amateur and professional users with the implementation of pay-per-view access to their content.

A range of cheap wearable technologies now exist to support life-logging. The Ucorder (UCorder, 2012) is wearable mini pocket camcorder aimed at the life logging market. Vicon (Vicon Motion Systems Ltd n.d.) produces cameras for motion capture applications that can process up to 1000 images a second to create data based on detailed motion analysis. This can be used by athletes, vets and engineers as a diagnostic or trouble-shooting tool to help improve performance. The Looxcie (Loxcie Inc., 2014) is a wearable Bluetooth camcorder costing $150. It is always recording and if you want to retain the last 30 seconds to just tap a button and it will save that moment' posting it online. You can also start and stop it manually just like an ordinary camcorder, reviewing the footage on your mobile phone. These are aimed at extreme sports people and groups of friends who just want to stay in touch, extending the group experience across geography and time.

Life-logging is not confined to humans. Researchers also apply this to animals such as primates. In this case the idea is to apply the paradigm to understanding the brain. At least one group of researchers led by Prof. Naotaka Fuji from RIKEN in Japan has developed a system called ULLp which stands for Ultimate LifeLog in primates. This combines data from the detailed recordings of the neocortical brain activity of monkeys along with simultaneous data about body movements, eye-movements and social interactions of monkeys. The ultimate goal is to be able to understand the working of the brain. Another element of this work is an initiative called Neurotycho (Neurotycho, n.d.), an online primate data sharing service which makes brain and behavioral data such as that generated by ULLp available to researchers all over the world so that to mine the data, formulate and check hypotheses and develop their own models of brain function base on the ULLp dataset.

DARPA ran a life logging project entitled LifeLog ("Lifelog", n.d.) until about 2004. The goal here was similar to other life logging projects, to gather together in one place all of the very heterogeneous data of someone's life, all the emails they sent or received, the place tickets they bought, purchases they made as well as a continuous record of their physiological data, blood pressure, blood sugar, body weight and temperature, with a view to searching and processing this data at some later stage. It appears that one of the reasons the project was cancelled was opposition from pressure groups and concerns about security. It seems clear that at some stage the issue of security will have to be addressed, but it should not hamper the kind of experimentation that is currently required to prove the key concepts, develop the systems and services for implementation and explore the ways in which this kind of activity can create value.

One of the most famous names in life logging however is Gordon bell, who as VP of Engineering at DEC oversaw the development of the VAX, but has since worked at Microsoft on subjects such as telepresence and as the experimental subject of the MyLifeBits (Microsoft, 2014) project. The goal of this project is to permanently record all of the images, sounds and documents of a human lifetime, in this case that of Gordon Bell. This presents challenges not only for recording and storing data but for searching it and visualizing the results of such as search in a useful format. The experiment has led to the concept of the "terabyte life", based on an estimate that the total of all recorded sights and sounds of an individual lifetime should require about 1 terabyte of storage. A book originally entitled "Total Recall: How the e-memory revolution will change everything" (Bell & Gemmell 2009) was republished in November 2010 as "Your life uploaded: The digital way to better memory, health and productivity" by Gordon bell and Jim Gemell (Bell & Gemmell, 2010) one of the original creators of the MyLifeBits project.

A related concept is the Lifestream ("Lifestreaming", n.d.), a term coined by David Gelernter author of a seminal work in the early history of the internet called Mirror Worlds (Gelernter, 1992), and creator of the original concept of "the cloud". For Gelernter a life stream is the collection of all ones documents and texts, images and videos, but organized as the mind organizes things (Brockman, 1999). A recent Singularity Hub article (Singularity Hub, 2010) estimates that by combining already available technologies that can recognize and tag faces in a photo, with imminent technologies for voice recognition and speech to text translation, star-trek like interrogation of one's life log may be a reality within 10 to20 years.

The most recent manifestation of life-logging and life streaming is the self-quantifying. The Quantified Self (Quantified Self Labs, 2012) is a movement that stared in California in 2008. Gary Wolf one of the founders of the QS movement explains its goals in a recent TED conference (Wolf, 2010). Since its foundation it has grown into a global organization with more than 5,000 members in 11 countries, in the Americas, Europe and Asia. The Brussels group held their first meeting (Meetup, 2011) in March 2011. The members share an interest in how to use the continuous measurement of any or all aspects of their lives, an activity known as self-quantification, to manage and improve various aspects of their lives. The QS website maintains a catalogue of more than 400 QS applications (Quantified Self Labs, 2011).

One of these is Moodscope (Moodscope Ltd, 2014) an online system for tracking your mood in real time. MercuryApp (MercuryApp, 2014) helps its clients gather data to understand what affects their mood and how to manage enabling them to live the happiest most enjoyable life possible. A company called Zeo provides a range of products and services around the subject of sleep.

A company called Jawbone has developed the UP wrist band iPhone app (Jawbone, 2014) that tracks your movements and sleep quality. For example it automatically records how many steps you have taken and hours of deep sleep and light sleep you have slept, all on a continuous

basis. When you plug it into an iPhone you get a voice read out of the data. The iPhone can be used to keep a photo journal of what you eat that is synchronized with the sleep an exercise data. Further applications allow you to mine this data or visualize trends over time. It is aimed at people who want to improve their performance over time, for example those who have difficulty sleeping and want to understand what mixture of sleep and exercise makes them feel most comfortable and happy.

A company called Asthmapolis (Propeller Health, 2013) provides tools to track manage and control Asthma. One of their products is an inhaler with a Wi-Fi enabled built in GPS system. It allows an individual user to understand where and at what time the attacks occur. It allows their physician to remotely monitor the condition. At a collective level it allows pubic authorities or a service provide to identify trend and even find root causes of Asthma attacks. This data can be displayed to someone with Asthma using a map based app on their iPhone. Inspired by a story (Acever, Grimalt, Sunyer, Anto, & Reed, 1991) of how emergency room records for asthma attacks in the city of Barcelona enabled the identification of the attacks as the offloading and storage of soybeans, the hope is that a large community of users of the Asthmapolis device will enable smart management of the condition in future.

A Wi-Fi weighing scale costing $160 was released by Withings (Withings, 2014b) in time for the 2011 Christmas gift market. When you step on this in your bare-feet it records your weight transmitting both your weight and body-mass statistics to a password protected website that can be consulted using your iPhone. This is aimed at sports people and families who want to monitor the weight, fat, muscle and body-mass index of the whole family with a view to managing diet and maintaining health and fitness. The same company produces baby-monitors and blood pressure monitors. An interesting phenomenon from an innovation perspective is the companies that are associated with this product using the data it generates as the basis for a wide range of value added health and lifestyle services (Withings, 2014a).

Telcare has developed what it claims is the world's first mobile phone enabled blood glucose meter. The product is called the Telcare BGM (Telcare Inc., 2014) and is aimed at people with diabetes. A device carries out the blood glucose measurement. The reading is then passed to an FDA approved server where all the sensitive health related data is stored. It can be accessed via an iPhone or mobile device. The data can be visualized, instructions passed and shared with a care-giver or family member.

Many of those who practice life-logging, life-streaming or any variation thereof may have come to this from extreme sports. Those involved in extreme sports love to share the moment. They attach small cameras to their skis, snow-boards and skate-boards, their mountain bikes, climbing equipment and scuba masks, their surf-boards, wind-surfers and hang-gliders, and of course they attach them to their sky-diving helmets. It helps them learn new moves and improve old ones. It allows them to capture intense moments of exhilaration, share them with others and in quiet moments remind themselves of how vividly they have lived.

Nike+ (Nike Inc., 2014) is a social networking service run by Nike that uses mobile apps to help people track their performance, formulate goals and associate with like-minded people. Of course one of the goals is to sell more Nike sports gear, but the use of iPhone apps and social networking makes it into an opportunity to achieve real health fitness, social lifestyle goals. Who knows how the future will evolve maybe Nike+ will evolve into a major performance lever for elderly people in 2020?

Last year Apple filed a patent for biometric ear buds that not only allows you to hear music on your iPhone or iPod, but will also detect blood oxygenation, body temperature and heart rate.

The CureTogether (CureTogether, 2014) website provides a venue for quantifiers as well as non-quantifiers to share experience and discuss approaches to dealing with over 590 different conditions including depression, anxiety, shyness, back-pain and migraine. The gathering and sharing of data, the mining of the data and the constant experimentation with sleep and diet, rest and exercise, all with a view to improving one's personal health or performance, is a form of citizen science ("Citizen science", n.d.), science that is done by involving ordinary citizens, often students and hobbyists, in the gathering of scientific data or the testing of scientific hypotheses, all with a serious scientific end. It resembles the use of games such as fold-it to explore protein folding, the classification of stars and galaxies.

Already there is an extraordinary range of products and services that measure data about ones bodily functions. The range of service will increase to include cognitive states and brain activity. Parameters that are currently self-reported such as mood or feeling of well bring will become increasing automated, being based on the ability of machines to read body language and interpret gestures, facial expressions and patterns of behavior.

The data streamed from wearable web cams for life logging will be automatically annotated for easy search. Image recognition systems will recognize meals, identify what is being consumer and in what quantity. Or maybe this will come from smart kitchenware. It will become increasingly easy to associate behaviors and content with healthcare outcome and the ability to life with a disability. Specialists will work with specialist service providers mining this data to develop and deliver improved diagnostic and treatment services based physical, cognitive and behavioral therapies.

Eventually this will work not only as assistive technologies for people who want to live independent lives as they grow old, but for younger people living with developmental disabilities such as ADHD and autism, enabling them to more easily enter the work force and live full, productive independent lives. It can also be applied to those with recurrent or occasional or temporary disabilities such as excessive shyness, self-destructive behavior, migraines, bouts of depression or anxiety, eating related disorders such as anorexia, bulimia or obesity, work related stress or nervous breakdown, dependence on drugs or alcohol.

This is a huge ambition and perhaps not all of it can be achieved by 2020, but much of it may, and there are many useful intermediate phases to work through before the ultimate goal can be achieved.

HUMAN FACTORS

Many of the solutions presented in research projects for health and social care services focus solely on technological challenges. Although technical challenges can be quite compelling and interesting for research in this area there is one important factor not to be missed. All current state of the art technologies used in health and social care domain need to address real peoples' needs. There should inevitably some focus on how each solution suggested is an applicable one and what practical issues may rise from the fact that in many cases they have to do with people that have limited or decreasing cognitive abilities such as memory, learning skills etc. Thus, the ease of use, the applicability and everyday lifestyle issues preventing it should be taken seriously under account.

The Problem with Wearable Computing

A technology often used for monitoring services for health and social care is wearable systems. There are currently a variety of projects dealing with research on how these wearable systems can be used in health services. Wearable systems suggested for elderly monitoring usually take the form of bracelets that are worn on ankles or wrists. There are already major developments in the area indicating the potentials for such kind of solutions

in health care monitoring especially for elderly people. However, most of the research does not seem to report on simple practical matters that may hinder the use of such devices for everyday life. People tend to take wearable devices when showering, or cooking or doing other jobs. Elderly people are often forgetful and forget to wear them back. In other cases such devices might annoy people that wear them and also it might be an indication of their condition stigmatizing them in social interactions.

In 2003 Kahterine Watier (Watier, 2003) in her MSc thesis on wearable systems and how early adopters where perceiving such devices, she was describing a gap in research pointing out that *"Most of the published research, which promotes wearable computers, is focused on improving the functional aspect of the technology (making it smaller, lighter, faster) and ignores the impact of human factors behind its adoption. If the attitudes and concerns of users are referenced, the tendency is for researchers to talk about how the users will only be interested in the technology if the functions become more efficient (making it lighter, easier to use, and more ambiguous - less geeky) rather than addressing the consumer attitudes and perceptions (their social distraction concerns, concerns about durability, etc.)"* Since then, there seems to be a little research on these human factors affecting adoption rates of solutions based on wearable systems and how such issues can be dealt with.

Wearable computing and relevant monitoring systems should provide solutions that are unobtrusive and easy to use so as to maximize their usability and impact. Unobtrusive means that person wearing such systems will not be annoyed in any undesired way by such devices. They should be able to even forget their existence in order to wear them all the time. Research on making such systems smaller and lighter might help in that direction, but it should always take more seriously human factors that will prevent its continually and seamless functionality. Future research programs should look into these dimensions of technology in order to make it more feasible and possible to be expanded in widely adopted solutions. Additionally, this is also a challenge for innovation in the area from the companies producing such wearable systems.

Smart Environments

Another area with interesting results in monitoring services is this of smart homes. In the past technologies for smart homes meant that a set of sensor would have to be wired into the house. This installation was a problem since it meant drilling holes into walls, getting cables inside them or under the floor and generally a general disturbance for the older adult living in the house. That is also a reason why many of the researches in the area where building their own testing house environments and bringing people to live into them. Wireless technology has lifted this significant barrier in installation of such a system. However it doesn't seem to have affected the cost barrier which is still high. Sensors like cameras, infrared movement sensors, bed sensors, water detecting sensors etc. can now be installed and connected wirelessly in a central monitoring system such as the one presented by Eric Gunther (Gunther, 2008).

However, research and development in the area of wearable systems often tends to underestimate issues of applicability, appropriateness and usefulness. As pointed out by Dan Ding et al (Ding et. al., 2011) in their review of available technologies for smart home environments "*More evidence on the appropriateness, usefulness, and cost benefits analysis of sensor technologies for smart homes is necessary before these sensors should be widely deployed into real-world residential settings and successfully integrated into everyday life and health care services*". Three years earlier in a study presenting a model for participatory formative model of evaluation of smart home environments the authors George Demiris et al (2006) conclude that "*Their (smart home sensors' for elderly) suc-*

cess depends not only on the technical feasibility of specific devices and sensors but also on the level of successful integration into everyday life and health care services. Thus, extensive and ongoing evaluation can reveal challenges and allow for participants to provide feedback and improve the overall system".

The challenge of successful integration in living environments is indicative of the problems that research is facing when trying to transfer ICT applications in real life. In general research tends to focus on the sensors efficiency, their durability, sustainability, accuracy and other technical aspects leaving out of the equation human factors. If sensors are placed in wrong places they might get disconnected, damaged, stop functioning due to a variety of reasons from cleaning up the house to pets fooling around with them and finally destroying them. This is one of the biggest challenges for the future of research and innovation in the area of smart homes for health care services for elderly. Maybe a different innovation model based on user cantered design and implementation would provide with answers and solutions easier than already existing ones.

Another issue also associated with smart home environments for health care of elderly has to do with the monitoring and caring services connected with them. How does such a health care service respond to malfunctioning of sensors? How should it respond to sensors being tampered and broken? How should it respond in danger alerts? What happens with false alarms? Should a caregiver be sent to home in all of these cases? If an elderly person gets visits all the time from a caregiver because his cat is tempering with sensors sending false alarms this is a case where care becomes annoying.

There is a wide area of research in this direction and questions like the latter should be addressed before such services are implemented widely. Let's not forget that it is a lot easier for a participant to accept such nuances in his personal life when he willingly participates in a study, but such problems in services would be unacceptable if they were provided under a subscription scheme.

Affective Smart Environments

Looking further into the user-friendliness aspect of the smart home solution we can understand that some of the possible problems of annoying residents of smart homes with false alarms could be avoided if sensor signals were reinforced with further information about the resident's status at the moment. What was his emotional state, what was he doing at the time the alarm went off, how is he reacting to what happened. Much of this information could be gathered by affective computing solutions.

In Universidad Carlos III de Madrid scientists developed a machine able to recognize a person's feelings (Universidad Carlos III de Madrid, 2011) based on his speech interaction with the machine. It can recognize anger, doubt and boredom and adjust the conversation accordingly. In Binghamton University scientist Lijun Yin is working with psychologist Peter Gerhardstein (Coxworth, 2011) collecting a large set of facial expression images and mapping them to emotions in order to produce software that will recognize emotion based on a person's facial expression. EU has also funded research in the area with HUMAINE being one the projects in that direction. HUMAINE project (European Commission, 2010) aims to lay the foundations for European development of systems that can register, model and /or influence human emotional and emotion-related states - 'emotion-oriented systems'. In general the area of affective computing is showing vast potential of recognizing emotion of people in the future.

One of the areas where affective computing solutions can be used is smart home environments for health care monitoring services. Such environments in the future could detect person's emotions and respond accordingly. If the person is feeling quite confident with what he is doing they could reduce assistance provided and if they show signs of anxiety, doubt or other disturbing feelings they could come up with appropriate responses. Smart homes of the future are expected to understand implicit user's behavior signs such as face expressions, movements, voice etc. and react accordingly. This technology could also provide monitoring and caring services with additional parameters when something unexpected happens to the person receiving care to evaluate the importance of a situation.

In such environments for example when a person for example wakes up and stays in bed because he is in pain it will trigger the appropriate alarms and reactions, while on the other hand it will not do anything if the person woke up and just enjoys a few more moments of relaxation in bed looking out the window. Sensors in bed will cooperate with wake-up alarm clocks and cameras or microphones in the room to detect which is the case.

Further research in the area of affective computing will boost the applications of smart home environments and not only. The applications of this technology can be numerous across many aspects of living apart from health-related services. A number of research issues should (better) be addressed, including privacy concerns, acceptance by users, integration of different emotion detection technologies, etc.

Beyond Appliances Communication

Smart home environments have already passed the boundaries of appliances interacting with the user. The wired model of a smart house is already giving place to the wireless one where sensor networks communicate with each other (Verwymeren, 2011)and together they reach certain decisions on the residents' activities within the house. So, instead of having a smart fridge detecting that there is no milk and suggesting to the user to order some we now have a network of appliances cooperating together. The smart home of the future will have appliances in the kitchen communicating with each other and acting as a whole. If for example the kitchen knows the diet program of the resident it can find out which ingredients are missing for coking the meals for the next 3 days. It could further communicate with the mobile device of the resident and the smart wallet application to decide and suggest to the resident what he needs to buy for the next days. It could send the list to the mobile phone, it could send an order to the super market or it could just inform the person by showing up the list in the TV screen when requested.

There are two issues in that picture though. The first has to do with the interaction with the person living in the house. People and especially older ones, will probably have problems if you introduce them with all this technology from one day to the other. Smart homes in reality will not be expected to be developed in one instance as in experiments taking place. A more possible model of building a smart home will be a gradual transition from the traditional home to the smart one by gradually introducing new devices and appliances to it. An ageing person will possibly not need all this technology in one day. He will rather gather it gradually by renewing appliances or installing parts of the smart environment gradually.

There is a need for provision in issues such as compatibility and communication of appliances and other devices installed in a smart home. Software architecture should be open to upgrades and there needs to be provision on methods, technologies and protocols for communication between various devices.

The second issue that has to be taken under account in developing parts (sensors, appliances etc.) for a smart home solution is its integration within an already existing and adapted network of devices. For example, one problem might be the degree of adaptability of each device according to the user. It's not worth buying and integrating a new TV in the grandpa's smart home if it cannot adjust its behavior to his needs. Interaction methods and adaptation of interaction should be followed seamlessly by all devices and appliances integrated in a smart home of the future. Smart environments in the future will need to deal with issues of new installations, new devices, new appliances and new interaction entities in general (e.g. a new companion robot, a new pet, a new person, a new mobile phone) in the house without troubling the resident.

Perceived Risks with Service or Companion Robots

One of the technologies already presented for health care, education and may other purposes is robotics. Latest developments in affective computing and robotics bring closer scenarios where robots will be one of the major solutions for caring services to elderly. In the University of Hertfordshire the project titled "ACCOMPANY" (University of Hertfordshire, 2011) aims to provide an assistance robot for elderly. As Dr Amirabdollahian states "*The envisaged relationship between the user and the robot is that of co-learner, whereby the robot and user provide mutual assistance and so that the user is not dominated by technology, but feels empowered by it. Our aim is to use the robot to increase independence and quality of life*". The relationship described is what the scientist believes that the use of the robot should be. However, there are still no clear regulations defining the limitations of use of robots.

In the University of Sheffield another top robotics expert, Noel Sharkey, (University of Sheffield, 2008) calls for international guidelines to be set for the ethical and safe application of robots before it is too late. According to Sharkey, robots will invade our lives soon in unprecedented numbers and they will be used for a variety of applications. It is essential though to get ready for the potential impact that these changes will have to communities. For example, an already exploited application is taking care of children, but as Noel Sharkey points out "*...because of the physical safety that robot minders provide, children could* *be left without human contact for many hours a day or perhaps for several days, and the possible psychological impact of the varying degrees of social isolation on development is unknown.".* Similarly he also describes a dark possibility for elderly *"These robots can help the elderly to maintain independence in their own homes, but their presence could lead to the risk of leaving the elderly in the exclusive care of machines without sufficient human contact."*

These concerns are issues that have to be researched and regulated before robots invade our lives and learn to depend on them. There is a need for further research on the effects that human-robot interaction can have in cases of companion or assistive robots and the potentials for the future of our societies. Especially when it comes to people with disabilities, developmental disorders and elderly where the social aspect should play crucial role in their lives it would be a major mistake if societies use robots as a way to "dumb" the difficulties of including them in the society.

On the other hand solutions of robotics such as telepresence robots might help in keeping contact with friends and family and not feel abandoned. However, there is no research yet that indicated the effects that such robot can have for elderly or people with cognitive disorders and disabilities. It is possible for people with cognitive disabilities to mix reality with virtual reality entities. The phenomenon of videogame addiction ("Video game addiction", n.d.) is already revealing psychological problems that can be caused by excessive interaction with video games where the user is one of the heroes and it could possibly give some lessons to the research on robotics.

There is a vast area of research that needs to address those issues in the coming years. Since robots are going to invade our everyday lives sooner or later it is better to know the potential dangers especially for those who can benefit the most from them.

Assistive Technologies for Caretakers

An aspect that is really interesting especially in the health and social care services is that there might be assistive technology solution that might not target the person with disability directly. For example Lockheed Martin originally developed the HULC (Human Universal Load Carrier) to assist soldiers during combat. It could be used to help lift heavy loads while exerting minimal effort, with soldiers currently going into combat with up to 130 pounds of combat gear. Also, it could be used as a framework for body armor or sensor arrays that would allow for better situational awareness during combat.

Lockheed Martin is also exploring exoskeleton designs to support industrial and medical applications. A typical application for such an exoskeleton would be to target persons with mobility impairments and help then stand on their feet. However it is also interesting to notice that since the exoskeleton allows people to augment their strengths and power it could easily be used in health care service by nurses who want to lift persons with paralysis or other impairments.

Another similar example is this of Toyota Partner Robots (TOYOTA, 2011). They can be used by caretakers to help them in lifting patients, helping them balance and walk. RIBA II by RIKEN (Riken, 2011) is also another similar robot for caretakers to help them lifting patients. It seems that lifting a patient can be a strenuous task for nurses that might need to do this up to 40 times per day in Japan. Caretakers and nurses often suffer from extended exposure to back injuries (Ergonurse, n.d.). Giving them technology such as this that helps them respond to such tasks easier is certainly for the benefit of person with disability too.

There are a lot of cases where new technologies can help caretakers perform their tasks more effectively. This is a market worth looking into in the future since the increasing costs for keeping a personal care assistant for elderly persons given the financial austerity situation currently experienced all over Europe. The use of technology to assist humans seems like an optimal solution and not as a compromise.

THE NEED FOR AFFORDABILITY

The Fashion Factor in Wearable Computing

One of the major problems with new technologies is their cost. In most cases building a smart home as the ones build for experiments or the ones adapted for research requires a lot of money for a single person to afford. Especially when we are referring to elderly and disabled who sometimes face also employment and employability problems and live on allowances. This is also the case for many wearable systems too.

One of the major ideas in the direction of making technologies for persons with disabilities affordable has to do with the idea of mainstreaming accessibility. The idea is to repurpose assistive devices and technologies for wider audiences. A recent example of that effect is with Siri (Apple, 2014a), the speech interfaces software integrated in iPhone 4S (Apple, 2014b). Up to now, the cost of having similar software on a PC or mobile device was something that only a few could afford. In fact, many people that could benefit from its use compromised by choosing other methods of interaction. Bringing Siri on one of the most popular phones (even if its cost isn't the lowest of all) made competition to seek and start providing similar applications lowering even more its cost. This rally for market share is going to constantly lower the cost to speech interface technologies making is even more affordable for Persons with disabilities.

The example with iPhone 4S brings up also another interesting discussion on how the cost of various technologies can be brought down. It's the

fashion factor and it's something that can really affect costs in wearable computing. When something becomes fashionable it almost immediately gains popularity and more potential buyers on the market. This in turn leads to lowering the cost to make it even more popular.

Wearable computing has already been connected with the fashion world and can benefit most from this relation. Appealing design of wearable computing and integration of such applications into fashion items can potentially multiple their market demand. Evidence of that combination happening are already existent such as the Ubiquitous Fashionable Computer Fashion Show In South Korea in 2006 (Avax News, 2011) which presented some really interesting wearable computing devices. Lately there is also increasing interest in wearable computing from major companies such as Apple, Google (Bliton, 2011) and Microsoft (Microsoft, 2014).

The DIY Factor in Smart Homes

Another interesting trend in AT that could also help in lowering costs of installation and maintenance especially for smart environment technologies is the Do It Yourself trend. In a research presented in ASSETS 2011 by Amy Hurst and Jasmine Tobias (Hurst & Tobias, 2011) a series of do-it-yourself assistive devices are presented and as explained the emergence of such solutions is reinforced lately from the increasing use of online communities and social networks that help in sharing knowledge and experiences and improve or create your own assistive devices.

In the case of smart homes Grad School Digital Imaging student Sam Cox (Fish, 2011) presents how he managed to enhance his home security with off the self-products combined under a common home network in order to communicate with each other. Such devices are already available in the market but they lack co-operation with other devices. Combining them and producing smart home applications can be fairly easy for someone with some technical knowledge and creativity. There are also a number of guides, videos, tutorials etc. in the web that can explain and guide anyone with some basic knowledge how to reproduce such solutions. Of course it is not expected from an 80 year old to have this knowledge and do such installations on his own, but it could be his child, grandchild or even a close friend in the neighbor that takes care of him that he/she could install such a system in the house for fairly simple functions such as fall detection.

DIY solutions for smart homes will benefit from protocols and general software required which can make the integration of appliances and devices possible. Once again the point of connectivity and communication between devices becomes crucial and it seems to be the cornerstone for success of such systems. Thus, there is once more evident a need for standards and compliance of major stakeholders to them.

The Problem of Adoption

A recent study by Eurostat reveals that almost 25% or European population has never accessed the Internet. The same study though shows that the percentage of people without access to the Internet has been decreased from 42% to 24% in the last 5 years. Thus, one can see two major facts in the study. The first is that there are still a large number of people that don't have internet access and the other is that the rate of increase in internet access is really fast. Looking further into the statistics of Eurostat one can see that people in age groups 55 to 64 and 65 to 74 (Eurostat, 2013a) the percentages are increased to 44% and 67% respectively in 2010 but we can also see a similar decrease with the one of the whole population (almost 20%) in that percentage over the past 5 years. As for eHealth services the percentage of population using the internet to seek health related information (Eurostat, 2013c) has raised over the past 5 years from 19% (2006) to 38% (2011).

A simple generalization of that fact would be to say that there is still a large part of the population that does not use ICT especially for elderly people. However, this is not always the case with all ICT. The report for example from WHO on mHealth (mobile eHealth) (WHO Global Observatory for eHealth. World Health Organization, 2011) services point out that usage and acceptance of mobile phones is generally higher than other ICT. For Europe the number of subscription per 100 habitants in 2009 was 125 (Eurostat 2013b) without any further analysis on age groups. TV is also another example of a device with wide adoption. Landline phones are also another similar example with wide adoption. So, although internet access adoption might not be high enough to call it widely adopted (especially among elderly), this is not the case with other ICT too.

Another interesting remark that can be done from the Eurostat report is that there is significant difference in internet access percentages between various European counties. While the Netherlands have 94% of their households accessing the internet in Greece only 50% of households have internet access. Although there is not a further explanation on the reasons of this phenomenon it is possible that both cultural and national policy aspects might have affected this difference.

Wide penetration of the internet in European households is closely linked with relevant national and regional policies. Good practice examples of such successful policies may be transferred to other countries. However, there is also a need to identify what are the cultural differences that lead to such different rates of adoption and what can be done to overcome them. Adoption might be one of the biggest barriers especially in the health-related services domain which deals a lot with elderly people resisting to change. Learning lessons from success stories in EU countries will be crucial for the success in others too.

E-HEALTH SERVICES BEYOND WWW

In another study conducted in 2008 by AARP (Barrett, 2008) aiming to profile elderly people especially in the group of 65+ there are some results that are remarkable. First of all 88% of elderly asked said that they were willing to use a computer to seek for health related information online. Among the reasons for using a computer to seek for information or stay in touch with family are "give my relatives piece of mind", "give me piece of mind", "make me safer" and "make me more comfortable" although there is still a 58% that believe that this is something they don't really need.

It is also evident that willing to use home safety devices exceeds knowledge of existence of such devices. However, this willingness is not as high as with computer use. Some of the biggest perceived barriers to using home safety devices are the cost of installation (81%) and maintenance (79%) and still another 70% still believe that these devices are something they don't really need. Interestingly they do also believe that using home safety devices will give piece of mind to relatives (82%) and make them feel safer (84%). Similarly costs are the main barrier for Health and Wellness devices and the most important reasons for adoption are still personal safety and peace of mind for friends and family. However, willingness and knowledge of such devices is generally lower than the other two categories.

Interestingly the Personal Emergency Response Systems (PERS) are very well known to them (91%) but they are really reluctant to use them (60%).

Another critical aspect in adoption of e-Health services is the perceived and real ease of use. Interestingly in almost all categories of e-Heath services presented in the previous research almost half the population of elderly believes that the devices will be difficult to learn on how to use. Although in some cases, such devices do not need any special interaction. It is also important to point out those introducing e-Health services within traditional means of communication and interaction with machines is a factor that could possible affect that perceived ease of use. A TV set for example that reminds you to take your pills is an example of an e-Health service provided through a widely adopted device and already known interface. The same goes for reminders using phone calls. Successful cases of devices for elderly that are easy to use (Taub, 2008) already exist and what is need is to follow such examples. Thus, it is important for future research to gracefully integrate services within already existing devices or using unobtrusive and easy to use devices.

The Case of M-Health Services Adoption

An emerging technology trend that made its appearance lately is the use of mobile devices and computing. Mobile devices are expected to be the tool for providing a variety of e-Health services in the future and the WHO observatory for e-Health services has published a report on mHealth services (WHO Global Observatory for eHealth. World Health Organization, 2011) and the potentials that mobile technology can have for health care services. However there is no special reference to people with disabilities or elderly within the health care solutions presented in the book. Some of the solutions are indeed focusing on monitoring elderly, medicine reminders for people with forgetfulness etc. The general conclusions are drawn on the basis of health care service that addresses problems both for people with and without disabilities.

When coming to elderly there are two different options and points of view on the future of health care services. One side supports that elderly are keen to adopting new technologies in general and this trend is rising fast as the Baby Boomers generation is reaching retirement ages. Adoption of mobile phones and especially smartphones within ageing population is a crucial point for the success of m-Health services. There is no point in developing m-Health services and applications if ageing population isn't going to use it. To this direction recent research presented by Nielsen (Srivastava, n.d.) shows that current adoption rate of mobile phones and especially smartphones is relatively small when compared to younger age groups. However, the study found an increase in smart phone purchases by 5% on the third quarter of 2011 that is characterized as a "wake-up call" by Don Kellogg of Nielsen. To that direction smart phone market is moving towards providing cheaper smartphones with social networking capabilities and standard features especially targeted for older adults such as bigger text. Supporting evidence also come from a study form the Pew Research Centre (Rock, n.d.) which shows a significant raise in usage of social networking sites by older adults that are often referred to as silver surfers. These technology trends show that upcoming ageing populations might be more used to using ICT in their everyday life thus making it easier to provide e-Health and m-Health services to them.

On the other hand studies such as the one by Kelly Quinn presented in the International Journal of Emerging Technologies and Society (Quinn, 2010) point out potential bias of studies that use ICT based tools to gather information about technology use by older adults. It is also clear in the study that there is a significant divide in technological sophistication between people younger than 55 and older than 55.

People younger than 55 who are going to be the future elderly generations show a better familiarization with ICT and its use in everyday life in contrast with those above 55 year old. Similar findings are also presented by Dr. Mireia Fernandez Ardevol (Fernández-Ardèvo, 2010) who presents a study about how elderly people use mobile phones. It is important to say that mobile phones among other ICT are adopted easier and in wider range by elderly. However the services used by elderly are fairly simple. They mainly use it for telephony and texting services.

The latter, indicate that there seems to be forming a trend among upcoming elderly genera-

tions in using smartphones and mobile devices in their everyday lives. However, there is still a significant lack of adoption of such technologies among already existing elderly generations. A point however worth taking note is that older adults are showing evidence of adoption of mobile phones although not especially smartphones. They also seem able to use them for simple tasks such as calling and in some cases texting with it. It is also important to point out that according to other studies a significant factor affecting acceptance of mobile phones by older people is the perceived ease of use that might not change easily even after year of usage of mobile phone. As pointed out in the conclusions of the study and that *"there are at least two ways to improve the overall confidence of older people in the MP (Mobile Phones): a) contrasting the importance of ease of use by improving long term usability of the MP, and b) given the relationships of Enjoyment and Self Actualization to PEU (Perceives Ease of Use), leveraging on hedonic and experiential aspect, and on functionalities enhancing self-realization in older people."*

A general conclusion from the debate on m-Health services can be that there are currently two age groups that can be significantly affected now and in the future by m-Health services but there seems to be a difference between them in lifestyles and especially in adoption of mobile phones and smartphones especially. What can be learned from that is that current development of m-Health services should base itself in fairly simple functions of mobile phones such as calling. For example, it is more probable that currently a medicine reminder service based on automatic calling machine that calls the patient to remind the medicines to take, will be more successful in being adopted be elderly. However, future trends will probably change so that mobile smart phone apps for reminder will be easier adopted in the future rather than the current automated calling system.

New Intuitive Interfaces for All Devices

In addition to adoption issues of mobile phones from elderly there are also issues that can affect efficiency and effectiveness of m-Health services that do not relate to ease of use and simplicity of such services. Older adults with dementia, forgetfulness, Alzheimer and similar cognitive conditions tend to forget their mobile phones around the house, in other places (friends' homes, parks, restaurants, etc.). It is essential though for mobile phone markets when targeting older adults to provide appropriate devices, easy to use, that recognize their owner, that know where they are and that can warn the owner in case they sense they will be forgotten.

An interesting point with mobile technologies and m-Health solutions is how the ease of use factor of a mobile device can be eliminated in providing such services. As already discussed simplicity in m-Health care services can affect adoption rates significantly. As pointed out in the WHO report on m-Health "*SMS was the most common phone feature used for appointment reminders.*" If the phone interface is simple enough to read SMS's then the over service usability increases. Getting new intuitive interaction mechanisms in mobile phones such as speech interaction (see Siri for iPhone 4S) can certainly make this interaction even easier. Improving interaction with mobile devices with more intuitive interaction mechanisms could lead mobile devices to becoming primal robot-like devices providing a whole lot of new range of monitoring, care and assistive services.

Concerns over Security and Privacy

Just about two years ago the Bureau of Justice Statistics in US released a report (United States. Bureau of Justice Statistics, 2007) about the crime against persons with disabilities. Some of the most interesting findings are the following:

- The age-adjusted rate of nonfatal violent crimes against persons with disabilities was 1.5 times higher than the rate for those without disabilities (32 per 1,000 persons age 12 or older compared to 21 per 1,000).
- The rate of violence did not differ by disability status for persons age 50 or older. Persons age 65 or older, with or without a disability, had the lowest rates of violent crime.
- Persons with cognitive disabilities had a rate of nonfatal violent crime higher than the rates for persons with other types of disabilities.

These facts reveal that people with disabilities have higher possibilities to be victimized in non-violent crimes and those with cognitive disabilities are at the outmost risk. In addition it is also evident that elderly, regardless of disability are also in the same group with people with disabilities as person with high possibilities of victimization. In other words, people with disabilities of all kinds and elderly are the most probable victims of nonviolent crimes. However, there is no evidence yet on what is the relation between people with disabilities and cyber-crime.

In another article (10TV, 2011) FBI says that cyber-crime is likely to rise to No.1 threat in a few years from No.3 that is currently is. FBI Supervisory Special Agent Robert White says that "*Given our connection to the Internet, and our infrastructure and everything being computerized, it also lends itself to possible cyber terrorism*". Finally Europol recently revealed that intends to host an EU cyber-crime center. As Troels Oerting, Europol's deputy chief says "*These attacks will only increase in the future, as our lives get more and more integrated to the Internet. How will this all work? What about the speed of mutual legal assistance, with these cumbersome and old-fashioned systems, where you have to send it to the ministry. New rules should be set up by this cyber center for us to exchange information very rapidly, not to take days and weeks"*.

The increase of cyber-crime and the high victimization of people with disabilities in nonviolent crimes cannot help but thinking that people with disabilities and especially those with cognitive ones can also be highly victimized in cyber-crime too. Although it is not yet studied extensively the transfer of the crime to the cyber world is very likely to follow the same rules. Therefore, there is a need for provision in that direction to be taken especially with health care systems.

Social Media as Protection Mechanism

Recently Facebook revealed a new tool for preventing suicides (Donald, 2011). It makes easier to spot persons expressing suicidal thoughts by allowing friends of the person to report that a comment or a post expresses suicidal thoughts. Facebook then sends an email to the person encouraging them to contact a suicide hotline or click on a link to start a confidential chat. Similarly it also allows people to report bullying and other offensive behavior and acts accordingly. In addition, police today has already used social media to prevent and investigate crimes in many cases ("Use of social network websites in investigations", n.d.).

Since reports show an increase in social networking adoption by elderly people it is possible to see in the future such tools to be able to report other forms of cyber-crime. If a friend of a person with disability or an elderly person suspects from discussions or posts that he has fallen victim of cyber-crime they could similarly report this to the respective social media and trigger an appropriate action.

Privacy vs. Health and Care Services

Technologies presented for health and social care are largely based on monitoring human activities and machines assisting Persons with disabilities in their lives. Since there is an evident need for such devices to be connected and communicate (from smart home appliances to wearable systems and robots) it is also obvious that they are creating a large stream of data related with our lives. The life-logging movement which is also presented and analyzed further in this section shows that this is an emerging trend. Recently in M.I.T. 100 students accepted to give up some of their privacy in exchange of a smartphone device (Markoff, 2008). Steve Steinberg, a computer scientist who works for an investment firm in New York says *"This is one of the most significant technology trends I have seen in years; it may also be one of the most pernicious."*.

Mining such digital trails of people with disabilities could help in detecting possible cyber-crime instances. If people with disabilities and elderly of the future live within connected environments taking care many of their needs an logging down most of their daily interaction it is easy to see to imagine possible applications for mining this information to detect instances of common crimes or cyber-crimes from his/her reactions.

One of the concerns of elderly people in adopting new technologies is the invasion to their privacy. This means that there should be real evidence that giving up some of their privacy could increase their security of health services. The combination of privacy concerns for health care services of the future with real benefits for elderly and their persuasion will be one of the biggest bets of future research. It should also be a very important factor to be taken under account in funding and promoting such research and maybe it is worth exploiting related legislative regulations to better ensure privacy in such occasions.

The abundance of connected devices in a smart environment providing health care services means that there are more potential opportunities for criminal attacks. The increase of online security issues and smart phone viruses (Williams, 2008) are already showing the potential of new ports opening to criminals from the variety of devices we are now using. Obviously a smart home environment with a series of appliances and sensors connected with the internet and possible robots taking care of a person with disabilities increases the opportunities for criminals to attack.

The future will need an even bigger effort to protect people with disabilities from online crime and it is essential that research in all the previous areas for health and social care services to take under account such issues. The movement of Google (Stevens, 2011) to develop an operating system for home devices shows one of the potential solutions. Developing antivirus software for such devices will be easier if they run common operating systems. Another possibility is to include protection mechanisms in the hardware as recently presented by McAfee (ASTALAVISTA, 2013).

Whatever the future sees in health and social care services security must remain one of the biggest issues and should always take under account in future research programs.

REFERENCES

Acever, M., Grimalt, J., Sunyer, J., Anto, J., & Reed, C. (1991). Identification of soybean dust as an epidemic asthma agent in urban areas by molecular marker and RAST analysis of aerosols. *The Journal of Allergy and Clinical Immunology*. doi: doi:10.1016/0091-6749(91)90309-C

Apple. (2014a). *Apple - iOS 7 - Siri*. Retrieved March 8, 2014, from http://www.apple.com/ios/siri/

Apple. (2014b). *Apple - iPhone*. Retrieved March 8, 2014, from http://www.apple.com/iphone/

Asperger Syndrome. (n.d.). *Wikipedia, the free encyclopedia*. Retrieved March 8, 2014, from http://en.wikipedia.org/wiki/Asperger_syndrome

ASTALAVISTA. (2013). *ASTALAVISTA - Cloud-Based Security Scans*. Retrieved March 8, 2014, from http://www.astalavista.com/

Attention deficit hyperactivity disorder predominantly inattentive. (n.d.). *Wikipedia, the free encyclopedia*. Retrieved March 8, 2014, from http://en.wikipedia.org/wiki/Attention_deficit_disorder

Autism rights movement. (n.d.). *Wikipedia, the free encyclopedia*. Retrieved March 8, 2014, from http://en.wikipedia.org/wiki/Autism_rights_movement

Autism spectrum. (n.d.). *Wikipedia, the free encyclopedia*. Retrieved March 8, 2014, from http://en.wikipedia.org/wiki/Autism_spectrum_disorder

Autisme Centraal. (n.d.). *Autisme Centraal | Welkom*. Retrieved March 8, 2014, from http://www.autismecentraal.com/index.html

Autistic Self Advocacy Network. (2014). *Autistic Self Advocacy Network | Nothing About Us Without Us*. Retrieved March 8, 2014, from autisticadvocacy.org/

Avax News. (2011, December 19). *Computer Fashion Show*. Retrieved March 8, 2014, from http://avaxnews.net/disgusting/Computer_Fashion_Show.html

Barrett, L. L. (2008). *Healthy @ Home*. Retrieved from http://assets.aarp.org/rgcenter/il/healthy_home.pdf

Belkin, L. (2010, April 20). *Parenting an Autistic Adult - NYTimes.com*. Retrieved March 8, 2014, from parenting.blogs.nytimes.com/2010/04/20/parenting-an-autistic-adult/

Bell, C. G., & Gemmell, J. (2009). *Total recall: How the E-memory revolution will change everything*. New York: Dutton.

Bell, C. G., & Gemmell, J. (2010). *Your life, uploaded: The digital way to better memory, health, and productivity*. New York: Plume.

Bipolar disorder. (n.d.). *Wikipedia, the free encyclopedia*. Retrieved March 8, 2014, from http://en.wikipedia.org/wiki/Bipolar_disorder

Bliton, N. (2011, December 18). *Disruptions: Wearing Your Computer on Your Sleeve*. Retrieved March 8, 2014, from bits.blogs.nytimes.com/2011/12/18/wearing-your-computer-on-your-sleeve/?_php=true&_type=blogs&_php=true&_type=blogs&_r=1

Brockman, J. (1999, December 31). *THE SECOND COMING — A MANIFESTO | Edge.org*. Retrieved March 8, 2014, from http://www.edge.org/conversation/the-second-coming-a-manifesto

Callejas, Z., Griol, D., & López-Cózar, R. (2011). Predicting user mental states in spoken dialogue systems. *EURASIP Journal on Advances in Signal Processing*. doi:10.1186/1687-6180-2011-6 PMID.24348546

Citizen science. (n.d.). *Wikipedia, the free encyclopedia*. Retrieved March 8, 2014, from http://en.wikipedia.org/wiki/Citizen_science

Coxworth, B. (2011, March 7). *What humans really want - creating computers that understand users*. Retrieved March 8, 2014, from http://www.gizmag.com/designing-computer-software-to-recognize-users-emotions/18078/

CureTogether. (2014). *Treatment Ratings and Reviews for 637 Conditions. Self Tracking. Free Tools to Help You Manage Your Health. | CureTogether.com*. Retrieved March 8, 2014, from http://curetogether.com/

DARPA LifeLog. (n.d.). *Wikipedia, the free encyclopedia*. Retrieved March 8, 2014, from http://en.wikipedia.org/wiki/LifeLog_%28DARPA%29

Diagonal View. (2009, July 7). *Amazing Robot Chef*. [Video file]. Retrieved from http://youtu.be/CNSKMGurrPI

Ding, D., Cooper, R. A., Pasquina, P. F., & Fici-Pasquina, L. (2011). Sensor technology for smart homes. *Maturitas, 69*(2), 131–136. doi:10.1016/j.maturitas.2011.03.016 PMID:21531517

Dodds, P. S., Harris, K. D., Kloumann, I. M., Bliss, C. A., & Danforth, C. M. (2011). Temporal patterns of happiness and information in a global social network: Hedonometrics and Twitter. *PLoS ONE*. doi:10.1371/journal.pone.0026752 PMID:22163266

Donald, B. (2011, December 13). *Facebook Aims to Help Prevent Suicide*. Retrieved March 14, 2014, from http://www.pddnet.com/news/2011/12/facebook-aims-help-prevent-suicide

DotComGuy. (n.d.). *Wikipedia, the free encyclopedia*. Retrieved March 8, 2014, from http://en.wikipedia.org/wiki/DotComGuy

Ergonurse. (n.d.). *Compression Force on the Back*. Retrieved from http://www.ergonurse.com/BackCompressionFlyer.pdf

European Commission. (2010, January 8). *European Commission: CORDIS: Projects: Search*. Retrieved March 8, 2014, from http://cordis.europa.eu/projects/rcn/71108_en.html

Eurostat. (2013a, October 17). *Individuals never having used the Internet*. Retrieved March 8, 2014, from http://epp.eurostat.ec.europa.eu/tgm/refreshTableAction.do?tab=table&plugin=1&pcode=tin00011&language=en

Eurostat. (2013b). *Individuals using the Internet for seeking health-related information*. Retrieved March 14, 2014, from http://epp.eurostat.ec.europa.eu/tgm/table.do?tab=table&init=1&language=en&pcode=tin00101&plugin=1

Eurostat. (2013c, October 17). *Mobile phone subscriptions*. Retrieved March 8, 2014, from http://epp.eurostat.ec.europa.eu/tgm/table.do?tab=table&plugin=1&language=en&pcode=tin00060

Fernández-Ardèvo, M. (2010). Interactions with and through mobile phones: what about the elderly population? In *Proceedings of ECREA Conference 2010*. ECREA. Retrieved from http://www.academia.edu/782946/Interactions_with_and_through_mobile_phones_what_about_the_elderly_population

Fish, E. (2011, June 27). *Home Automation: Inside a DIY Smart House | TechHive*. Retrieved March 8, 2014, from http://www.techhive.com/article/231260/home_automation_inside_a_diy_smart_house.html

Gelernter, D. (1992). *Mirror Worlds: Or the Day Software Puts the Universe in a Shoebox. How It Will Happen and What It Will Mean*. New York: Oxford University Press.

Gunther, E. W. (2008, January 30). *Smart Grid: Wireless home sensor network finally possible*. Retrieved March 8, 2014, from http://www.smartgridnews.com/artman/publish/article_399.html

Harmon, A. (2004, May 9). *Neurodiversity Forever, The Disability Movement Turns to Brains - New York Times*. Retrieved March 14, 2014, from http://www.nytimes.com/2004/05/09/weekinreview/neurodiversity-forever-the-disability-movement-turns-to-brains.html?pagewanted=all&src=pm

Harmon, A. (2011a, September 17). *Autistic and Seeking a Place in an Adult World - NYTimes.com*. Retrieved March 8, 2014, from http://www.nytimes.com/2011/09/18/us/autistic-and-seeking-a-place-in-an-adult-world.html?ref=us&pagewanted=all

Harmon, A. (2011b, December 26). *Navigating Love and Autism - NYTimes.com*. Retrieved March 8, 2014, from http://www.nytimes.com/2011/12/26/us/navigating-love-and-autism.html?_r=1&nl=todaysheadlines&emc=tha2&pagewanted=all

Hurst, A., & Tobias, J. (2011). *Empowering individuals with do-it-yourself assistive technology*. doi:10.1145/2049536.2049541

ISNT. (2002). *Institute for the Study of the Neurologically Typical*. Retrieved March 14, 2014, from http://isnt.autistics.org/

Jawbone. (2014). *UP24 by Jawbone | Wristband + App. | Track how you sleep, move and eat*. Retrieved March 8, 2014, from https://jawbone.com/up

Jennifer Ringley. (n.d.). *Wikipedia, the free encyclopedia*. Retrieved March 8, 2014, from http://en.wikipedia.org/wiki/JenniCam

Joshi, P. (2011, November 29). *Finding Good Apps for Children With Autism - NYTimes.com*. Retrieved March 8, 2014, from gadgetwise.blogs.nytimes.com/2011/11/29/finding-good-apps-for-children-with-autism/

Justin.tv Inc. (2014). *Watch Live Video*. Retrieved March 8, 2014, from http://www.justin.tv/

Lifelog. (n.d.). *Wikipedia, the free encyclopedia*. Retrieved March 8, 2014, from http://en.wikipedia.org/wiki/Lifelog

Lifestreaming. (n.d.). *Wikipedia, the free encyclopedia*. Retrieved March 8, 2014, from http://en.wikipedia.org/wiki/Lifestreaming

Looxcie, Inc. (2014). *Looxcie: Wearable Streaming Cameras for Consumers & Business*. Retrieved March 14, 2014, from http://www.looxcie.com/

Mad Pride. (n.d.). *Wikipedia, the free encyclopedia*. Retrieved March 8, 2014, from http://en.wikipedia.org/wiki/Mad_Pride

Markoff, J. (2008, November 29). *You're Leaving a Digital Trail. What About Privacy? - NYTimes.com*. Retrieved March 8, 2014, from http://www.nytimes.com/2008/11/30/business/30privacy.html?th=&emc=th&pagewanted=all

Mathers, C. Fat, D. M., & Boerma, J. T. (2008). The global burden of disease: 2004 update. Geneva, Switzerland: World Health Organization.

Meetup. (2011, March 8). *Brussels Quantified Self Show and Tell 2011 #1 - Quantified Self Show & Tell Brussels (Brussels)- Meetup.* Retrieved March 8, 2014, from http://www.meetup.com/Quantified-Self-Show-Tell-Brussels/events/15876800/

Mental Health Foundation. (n.d.). *Mental Health Statistics: UK & Worldwide.* Retrieved March 8, 2014, from http://www.mentalhealth.org.uk/help-information/mental-health-statistics/UK-worldwide/

MercuryApp. (2014). *MercuryApp. | Track your feelings and make better decisions!* Retrieved March 8, 2014, from https://www.mercuryapp.com/

Microsoft. (2014). *MyLifeBits - Microsoft Research.* Retrieved March 8, 2014, from http://research.microsoft.com/en-us/projects/mylifebits/default.aspx

Moodscope Ltd. (2014). *Moodscope - Lift your mood with a little help from your friends.* Retrieved March 8, 2014, from https://www.moodscope.com/

Neurodiversity. (n.d.). *Wikipedia, the free encyclopedia.* Retrieved March 8, 2014, from http://en.wikipedia.org/wiki/Neurodiversity

Neurotycho. (n.d.). *Welcome to Neurotycho! | neurotycho.org.* Retrieved March 8, 2014, from http://neurotycho.org/

New York Times. (2011, November 29). *Apps for Autistic Children - NYTimes.com.* Retrieved March 8, 2014, from parenting.blogs.nytimes.com/2011/11/29/apps-for-autistic-children/?_php=true&_type=blogs&_r=0

Nike Inc. (2014). *Nike+.* Retrieved March 8, 2014, from https://secure-nikeplus.nike.com/plus/#//dashboard/

Persyn, J. (2006, April 10). *jurriaanpersyn.com — Designing 'Autism-friendly' websites, principles and guidelines.* Retrieved March 8, 2014, from http://www.jurriaanpersyn.com/archives/2006/04/10/designing-autism-friendly-websites-principles-and-guidelines/

Propeller Health. (2013). *Propeller Health - The leading mobile platform for respiratory health management.* Retrieved March 8, 2014, from http://propellerhealth.com/

Prosopagnosia. (n.d.). *Wikipedia, the free encyclopedia.* Retrieved March 8, 2014, from http://en.wikipedia.org/wiki/Prosopagnosia

Quantified Self Labs. (2011). *Quantified Self Guide.* Retrieved March 8, 2014, from http://quantifiedself.com/guide/

Quantified Self Labs. (2012). *Quantified Self | Self Knowledge Through Numbers Quantified Self | Self Knowledge Through Numbers.* Retrieved March 8, 2014, from http://quantifiedself.com/

Quinn, K. (2010). Methodological Considerations in Surveys of Older Adults: Technology Matters. *International Journal of Emerging Technologies and Society, 8*(2), 114–133.

Redmond, W. (2011, August 3). *Dressing for the Future: Microsoft Duo Breaks Through with Wearable Technology Concept.* Retrieved March 8, 2014, from http://www.microsoft.com/en-us/news/features/2011/aug11/08-03printingdress.aspx

Riken. (2011, August 2). *RIBA-II, the next generation care-giving robot | RIKEN.* Retrieved March 8, 2014, from http://www.riken.jp/en/pr/press/2011/20110802_2/

Rock, M. (n.d.). *Half of U.S. Use Social Networks, Older Population Catching Up | Mobiledia.* Retrieved March 8, 2014, from http://www.mobiledia.com/news/105257.html

Singularity Hub. (2010, July 20). *Your Entire Life Recorded – Lifelogging Goes Mainstream | Singularity Hub*. Retrieved March 8, 2014, from http://singularityhub.com/2010/07/20/your-entire-life-recorded-lifelogging-goes-mainstream/

Smith, K. (2011, September 5). *Mental disorders affect more than a third of Europeans: Nature News*. Retrieved March 8, 2014, from http://www.nature.com/news/2011/110905/full/news.2011.514.html

Sobocki, P., Jonsson, B., Angst, J., & Rehnberg, C. (2006). Cost of depression in Europe. *The Journal of Mental Health Policy and Economics*, *9*(2), 87–98. PMID:17007486

Srivastava, K. (n.d.). *Phone Makers Focus on Elderly | Mobiledia*. Retrieved March 8, 2014, from http://www.mobiledia.com/news/115093.html

Stevens, T. (2011, May 10). *Google announces Android@Home framework for home automation*. Retrieved March 8, 2014, from http://www.engadget.com/2011/05/10/google-announces-android-at-home-framework/

Stickam (n.d.). *Goodbye*. Retrieved March 14, 2014, from http://www.stickam.com/

Taub, E. (2008, August 27). *Basics - For the Advanced in Age, Easy-to-Use Technology - NYTimes.com*. Retrieved March 8, 2014, from http://www.nytimes.com/2008/08/28/technology/personaltech/28basics.html?th&emc=th

Telcare Inc. (2014). *Telcare | Telcare Blood Glucose Monitoring System and myTelcare*. Retrieved March 8, 2014, from http://www.telcare.com/

Tourette syndrome. (n.d.). *Wikipedia, the free encyclopedia*. Retrieved March 8, 2014, from http://en.wikipedia.org/wiki/Tourette_syndrome

TOYOTA. (2011, November 1). *TMC Shows New Nursing and Healthcare Robots in Tokyo | Toyota Motor Corporation Global Website*. Retrieved March 8, 2014, from http://www2.toyota.co.jp/en/news/11/11/1101.html

10. TV. (2011, July 27). *FBI: Cyber Crime Will Soon Be Agency's Biggest Threat | WBNS-10TV Columbus, Ohio*. Retrieved March 8, 2014, from http://www.10tv.com/content/stories/2011/07/27/stories-columbus-FBI-cyber-crime.html

UCorder. (2012). *uCorder | Record Your Life | Wearable Mini Pocket Camcorder*. Retrieved March 8, 2014, from http://www.ucorder.com/

United States Bureau of Justice Statistics. (2007). *Crime against people with disabilities*. Retrieved from http://www.bjs.gov/content/pub/press/capd07pr.cfm

Universal Studios Home Entertainment. (2010). *A Beautiful Mind on DVD | Trailers, bonus features, cast photos & more | Universal Studios Entertainment Portal*. Retrieved March 8, 2014, from http://www.universalstudiosentertainment.com/a-beautiful-mind/

Universidad Carlos III de Madrid. (2011, November 21). *Machines Able to Recognize a Person's Emotional State*. Retrieved March 8, 2014, from http://www.pddnet.com/news/2011/11/machines-able-recognize-persons-emotional-state

University of Hertfordshire. (2011, February 12). *Robotic Companions for Older People*. Retrieved March 8, 2014, from http://www.pddnet.com/news/2011/12/robotic-companions-older-people

University of Sheffield. (2008, December 21). *British Scientist Warns We Must Protect The Vulnerable From Robots -- ScienceDaily*. Retrieved March 8, 2014, from http://www.sciencedaily.com/releases/2008/12/081218141724.htm

Use of social network websites in investigations. (n.d.). *Wikipedia, the free encyclopedia*. Retrieved March 8, 2014, from http://en.wikipedia.org/wiki/Use_of_social_network_websites_in_investigations

Verwymeren, A. (2011, August 3). *The Home of the Future Is Almost Here | Fox News*. Retrieved March 14, 2014, from http://www.foxnews.com/leisure/2011/08/03/home-future-is-almost-here/

Vicon Motion Systems Ltd. (n.d.). *Vicon | Homepage*. Retrieved March 14, 2014, from http://www.vicon.com/

Video game addiction. (n.d.). *Wikipedia, the free encyclopedia*. Retrieved March 8, 2014, from http://en.wikipedia.org/wiki/Video_game_addiction

Watier, K. (2003, April 19). *Marketing Wearable Computers to Consumers*. Retrieved March 8, 2014, from http://www.scribd.com/doc/49892917/Marketing-Wearable-Computers-to-Consumers

WHO Global Observatory for eHealth, World Health Organization. (2011). *mHealth: New horizons for health through mobile technologies*. Retrieved from http://www.who.int/goe/publications/goe_mhealth_web.pdf

Williams, C. (2008, February 8). *Smartphone virus attacks soar - Telegraph*. Retrieved March 8, 2014, from http://www.telegraph.co.uk/technology/google/8310689/Smartphone-virus-attacks-soar.html

Withings. (2014a). *Withings - Partner apps*. Retrieved March 8, 2014, from http://www.withings.com/en/app/partners

Withings. (2014b). *Withings - Smart products and apps - Homepage*. Retrieved March 8, 2014, from http://www.withings.com/

Wolf, G. (2010, September 27). *Gary Wolf: The quantified self*. [Video file]. Retrieved from https://www.youtube.com/watch?v=OrAo8oBBFIo&feature=youtu.be

World Health Organization. (2011). *Mental health atlas 2011*. Retrieved from http://whqlibdoc.who.int/publications/2011/9799241564359_eng.pdf

KEY TERMS AND DEFINITIONS

Affective Environments: Environments with appropriate sensors to detect and respond to human emotions and stimuli.

Behavioral Disorders: Behavior Disorders or BD are conditions that are more than just disruptive behavior.

Cognitive Disorders: Cognitive disorders are those that center around the brain's ability to remember and process information.

E-Health: E-Health (also written e-health) is a relatively recent term for healthcare practice supported by electronic processes and communication, dating back to at least 1999.

Health Services: Health care (or healthcare) is the diagnosis, treatment, and prevention of disease, illness, injury, and other physical and mental impairments in humans.

Life Logging: Life logging is the process of tracking personal data generated by our own ... usage activity.

M-Health: An umbrella term for wireless devices that are used in healthcare.

Privacy: The state of being alone: the state of being away from other people.

Quantified Self: The Quantified Self is a movement to incorporate technology into data acquisition on aspects of a person's daily life in terms of inputs (e.g. food consumed, quality of surrounding air), states (e.g. mood, arousal, blood oxygen levels), and performance (mental and physical).

Robotics: The science or study of the technology associated with the design, fabrication, theory, and application of robots.

Smart Home Environments: The concept of smart environments evolves from the definition of Ubiquitous computing that, according to Mark Weiser, promotes the ideas of "a physical world that is richly and invisibly interwoven with sensors, actuators, displays, and computational elements, embedded seamlessly in the everyday objects of our lives, and connected through a continuous network.

ENDNOTES

[1] Attention deficit hyperactivity disorder (ADHD, similar to hyperkinetic disorder in the ICD-10) is a psychiatric disorder of the neurodevelopmental type in which there are significant problems of attention, hyperactivity, or acting impulsively that are not appropriate for a person's age. These symptoms must begin by age six to twelve and be present for more than six months for a diagnosis to be made. In school-aged individuals the lack of focus may result in poor school performance. ("Attention deficit hyperactivity disorder," 2014)

[2] Alzheimer's disease (AD), also known in medical literature as Alzheimer disease, is the most common form of dementia. There is no cure for the disease, which worsens as it progresses, and eventually leads to death. It was first described by German psychiatrist and neuropathologist Alois Alzheimer in 1906 and was named after him. Most often, AD is diagnosed in people over 65 years of age, although the less-prevalent early-onset Alzheimer's can occur much earlier. In 2006, there were 26.6 million people worldwide with AD. Alzheimer's is predicted to affect 1 in 85 people globally by 2050. ("Alzheimer's disease," 2014)

[3] Asperger syndrome (AS), also known as Asperger disorder (AD) or simply Asperger's, is an autism spectrum disorder (ASD) that is characterized by significant difficulties in social interaction and nonverbal communication, alongside restricted and repetitive patterns of behavior and interests. It differs from other autism spectrum disorders by its relative preservation of linguistic and cognitive development. Although not required for diagnosis, physical clumsiness and atypical (peculiar, odd) use of language are frequently reported. ("Asperger syndrome", n.d.)

[4] The autism spectrum or autistic spectrum describes a range of conditions classified as neurodevelopmental disorders in the fifth revision of the American Psychiatric Association's Diagnostic and Statistical Manual of Mental Disorders 5th edition (DSM-5). The DSM-5, published in 2013, redefined the autism spectrum to encompass the previous (DSM-IV-TR) diagnoses of autism, Asperger syndrome, pervasive developmental disorder not otherwise specified (PDD-NOS), childhood disintegrative disorder, and Rett syndrome. These disorders are characterized by social deficits and communication difficulties, stereotyped or repetitive behaviors and interests, and in some cases, cognitive delays. ("Autism spectrum", n.d.)

[5] Bipolar disorder (also known as bipolar affective disorder, manic-depressive disorder, or manic depression) is a type of mental illness, specifically a mood disorder, characterized by episodes of an elevated or agitated mood known as mania that often alternates with episodes of depression. These episodes can impair the individual's ability to function in ordinary life. About 3% of people have bipolar disorder worldwide, a proportion consistent for both men and women and across racial and ethnic groups. The disorder is the sixth leading cause of disability. The cause is not clearly understood, but both

[6] genetic and environmental risk factors are believed to play a role. Treatment commonly includes mood stabilizing medication and psychotherapy. ("Bipolar disorder", n.d.)

Tourette syndrome (also called Tourette's syndrome, Tourette's disorder, Gilles de la Tourette syndrome, GTS or, more commonly, simply Tourette's or TS) is an inherited neuropsychiatric disorder with onset in childhood, characterized by multiple physical (motor) tics and at least one vocal (phonic) tic. These tics characteristically wax and wane, can be suppressed temporarily, and are preceded by a premonitory urge. Tourette's is defined as part of a spectrum of tic disorders, which includes provisional, transient and persistent (chronic) tics. ("Tourette syndrome", n.d.)

[7] Prosopagnosia (Greek: "prosopon" = "face", "agnosia" = "not knowing"), also called face blindness, is a cognitive disorder of face perception where the ability to recognize faces is impaired, while other aspects of visual processing (e.g., object discrimination) and intellectual functioning (e.g., decision making) remain intact. The term originally referred to a condition following acute brain damage (acquired prosopagnosia), but a congenital or developmental form of the disorder also exists, which may affect up to 2.5% of the population. ("Prosopagnosia", n.d.)

Chapter 7
Transport and Mobility

ABSTRACT

One of the most common needs for persons with disabilities and elderly is the need for transportation and mobility. It is a need that penetrates many aspects of a person's life. From travelling to another city or country, commuting to work, or travelling within your city and being able to navigate in indoor environments such as a shopping mall, a museum, or even your own home, transportation and mobility are needed. This chapter focuses and discusses issues, technologies, and applications for enhancing the accessibility in transportation and mobility together with new ideas such as the idea and trend of telepresence that could be helpful for a large group of people apart from people with disabilities. Technologies and applications discussed include driverless transportation, indoor navigation, smart assistive technology devices for mobility and navigation such as smart wheelchairs, exoskeletons, smart white canes, etc.

MOBILE TELEPRESENCE ROBOTS

In 2010 the New York Times ran an article entitled The Boss Is Robotic, and Rolling-Up behind You (Markoff, 2010). It described the current state of the art in mobile telepresence robots. It referred explicitly to models that were already available in the marketplace. The Vgo by Vgo communications (VGo Communications, Inc., 2013), the Tilr by Robodynamics, Texal by Willow Garage (Willow Garage, 2008), the RP71 by InTouch Health (InTouch Technologies, Inc., 2014) and the QB by Anybots (Anybots Inc., 2014) for a price anywhere in the range of $5,000 to $15,000.

Other companies involved in this business include Mobile Robots Inc. (Adept Mobilerobots LLC, 2013) a division of Adept Technologies (Adept Technology Inc., 2014). A number of EU providers have also entered the sector to much acclaim, for example Jazz (Robots Dreams, 2011a) by the French robotics company Gostai (Gostai, n.d.).

The QB which costs the same as a small car is based on Segway technology and is the closest so far to being 'untippable'. One of the big challenges of the future is to make them robust enough to be able to navigate outside in the real world where they may be jostled by humans in a crowd, knocked over by school boys or the bustle of modern life.

There is a fine line between telepresence robots and humanoid service robots. The highly emotive Reeti (Robots Dreams, 2011b) by Robopec (Robopec, 2010) and a female humanoid called Robixa (Robots Dreams, 2011c) are intended for

DOI: 10.4018/978-1-4666-6130-1.ch007

meeting and greeting, acting as sales assistants or presenting products, for example in trade expos for greater impact. These devices are used for surveillance, as well as for high end sales and marketing.

In a report in Wall Street Journal (Glazer, 2012) the telepresence robots of Vgo and Anybots are presented through a variety of cases. A guy from Belgium describes how he uses Vgo to cooperate and work with people in the US, a grandmother used the QB from Anybots to attend her son's wedding in Paris and a student at Princeton shows how he uses it to get to his local tacos restaurant and place orders.

These examples show that telepresence robots are already used by people to get together with relatives and friends, cooperate at work and even for fun. Most vendors of telepresence systems claim that they can be used by anyone with a disability, sick or in care, to fulfil similar needs such as attend meetings, visit friends, attend class or generally make up for any normal lack of mobility. However, so far we have not hear of them being used in any systematic way in care-homes for the elderly or in the homes of people with disabilities.

The Issue with Cost

The high end QB is mainly aimed at corporate executives. A technology that allows a boss to visit 5 or 6 factory or supplier sites, many thousands of miles apart in a single day, is easily worth a $15,000 price tag when compared to time saved and the accumulated cost of flights, hotels and company service cars.

For now there is a certain novelty attached to it. It is clear however that low cost will be an important issue in opening up the use of these devices to a larger market. Engineering websites claims that you can build your own using off the shelf parts for about $1,000 and more recent models such as the Mantarobot (VGo Communications, Inc., 2013) aims to compete on price at $3,500 per unit.

Virtual presence solutions demonstrate the power that such innovation models can have in lowering the cost in expensive (at least up to now) alternatives which are targeting specific groups of people. Bringing further down the cost will make such AT more affordable to people with disabilities that are already facing problems with employment rates and low income. In addition, it also accelerated the speed of research and development for newer, better solutions in the future.

The Notion of Presence

Some commentators claim that this technology is trivial being merely video conferencing with some bells and whistles and that it does not offer any advantage, however researchers at the Stanford based Centre for Work, Technology and Organization (Stanford University, 2008) point out that most teleconference systems are designed for use in meetings, but that is not where most work gets done. In this sense robotic telepresence is a big step forward. Colin Angle, chief executive of iRobot (IRobot Corporation, 2013) one of the largest robot manufacturers claims that "*the beauty of mobile telepresence is it challenges the notion of what it means to be somewhere.*"

What this statement shows is that in some cases solving a problem might not actually mean going along traditional ways of thinking. Innovation has to challenge traditional notions such as this of presence by introducing technology. This kind of innovation might be more difficult to pursue and encourage its take up, nevertheless this doesn't mean that future research has to stay away from it.

SMART WHEELCHAIRS AND THEIR ISSUES

A smart wheelchair is any motorized platform with a chair designed to assist a user with a physical disability, where an artificial control system augments or replaces user control. Its purpose is to reduce or eliminate the user's task of driving a motorized wheelchair. Usually, a smart wheelchair is controlled by a computer, has a suite of sensors and applies techniques in mobile robotics, but this is not necessary. The interface may consist of a conventional wheelchair joystick, or it may be a "sip-and-puff" device or a touch-sensitive display connected to a computer. This is different from a conventional motorized or electric wheelchair, in which the user exerts manual control over motor speed and direction via a joystick or other switch- or potentiometer-based device, without intervention by the wheelchair's control system.

Smart wheelchairs usually employ sonar, infrared sensors or laser rangefinders to detect obstacles and modify the user's intended drive command to ensure that the platform does not collide with them. Some smart wheelchairs may be equipped with robotic manipulators, used to manipulate common household objects or grasp door handles, for example, and some may employ computer vision techniques to visually detect obstacles or landmarks to assist in navigation.

Smart wheelchairs are designed for a variety of user types (Kuipers, n.d.). Some platforms are designed for users with cognitive impairments, such as dementia, where these typically apply collision-avoidance techniques to ensure that users do not accidentally select a drive command that results in a collision. Other platforms focus on users living with severe motor disabilities, such as cerebral palsy, or with paraplegia, and the role of the smart wheelchair is to interpret small muscular activations as high-level commands and execute them. Such platforms typically employ techniques from artificial intelligence, such as path-planning, artificial reasoning, and behaviour-based control.

For example, a team of researchers is currently looking to translate that success to the medical field by building smart wheelchairs with artificial intelligence (Greenemeier, 2009) that uses lasers, sensors and mapping software

to operate and navigate powered chairs for riders who cannot do so on their own. With help from a five-year, $480,000 National Science Foundation grant, a team of researchers led by John Spletzer, an associate professor of computer science and engineering at Lehigh University in Bethlehem, Pa., has developed a prototype chair designed specifically for negotiating sidewalks, parking lots and other outdoor areas.

The MIT Intelligent Wheelchair Project (The MIT Intelligent Wheelchair Project, n.d.) also aims to enhance an ordinary powered wheelchair using sensors to perceive the wheelchair's surroundings, a speech interface to interpret commands, a wireless device for room-level location determination, and motor-control software to affect the wheelchair's motion.

Another wheelchair system developed to help shoppers in Japan uses GPS, 3D personal positioning technology. The shopper is able to reserve the wheelchair using their smart phone. The wheelchair autonomously goes to meet the shopper when they arrive at the mall. The shopper is then able to control it using a Wii device. One of the design goals of this system is to enable the elderly the shopper to navigate the complex crowded and possible dangerous space with confidence and in safety. The system called the Ubiquitous Networked Robot was developed by ATR research centre in Japan (Advanced Telecommunications Research Institute International(ATR), 2012) and a YouTube video (Youtube, 2011) demonstrates the system and its major features. The wheelchair uses voice recognition and is able to understand remarks by a user such as "I forgot to buy a notebook, I would like to go back and get one" replying in a conversational tone and bring the shopper back in to the shop so that they can complete their shopping trip.

Current research on smart wheelchairs focuses on building intelligence into them in order to navigate around obstacles_(Herman, 2011), autonomously reach pre-set locations, use alternative means of steering (Grabianowski, 2007) (e.g. voice control), extend functionalities (e.g. with robotic arms) etc.

The user of a wheelchair may still feel helpless when it comes to other matters of daily living, apart from purely mobility. For example, users may want to plan routes for boarding a public transport that is disabled-friendly, in order to reach a destination. Or they may want to find information about a product at a supermarket that is out of reach to them, or find some other information that may be available on the Internet but that the user cannot access due to his/her physical difficulties on accessing such information on the move.

Future research on smart wheelchairs could therefore focus on integrating better access to information on the computing cloud for different types of disabilities (e.g. upper-limbs, etc.) in addition to motor disabilities, in order to give users better control over their daily activities, by leveraging the information that is available or can become available on the cloud.

There have been many 'smart wheelchair' projects. There are two general models to follow. One direction is where the mobility function of the wheelchair is developed to enable it to climb stairs or navigate uneven ground. Another is to add extra functions to the chair, in particular navigation functions. We will discuss this in more detail later.

The approach in developed economies is to add capabilities. Many new wheelchair projects target the needs of developing economies. In this case there is a need to operate without electricity or at least a guaranteed electricity supply. Cost and ease of maintenance is also an issue.

One strategy is to create frames into which someone insert their own chair or attach standard bicycle wheels. Another is to use a ratchet in addition to a wheel device for making the wheels turn. The problem is that few footpaths exist in developing countries. Mobility means being able to move on grass, over gravel and through mud. These issues will continue to be an important focus of development for so called bottom of the pyramid markets for these devices.

The Lesson from The iBOT Story

Most wheelchairs cannot be used on uneven ground. They are good on sidewalks as long as there are no steps. Ideally sidewalks should have ramps that allow the user to mount and dismount the side walk crossing the road at the appropriate place, but many sidewalks and public spaces are not suitable for the use of a wheelchair. Of course stairs without lifts are another problem as are escalators and all of these obstacles remain constraints for wheelchair users in many urban areas.

Dean Kamen saw that the technologies he employed in the Segway technologies could be used to develop a new kind of electric wheel-chair that would overcome these obstacles. Eventually he developed a product called the iBOT that was able to do all of these things. The iBOT mobility system (Segway, 2003) was just as surprising as the Segway device itself. It could switch dynamically from a 4-wheel mode to a 2-wheel mode of operation, maintaining its balance in a counterintuitive way just as the Segway does. Not only could it navigate sidewalks without ramps, stairs and escalators, it could also raise the user up and down varying their position so that they could adjust their height to the correct level for sitting at a table or working at a desk. The iBOT enabled users to reach objects stored on shelves or in cupboards. It gave the users unprecedented freedom at a cost of $25,000.

Because it was intended for use as a wheelchair for people with disabilities, weakness after an operation or course of chemo-therapy, or need to reduce stress due to cardiovascular disease, it was considered a medical device. It therefore had to go through an expensive process of evaluation by the FDA before being certified as being suitable for medical use. It was commercialized through a company called Independence Technologies (Independence Technology, L.L.C., 2001) established in 1999 and later taken over by Johnson & Johnson. The device was offered both in the US and the UK. Independence Technology was shut down ten years later in January 2009. Johnson

& Johnson now controls the iBOT intellectual property. The reason given for the shut-down was that demand was poor. Apparently they only sold 400 units in 2007. Owners also had difficulties getting reimbursed by Centres for Medicare and Medicaid Solutions.

Apparently Dean Kamen once gave a talk at Georgia Tech and there was interest among robotics experts in using the iBOT as a platform for new smart-wheelchair technologies. A blogger recounts (Deyle, 2009) that according to Kamen, since the device has been registered as a medical device, no one can use it without a prescription from a doctor and without undergoing training. He explained that although he would like to sell iBOTs to robotics scientists, the laws governing the use of such medical devices effectively stopped him. If he went ahead they would lose the certification that they paid so much and waited so long to obtain.

Regulator issues are of particular importance when dealing with devices intended for medical-related use.

Ways to Help Smart Wheelchairs Take Off

We have discussed the iBOT form the US, but there are European smart-wheelchair models as well. The TopChair (Topchair, n.d.) range from France uses a caterpillar system for climbing stairs. There are many variations on the wheelchair (1800wheelchair.ca Inc., 2014) for example wheelchair bicycles, even tandem bicycles for use with an assistant, as well as EV cars for wheelchair users such as the Kenguru (Kenguru, n.d.) or the AMKAR (Youtube, 2009a). There are also examples of solar powered wheelchairs and wheelchairs for dogs.

Toyota has produced a range of unique new mobility devices one called the winglet (Youtube, 2008) that has already been used as the basis for new robotic mobility devices. Along with the winglet it has also created the i-Real (Youtube, 2009c) intended for personal mobility in urban

spaces and first demonstrated in 2007. Honda has created a similar concept device called the U3-X (Youtube, 2009b). Competition in the EV car industry is bound to drive prices down and there seems to be a convergence of sorts between car and wheelchair concepts drive by the new design and engineering possibilities that EV technology provide as well as the need to create smaller more energy friendly forms for urban living.

Many examples of smart wheelchairs are intended for non-disabled users but can be used with relatively minor modifications by people with disabilities too. Next generation wheelchair devices might be no different from next generation personal mobility devices. In this direction it might be possible to develop a new generation or high performance e-access devices by encouraging UD devices based on the convergence phenomenon with emerging European EV makers, for example with companies such as River Simple of the UK or EVbike and scooter makers form Italy.

The Paralympic Games has done a lot for wheelchair users. In addition to providing wheelchair users with new heroes the demands of sports has led to light, highly manoeuvrable high-performance wheelchairs. It is possible that the growing popularity of the Paralympic games and the rapid development of the electric vehicle industry, in addition to pressure from makers in emerging economies such as China and India will lead to further progress in future.

One of the most innovative new products in relation to the wheelchair is a device called a Whill that can transform any wheelchair into an electric mobility vehicle. The story as told by Japanese Trends is especially interesting as it required only about €10,000 in seed funding to develop, almost all of which was raised using the Japanese crowd-funding system called campfire.

The White Cane of the Future

A blind or visually-impaired person currently relies on white canes to get tactile information about his/her immediate surroundings and navigate around his/her immediate environment. The information that the user receives from this tool can be greatly enhanced with the use of electronic means (RFID, Laser technologies) while also potentially using the power of cloud computing to enhance the information that a cane can provide.

A white cane is used by many people who are blind or visually impaired both as a mobility tool and as a courtesy to others. Not all modern white canes are designed to fulfill the same primary function, however: There are a number of varieties of this tool, each serving a slightly different need:

- **Long Cane:** This "traditional" white cane, also known as a "Hoover" cane, after Dr. Richard Hoover, is designed primarily as a mobility tool used to detect objects in the path of a user. Cane length depends upon the height of a user, and traditionally extends from the floor to the user's sternum.
- **"Kiddie" Cane:** This version works in the same way as an adult's long cane, but is designed for use by children.
- **Identification Cane ("Symbol Cane" in British English):** The ID cane is used primarily to alert others as to the bearer's visual impairment. It is often lighter and shorter than the long cane, and has no use as a mobility tool.
- **Support Cane:** The white support cane is designed primarily to offer physical stability to a visually impaired user. By virtue of its colour the cane also works as a means of identification. This tool has very limited potential as a mobility device.

Engineering students at Central Michigan University have developed a new RFID-enabled Smart Cane (Schwartz, 2009) to help blind students move more freely on campus. The Smart Cane is equipped with an ultra-sonic sensor that works together with a miniature navigation system contained within a shoulder bag worn by the user. The navigation system receives information from RFID-embedded mini flags planted along campus walkways. When the user gets too close to a flag a speaker located on the bag strap issues an audio alert that tells the user which way to move.

In addition, an associate professor of applied science at the University of Arkansas who has been working on a white cane which utilizes laser technology in order to deliver the layout of the land to users. A Flash LADAR (Coxworth, 2010) (laser detection and ranging) three-dimensional imaging sensor will be the main star behind recreating a detailed model of the user's environment. It is capable of taking in just about everything simultaneously, within sequential floodlit exposures that typically lasts less than a nanosecond each, making it suitable for those who are always on the move.

In future visually impaired people need to be able to better navigate around their surroundings, and to do this, they need better tools and environmental information that communicates with these tools. Current research on RFID and Laser-enhanced white canes is a step towards bridging this gap. Environmental information that can assist users to better navigate including pre-navigation information (e.g. information on weather conditions, traffic conditions, public transport disruptions, etc.), and on-the-route information (e.g. public transport arrival information, information on road hazards such as potholes, etc.) is crucial. This information may be provided to the user by means other than a smart cane or by smart cane extensions (e.g. a speech interface or audible signals). In addition, information from the computing cloud can also be downloaded to the smart cane or its extensions, in order to enable the user to better navigate in his/her surroundings inside and outside the home.

Exoskeletons and a Substitute for Wheelchair

In the chapter of exoskeletons earlier in this report there are a number of examples already presented.

Some of the projects presented show the potential of exoskeletons for helping people with mobility impairments.

eLEGS by UC Berkley is such an example. eLEGS is aiming to help paraplegics and those with mobility disorder to stand and walk. eLEGS. A similar project called Austin (Berkeley Robotics & Human Engineering Laboratory, n.d.) is also aiming to help individuals with mobility impairments to walk. However, the project also represents a series of technologies that lead to low cost and therefore accessible exoskeletons.

Another solution is also presented by Bionics Research Inc. which presented an exoskeleton for persons with mobility impairments called ReWalk (Bionics Research, Inc., 2013). In Japan one of the most known examples of exoskeletons is HAL (Hybrid Assistive Limb) which is developed in the Tsukuba University and aims to assist people with mobility impairments to improve their capabilities. HAL 5, the latest version of those exoskeletons, is a full-body exoskeleton for the arms, legs, and torso and is currently capable of allowing the operator to lift and carry about five times as much weight as he or she could lift and carry unaided.

In Europe, two programs worth referring are the AVATAR exoskeleton which is expected to be commercialized by 2016 and it is designed by TECIP (Information Technology and Perception) of the Sant'Anna Institute in Pisa (Instituto TeCIP, 2014). The Italian Ministry for Defence who financed research are aiming at an exoskeleton to help soldiers or civil protection personnel engaged in rescue operations in unstructured environment. Aside from civil protection, other field of operations might cover engineering in heavy manufacturing. In France, engineering company RB3D (RB3D, 2011) has developed Hercules, a battery powered robotic exoskeleton that can carry 100 kg at regular walking speed.

Exoskeletons for the disabled or injured and for rehabilitation in post-traumatic or chronic conditions have been the object of several research programmes. Though substantial advances have been done in energy actuators technologies enabling patients to perform movement, the acceptance of such systems is still limited due among others to usability and cosmetics or aesthetic reasons. According to a 2011 study by Rocon and Pons (Exoskeleton in Rehabilitation Robotics), "patients said the use of such device should cause social exclusion". Technologies like magneto-rheological fluids (MRFs) or Electro Active Polymer Actuators (EAP) are likely to overcome some of the current bottlenecks towards a better usability of exoskeletons or artificial limbs.

As research advances in exoskeletons for rehabilitation of chronic conditions there is a need to take care of aesthetics issue in order the results to gain traction in the market easier. A person with a mobility impairment using a wheelchair will probably resist the change to such a system especially if he/she needs help in fitting it properly to use. Moreover using such systems will probably make him/her look awkward and probably his/her social circles will need time to adapt to the change. These are issues that need to be addressed if we want to reach a stage where exoskeletons will replace wheelchairs.

The possibility of a future where wheelchairs will be totally replaced by exoskeletons is to bring a series of other consequences but first of all needs to bring down the cost of such systems. Austin (Berkeley Robotics & Human Engineering Laboratory, n.d.) presented earlier is a first step in that direction but need to be followed by other in the domain to have a more significant impact. Open sourcing software and hardware for such systems together with technologies such as 3D printing might lead to that direction easier.

However in a potential future world where wheelchairs are not used any more there will be no need for ramps in buildings and for similar adjustments in buildings. Similar needs will extinct also for vehicles and means of transportation in general. However, there might be the need for different provision in the case of exoskeletons.

Research has to identify those potential needs in order to be prepared when these needs come up.

THE FUTURE OF GUIDE-DOGS AND OTHER PETS

Animals can be trained to do a wide range of tasks to assist their master. But the emotional bond between the animal and the person being assisted is also very close. They are also of great importance as companions and providers of emotional support and not just as provides of physical help. Nevertheless in view of the fact that one of the most important uses of animals in the context of assistance for people with disabilities is the guide-dog for the blind and as such it is a help in navigating public spaces and facilitating communication with others.

The use of assistance animals by disabled people is not new at all. Guide dog use began in Germany in the 1920's for veterans of World War I who lost their sight. In 1929, the Seeing Eye (The Seeing Eye, Inc.,, 2014) became the first group in the United States to breed, raise, and train guide dogs. Although the formal training of guide dogs dates back 75 years, training only became more widespread in the last 30 years and there are many groups raising and training these dogs.

Disabled people today rely on animals for a variety of reasons (Adams & Rice, 2011), as guiding animals, hearing animals, Service Animals, Seizure Alert Animals, and as Social or Therapy Animals. The communication with animals is provided mainly by training animals to do with they are supposed to.

Today, animals provide therapeutic benefits to humans with physical and mental illnesses as well as provide assistance to people with disabilities. The most commonly recognized assistance animals are dogs. Due to their social nature, dogs are wonderful pets, companions, and protectors for many people. Dogs work closely with people in a variety of areas including law enforcement,

search and rescue, and farming. As assistance animals, dogs provide help for the visually and hearing impaired, serve as an alert system for impending seizures, and offer additional strength and mobility for the physically disabled. Dogs also provide comfort for some people suffering emotional difficulties.

There are many other animal species that provide therapeutic benefits to people. The Americans with Disabilities Act (ADA) specifically defines a service animal as a "*guide dog, signal dog, or other animal individually trained to provide assistance to an individual with a disability.*" Some of these "other animals" that assist people with disabilities are monkeys, birds, pigs, and horses. An even greater number of animal species serve as therapy animals, including rabbits, hamsters, and snakes. In March 2011, the ADA definition of service animal changed (US Dept. of Justice, 2012) as a result of a revision made by the Department of Justice. The key changes it the Act as pointed out in the Service Dog Central (Service Dog Central, 2013) are:

- Only dogs will be recognized as service animals.
- Service animals are required to be leashed or harnessed except when performing work or tasks where such tethering would interfere with the dog's ability to perform.
- Service animals are exempt from breed bans as well as size and weight limitations.
- Though not considered service animals, businesses are generally required to accommodate the use of miniature horses under specific conditions.

Human-animal communication is the communication observed between humans and other animals, from non-verbal cues and vocalizations through to, potentially, the use of a sophisticated language.

Human-animal communication is easily observed in everyday life. The interactions between pets and their owners, for example, reflect a form of spoken, while not necessarily verbal, dialogue. A dog being scolded does not need to understand every word of its admonishment, but is able to grasp the message by interpreting cues such as the owner's stance, tone of voice, and body language. This communication is two-way as owners can learn to discern the subtle differences between barks and meows (one hardly has to be a professional animal trainer to tell the difference between the bark of an angry dog defending its home and the happy bark of the same animal while playing).

Achieving a deeper level of communication between animals and humans has long been a goal of science. Perhaps the most famous example of recent decades has been Koko (The Gorilla Foundation, 2010), a gorilla who is supposedly able to communicate with humans using a system based on American Sign Language with a "vocabulary" of over 1000 words.

However, this kind of interacting and communication takes years for a person to learn. Thus, an easier and quicker way to understand animals has to be found in order to improve this communication. One of the examples where technology helped in that direction is this of the Takara Bow-Lingual (CNN, 2003). A Japanese toy maker company's device which sold thousands of pieces claiming that it can interpret dogs barks.

In the context of this scenario, improved communication between disabled and their assistance pets is supposed to take place aiming to support the independent living and increased mobility of disabled or older people. Since a set of drivers identified in the First Interim Report ("Economic turbulence and uncertainty in the EU", "Increase of median ages", "Towards independent living and active ageing") seem to result in the increase of demand for Personal Care Assistance services over the next three decades while at the same time the persons in the personal care services business is expected to decrease due to cuts in public expenses for health and social care services.

The history of service animals shows that there is a trend for having a pet at home especially in cases of people with disabilities or older persons. Thus, it is not hard at all to try and assign care tasks to a pet that may become some type of assistance pet helping persons who are disabled, chronically ill or simply old with their activities of daily living (ADLs) whether within the home, outside the home, or both. Such pets may assist their owners with personal, physical mobility and therapeutic care needs, usually as per care plans established by a rehabilitation health practitioner, social worker or other health care professional.

In future new computing advances open the way for increased communication with the animals, e.g. instead of training dogs as guides for the disabled, BCI interfaces can be used to guide the dog in a particular direction, or sensors can detect the mental state of an animal to e.g. guide for an imminent danger ahead.

THE US MILITARY UNMANNED SYSTEMS ROADMAP

In 2007 the US Department of Defence has published a roadmap (United States. Department of Defense, 2007) for the development of its unmanned systems over a 25 year period from 2007 to 2032. Many of the projects in this document are a continuation of on-going work. The BEAR system for example, a Battlefield Extraction Assist Robot is intended to help in the removal of a wounded or disabled soldier from the line of fire to a place where it can receive the first line of treatment. In 2007 at the time of writing the report this system had already gone through 3 successive prototypes and was already capable of picking up and carrying a person, weighing more than 200kg including combat gear, over rough terrain. Experts familiar with the projects explain that these functions are already well developed, and that the next step would be a prototype capable of going into the field, identifying a body and deciding what to actions to take. That person was of the opinion that this kind of technology could be deployed within the next 5 years. The BEAR system is being developed by a company called Vecna Technologies (Vecna Technologies, Inc., 2013) a supplier of advanced technology systems for medicine, business and military use in both developed and developing country environments. The BEAR is not its only foray into robotics. Vecna also produces the QC Bot, a hospital courier, telepresence and patient self-service robots, intended to improve efficiency, reduce medical error, and increase both patient and staff satisfaction.

Since the US DoD roadmap (United States. Department of Defense, 2007) for unmanned systems was written, the issue of machine ethics has come to the fore. Once a robot or autonomous vehicle is able to sense, think and act, the issue of what is right or correct in any circumstance becomes very important. For example, how are we sure that the route selected from a smart wheelchair for a mobility impaired person is the one that person wants. What happens when people change mind while on the go? How much control will machines allow on them? Could a mobility impaired person guide his wheelchair through a course full of obstacles when the machine's reasoning suggest otherwise? In general the issue of machine ethics and level of control people will have over them is a crucial one and needs special attention in some solutions described earlier

Driverless Transport and Self-Drive Vehicles

In November 2011 Paris introduced a new driverless train on metro line 1 from La Défense to the Château de Vincennes, one of its busiest lines carrying 750,000 passengers a day. Already in 1998 Paris introduced a fully automated underground train system on line 14. This new line built from scratch extending the Paris metro system, is believed to be the first driverless underground rail system in the world. Spain and Denmark also

have driverless metropolitan rail lines. Driverless shuttle-bus systems already exist. Heathrow recently introduced one to bring passengers from one terminal to another. A Dutch company called 2getthere (2getthere, 2012) develops and markets such systems. It refers to these transport systems as "Automated People Mover Systems". It has developed the ParkShuttle system for Group Rapid Transit markets, and the CyberCab system for Personal Rapid Transit markets. ParkShuttle was first demonstrated in Rivium near Rotterdam and at Masdar in the UAE in 2005.

Driverless helicopters and planes (drones) originally developed for use by the military, are routinely deployed by US and Israeli forces around the world. This technology is also used by civilian police forces in countries like the UK, for traffic and crowd monitoring as well as hot pursuit of criminals and gangs.

Commercial aviation has for many years used auto-pilot systems that 'drive' the plane while pilots rest or carry out other tasks. The number of pilots in planes has consistently reduced over the years. One industry executive recently remarked that modern airlines no longer need pilots in the cockpit that navigators have already been eliminated and co-pilots will probably go too, that the only reason pilots will be retained is to reassure passengers and intervene in the event of an emergency.

The history of self-drive or autonomous cars really starts in about 1994 with the first demonstration of autonomous or semi-autonomous driving on public roads by Daimler Benz and Mercedes Benz. Google has received lots of publicity for its demonstration of self-drive cars (Herman, 2011). The Google self-drive car project run out of Google X-Labs is a spin off from the DARPA grand challenge. DARPA continues to fund research on autonomous vehicles but the focus is now on off-road autonomy. VisLab (Vislab, 2010) of Italy organized the Intercontinental Autonomous Challenge and in 2010 accompanied 4 self-drive vans that drove 13,000kms from Italy to Shanghai to attend the world expo.

The mining company Rio Tinto (Rio Tinto, n.d.) has experimented with self-drive trucks for a number of years and has signed an agreement to buy 150 autonomous trucks for purchase in the period 2012 to 2015.

Driverless cars have already been successfully demonstrated on both US and European roads. Thanks at least in part to the lobbying efforts of Google, the state of Nevada in the US has been authorised to prepare rules and regulations governing the use of driverless cars in its roads. It is likely at least in a first stage that such cars will require someone on board with a valid driving license, but it is expected that this will already be possible from sometime in 2012.

According to press release General Motors may already be selling self-drive cars, originally referred to as GPS cars, by 2018.

An EU funded project called SARTRE or Safe Road Trains for the Environment (SARTRE-Consortium, n.d.) has already demonstrated self-drive vehicles, with a view to enabling the platooning of vehicles on public roads as a strategy for saving energy. The consortium has already demonstrated self-driven vehicles on EU roads and expects to have demonstrated the platooning of up to 5 vehicles by 2012. This technique eliminates drag through aero-dynamic effects and reduces the power needed for transport. The consortium estimates that up to 20% energy savings can be made on long journeys with the use of such technology. The consortium claims (Telegraph, 2010) that this could be a feature of European roads within the next 10 years.

One of the issues linking the ability to drive with the ageing of EU society is the fact that there is no age after which one cannot drive. Once someone has passed a test and is able to drive there is no re-evaluation of the person's fitness to dive as they get older. Although drivers tend to get better with experience, and older ones tend to be safer drivers, the risk of accident does increase as

their eye-sight and reflexes decline. Going a step further, one might see in the future the possibility of such self-drive cars to be used by persons with visual impairments or even blind.

The need to interact with machines in an intuitive robust and human way seems important for the future of these e-access technologies. It is shared by all areas of application such as ATM machines, humanoid companion and service robots, vending machines, modern check-out or ordering systems in large scale retail and fast-food restaurant environment.

Note that Mercedes plans to equip its 2013 model S-Class cars with a system (Auto Express, 2011) that allows it to drive autonomously through city traffic at speeds of up to 40 km/h.

Automobile Technologies for Security and Performance

Every year in Europe there are about 1.5 million accidents and 35,000 deaths on the road. 97% of these accidents are caused by driver error. For every person killed, 4 are permanently disabled, 10 are seriously injured and require long recovery times, while 40 have minor injuries. A considerable effort has been made over the last 10 years by automobile companies to develop network based technologies that are intended to reduce the possibility of accidents. These technologies aim to reduce driver stress, avoid accidents, guard against behaviours that are more likely to lead to accidents, as well as intervene automatically in a critical situation by slowing, braking, honking, flashing or taking necessary evasive action.

Drivers of the future will effectively have virtual co-drivers. They will be able to hand over the task of driving to the car, just as pilots of planes already hand-over controls to the auto-pilot. Remote control of a vehicle by a human assistant is also possible. Some such technologies are already used by military, security and policing services around the world. Others are currently being developed.

These are e-Assistive technologies and aside from increased safety, one of the motivations for developing these technologies is the expectation that roads and traffic will continue to become more crowed and more complex while the population ages.

The EU funded HAVE-IT (HAVEit - Highly Automated Vehicles for Intelligent Transport, n.d.) project (Highly Automated VEhicles for Intelligent Transport) has demonstrated many of these technologies in a range of different vehicles. This general category of technology is referred to as ADAS or Advanced drivers Assistance System technology. They include in-vehicle navigation system and pedestrian protection systems.

It is easy to see these as precursors for personal navigation systems suitable for people with disabilities or pedestrian protection systems that are employed by electric assistive mobility technologies on sidewalks as well as autonomous humanoid robots. The long term vision of those involved in such research is the development of the self-drive car, a car that drives itself without any human intervention at all.

The Segway Story and the Obstacle in Its Adoption

The Segway PT (Segway Inc., 2014) or personal transport system was developed by Dean Kamen and released for sale to the public in 2002. It was hailed as a revolution in personal transport. It was quite unusual in that it features two wheels placed side-by-side, instead of for or two in line as you have for bikes and scooters. In fact when the Segway was introduced at first it was also presented as providing an e-assistive technology solution for people with health problems for example for patients who have undergone heart or lung transplants and have to keep their efforts to a minimum despite any need for mobility they might have.

When it was first developed it was not allowed either on roads or on sidewalks. It could only be used on private property. Although it is two wheeled it is not a bicycle and not obviously a road vehicle. Being powered by battery and capable of up to 20kmph, neither is it obviously not a vehicle and so it not allowed on sidewalks. A lot of work was required before it was allowed on US sidewalks. The breakthrough came in 2001 when the first state bill was passed allowing for a new category of devices called an Electric Personal Assistive Mobility Device or EPAMD to be used on sidewalks throughout the state. By the end of 2002 this was also possible in 30 other states. Without the passage of these laws the device could only have been used at home or in the park.

The selling point of the device was that it was green, very easy to use and took up very little space. Dean Kamen, with his background in medical innovation considered that it would be very attractive as an assistive technology for people, for example for people with cardio-vascular disease or following a lung transplant. There is no doubt that it provides a transport and mobility solution that is very attractive in cities where space is scarce, both noise and fuel pollution need to be controlled and the widest possible variety of transport options is desirable. This was not so easy however. Many associations representing people with disabilities in the US opposed allowing it on sidewalks fearing that it would pose a danger. Many municipalities even the City of San Francisco opposed its use on side-walks even though state laws allowed it. In the Netherlands its use on sidewalks is permitted, but only for people with certain disabilities or medical conditions. A list and history of restrictions on Segway use is published on Wikipedia. The situation is quit complex and not at all uniform across Europe. At first its use was tolerated in the Netherlands. Then in 2007 its use was banned on roads. Since 2008 however anyone over the age of 16 can use it on roads as long as they purchase a special insurance.

The Segway is an example of an assistive technology that is suitable for both disabled and non-disabled users. Designing technologies so that they can be used in this way is a good way to increase the possibility of success by expanding the range of markets it can serve. It is clear however that the possibility of restriction on use is a threat to adoption and may need to be addressed in future EC research and innovation programs. There should be some lessons in the Segway story of adoption for the future of e-Assistive transport and mobility devices in Europe.

PUBLIC TRANSPORTATION INFRASTRUCTURE

Navigation

There are already many outdoor navigation systems available in the market, which work on GPS and GIS technologies linked with Global Navigation Satellite System (GNSS). However, such technologies cannot be used for indoor navigation since buildings block them. For effective indoor navigation any system developed should perform accurately, three basic tasks (Mehta, Kant, Shah, & Roy, 2011): a) Determining the position and orientation of user in the indoor environment, b) calculating the path to destination (i.e. Navigation), c) communicating seamlessly with the user.

Indoor Navigation Based on RFID and NFC

There are significant solutions suggested so far for indoor positioning and orientation. For example, mobile phones with NFC (near field communication) hardware intercommunicating with well-defined RFID tags. Such existing indoor navigation systems typically rely upon augmenting the physical infrastructure with identifiers such as RFID tags. While RFID tags might be cheap, a large amount of them is required to cover a whole building. Although it is possible to install tags under carpets, hallways or large open spaces with concrete door or tiles make such installation challenging and expensive (Spletzer, n.d.). Furthermore, RFID tags are not addressing moveable objects.

Nokia Research has been working on an indoor navigation concept that takes GPS-style navigation to the next level. It works indoors and it is accurate to 30cm, which is more than enough to enable precise location-based services within a building, or even within a store. This indoor navigation relies on positioning beacons (i.e. a transmitter at a known location, which transmits its location) but it is a proprietary system that doesn't allow interoperability with other mobile devices from other vendors. Furthermore, such a system in order to have some value, it requires the development of indoor maps, i.e. indoor maps for each and every place that will be equipped with such a technology (e.g. in airports, malls and shopping centres, public buildings and in private ones. Again such technology doesn't consider movable objects that maybe a barrier specifically for people with sight loss.

The problems of RFID based indoor navigation systems demonstrate that covering an indoor space with landmark sensors could require a large amount of money and also needs provision and study of the places where the sensor will be placed in order to be functional in long term. It might also require often maintenance and checks to ensure its functionality. Therefore the installation of such systems is not followed widely.

Indoor Positioning Based on Wi-Fi

Lately, a number of positioning techniques have been developed for indoor environments (e.g., the methods based on Wireless Local Area Networks (WLAN), Bluetooth, Radio Frequency Identification (RFID), Ultra Wideband (UWB), infrared and ultrasound, etc.). Among these techniques, the approach on the basis of exploiting 802.11 WLAN (Wi-Fi) is attractive, which is expected to yield a cost-effective and easy-accessible solution (Chai, Zhou, Chen, Nies, & Loffeld, 2011). For example, an experimental system was recently developed (Lin, Shieh, Tu, & Pan, 2012), it makes use of Received Signal Strength (RSS) Index value of low-power active RFID (Radio

Frequency Identification) for movement detection. Besides, it adopts ZigBee wireless transmission technology as reference nodes for positioning detection. Information gathered by reference points is delivered to the server through the Internet. All positioning information is computed by the server through some positioning algorithm using the average values of signals and results can be accessed through the networked computer or mobile device with Wi-Fi functionality.

Furthermore, all modern smartphones have Wi-Fi built in, and wireless networks are common enough in indoor spaces that an app could easily scan for known access points and calculate your position using trilateration (trilateration is the process of determining absolute or relative locations of points by measurement of distances, using the geometry of circles, spheres or triangles). This is currently enabled in open operating systems of smart phones, e.g. in Android ones. As an alternative, there are some Wi-Fi installations in buildings, such as the ones based on Cisco MSE (Cisco, n.d.) that can determine the location of any wireless device in the building. The Wi-Fi access points receive the Wi-Fi signals created by the mobile phone and then estimate its position via trilateration.

The American Museum of Natural History (Apple, 2013a) has developed their own interactive Museum explorer that can be downloaded in an iPhone and based on Wi-Fi based positioning and navigation (see previous section for more info on this technology) to find your current location within the Museum, explore an interactive map, listen to digital guides and get real-time directions to your next exhibit, a café, or anywhere else in the Museum using the quickest route.

Also Google announced in November 2011 (Google, 2011) the new version of its Maps app for Android. The mapping and navigation software got indoor maps and navigation, allowing you to find your way around malls, airports, IKEAs and the list is expanding. Google Maps 6.0 is also said to be able to detect on what floor of the building you are and adjust the map data appropriately, so you will only be seeing what's around you. According to the developers, the location algorithm is finely tuned, so it should work as well indoors as it does outdoors. In this way, there are already applications developed that can give spoken walking directions from Google maps (Purewal, 2010) (e.g. Walky Talky, Intersection Explorer) and can be of tremendous help to people with sight loss or navigation problems such as elderly people with dementia, Alzheimer or people with learning disabilities.

Given the widespread use of Wi-Fi in indoor spaces an indoor positioning solution based on Wi-Fi might be more feasible and cost effective than the one presented earlier based on sensors. It demonstrates that in order for an indoor navigation system to be successful there are two critical parameters.

- Not repairing any additional installation by using existing infrastructure on a building.
- Not requiring special devices and sensor systems on the client.

Although solutions like Wi-Fi positioning and navigation seem to be ideal for indoor spaces especially when it comes to public spaces, large stores, shopping malls, museums, theatres, airports etc. there are still a number of issues to deal with in the next years. In his article Nick Farina (Farina, 2011) describes those issues quite clearly.

Current location cannot be estimated accurately by indoor positioning systems based on trileration; therefore systems developed for indoor navigation should be designed in a way to compensate for that. This could be done by using data from other sensors like accelerometers, compasses etc. but in any case there is a need for further research in that direction to improve indoor positioning.

Computer Vision

Sensor-based solutions employ sensors, such as cameras that can detect pre-existing features of indoor spaces, such as walls or doors. For instance, a camera system matches physical objects with objects in a virtual representation of the space to locate the user. However, cameras require good lighting conditions, and may impose a computational cost prohibitive for portable devices. An alternative makes use of a 2D laser scanner. This method (Fallah, Apostolopoulos, Bekris, & Folmer, 2012) achieves 3D pose estimation by integrating data from inertial sensors, i.e. motion sensors (e.g. accelerometers) and rotation sensors (e.g. gyroscopes) that most smart phones are equipped, the laser scanner, and knowledge of the 3D structure of the space.

While this method achieves accurate localization, it relies on pre-existing knowledge and representation of the 3D space and computational power. All these are currently impede mobility of users with visual impairments as well as elderly users with Alzheimer and dementia. However, 3D representation may not be such a barrier and a challenge now, since Google recently announced the availability of indoor maps for several airports and malls in US and furthermore 3D models of indoor spaces are becoming available (e.g. see this example here) but also can be created with little effort using tools such as Google Sketchup (Trimble Navigation Limited, 2013).

In general, 2D laser scanners also have been widely used for accomplishing mapping of large environments and localization in highly dynamic environments. However, using only one 2D laser scanner could be insufficient and less reliable for accomplishing tasks in 3D environments. The problem could be solved using multiple 2D laser scanners or a 3D laser scanner for performing 3D perception. Unfortunately, the cost of such 3D sensing systems is still too high. Alternatively a 2D laser scanner and a stereo camera[1] (Lin, Chang, Dopfer, & Wang, 2012) for accomplishing simultaneous localization and mapping (SLAM) in 3D indoor environments in which the 2D laser scanner is used for SLAM and the stereo camera is used for 3D mapping are examined with some promising results.

Recently in the latest ASSETS conference a computer vision system was presented (Viswanathan, Little, Mackworth, & Mihailidis, 2011) for helping elderly people with cognitive impairments to navigate better in indoor spaces avoiding obstacles. In another solution presented (Ko, Ju, & Kim, 2011) a system based on colour codes simply printed out on paper was used to help visually impaired person navigate within buildings. The presentations raised the discussion of how computer vision could potentially provide solutions based solely on identifying objects and estimating position based on them. The problems and cost of systems based on additional installation even if this is printed colour codes were also pointed out as a potential barrier from introducing such systems widely.

Computer vision is a technology that is based primarily on a simple and widely used sensor present in almost all mobile devices nowadays, the camera. However it is limited from computational power that requires. Given the evolution of computational power and the increase in network speeds it is possible to see such systems emerge in the next years enabled by these developments. It is also possible to see cloud based solutions since large and complex computational algorithms could take place in large systems on the cloud and return results to the user. The simplicity of the sensor and the wide adoption and use of it makes computer vision a very promising technology for the future especially for people with disabilities.

The Indoor Navigation Products War and Interoperability Issues

There are already a number of different solutions presented for indoor navigation. In addition to them there are also many more. For example, it was not before the beginning of 2011 that the first mobile shopping applications reaching consumer markets such as the Sam's Club mobile app (Sam's West, Inc., 2010) that provides indoor navigation to specific items and shops in some selected American shopping malls. In the same manner

FastMall app (Apple, 2013b) for smart phones is linked with interactive maps that you download and use them for finding your way within specific shopping malls in more than 31 countries. In contrast to traditional mobile shopping and mapping apps, FastMall is based on MapOS platform that provides turn-by-turn walking directions for any venue without requiring a global positioning system (GPS), WIFI connection, or an Internet signal. Similar applications are Meijer Find It (Meijer, Inc, 2014) and Micello Maps (Micello, Inc., 2010).

GloposMPS (GloPos Technologies, 2009) is a software-based technology, providing positioning accuracy (around to 12 meters accuracy) both outdoors and indoors by requiring only mobile network information and in this way it can be used for all kinds of mobile phones. However, it is mostly used for location of positioning rather than for navigation.

A very interesting development in indoor navigation was recently presented in World mobile Congress by CSR (CSR, 2012). The systems presented is demonstrating one of the industry's most recent technological advancements that "fuses" satellite signals, multiple radio signals, sensor inputs and other location data to make extremely reliable and accurate indoor location and navigation a reality. Such systems employing a variety of solutions and technologies could be a way forward to break the fragmentation that seems to appear in the market.

The different technologies, sensors required, installations and mappings in building required for each system and application presented lead to inevitable observation that indoor navigation is a market and research area highly fragmented. However it is not possible to expect users run 20 different apps on their mobile devices in order to get indoor navigation depending on the place they are. People need to know how to get from point A to point B. They simply do not care what kind of technology is used or what kind of sensors and installation is required. Therefore future indoor navigation systems will have to take this under account and provide a higher degree of interoperability with different technologies. It is also important to point out that they should integrate gracefully with already existing outdoor navigation systems in order to provide a better, seamless navigation in all places.

Integration with Dynamic Data

A very interesting point raised by Nick Farina in his article (Farina, 2011) on the problems of indoor navigation is the potentials of indoor navigation if integrated with dynamic data. People in a large store will not just need to navigate in it but accomplish specific tasks (i.e. find a specific product). Linking the navigation system with data such where each product is placed then navigation is taking a whole new direction.

Future indoor navigation systems will integrate with dynamic data to provide an even better experience of indoor navigation. In that context it is easy to imagine an indoor navigation system guiding a student with visual impairments form auditorium to laboratories and various classes depending on his course lessons followed and timetables.

REFERENCES

1800wheelchair.ca Inc. (2014). *Modern Wheelchair Inventions*. Retrieved March 9, 2014, from http://www.1800wheelchair.ca/ news/post/modern-wheelchair-inventions.aspx

2getthere. (2012). *2getthere*. Retrieved March 9, 2014, from http://www.2getthere.eu/

Adams, K., & Rice, S. (2011, September 19). *Brief Information Resource on Assistance Animals for the Disabled*. Retrieved March 9, 2014, from http://www.nal.usda.gov/awic/companimals/assist.htm

Adept Mobilerobots, L. L. C. (2013). *Intelligent Mobile Robotic Platforms for Research, Development, Rapid Prototyping*. Retrieved March 9, 2014, from http://www.mobilerobots.com/Mobile_Robots.aspx

Adept Technology Inc. (2014). *Adept Technology, Inc*. Retrieved March 9, 2014, from http://www. adept.com/

Advanced Telecommunications Research Institute International (ATR). (2012). *ATR? Advanced Telecommunications Research Institute International*. Retrieved March 9, 2014, from http://www.atr.jp/ index_e.html

Anybots Inc. (2014). *Anybots | ANYBOTS® Virtual Presence Systems. It's You, Anywhere?* Retrieved March 9, 2014, from https://www. anybots.com/

Apostolopoulos, I., Fallah, N., Folmer, E., & Bekris, K. E. (2012). *Integrated online localization and navigation for people with visual impairments using smart phones*. doi:10.1109/ ICRA.2012.6225093

Apple. (2013a, March 20). *Explorer: The American Museum of Natural History on the App. Store on iTunes*. Retrieved March 9, 2014, from https:// itunes.apple.com/us/app/explorer-american-museum-natural/id381227123?mt=8

Apple. (2013b, November 14). *FastMall - Shopping Malls, Community & Interactive Maps on the App. Store on iTunes*. Retrieved March 9, 2014, from https://itunes.apple.com/us/app/fastmall-shopping-malls-community/id340656157?mt=8

Auto Express. (2011, November 14). *New Mercedes S-Class to drive itself | News | Auto Express*. Retrieved March 9, 2014, from http:// www.autoexpress.co.uk/mercedes/s-class/35181/ new-s-class-drive-itself

Berkeley Robotics & Human Engineering Laboratory. (n.d.). *Austin | Berkeley Robotics & Human Engineering Laboratory*. Retrieved March 9, 2014, from http://bleex.me.berkeley.edu/research/ exoskeleton/medical-exoskeleton/

Bionics Research, Inc. (2013). *Bionics Research ReWalk? U.S. - the wearable bionic suit*. Retrieved March 9, 2014, from http://rewalk.us/

Chai, W., Zhou, J., Chen, C., Nies, H., & Loffeld, O. (2011). Continuous Indoor Localization and Navigation Based on Low-cost INS/Wi-Fi Integration. *International Conference on Indoor Positioning and Indoor Navigation*. Retrieved from http://ipin2011.dsi.uminho.pt/PDFs/ Short-paper/11_Short_Paper.pdf

Cisco. (n.d.). *Cisco Mobility Services Engine - Products & Services - Cisco*. Retrieved March 9, 2014, from http://www.cisco.com/ c/en/us/ products/wireless/ mobility-services-engine/ index.html

CNN. (2003, March 24). *CNN.com - Dog translation device coming to U.S. - Mar. 24, 2003*. Retrieved March 9, 2014, from http://Ed.cnn. com/2003/ TECH/biztech/03/24/tech.dogs.language.reut/

Coxworth, B. (2010, October 4). *Developing a 'smart cane' for the blind*. Retrieved March 9, 2014, from http://www.gizmag.com/ smart-cane-uses-laser-range-finder/16562/

CSR. (2012, February 27). *CSR Demonstrates Breakthrough Indoor Navigation Accuracy at Mobile World Congress 2012*. Retrieved March 9, 2014, from http://www.csr.com/news/pr/release/706/en

Dept, U. S. of Justice. (2012). *Text of the Revised Title II Regulation*. Retrieved March 9, 2014, from http://www.ada.gov/regs2010/ titleII_2010/ titleII_2010_withbold.htm

Deyle, T. (2009, February 11). *iBOT Discontinued -- Unfortunate for the Disabled but Perhaps a Budding Robotics Opportunity? | Hizook*. Retrieved March 9, 2014, from http://www.hizook.com/ blog/2009/02/11/ibot-discontinued-unfortunate-disabled-perhaps-budding-robotics-opportunity

Fallah, N., Apostolopoulos, I., Bekris, K., & Folmer, E. (2012). *The user as a sensor: navigating users with visual impairments in indoor spaces using tactile landmarks*. doi:10.1145/2207676.2207735

Farina, N. (2011, October 11). *Why indoor navigation is so hard - O'Reilly Radar*. Retrieved March 9, 2014, from http://radar.oreilly.com/2011/10/indoor-navigation.html

Glazer, E. (2012, March 9). *What Does It Say When a Robot Is the Life of a Party? - WSJ.com*. Retrieved March 9, 2014, from http://online.wsj.com/news/articles/SB10001424052970203458604577265321595882542?KEYWORDS= vgo&mg=reno64-wsj&url= http%3A%2F%2Fonline.wsj.com%2 Farticle%2FSB 1000142405297 0203458604577 2653215958825 42.html%3FKEYWORDS%3Dvgo

GloPos Technologies. (2009). *Glopos - Glopos*. Retrieved March 9, 2014, from http://www.glopos.com/

Google. (2011, November 29). *Official Google Blog: A new frontier for Google Maps: mapping the indoors*. Retrieved March 9, 2014, from http://googleblog.blogspot.gr/2011/11/ new-frontier-for-google-maps-mapping.html

Gorilla Foundation. (2010). *Gorilla Foundation - Koko the Gorilla*. Retrieved March 9, 2014, from http://www.koko.org/friends/index.html

Gostai. (n.d.). *Gostai*. Retrieved March 9, 2014, from http://www.gostai.com/

Grabianowski, E. (2007, November 16). *HowStuffWorks How Thought-Controlled Wheelchairs Work*. Retrieved March 9, 2014, from http://computer.howstuffworks.com/audeo.htm

Greenemeier, L. (2009, December 14). *On a Roll: Autonomous Navigation Lasers and Robotics Push Smart Wheelchair Technology to the Cutting Edge [Slide Show] - Scientific American*. Retrieved March 9, 2014, from http://www.scientificamerican.com/ article/smart-wheelchair/

HAVEit - Highly Automated Vehicles for Intelligent Transport. (n.d.). *HAVE IT Website*. Retrieved March 9, 2014, from http://www.haveit-eu.org/displayITM1.asp?ITMID=6&LANG=EN

Herman, J. (2011, March 4). *Google's self-driving car. In action - SmartPlanet*. Retrieved March 9, 2014, from http://www.smartplanet.com/blog/ thinking-tech/googles-self-driving-car-in-action/6422

Independence Technology, L. L. C. (2001). *Independence Technology, L.L.C.* Retrieved March 9, 2014, from http://www.ibotnow.com/

Instituto TeCIP. (2014). *Scuola Superiore Sant' Anna - Instituto TeCIP*. Retrieved March 9, 2014, from www.sssup.it/ist_home. jsp?ID_LINK=10509&area=199

InTouch Technologies, Inc. (2014). *InTouch Health*. Retrieved March 9, 2014, from http://www.intouchhealth.com/

IRobot Corporation. (2013). *iRobot Corporation: Robots that Make a Difference*. Retrieved March 9, 2014, from http://www.irobot.com/us

Kenguru. (n.d.). *Kenguru - The car you have all been waiting for*. Retrieved March 9, 2014, from http://www.kengurucars.com/

Ko, E., Ju, J. S., & Kim, E. Y. (2011). *Situation-based indoor wayfinding system for the visually impaired*. doi:10.1145/2049536.2049545

Kuipers, B. J. (n.d.). *Intelligent Wheelchair Resources*. Retrieved March 9, 2014, from http://www.cs.utexas.edu/ ~kuipers/wheelchair.html

Lin, K. H., Chang, C. H., Dopfer, A., & Wang, C. C. (2012). Mapping and Localization in 3D Environments Using a 2D Laser Scanner and a Stereo Camera. *Journal of Informaiton Science and Engineering, 28*, 131–144.

Lin, Y. C., Shieh, C. S., Tu, K. M., & Pan, J. S. (2012). Implementation of Indoor Positioning Using Signal Strength from Infrastructures. *Intelligent Information and Database Systems, 7198*, 206–215. doi:10.1007/978-3-642-28493-9_23

Markoff, J. (2010, September 4). *Smarter Than You Think - The Boss Is Robotic, and Rolling Up Behind You - NYTimes.com*. Retrieved March 9, 2014, from http://www.nytimes.com/2010/09/05/science/05robots.html?_r=0

Mehta, P., Kant, P., Shah, P., & Roy, A. K. (2011). *VI-Navi: a novel indoor navigation system for visually impaired people*. doi:10.1145/2023607.2023669

Meijer, Inc. (2014). *download Meijer mobile apps - Meijer and Meijer Pharmacy*. Retrieved March 9, 2014, from www.meijer.com/content/ content.jsp?pageName=mobile_app

Micello, Inc. (2010). *Micello*. Retrieved March 9, 2014, from http://www.micello.com/

MIT Intelligent Wheelchair Project. (n.d.). *Intelligent Wheelchair Project at MIT*. Retrieved March 9, 2014, from http://rvsn.csail.mit.edu/wheelchair/

Purewal, S. J. (2010, October 12). *Two Google Apps Help Blind Navigate | TechHive*. Retrieved March 9, 2014, from http://www.techhive.com/article/207500/ Two_Google_Apps_Helps_Blind_Navigate.html

RB3D. (2011). *RB3D, solution mécatronique de prévention des TMS*. Retrieved March 9, 2014, from http://www.rb3d.com/

Rio Tinto. (n.d.). *Home - Rio Tinto*. Retrieved March 9, 2014, from http://www.riotinto.com/

Robopec. (2010). *Robopec - Conception et réalisation de systèmes mécatroniques et de leur intelligence embarquée et développement logiciel*. Retrieved March 9, 2014, from http://www.robopec.com/

Robots Dreams. (2011a, April 1). *GOSTAI JAZZ Telepresence Robot at InnoRobo 2011*. [Video file]. Retrieved from https://www.youtube.com/watch?v=T7ya6JOAbp0

Robots Dreams. (2011b, March 29). *Le REETI - Expressive Robot from robopec*. [Video file]. Retrieved from https://www.youtube.com/watch?v=3A8KRch-tR0

Robots Dreams. (2011c, March 30). *Robbixa Female Robot at InnoRobo 2011*. [Video file]. Retrieved from https://www.youtube.com/watch?v=4PYxRnQnxow

Sam's West, Inc. (2010). *Sam's Club Mobile - Home*. Retrieved March 9, 2014, from www3.samsclub.com/mobile

SARTRE-Consortium. (n.d.). *The SARTRE project*. Retrieved March 9, 2014, from http://www.sartre-project.eu/ en/Sidor/default.aspx

Schwartz, A. (2009, August 3). *Smart Cane Makes it Easy for the Blind to Get Around | Fast Company | Business + Innovation*. Retrieved March 9, 2014, from http://www.fastcompany.com/ 1323616/smart-cane-makes-it-easy-blind-get-around

Segway. (2003). *The iBOT*. Retrieved March 9, 2014, from https://www.msu.edu/ ~luckie/segway/iBOT/iBOT.html

Segway Inc. (2014). *Segway Personal Transporters for Individuals*. Retrieved March 9, 2014, from http://www.segway.com/individual

Service Dog Central. (2013). *How was the definition of service animal changed July 23, 2010? | Service Dog Central*. Retrieved March 9, 2014, from http://www.servicedogcentral.org/ content/changes

Spletzer, J. R. (n.d.). *John R. Spletzer Home Page*. Retrieved March 9, 2014, from http://www.cse.lehigh.edu/~spletzer/

Stanford University. (2008). *Work, Technology & Organization*. Retrieved March 9, 2014, from http://www.stanford.edu/ group/WTO/cgi-bin/index.php

Telegraph. (2010, January 3). *'Self-drive cars on roads within 10 years' - Telegraph*. Retrieved March 9, 2014, from http://www.telegraph.co.uk/news/uknews/road-and-rail-transport/6926514/Self-drive-cars-on-roads-within-10-years.html

The Seeing Eye, Inc. (2014). *Guide dogs for people who are blind or visually impaired | The Seeing Eye, Inc.* Retrieved March 9, 2014, from http://www.seeingeye.org/

Topchair. (n.d.). *TOPCHAIR a Powered Wheelchair. The only Stair Climbing Wheelchair capable of going up and down straight stairs and pavements / side walks without assistance.* Retrieved March 9, 2014, from http://www.topchair.fr/en/

Trimble Navigation Limited. (2013). *SketchUp | 3D for Everyone*. Retrieved March 9, 2014, from http://www.sketchup.com/

United States Department of Defense. (2007). *Unmanned systems roadmap: 2007-2032*. Retrieved from http://www.fas.org/irp/ program/collect/usroadmap2007.pdf

Vecna Technologies, Inc. (2013). *Vecna | Better Technology, Better World*. Retrieved March 9, 2014, from http://www.vecna.com/

VGo Communications, Inc. (2013). *VGo robotic telepresence for healthcare, education and business*. Retrieved March 9, 2014, from http://www.vgocom.com/

Vislab. (2010). *Intercontinental Challenge*. Retrieved March 9, 2014, from http://viac.vislab.it/

Viswanathan, P., Little, J. J., Mackworth, A. K., & Mihailidis, A. (2011). *Navigation and obstacle avoidance help (NOAH) for older adults with cognitive impairment: a pilot study*. doi:10.1145/2049536.2049546

Willow Garage. (2008). *Willow Garage*. Retrieved March 9, 2014, from http://www.willowgarage.com/

Youtube. (2008, August 1). *Toyota's Winglet robotic transporter*. [Video file]. Retrieved from https://www.youtube.com/ watch?v=DSka-3uHcDw

Youtube. (2009a, August 17). *Electric Car-Amkar Wheelchair Access Version Get yours at Monmouth Vans-Wall, NJ (800) 221-0034*. [Video file]. Retrieved from https://www.youtube.com/watch?v=l-J5Sc6zWKc

Youtube. (2009b, September 24). *Honda U3-X - a Japanese take on the Segway*. [Video file]. Retrieved from https://www.youtube.com/watch?v=ghedatUdj3E

Youtube. (2009c, October 22). *The TOYOTA i-REAL personal mobility vehicle @ NAGOYA, Centrair International Airport*. [Video file]. Retrieved from https://www.youtube.com/watch?v=fmoTLoJzluI

Youtube. (2011, March 18). *Robotic wheelchair takes elderly customers shopping*. [Video file]. Retrieved from http://youtu.be/1V78KPs8Y44

KEY TERMS AND DEFINITIONS

Blind: Sightless.

Exoskeletons: An exoskeleton is the external skeleton that supports and protects an animal's body, in contrast to the internal skeleton (endoskeleton) of, for example, a human.

Indoor Navigation: An indoor positioning system (IPS) or micromapping is a network of devices used to wirelessly locate objects or people inside a building.

Mobility: The ability to move freely.

Mobility Impaired: Inability to function normally, physically or mentally; incapacity.

Navigation: The process or activity of accurately ascertaining one's position and planning and following a route.

Public Transportation: a system of vehicles such as buses and trains that operate at regular times on fixed routes and are used by the public.

Smart Wheelchair: A smart wheelchair is any motorized platform with a chair designed to assist a user with a physical disability, where an artificial control system augments or replaces user control.

Smart White Cane: Mobility aid for people with vision impairments equipped with extra functionalities.

Telepresence: The term used to describe a set of technologies, such as high definition audio, video, and other interactive elements that enable people to feel or appear as if they were present in a location which they are not physically in.

Telepresence Robots: A remote-controlled, wheeled device with a display to enable video chat and videoconferencing, among other purposes.

Transportation: Any device used to move an item from one location to another.

Visually Impaired: Having impaired vision; partially sighted.

ENDNOTES

[1] Wikipedia definition: A stereo camera is a type of camera with two or more lenses with a separate image sensor or film frame for each of the two lens. This allows the camera to simulate human binocular vision, and therefore gives it the ability to capture three-dimensional images, a process known as stereo photography.

Chapter 8
Training, Teaching, and Learning

ABSTRACT

We are constantly being educated, learning, and getting training for new skills. People with disabilities and the elderly are no exception to this rule. Moreover, they might need additional training and education on how to use assistive technologies and how to cope with the everyday aspects of overcoming their problems. This chapter focuses on education and training and presents technologies, policies, challenges, and opportunities that lie ahead for accessibility in education and training. It presents the different aspects and the different potential solutions based on the level of education trying to cover this need throughout the lifespan of a person. Finally, it finishes by discussing common problems and issues in research for accessible and inclusive education in order to provide useful suggestions and lessons to be had for the future.

INTRODUCTION

People are being educated throughout their lives. However, education needs change from time to time depending on the age and needs of the person. A young children in preschool age needs to learn about basic social skills such as how to communicate with others, how behave in a group of people, how to collaborate with them, how to follow orders and instructions, etc. Following that, in the primary school, children learn about reading and writing, basic mathematics and physics, arts, etc. Their knowledge on various subjects is further improved and enriched during secondary school education leading to higher education in universities and colleges where they excelled at knowledge is on a specific subject getting prepared for the job market. Many people think that education stops after graduating the University. However, this is not the case nowadays. People in their jobs need to get training on new technologies and new methods in order to constantly improve their performance. The rapid growth of technology and science generates this cause and needs for education and training almost in all professions.

Apart from former education provided through traditional educational systems, people get educated in a variety of other ways for many other reasons. They learn how to get dressed, how to keep their personal hygiene, they take up hob-

DOI: 10.4018/978-1-4666-6130-1.ch008

bies, they learn how to cook and generally they constantly need to learn about new students or how to improve already existing ones. In addition to improving our learning everyday life skills, people also need to adapt their skills according to their changing capabilities. Ageing persons for example, might need to change the way they read due to decreasing visual capabilities, or the way they watch the TV due to decreasing hearing capabilities.

Moreover, the fact of a sudden disability due to an accident also generates additional educational and training needs. A person who lost his sight needs to learn how to read and write in Braille or how to use his white cane. A person becoming hearing impaired or deaf might need to learn sign language and the person becoming motor disabled will it learn how to use his wheelchair. In addition, every person becoming disabled due to an accident will also need change and adapt his/her behavior and habits according to his/her new needs. The following sections try to exploit potential future ways of teaching, training and educating people with disabilities throughout their lives and according to their period-specific needs.

Looking at the overall picture of education we can see three main different roles. The first is the one of the learner, either this is a pupil, student, worker or whatever else. The second is the role of the educator which includes teacher, professors, trainers etc. Finally there is also the role of learners' sponsors meaning the persons who are interested in learners' education and training such as parents of children in schools, employers of persons being trained for a job, close relatives or friends taking care of a person's education etc.

Having distinguished these roles we can separate the user needs for education based on them.

Learners need to:

- Communicate and collaborate with educators and peers.
- Discover, access and use teaching material.
- Be able to use and participate in assessment procedures for their learning experience.

Educators need to:

- Communicate and collaborate learners and sponsors.
- Communicate and collaborate with other educators and persons in other professions.
- Discover, produce, access and use teaching material and information related with various teaching methods.
- Access and use appropriately information about each learners educational background and needs.
- Assess learners achievements and needs.

Sponsors need to:

- Communicate and collaborate with educators, peers, learners and persons in other related professions.
- Access information about learners assessment and learning experience.

The needs presented earlier lead to a variety of accessibility issues when either the learner the educator or the sponsor is a person with disability. However, the issues that a disability generates for an educator overlap with the needs of employees with disabilities discussed in the employment, employability and entrepreneurship chapter. Therefore, they are not the main focus in this chapter.

For learners:

- The ability to use effectively new technologies used in educational settings together with AT to communicate and collaborate with educators and peers throughout the whole educational period (primary, secondary schools, tertiary education, vocational training etc.). This also involves the ability to use AT in classrooms, libraries, auditoriums and other educational settings.
- The ability to access and use effectively teaching material which is not appropriate for use depending on their capabilities (e.g.

a blind student having to read a textbook etc.).

- The ability to use and participate equally in assessment procedures (e.g. taking tests, writing essays, working on assignments, working on projects, etc.).
- How a learner with disabilities can be assessed using alternative ways accommodating his/her capabilities but maintaining respective standards with other learners. (e.g. How much more time does a blind person need to take a test when using a screen reader? What kind of questions can assess the achievements of a learner with cognitive disabilities? How do they correspond with the expected learning outcomes of other learners?).

For educators:

- There is a need for educators to know (possibly through training or other available resources) and be able to collaborate and communicate with learners with disabilities that use AT.
- They need to be able to collaborate and consult with appropriate experts when they are facing students with disabilities that need different teaching methods or tools.
- The ability to produce easily (sometimes even automatically) teaching material that is accessible in various forms.
- The knowledge about and ability to use various teaching methods (sometimes in collaboration with other peers, "collaborative teaching" settings) and adapt them according to various learners needs at the same time.
- There is a need for tools to assist in assessment of various learners depending on their capabilities. (e.g. to produce or alter tests in appropriate ways for respective learners, to suggest and produce alternative ways of assessment, to be able to assess appropri-

ately each learners learning outcomes according to his/her capabilities).

For sponsors:

- They need to be able to communicate and collaborate appropriately with learners with disabilities using AT.
- The ability to be trained and consult with experts on how to communicate and how to encourage (and possibly participate) in the education process of the learner.
- They need to provide all kind of useful information for their learners needs and capabilities to educators and collaborate with them in the education process while at the same time ensure privacy of the provided information.
- Assessment feedback for the learners learning achievements should be provided to sponsors and used appropriately. This might also involve further consultation with educators and experts on how to respond to assessment feedback.

At the World Education Forum (World Education Forum, 2000) that took place in Dakar in 2000, 164 governments pledged to achieve "Education for All" (EFA) and identified six goals (UNESCO, n.d.c) to be met by 2015. UNESCO, which is the leading agency in that movement, focuses its activities on five key areas: policy dialogue (UNESCO, n.d.f), monitoring (UNESCO, n.d.e), advocacy (UNESCO, n.d.a), mobilization of funding (UNESCO, n.d.d) and capacity development (UNESCO, n.d.b). Inclusive education covers a broad range of problems in accessing education such as children living in areas of conflict, cultural issues, gender issues etc. Including children with disabilities in inclusive learning environments is just a part of it. However, the techniques and methods that can be used to include all children in education remain the same. To that direction UNESCO has already published a guide for teachers titled "Understanding and Responding to Children's Needs in Inclusive Classrooms" (McConkey, Roy, 2003) where it explains various possible problems that a kid might have in a class due to a disability or various other chronic illnesses and offers a variety of possible solutions that the teacher might exploit in order to facilitate learning for those children. In another document titled "Changing Teaching Practices: using curriculum differentiation to respond to students' diversity" (United Nations Educational Scientific and Cultural Organisation, 2004) UNESCO offers a more extensive guide on techniques for curriculum differentiation that can be employed by teachers to help them include all children in education. Effective policies and practices for inclusive education are also explained and presented in the article by Cor J.W. Meijer in 2010 (Meijer, 2010).

In Europe, the European Agency for Development in Special Needs Education, which is an independent and self-governing organization established by EU member countries to act as a platform for collaboration in the field of special needs education, has published a series of documents on various issues of inclusive education. In the report "Inclusive education and classroom practices" (Meijer, 2003) they refer to useful and successful practices that can be used to implement inclusive education in practice and in "Key Principles for Promoting Quality in Inclusive Education" (European Agency for Development in Special Needs Education, 2009) a set of recommendations is provided for policy makers. In another report titled "Inclusive Education and Classroom Practice in Secondary Education" (Meijer, 2005) a set of practices to implement inclusive education in secondary schools is provided through case studies in 14 EU countries and the report "Assessment in Inclusive Settings - Key Issues for Policy and Practice" (Watkins, Amanda, 2007) focuses on practices of assessment that can be employed for inclusive education. Finally, the report "Special Needs Education Country Data 2010" (Watkins, 2011b) shows the current status in education of

pupils in primary and secondary schools in EU countries. In US the National Center of Universal Design for Learning (UDL)("Universal Design for Learning," 2014) is embracing the framework that provides guidelines for the development of curricula that are inclusive. UDL is based on following 3 basic principles:

- Provide multiple means of representation
- Provide multiple means of action and expression
- Provide multiple means of engagement

These principles and guidelines are in the same wavelength as the suggestions and guides of the previous reports from UNESCO and the European Agency for Development in Special Needs Education.

Inclusive education might be a goal for 2015 according to UNESCO but the report shows the current statues in practices followed in EU countries. Currently there are 3 kinds of settings for providing education to pupils with Special Education Needs (SEN). The first is through segregated special schools for pupils with SEN, the second is through segregated special classes in mainstream schools and the third is through classes with fully inclusive settings. The report reveals that there is a lot to be done to reach the level of full inclusive learning environments becoming the standard of providing education to students with SEN. Amongst the Europeans Agency reports though there is also a very interesting report titled "ICTs in education for people with disabilities" (Watkins, 2011a) presenting case studies of ICTs being used to facilitate inclusive education settings for people with disabilities.

The following sections focus on policies, techniques and practices presented in the previous documents aiming to facilitate different educational needs presented earlier in different stages of a person's life starting from education in schools and going all the way to their retirement from work and ageing.

PRE-SCHOOL EDUCATION

Pre-school education in kindergartens aims to educate children in terms of basic social skills and understanding of their environment. Children how to collaborate and work in teams, how to behave in groups, how to communicate with peers, how to follow orders and instructions etc. Main tools of education in that age are games, toys and general fun and engaging ways and method in order to attract young children' attention and communicate effectively the learning objectives.

The Lack of Centralized Guidance and Advice

Looking at the matrix of needs we can understand that there are some needs that are more important than others in education of pre-school age. Most important of all is the need for communication and collaboration amongst all stakeholders. In communication of the child with its environment currently there is a wide variety of AT for all kinds of disabilities. However, there is no guidance or information on which tools and technologies can be used by pre-school children, how easy can they be used and if they really help them. GreatSchools (Raskind & Stanberry, n.d.) has also a quite extensive guide of assistive technologies for each kind of disability. However, once again it is not clear how they can be used in different education levels. An interesting attempt to present available AT solutions for children in early ages is done by the Let's Play project (Let's Play! Projects, 2004) from the "School of Public Health and Health Professions" (University of Buffalo, 2014) from University at Buffalo. The latter cases reveal a lack of centralized, credible source of information in that area such as large international organizations.

An interesting and relatively exhaustive attempt has been made by AbilityNet (AbilityNet, 2013), a UK national charity helping disabled adults and children use computers and the internet by adapting and adjusting their technology.

AbilityNet has already two projects running for pre-school education. In particular, the Play AT IT AbilityNet (AbilityNet, 2009d) project aimed to help raise awareness and opportunities for Nurseries and Pre-school Education Professionals to gain further support, training and awareness of Accessible Technology. AbilityNet worked in nine English regions, 18 Nurseries and 36 Local Authority Early Years Team to provide inclusive play opportunities to children with disabilities. To achieve that they provide training and support directly to the nurseries or children's centers who have received AT kits. AbilityNet will also be offering training, support and access to an extensive Loan Bank of assistive ICT equipment to 36 local authority Early Years teams and portage services. A similar project is also running in Northern Ireland titled "Play AT ICT Northern Ireland" AbilityNet (AbilityNet, 2009c)providing support to 27 participating nurseries and children centers. Over the next 2 years the project is also looking to engage a further 50 Nurseries with equipment, assessment, support and training. Their knowledge on AT and its usage in various situations is presented in factsheets and skill sheets (Play AT IT factsheets AbilityNet (AbilityNet, 2009a), Play AT ICT Northern Ireland factsheets and skill sheets(AbilityNet, 2009b),).

One major issue in the area of AT for pre-school children remains the cost of such solutions. The limited financial resources are usually preventing ordinary families and schools from buying such solutions. The relatively small size of this target group and their specialization makes it difficult to lower their cost thus in many cases such AT may become inaccessible for children that need it.

Apart from the technology itself, training, support and information about which AT is suitable in each case and how it should be used is limited and scattered around in pieces. A professional searching for such information can be lost in an ocean of documents, sites, companies and products that may discourage him form further involvement. The biggest problems as discovered from our research are not the technologies themselves but rather access to information about them and access to them. Thus, the actual challenges for technology is not how ICT can help communication and learning process of children with disabilities but rather how technology can help in wider access to AT for early childhood and better information dissemination between professionals, educators and sponsors.

Another crucial aspect in early childhood education is the need for assessing learners' needs. Children at that age are not able to communicate effectively with educators and parents and express their needs in an articulate form. Thus, educators and parents need to collaborate with experts in assessing disabilities especially in early childhood in order to provide the appropriate solutions. Thus, the communication channels discussed earlier should also facilitate collaboration too. Collaboration of experts with educators and parents in this early stage can be very crucial for early intervention.

PRIMARY AND SECONDARY SCHOOL EDUCATION

Supporting Collaborative Teaching

Both UNESCO and the European Agency presented earlier set as target inclusive education. To achieve that target they both set through various documents a set of principles and techniques that could be followed. One of the techniques already tested and working in many cases during the past 2 decades is co-operative teaching. It is also referred to as collaborative teaching or co-teaching and it is when two teachers are co-operating and teach at the same time in one classroom.

Co-teaching can follow five different models (Mason, 2010).

- one leads, one supports
- parallel teaching – teaching the same content to two groups, each taught by one of the co-teachers
- alternative teaching where one co-teacher teaches alternative content or using an alternative approach
- learning centers
- true team teaching that involves co-planning and shared responsibility for all aspects of instruction

There is a variety of cases of co-operative teaching such as in Norwood Elementary, in Baltimore (Heitin, 2011), that could not all be covered in the context of this book. There are also examples and information on how to use technology in a classroom with 2 teachers (Mason, 2010). They all prove the value of the technique, not only for children with disabilities, but also for children with learning difficulties, ADHD, autism, dyslexia etc. However, as valuable as this technique might be it is not a widespread solution. Rules and regulations of educational systems, lack of support from principals and lack of co-operation skills from teachers and lack of funding are some of the main problems (Heitin, 2011) preventing co-teaching to spread widely, at least for including pupils with disabilities in general classrooms.

Although there are already ideas on how to use technology in co-teaching environments, most of them are focusing on how to disseminate and use technology such as computers, electronic whiteboards, hand-held devices etc. in classrooms. There is little research and development on software and use of technologies for teacher that co-teach. An example of software aimed to assist co-teachers to improve and make their work easier is the Co-Teaching Solutions Systems Package which includes software for evaluating co-teaching from observers and toolbox providing teachers with resources, methods, strategies that they can follow in co-teaching. Such solutions, if provided open to educational systems, teachers, principals and other stakeholders could provide a better platform to educate teachers on how to co-operate and improve their teaching through co-teaching.

In that context, there is already a variety of Learning Management and Course Management systems for organizing, publishing and using teaching material. Such systems already allow more than one teachers to work together on producing and publishing content for a specific lesson. Why not incorporate into them solutions and tools for co-teaching as well?

Co-teaching requires both teachers to be present in the classroom and co-operate during the lesson. However, in cases of students with disabilities the second teacher needs to have some specific knowledge of how to handle and communicate with the student, for example if necessary using sign language. This means that teachers for students with disabilities might be needed in different places during the same day. On the other hand it means that a sign language reader could enable any teacher to work with students reliant on the use of sign language.

Robots as Assistive Teachers

In Korea a new model of co-teaching is used. They plan to have a robot in each kindergarten classroom by 2013 (Saenz, 2010) helping in teaching English. Robots like EnKi can serve as valuable portals for telepresence. In that capacity it allows Korea to hire English speakers around the world to teach in their classrooms at a fraction of the price of traditional instructors who are shipped into the country.

Telepresence robots can also serve in the case of students with disabilities allowing teachers to be present in many classrooms during the same day. This way the cost of co-teaching for students with disabilities could be lowered significantly to allow co-teaching to spread easier.

Networking for Collaborative Teaching

One of the key issues in co-teaching is the exchange of information and co-operation between wide networks of professionals in the educational sector. Being able to exchange information with other teachers, connect and find teachers for specific cases of students with disabilities and sharing good practices has already been proved to help in improving inclusive education in general. UNESCO in their document "ICTs IN EDUCATION FOR PEOPLE WITH DISABILITIES" (Watkins, 2011a) conclude that one of the major areas that ICTs can help in inclusive education is supporting international co-operation and practice exchange (p. 92).

There is a need for more co-operation networks in teaching at international level. eTwinning (ETwinning, n.d.) is one of the biggest European teacher's networks and recently the Tellnet project (Tellnet, n.d.) organized a workshop to sketch out prospective scenarios about the role of teachers' networks in 2025 for teachers' professional development together with the Institute of Prospective Technology Studies in Sevilla, Spain (European Commission, Joint Research Centre, Institute for Prospective Technological Studies.,2009). The document "Teacher Collaboration Networks in 2025" (Bacigalupo, Margherita. Cachia, Romina, 2011) that was produced from the workshop describes the benefits for teachers from such social networks and presents possible future solutions in that direction. However it might be useful to exploit increase participation through various policies and maybe categorize/organize better teachers for students with disabilities

Personalization in Computer Supported Collaborative Learning (CSCL)

Another interesting technique for inclusive education is collaborative learning. This is when a group of people learn something together which means that people have to depend on and help each other during the learning process. There are many different ways to implement collaborative learning and the introduction of technology in that technique has already lead to the development of a specific domain of collaborative learning called computer supported collaborative learning (CSCL). The SharedExperience project which launched in 2007 is aiming to provide a platform for sharing experiences in teaching and learning and have already developed a quite explanatory table of different technologies for CSCL. A quick look at the table reveals that most of the technologies now used for CSCL are based on the web. Social bookmarking, Social networking and learning management systems, Blogs, Wikis, Social media sharing and mashups are all web based solutions for facilitating collaborative learning.

A crucial aspect for accessible CSCL is actually web accessibility. Since social media and networks seem to heavily affect CSCL technologies, the accessibility of social networks and related applications is one of the major issues of web accessibility related with CSCL. Current social media content, blogs and Wikis etc. already pose problems for persons with disabilities so there is a need for increased awareness in the area, to help students with disabilities participate easier in CSCL activities.

Another aspect in such solutions is that the content is usually produced by their users. Thus, there is also a need for either increased awareness amongst users of the problems caused by content that is not accessible. Another approach in that direction could also be the development of such tools in the future to prevent users from creating and publishing inaccessible content.

A category of CSCL solutions is also synchronous communication and conferencing tools. Currently, major players in the area of Learning Management Systems and Course Management Systems are offering such tools with in their platforms. Blackboard, (BlackBoard, 2013b) being one of them, offers "Blackboard Collaborate" (BlackBoard, 2013a) in that direction, Adobe (Adobe Systems Inc., 2014a) has "Adobe Connect" (Adobe Systems Inc., 2014b) while traditional teleconferencing applications such as Skype (Microsoft, 2014a) and Meebo (Meebo, n.d.) can also be used for the same purpose.

There is no indication on how accessible are these kinds of services. For example how does a person who is blind participating in a teleconference understand what is shown by the teacher who is sharing his desktop. Either the teacher has to know that there is a student who cannot see the presentation and describe it or the person is excluded from the learning process. The development of new ways of interaction with ICT such as speech recognition and gesture recognition might also help in making such tools more accessible for Persons with disabilities. In addition there is a need for personalization of the interface and the whole experience according to a user's needs. For example a student who is deaf should be able to have automatically enabled the transcripts feature of the tool in order to follow the conversation online.

Virtual Reality CSCL

Another interesting trend in CSCL is the use of virtual worlds and gaming. Currently, there is a variety of applications on the web offering educational virtual worlds for kids that require children to complete projects and tasks, play games and throughout this process learn a variety of subjects. Web sites like JumpStart (Knowledge Adventure, Inc., 2014), Club Penguin (Disney Canada Inc., 2014), Webkinz World (Webkinz, n.d.), National Geographic Animal Jam (National Geographic

Society and Smart Bomb Interactive, Inc., 2013) etc. offer various educational games, quizzes and activities in the context of a virtual world where children are learning while playing. However, there are still questions on how accessible are these kind of applications for children with disabilities.

As already presented in the consumer and lifestyle section there are already a variety of technologies for rendering virtual reality scenes such as OpenGL (Khronos Group, 2014), Direct3D (Microsoft, 2006), Java3D and VRML (Bell, Parisi, & Pesce, 1995). In addition, major companies in the ICT industry such as Sony are investing on virtual reality gear such as the new head mounted display by Sony introduced lately (Shapiro, 2011). HMZ-T3W (Hartien, 2013) as it is called, costs $800 and is able to display 2D and 3D immersive scenes. The small screens in the device are equivalent of having your very own 150 inch movie screen only twelve feet away. It also a built-in virtual 5.1 surround sound headphones which can simulate a movie theatre's surround sound. Similar devices have also been presented by other manufacturers such as the WRAP1200 by Vuzix and the ST1080 by SiliconMicroDisplay (Silicon Micro Display, Inc., 2012).

The devices presented earlier are mainly used for output of virtual reality scenes. However, a complete virtual reality system must also use some kind of input devices beyond the traditional keyboard and mouse. Advances in that area can be seen by Microsoft which presented Kinect (Microsoft, 2014c), a camera based device which can recognize body movements, gestures and faces and provide an interaction with an Xbox (Microsoft, 2014d). device through them. Microsoft also released an API for developers in order to take advantage of Kinect's potentials by developing their own applications. From then on there's been a variety of applications coming from various developers allowing people to control and interact with their computers through movements and gestures. In August, Apple has also filed a patent (Pachal, 2011) for a similar system allowing users to control their

devices through movements showing that motion control of devices is a possible emerging trend of the future. Going some steps further in that direction some months ago, Gallotti, Raposo & Soares (Gallotti, Raposo, & Soares, 2011) presented in a research paper a virtual reality glove (v-Glove) able to simulate touch through haptic feedback.

The developments presented earlier show that the future might see virtual educational worlds being accessible in additional modalities other than the current visual one. This way virtual reality might become more accessible to persons with disabilities. Having said that it might also be useful to investigate the benefits in social and interpersonal skills of children with disabilities through virtual worlds and if they can really help them in the real world

Augmented Reality in CSCL

Games can also be designed to promote positive interdependence. This is when students are working in groups to complete a task or a project and they have to rely on each other to succeed in completing it. Games can assign to students different roles or different parts of information and asked to collaborate in order to achieve a task. Including students with disabilities in such a process makes them feel useful in society and can increase their confidence and self-esteem. However, the nature of tasks and roles given to each member of the group and especially to children with disabilities should be so that conform with his/her abilities. Personalization of computer games in networks could lead to games taking under account a user's profile in order to assign specific tasks, roles, or pieces of information in the general game context. Such games could be very useful tools for educators in classroom settings making the learning process more engaging for everyone.

Apart from virtual reality technologies already presented to support such games there is also an emerging trend or Augmented Reality based games. In Radford University, the project called

Radford Outdoor Augmented Reality (National Science Foundation, n.d.b) designed two games (National Science Foundation, n.d.a) based on augmented reality. They gave students mobile devices with the respective software and assigning specific roles or pieces of information to each of them and asked them to complete specific tasks. However, they had to combine their information and roles to achieve the final goal. The outcomes showed AR has the potential to impact several areas of learning.

From the accessibility perspective such augmented reality educational games can help children with disabilities in their social interactions and cooperation as long as they can access and use AR information and resources.

Personalized Education

In all previous examples one of the key factors for inclusive education is the ability to adapt teaching methods, materials, tasks etc. according to learners' needs and profile. Either by having a co-teacher, a robot co-teacher, a traditional CSCL system, a teleconference based CSCL system or an AR based CSCL system the key factor for success is to adapt teaching methods and learning objectives according to students' needs and performance. Educators need to know how well students perform, what are their strengths and weaknesses and focus on them. This means that the learning process has to be adapted for each student individually and the traditional model of one-size-fits-all teaching and learning should be abandoned. Given however the ratio of teachers to students in schools this means that educators need tools to help them in adapting their teaching methods according to each student. They need tools to support personalized learning and assessment of their students in order to provide better personalized education services.

Today's technology with all these online courses, teaching material, educational games makes quite easy for educators to track their students'

progress and find out what is needed for each of them. As Darell M. West presents it in his paper titled "Using Technology to Personalize Learning and Assess Students in Real-Time" (West, 2011):

Imagine schools where students master vital skills and critical thinking in a personalized and collaborative manner, teachers assess pupils in real-time, and social media and digital libraries connect learners to a wide range of informational resources. Teachers take on the role of coaches, students learn at their own pace, technology tracks student progress, and schools are judged based on the outcomes they produce. Rather than be limited to six hours a day for half the year, this kind of education moves toward 24/7 engagement and learning fulltime.

This kind of education described is student oriented and adapted according to each individual. In his paper West presents a variety of cases that support this kind of personalization in education and their achievements. One of the best examples is School of One ("School of one", n.d.) in New York. Students in School of One are not arranged in classrooms where they follow a specific subject according to a schedule as it happens in ordinary schools. They each get a different set of activities for each day based on their progress. This happens because School of One learns about the specific academic needs of every student and then accesses a large bank of carefully reviewed educational resources, using sophisticated technology to find the best matches among students, teachers, and resources. In addition, School of One's learning algorithm takes up-to-date data about students' performance and available materials, and creates a unique schedule for every student, every day. This way, individual students are moved ahead only after they've demonstrated mastery. Currently the program is running in three middle schools for the subject of math. However, the funding received and the initial outcomes encourage its expansion in more subjects and schools.

Another similar example is the High Tech High (HTH) (High Tech High, 2000) program running in 11 public charter schools in Chula Visa and San Diego, California. Students at HTH follow personal interests and develop personal portfolios of projects demonstrating their progress in various subjects. Apart from personalization, HTH has also 2 more basic design principles: adult world connection which is implemented by encouraging students to work on companies in internships and "shadow" projects and Common Intellectual Mission which doesn't separate between college preparation and technical education. The program uses a variety of teaching models assigning a staff advisor to each student who is responsible for the student and keeping contact with the family. Students with special needs receive special attention and are provided with available assistive technologies and solutions to facilitate their learning.

The iZone (NYC Department of Education, n.d.) in New York City is a program that aims to investigate innovative teaching and learning practices in schools based on digital learning. The K12 Company (K12 Inc., 2014) is also another example of personalized learning. In K12 students can enroll in virtual online schools connected public school programs. The program offers personalized learning services for students who want some extra help, feel bored by the pace followed in the classroom or for any other reason they might feel that the education received in classroom doesn't satisfy their needs.

In general, we can see that personalized learning is a trend in education that seems to spread a lot easier with the use of technology. This personalization, if implemented appropriately, could also help children with disabilities in their education too. They could receive special help on how to use assistive technologies, they could follow subjects on their own pace, get in groups with other students who might have similar problems in same subject and in general follow an educational program tailored to their needs and capabilities. In such an environment children with disabilities would

be included gracefully in a learning environment encouraging collaboration with other students while in parallel motivating them for personal development and learning goals achievement. However, there is a need for research in the area to include even more children with disabilities in these personalized learning schemes in order to identify problems and solutions for them.

Learning Analytics

A keystone need for personalized learning systems and curriculum differentiation has to do with assessment of learners' progress. Assessment has to take under account specific factor for each student and adapt accordingly. Using technologies to assess students' progress can have a series of benefits (Russel, 2013) but most importantly it can support easier the adaptations needed for assessment for students with disabilities. Designing assessments for students with disabilities has to take under account various factors (The University of Strathclyde, 2004) such as time, place, objectives etc. in order to be in equal terms with other peers.

Modern solutions of personalized learning presented earlier already employ a set of assessment techniques usually through online tests, quizzes and games that allow the systems to understand the learners' progress and adapt the rest of his curriculum accordingly. Using online tests, quizzes, games etc. for assessing daily progress of students can also lead to one of the first steps for achieving what is presented in "Horizon 2011" (New Media Consortium. EDUCAUSE (Association), 2011) report as learning analytics. Similar to Web analytics such as Google analytics (Google, 2014a) which can capture a web-site's users' interactions, preferences, visits, times etc. and produce graphs that visualize the use of a web site online assessments can also be used to analyze and produce similar reports for a learner, his progress, his strengths and weaknesses etc.

Since much of the assessment and teaching material is in digital form in online courses, tests, quizzes etc. there are already existing analytics tools aimed mainly for web-site usability testing and evaluation that could also be used in the direction of gathering learning analytics data. Solutions such as Mixpanel analytics (Mixpanel, n.d.) and Userfly are already used in commercial sites for usability evaluation d could also be used in learning analytics situation easily. An example of tool developed especially for learning analytics is Socrato (Socrato, 2013) which can generate diagnostic and performance reports for students. Loco-analyst (LOCO-Analyst, 2014) can also provide feedback for educators on how a web-based course is used in order to improve it and ROLE is a platform that also enables students to get the feedback from their learning analytics.

The future might change the school into a wired school model where student complete various learning activities such as following classes, working in groups for projects and problem solving, working with teachers in small groups for specialized training and teaching in subjects that are difficult for them, consult with teachers on their assessments, projects, lessons, resources etc. All this action and interaction with various devices and interfaces will be recoded and analyzed so that it is easy for teachers to point out the potential problems for each kid, adapt their teaching methods and teaching material in order to improve the learning outcomes from the whole school education/learning experience. Coupled with modern profiling systems the systems itself could suggest and support decision making for teachers giving them additional information such as what kind of disability the kid has, how they should work with him to achieve the most from its education, what kind of AT tools are best suited for him etc.

Affective Computing For Learning Analytics

When looking at the learning analytics trend from the accessibility perspective it would probably be

even more useful for educators to also include feedback of implicit students' interaction with learning systems. One of the best practices for assessing a students' progress and needs is by observing him while working on the class. This way the student not knowing that he is assessed performs naturally and shows more obvious signs of problem he might have. However, observing students in an environment such as the one described earlier might be difficult for teachers that will have to devote their time in various other tasks too. Thus, it would be helpful if the learning environment itself observes each student's behavior. Affective computing is a technology where computers can understand emotions of people based on their implicit user input through facial expression, voice recognition, body language etc. There is already research in the area such as the Affective AutoTutor by D'Mello, Lehman and Graesser (D'Mello, Lehman, & Graesser, 2011) which seemed to improve the learning for low-domain knowledge learners, particularly at deeper levels of comprehension. Similar research in the Institute for Neural Computing at the University of California on San Diego (Littlewort, Bartlett, Salamanca, & Reilly, 2011), demonstrates how facial expression can indicate various emotions of students during problem solving tasks. In another research presented in the 20th Australasian Conference on Computer-Human Interaction (Perera, Kennedy, & Pearce, 2008) it is demonstrated how user agents can affect users' performance and satisfaction can change depending on how friendly the user agent is. In general there is a lot of research in the area of affective (or emotive) computing in relation to learning process and it seems as one of the promising technologies for helping students achieve better learning outcomes.

Especially in the cases of children with disability where interactions with ICT might be difficult, boring or tiresome and confusing having systems that could automatically recognize such behavior and adapt accordingly could prove very beneficial. So in the previous example of the wired school providing constant learning analytics data to teachers, emotive computing could also be used in ICTs to improve interaction and engagement in the learning process. For example, when a student who is deaf and reading a textbook chapter on Newtonian physics shows signs of boredom, the system could automatically change its method and instead of continuing with the textbook it could interrupt and use a game in order to attract his attention and connect the applications of Newtonian physics to real life.

All this learning analytics data and information could also be available to the parents of a child engaging them in the learning process. The learning process will not stop in school. It will continue throughout the day with a variety of other activities which could also connect learning with real life issues and problems. For example, math could also be practiced during a visit on a shopping mall by giving the child real life situations to use them. This will engage parents in games, problem solving situation, projects, involving them actively in the learning process. This involvement would also provide teachers with additional feedback on students' behaviors and teachers could also cooperate this way with parents to adapt teaching methods accordingly. Especially in cases of children with disabilities the involvement of parents is crucial and could provide educators with valuable feedback on learning behavior of children.

Social Media in Schools

Apart from getting education in traditional subjects such as reading, writing, mathematics, science etc. school education also provides a great deal of education in social skills. Students in schools learn basic social skills such co-operation and communication with peers, standing up for their rights, accepting differences in peoples' social background etc. Social media being an emerging trend today have also penetrated students' population. Research show that students want their schools to use social media for their educa-

tion (KQED Inc., 2014), challenging this way the boundaries between personal and professional life of educators. Social media are also affecting school education in many other ways (Bernard, 2010) such as changing the communication between parents and children, providing more opportunities for class activities and connecting teachers with their classrooms. One of the most important aspects though, that needs attention is the effect that social media can have in the phenomenon of bullying.

Social media helped bullying spread beyond school boundaries. Bullying today doesn't stop when a student leaves school and goes home. It can continue over social media with comments, rumor spreading, uploading photos etc. It also appears that cyber-bullying is even more dangerous than bullying since according to recent studies (Moyer, 2010) cyber-bullies and their victims have higher suicide rates than their peers. It also appears to be a phenomenon spreading quickly as technology penetrates students' lives. The same study revealed that 58% of 12-year-olds owned a cell phone in 2009, up from only 18% in 2004. Research (Didden et al., 2009) also shows that cyber-bullying and bullying is prevalent among students with intellectual and developmental disability in special education settings and that is spreading silently as an epidemic (AbilityPath.org, 2011).

However, another study (Watters, 2011) reveals that educators in schools are not up to speed with the developments. In a recent study, only half of teachers believed that schools are doing enough to educate students on online safety issues. Despite that, a much larger percentage of school administrators thought that education on online safety provided is enough. Another interesting finding is that a little over half of teacher felt equipped to talk to students about safety and privacy online and about cyber-bullying.

It is evident that educational systems need to get up to speed with developments in online safety and privacy issues and educators need to get up to date with such issues. Technology and social media themselves can also help in that direction.

There are already applications (Bernard, 2010) which help in detecting cyber-bullying and inform parents and teachers respectively.

Most of these applications monitor the online activity on children' computers, smart phone and tablets, with a view to alerting teachers and parents when potential harassment is taking place. Cyber-bullying is an epidemic that spreads silently and needs to be addressed both for students with and without disabilities equally. Perhaps, an additional solution to already existing programs and applications for detecting cyber-bullying could be the enhancement with users' disability profiles to help identifying easier bullying happening to children with disabilities.

THIRD LEVEL EDUCATION

Higher education has many similarities with school education in techniques and practices that could be exploited in the learning process but the main difference is that students in higher education tend to be more independent from their parents/sponsors. Thus, supervision of students' progress by their parents is not as crucial as in school education. However, the role of sponsor is usually played by students themselves so there is an increased need for self-assessment and self-improvement techniques in higher education. Additionally, there is also a difference in students-to-educators ratio. Professors are not as close to students as teachers in schools leaving students with more space for initiative and creativity. This means that higher education environment fosters independency of students in their learning process. Independence in their learning process is also followed by independence in their everyday life. It is usually the age where students start to live on their own and manage real-life issues that were once handled by their parents or guardians. However, independency does not mean that collaborative learning methods or collaboration with peers is not supported. Students form their own identity while working in groups and learning to cooperate in a professional level.

From the point of accessibility in higher education a recent study published by Sachs and Schreuer (Sachs & Schreuer, 2011) and reports bye OECD shows that enrolment of students with disabilities in higher education is lower than expected and that is followed by high first year dropout rates. It also showed that although achievements of students with disabilities are not remote to achievements of the rest of students, students with disabilities devote more time and effort and participated in fewer extra-curriculum and social activities. However, the use of ICT shows improvement in the overall learning experience for students in higher education. The impact of accessible ICT through assistive technology both in education and in employment is also reported in other research by Dorwick et al. (2005) and Schreuer et al. (2006). One of the major barriers in inclusive education in higher education is reported to be the ignorance of faculty members and administration on issues about disabilities and how to provide solutions. In studies by Barazandeh (2005) and Kraska (2003) it is found that only 50% of students with disabilities felt that faculty members understood their needs and that only 25% of faculty members were willing to change their teaching material and methods in order to accommodate their needs. The majority of students with disabilities (82%) reported that faculty members needed to learn more about disabilities.

Looking at this evidence one can identify that technology can help in inclusive higher education but there is a definite need for raising awareness amongst the academic community on accessibility issues and how technology can help overcoming them. Inclusive education initiatives on an International level such as the International Initiative for Inclusive Education (Equity Alliance, 2011), on a national level such as the National Inclusive Education Initiative or Inclusive Education Canada (Inclusive Education Canada, n.d.), together with international human rights associations such as

UNESCO Enable (UN Enable, 2008) and AT ICT initiatives such as G3ICT (The Global Initiative for Inclusive ICTs, 2014), can help in that direction but what is needed is initiatives and research that takes place in higher education institutes to promote various AT.

The Case of Speech Recognition in Universities

An interesting example of promoting an emerging technology that could help in higher education becoming accessible for a more people is the Liberated Learning Consortium which is promoting the use of speech recognition technology in education. The Liberated Learning Consortium is an international research network aiming to advanced speech recognition technologies so that they can be used in learning environments to improve accessibility. The universities and companies involved in this consortium (Liberated Learning, 2014) are implementing solutions based on speech recognition technologies in learning environments. In one of their projects called Youth Initiative (Liberated Learning, 2010) running in Canada, students with disabilities of postsecondary school are given access to a cloud-based service allowing them to use speech recognition software to transcribe previously inaccessible letters. In another project called Synote (University of Southampton, 2011) developed by the University of Southampton, students are able to search, exploit, manage and annotate lecture transcripts. This way, not only students with disabilities could access lectures and use them, but also any other student could use transcripts to have better access to lecture notes and material.

Experience form running and past speech recognition projects in higher education shows both positive and negative signs. In most of the cases negative signs have to do with infrastructure and software problems causing it to stop running during a lecture and resulting in incomplete lecture files. Current research is also focusing on problems related to multiple speakers discussing in a classroom environment. Apart from recognizing speech from multiple speakers, the problem also involves issues of sound quality and how can you capture multiple speakers' speech in a large auditorium environment without requiring any specific microphone infrastructure installation. Interesting ideas in that direction involve even the use of mobile devices to be used as microphones from students in a large classroom/auditorium environment.

The Additional Value of Assistive Solutions

A very important factor that could increase the uptake of usage of speech recognition technology in classes could be the additional value that automatic transcripts and caption can add to educational material. Nowadays, almost all higher education institutes provide their student with online teaching materials such as lecture notes, presentations, sources and even lectures themselves. So, having live lecture transcripts as an additional teaching material is something that could benefit all students. In addition, combining lecture transcripts with lecture video or audio could definitely help students, apart from those with hearing impairments, by adding value to lecture video or audio. Students for example could search for a specific part of the lecture based on transcripts using technologies such as that developer in the Synote (University of Southampton, 2011) project, or find out lectures in other courses that deal with similar subjects.

The idea of adding automatic transcripts in lectures could also evolve even more if integrated with other technologies too. Since many lecturers are already using some kind of presentation software such as PowerPoint, an additional layer of audio description could also be automatically produced during the presentation. Software for screen capturing like Camtasia Studio (TechSmith, 2014b), CamStudio (CamStudio.org, 2013),

SnagIt (TechSmith, 2014a) etc. could evolve even more to capture events during the presentation such as slide change, pointer movement, animation etc. and provide additional text streams explaining actions and images on screen. These text feeds could be then used by text to speech technology to produce additional synchronized audio description feed for the presentation while this is happening.

Social Media as an Assistive Technology

Similar feeds now can be produced and synchronized to lectures using for example Twitter. Free Power Point Twitter tools is a suite of programs by SAP (Business Analytics, 2013) that can be used by lecturer as well as by any other presenter to either Tweet automatically texts during a presentation, get slides with comments, get online voting results during the presentation etc. Students can follow these tweets for additional resources and comments on a presentation. In addition there are examples (Ferenstein, 2010) that Twitter is used for engaging students in lectures with live commenting from students or questions send by twitter while the presentation is taking place etc.

The trend of using Twitter and other social media during lectures could provide many benefits both for student with disabilities and for students without disabilities. Students for example with speech impairment could comment or pose questions without problems. Students who are blind could follow streams for audio descriptions of slides presented in a presentation. If for example a slide show a graph representing specific statistics this could be tweeted during the lecture and read through the students mobile phone or laptop using the respective screen reader software. Other benefits include that these twitter streams could also be included as additional information layers in a recorded lectures and be used either for book marking, searching or sharing applications.

The trend of social media seems to affect heavily higher education. Actually social media can be used for many purposes even from schools (Hartstein, 2011) but in higher education uses are even more. Social media can be used for sharing information with students, communication with students, tutoring, research etc. Some examples are presented by Justin Marquis in his blog (Marquis, 2011). In fact, there are so many different ways to use social media that enumerating them in this book is impossible. The blog post called "Over 100 ideas for using Twitter in the Classroom" (Walsh, 2010) proves that by refereeing to more than 100 uses only for Twitter (Twitter, 2014). Let alone, Facebook, LinkedIn (LinkedIn, 2014), Google+ (Google, 2014b), YouTube (Google, 2014c), blogs, podcasts, wikis etc. In addition, recent research is proving that the use of social media by students does not affect negatively their performance. The study shows that it is the way that students use social media that affects most their performance rather than the fact of using it. On the other hand, while nearly every student is using social media, other studies show (Tinti-Kane, Seaman, & Levy, 2010) that the acceptance and usage of them in education by educators doesn't seem to show a similar uptake. The trend seems to be fighting with educators' skepticism and possibly unwillingness to change teaching tools and methods, but gains steadily more ground.

However, there are no studies on how many students with disabilities are using social media. Which ones they prefer, how they prefer accessing them (mobile, desktop), what are they using them for etc. There is also lack of data from already existing studies on how many students with disabilities were included in the studies and particular problems referred to them. Major players are showing some interest on accessibility since Facebook was recently hiring accessibility experts and according to a brief history of Facebook's communication with AFB (SimplyRaydeen, 2009) and according to AFB's blog they were open to discuss accessibility problems (BIK project, 2014) and committed to work on finding solutions. Google who just recently launched their own social network platform stated that Google+ was built from scratch with accessibility in mind and calls for users to bring up accessibility issues in order to deal with them. A recent survey by WebAIM (WebAIM, 2009) also shows trends and habits among screen reader users who also report their perception of accessibility of various social media. In general the most accessible social site seems to be Twitter, possibly because of the simplicity of its interface and structure.

Future developments in social networking tools should definitely take under account accessibility issues since there usage could become a very useful tool both for education and for other purposes too. Thus, to enable this kind of tools and make persons with disabilities more active and give them an even louder voice in the web, social networking should become more accessible through appropriate policy enforcement.

The Use of Tablets in Education

Another interesting technology trend that begins to form in education is the use of e-readers and tablets in classroom as teaching tools. There are already many reasons (Madan, 2011) why tablets would fit and could be used easily in education. Tablets can spice up and make more interesting the already existing textbooks, there is already much educational software developed for tablets, they fit students lifestyle who are already using smartphones and are quite familiar with using similar interfaces and their prices are getting lower. However, there are also important barriers in scaling up the use of tablets in national level, cost being the biggest of them all and pressing for action from policy makers. In fact, South Korea (Murray, 2011), India (Qing, 2011) and Kazakhstan (Drinkwater, 2010) have already announced programs that set targets for rolling out tablets in universities and schools.

From the accessibility point of view, tablets already come with a variety of assistive software such as VoiceOver (Apple, 2014) or Talkback

(Warrior, 2011), allowing access to persons with disabilities. In addition there are already many apps (Disabled World, 2014) for people with disabilities. Some of them are also targeted for users with cognitive disabilities or other learning difficulties (Swanson, 2011).

The plethora of apps for people with disabilities proves that there is potential for providing both teaching material and teaching tools (as educational apps) that do not exclude students with disabilities from the learning process. However, there is a need to make sure of the potential accessibility issues before introducing a device in education for wide use. The case of Kindle e-readers and the law that was introduced for their use in education (Schaffhauser, 2010) is one of the examples of how legislation and national policies should take care for accessibility before spreading widely the use of an inaccessible device.

Tactile Screens for Students with Disabilities

A technology lately introduced in touch screen interfaces that could potentially increase even more accessibility of such devices is tactile touch screens. There are already a number of companies specializing in that direction with major players taking also interest in the technology. Samsung has presented Senseg (Senseg, 2011) a product for tactile touch screens which as they say is quite expensive. Currently they are looking for partnerships with other device manufacturer such as Toshiba who already hopped on board to take advantage of the solution by embedding it to their products. Apple was recently granted a patent (Wong, 2011) for tactile touch screens and there is a lot speculation about its next product that will use this kind of technology. Microsoft has also filed a patent for tactile touch screens (Dillow, 2010) but the technology introduced is aiming large touch screen interfaces like Microsoft's Surface (Microsoft, 2014b). Other solutions available are introduced by smaller companies like Immersion

(Immersion Corporation, 2013). However, a common issue for all the technologies and solutions for tactile interfaces introduced is their cost. As a new technology in the market it is expected to be rather expensive initially for wide adoption in education systems. The development of applications and the increase in its utility could potentially lower down the cost to reasonable levels.

Obviously, tactile touch screens when introduced in tablets, smartphones or even Surface-like devices will be able to provide a plethora of accessibility solutions (Rock, n.d.) for persons with disabilities. The most obvious ones have to do with persons who are blind but more research could reveal potential benefits for other groups too such cognitive impaired persons. In education the introduction of tablets with tactile screens in schools could potentially solve a lot of problems existing now in teaching in large auditoriums. The most important one could be the presentation of drawings, sketches and graphs used by educators either in traditional or in interactive whiteboards. The wired university auditorium of the future could possibly include technology that will transfer the drawings form the whiteboard on a tactile touch screen of a student who is blind.

Opening Higher Education and Distance Learning

Another very interesting innovation in education that is emerging especially in higher education is what is called democratization of education. It started some years ago with the introduction of Open University in UK (Open University, 2014a). The Open University contrary to what was the norm up to date is accepting students without any specific qualification criteria opening up access to higher education. Students can choose from a variety of courses offered and study from their own home though distance learning technologies. What is important from the accessibility point of view is that the Open University has "...*over 12,000 students with a disability, health condi-*

tion, mental health difficulty or specific learning difficulty (such as dyslexia) study at the OU" according to their site (Open University, 2014b). Other interesting initiatives for opening access to higher education learning were recently announced and deployed by MIT and University of Stanford. The University of Stanford has already opened access to lectures of three courses and plans to now open access to even more in the following semester. MIT has recently announced a new open source learning initiative called MITx (MIT News office, 2011). The examples indicate a trend for opening access to higher education learning through distance learning applications and technologies. This could prove to be of significant importance for people with disabilities that are often discouraged by the barriers confronted with access to the university itself. It could be access to the campus, within the campus reaching the classrooms, following lectures live, participating in extra-curriculum activities etc. All this fuss and problems that might seem trivial can discourage a person with disability when he has to deal with them every day. So, opening up access to education could also give many people with disabilities a second chance to higher education.

A reason why Universities start investing in distance learning courses is also the cost. Distance learning doesn't need classrooms or labs and consequently is not limited by such factors. The potential audience for an online lecture could be hundreds of thousands of people all over the world whereas the same lecture could be followed only by a limited number of students in a classroom or auditorium environment. However, there are cases in higher education where presence in a specific place could be off importance and could not be substituted by distance learning techniques such as attending a lab session.

As already explained earlier, access to universities, even if there is increasing awareness and provision, still poses problems in many cases. A technology that could help in that direction could be that of telepresence robots. Telepresence robots presented also in previous sections such as those provided by Anybots (Anybots, 2014) and Vgo Communications (VGo Communications, Inc., 2013) could potentially be used within a university environment so that students with disabilities can attend lectures, lab sessions, workshops etc. by using a telepresence robot.

Producing and Repurposing Content for Open Distance Learning

As distance learning and open learning technologies get more traction there will be a need for educators to produce more teaching material and a lot easier. Capturing a lecture with software like Camtasia Studio (TechSmith, 2014b), CamStudio (CamStudio.org, 2013) or SnagIt (TechSmith, 2014a), could be already quite easy. However, content produced with such software could be very inaccessible. On the other hand a lecture presentation file on its own might quite accessible but without being able to access the actual lecture loses some of the information. Being able to access the lecture video and the presentation file at the same time could be very helpful for students with visual impairments. In parallel, a text stream of tweets about the lecture, comments and questions could also add more value and interactivity to the lecture. All this and many more layers of information that could accompany a lecture video such as live transcripts or captions, additional resources for specific issues discussed during the lecture etc. could make easier the learning experience for a student with disabilities and enhance even more the experience for the rest of the students. Thus, there is a need for media and media production and consumption tools that could easily tailor all this information together, publish it and use it as needed.

There are already media formats that could tie media such as video or audio with additional metadata. Having all this additional information as metadata layers could enrich significantly the learning experience. Imagine for example the auditorium of the future capturing the video feed of the lecture, synchronizing it with events in the presentation such as slide or text and image transitions, tying also events in social media such as posts on the lecture's Facebook page or on Twitter, following and capturing audience responses to questions, level of attention and mood during the lecture from various students interactions, producing and adding audio transcripts and finally producing an overall media content file that includes all the above meta information. The content is also automatically broadcasted though internet, so that it can be followed live by students at their home. Additionally the educator after some editing and corrections on the content also uploads the lecture content on the university's media server. Students that either have attended the lecture or not could then have access from a special media player that could allow them to configure which layers of content to see and which not adapting this way the presentation to their needs.

Another issue that follows also the problems described earlier is technologies that can help in repurposing of existing content. For example, how can a textbook written in a word processor are easily transferred to material for a web page? How accessible this web page will be? How easily the textbook can be used from an e-Reader, a tablet or a mobile phone? Although technologies and standards in the filed have evolved there are still important issues in repurposing of content even for the already existing technologies. New technologies will amplify these problems if standards common practices are not followed.

Personalizing Assessment

Another need not examined so far in higher education is the one for assessment of learning progress. In the previous section of school education the technology of learning analytics was presented and examined in relation to students with disabilities. The main difference between school and higher education assessment is that the first one is mainly targeted to educators who follow students' progress and adapt their teaching methods and tools, whereas in higher education it should be intended mainly for use by students themselves. Students seeing learning analytics reports should be able to see their progress compared to other students following the same subject and adjust accordingly their own learning tools and methods. It could be that the tools themselves provide them with decision support mechanisms and provide them with possible solutions in adjusting their learning experience.

In the case of students with disabilities however, learning analytics should also take under account disability in the learning process. As already explained (The University of Strathclyde, 2004) assessment of students with disabilities might need adaptations in time, nature, objectives on order to be on equal basis with other students. Learning analytics tools should know and take under account those factors in order to provide information that is in comparison with the rest of the students. For example, knowing that a student who is blind take more time to read through a page of a textbook and this time might also increase in case there are math involved, the tool should adapt the time needed for the student who is blind in similar scale with the rest of the students in order to show him that he is following at the same pace. In that direction there is a need for more research to understand even better how these adaptations work.

LIFELONG LEARNING FOR LIVING AND WORKING

Some might say that learning is a process that ends with the graduation from a university. These ideas now belong to the past. People are required throughout their life to constantly learn new skills, new tools, new methods etc. Current work environments and the rapid changes in technology and science require persons in almost all professions to stay up to date with trends, news and developments in their area of interest. Thus, there is a need for constant learning in all stages of life of a person. Vocational education and training though doesn't necessary follow traditional educational schemes of educators teaching in a classroom a group of learners. In many cases this training is happening in a self-training mode. People follow self-training courses or tutorials and learn new skills. As all other people, persons with disabilities also need this kind of vocational training and education to develop professionally as their colleagues. So, it is essential to ensure that this kind of training and education is accessible to persons with disabilities too. However this section will not analyze further such issues because they are very well analyzed at the section on employment and employability.

Disability however, has another additional connection with education and training. People who are disabled from birth or become disabled in young ages as already explained should be included in general educational systems. People with disabilities whether they are born with them or whether they become disabled later in life need to learn additional skills for their everyday living. They mainly have to learn how to adapt old habits and skills in ways that fit their current status. For example, a person who is left blind after an accident in work environment will need to learn how to cook, take care of his personal hygiene, walk and orientate within the home or city environment, use a white cane, read Braille etc. This indicates that a disability itself is also a source for new educational and training needs.

Similarly, there is a gradually increasing need of training for an ageing population with decreasing capabilities. Ageing people, with decreasing capabilities in hearing, seeing, remembering, etc. need a gradual training to adapt their lifestyles to their new capabilities. These training needs in some cases resemble the needs of a person that becomes disabled due to an accident or illness.

Today there are an increasing number of AT solutions for all kinds of disabilities and possible problems. National policies on how to help people with disabilities getting appropriate training vary from country to country within the EU. ViPi (ViPi project, 2011) an EU program recently funded by EU stresses out in its launch announcement that *"Recent studies conducted by various projects such as ACCESSIBLE and AEGIS have highlighted that people with disabilities (persons with disabilities) can benefit enormously from digital competences which are core life and employability skills (see Lisbon Objectives). However, same and other studies revealed also that the main barrier is the lack of specific training support or material. "*. Projects like ViPi which aims to provide people with disabilities a platform with training material on ICT usage and trainers to upload training courses, games and material can help in connecting people with disabilities with trainers.

However, the aim of the project is to provide a platform for training Persons with disabilities on using ICT. As already highlighted there is also a need for training on everyday issues and tasks and the use of various other AT devices. Although, there are a number of other projects fostering research and development in the area of assistive ICT such the ETNA (European Thematic Network on Assistive Information Technologies, 2013), ATIS4ALL (ATIS4All, n.d.), AAATE (Association for the Advancement of Assistive Technology in Europe, 2014), FAST (FAST, 2014) etc., there are limited resources on centers and organizations that provide training to people with disabilities, advice on assistive technologies available etc. such as the Danish Centre of Assistive Technology or the Queen Elizabeth's Foundation (Queen Elizabeth's Foundation for Disabled People, 2014). People with disabilities searching for information on special education and training and advice centers are often overwhelmed with fragmented information from various sources which might disorientate and discourage them from looking further into it.

In the area of lifelong learning there is a need for better organization and a central information

point on various sources, organizations, centers and the services different learning solutions provide. Future policies should look further into providing centralized information of resources available for training for living. This gathering of information will also bring to front differences in resources available among EU countries and policies followed and will also help EU to form a better overall policy on training for living resources for people with disabilities.

To this direction current educational institutes could play a significant role. There are already a number of universities for example with specific offices that offer support training and support services for students with disabilities. Opening such centers and activities to the wider audience outside a university's or an educational institute's limits, could generally help people with disabilities and connect innovation and research happening in those institutes with wider audiences.

Smart Homes Training Persons with Disabilities

People learning to live with a disability are usually beginning the adaptation process within the home environment. Advances in the area of smart homes reveal that there might be potential for providing such training services through smart home environments. Smart home projects such as the I2Home (I2Home, n.d.) which presented an EU smart-home concept (Adams-Spink, 2010) show that disabled users could benefit in everyday activities, health and social care services with the assistance of smart homes. Although, there is no indication up to now on how such smart environments can also be used for training of people acquiring a disability to be trained in their everyday-life activities, one can see the potentials. When the smart-home will know that the person in the home is someone who recently became deaf from an accident it could adjust appropriately various functions to train the person on sign language. For example it could provide small video clips of an avatar showing him sing language expressions related to his current activity. When cooking, it could show him in a display on the fridge how the expression "I am cooking" is in sign language.

However as explained in his web site on smart homes Guy Dewsbury (HomeToys, 2013) smart homes have to deal with a variety of issues in order to become widely adopted. The four major categories that can group these issues are:

- Fitness for Purpose
- Trustworthiness
- Usability
- Adaptability

In an interview he also says that *"What is evident is that there are a small number of people in the UK who are working closely in this area and developing new solutions and changing the way we can think about how technology can support people. If their work gets into the public domain and is publicized correctly then the future is very bright. I also should say that manufacturers of smart home technology should also come on board and begin to consider lowering their prices as this would make this option more viable in the long term. I personally see the future as very good indeed. I can see a future where smart homes are standard and not unique."*

Gaming For Training Persons with Disabilities

An interesting trend emerging in training both for vocational training and for general training for a variety of reasons has to do with gaming. Serious games is a category of games that aims to educate and train people through games that are more engaging and fun as a learning process than reading books and other traditional ways of learning. Games like IBM CityOne (IBM, n.d.), FloodSim (Playgen.com, 2012), PeaceMaker (ImpactGames LLC, 2010), A force more powerful

(A Force More Powerful, n.d.) etc. teach people issues in civil engineering, peaceful negotiations, nonviolent methods of fighting for rights etc. Serious games are also used for vocational training such as Microsoft's Flight Simulator (Microsoft, 2013) which is used for training on civil aviation rules.

The trend has also started getting exploited for people with disabilities too. Projects like GOAL NET, GOAT (Game On Extra Time, n.d.) and RECALL – KA3 (RECALL KA3 LLL project, 2012) project have already started investigating the potentials of serious games in training people with disabilities. The games produced from these programs are used to educate people with sensory or cognitive disabilities in a variety of skills either for employment or for their everyday life. The CapAbility Games Research Group (CapAbility Games Research Group, n.d.) in Rensselaer Polytechnic Institute is a research group aiming to provide persons with disabilities with games that train them in basic life skills such as personal care, job readiness, money management, household management and other areas.

A crucial aspect pointed out by David Brown and Penny Standen in their interview for Platform Online (Lee, 2010) is that in serious games the players can repeat an action over and over again and learn from the results of each action. For example, it can describe and simulate the consequences of crossing a street without paying attention to the traffic lights without actually getting the person in danger.

Serious games have already started evolving by using advances in Virtual and Augmented Reality technologies. Virtual reality and immersive environments allow serious game developers to reproduce whole environments and use them for training people with disabilities. There is already evidence that games using immersive environments can be more effective and engaging for learners, but there is also quite a lot ground to be covered in research and development. Some of the problems referred to the paper of Adamo-Villani, Carpenter and Arns are also the cost of equipment and potential health and safety issues from the usage of equipment such as head mounted displays. The paper was presented in 2007 and now costs are getting lower in VR devices (see Consumer and Lifestyle section) however there is still a lot of research needed on how VR systems can become accessible to persons with disabilities.

The rise of mobile devices and mobile computing though brought to light another interesting technology for serious games. Augmented Reality (AR) can be easily used from a person's mobile device and one of the major application it is used is gaming. This makes possible the development of serious games for training persons with disabilities while interacting with their everyday real life environments.

For example, a treasure-hunting game for blind persons in their city could train them to orientate and navigate in city environments. However, this is an area that now starts getting exploited. Comparing VR and AR we can see that future AR solutions for serious games could emerge easier and have a greater impact since their ease of access and use is significantly better than VR ones. However, VR has the advantage of simulating circumstances and environments that are probably dangerous for training in reality.

A lot of serious games are developed to educate people in a variety of social skills such as conflict management and cultural differences. This means that serious games could be used not only for training persons with disabilities. They could also be user to educate and train societies on problems of persons with disabilities. This could lead to societies of the future with better understanding of people with disabilities needs and consequently more sympathetic for them. For example, a VR game simulating your moving around the city using a wheelchair could get a lot of people to understand the problems they are causing to motor impaired person when parking in their parking spaces or in front of ramps on pavements. An additional incentive to that kind

of games can be given if combined with social networking media.

A game that gets you various situations where you need to help and interact with a person with disability and giving points depending on your reactions could give you an incentive to prove to your friends how good you are in such situations and could help you find out possible misconceptions of what an appropriate behavior to a Persons with disabilities is. It could also help people recognize easier disabilities (especially in cases of cognitive ones) by learning more about them during the game.

Mobile Device as a Trainer

Similarly to persons acquiring a disability due to an accident or illness there is also a large part of ageing population who have gradually decreasing capabilities reaching slowly towards disability levels. One of the biggest fields of research and market in that direction has to do with brain training apps and cognitive therapy. Companies like Lumocity (Lumosity, n.d.) provide a series of mobile apps that can be used for training peoples' brains through variety of games. Mobile app markets are now flooded by games for brain training such as Sudoku and other kinds of puzzles, memory games, word games etc. Although there is a debate whether such apps and brain games in general improve cognition (Harrell, 2010), it is evident that people practicing in a specific skill through games get better on it. Other issues with mobile games pointed out in a study on the University of Belfast (O' Brien, 2011) are mainly usability and poor communication issues as de-motivation factor for continuing playing such games.

The brain training apps trend and cognitive therapy through brain games is an area still to be exploited and it is further analyzed in the health and social care section. However, it is crucial to point out that mobile brain games for seniors is an area that faces a bigger challenge, namely how to motivate elderly to use smartphones in the first place? Some argue that future elderly generation will be used in smartphones usage and will want to continue using them but there is still no strong evidence of this happening. So some of the questions rising form mobile brain games for elderly are:

TEACHING AND LEARNING INNOVATION ISSUES

Issues of Action Research

The main method of research employed by people involved in fields such as education and management is Action Research ("Action research", n.d.), also often referred to as Participatory Action Research ("Participatory action research", n.d.). For those who practice AR or PAR, research in the form of experimentation and reflection is embedded into their everyday work. As they work they constantly experiment with new tools, textbooks, ways of teaching or ways of working in a learning environment. In principle, every act of work can be seen as an experiment and provide food for reflection on the result. Working with colleagues or on one's own is possible to draw conclusions, design new experiments and steadily improve outcomes over time.

This is very different from the way research is done in chemistry or physics. One hydrogen atom is just like any other and a chemist reasonably expects the properties of one to be identical with the properties of another. The same does not apply in areas such as teaching, medicine or management. No two teachers or students are alike. No two classes are ever the same. The curriculum constantly evolves. An experiment in learning modifies both the teacher and the student so that the 'same' experiment can never even be performed on the same teacher-student pair. When an experiment is repeated, the teacher becomes more experienced, the student will have learned something new, and so it becomes impossible

to carry out the exact same experiment with the exact same set of conditions.

The same argument holds in the case of e-access research and development. Technologies intended to help someone with a disability face the challenge that disability is a vague and expanding concept. Every disabled person is first of all a person with their own unique set of qualities, all of which come into play when they use an assistive technology. Some disabled people are able to run faster than most non-disabled people. Few non-disabled people will ever compose music as innovative and enduring as Beethoven did despite being deaf.

Despite this difficulty real progress is possible. A large body of practice has developed over the years to support research and progress in areas such as teaching and learning. It may be desirable in future ICT programs to give explicit weight to the research methods of the social sciences such as Action Learning, in the application of ICT to domains such as e-access ICT research for teaching, training and learning.

The techniques of AL, AR and PAR are routinely used in the development of domains such as technologies for teaching and learning and many of the research presented in this section is based on these principles. However, the pace of change is furious. There may be a need to ensure that people with disabilities are systematically included in this kind of research effort so that the requirements of people with special needs are fully considered in future research programs.

The Hawthorne Effect

Another issue that needs attention in research related with education, teaching and learning is the Hawthorne effect. Lots of business books deal with this, as well as magazines such as the Harvard Business Review (Harvard Business Review, 2008), but it is not difficult concept and Wikipedia explains it very well ("Hawthorne effect", n.d.). It is a kind of placebo effect, whereby the productivity of a group under study improves merely because of the attention being paid to it by management. A manager who does not know about the Hawthorne effect will easily mistake what is in reality only a short term productivity boost, for a permanent productivity boost, brought about by the clever nature of the manager's intervention.

The phenomenon was discovered by Henry Landsberger in Chicago in the 1950s when he analyzed the results of work productivity experiments carried out at Hawthorne works in 1924-1932. There is still some discussion among experts as to what is the real cause of the Hawthorne effect, though the phenomenon itself seems to be real and has been borne out by many subsequent experiments.

In the case of accessibility research especially related with education and learning this could also be the case in some situations. People with disabilities might seem to benefit for the period that the study runs. However, looking at long term results of a research might prove that the benefits and boost in learning achievements was just temporary due to the Hawthorne effect. It should be pointed out that positive outcomes from research in education should provide evidence that the learning experience itself was improved not just by boosting the results in short term exams but by providing lasting outcomes. A person who improves his learning experience is expected to boost his performance in long term and show evidence of lasting effects. Thus, it is essential that research programs related with people with disabilities in education take under account this factor and examine carefully their results.

Scaling Up

Finally when it comes to education research and innovation one of the biggest problems is scaling up.

During the research for this section we came across numerous cases of education innovations and research that was applied locally on a number of schools, universities and educational institutes but stayed there. It never succeeded in scaling up and reforming education systems, practices, methods etc. One of the reasons might be explained by the Hawthorne effect presented earlier but this is not always the case.

A variety of reasons are presented in an article in Education Week by Rick Hess (Hess, 2011). One of the most important issues presented is funding. Research and innovation is easy to get funding when it is about a small number of cases. However, when scaling a lot more funding should be found and national policies usually lack the ability and willingness to support it. Other issues presented are increased experts interest in research which fades out when scaling, increased enthusiasm which also fades out when confronting problems in scaling and need for changes in accommodation which may prove difficult to meet when scaling. However in his response, Robert Slavin (Slavin, 2011) points out that education innovation can thrive when it:

- Produces strong evidence of effectiveness
- Can be funded by stable sources
- Is supported by strong organizations and committed networks of dedicated educators
- Communicates a very strong and clear vision of the future and the path to get there
- Provides intensive professional development for educators in early years of implementation while in parallel ensures the maintenance of quality for the future.

Given those factors we can understand the problems that some of the scenarios presented in this section might have in scaling up. Despite that, this book intends to provide a variety of scenarios for the future of education for persons with disabilities and become the starting point of discussions which will lead to specific recommendations. So, it's worth investigating as many options as possible.

REFERENCES

K12 Inc. (2014). *K12 | Online Public School, Online High School, Online Private School, Home-schooling, and Online Courses options*. Retrieved March 10, 2014, from http://www.k12.com/

I2Home. (n.d.). *i2home > Home*. Retrieved March 10, 2014, from http://www.i2home.org/

A Force More Powerful. (n.d.). *A Force More Powerful*. Retrieved March 10, 2014, from http://www.aforcemorepowerful.org/game/index.php

AbilityNet. (2009a). *Factsheets - Play AT IT*. Retrieved March 9, 2014, from http://www.abilitynet.org.uk/play/factsheets.htm

AbilityNet. (2009b). *Factsheets and Skillsheets - Play AT ICT Northern Ireland*. Retrieved March 9, 2014, from http://www.abilitynet.org.uk/playni/factsheets.htm

AbilityNet. (2009c). *Play AT ICT Northern Ireland*. Retrieved March 9, 2014, from http://www.abilitynet.org.uk/playni/

AbilityNet. (2009d). *Play AT IT*. Retrieved March 9, 2014, from http://www.abilitynet.org.uk/play/

AbilityNet. (2013). *Welcome to AbilityNet | AbilityNet*. Retrieved March 9, 2014, from http://www.abilitynet.org.uk/index.php

AbilityPath.org. (2011, February 15). *Silent Epidemic of Bullying Against Children With Special Needs*. Retrieved March 10, 2014, from http://www.disabled-world.com/disability/education/special/bullying-special-needs.php

Action research. (n.d.). *Wikipedia, the free encyclopedia*. Retrieved March 10, 2014, from http://en.wikipedia.org/wiki/Action_research

Adams-Spink, G. (2010, February 15). *BBC News - EU smart-home concept shown off*. Retrieved March 10, 2014, from http://news.bbc.co.uk/2/hi/8495479.stm

Adobe Systems Inc. (2014a). *Adobe*. Retrieved March 9, 2014, from http://www.adobe.com/

Adobe Systems Inc. (2014b). *Web conferencing software - video conferencing - webinars | Adobe Connect 9*. Retrieved March 9, 2014, from http://www.adobe.com/products/adobeconnect.html

Alliance, E. (2011). *Equity in Inclusive Education Global Initiative | The Equity Alliance at ASU*. Retrieved March 10, 2014, from http://www.equityallianceatasu.org/ii

Analytics, B. (2013). *PowerPoint Twitter Tools | Business Analytics*. Retrieved March 10, 2014, from http://timoelliott.com/blog/powerpoint-twitter-tools/

Anybots. (2014). *Anybots | ANYBOTS® Virtual Presence Systems. It's You, Anywhere?* Retrieved March 10, 2014, from https://www.anybots.com/#front

Apple. (2014). *Apple - Accessibility - iOS*. Retrieved March 10, 2014, from http://www.apple.com/accessibility/ios/

Association for the Advancement of Assistive Technology in Europe. (2014). *Welcome to AAATE! | Association for the Advancement of Assistive Technology in Europe*. Retrieved March 10, 2014, from http://www.aaate.net/

ATIS4All. (n.d.). *Home page - ATIS4all*. Retrieved March 10, 2014, from http://www.atis4all.eu/

Bacigalupo, M., & Cachia, R. (2011). *Teacher collaboration networks in 2025: What is the role of teacher networks for professional development in Europe? notes from the workshops held on the 6th and 7th June 2011 at the Institute for Prospective Technological Studies of the European Commission Joint Research Centre*. Retrieved from http://ftp.jrc.es/EURdoc/JRC67530_TN.pdf

Barazandeh, G. (2005). Attitudes Toward Disabilities and Reasonable Accommodations at the University. *The UCI Undergraduate Research Journal*, 1-11. Retrieved from http://www.urop.uci.edu/journal/journal05/01_barazandeh.pdf

Bell, G., Parisi, A., & Pesce, M. (1995, November 9). *VRML 1.0C Specification*. Retrieved March 9, 2014, from http://www.web3d.org/x3d/specifications/vrml/VRML1.0/index.html

Bernard, S. (2010, December 10). *5 Apps That Could Help to Stop Cyberbullying | MindShift*. Retrieved March 10, 2014, from http://blogs.kqed.org/mindshift/2010/12/5-apps-that-could-help-to-stop-cyberbullying/

BIK project. (2014). *BIK BITV-Test | Articles | Tests - The accessibility of Facebook*. Retrieved March 10, 2014, from http://www.bitvtest.eu/articles/article/lesen/fb-accessibility.html

BlackBoard. (2013a). *Blackboard Engaging Online Collaborative Learning | Blackboard Collaborate*. Retrieved March 9, 2014, from http://www.blackboard.com/Platforms/Collaborate/Products/Blackboard-Collaborate.aspx

BlackBoard. (2013b). *Blackboard*. Retrieved March 9, 2014, from http://uki.blackboard.com/sites/international/globalmaster/

CamStudio.org. (2013). *CamStudio - Free Screen Recording Software*. Retrieved March 10, 2014, from http://camstudio.org/

CapAbility Games Research Group. (n.d.). *CapAbility Games Research Group*. Retrieved March 10, 2014, from http://www.arts.rpi.edu/~ruiz/capAbilityGamesOverview_files/capAbilityGamesOverview.htm

D'Mello, S. K., Lehman, B., & Graesser, A. (2011). *A Motivationally Supportive Affect-Sensitive AutoTutor*. doi:10.1007/978-1-4419-9625-1_9

Didden, R., Scholte, R. H., Korzilius, H., Moor, J. M., Vermeulen, A., O'Reilly, M., & Lancioni, G. E. (2009). Cyberbullying among students with intellectual and developmental disability in special education settings. *Developmental Neurorehabilitation*. doi:10.1080/17518420902971356 PMID:19466622

Dillow, C. (2010, December 1). *Microsoft Building Shape-Shifting Touchscreen For True Tactile Touch Tech | Popular Science*. Retrieved March 10, 2014, from www.popsci.com/technology/article/2010-12/patent-filing-reveals-microsofts-novel-attempt-true-tactile-touchscreen-tech

Disney Canada Inc. (2014). *Club Penguin | Waddle around and meet new friends*. Retrieved March 9, 2014, from http://www.clubpenguin.com/

Dorwick, P. W., Anderson, J., Heyer, K., & Acosta, J. (2005). Postsecondary education across the USA: Experiences of adults with disabilities. *Journal of Vocational Rehabilitation*, 22(1), 41–47.

Drinkwater, D. (2010, November 14). *Kazakhstan to bring tablets to all school children by 2020 | TabTimes*. Retrieved March 10, 2014, from http://tabtimes.com/news/education/2011/11/14/kazakhstan-bring-tablets-all-school-children-2020

Enable, U. N. (2008). *UN Enable - Work of the United Nations for Persons with Disabilities*. Retrieved March 10, 2014, from http://www.un.org/disabilities/

ETwinning. (n.d.). *eTwinning - Homepage*. Retrieved March 9, 2014, from www.etwinning.net/en/pub/index.htm

European Agency for Development in Special Needs Education. (2009). *Key principles for promoting quality in inclusive education: Recommendations for policy makers*. Retrieved from http://www.european-agency.org/sites/default/files/key-principles-EN.pdf

European Commission, Joint Research Centre, Institute for Prospective Technological Studies. (2009). *IS UNIT WEB SITE - IPTS - JRC - EC*. Retrieved March 9, 2014, from http://is.jrc.ec.europa.eu/pages/EAP/eLearning.html

European Thematic Network on Assistive Information Technologies. (2013). *Homepage - ETNA*. Retrieved March 10, 2014, from http://www.etna-project.eu/

FAST. (2014). *FAST - Foundation For Assistive Technology*. Retrieved March 10, 2014, from http://www.fastuk.org/home.php

Ferenstein, G. (2010, March 1). *How Twitter in the Classroom is Boosting Student Engagement*. Retrieved March 10, 2014, from http://mashable.com/2010/03/01/twitter-classroom/

Gallotti, P., Raposo, A., & Soares, L. (2011). *v-Glove: A 3D Virtual Touch Interface*. doi:10.1109/SVR.2011.21

Game On Extra Time. (n.d.). *Game On Extra Time*. Retrieved March 10, 2014, from http://goet-project.eu/

Global Initiative for Inclusive ICTs. (2014). *G3ict: The Global Initiative for Inclusive ICTs*. Retrieved March 10, 2014, from http://g3ict.com/

Google. (2014a). *Google Analytics Official Website? Web Analytics & Reporting*. Retrieved March 10, 2014, from http://www.google.com/analytics/

Google. (2014b). *Google+*. Retrieved March 10, 2014, from https://plus.google.com/?

Google. (2014c). *YouTube*. Retrieved March 10, 2014, from https://www.youtube.com/

Harrell, E. (2010, April 20). *Study: Brain Games Don't Boost Overall Mental Function - TIME*. Retrieved March 10, 2014, from http://content.time.com/time/health/article/0,8599,1983306,00.html

Hartien, R. (2013, July 10). *Sony HMZ-T3W Headmount Gets In, and On, Your Face | Sony*. Retrieved March 10, 2014, from http://blog.sony.com/2013/10/sony-headmount/

Hartstein, D. (2011, April 26). *How Schools Can Use Facebook to Build an Online Community*. Retrieved March 10, 2014, from http://mashable.com/2011/04/26/facebook-for-schools/

Hawthorne effect. (n.d.). *Wikipedia, the free encyclopedia*. Retrieved March 10, 2014, from http://en.wikipedia.org/wiki/Hawthorne_effect

Heitin, L. (2011, October 12). *Education Week Teacher Professional Development Sourcebook: Pairing Up*. Retrieved March 9, 2014, from http://www.edweek.org/tsb/articles/2011/10/13/01coteach.h05.html

Hess, R. (2011, December 5). *Why Education Innovation Tends to Crash and Burn - Rick Hess Straight Up - Education Week*. Retrieved March 10, 2014, from http://blogs.edweek.org/edweek/rick_hess_straight_up/2011/12/why_education_innovation_tends_to_crash_and_burn.html

High Tech High. (2000). *High Tech High*. Retrieved March 10, 2014, from http://www.hightechhigh.org/

HomeToys. (2013). *AV and Automation Industry eMagazine - Hometoys Interview - Guy Dewsbury Smart Homes for Disabled People in the UK | HomeToys*. Retrieved March 10, 2014, from http://hometoys.com/emagazine.php?url=/ezine/09.05/dewsbury/index.htm

IBM. (n.d.). *IBM INNOV8: CityOne*. Retrieved March 10, 2014, from http://www-01.ibm.com/software/solutions/soa/innov8/cityone/index.html

Immersion Corporation. (2013). *TouchSense Tactile Feedback Systems*. Retrieved March 10, 2014, from http://www.immersion.com/products/touchsense-tactile-feedback/

ImpactGames LLC. (2010). *PeaceMaker Home: PeaceMaker - Play the News. Solve the Puzzle.* Retrieved March 10, 2014, from http://www.peacemakergame.com/

Inclusive Education Canada. (n.d.). *Inclusive Education Canada.* Retrieved March 10, 2014, from http://inclusiveeducation.ca/

Khronos Group. (2014). *OpenGL - The Industry Standard for High Performance Graphics.* Retrieved March 9, 2014, from http://www.opengl.org/

Knowledge Adventure, Inc. (2014). *Fun Games for Kids | Free 3D Games Online | JumpStart.* Retrieved March 9, 2014, from http://www.jumpstart.com/

KQED Inc. (2014). *Children and Media | MindShift.* Retrieved March 10, 2014, from http://blogs.kqed.org/mindshift/feature/children-and-social-media/

Kraska, M. (2003). Postsecondary Students with Disabilities and Perceptions of Faculty Members. *The Journal for Vocational Special Needs Education, 25*(2), 11–19.

Learning, L. (2010). *Liberated Learning Project - Speech Recognition Technology in the Classroom - Halifax, Nova Scotia.* Retrieved March 10, 2014, from http://transcribeyourclass.ca/index.html

Learning, L. (2014). *Partners | Liberated Learning.* Retrieved March 10, 2014, from http://liberatedlearning.com/?page_id=99

Lee, A. (2010, February 1). *Interview: David Brown & Penny Standen | Platform Online.* Retrieved March 10, 2014, from http://platform-online.net/2010/02/interview-david-brown-penny-standen/

Let's Play! Projects. (2004). *Welcome to the Let's Play Projects!* Retrieved March 9, 2014, from http://letsplay.buffalo.edu/index.html

LinkedIn. (2014). *World's Largest Professional Network | LinkedIn.* Retrieved March 10, 2014, from https://www.linkedin.com/

Littlewort, G. C., Bartlett, M. S., Salamanca, L. P., & Reilly, J. (2011). *Automated measurement of children's facial expressions during problem solving tasks.* doi:10.1109/FG.2011.5771418

LOCO-Analyst. (2014). *LOCO-Analyst.* Retrieved March 10, 2014, from http://jelenajovanovic.net/LOCO-Analyst/

Lumosity. (n.d.). *Brain Games & Brain Training - Lumosity.* Retrieved March 10, 2014, from http://www.lumosity.com/

Madan, V. (2011, May 16). *6 Reasons Tablets Are Ready for the Classroom.* Retrieved March 10, 2014, from http://mashable.com/2011/05/16/tablets-education/

Marquis, J. (2011, September 8). *Using Social Media in the Higher Education Classroom - OnlineUniversities.com.* Retrieved March 10, 2014, from http://www.onlineuniversities.com/blog/2011/09/using-social-media-in-the-higher-education-classroom/

Mason, C. Y. (2010). *Co-Teaching with Technology: The Power of? 3?* Retrieved March 9, 2014, from http://www.edimprovement.org/wp-content/uploads/2010/09/Co-Teaching-with-Technology.pdf

McConkey, R. (2003). *Understanding and responding to children's needs in inclusive classrooms: A guide for teachers.* Paris: UNESCO.

Meebo. (n.d.). *Meebo: More of What You Love.* Retrieved March 9, 2014, from https://www.meebo.com/

Meijer, C. J. (2003). *Inclusive Education and Classroom Practice.* Retrieved from http://www.european-agency.org/sites/default/files/iecp-en.pdf

Meijer, C. J. (2005). *Inclusive Education and Classroom Practice in Secondary Education.* Retrieved from http://www.european-agency.org/sites/default/files/iecp_secondary_en.pdf

Meijer, C. J. (2010, February). *Special Needs Education in Europe: Inclusive Policies and Practices | Meijer | Zeitschrift für Inklusion.* Retrieved March 9, 2014, from http://www.inklusion-online.net/index.php/inklusion-online/article/view/136/136

Microsoft. (2006, November 10). *Download DirectX Software Development Kit from Official Microsoft Download Center.* Retrieved March 9, 2014, from http://www.microsoft.com/en-us/download/details.aspx?id=9977

Microsoft. (2013). *Microsoft Games.* Retrieved March 10, 2014, from http://www.microsoft.com/games/

Microsoft. (2014a). *Skype - Free internet calls and online cheap calls to phones and mobiles.* Retrieved March 9, 2014, from http://www.skype.com/

Microsoft. (2014b). *Microsoft Surface Tablets - The Windows Tablet That Does More.* Retrieved March 10, 2014, from http://www.microsoft.com/surface/en-US

Microsoft. (2014c). *Xbox Kinect | Full Body Gaming and Voice Control - Xbox.com.* Retrieved March 10, 2014, from http://www.xbox.com/en-US/kinect

Microsoft. (2014d). *Xbox | Games and Entertainment on All Your Devices - Xbox.com.* Retrieved March 10, 2014, from http://www.xbox.com/en-US/

MIT News Office. (2011, December 19). *MIT launches online learning initiative - MIT News Office.* Retrieved March 10, 2014, from http://web.mit.edu/newsoffice/2011/mitx-education-initiative-1219.html

Mixpanel. (n.d.). *Mixpanel | Mobile Analytics.* Retrieved March 10, 2014, from https://mixpanel.com/

Moyer, C. S. (2010, November 15). *Cyberbullying a high-tech health risk for young patients - amednews.com.* Retrieved March 10, 2014, from http://www.amednews.com/article/20101115/profession/311159961/2/

Murray, P. (2011, October 25). *South Korea Says Good-Bye To Print Textbooks, Plans To Digitize Entire Curriculum By 2015 (video) | Singularity Hub.* Retrieved March 10, 2014, from http://singularityhub.com/2011/10/25/south-korea-says-good-bye-to-print-textbooks-plans-to-digitize-entire-curriculum-by-2015-video/

National Geographic Society and Smart Bomb Interactive, Inc. (2013). *Animal Jam - Animal Jam - Meet friends, adopt pets, and play wild!* Retrieved March 9, 2014, from http://www.animaljam.com/

National Science Foundation. (n.d.a). *ROAR - Games.* Retrieved March 10, 2014, from http://gameslab.radford.edu/ROAR/games.html

National Science Foundation. (n.d.b). *ROAR - Home.* Retrieved March 10, 2014, from http://gameslab.radford.edu/ROAR/

New Media Consortium EDUCAUSE (Association). (2011). *The horizon report: 2011 ed.* Retrieved from http://www.nmc.org/pdf/2011-Horizon-Report.pdf

NYC Department of Education. (n.d.). *iZone NYC.* Retrieved March 10, 2014, from http://izonenyc.org/

O' Brien, D. (2011, February 10). *Brain Training Games for Seniors: Looking for the best brain training app. | SharpBrains.* Retrieved March 10, 2014, from http://sharpbrains.com/blog/2011/02/10/brain-training-games-for-seniors-looking-for-the-best-brain-training-app/

Open University. (2014a). *Distance Learning Courses and Adult Education - The Open University.* Retrieved March 10, 2014, from http://www.open.ac.uk/

Open University. (2014b, February 4). *Services for Disabled Students - Study Support - Open University*. Retrieved March 10, 2014, from http://www2.open.ac.uk/study/support/disability/orientation

Pachal, P. (2011, December 9). *Will Apple iTV Trade the Remote for Kinect-Like Control?* Retrieved March 10, 2014, from http://mashable.com/2011/12/09/apple-itv-gestures/

Participatory Action Research. (n.d.). *Wikipedia, the free encyclopedia*. Retrieved March 10, 2014, from http://en.wikipedia.org/wiki/Participatory_action_research

Perera, N., Kennedy, G. E., & Pearce, J. M. (2008). *Are you bored? Maybe an interface agent can help*. doi:10.1145/1517744.1517760

Playgen.com. (2012). *FloodSim | PlayGen*. Retrieved March 10, 2014, from http://playgen.com/play/floodsim/

Qing, L. Y. (2011, October 5). *India to debut $45 Android tablet for education | ZDNet*. Retrieved March 10, 2014, from http://www.zdnet.com/india-to-debut-45-android-tablet-for-education-2062302369/

Queen Elizabeth's Foundation for Disabled People. (2014). *Residential care for disabled people | Queen Elizabeth's Foundation for Disabled People*. Retrieved March 10, 2014, from http://qef.org.uk/our-services/

Raskind, M., & Stanberry, K. (n.d.). *Assistive technology for kids with learning disabilities: An overview - Assistive technology | GreatSchools*. Retrieved March 9, 2014, from http://www.greatschools.org/special-education/assistive-technology/702-assistive-technology-for-kids-with-learning-disabilities-an-overview.gs

RECALL KA3 LLL Project. (2012). *RECALL - KA3 project*. Retrieved March 10, 2014, from http://recall-project.eu/

Review, H. B. (2008, July). *A Field Is Born - Harvard Business Review*. Retrieved March 10, 2014, from http://hbr.org/2008/07/a-field-is-born/ar/1

Rock, M. (n.d.). *New Touch Screens Allow Blind to Read Braille | Mobiledia*. Retrieved March 10, 2014, from http://www.mobiledia.com/news/97666.html

Russel, C. (2013, March 25). *Selecting Assessment Technologies | UNSW Teaching Staff Gateway*. Retrieved March 10, 2014, from http://teaching.unsw.edu.au/assessment-technologies

Sachs, D., & Schreuer, N. (2011). Inclusion of Students with Disabilities in Higher Education: Performance and participation in student's experiences. *Disability Studies Quarterly*, *31*(2). PMID:21966179

Saenz, A. (2010, November 2). *A Robot in Every Korean Kindergarten by 2013? | Singularity Hub*. Retrieved March 9, 2014, from http://singularityhub.com/2010/11/02/a-robot-in-every-korean-kindcrgarten-by-2013/

Schaffhauser, D. (2010, June 29). *Department of Ed Lays Down Law on Kindle E-Reader Usage -- Campus Technology*. Retrieved March 10, 2014, from http://campustechnology.com/articles/2010/06/29/department-of-ed-lays-down-law-on-kindle-e-reader-usage.aspx

School of One. (n.d.). *Wikipedia, the free encyclopedia*. Retrieved March 10, 2014, from http://en.wikipedia.org/wiki/School_of_one

Schreuer, N., Rimmerman, A., & Sachs, D. (2006). Adjustment to severe disability: Constructing and examining a cognitive and occupational performance model. *International Journal of Rehabilitation Research. Internationale Zeitschrift fur Rehabilitationsforschung. Revue Internationale de Recherches de Readaptation*. doi:10.1097/01.mrr.0000210053.40162.13 PMID:16900040

Senseg. (2011). *Senseg*. Retrieved March 10, 2014, from http://senseg.com/

Shapiro, L. (2011, November 16). *Sony's 3D Headset: Virtual Reality Goes Mainstream | Sound & Vision*. Retrieved March 10, 2014, from http://www.soundandvision.com/content/sonys-3d-headset-virtual-reality-goes-mainstream

Silicon Micro Display, Inc. (2012). *ST1080 features, 1080p hmd features, hmd specs | SiliconMicroDisplay, Silicon Micro Display, SMD - Silicon Micro Display*. Retrieved March 10, 2014, from http://www.siliconmicrodisplay.com/st1080-features.html

SimplyRaydeen. (2009, April 9). *Facebook - Accessibility*. Retrieved March 10, 2014, from http://www.simplyraydeen.com/faq/48-web-site-accessibility/71-facebook-works-with-the-blind-on-accessibility

Slavin, R. (2011, December 8). *How Education Innovation Can Thrive at Scale - Sputnik - Education Week*. Retrieved March 10, 2014, from http://blogs.edweek.org/edweek/sputnik/2011/12/how_education_innovation_can_thrive_at_scale.html?cmp=ENL-EU-VIEWS2

Socrato. (2013). *Learning Analytics and Test Scoring Software | Socrato*. Retrieved March 10, 2014, from http://www.socrato.com/

Swanson, G. (2011, December 17). *Apps in Education: Monster List of Apps for People with Autism*. Retrieved March 10, 2014, from http://appsineducation.blogspot.gr/2011/12/monster-list-of-apps-for-people-with.html

TechSmith. (2014a). *Screen Capture Software for Windows, Mac and Chrome | Snagit*. Retrieved March 10, 2014, from http://www.techsmith.com/snagit.html

TechSmith. (2014b). *TechSmith | Camtasia, Screen Recorder and Video Editor*. Retrieved March 10, 2014, from http://www.techsmith.com/camtasia.html

Tellnet. (n.d.). *TellNet - Welcome*. Retrieved March 9, 2014, from http://www.tellnet.eun.org/web/tellnet,jsessionid=0EAF6638D4D5B887A228FE6E263D3716

Tinti-Kane, H., Seaman, J., & Levy, J. (2010, April 29). *Pearson Social Media Survey 2010*. Retrieved March 10, 2014, from http://www.slideshare.net/PearsonLearningSolutions/pearson-socialmedia-survey2010

Twitter. (2014). *Twitter*. Retrieved March 10, 2014, from https://twitter.com/

UNESCO. (n.d.a). *Advocacy | Education | United Nations Educational, Scientific and Cultural Organization*. Retrieved March 9, 2014, from http://www.unesco.org/new/en/education/themes/leading-the-international-agenda/education-for-all/advocacy/

UNESCO. (n.d.b). *Capacity Development | Education | United Nations Educational, Scientific and Cultural Organization*. Retrieved March 9, 2014, from http://www.unesco.org/new/en/education/themes/leading-the-international-agenda/education-for-all/capacity-development/

UNESCO. (n.d.c). *EFA Goals | Education | United Nations Educational, Scientific and Cultural Organization*. Retrieved March 9, 2014, from http://www.unesco.org/new/en/education/themes/leading-the-international-agenda/education-for-all/efa-goals/

UNESCO. (n.d.d). *Funding | Education | United Nations Educational, Scientific and Cultural Organization*. Retrieved March 9, 2014, from http://www.unesco.org/new/en/education/themes/leading-the-international-agenda/education-for-all/funding/

UNESCO. (n.d.e). *Monitoring | Education | United Nations Educational, Scientific and Cultural Organization*. Retrieved March 9, 2014, from http://www.unesco.org/new/en/education/themes/leading-the-international-agenda/education-for-all/monitoring/

UNESCO. (n.d.f). *Policy dialogue | Education | United Nations Educational, Scientific and Cultural Organization.* Retrieved March 9, 2014, from http://www.unesco.org/new/en/education/themes/leading-the-international-agenda/education-for-all/policy-dialogue/

United Nations Educational Scientific and Cultural Organisation. (2004). *Changing teaching practices: Using curriculum differentiation to respond to students' diversity.* Retrieved from http://unesdoc.unesco.org/images/0013/001365/136583e.pdf

University of Buffalo. (2014). *School of Public Health and Health Professions.* Retrieved March 9, 2014, from http://sphhp.buffalo.edu/

University of Southampton. (2011). *Synote Home Page.* Retrieved March 10, 2014, from http://synote.org/synote/

University of Strathclyde. (2000). *Alternatives to what is assessed - Teachability: Creating accessible examinations and assessments for disabled students.* Retrieved March 10, 2014, from http://www.teachability.strath.ac.uk/chapter_8/reflectingonpractice8c.html

University of Strathclyde. (2004). *Alternatives to what is assessed - Teachability: Creating accessible examinations and assessments for disabled students.* Retrieved March 10, 2014, from http://www.teachability.strath.ac.uk/chapter_8/reflectingonpractice8c.html

VGo Communications, Inc. (2013). *VGo robotic telepresence for healthcare, education and business.* Retrieved March 10, 2014, from http://www.vgocom.com/

ViPi Project. (2011, January 8). *ViPi.* Retrieved March 10, 2014, from http://www.vipi-project.eu/

Walsh, K. (2010, February 7). *Over 100 ideas for using Twitter in the Classroom.* Retrieved March 15, 2014, from http://www.emergingedtech.com/2010/02/100-ways-to-teach-with-twitter/

Warrior, P. (2011, May 24). *TalkBack for Android (reviewed).* Retrieved March 10, 2014, from http://www.appszoom.com/android_applications/tools/talkback_eq.html

Watkins, A. (2007). *Assessment in inclusive settings: Key issues for policy and practice.* Retrieved from http://www.european-agency.org/sites/default/files/Assessment-EN.pdf

Watkins, A. (2011a). *ICTs in Education for People with Disabilities: Review of innovative practice.* Retrieved from http://www.european-agency.org/sites/default/files/ICTs-in-Education-for-people-with-disabilities.pdf

Watkins, A. (2011b). *Special Needs Education, Country Data 2010.* Retrieved from http://www.european-agency.org/sites/default/files/SNE-Country-Data-2010.pdf

Watters, A. (2011, March 19). *How Well Are Schools Teaching Cyber Safety and Ethics? | MindShift.* Retrieved March 10, 2014, from http://blogs.kqed.org/mindshift/2011/05/how-well-are-schools-teaching-cyber-safety-and-ethics/

WebAIM. (2009). *WebAIM: Screen Reader User Survey #2 Results.* Retrieved March 10, 2014, from http://webaim.org/projects/screenreadersurvey2/

Webkinz. (n.d.). *Welcome to Webkinz? - a Ganz website.* Retrieved March 9, 2014, from http://www.webkinz.com/

West, D. M. (2011). *Using Technology to Personalize Learning and Assess Students in Real-Time.* Retrieved from http://www.brookings.edu/~/media/research/files/papers/2011/10/06%20personalize%20learning%20west/1006_personalize_learning_west.pdf

Wong, G. (2011, June 4). *Apple granted patent for? bumpy? tactile touchscreens | Ubergizmo.* Retrieved March 10, 2014, from http://www.ubergizmo.com/2011/04/apple-patent-tactile-touchscreens/

World, D. (2014). *Health and Disability Apps for iPhone Android and Mobile Devices - Disabled World*. Retrieved March 10, 2014, from http://www.disabled-world.com/assistivedevices/apps/

World Education Forum. (2000). *WEF (The Conference)*. Retrieved March 9, 2014, from http://www.unesco.org/education/wef/en-conf/index.shtm

KEY TERMS AND DEFINITIONS

Computer Supported Collaborative Learning: Computer-supported collaborative learning (CSCL) is a pedagogical approach wherein learning takes place via social interaction using a computer or through the Internet.

Distance Learning: Distance learning, sometimes called e-learning, is a formalized teaching and learning system specifically designed to be carried out remotely by using electronic communication.

E-Learning: Electronic learning; using computer technology for education.

Inclusive Education: Inclusion in education is an approach to educating students with special educational needs.

Learning Analytics: Learning analytics is the measurement, collection, analysis and reporting of data about learners and their contexts, for purposes of understanding and optimising learning and the environments in which it occurs.

MOOC: A massive open online course (MOOC) is a free Web-based distance learning program that is designed for the participation of large numbers of geographically dispersed students.

Personalized Education: Personalized Learning is the tailoring of pedagogy, curriculum and learning environments by learners or for learners in order to meet their different learning needs and aspirations. Typically technology is used to facilitate personalized learning environments.

Chapter 9
Employment, Employability, and Entrepreneurship

ABSTRACT

Employment and employability are some of the most important problems that people with disabilities face throughout their lives. Employers are often afraid or unaware of the abilities that people with disabilities might have for a specific position, and they misjudge and mistreat them. Such perceptions need to change, and new technologies and trends in the work environment such as the Bring Your Own Device can help in improving conditions for people with disabilities. Moreover, the need for more inclusion and assistive technologies in work environments is now becoming more evident by the ageing population that is still employed due to the increase of retirement age in many countries. This chapter discusses those issues and how technology together with relevant policies can help in decreasing unemployment rates for people with disabilities.

INTRODUCTION

In September-October 2011 the Economics Intelligence Unit (The Economist Group, 2014) surveyed 567 executives from all major industry sectors and all parts of the globe, for their opinions on how technology would change business between now and 2020. The survey entitled "Frontiers of Disruption: The next decade of technology in business" (The Economist Group, 2011) was released in 2012 and is available on the website of the Economist.

Almost 60% of executives feel that the vertical markets in which they will operate in 2020 will bear little or no resemblance to those in which they operate today. 70% expect to see a high degree of convergence between previously distinct business sectors. Many fear that their own company may no longer exist in 2020.

More than half of ICT executives fear that their company will not be able to keep up with change and will have lost their competitive edge by 2020. Apart from education and public administration, executives in all sectors consider that the main drivers of change will be:

- A relentless drive for efficiency and
- accelerated rates of change to business models,
- enabled by big-data.

DOI: 10.4018/978-1-4666-6130-1.ch009

Table 1. Trends on the main sources of ideas (The Economist Group, 2011)

Main Source of Ideas	2011		2020		Trend
	%	Rank	%	Rank	
R+D Department	38%	1	18%	3	▼
Customers	21%	2	30%	1	▲
Competitors	13%	3	8%	5	▼
Employees (non R+D related)	12%	4	7%	6	▼
Online Communities	6%	5	19%	2	▲
Emerging Markets	5%	6	9%	4	▲
Partners	4%	7	6%	7	▲
Other Industries	1%	8/9	2%	8	▲
Don't Know	1%	8/9	1%	9	▼

All of these changes, especially the increasingly rapid change in business models will increase the need for training and learning on the job, at all levels of the organization.

Overall executives believe that people will work longer hours than today and more years, mainly out of necessity due to the erosion of pensions.

This suggests that over the next 10 years, we will see not only the ageing of society, but the ageing of the work-force. The challenge of maintaining the productivity of workers as they age despite a natural decline in physical and even cognitive capabilities will become more important, as it will have a bigger impact on overall competitiveness of the company.

80% of executive across all domains and regions either agree or strongly agree that the working environment will become almost entirely virtual. In other words almost all data and information people work with will be in electronic format. Many believe that there will be a vast reduction or even a disappearance of non-digitized information in the work-place. Most workers will rely on a single network-enabled, cloud-connected device.

This suggests that the ability to efficiently and competently use this main access device may be a deciding factor in the employability of the worker. It suggests that by 2020 the access gap could become an even greater barrier to work-force entry or promotion for people with disabilities than it is today.

Despite most work being conducted in a virtual environment, this does not mean that most work will become telework. 50% of executives surveyed either disagree or strongly disagree with the assertion that the majority of workers will work from home rather than a traditional office.

The barriers to employment experienced by people with mobility problems will remain and will not be rendered insignificant by a teleworking trend.

One of the biggest and most significant shifts however is a shift in how innovation happens. When asked to rate the most important source of innovative ideas now and in 2020, the response of the executives surveyed showed *a major shift away from R+D as the major source of ideas* to customers - both B2B and B2C, online communities an emerging markets.

A combination of the internet, online communities and big-data will reduce the information asymmetry between the company and its clients or customers. This means that customer will know more about companies and companies in principle will know more about clients, enabling them to better segment and target new products and marketing campaigns

This suggests a far more important role for marketing, design and user-led approaches to support for innovation on accessibility issues in the future that in the past. This means that R&D in future may play a role sub-ordinate to marketing and development. Maybe R&D will be replaced by an M&D structure. Research will pay a greater role in strategy, human resource development and the procurement of knowledge outside the organization.

In the event "EU2050: Europe's tech revolution" (Debating Europe, 2012), of the think-tank called "Friends of Europe" (Friends of Europe, n.d.) a discussion took place for the future of Europe in the technology domain. The main panellists were Professor Anne Glover, Chief Scientific Advisor to the European Commission President, and Dan Reed, Corporate Vice President of the Technology Group at Microsoft Research.

The discussion led to issues of productivity in work and assistive technologies although this was not the main subject. It is interesting to see that important people in the technology domain such as Dan Reed think that when we are 80 or 90 years of age *"assistive technologies will make all the difference between most of us living active, interesting independent lives or depending on someone else and living in an institution."* In addition Anne Glover said that *"Ageing will be a burden unless technology can help to keep people more active and more socially connected…'.* This shows that people in the technology domain are already thinking about ageing and take it seriously under account. It is therefore an issue not to be neglected.

They also identified that the pace of change will have a big impact on areas like learning and training, which are critical to employment and employability. They predict that training will become more just-in-time training. Meaning that you won't have the time to train yourselves in using a new system, application or whatever new technology arises. This training will have to happen in parallel with using and producing

value out this use. For this however to happen in a graceful way for persons with disabilities new technology solutions will have to adapt in real time to the needs of someone with a disability.

Finally, supporting the previous points about customer and the market being the major driver for innovation in the future Ann Glover answering a question about *"How can we keep innovative when society is getting old and people increasingly resist change"* suggested that change is frustrating only because we (consumers/customers) are not consulted. If we are involved in it, it is different. It is part of our lives. Technology is already a big part of our lives and like it or not as we get older technology is going to increasingly be a part of our lives. This means that companies will have to get even closer to customers and their needs if they want to succeed. So customers will increasingly pay a significant role in that change and thus accept it easier.

EMPLOYABILITY

There are some very good examples of people who overcome disabilities and lead exceptional working lives. The areas that these people come from include amongst others politics, journalism, sports (e.g. by people with loss of limbs), mathematics (blind geometers), music (deaf and blind persons), or architecture (blind persons). Django Reinhardt one of the greatest ever Jazz guitarists played with only two fingers after an accident in a fire when he was very young. The examples are many and varied and include:

- People with Vision problems (Disabled World, 2008) include Louis Braille (inventor), Stevie Wonder, Ray Charles and Andrea Bocelli (music), David Blunket (UK ex-minister), Zohar Sharon (pro golfer), Leonhard Euler (mathematician), Peter White (journalist), Christopher Downy (Rains, 2011) (architect).

- People with Hearing problems include Thomas Edison (inventor) and Ludwig van Beethoven (music composer, who composed his greatest music late in life while being profoundly deaf).
- People with mobility problems such as the cosmologist Steven Hawking, as well as famous athletes and sex-symbols Oscar Pistorius and Aimee Mullins.

In particular the Paralympics movement has done a great deal to improve awareness and acceptance of diversity, and reinforce the message that people with disabilities are just people with different abilities, many of whom have great drive and ambition and can achieve levels of excellence in anything they chose to do.

People who are blind or visually impaired can in fact perform almost any job one can imagine (American Foundation for the Blind, 2013): lawyer, artist, accountant, secretary, customer service representative, food service worker, factory worker, financial analyst, teacher, medical transcriptionist, day care worker, counsellor, computer programmer, cook, salesperson, clerk, and more. There are even jobs for the blind as police detectives (Soares, 2007). The possibilities are tremendous and there is certainly a departure from the times when blind people were only considered for a limited number of niche jobs such as massage and piano tuning (School of Piano Technology for the Blind, 2014).

People who are blind or visually impaired have a wider array of career possibilities than ever before in history because of a combination of events since the passage of the Rehabilitation Act of 1973 (in the US). Legislative and societal changes have reduced discrimination toward visually impaired workers as attitudes toward people with disabilities generally have improved. Employers, especially in midsized and large businesses, routinely follow equal employment opportunity practices and have diversity and disability-accommodation processes in place.

In Europe, organisations like the EBU (European Blind Union) (EBU, n.d.b) have an employment website, which includes "Categories of jobs undertaken by blind and partially sighted people" (EBU, n.d.a), as well as "Other sources of information about employment for visually impaired people in Europe" (EBU, n.d.c). The latter of this includes a variety of sources for the employment of blind or partially-sighted people, including relevant (EU) legislations and policies.

Deaf people can also do most of the jobs that non-deaf people can do (Gallaudet University, 1998). For most occupations one can think about, one will probably find a deaf person or someone who is hard of hearing person who does that work or has done it. More employers are realizing that hearing is not necessary for every job. They see how their deaf colleagues do their work just as well as those with hearing can. And now deaf and hard of hearing people have more choices for schools and training programs where they learn skills for different jobs. These changes are important for deaf and hard of hearing students who are in school now. They can choose from many more careers. Some aim for careers seldom tried by deaf people in the past. About 20 years ago, for example, only a few deaf people went to law school. Today in the US, deaf lawyers work for the federal government and in private corporations. Some have their own law practices. At least one of them is a judge (Sloan, 2010). In the US there are also courtroom simulations by deaf high-school students (Civication, Inc., 2012) who are thinking about following a career in law.

Several organizations are helping employers learn how to change the workplace appropriately for their employees with hearing loss. This training teaches employers about deafness and hearing loss, about the skills and achievements of deaf and hard of hearing workers, and about simple ways to improve communication. In addition, universities like the University of Central Lancashire in the UK now offer deaf studies (Atherton, 2008), which are about deaf people, and teach things anybody who wants to work with deaf people needs to know.

Similar considerations apply to people with other types of disabilities (e.g. kinetic, mental, etc.). In fact, there are already world-wide a number of job search and career services aimed directly towards the disabled persons (e.g. disabledperson.com (Disabled Person, Inc., 2014), reemploy (Reemploy, 2014), job access (Jobaccess.co.za, 2012), Disabled Workers Co-operative (Disabled Workers Co-operative Ltd, 2004)), or indeed printed publications for careers for disabled people (EOP, Inc., 2012).

There is also the business case on employing disabled people. Many employers do care about their image, because a poor image is bad for business. The other reason for employing disabled people relates more directly to the 'bottom line'. Governments have spent years trying to convince businesses that there are good business reasons for recruiting disabled people, or retaining people who become disabled while at work. The arguments stressed by organisations such as the UK's Employers Forum on Disability (Business Disability Forum, 2014) are that someone with a disability:

- Is not less productive or reliable than non-disabled people.
- Often stay longer with an employer (are more loyal) and contrary to popular misconceptions take less time off.
- Along with their families they constitute a significant potential market and employing them may help target this segment.
- Having an effective diversity policy is good for staff morale as well as for the reputation of the organisation.

The Perception of Employers about Assistive Technologies in the Workplace

With regards to the use of computers, specialist and adapted equipment can make using computers easier whether at home, at work, in school at college or university. For example, for blind or visually-impaired people there are different types of computer screen readers available. Some relay back to the user, via a synthetic voice, what is being typed. Others read what is on a webpage. One can also get readers that have a Braille output device. Magnification software products can enlarge a particular part of a computer screen; closed circuit camera systems can magnify print and text and then display an enlarged version on a television or computer screen. There are also 'standalone' portable versions, which do not require a television or computer. Stickers can also be put onto standard keyboard keys that either present the letters and numbers as Braille or simply increase the size of the characters.

In general, blind or visually-impaired people currently have a range of gadgets (Steph, 2010) in their disposal for day-to-day and work activities, such as:

- Braille-touch mobile phones.
- The "Eye Stick" a white cane with a lens at the end being able to recognise features such as traffic lights and stairs.
- Tactile Flash Cards for learning, watches that can be "felt" and Braille e-books.
- Sign-Language Voice Translators for communicating with the deaf.
- Navigation Bracelets that use GPS, take voice commands and provide audio and haptic feedback to provide the blind with a level of independence.
- Touch Colour Paining Tablet (using thermal energy and a hand-held colour wheel to create works of art by blind people).
- Colour Sensors that help see with sounds by associating each colour with a particular sound.
- There is even a Braille Polaroid Camera that acts as an instant Braille printer, translating the basic shape of an object into texture so that the blind can collect "images" in an album.

For users with a physical disability, there is also equipment to help them use a computer, for example:

- A larger keyboard may help if one has difficulties with dexterity.
- Devices that replace keyboards but are smaller and need less effort to press the keys.
- An 'on-screen keyboard' means one only needs a mouse to select characters on the screen.
- Alternatives to the standard mouse such as joysticks or tracker balls, and which can be easier to control and use.
- Pointers and sticks are available that can be attached to the head and used to press keys on a keyboard.
- Predictive text can help increase the rate of typing - after typing two or three letters, one is given a selection of words to choose from.

A long list of already available Assistive Technology devices (AbleData, n.d.b) that provide benefits to people with disabilities in a variety of situations, including at the workplace and when using a computer, are supplied by Able Data (AbleData, n.d.a), whose aim is to provide objective information about assistive technology products and rehabilitation equipment. It features almost 40,000 product listings, including information of the companies producing them. These products are split into 20 categories, including categories for specific disabilities, communications, the use of computers, environmental adaptations, orthotics, prosthetics, transportation, and the workplace. Similar sites such as Enabling Devices (Enabling Devices, 2014) offer similar, but more limited services on information for AT for the disabled.

It is beyond the scope of this report to examine these exhaustively but we provide some indicative examples. ICT tools, that can help PC users with dyslexia include:

- Kurzweil 3000 (Kurzweil, n.d.b): Designed by the "Kurzweil Educational Systems" company, the system provides text to speech facilities. It offers a combined scanning and reading application that lets convert printed text into audio feedback. Because of its accurate and reliable OCR engine, Kurzweil 3000 is capable of reproducing text on screen, with pictures, as it appears on paper. It also helps reading and learning to read by highlighting both the line and word as it is read, which can be useful for people with dyslexia. It costs in the order of €1,000.
- BigKeys keyboards (BigKeys Keyboards, 2014): Keyboards with extra-large keys, designed by the BigKeys company. Especially the versions with coloured keys and an ABC key layout may be useful for someone with dyslexia. They cost in the order of €100.
- WebspirationPro (Inspiration Software, Inc., 2014a): Designed by the Inspiration company (Inspiration Software, Inc., 2014b), it is targeted to business professionals and college students. WebspirationPro is a visual thinking and cloud-computing productivity tool. Because of its visual mind-mapping capabilities, it can be used by people with dyslexia as well. Single user licenses are in the order of €40.

Specific ICT tools that can help users with visual impairments include:

- Aladdin Genie Pro CCTV (Telesensory, 2008a): Designed by the Telesensory (Telesensory, 2008b) company, it is a colour desktop CCTV that links to a VGA monitor or computer with 5.5X - 50X magnification on a 17" monitor. It is an electronic magnifier designed to assist those with visual impairments who want to use a separate monitor or computer to view items. It costs in the order of €2,500.

- BigKeys – LX Black Keys QWERTY (BigKeys Keyboards, 2014): Similar to the ones described for the users with dyslexia, they can also be used by people with visual impairments.
- DECtalk Express (SpeechFX Inc., 2013): Produced by the SpeechFX company, this is a basic portable voice synthesizer with internal NICAD batteries. It can be connected to any PC or compatible laptop computer via a serial interface. A battery charger, carrying case and headphones are included. It costs around €900 per piece.
- JAWS for Windows (Freedom Scientific, Inc., 2014b): Developed by Freedom Scientific (Freedom Scientific, Inc., 2014a), this is a screen reader which makes on-screen information accessible through speech output (via loudspeaker or headphones) or Braille displays. JAWS for Windows supports a range of hardware synthesizers including DECtalk, and costs around €800.
- ZoomText Magnifier / Screen Reader (Zoomtext, 2014b): Developed by the ZoomText company (Zoomtext, 2014b), this is a screen magnification package that combines magnification software with a built-in document reader. It also adds speech output using any sound card or a speech synthesizer. Magnification ranges from 2 to 16 times, controllable via the keyboard or the ZoomText control panel. It costs around €750.
- Kurzweil 1000 (Kurzweil, n.d.a): Designed the "Kurzweil Educational Systems" (Kurzweil, n.d.c), it is a scanning, reading and writing software program for use by people who are blind or visually impaired. It works on a PC in conjunction with a flat-bed scanner and synthetic speech. Scanned

text is converted into speech. The product costs around €750.

Specific ICT tools that can help users with muscular disabilities are as follows:

- REACH Keyboard Interface Bundle (Gus Communication Devices Inc., n.d.): Developed by GUS Communication Devices Inc. (Gus Communication Devices Inc., 2012), it uses a single switch placed near the finger, toe, or anywhere one has voluntary muscle control, enabling the person to control the computer, speech software, cruise the internet, send email and do just about anything on the computer. It costs around €750.
- SmartNav AT Headmouse (Gus Communication Devices Inc., n.d.): Also developed by GUS Communication Devices Inc., it allows hands-free cursor control of a computer by naturally moving the head. It includes dwell clicking software and an on-screen keyboard, allowing for complete cursor control specifically for people with amyotrophic lateral sclerosis (ALS), spinal cord injuries, muscular dystrophy, and other special needs. It costs around €600.
- HeadMouse Extreme (Origin Instruments Corporation, 2011): Developed by the Origin Instruments (Origin Instruments Corporation, 2014) it takes the place of a mouse by translating the movements of a user's head into proportional movements of the computer mouse pointer on the screen. It is a good solution for people who cannot use or have limited use of their hands, and costs around €750.
- Sip/Puff solutions (Origin Instruments Corporation, 2013): Also developed by the Origin Instruments (Origin Instruments Corporation, 2014) they are ideal for people who have limited or no motor capabil-

ity to operate switch-activated devices, including computers, augmentative communication devices, adapted toys, environmental control systems and devices accessed or controlled by scanning. Sip/Puff technology is also popular for wheel chair navigation. Prices start from around €230.

Apart from the above tools, there are also other tools and policies that can support the disabled in the workplace, for example,

- Telepresence robots for moving around (e.g. for the physically disabled)
- Telecommuting (working from home)
- Voice interaction (doing away with the keyboard and mouse and instead interacting with the computer by voice)
- Brain interaction (using brainwaves to communicate with the computer)
- Internet and intranet (design and compliance with accessibility guidelines)
- Productivity software (word, spread sheets, power-point, etc. specifically tailored for the disabled)
- Searching, browsing, selecting, editing documents (tailored for the disabled)

Working collaboratively across various boundaries can also have a major impact on productivity, particularly where knowledge is successfully transferred. Assistive technology is one area that is often overlooked, but could provide many solutions to everyday issues that have the potential to benefit many within the business and community sectors. According to Microsoft's Accessibility Guide (Microsoft, 2014), accessible (assistive) technologies can enhance the productivity for all employees (through better collaboration and communication), reduce costs of time lost and money spent when an employee develops a temporary disability, and attract new customers by providing products and services that appeal to a broader

range of customers (through businesses market insights provided by disabled people).

There currently exists a wide range of tools and gadgets (some simple and others more complicated) to enable disabled employees to carry out their work (e.g. on the computer or the Internet). However, in many cases employers may view these tools as an overhead or additional effort in procuring and installing them. It is therefore a matter of research and policy initiatives to examine how best to introduce to a larger scale ICT and AT tools in the workplace to enable more people with disabilities to become employed and run a successful professional career.

The Value of Assistive Technologies in the Workplace

While finding a precise cost per employee for assistive technology can be difficult, studies put the average one-time cost at around $500 to $600 per individual. In some cases, it may cost even less because many disabled workers already have the equipment and the software they need to perform their job duties through health insurance and government programs. While popular text reader packages may carry price tags of more than $1,000 per user, multiple licenses can reduce the cost. These are figures for the US. We did not come across similar studies for the EU.

Online tools such as Hire Gauge (Think Beyond the Label, 2012) help employers calculate the return on the investment an organization can generate from hiring qualified workers with disabilities. For a typical large business in the US, this can mean nearly $32,000 in tax credits, deductions and hiring cost savings – not to mention the additional benefits of diversity in the workplace, from employee morale and loyalty, to the opportunity to tap new markets. Once more this is specific to the US. We have not found information on whether or not such incentives exist in the EU.

Many tools and approaches that are good for inclusion are also good for productivity. Clearly, assistive technologies can help disabled staff be more productive and effective. Demonstrating the power of productivity tools to business is becoming a fast growing area for the ICT Service Industry and at the same time starts to address the issue of accessibility for staff and customers alike.

In the US Microsoft has a network of stores dedicated to the issue of accessibility. It does not have such a network in the EU.

People with Disabilities Working in Call Centres

Call centres are one particular example of a business area where disabled people with a variety of disabilities can be employed and succeed in their careers, and therefore are mentioned here. One example is in the city of Chembur (Kumaran, 2011), India's first dedicated call centre employing the physically disabled. The centre will answer queries and register complaints of consumers based in north India, Gujarat, Rajasthan and Madhya Pradesh. Once the call centre is fully operational with 120 employees, it is expected to cater to about 10,000 customer calls in a day.

A similar story exists in Israel, where a unique call centre called Call Yachol (Yachol call, n.d.) was founded in 2008 and run with the vision of offering employment to a large number of people with various types of disabilities. Its call centre representatives are aged 20 to 65, most of them with some kind of disability (but without cognitive impairment). What is particularly unique is that it is run totally as a for-profit commercial venture and not as a charity. Located in Rishon LeZion, Israel, it is a great example of how minor adjustments, accommodations, and support can allow disabled people to be fully productive members of society and the workforce. Psychologist Gil Winch, founder of the venture, says there is no reason for these employees' mental or physical limitations to keep them from excelling on the job. But most have suffered from being shunned by mainstream employers and lack self-confidence in their poten-

tial. Up to 90% of severely disabled adults in Israel face chronic unemployment. Winch implemented a parent-based management model where workers are given affection and have scheduled time for team fun. The unusual arrangement has garnered interest from people in several countries looking to replicate the idea.

In Turkey, the Happy Disabled Call Centre (Microsoft, 2008) was established by the Foundation for Disabled People with the support of Microsoft. The business need it addresses is to create a database of 9 million disabled people in Turkey and become a resource centre about disability issues. The aim is to provide structured information about disability issues for clients, public authorities, corporations, and other organizations in Turkey. They currently employ 20 people in the call centre, 10 of whom have disabilities.

Call centres are just an example of how persons with disabilities given the proper circumstances and environment can excel in their jobs. However there is a need for better identification of such jobs and work environments that favour employment of persons with disabilities with minor adaptations. This could help both in better legislation promoting employability of persons with disabilities in these areas while also helping persons with disabilities in their career orientation by providing list of opportunities where they can feel productive and not restricted in their job

EMPLOYMENT

The Numbers Tell All

Despite the positive messages from the perspective of the employability of disabled people, people with disabilities are disadvantaged in the labour market (World Health Organization. World Bank, 2011). For example, their lack of access to education and training or to financial resources may be responsible for their exclusion from the labour market – but it could also be the nature of the workplace or employers' perceptions of disability and disabled people. Social protection systems may create incentives for people with disabilities to exit employment onto disability benefits. Our distinct impression is that more research is needed on factors that influence labour market outcomes for persons with disabilities.

The degree of education and the level of qualification (Greve, 2009) have, as in the core of the labour market, a clear impact on types of jobs and on security of employment. Education must be understood in the broad sense, starting from primary education and continuing through life-long learning. Concerns are raised when people with disabilities very rarely participate in adult education.

Indeed, for many disabled people life-long learning as adults becomes increasingly important to labour market integration as, when for example the onset or progression of impairment changes the opportunities for certain types of jobs over time. Education is therefore a key area in ensuring equal opportunities where future EU initiative may be effective, including opportunities for lifelong learning to facilitate easier access to the labour market where disability occurs during the life-cycle.

The Need for Better Statistical Data

In many countries data on the employment of people with disabilities are not systematically available. In fact finding reliable disability statistics - especially reasonably current ones - can be a challenge (Dority, 2009). Amongst other reasons for this, the term 'disability' can be given wide interpretations, different governmental organisations may only track specific aspects of disability, tracking disability statistics has been infrequent and in many cases inconsistent, and there is also inconsistency among reporting agencies in how they define their data.

Analysis of the World Health Survey results for 51 countries undertaken in WHO's and World Bank's 2011 World Report on Disability (World Health Organization. World Bank, 2011), gives employment rates of 52.8% for men with disability and 19.6% for women with disability, compared with 64.9% for non-disabled men, and 29.9% for non-disabled women. A recent 2010 study (Organisation for Economic Co-operation and Development, 2006) from the Organization for Economic Co-operation and Development (OECD) showed that in 27 countries, working-age persons with disabilities experienced significant labour market disadvantage and worse labour market outcomes than working-age persons without disabilities. On average, their employment rate, at 44%, was only half that for persons without disability (75%). The inactivity rate was about 2.5 times higher among persons without disability (49% and 20%, respectively).

In Europe in particular, according to the "Mobility and Integration of People with Disabilities into the Labour Market" report (Eichhorst et. al., 2010) report, the EU-wide employment rate of disabled people in 2007 was approximately 20 percentage points lower than the rate of the non-disabled people. For all European countries investigated, the employment rate of people (between the ages of 15-64) with no limitations in activities because of health problems (65.1%) was higher compared to the rates of people who are limited (52.4%) or strongly limited (26.2%) in the severity of their disability. However, the EU average (excluding France and Malta) covers a variety of gaps in employment rates: of the 25 EU Member States analysed, 14 had a difference in employment rates between the non-disabled and the disabled which ranged above the average European difference. A particularly high difference was observed in Romania, where the non-disabled had on average an employment rate which was 31.0 percentage points higher than the one of the disabled.

It is evident that the statistical analyses provided in the reports do not help policy makers to understand the reasons for the problems. Therefore, there is a need to identify what kind of data on the employment of people with disabilities in Europe needs to be collected. In addition there is also a need to identify specific variables in order to determine causes and effects, enablers and disablers, advantages and disadvantages for the employment of people with disabilities. Finally there is also a need for harmonisations over the legislative definition of "disability" for employment. In general, to get more accurate and clear data there is a need for better statistical data collection in that domain.

In developing countries, employment rates of disabled youth in particular are rarely tracked. According to the Asia Pacific Disability Rehabilitation Journal's 2004 article "Adolescents and youth with disability: issues and challenges" (Groce, 2004) however, if the general pattern of unemployment and underemployment for the rest of the disabled population holds true, it can be anticipated that unemployment rates among youth with disability will be the higher than for all other young people. Rates of unemployment among adults with disability vary from country to country, but on average, tend to be about 40-60% higher than for the non-disabled population. This is true even in developed countries with sophisticated school-to-work programmes and reserved employment schemes. Furthermore, even when they enter the work place, adolescents with disabilities often find they have little margin for error. Unlike non-disabled adolescents who frequently fail at a first job or apprenticeship, adolescents with disabilities are rarely allowed to explore their options. Should they not succeed in an initial apprenticeship or be fired from their first job, those around them are quick to label them unemployable and refuse to let them try again.

In the same Asia Pacific Disability Rehabilitation Journal article, it is mentioned that "*unemployment among disabled young women in all societies, averages 50% higher than unemployment among comparably educated disabled young men...*" which itself is double that of their non-disabled

male peers. Disabled young people from ethnic and minority communities also routinely have unemployment rates that are significantly higher than those of their non-minority disabled peers.

Statistics regarding the employment of people with disabilities, broken down by type of disability, are only available for the US (Cornell University, 2013). Comparative statistics do not exist for Europe or indeed for most parts of the world.

The term 'disability' is so broad as to be unhelpful. The specific problems faced by someone who is confined to a wheelchair are very different to those faced by someone with limited eye-sight, are very different from someone with autism spectrum disorder, anxiety or depression. The perception of the difficulty of employment will probably be different as well.

The task of objectively demonstrating how a person with a disability can work as productively as anyone else is different too, as are their requirements in terms of specifically adapted assistive technology. It seems that better statistics and productivity research would help both entrepreneurs in assistive technologies and employers employing people with disabilities by lowering the cost of market segmentation and enabling actors to better target their efforts and messages concerning different segments of this potential workforce.

Data reported from the Cornell University Employment and Disability Institute (Cornell University, 2014) in the US (see table below) show indeed that people with disabilities have on average less than half the employment rate of their non-disabled counterparts. Men (with or without disabilities) always tend to fare better than women with regards to employment. It is also interesting to note that disabled people with a BA or higher degree have approximately 2.5 more chances than those with less than a high school education (22.8% compared to 54.8%) of finding employment. *Education (especially tertiary) therefore appears to be an important factor in increasing the employment chances of people with disabilities.*

Table 2. The percentage of non-institutionalized, male or female, with or without a disability, ages 21-64, with all or specific education levels in the United States who were employed in 2009 (Source: Cornell University Employment and Disability Institute – Disability Statistics (Cornell University, 2013))

Disability Type	Men & Women – All Education Levels	Men – All Education Levels	Women – All Education Levels	Men & Women – Less than a High School Education	Men & Women – a BA degree or higher
Without	76.8%	81.9%	71.8%	54.7%	82.3%
Any	36%	39%	33%	22.8%	54.8%
Visual	38.7%	42.3%	35.3%	26.6%	59.7%
Hearing	52.8%	56.2%	47.0%	32.8%	69.6%
Ambulatory[1]	26.4%	26.4%	26.3%	15.9%	44.2%
Cognitive[2]	24.9%	26.5%	23.2%	16.4%	38.7%
Self-care disability[3]	17.3%	19.0%	15.8%	10.7%	33.8%
Independent Living disability[4]	17.2%	18.7%	16.0%	11.7%	29.4%

It is also interesting to notice that people with hearing impairments have the highest level of employment, while people with ambulatory impairments have one of the lowest (26.4% for all employment levels). This is surprising given that in an age where so much work relies mainly on the ability to work at a screen, use a phone and discuss with colleagues, where Teleworking is so cheaply available and even encouraged, one naively expects that the segment of people in a wheelchair should have the highest level of employment, and participate in most professions at least to the same extent as their non-disabled peers.

Due to the legal-administrative nature of the definition of a disability, and essential differences throughout the European Union in how these are recognised for the purposes of each national healthcare system, it would also be useful to develop population statistics that look at the broader issue of ability rather than the strictly legal issue of disability. The idea is to randomly sample a population, to determine where each person lies on the entire spectrum of ability, and not just whether or not the person is recognised by the national healthcare system as being eligible for assistance on the basis of disability. This could be done in the case of eye-sight for example. Ideally

this would independently assess the productivity of the person as well as their employment status and their sector of activity.

Although the remarks on statistics may not seem directly relevant to future ICT research and innovation programs, they are of potential importance if they help to target research and innovation efforts towards better defining challenges with higher impact probabilities. To have the maximum effect, we would suggest that the most useful results might derive from the involvement of people with expertise in the marketing of relevant technologies, or to ageing demographics or other relevant groups, in collaboration with social scientists and economists interested in the disabilities as an academic pursuit.

Employment for Persons with Cognitive and Intellectual Impairments

From the limited data available in Europe, it is mentioned that the employment rate also varies considerably for people with different disabilities, with individuals with mental health difficulties or intellectual impairments experiencing the lowest employment rates[5].

A British analysis (Jones, Latreille, & Sloane, 2006) found that people with mental health difficulties faced greater difficulties in gaining entry into the labour market and in obtaining earnings compared with other workers. Another study (Verdonschot et.al., 2009) found that people with intellectual impairments were three to four times less likely to be employed than people without disabilities – and more likely to have more frequent and longer periods of unemployment. They were less likely to be competitively employed and more likely to be employed in segregated settings.

Many disabilities actually arise through work. This is less likely due to industrial accidents than in the past, though the incidence of back-pain, depression and physical ailments such as Carpal Tunnel Syndrome seem quite important.

The issue of cognitive, behavioural or psychological difficulties arising in mid or late career is especially interesting as it raises the possibility of a role for the employer in prevention. It is in the interest of employers, employees and society in general to preserve the earning capability of individual and increase it throughout the whole career, especially at a time when late career lay-offs seem to be on the increase. The kind of issues we have in mind are all types of causes of absenteeism, such as drug dependency, alcohol abuse, stress or anxiety form overuse, the phenomenon of burn-out or nervous breakdown. Although the root cause of many of these may be poor management or an abusive organisational culture, many of these conditions could benefit from active management for example using new assistive technologies for cognitive, behavioural therapies, as well as social network inspired communities and support groups.

The Problem with Identifying the Types of Jobs Proffered

With regards to the types of jobs and sectors of employment for disabled people, there is again lack of current and detailed data in this theme (including Europe), not least because many disabled people employed in the ordinary labour market are not recognised or measured in reported figures (e.g. because they are not recorded as having work limitations or receiving specific support services). The table below summarises the available evidence from Europe in 2002, which also highlights an absence of knowledge about the employment sectors of very many disabled people.

Due to the paucity of data in the EU (as indicated in the table above) it is difficult to reach conclusions on the types of professions preferred by disabled people. More research is needed in this area, together with the industries where disabled people choose to work. This statistical analysis could also help in identifying in which jobs persons with specific disabilities succeed better and make this way easier the expansion of the example of call centres referred earlier in the chapter.

Education for People with Disabilities

By the time children with a disability reach early adolescence, the vast majority find themselves far behind the educational and skill levels of their non-disabled peers. Cases exist where disabled high school students are not allowed to enrol in the full range of academic courses. Difficulties in access to education have immediate relevance to disabled young people. At an age when non-disabled individuals are beginning to define themselves through their anticipated careers, most disabled young people enter the workforce unprepared. In the current economic climate, young people are also at a high risk of unemployment, partial employment or full employment at lower wages than ever before.

In a number of countries, it is unlawful for schools and other education providers to discriminate against disabled pupils, students and adult learners. In the UK for example (UK Government Digital Service, 2013), the Equality Act 2010 has increased protection for disabled learners against unfair treatment, which could amount to (direct

Table 3. Types of jobs and sectors of employment of disabled people in 2002 (Source: The labour market situation of disabled people in European countries – ANED VT/2007/005 (Greeve, 2009))

Area	Legislators, senior officials and managers	Professionals	Technicians and associate professional	Clerks	Service workers and shop and market sales workers	Skilled agricultural and fishery workers	Craft and related trades workers	Plant and machine operators and assembler	Elementary occupations	Unknown	Total
EU (25)	12.7	10.2	11.1	12.5	11.9	15.7	11.8	13.9	15.8	23.4	16.2
EU (15)	14.4	12.0	13.3	14.4	13.7	17.8	13.8	15.9	17.0	24.6	17.8

or indirect) discrimination, discrimination arising from a disability, or harassment.

At the international level, the United Nations Convention on the Rights of Persons with Disabilities (Article 24) strengthens the principles of non-discrimination and promotes equal opportunities in education at all levels. Sixteen European countries have already ratified the UN Convention, including Austria, Belgium, Czech Republic, Denmark, France, Germany, Hungary, Latvia, Lithuania, Portugal, Slovakia, Slovenia, Spain, Sweden and UK (although the UK reserved its right to maintain special schools) The European Union concluded the convention in December 2010 and ratification is about to happen in many other countries, such as Cyprus, Estonia, Finland, Greece, Iceland, Ireland, Malta, the Netherlands, Norway and Poland.

The 2011 ANED report on "Inclusive Education For Young Disabled People In Europe: Trends, Issues And Challenges" (Ebersold, Schmitt, & Priestley, 2011) argues that with regards to the access to higher education for the disabled people, this is no longer a utopia and concern about provision for them is taking on a high profile. There has been a noticeable rise in enrolment for around a decade in many OECD member countries. In Sweden, the number of Students with Disabilities (SWD) enrolled at university rose by 125% from 1993 to 1999; in Ontario, Canada, SWD enrolments at university have risen from 1,668 in 1989/90 to 6,883 in 2000/01 (Ministry of Educa-

tion). Enrolment in colleges has also risen, from 3,501 in 1989/90 to 12,491 a decade later. In France the Ministry of Education figure for SWD enrolment at university in 1993/94 was 3,601. By 2000/01 the figure had risen to 7,029. According to the Ministry of Education, most SWD wanting a place at university would be accepted.

More recent data Europe-wide on the participation of disabled students (undergraduate and postgraduate) in Higher Education are not readily available. Data are only available for some European countries e.g. Ireland, where the total number of students with disabilities rose from 1,410 in 1999 to 6,321 ten years later (2009). Specific Learning Difficulties was the most widespread disability (61%) of SWD in 2009, followed by Significant On-going Illnesses (10%), Mental Health (8%), Physical or Mobility Disabilities (7%), Deaf/Hard of Hearing (4%) and Blind/Visually Impaired (3%). The most common subjects studied were Social Science, Business & Law (25.9%), Humanities & Arts (18.9%), Science (15.9%), Health & Welfare (14.7%), Engineering, Manufacturing and Construction (13.5%), Education Science (5.4%).

For business studies in particular, there are also business schools classes (e.g. for disabled US soldiers) (Philadelphia, 2008) coming back from the battlefield (e.g. in Iraq), while business schools across the globe are making their services available to disabled students as well. This means that disabled students can also have the opportunity to become future business leaders or entrepreneurs, or otherwise take an active part in business activities.

Disabled children / youth with no or poor education fare worse in their working lives, have increased job insecurity and less income than disabled people with higher levels of education. This use case envisages the EU gathering more comprehensive data on the link between the level and quality of education received by disabled people, and the type and quality of jobs they subsequently obtain. It also envisages examining whether the current policies, AT and support received by disabled students are sufficient or more measures needs to be taken. It also presupposes monitoring mechanisms to make sure the individual performs according to his/her capabilities in education and that any changes in the status of disability are diagnosed well in advance, so that the individual's performance and well-being are not affected. This kind of policy could lead to identifying problems, provide better directions to persons with disabilities and in long term increase their employment rates.

Job Mentoring For and By People with Disabilities

Although the concept of job mentoring is recognised worldwide as evidenced by the International Mentoring Network Organization, it must nevertheless be noted that well-organised mentoring programs to aid the disabled in their pre- and during-work life are not generally available. There are some isolated initiatives like the Chemists with disabilities (American Chemical Society, 2011) that are not mentoring networks per se, but may, amongst other activities, also offer some informal mentoring opportunities to their members. Isolated initiatives also include EU projects like the M-NET EOP project (Mentoring Network for Equal Employment Opportunities, 2009) whose main aim is to develop and evaluate a web based training resource for employers and entrepreneurs

who wish to establish new businesses atmosphere offering environmental products and services. As part of this project, project managers of companies set out to find mentors for the disabled candidates. Each mentor is to be coupled with a disabled employee in a field chosen by the disabled person. Closely linked to the mentoring programme, the project also seeks to establish an employer's network for disability. This network is to consist of companies with a positive attitude towards the employment of disabled people.

The creation of this network would enable employers to share experiences as well as best practices concerning the employment of disabled people. This could also lead in changing the perception of employers on the subject of employing a person with disability. Consequently, market's perception on persons with disabilities will change gradually to the degree where a disability will not be such a significant barrier for employment.

Ageing and Unemployment

During past recessions, older workers simply would have retired rather than searching ads and applying for jobs. But these days, with outstanding mortgages, bank loans and high medical bills, many of them can't afford to be out of work (Ansberry, 2009). The number of unemployed workers 75 and older increased in the US to more than 73,000 in January 2009, up 46% from the prior January. Among workers 65 and older, the jobless rate stood at 5.7%. That was below the national average, but well above what it was in previous recessions, including the recession of 1981, when it reached at 4.3%.

On a more global scale, according to a 2006 OECD report (Keese, 2006) population ageing is one of the most important challenges facing OECD countries. Over the next 50 years, all OECD countries will experience a steep increase in the share of elderly persons in the population and a large decline in the share of the population of prime working-age. Consequently, in most countries, the number of workers retiring each year will increase sharply and eventually exceed the number of new labour market entrants.

If there is no change in work and retirement patterns, the ratio of older inactive persons per worker will almost double from around 38% in the OECD area in 2000 to just over 70% in 2050. In Europe, this ratio could rise to almost one older inactive person for every worker over the same period.

Ageing on this scale would place substantial pressures on public finances and reduce growth in living standards. For instance, on the basis of unchanged participation patterns and productivity growth, the growth of GDP per capita in the OECD area would decline to around 1.7% per year over the next three decades, about 30% less than its rate between 1970 and 2000.

There is therefore substantial scope for promoting employment of older workers, although the situation varies across countries. In 2004, less than 60% of the population aged 50-64 had a job, on average in the OECD, compared with 76% for the age group 24-49. The figure varies from less than 50% in certain countries to more than 70% in others. There are numerous work disincentives and employment barriers facing older workers which often result in early exit from the labour market. It is indeed remarkable that, despite sustained increases in longevity, the effective age at which workers retire has tended to follow a downward trend in virtually all OECD countries, at least until recently. Thus, the number of years that workers can expect to spend in retirement has risen considerably – for men, from less than 11 years on average across the OECD in 1970 to just under 18 years in 2004 and, for women, from less than 14 years to just under 23 years.

In Europe in particular, the EU-27 employment rate for older workers (aged between 55 and 64) reached 46.3% in 2010. Apparently, official data with regards to the employment of the elderly past the statutory retirement age do not exist.

The main pathways for exiting early from the labour market differ across countries. In some countries, this occurs mainly through provisions in the pension system or through formal early retirement schemes. In other countries, it is through disability and other welfare benefits. In all countries, early exit from the labour market tends to be a one-way street, with very few older workers returning to employment – in general, fewer than 5% of those inactive aged 50-64 are in jobs one year later.

Part of the problem with the higher unemployment rate of the elderly may lie in their limited knowledge and use of the Internet. The Irish Commission for Communications Regulation (Comreg) (Commission for Communications Regulation, 2014) reported in March 2007 (Commission for Communications Regulation, 2007) that 98% of Irish people aged between 65 and 74 years of age do not use the Internet. Although the figures emanating from many other Western societies are not as severe, they paint a similar and troubling picture. The UK's National Audit Office has reported in 2007 (Great Britain. National Audit Office, 2007) that the overwhelming majority of over 65s have never logged on. A recent survey (Fox, 2006) by the Pew Internet & American Life Project in 2006 found that just 34% of Americans aged 65 or older go online. This compares with near universal use by those under the age of 60.

Statistics show that education and familiarization of elderly with Internet and other new technologies could result in longer work life. Therefore there is a need for policies to encourage such education to help re-entry of retired people in the work-force. In addition, there is also a need to identify, independently of the politics of retirement and benefits, the barriers to successful late-life work transition.

The current economic conditions mean that many elderly people may not afford to be out of work, even with receiving additional benefits such as for retirement or disability. Some people may also simply enjoy the stimulation and challenge provided by a job. On the other hand, older people who lose their job find it more difficult than their younger counterparts to find alternative employment.

Coupled with the fact that the world's population (including Europe) is getting older and it will become increasingly difficult to provide financially for these people once they retire, it becomes imperative to consider the employment of elderly people, not just of those before retirement age, but also of those past-retirement who wishes to remain employed.

LEGISLATION AND POLICIES FOR EMPLOYMENT

Corporate Social Responsibility for the Disabled

CSR is often cited as a major driver of social inclusion (Travability Pty Ltd, 2013). CSR is perhaps more misunderstood than environmental sustainability was 10 years ago. CSR does generate significant amounts of funds for social activities but does not always result in fundamental cultural change. It may look good on the annual report or make the directors feel good about their organization, but if it is being discriminatory in the way it treats its customers or employees then the motives do not lead to a change in corporate behaviour.

The fundamental question is why. CSR perpetuates the social model and the basic rights issues surrounding it. When change is driven by rights, government legislation and compliance, then the outcome will always be procedures to ensure those obligations are met. Seldom is the associated expenditure on infrastructure, manuals and training seen as an asset that will lead to an economic return or a competitive advantage. When it comes to accessible infrastructure we see time and again great infrastructure with little or no marketing to inform people of its existence. The disabled community complains about the lack of infrastructure and industry bemoans the poor utilization and over-regulation.

In 2002 in the UK, the Employer's Forum on Disability has conducted an audit (Business Respect, 2002) on the Corporate Social Responsibility reports of 50 leading British and global companies, analysing how they approached disability and treated disabled customers and staff. As few as 12% included any mention of disability as part of the company's corporate responsibility strategy.

More recently in 2009, the Spanish organisation Fundación ONCE (Fundacion ONCE, n.d.b) published a Guide on Corporate Social Responsibility and Disability (CSR-D), applicable to companies at European level. The guide (Fundacion ONCE, n.d.a) was developed within a number of awareness-raising activities addressed to economic and social stakeholders and promoted as part of the Operative Programme on the Fight Against Discrimination, co-financed by the European Social Fund. The objective of this programme is the social and labour participation of people with disabilities.

CSR for people with disabilities could become in important driver towards increasing employment of persons with disabilities. This is an area that has to be exploited more rigorously in the future.

General Disability Policies

An updated 2010 OECD report on Disability and Work (Organisation for Economic Co-operation and Development, 2006) argues that in many of the examined countries[6], disability policy has advanced considerably during the past decade. However, changes in outcomes have not kept pace with changes in policy development. Disability appears to be a moving target for policy makers, requiring i) more rigorous implementation of rules and recent changes and ii) additional and more comprehensive reform.

Moreover, things have become even more complicated in recent years because of the growing weight of a wide range of mental health problems in the inflows to sickness and disability systems.

The latter phenomenon is not yet well understood and the OECD launched a country review exercise to analyse it and evaluate which policies might help to counteract it. Mental health sufferers are consequently targeted in a recent 2011 OECD report (Organisation for Economic Co-operation and Development, 2012) on the topic of mental ill-health and work. In this report it is argued that people with severe mental disorders are too often too far away from the labour market, and need help to find sustainable employment. The majority of people with common mental disorder, however, are employed but struggling in their jobs. Neither are they receiving any treatment nor any supports in the workplace, thus being at high risk of job loss and permanent labour market exclusion. This implies a need for policy to shift away from severe, to common mental disorders and sub-threshold conditions; away from a focus on inactive people to more focus on those employed; and away from reactive to preventive strategies. The report in particular cites that today, between one-third and one-half of all new disability benefit claims are for reasons of mental ill-health, and among young adults that proportion goes up to over 70%.

Mental disorders can be segregated into severe and common ones. People with severe mental disorders (requiring frequent clinical intervention) are usually far away from the labour market, and need help to find sustainable employment. On the other hand, people with common mental disorders (such as mild depression, anxiety, etc.) are mostly employed, but struggling in their jobs. They are also not receiving any treatment or support in the workplace, thus running the risk of job loss and potentially permanent exclusion from the labour market.

It may therefore be necessary to shift the focus of disability policies away from severe and towards common mental disorders; also away from reactive to preventive strategies, as the latter can be much less costly to address.

Outcomes and Challenges of Disability Policies

With regards to the social and economic outcomes of disability policy, the 2010 OECD report argues that spending on disability benefits (for people who are not working) has become a significant burden to public finances in most OECD countries and hinders economic growth as it reduces effective labour supply. Some statistics to substantiate this are as follows:

- Public spending on disability benefits totals 2% of GDP on average across the OECD, rising to as much as 4-5% in countries such as Norway, the Netherlands and Sweden.
- Around 6% of the working-age population rely on disability benefits, on average, and up to 10-12% in some countries in the north and east of Europe.

Most importantly, disability benefit take-up is a one-way street. People almost never leave disability benefits for a job, and if they leave the disability benefit scheme before retiring, they are far more likely to move onto another benefit.

A big challenge facing governments is then how best to reform tax and benefit systems for persons with disability with a view to providing appropriate financial incentives to take up jobs, remain in work and increase work effort. This issue has not received enough attention so far, although some countries have recently started to address it, e.g. with in-work payments in the United Kingdom and Ireland and a benefit which depends on the individual's work effort in the Netherlands.

Treatment of Disabled People in the Workplace

With regards to equality policies, in the UK the Equality Act 2010 (Great Britain. Equality and Human Rights Commission, author, 2011) has been passed to warrant against unlawful discrimination at employment. For persons with disabilities, in order to make sure that they have the same access, as far as is reasonable, to everything that is involved in getting and doing a job as a non-disabled person, an employer must make reasonable adjustments. Reasonable adjustments should also be put in place if someone becomes disabled while in work or if their needs change or they move to a different role.

In addition, a 2011 revised edition of UK's TUC (Trade Union Congress) report on Disability and Work mentions that the underpinning principle of disability discrimination law is the understanding that, unlike all the other strands of equality law, disability discrimination law does not work on the basis of treating everyone the same. On the contrary, it relies on grasping the understanding that, because of the numerous barriers faced by so many disabled people, *the only way to achieve an equal outcome may be to treat disabled people more favourably.*

It may be hard to persuade workplace representatives, who have been brought up on the principle that trade unionism involves treating all their members the same, to understand that (some) disabled members may require to be treated better than their colleagues, if an equal outcome is to be obtained. That's why when training in equality law is provided for workplace representatives, it is strongly recommended that the different way in which the law treats disability is clearly explained. It may be even harder to persuade the employer – especially as represented at line management level, where key decisions are made, and where there is less likelihood of training having been provided on this subject.

Some of the initiatives regarding the equality of disabled people in the EU countries require not that disabled people are given the same status as non-disabled people, but that they are treated more favourably than their non-disabled colleagues. The reasoning behind this difference is that disabled people face additional barriers which must be overcome for their successful integration in the workplace.

On the one hand, this may initially pose a problem to workplace representatives or trade unions which are used to the principle of treating all employees the same. On the other hand, employers or line managers may also not be convinced of the principle of treating disabled employees more favourably, and this must be communicated to them.

Disability Acts

At EU level, in 2010 the EU published a "Disability Strategy: 2010-2020" (European Commission, 2010), covering amongst others areas in employment, education and training, and social protection. In January 2011 Viviane Redding promised to put forward an EU "Disabilities Act" by the end of 2012. The 2010-2020 Disability Strategy aims to provide Member States with analysis, political guidance, information exchange and other support on the area of the employment of the disabled people. It will improve knowledge of the employment situation of women and men with disabilities, identify challenges and propose remedies. It will pay particular attention to young people with disabilities in their transition from education to employment. It will address intra-job mobility on the open labour market and in sheltered workshops, through information exchange and mutual learning. It will also address the issue of self-employment and quality jobs, including aspects such as working conditions and career advancement. The Commission will step up its support for voluntary initiatives that promote diversity management at the workplace, such as diversity charters signed by employers and a Social Business Initiative.

Worldwide there are also various Disability Discrimination Acts (e.g. Section 508 in the US) that dictate that new websites and staff intranets should be developed to be accessible (Riverdocs Bureau Service, 2011) and usable for disabled users; and reasonable adjustments should be made to existing sites to ensure that they are accessible and usable for disabled users. In determining what adjustments are reasonable, the cost is likely to be taken into account by a court. However, due to the internal nature of these sites, it is difficult to determine the rates of compliance of companies and whether they tend to comply more with their public web sites as opposed to their internal web sites.

ENTREPRENEURSHIP

Status of Disabled Entrepreneurship

In the UK, organisations like "Disabled Entrepreneurs" (Disabled Entrepreneurs, 2012) exist with the objective of providing assistance and support to disabled people who are thinking of becoming (or are already) an entrepreneur. Similar organisations also exist in the US, e.g. Disabled Businesspersons Association (Disabled Businesspersons Association, n.d.), a charitable organization dedicated to assisting enterprising individuals with disabilities maximize their potential in the business world, and work with vocational rehabilitation, government and business to encourage the participation and enhance the performance of the disabled in the workforce.

Even when the economy was strong, three-fourths of the people with moderate to severe disabilities remained unemployed (Diversity World, 2014). Not surprisingly, many people with disabilities see small business ownership as their chance for economic self-sufficiency.

Funding for disabled entrepreneurs is an important area to look at, as according to the U.S. Department of Census, people with disabilities are almost twice as likely as non-disabled individuals to start a business (US Small Business Administration, n.d.). In addition, almost 15% of working disabled people are self-employed compared to under 10% of non-disabled working people.

Nevertheless, building a business from nothing, particularly as a disabled person, presents unique challenges, not least of which are attitudinal barriers; the potential loss of benefits; the lack of assets to use as collateral; and perceived lack of access to programs that promote self-employment and small business development.

Despite the challenges, the success rate among disabled small business owners (in the US at least) is unprecedented. Looking at statistics from the Disabled Businessman's Association (Virginia Commonwealth University, 2013) - they estimate that *40% of home-based businesses are operated by people with disabilities.*

In more concrete terms, research by Thomas Cooney (Cooney, 2008) from the Dublin Institute of Technology has indicated that in the United States, based on the 1990 national census, people with disabilities had a higher rate of self-employment (12.2%) than people without disabilities (7.8%), with approximately 40% of the disabled self-employed having home-based businesses. By the time of the 1994 national census, the number of people with disabilities who were self-employed had risen to 14%. Moreover, nearly as many people with disabilities reported being self-employed as reported working for federal, state, and local government combined. 14.6% of men with disability were self-employed compared with 9.6% of men with no work disability, while 9.0% of women with disability were self-employed compared with 5.6% of women with no work disability.

Cooney also cites that for people with disabilities in the UK in 2003, 18% of disabled men and 8% of disabled women were self-employed, compared to 14% and 6% of non-disabled men and women respectively. Both disabled self-employed men and disabled self-employed women were older, on average, than their non-disabled counterparts (49% compared to 43% for men, 45% compared to 42% for women). In addition, a higher proportion of disabled self-employed men and disabled self-employed women had no educational qualifications (20% and 12% respectively) compared to non-disabled self-employed

(13% and 10% respectively), while a smaller proportion of disabled self-employed people lived in households containing children, compared to non-disabled self-employed people (this is partly due to the different age profile of the two populations). Disabled men and women had also been self-employed longer (13.1 years on average for men, 8.4 years for women) in comparison to non-disabled men and women (11.3 years for men, 7.9 years for non-disabled women), although this finding was partly explained by the fact that disabled self-employed are also older on average.

In terms of classifying people's disabilities, men and women with musculosketal problems, and women with mental health problems, were particularly likely to be self-employed, while men with sensory impairments were relatively unlikely to be self-employed. Furthermore, the report highlighted that people with disabilities bring lower human capital to their employment than non-disabled people, and that self-employed disabled men report lower incomes from self-employment than their non-disabled counterparts. These findings give significant insights into the characteristics of self-employed disabled people in the U.K., and indeed can also be used as a guideline regarding the likely positions in other countries.

With regards to the self-employment of disabled people in other EU countries, according to a 2010 EU-sponsored research report entitled "The Mobility and Integration of People with Disabilities into the Labour Market", (Eichhorst, et. al., 2010) high rates of self-employment for the disabled as well as for the non-disabled are predominantly found in southern Member States such as Greece (26.7% of non-disabled people as part of total non-disabled working population, 40% of disabled people as part of total disabled working population), Italy (17.6% for non-disabled people, 20.3% for disabled people), Portugal (13.8% for non-disabled people, 27.3% for disabled people) and Spain (13.3% for non-disabled people, 16.5% for disabled people). With the EU average at 12.2%

for non-disabled people in self-employment and 12.7% for disabled people, countries with above average figures were also Romania (21% for non-disabled people, 27.8% for disabled people), Cyprus (12.1% for non-disabled people, 24.9% for disabled people) and Poland (15.8% for non-disabled people, 22.3% for disabled people).

Self-employment may be an alternative pathway towards labour market integration, in particular for the disabled, as discrimination and accessibility restrictions imposed by employers may be less of an issue. So far, no consistent strategy to foster the integration of disabled people through supported start-up incentives exists at the European level. Only three Member States, Portugal, Slovakia and Sweden, currently provide for labour market interventions which can be categorized as start-up incentives specifically targeted at the disabled. The fraction of disabled entrants into these interventions relative to the non-disabled are, however, fairly small and amounted to only 0.7% in Portugal, 2.7% in Slovakia and 11.0% in Sweden in 2008.

The lowest self-employment rates for both groups are observed in Germany, Denmark and Estonia. In Germany, 5.8% of the non-disabled and 2.8% of disabled people are self-employed. In Denmark, the observed self-employment rate of the non-disabled is 5.7%, whereas it is 2.3% for the disabled people. Rates for the self-employed Estonians are 4.7% and 3.3%, respectively.

It must be mentioned however, that the number of people with disabilities who are self-employed may be even higher in some countries as some people with disabilities will not report themselves as being self-employed as they perceive that it might negatively affect their welfare benefits. This so called 'welfare trap' is a particularly difficult situation as some people with disabilities do generate income from self-employment, but since they would lose their benefits if they exceeded a certain income threshold, they may underplay their self-employment income in order to maintain their welfare entitlements.

Mompreneurs and Carepreneurs

Although this is a US phenomenon, it is interesting to note a particular type of entrepreneur known as the so-called mompreneur. Mompreneurs or mom-inventors, who go ahead and commercialize their inventions, may provide a lesson for people with disabilities and those who care for them. No one is more acutely aware of the challenges and frustrations of caring for children than moms. They are expert in the things that children find difficult to do and they spend much of their time putting things right or cleaning up after them.

A website called Mom Inventors (Mom Invented, 2014) supports Moms who have product ideas. It provides advice on how to develop the idea. It assists with product evaluations. It lists products and businesses. It allows Moms to post needs asking for an entrepreneurial solution. Other sites include Mogul Moms (The Mogul Mom, 2014) which gives advice on how to kick-start one's business for as little as $1,000, and The Busy Mom Boutique (The Busy Mom Boutique, 2014) which claims that all products are mom invented and Mom approved.

Companies such as Whirlpool have in the past tried to tap into the knowledge and insights of Moms. They make most of the buy decisions for household products. They know what they want and are a source of ideas for future products. In the period from 2004 to 2008 Whirlpool ran a Mother of Invention (Harbor, 2008) grant program to encourage mothers to come forward with their ideas for new products. The 2008 winner received $20,000 plus advice from Whirlpool on how to launch a new business based on a product idea called MEDPACK for a compact temperature controlled medicine case, of use to people who had to bring temperature sensitive medicines with them as they go throughout their day.

There may be a lesson for us in this. Perhaps other categories of carers, those who care for the elderly or those who care for people with disabilities (carepreneurs), could be explicitly involved in programmes or initiatives intended to help. Writing in the Baltimore Sun (The Baltimore Sun, 2011), the President of the Health Facilities Association of Maryland, pointed out that with unemployment in the US at 9%, with drastic cuts to healthcare budgets and a growing need for long-term or rehabilitative care by people of all ages, there was a need for a much more entrepreneurial approach to care. He called for more "carepreneurs". This term may point to a trend as Nurse Next Door now organizes an annual conference called "Growing Carepreneurs" (Nurse Next Door, 2011).

Nurse Next Door (Nurse Next Door Home Care Franchise., 2014) was founded in 2001 and has grown into one of the most successful homecare businesses in Canada. It has recently adopted a franchise model. It now has more than 50 locations and has expanded to the US. It provides home care to people of any age. The success of the model relies also on the support it provides to franchisees. Not just in terms of training and help getting started, but in terms of help-line support and night-time support that allows the franchisees to take time off from the burden of 24/7 care giving.

Entrepreneurship might be a natural choice for people with disabilities, due to the freedom and flexibility it offers to these people with regards to the working environment and conditions of work. The statistics certainly confirm the preference of self-employment by people with disabilities, as compared to their non-disabled peers.

The future might see the EU supporting entrepreneurship and self-employment through policies and grants, but also through educating the public of the benefits of entrepreneurship of the disabled in order to increase their business. This use case also envisages promoting synergies between entrepreneurs and large organisations (similarly to initiatives like the FairTrade ("Fair trade", n.d.)) for the benefit of the disabled people (as compared to the benefit of the poor in the FairTrade example).

Promoting this type of entrepreneurship may involve initiatives like incubators, soft loans, venture capital, prizes, advice and support (e.g. as currently carried out in EU's "Encouraging Women Entrepreneurs" programme (European Commission: Enterprise and Industry, 2013)). High-profile media models such as "Dragons Den" or "The Apprentice" could be exploited in order to highlight the achievements and capabilities of disabled people and generalize an understanding of the specific challenges they face.

It also implies that late-entrepreneurs (older people or retired people, not just young and straight out of university cases) are not excluded from support. It also involves initiatives that target the area of design marketing and communication, in order to bring into the foreground the entrepreneurial activities carried out by and for people with disabilities.

REFERENCES

AbleData. (n.d.a). *AbleData: Assistive Technology Products, News, Resources*. Retrieved March 10, 2014, from http://www.abledata.com/abledata.cfm

AbleData. (n.d.b). *AbleData: Products*. Retrieved March 10, 2014, from http://www.abledata.com/abledata.cfm?pageid=19327&ksectionid=19327

American Chemical Society. (2011). *Chem. with Disabilities - Division of Professional Relations*. Retrieved March 10, 2014, from http://prof.sites.acs.org/chemwithdisabilities.htm

American Foundation for the Blind. (2013). *Careers for Blind and Visually Impaired Individuals - American Foundation for the Blind*. Retrieved March 10, 2014, from http://www.afb.org/info/living-with-vision-loss/for-job-seekers/for-family-and-friends/careers-for-blind-and-visually-impaired-individuals/1235

Ansberry, C. (2009, February 23). *Elderly Emerge as a New Class of Workers -- and the Jobless - WSJ.com*. Retrieved March 10, 2014, from http://online.wsj.com/news/articles/SB123535088586444925?mg=reno64-wsj&url=http%3A%2F%2Fonline.wsj.com%2Farticle%2FSB123535088586444925.html

Atherton, M. (2008, February 1). *Deaf studies - A-Z Careers - Career Planning - The Independent*. Retrieved March 10, 2014, from http://www.independent.co.uk/student/career-planning/az-careers/deaf-studies-671539.html

Baltimore Sun. (2011, October 24). *Medicare and Medicaid cuts: Nursing and rehabilitation centers are at risk again - Baltimore Sun*. Retrieved March 10, 2014, from http://articles.baltimoresun.com/2011-10-24/news/bs-ed-long-term-care-20111023_1_state-cuts-nursing-and-rehabilitation-health-facilities-association

BigKeys Keyboards. (2014). *BigKeys Company - BigKeys LX*. Retrieved March 10, 2014, from http://www.bigkeys.com/productcart/pc/viewCategories.asp?idCategory=2

Business Disability Forum. (2014). *Welcome to Business Disability Forum*. Retrieved March 10, 2014, from http://businessdisabilityforum.org.uk/

Business Respect. (2002, July 14). *CSR News - UK: Top companies acclaimed for Attention to Disability*. Retrieved March 10, 2014, from http://www.businessrespect.net/page.php?Story_ID=484

Busy Mom Boutique. (2014). *The Busy Mom Boutique: Mom-Invented Products for Maternity, Baby & Beyond*. Retrieved March 10, 2014, from http://www.busymomboutique.com/

Civication, Inc. (2012). *Deaf Justice | Civication, Inc. | Promoting Civic Learning and Civil Responsibility*. Retrieved March 10, 2014, from http://www.civication.org/blog

Commission for Communications Regulation. (2007). *The Internet and Broadband Experience for Residential users: A Communications Survey Report based on the Trends Survey Series* (07/12). Retrieved from http://www.comreg.ie/_fileupload/publications/ComReg0712.pdf

Commission for Communications Regulation. (2014). *Commission for Communications Regulation - ComReg*. Retrieved March 10, 2014, from http://www.comreg.ie/

Cooney, T. (2008). Entrepreneurs with Disabilities: Profile of a Forgotten Minority. Dublin Institute of Technology: ARROW@DIT, 4(1), 119-129.

Cornell University. (2013). *Disability Statistics*. Retrieved March 10, 2014, from http://www.disabilitystatistics.org/reports/acs.cfm?statistic=2

Cornell University. (2014). *Employment & Disability Institute (EDI), Advancing knowledge on disability & employment issues*. Retrieved March 10, 2014, from http://www.ilr.cornell.edu/edi/

Debating Europe. (2012, March 21). *EU 2050: Europe's Tech Revolution? Debating Europe*. Retrieved March 10, 2014, from http://www.debatingeurope.eu/2012/03/21/eu-2050-europes-tech-revolution/#.Ux3-oPmSyQI

Disabled Businesspersons Association. (n.d.). *About The DBA - Disabled Businesspersons Association Disabled Businesspersons Association | Serving the needs of America's enterprising disabled, and professionals in rehabilitation. Since 1985*. Retrieved March 10, 2014, from http://disabledbusiness.org/

Disabled Entrepreneurs. (2012). *Home | Disabled Entrepreneurs - Inspiring Potential*. Retrieved March 10, 2014, from http://www.disabledentrepreneurs.co.uk/

Disabled Person, Inc. (2014). *Disabled Person: Home*. Retrieved March 10, 2014, from https://www.disabledperson.com/

Disabled Workers Co-operative Ltd. (2004). *Jobs for Disabled People - Employment - Disabled Workers Co-operative*. Retrieved March 10, 2014, from http://www.disabledworkers.org.uk/careers/

Disabled World. (2008, January 20). *Famous Blind and Vision Impaired Persons*. Retrieved March 10, 2014, from http://www.disabled-world.com/artman/publish/famous-blind.shtml

Diversity World. (2014). *Self-Employment for People with Disabilities*. Retrieved March 10, 2014, from http://www.diversityworld.com/Disability/selfempl.htm

Dority, K. (2009, May 21). *FreePint: Disability Statistics: Challenges and Sources [ABSTRACT]*. Retrieved March 10, 2014, from http://web.freepint.com/go/blog/3933

Ebersold, S., Schmitt, M. J., & Priestley, M. (2011). *Inclusive Education For Young Disabled People In Europe: Trends, Issues And Challenges*. Retrieved from Academic Network of European Disability website: http://www.disability-europe.net/content/aned/media/ANED%202010%20Task%205%20Education%20final%20report%20-%20FINAL%20(2)_0.pdf

EBU. (n.d.a). *Categories of jobs undertaken by blind and partially sighted people | EBU Job Website | Employment, rehabilitation and vocational training | Working Areas | European Blind Union*. Retrieved March 10, 2014, from http://www.euroblind.org/about-ebu/ebu-employment-website/blind-and-partially-sighted-people/

EBU. (n.d.b). *European Blind Union*. Retrieved March 10, 2014, from http://www.euroblind.org/

EBU. (n.d.c). *Useful links | Resources | European Blind Union*. Retrieved March 10, 2014, from http://www.euroblind.org/resources/useful-links/#Employment

Economist Group. (2011, November 16). *The Economist Insights? Expert Analysis and Events | Frontiers of disruption*. Retrieved March 10, 2014, from http://www.economistinsights.com/technology-innovation/analysis/frontiers-disruption

Economist Group. (2014). *Country, industry and risk analysis from The Economist Intelligence Unit*. Retrieved March 10, 2014, from http://www.eiu.com/Default.aspx

Eichhorst, Kendzia, Knudsen, Hansen, & Vandeweghe. (2010). *The mobility and integration of people with disabilities into the labour market: Based on a study conducted for the European Parliament under contract IP/A/EMPL/FWC/2008-002/C1/SC4*. Retrieved from http://www.iza.org/en/webcontent/publications/reports/report_pdfs/iza_report_29.pdf

Enabling Devices. (2014). *Enabling Devices - Assistive Technology - Products for People with Disabilities*. Retrieved March 10, 2014, from http://enablingdevices.com/catalog

EOP, Inc. (2012). *Equal Opportunity Publications - Magazines Page - Careers & the Disabled*. Retrieved March 10, 2014, from http://www.eop.com/mags-CD.php

European Commission. (2010). *People with disabilities have equal rights: The European Disability Strategy 2010-2020*. Retrieved from http://eur-lex.europa.eu/LexUriServ/LexUriServ.do?uri=COM:2010:0636:FIN:EN:PDF

European Commission. Enterprise and Industry. (2013, April 15). *Encouraging women entrepreneurs - Small and medium sized enterprises - Enterprise and Industry*. Retrieved March 10, 2014, from ec.europa.eu/enterprise/policies/sme/promoting-entrepreneurship/women/index_en.htm

Fair trade. (n.d.). *Wikipedia, the free encyclopedia*. Retrieved March 10, 2014, from http://en.wikipedia.org/wiki/Fair_trade

Fox, S. (2006, April 11). *Are Wired Seniors Sitting Ducks? | Pew Research Center's Internet & American Life Project*. Retrieved March 16, 2014, from http://www.pewinternet.org/2006/04/11/are-wired-seniors-sitting-ducks/#fn-836-1

Freedom Scientific Inc. (2014a). *Products for low vision, blindness, and learning disabilities from Freedom Scientific*. Retrieved March 10, 2014, from http://www.freedomscientific.com/default.asp

Freedom Scientific, Inc. (2014b). *JAWS Screen Reading Software by Freedom Scientific*. Retrieved March 10, 2014, from http://www.freedomscientific.com/products/fs/jaws-product-page.asp

Friends of Europe. (n.d.). *Friends of Europe | Home*. Retrieved March 10, 2014, from http://www.friendsofeurope.org/Home/tabid/1124/Default.aspx

Fundacion, O. N. C. E. (n.d.a). *Miguel Carballeda Piñeiro - Prologues - CSR-D Guie corporate social responsibility and disability of Fundación ONCE*. Retrieved March 10, 2014, from http://rsed.fundaciononce.es/en/prologos.html

Fundacion, O. N. C. E. (n.d.b). *Portada - Fundación Once*. Retrieved March 10, 2014, from http://www.fundaciononce.es/EN/Pages/Portada.aspx

Gallaudet University. (1998). *Jobs and Careers of Deaf and Hard of Hearing People*. Retrieved March 10, 2014, from http://www.gallaudet.edu/clerc_center/information_and_resources/info_to_go/transition_to_adulthood/working_and_careers/jobs_and_careers_of_dhoh_ppl.html

Great Britain Equality and Human Rights Commission. (2011). *Equality Act 2010: Summary guidance on employment*. Retrieved from http://www.equalityhumanrights.com/uploaded_files/EqualityAct/ea_employment_summary_guidance.pdf

Great Britain National Audit Office. (2007). *Government on the internet: Progress in delivering information and services online*. Retrieved from http://www.nao.org.uk/report/government-on-the-internet-progress-in-delivering-information-and-services-online/

Greve, B. (2009). *The labour market situation of disabled people in European countries and implementation of employment policies: a summary of evidence from country reports and research studies*. Retrieved from http://www.disability-europe.net/content/aned/media/ANED%20Task%206%20final%20report%20-%20final%20version%2017-04-09.pdf

Groce, N. E. (2004). *Adolescents and youth with disability: issues and challenges*. Asia Pacific Disability Rehabilitation Journal.

Gus Communication Devices Inc. (2012). *Gus Communications Devices-Name brand speech aids at discounted prices*. Retrieved March 10, 2014, from http://www.gusinc.com/2012/Home.html

Gus Communication Devices, Inc. (n.d.). *Computer Access*. Retrieved March 10, 2014, from http://www.gusinc.com/2012/Computer_Access.html

Harbor, B. (2008, September 18). *Whirlpool Brand Business Grant Recognizes Innovative Moms | FinancialContent Business Page*. Retrieved March 10, 2014, from http://markets.financialcontent.com/stocks/news/read?GUID=6604909&ChannelID=3197

Inspiration Software, Inc. (2014a). *WebspirationPRO | inspiration.com*. Retrieved March 10, 2014, from http://www.inspiration.com/WebspirationPRO

Inspiration Software, Inc. (2014b). *Inspiration Software, Inc. - The Leader in Visual Thinking and Learning | inspiration.com*. Retrieved March 10, 2014, from http://www.inspiration.com/

Jobaccess.co.za. (2012). *People With Disabilities, Disabled People, Disbility, People With Disabilities, Jobs, PWD, Search Hundreds Of Jobs Within The South Africa*. Retrieved March 10, 2014, from http://www.jobaccess.co.za/

Jones, M. K., Latreille, P. L., & Sloane, P. J. (2006). *Disability, gender, and the British labour market*. Oxford Economic Papers-new Series.

Keese, M. (2006). *Live longer, work longer*. Retrieved from http://www.oecd.org/employment/livelongerworklonger.htm

Kumaran, U. (2011, April 1). *India's first call centre for the disabled launched in Chembur | Latest News & Updates at DNAIndia.com*. Retrieved March 10, 2014, from http://www.dnaindia.com/mumbai/report-india-s-first-call-centre-for-the-disabled-launched-in-chembur-1526860

Kurzweil. (n.d.a). *Kurzweil 1000 | Assistive Technology for Vision Impaired*. Retrieved March 10, 2014, from http://www.kurzweiledu.com/kurzweil-1000-v12-windows.html

Kurzweil. (n.d.b). *Kurzweil 3000: Kurzweil Educational Systems*. Retrieved March 10, 2014, from http://www.kurzweiledu.com/products/k3000-win.html

Kurzweil. (n.d.c). *Text to Speech, Literacy Software | Kurzweil Educational Systems*. Retrieved March 10, 2014, from http://www.kurzweiledu.com/default.html

Mentoring Network for Equal Employment Opportunities. (2009). *M-NET EOP - what is m-net-eop*. Retrieved March 10, 2014, from http://www.mneteop.eu/

Microsoft. (2008). *Happy Disabled Call Center by the Foundation for Disabled People*. Retrieved from http://download.microsoft.com/download/4/2/5/42519e83-2902-4041-bc5f-0bc-7ca51b8e9/fiziksel_engelliler_vakfi_-_turkey.pdf

Microsoft. (2014). *The Business Value of Accessible Technology*. Retrieved March 10, 2014, from http://www.microsoft.com/enable/business/value.aspx

Mogul Mom. (2014). *The Mogul Mom | For moms running a business, raising a family and rocking both*. Retrieved March 10, 2014, from www.themogulmom.com/

Mom Invented. (2014). *Mom Invented: Business Advice & Inventing Help for Women Entrepreneurs*. Retrieved March 10, 2014, from http://www.mominventors.com/

Nurse Next Door. (2011). *Growing Carepreneurs: 2011 Annual Conference*. Retrieved March 10, 2014, from https://www.facebook.com/media/set/?set=a.10150375808544668.373474.92317029667&type=3

Nurse Next Door Home Care Franchise. (2014). *Nurse Next Door Home Care Franchise? Home Health Care Franchising Opportunity*. Retrieved March 10, 2014, from http://www.nursenextdoor-franchise.com/

Organisation for Economic Co-operation and Development. (2006). *Sickness, disability, and work: Breaking the barriers*. Retrieved from http://www.oecd-ilibrary.org/social-issues-migration-health/sickness-disability-and-work-breaking-the-barriers_9789264088856-en

Organisation for Economic Co-operation and Development. (2012). *Sick on the job? A myths and realities about mental health and work*. Retrieved from http://www.oecd-ilibrary.org/social-issues-migration-health/mental-health-and-work_9789264124523-en

Origin Instruments Corporation. (2011). *HeadMouse® Extreme [HM-0204-SP]: Shop at Origin Instruments*. Retrieved March 10, 2014, from http://shop.orin.com/shop/index.php?main_page=product_info&products_id=1

Origin Instruments Corporation. (2013). *Sip/Puff Switch*. Retrieved March 10, 2014, from http://www.orin.com/access/sip_puff/

Origin Instruments Corporation. (2014). *Origin Instruments Corporation*. Retrieved March 10, 2014, from http://www.orin.com/

Philadelphia, D. (2008, September 15). *Business school retrains disabled Iraq veterans - Sep. 15, 2008*. Retrieved March 10, 2014, from http://money.cnn.com/2008/09/11/smallbusiness/bschool_to_iraq.fsb/index.htm

Rains, S. (2011, April 26). *Notes from the First-ever International Blind Architects Conference - Part 1 - Rolling Rains Report*. Retrieved March 10, 2014, from http://www.rollingrains.com/2011/04/notes-from-the-first-ever-international-blind-architects-conference.html

Reemploy. (2014). *Remploy | Home*. Retrieved March 10, 2014, from http://www.remploy.co.uk/

Riverdocs Bureau Service. (2011). *Corporate Intranets - web accessibility legal briefs - from Outlaw.com*. Retrieved March 10, 2014, from http://riverdocs.com/accessibility/legal/corporate_intranets.html

School of Piano Technology for the Blind. (2014). *Careers for the Blind and Visually Impaired*. Retrieved March 10, 2014, from http://pianotuningschool.org/

Sloan, K. (2010, October 11). *Wisconsin judge overcomes hearing impairment | National Law Journal*. Retrieved March 10, 2013, from http://www.nationallawjournal.com/id=1202473099157?slreturn=20140210140521

Soares, C. (2007, November 23). *Move over Poirot: Belgium recruits blind detectives to help fight crime - Europe - World - The Independent*. Retrieved March 10, 2014, from http://www.independent.co.uk/news/world/europe/move-over-poirot-belgium-recruits-blind-detectives-to-help-fight-crime-760087.html

Speech, F. X. Inc. (2013). *SpeechFX Inc Home Page*. Retrieved March 10, 2014, from http://www.speechfxinc.com/

Steph. (2010, April 5). *12 Ingenious Gadgets & Technologies Designed for the Blind | Urbanist*. Retrieved March 10, 2014, from http://weburbanist.com/2010/04/05/12-ingenious-gadgets-technologies-for-the-blind/

Telesensory. (2008a). *Genie Pro: Description*. Retrieved March 10, 2014, from http://www.telesensory.com/product.aspx?category=desktop&id=11

Telesensory. (2008b). *Telesensory Video Magnifiers help people with Low Vision read again*. Retrieved March 10, 2014, from http://www.telesensory.com/

Think Beyond the Label. (2012). *Think Beyond the Label | Evolve Your Workforce*. Retrieved March 10, 2014, from http://www.thinkbeyondthelabel.com/

Travability Pty Ltd. (2013). *Changing the demand drivers for the provision of products and services in Inclusive Tourism: The Why and How*. Retrieved March 10, 2014, from http://travability.travel/papers/occasional_4.html

UK Government Digital Service. (2013, November 8). *Disability rights - GOV.UK*. Retrieved March 10, 2014, from https://www.gov.uk/rights-disabled-person/education-rights

US Small Business Administration. (n.d.). *SBA.gov*. Retrieved March 10, 2014, from http://www.sba.gov/community/blogs/community-blogs/small-business-matters/disabled-entrepreneurs-resources-and-tips-highly-successful-business-grou

Verdonschot, M. M., Witte, L. P., Reichrath, E., Buntinx, W. H., & Curfs, L. M. (2009). Community participation of people with an intellectual disability: a review of empirical findings. *Journal of Intellectual Disability Research*. doi: doi:10.1111/j.1365-2788.2008.01144.x PMID:19087215

Virginia Commonwealth University. (2013, July 12). *VCU WorkSupport*. Retrieved March 10, 2014, from http://www.worksupport.com/resources/viewContent.cfm/295

World Health Organization. World Bank. (2011). *World report on disability*. Retrieved from World Health Organization website: http://whqlibdoc.who.int/publications/2011/9789240685215_eng.pdf

Yachol call. (n.d.). Retrieved March 10, 2014, from http://www.callyachol.co.il/eng/

Zoomtext. (2014a). *Willkommen bei Zoomtext*. Retrieved March 10, 2014, from http://www.zoomtext.de/

Zoomtext. (2014b). *ZoomText Magnifier/Reader 10 Bildschirmvergrößerung*. Retrieved March 10, 2014, from http://www.zoomtext.de/produkte/zt/ztms/index.html

KEY TERMS AND DEFINITIONS

Ageing Population: Population ageing is a phenomenon that occurs when the median age of a country or region rises due to rising life expectancy and/or declining birth rates.

Assistive Technologies: Assistive Technology is an umbrella term that includes assistive, adaptive, and rehabilitative devices for people with disabilities and also includes the process used in selecting, locating, and using them.

Bring Your Own Device: a trend of employees bringing and using their own devices to work environments.

Disability Acts: A legal document describing legal rights of persons with disabilities.

Disability Policies: policies about persons with disabilities.

Employability: set of achievements – skills, understandings and personal attributes – that make graduates more likely to gain employment and be successful in their chosen occupations, which benefits themselves, the workforce, the community and the economy.

Employment: The state of being employed.

Entrepreneurship: the state, quality, or condition of being an entrepreneur, an organizer or promoter of business ventures.

Job Mentoring: Mentoring is to support and encourage people to manage their own learning in order that they may maximise their potential, develop their skills, improve their performance and become the person they want to be.

Unemployment: The state of being unemployed, especially involuntarily.

ENDNOTES

[1]   Question asked: Does this person have serious difficulty walking or climbing stairs?

[2]   Question asked: Because of a physical, mental, or emotional condition, does this person have serious difficulty concentrating, remembering, or making decisions?

[3]   Question asked: Does this person have difficulty dressing or bathing?

[4]   Question asked: Because of a physical, mental, or emotional condition, does this person have difficulty doing errands alone such as visiting a doctor's office or shopping?

[5]   Thornicroft G. Shunned: discrimination against people with mental illness. London, Oxford University Press, 2006.

[6]   Australia, Canada, Denmark, Finland, Ireland, Luxembourg, the Netherlands, Norway, Poland, Spain, Sweden, Switzerland and the United Kingdom.

Chapter 10
Consumer and Lifestyle

ABSTRACT

Consuming is an important aspect of our lives. It is part of our lifestyle. People with disabilities and the elderly, however, face problems in everyday transactions in shops, ATMs, vending machines, etc. This chapter focuses on presenting the potential technological applications and suggested policies that might help to overcome many of those problems. Issues and technologies related with the shopping experience, consuming services, using ATMs and vending machines, and also related lifestyle trends that might affect accessibility are presented and analyzed in order to provide the reader with the big picture on how accessibility solutions could become mainstream and used by greater audiences.

THE SHOPPING EXPERIENCE

Shopping in large stores may these be super markets, utility stores, toy stores etc. is an experience with many similarities across the areas. People when entering such a store select a trolley or some kind of basket to collect their products to buy. They browse through large aisles tagged with large signs categorizing products under specific categories. While browsing them, they may use a shopping list or just grab whatever attracts their attention and they need drop it to the trolley or basket and continue. In other cases they might stand in front of shelves with similar products from different brands and compare prices, product characteristics displayed in labels in order to decide whether to buy or not each product. In some cases they might also grab a product, examine its package, physical properties, information on the

package etc. in order to decide buying it or not. Finally they usually exit the shop after paying in cash or using credit cards in a cashier.

The Smart Shelves

The picture described was a usual and familiar in the past and may still be like this in many cases. However there are already signs and evidence of that process changing though the introduction of new technologies and ICT. ShelfX (ShelfX, 2013) is a company based in US providing customers with solutions on inventory management. Their products included systems such as ShelfX Smart Shelves, the ShelfX Software and Server platform, the ShelfX Cards and Kiosks and the ShelfX App that combine to form a self-checkout solution for retailers worldwide. Their latest product, ShelfX Smart Shelves is using NFC and

DOI: 10.4018/978-1-4666-6130-1.ch010

RFID technologies in order to provide customers with information about products while they are browsing a large grocery stores, big box store, super market etc. When approaching a shelf the customer equipped with an NFC enabled phone or a specific loyalty card, the shelf and its products can greet him in person and provide with all available information for the customer. By lifting up the product, the amount can be automatically added on the checkout and the store's inventory can be updated appropriately. Similar inventory management solutions provided by other companies such Imagine Retail (Imagine Retail, 2011) or Analytica (Analytica, n.d.) are mainly focused on inventory control and facilitating the retailer. However, as more NFC and RFID sensors will be included in mobile phones such businesses will start to think about the customer too.

In France, a Supermarket called "Groupe Casino"(Groupe Casino, n.d.) has already started testing a NFC based system that allows customers with visual impairments and elderly to scan and read in larger fonts product details through their phone. As RFID journal (Swedberg, 2011) describes in their article the systems tested is just a start for series of applications that can be introduced later. As pointed out in the article, Thibault de Pompery, the creative director of Groupe Casino's innovation department says that "*What's interesting is that everything can be done on a single device*". This means that such solutions could potentially help a lot more customers, including visually disabled that can now learn more about a particular product and make purchases. According to Tim Baker, Think&Go's NFC marketing director "*The technology may provide other options as well, such as enabling a company like Casino to set up a store containing very little product, with shelves stocked simply with empty packaging fitted with RFID labels. At such sites, shoppers could select the items they would like to purchase and then have them delivered, or can pick them up at a separate drive-through location. Such solutions might be popular for*

customers without cars, he notes, or those living in city centers, far from the supermarkets more typically located in suburbs"

In the future NFC enabled mobile phones could also carry profile information about their owner. Combine that with tagging products with accessibility related information such as if it is appropriate or operable by persons with specific disabilities, which kinds of disabilities might it provide assistance to, etc. and you could get a much richer, easier and enjoyable shelf browsing experience for persons with disabilities. What is needed to achieve such a state is the development of appropriate profiling schemas to describe the capabilities of a person and the appropriate schemas to describe products accessibility compliance information. That may sound easy but in order to be successful it has to be implemented in a wide range. We cannot expect competitors in the area to come up with the same idea when providing profiling schemas for such a vague and complex matter. There will definitely be a bunch of different solutions that might lead to nuisance for users such as having to use a specific mobile app for each store which would have to keep your profile information but in a different format. In the end of the day end-users might be confronted with such a redundancy of apps and profiling information in their mobiles that they will stop using them all.

Shopping Baskets

Shopping experience continues by collecting products that the customer needs in a shopping basket. Technologies of RFID and NFC are already tried out in some stores in order to make the shopping basket a smarter item in the shopping experience. In Spain the Tomas Morcillio Industrials company is already producing plastic trolleys named "Polycart" (Industrias Tomás Morcillo, S.L., 2014) that can be used for automatic scanning of RFID tags of the products inside the trolley. Such trolleys could be used in stores to implement unattended stores such as the ones described by Athul Rathore and Raul Valverde in their paper "An RFID based E-commerce solution for the implementation of secure unattended stores" (Rathore & Valverde, 2011).

Being able though to connect your mobile device with your shopping basket in a store, could provide a whole range of new applications useful for every customer. Imagine getting into a store and taking a Bluetooth-enabled shopping basket with an RFID scanner. You then connect it with your mobile device where an application has stored your shopping list. Each item picked up and placed in the basket would be automatically checked-off your list. This shopping list application could also be connected with the browsing app presented earlier so that it could filter out and give you information when you are crossing shelves with products in your shopping list. A person for example with visual impairments could get into such a store, get a smart shopping basket and connect it to his/her mobile device. While browsing through the supermarket's aisles the mobile device would recognize what products are around. Thus, when the person crosses the aisle with dairy products the application could inform him/her that: "You are near the dairy products shelves. According to your shopping list you need 2 bottles of milk that you can find in about 3 meters."

It is necessary at this point to make clear that by the term mobile device we now tend to mean a mobile phone. However, the same application running now on a mobile phone could generally be available to other devices we will carry with us tomorrow. It could be a personal robot or a wearable device such as a pair of glasses. The device is not what is important in the use case described. The key point for the success of such a system is to provide means and standards for the communication between different applications, sensors, and devices. So developers of applications, sensors or devices in the future will have to think that if they want their product to be successful it should be able to cooperate and communicate with the largest possible number of other components.

Our Next Generation Wallets

After filling up their basket, customers are going through the checkouts where the paying process takes place either in cash or using a credit card. In many cases stores are also issuing loyalty cards to customers giving them special offers in exchange of the information they are providing when using the card. The latest trend in payment is mobile payment. Major players in the mobile computing domain have shown interest in the area of mobile payments with Google entering the competition by introducing Google wallet (Google, 2014a). According to Google, their vision is that Google wallet will "*eventually hold many if not all of the cards you keep in your leather wallet today.*" Meaning that "*Eventually your loyalty cards, gift cards, receipts, boarding passes, tickets, even your keys will be seamlessly synced to your Google Wallet. And every offer and loyalty point will be redeemed automatically with a single tap via NFC.*" Google wallet is based on NFC and requires a phone with a NFC sensor. However, using it is such a simple process as the only thing needed is a tap of your mobile phone in the respective machine.

On the other hand, in the US another company called Square (Square, 2014a) has already introduced mobile payments some time ago and now reached the level of processing $4 Million each day (Rao, 2011b). They have already shipped 500.000 card readers to shops (Rao, 2011a) and lately they introduced a new app called the "Card case" (Square, 2014b). With that customers of specific shops can open tabs on them to charge their purchases. So when going to the checkout the customer just says on which account they have to charge the purchase and it's done! In addition, stores, shops, cafes, etc. can know when a customer is on their shop and treat him with offers according to his previous purchases.

The trend of mobile payments is escalating to a war between these two companies and the aspects of the war are well explained in the infographic presented in the article of Australian Anthill (Murray, 2011). In any case, such a competition can lead to better services for customers. However, how could this trend benefit disabled or impaired customers of stores?

The fact of being able to pay with a single tap of your phone or by telling your name to the checkout is already making the process a lot easier. Combined with solutions already presented earlier such as the smart shopping basket and the shopping list app in a mobile phone it could lead to being able to checkout from a store simply by passing through the exit doors.

However, although the simplification of the payment process is a large step towards accessibility, the even bigger benefit for persons with cognitive impairments and older people can come from the adaptations of such an application according to the user's profile. Smart wallet apps combined with personalization features could evolve in some kind of financial guardian angels for people with cognitive disabilities, dementia, forgetfulness, etc. They could inform such persons of their previous purchases, their needs, and help them complete a shopping process without the dangers of buying redundant products, spending more than they can afford according to their income, being tricked in the checkout, etc. A possible picture of the future might be an 80 year old person with dementia going to the supermarket and while browsing the shelves and picking up stuff the mobile phone would advise him: "You probably don't need another bottle of orange juice. You already bought a six-pack 2 days ago from the convenient store next to your home. I think you might need some apples though because last time you bought was 2 weeks ago and you have them in your list."

It is worth to research privacy issues raised by the combination of mobile payment apps with the accessibility profiling, and also explore its implications, i.e. whether it is possible that mobile payment apps will provide their data to platforms for other applications and how can current legislation handle such issues, what new legislation is needed to cover those aspects etc.

Finally, it is highly important to investigate technologies and applications that can make mobile payments safer for persons with disabilities (voice recognition, fingerprint recognition, retina recognition, etc.).

Shopping in Between...

Shopping in stores of the future might also evolve in other directions too. Tesco (Tesco, 2014), one of the largest supermarket chains in UK, has already conducted tests in Korea though the Home Plus (Home Plus, n.d.) supermarket chain that they own per 95%. They displayed large grocery store shelve pictures in billboards in metro stations. Products on the display where tagged with QRCodes that customers could scan and include them in their shopping baskets. Finishing their shopping they could place an order to the supermarket through the internet and arrange its delivery wherever they wanted (home, work, etc.). According to NFCWorld (Clark, 2011) "*10,287 consumers visited the online Home Plus mall during the visit, the number of newly registered online shoppers increased by 76% and sales increased by 130%.*" This shows that shopping of the future might not even take place in stores. People could use such kind of solutions to do their shopping while on the go to their work and arrange for delivery at home when they return.

Advertisement billboards, windows in transportation media, walls in metro stations and any other kind of surface or place could potentially become a representation of a store offering the convenience of shopping while on the go through augmented reality. Looking this kind of trend from the accessibility perspective we understand that all this peripheral information and opportunities in the augmented world might not be accessible or might cause other problems for persons with disabilities. For example, a blind person could miss the information that there is a virtual grocery shop in the wall of the metro station. A person with cognitive disabilities, dementia, forgetfulness etc. might use this kind of shops more than needed or might confuse the products displayed (since they will not be able to feel them in other ways) and order redundant products.

On the other hand, augmented reality today can be triggered and based on a variety of technologies such as GPS, NFC, RFID, QRCodes etc. This means that in the future the potential amount of information available around us in the augmented reality world might become overwhelming, confusing and even annoying under certain circumstances. This confusion and annoyance can be even stronger for persons with disabilities. Thus, a filtering of that information is necessary in order to make it useful for them. Devices such as mobile phones, personal robots etc. which contain a variety of sensors and will probably be able to store profiling information for their owner, could be used as platforms for the development of smart applications able to realize the context where the user is and filter accordingly the information flow. For example, if the phone knows the weather conditions are good on a sunny Sunday and its blind owner is strolling along the city streets it could understand that it is appropriate to inform him of surrounding wall stores, advertisements and general information that he might need. On the contrary, the next morning when the same person will be hurrying down the metro station 10 minutes before having to be in his work it will probably cut off any unnecessary peripheral information.

Research is needed for exploring the potential of synergies, combination and interoperability of technologies such as RFID, NFC and GPS to be combined in applications that will provide seamless surrounding information control.

Social Shopping

Social media have also intruded the shopping experience a lot. Social shopping is a trend with many different views and aspects. One of them is the daily deals trend. Sites like Groupon (Groupon, n.d.) and LivingSocial (Living Social Inc., 2014) are considered as social shopping sites because they bring out deals that have to reach a certain number of buyers to be valid. Thus, people buying from such sites tend to share their purchases from the site to spread the word and get the offer. The trend apparently attracted major players in the area and Google has recently announced the launch of Google Offers (Google, 2014b), Facebook also introduced Facebook Deals (Fougner, 2011)and Microsoft collaborated with The DealMap (PR Newswire, 2011)to bring similar offers to Bing.

However, these developments also mixed the social shopping trend with the trend of mobile computing. Instead of looking for deals while you browse the web, applications such the Facebook app for mobile devices (iPhone, Android, Windows Phone) is integrated with Facebook Deals when a user is using Facebook Places to sign in to specific locations. Similarly Google Offers also introduced a mobile device app_(Patel, 2011), while companies such as Facebook, Google and Microsoft are already battling at the social media field with respective web applications and getting involved in the social shopping trend shows its importance for businesses and its potentials.

Apart from the deals aspect in social shopping there is also another significant trend involving mobiles, social media and shopping. The fact that people can share their shopping experience as it happens through their mobile phones, leave comments on a store's web site about their process, staff's behavior, what they tried and liked, what they bought etc. According to a recent study of ListenLogic_(Perry, 2009) 25% of shopping conversations taking place online happen while customers are in the store. It shows that the whole idea of going to the shops with friends is transferring to another level. People are sharing their shopping experience almost real-time and they can have almost real time feedback and conversations on that. Actually, just a few months ago a new web site (Bryne, 2011) called Shop-WithYourFriends (SWYF, 2014) introduced the idea of real-time co-shopping online. Visitors of ShopWithYourFriends (SWYF, 2014)can invite their friends from social media such as Facebook and Twitter to share a common shopping space where they can place suggestions, mix and match clothes and discuss choices online. It's almost like going to the shops with friends but without being collocated this time.

The idea could go even further and in the future we definitely expect such applications to come into mobiles. More applications like the Select2gether (Marketwire, 2011)will appear allowing groups of friends to virtually go shopping in various places at the same time and discuss and exchange information during that process. A picture of the future could be a group of girls in their twenties arranging meetings for shopping but without being at the same place. Instead they just log on to a specific web-site or mobile app at that time and while wondering, trying and buying things they could share photos, videos, product information etc. and exchange opinions helping each other to decide.

This kind of social real time shopping applications can prove really helpful in cases of persons with disabilities too. They could have this way a real-time advice from friends on what to buy and probably they could also have real-time advice and information exchange about products and their accessibility with friends having similar disabilities or impairments with them. Thus the latter picture could also be that of a blind person walking on a shopping mall alone and buying clothes, based on his friends' opinions on the mobile app. Similarly a person with hearing impairments could walk into an electric appliances store and choose his new TV set based on guidance and advice from

friends in the "People with hearing impairments" Facebook group. No need to mention that persons with agoraphobia or depression can be vastly helped to overcome their problems and deal with the difficulties of the shopping experience.

Virtual Reality Shops and the Lessons from Online Shops

Shopping together without being collocated can also be a feature of future virtual reality shopping malls. There are already a bunch of libraries widely used such as OpenGL_(Khronos Group, 2014), Direct3D_(Microsoft, 2006), Java3D (Oracle, 2013) and VRML (Bell, Parisi, & Pesce, 1996) for rendering 3D virtual reality scenes. In addition, major companies in the ICT industry such as Sony are investing on virtual reality gear such as the new head mounted display by Sony introduced lately (Shapiro, 2011). HMZ-T1 (Hollister, 2011) as it is called, costs 799,99$ and is able to display 2D and 3D immersive scenes. The small screens in the device are equivalent of having your very own 150 inch movie screen only twelve feet away. It also a built-in virtual 5.1 surround sound headphones which can simulate a movie theatre's surround sound. Similar devices have also been presented by other manufacturers such as the WRAP1200 by Vuzix and the ST1080 by SiliconMicroDisplay (Silicon Micro Display, 2012).

The devices presented earlier are mainly used for output of virtual reality scenes. However, a complete virtual reality system must also use some kind of input devices beyond the traditional keyboard and mouse. Advances in that area can be seen by Microsoft which presented Kinect (Microsoft, 2014), a camera based device which can recognize body movements, gestures and faces and provide an interaction with an Xbox_(Microsoft, 2014) device through them. Microsoft also released an API for developers in order to take advantage of Kinect's potentials by developing their own applications. From then on there's been a variety of applications coming from various developers allowing people to control and interact with their computers through movements and gestures. In August, Apple has also filed a patent (Pachal, 2011)for a similar system allowing users to control their devices through movements showing that motion control of devices is a possible emerging trend of the future. Going some steps further in that direction some months ago, Gallotti, Raposo & Soares (2011) presented in a research paper a virtual reality glove (v-Glove) able to simulate touch through haptic feedback.

Having seen the latest developments in virtual reality gear and related software libraries, one can see that the future might see a wider spread of virtual reality interfaces in various aspects of life, shopping being one of them. Virtual reality shops and shopping malls are around for some years now and Trillenium (Trillenium d.o.o., 2012) is just an example of them. People can go in such virtual reality shopping malls from the comfort of their office by logging in the site and find their friends, go for shopping or even hang around to socialize.

The developments in virtual reality devices might bring such experiences more close to virtual reality experiences seen in science fiction movies. People wearing their head mounted displays and virtual reality gloves sitting in front of their computer camera and virtually walking around in shopping centers.

This picture however might seem as an opportunity for some people and as a nightmare for other. For example, a person with mobility impairment might find in such a solution a very pleasant and enjoyable shopping experience. On the other hand, if virtual reality shopping malls are developed in a visual-dependent way not enhancing alternative representations of their environment they might become a problem for people with visual impairments. Even in their current state, head mounted displays are difficult to be used by people wearing glasses.

With the right provision though (i.e. including textual alternatives for objects or places, including

sound signals for specific actions etc.) a walk in a virtual reality shopping mall might become a pleasurable experience for blind persons as well. Moreover, it might also provide opportunities for even richer and better experience through devices such as VR gloves with haptic feedback. In that case a blind person visiting a VR automobile shop with his family could possibly feel the shape of vehicles, explore their interior design etc. without leaving his chair.

The situation might remind the current status of web accessibility. Current web technologies allow for web sites to be built in ways that are usable and accessible by the widest range of user's possible. However the long history of its evolution which did not pay the appropriate attention to accessibility made it both and dream and a nightmare for persons with disabilities. It is possible to get in to the most remote store and shop in the world and find the products you want to buy while at the same time it might be close to impossible to read the web page from the shop in your neighbor.

Virtual Reality due to its multi-modality of interaction with the user is a field of research where either big steps or big pitfalls may arise for eAccessibility. It is an area worth spending some attention for the future however it certainly needs some guidance and provision in order to avoid the pitfalls. If we are going to build a virtual reality world for the future then certain lessons from the trajectory of other technologies such as the web will be useful for eAccessibility. The problems of web accessibility today might become the problems of the virtual reality of the future if the right provision and attention is not paid.

It is worth to explore the various metaphors for representing virtual and augmented reality concepts, entities and properties, as well as to investigate the applicability of interaction techniques used in the real world and how these can be represented in the virtual one.

CONSUMING SERVICES

Consuming doesn't always involve shopping for goods in stores. People are also consuming when they buy and use a service, such as going to a bar for a drink, going to a restaurant for food or even going to the bank to make a deposit. Services may also be involved within the shopping process of products described earlier. Many shops provide services for delivery of products at home, services in cases of changing a bought product or returning one, services for after sales support for their product etc.

People with disabilities need to be able to use these services as everybody else. However, that is not always the case. Starting from the food and beverage services provided in various places a common picture in many places is for persons with disabilities to enter and leave the place the same time because they recognize that the place is not accessible. Very often, such places don't have wheelchair access for persons with mobility impairments. In other cases, the staff working in such places might not behave properly in assisting and servicing the person with disability. For example, a blind person enters a restaurant and sits on a table. The waiter goes to him and realizing that he is blind offers to read the menu to him and explain whatever questions he has. After several minutes the waiter gets the order and goes back to the kitchen. When the order is ready the waiter goes as usual with his disk on the table, places the plates with the main course and salad and the glass of wine in front of him and leaves the table as in any other case. However, the waiter could help the person even more by staying and explaining where each plate and glass is placed on the table. Even more he could have also described how various food elements are arranged in the plate (i.e. the steak is on the right and the potatoes on the left of the plate in front of you).

In such cases it is the lack of training and experience in similar situations that leads to such mistreatments and awkward behaviors. So the question is how can such training and education be provided when needed? How can the waiter in the previous example know beforehand how to behave in such a case? The simplest answer is through trial and error. If the blind person visits the restaurant every week and he serves him every week then inevitably he will learn how to treat him. But this not always the case. Some people might be offended, other might be too shy to ask for extra help, and many might not come back to the place (at least not alone). On the other hand, the personnel working in such jobs are quite often temporary and even when they learn from such experience they might move to another job after that. Thus it is quite optimistic to hope that in 10 years' time every person working in the services sector will be educated properly on how to behave to persons with disabilities. This scenario also falls under the education and training cluster where it is elaborated even more.

Tagging Places

One of the solutions for the problem described might come from what was also described earlier by using augmented reality technologies that will work in combination with mobile devices that keep their users' profile. As already described earlier items of the real world might be tagged with extra information for people that want to use them through their mobile devices (or any other AR device).

This tagging could also include places that provide services such as bars, restaurants, hotels, banks, etc. So why not tag a place with accessibility related information? For example a bar's profile on FourSquare (Foursquare, 2014), Google places (Google, 2014c), or Facebook locations (Facebook, 2014) might be enriched with accessibility related information such as if it provides wheelchair access, or how their personnel are behaving towards persons with disabilities. Such information could be helpful in case a person with a disability wants to decide whether to visit or not a place. Even better, if the mobile device knows the person's profile and requirements it could also provide suggestions of places where the person could go based on his profile and the place's accessibility profile.

The even bigger benefit however could become by having specific machine understandable languages to describe this kind of information similar to what we do today with books and Dublin Core ontology. An ontology or a set of ontologies describing specific accessibility features and the limitations of specific disabilities could also be described and connected with specific accessibility features. This kind of common maybe standardized description for disabilities and features of the real world that relate to them could lead to a realm of applications not only for places but for any kind of product or service is available to people.

Presence Technologies in Service Consumption

People are used to using presence technologies in chat or telecommunication programs on their computers. Almost every user of Skype, MSN Messenger and other similar tools know how to change their online status from online to offline, away, invisible etc. This kind of battles allows other people to know whether the person is sitting on the computer or not. Similarly, nowadays mobile phone applications such as Foursquare, Google Places or Facebook Places allow users to sign in various places announcing their presence there. In order for this to happen, people need to be connected to the Internet through their mobile devices and use the appropriate application. These presence technologies also allow the personnel in the respective places to know when a person is on its place.

However, there are also a number of technologies available that would make these signing in places automatic and without requiring Internet connectivity. Announcing that the person signed in a restaurant and having the person's profile on

the mobile device could allow the personnel on the restaurant to know beforehand the person's needs and adapt their behavior accordingly. In that direction, the software running at the restaurant would provide the waiter with specific advice on how to serve the specific customer.

So, in the previous example of a blind person entering a restaurant, when the person sits on the table, he/she leaves his mobile phone on top of the specific device and communicates in the restaurants software his profile. The waiter sees a modification on the software and planning at the checkout desk and this is information on how to serve a specific person. For example, the software might inform the way that that he needs to explain to the blind person where each plate is placed on the table and how the food is put on the plate. In the case of an elderly person with forgetfulness, entering the same restaurant the phone might communicate to the restaurant specific foods that are not allowed to him due to his diet. In that case, if the person orders something that is not allowed to eat the waiter might remind and explain to him that this might cause problems for his health and provide alternatives.

Personal Assistance Robots in Consuming Services

The case of advanced ATM systems developed by ICICI in India, shows that alternative means of interacting with ATM systems are also attractive, useful and even necessary alternatives, for non-disabled users, especially for those occasionally faced with situational disabilities due to problems of language, culture or level of digital literacy.

Apart from decision support services and adapting services according to user needs, another interesting technology emerging in the area of services has to do with robotics. Currently, there are a number of cases where robots are used to serve people in specific situations. As already referred in the first section a company based in South Korea named KIST (KIST, n.d.) has led the development of a humanoid teaching robot (Mangu-Ward, 2011) called Erki_(Plasticpals, 2010), which has been under trial for about a year now as an assistant in primary school teaching. Using robots as assistants in public places can be quite challenging. There are a number of issues to take under account apart from the interface and the communication of the robot with humans. For example, how will the robot operate in a situation where a group of students try to vandalize it, what happens when a part of the robot breaks down, how often and how long does it need to be recharged?

Apart from practical matters need to be addressed in such use of robots there are also a number of other issues on how people can accept robots as assistants in their everyday life tasks. BBC in an article about the problems of deploying robots as assistants in Japan focuses on some very important issues on the subject. One of them is the cost of such robots and to that direction last May, Willow Garage_(Willow Garage, 2014b), a California based maker of robot hardware and software, released a test version of its personal robot platform. PR2 (Willow Garage, 2014a) as this robot is called, has two arms, a variety of sensors, processors and a hard disk and comes for the price of 400.000$. The cost is obviously prohibitive for anyone to buy such a robot but the target for PR2 is to become a platform for testing a series of applications developed in different research centers. Samsung Electronics (Samsung, 2014) has already started using PR2 in their research for personal robots_(Schwartz, 2010). The Bosch Research and Technology Centre (Bosch, n.d.) have also begun a two-year project to enhance PR2 with even more sensors(Bosch, 2010) in order to improve its performance and reliability. Other institutes taking part in beta testing of PR2 (Willow Garage, 2010) and using it for research include Georgia Institute of Technology with the proposal "Assistive Mobile Manipulation for Older Adults at Home", MIT CSAIL with the proposal "Mobile Manipulation in Human-Centred Environments", Stanford University with the proposal

"STAIR on PR2", University of Pennsylvania with the proposal "PR2GRASP: From Perception and Reasoning to Grasping" and many more.

Having a common platform for developing all these applications by different institutes can lead to rapid innovation in robotics since the combination and integration of all these projects under a common platform adds significant value to the product itself. In addition, this added value also broadens the target group of persons that will potentially use such a robot which in turn can have significant impact on its cost. It also demonstrates a new way of innovation in robotics under common platforms that can be used for development of various applications.

The future might see robots like PR2 being able to adjust to various circumstances and being used for different purposes according to the software and the applications installed on them. Therefore a PR2 version with improved social skills software might be used easier in open environments such as hospitals, nursing houses, taking care of elderly, etc. Another version of PR2 with improved navigation software might also be used for guidance of blind persons in open environments. Connecting this kind of innovation with consuming and using services robots might become helpful assistants for persons with disabilities both in their close home environment and for open environments requiring more social and interpersonal skills. For example, in the case of the elderly person walking in the restaurant and ordering a course he is not allowed to eat, the robot might act as a friend would do in such a case. It could remind the person of his condition and doctor's advices about his diet and provide alternatives.

ATMS AND VENDING MACHINES

In September 2010, the European Journal of e-Practice published an article on the "Present and future of eAccessibility in public digital Terminals" (Torena et al., 2010) in which it compared approaches in Europe, the US, Canada and other countries to conclude that despite efforts at EU level, the current level of accessibility of ATMs and other self-service devices by people with disabilities was inadequate.

The study notes that where solutions exist they offer narrow or limited accessibility options. They are often highly tailored to specific devices or system. Their activation requires the use of arcane codes and protocols that are not generally known or available, that are hard to remember, and that are different from system to system. This is the result of a general lack of standards and interoperability solutions.

In the following paragraphs we try to present the most important issues, messages and possible evolutions for ATMs in the future in relation with accessibility

The Need for ATMs and the Predictions for Cash in the Future

ATMmarketplace.com,(Networld Media Group, 2014) in collaboration with the ATM Industry Association (ATM Industry Association, 2014), has just released the third edition of the ATM Future Trends Report 2012. The survey represents a cross-section of the financial services industry from banks, credit unions, EFT networks, transaction processors, ATM manufacturers and independent ATM deployers.

Amongst predictions and spotting of five-year trends, opportunities and challenges for the ATM industry, the survey recognizes that:

- Mobile technology will have the greatest impact on the global ATM industry. Mobile payment systems will be an additional and growing element of the overall ICT-enabled environment but interoperability, roaming charges, local monopolies will remain for a long time as barriers to adoption of these alternatives. However people with accessibility problems may be

lead users of such systems that will replace traditional ATMs in the years to come.

- Despite some extreme forecasts that foresaw a decline in the significance of ATMs (same as it happened in the computers with the – at least for the time – unmet prophecies of the disappearing computer), traditional ATM use might decline but will not disappear. We should not forget that one of the essential elements of the ATM is that it stocks bills (notes, paper money) and can both receive and deliver it; a smartphone or a tablet cannot do that - maybe with e-cash of some form but not of the type we are used to and expect to experience things for the next years to an horizon till 2020.

- Quite the opposite, cash is still the king and the expectation is that cash withdrawals will grow at a level of 8%, while as the only sure thing is the disappearing branches, there will be a strong increase in the number of ATMs, so there will be more ATM transactions per person and more cash in circulation.

On the whole, however, cash will not disappear any time soon as it is still needed by small shops because transaction charges of card companies are high, and also because most economies depend to an increasing extent on cash-intensive activities. It is still necessary when traveling so people will continue to need places where they can get cash and businesses will continue to need places where they can deposit it for many years to come and well beyond 2020. In the light of the above the accessibility of ATMs will still be an issue in 2020 so we still need to address it.

The vision of the disappearing ATM may be regarded as a vision that is set as the ultimate goal of several organizations' research agendas but neither the ICT industry nor the research community should bet on it.

The age of cashless transactions will start to leave its early adopters phase and aim to stabilize its position in the consumer markets – denoting, of course, not the end of money as much as the end of physical currency as we know it and the beginning of an economy of networked and intangible / immaterial payments.

Accessibility Conformance

March 15 of 2012 was the compliance day in the USA, where under the US federal law, ATMs must be ADA compliant by this date. Main points of the 2010 ADA compliance standards (Department of Justice, 2010)are the following:

- **Voice Guidance:** All ATMs must be speech enabled to service visually impaired consumers. Because speech output is considered by the ADA to be an auxiliary aid or service, implementation is required unless doing so would create an undue burden or expense.
- **Height and Reach:** To ensure consumers can easily access input controls, an ATM's reach must equal 48 inches.
- **Input Device:** Input device controls must be tactually discernible, which means key surfaces must be raised above surrounding surfaces to serve visually impaired consumers.
- **Numeric Keypads:** The ATM's keypad must be arranged in a twelve-key ascending layout, such as telephone keys, or descending, such as a computer number pad layout.
- **Function Keys:** Function keys must be designed to contrast visually from their background surfaces.
- **Display Screen:** For visibility from a point located 40 inches above the center of the floor in front of the ATM, characters on the screen must be in sans serif font, a minimum of 3/16 inch high, and contrast with their background.

- **Braille Instructions:** Braille instructions to initiate the voice guidance feature must also be provided.

However, it is interesting how the expanding functionality of ATMs is examined from the accessibility point of view: in the Advisory 220.1 it is stated, amongst others, that "*it is unacceptable for the accessible ATM only to provide cash withdrawals while inaccessible ATMs also sell theatre tickets*". So, the accessibility requirements are not defined with respect to some default idea about what an ATM used to do in the past, but also about it does for the mainstream categories of its users now, so that there is no space for creating or facilitating any type of exclusions.

The lesson to be learned here is that if the accessible ATM "solution" provided by the vendor is not "complete" it is not an acceptable solution. So while this may be seen as a weakness in compliance at the ATM machine manufacturer level, there are other levels of compliance needed at the vendor level: if the most advanced accessible ATM machine is offered by a manufacturer, but the vendor fails to have it placed in an accessible place then the result is lack of compliance. So it is an entire value chain that one should look at and not only part of the ATM design and manufacture processes.

Examples of Accessibility in ATMs

An encouraging element is that accessibility of ATMs has been at a great extent a European issue and the pioneering country in this seems to be Spain. More specifically:

- La Caixa (La Caixa, n.d.)is a caja with a long history of pioneering self-service and new technologies; it has introduced the highly successful 'Punt Groc' (yellow dot) ATMs which were launched in 2008 following three years of extensive research involving 2,000 interviews, focus groups and careful analysis of the interaction between the machines, customers and branch staff. All the features of the fascia, and the physical environment of the ATM were redesigned as a result, and both customers and non-customers are able to use the rich portfolio of lifestyle functionality such as bill payment or the selection and purchasing of tickets for events offered by the Punt Groc outlets.

- A more radical concept has been introduced recently by the Spanish banking group BBVA(Banco Bilbao Vizcaya Argentaria S.A., 2014). In early 2007 BBVA asked IDEO (IDEO, 2014) to re-think their self-service channel from scratch. The question was not how to further automate the teller, but rather how to humanize the machine. The result of that work is the vision for a totally new self-service experience: an ATM (IDEO, 2010)built from user up, rather than components down. In 2009 the first pilot units have been installed, while BBVA prepares to roll out the ATM across its Spanish branches. The system reduces the complexity of the interaction process between human and the ATM machine, while usability and good design are increasing the accessibility to groups that would not be inclined to use them.

Across Europe everything from ticket sales, vending machines and automated kiosks will be integrating wireless, cashless services (Hanlon, n.d.). With the click of a 3G/4G mobile phone consumers will shop without physical cash so payment will not be part of the interaction dialogue. Same as with the drag-and-drop (originally called 'click-and-drag') action that changed the way that users interacted with home and office computers, cashless transactions will inaugurate the time of direct manipulation in the retail and service business: people will only need to express their intention through a gesture, an eye-gaze, a thought or a hand-movement in order for a transaction to be completed. Such direct manipulation interfaces in the physical ("real") world will be increasing the accessibility chances for many different categories of users as there will be offered a plethora of access modalities that will help people use the various devices, equipment and machines.

ATMs increase their accessibility features and are facilitating interactions with groups that were facing increased difficulties in accessing their functionality: elderly people are finding an easier-to-use interface with no complicated interaction dialogues, even small children that want to reload their phone-cards using some prepaid credit card are capable to do so without needing to enter into a sophisticated interaction. Same also for wheelchair users that have been unable to access functions without asking for support from others.

The Cost Problems and Next Generation ATMs

The concern of increased costs for designing new, improved and more accessible ATMs is justified from the trends mentioned above: despite the proliferation of e-banking, Web-banking and m-payments, automated tellers need to be able to match the Web experience to stay relevant: the more accessible and user-friendly the ATM, the more likely it will attract customers.

At some level of abstraction, ATMs can be approached as a special type or category of the general class of automated vending machines, self-ordering systems in restaurants and self-check-out systems in supermarkets, and their interfaces and the overall access-to-service dialogues may be examined in parallel, being part of the overall e-commerce and consumption trends and lifestyles. In addition to this, the ATM world is growing rapidly to include increasingly complex and functional vending, POS and automated retail functions. In this picture, ATMs are there to serve several other purposes than withdrawing and depositing money: people use ATMs so that they can buy tickets for concerts, pay electricity bills or telephone bills through the ATM. So, while accessibility may not have been considered as a priority issue till today, but for sure there will be an increase in the demand for accessible ATM interactions.

ATMs become service access and service delivery points for several other e-commerce transactions, while there is a mutual transfer and exchange of functionalities between vending machines that assimilate also parts of what was considered as ATM function and vice versa.

Especially with the proliferation of RFID and NFC technologies, vending machines can be enriched with new functionality so that people can use them also for paying their invoices without having to go to a bank or an ATM. It should be noted, however, that large companies are delivering their invoice to the customer via the bank and the payment is either made directly or the customer simply approves it. This forms a further simplification of payment systems that should not be ignored at all.

ATMs, vending machines and self-check-out systems will be capable to recognize the customer who carries a smart card with an RFID chip, or by getting customer profile data from his mobile phone, and we shall be able to experience some first pilots and commercial prototypes of ATMs that read the thought of the customer. This may offer a way out to the difficulties faced today with the authentication process while it demonstrates quite well the fact that technology both creates and destroys access needs.

Judy walks after a tiring day in the office back to her home. She is thirsty and passes by an intelligent vending machine. The machine includes an NFC reader recognized by Judy's mobile phone. So, she is alerted that she can get a can of Irn Bru – otherwise she is not told anything (unless she accepts to receive ads and promotion messages from companies that promote their products through m-marketing). So as she wants to buy the product (Irn Bru) from the vending machine, a web app is downloaded to her device (may not necessarily be

a smart phone) when she approaches the vending machine and she place her order. When the time comes for payment, she only needs to hold her device near the vending machine and give the order to pay. Now she can enjoy her drink!

In the above use case, the central idea is to have the ATMs or the vending machines getting their interface to the user's personal device (a mobile phone, a service robot, a set of eye glasses or anything 'entitled' by the user for representing him / her for the conduct of a transaction). The device 'knows' their needs and provides them with the appropriate interaction modalities. In this case, there is no need to include natural language processing and speech recognition in an ATM; you only need to show the screen of the ATM in the user's mobile and let the user interact with his personal device for selecting, performing and completing the transaction.

LIFE STYLE TRENDS

Online Self-Help Communities

Internet made possible for many people all over the world sharing common problems, ideas, interests to connect with each other, exchange information, experiences, help each other etc. Online communities can be found for almost any purpose and interest. People with disabilities are also a group of people with common interests and concerns who can use such tools for communication with other people dealing with the same problems, exchange information and help each other. Looking for online communities for people with disabilities in the internet one can get lost in the amount information available. Disabled World (Disabled World, n.d.) and Daily Strengths support groups (DailyStrength, Inc, 2012) are just some examples of them. Other communities might also have a more local focus such as the DAWN Ontario Women With disabilities (DisAbled Women's Network Ontario, 2006) which focuses on women with disabilities leaving in Ontario. People that need to find relative information on such communities might also refer to relative directories' such as Disabilities Online (Online Directory, n.d.) directory etc. Social networks that emerged lately have also helped in forming such communities since forming a Facebook group for a specific group is a simple process that anyone can do.

Looking into the direction of online communities from the consumer and lifestyle perspective we can see how such communities may help people with disabilities to decide on buying specific AT devices, and other products in general. Combined with mobile computing and applications that are emerging such as Foursquare, Google Places and Facebook Places, these communities can become quite location-based and dynamic. For example, every person with a disability visiting places in a specific city and leaving messages about their accessibility automatically enters himself in a dynamic online community of people singing in to places in that city and leaving related comments. Making these dynamic groups more formal and tightly connected can lead them to having even bigger power. For example, currently there is no specific way on how to inform about accessibility issues other than simple comments. However an add-on application in such services, providing better cataloguing, indexing and searching n such kind of information might lead to even stronger connection of the community explained earlier.

Collaborative Consumption

Online communities, the power of a group of people getting together for a common purpose even if they are not in the same place and social networking sites are leading people to trust more each other and form new kinds of relationships in that direction. The phenomenon called "the wisdom of crowds" got a totally new dynamic with the evolution of web and it can be seen in its glory in places like Wikipedia where thousands of people are collaborating, by sharing information

and constantly updating the largest encyclopaedia in the world. People using the internet are not anymore passive consumers of information but also active creators and distributors of it. They share it on Facebook, Google+, Twitter, they upload videos on YouTube and in general they produce and distribute information as much as they consume it too. So, there is a new generation of people that are now growing up and learn to live in a totally different way than the previous ones. It's called the digital natives (Bennett, Maton, & Kervin, 2008) and it's the generation of people that are growing up with all this share-enabling technology around them. The trend of sharing, contributing in large schemes where collective wisdom can lead to ideas such as Wikipedia has also made people more open to trust total strangers in the web. When a person wants to buy something from EBay (eBay, 2014)for example can have a look at other users' opinion by looking at his trustiness score. This way a new kind of trust between people is formed based on the wisdom of crowds. In parallel with these changes in lifestyle, social structures and trust between people, societies today are faced with the phenomenon of a global economic recession which leads people to invent and discover new ways to collaborate, help each other and consume. In addition, the world today is also faced with the biggest challenge in history against climate change. People start realizing that the model of hyper-consumption leads to so many problems both for the economy and the environment itself and start thinking of ways to change it.

So, the restructure and the new belief in communities, the ease of creating online communities and their power, the amount of peer to peer social networks and real-time technologies are beginning to form a new way of consumption called collaborative consumption. Collaborative consumption is also driven and reinforced by the need to face great environmental challenges and the shock in consumer behaviors from a global economic recession.

Signs of the change towards this kind of consumer behavior can be found anywhere. And according to Rachel Botsman (Botsman, 2010), writer of the book titled "What's Mine Is Yours: The Rise of Collaborative Consumption" (Collaborative Consumption, n.d.), can be categorized in three major categories. The first category of collaborative consumption schemes is redistribution markets. Sites like SwapStyle (Swapstyle, n.d.), BookMooch_(BookMooch, n.d.), NeighBorrow(Neigborrow, n.d.) etc. are allowing people all over the world to share, swap and exchange products that they used and no longer need such as books, clothes, CDs, DVDs, Games, bags, accessories etc. The second category under collaborative consumption has to do with collaborative lifestyles. This is when people with various interests and needs get together to share skills, time, money and help each other. Landshare (Landshare, n.d.)is such an example where people who own a piece of land can meet people who want to use the land to grow their food. This way, people can make profit and put to actual use their land without having the knowledge or experience of how to do so. Another similar example is Zopa (Zopa Ltd., 2014)where people who want a loan can go and get it from a person in the community who volunteers to lend. The final category of collaborative consumption is product service systems where people share access to products through service schemes. For example, people sharing their cars through sites like Zipcar (Zipcar, Inc, 2014)and Goget (GoGet CarShare, 2014) or their homes to people that want to come for vacations through sites like CouchSurfing (Couchsurfing International, Inc., 2014) or Tripping_(Tripping International, 2014). This category is usually about sharing product with high idling capacity.

The success and the transition to that kind of consumer behavior can be seen in the experiment organized be Zipcar called Lowcardiet. They ask car owner to give up their car keys and use cars whenever absolutely necessary for one month.

The statistics shown on their page indicate the benefits and the changes that this behavior is bringing to people and the environment. In 2009, apart from the decrease in miles driven by cars, the increase in miles walked and biked and the pounds lost by participants in the experiment, 61% of the people taking part in the experiment said that they planned to get rid of their cars and go car free from then on.

Looking at this trend from the accessibility point of view it's highly likely that such collaborative consumption schemes might also come up especially adapted for persons with disabilities. For example, car sharing for persons with motor or visual impairments where people would share their cars, helping them in transportation. Another example could be people knowing sign language offering their skills and time to people with hearing impairments when they need to go to school or university. This way both people with disabilities and elderly would be happier and the rest of the community could find easier channels to help them without any intermediate formal groups or associations. Finally AT used by persons with disabilities could also be offered for exchange when not needed any more or not used. For example, people exchanging or giving away their wheelchairs, white canes, crouches etc. when buying new ones.

Social Media Activism for Accessibility

Having analyzed the new consumer behavior emerging from the combination of new technologies, environmental concerns and economic recession, we should also take a look at what is the potential impact of social media and online communities in businesses today. Large companies today invest a lot of money on social media advertising and develop strategies on how to listen and get feedback from their customers over the net. They can track blog posts, tweets, Facebook posts referring to them and analyze what is been said about their company. Marks & Spencer explain why and how they do so in an article on retail week (Perry, 2009). Companies care about their brand names and reputation and their public relation departments use increasingly social media to engage and listen to their customers. The reason that PR departments are paying so much attention to social media is the potential damage to their brand name and reputation that a PR or social media crisis can have. Toyota's example of the impact that a recall of 2.3 million cars had in social media (Wasserman, 2011) and how they managed the crisis is a lesson to be learned for many other companies. In other cases, it takes only a few tweets and posts that get reproduced massively in short time that can have a negative impact on a brands name. In the case of Ann Taylor Inc. customers complaint about the LOFT's new silk cargo pants (Marcus, 2010). The complaints got publicity and the company had to respond by changing their advertisements using employees in the photos wearing the pants. Similarly, when a passenger of Southwest airlines tweeted that the company asked him to purchase a second ticket because he was too fat the fact was rapidly picked up by followers and gained publicity which the company manages to handle due to their strategy for listening to what was being said on the web about them. In their analysis of social media crisis,(Swallow, 2011) Altimeter Group report that *"In all 50 social media crises cases, some sort of change was seen at the involved companies, with 52% of social media crises resulting in significant change by the companies; 40% of crises resulting in a change (of some lesser magnitude) by the companies and 8% of crises impacted the short-term finances of companies."*

The latter show the significance and the power that people can have through social media on companies. Such complaints and bad publicity for companies can also come from people with disabilities. People with disabilities using social media and publishing experiences in their interactions with companies could lead also to changes in their favour. Since this is already happening for a number of issues why doesn't it happen yet for cases of bad behavior to persons with disabilities?

Inclusion in Product Design

Having seen the potential impact that social media activism can have in businesses behavior towards customers it is also very important to point out the fact that an increasing number of companies are now using the internet, social media and other strategies to involve customers in their product design process. IBM explains how user-centered design works (IBM, 2013) as a process for product design and states that IBM is using such design methods for their products. Another example of how user-centered design used by companies in their product design is the company called "User-centered Design" (User-Centered Design, Inc., n.d.). The company has clients from the industry, government and education sector in the US and states that the key principles in their work are Usability, Suitability, and Accessibility Design & Evaluation. Another very interesting trend emerging in job market is the request for user-experience experts. The graph from indeed. com (Indeed, 2014) shows the constantly rising demand for user-experience experts in the job market. This means that an increasing number of businesses are investing in user-centered design methods for their products taking under account their customers' needs and opinions.

The web and more specifically the social web made the interaction between businesses and customers more personal. As already pointed out, businesses started listening to their customers opinions and respond to them. Apart from social media one of the most interesting trends in user-led innovation is the one of crowd sourcing product design through competitions. For example, in NamingForce (NamingForce.com, 2014) people can participate in competitions to name new products and in IdeaOffer participants get rewarded by companies for their ideas to improve, change, name or market their products. This way, businesses are involving customers actively in the design process of their products putting their ideas and opinions into practice.

In a world that innovation is going to be increasingly led be customers and consumers of products and services it would be disastrous for persons with disabilities not to have a presence in that user led innovation. Given the appropriate tools persons with disabilities can now increase their visibility and participation in user-centered design and innovation. Therefore, it is crucial to encourage businesses and markets to include persons with disabilities in the user-centered design processes though a variety of policies. A more thorough analysis of this trend is done in the democracy and citizenship chapter.

REFERENCES

Analytica. (n.d.). *Analytica | Data Integration*. Retrieved March 11, 2014, from http://www2. analytica-usa.com/

ATM Industry Association. (2014). *ATM Industry Association*. Retrieved March 11, 2014, from https://www.atmia.com/

Banco Bilbao Vizcaya Argentaria, S. A. (2014). *BBVA*. Retrieved March 11, 2014, from http:// www.bbva.com/TLBB/tlbb/esp/index.jsp

Bell, G., Parisi, A., & Pesce, M. (1996, January 25). *VRML 1.0C Specification*. Retrieved March 11, 2014, from http://www.web3d.org/x3d/specifications/vrml/VRML1.0/index.html

Bennett, S., Maton, K., & Kervin, L. (2008). The digital natives debate: A critical review of the evidence. *British Journal of Educational Technology*, *39*(5), 775–786. doi:10.1111/j.1467-8535.2007.00793.x

BookMooch. (n.d.). *BookMooch: trade your books with other people*. Retrieved March 11, 2014, from http://bookmooch.com/

Bosch. (2010, June). *Robert Bosch LLC. - Media Center*. Retrieved March 11, 2014, from http:// www.bosch-press.com/tbwebdb/bosch-usa/en-US/PressText.cfm?id=418

Bosch. (n.d.). *Bosch - Bosch Research and Technology Center*. Retrieved March 11, 2014, from http:// www.bosch.us/content/language1/html/rtc.htm

Botsman, R. (2010). *The case for collaborative consumption*. Retrieved from http://www.ted.com/ talks/rachel_botsman_the_case_for_collaborative_consumption

Bryne, C. (2011, March 9). ShopWithYourFriends brings you real-time, social shopping. *VentureBeat*. Retrieved from http://venturebeat. com/2011/03/09/shopwithyourfriends-real-time-social-shopping/

Caixa, L. (n.d.). Prehome. *la Caixa*. Retrieved March 11, 2014, from http://www.laCaixa.com/ index.html?Origen=Facebook-Like-Prehome-es

Casino, G. (n.d.). *Groupe Casino*. Retrieved March 11, 2014, from http://www.groupe-casino.fr/en

Clark, S. (2011, June 23). Tesco Korea points to the future of mobile grocery shopping. *NFC World*. Retrieved from http://www.nfcworld. com/2011/06/23/38280/tesco-korea-points-to-the-future-of-mobile-grocery-shopping/

Collaborative Consumption. (n.d.). Collaborative Consumption - Sharing reinvented through technology. Watch Rachel's TED Talk. *Collaborative Consumption*. Retrieved March 11, 2014, from http://www.collaborativeconsumption.com/

Couchsurfing International, Inc. (2014). *Welcome to Couchsurfing! - Couchsurfing*. Retrieved March 11, 2014, from https://www.couchsurfing.org/

DailyStrength, Inc. (2012). *Online Support Groups For Seniors - DailyStrength*. Retrieved March 11, 2014, from http://www.dailystrength.org/support-groups/Seniors

Department of Justice. (2010). *2010 ADA Standards for Accessible Design*. Department of Justice. Retrieved from http://www.ada.gov/regs2010/2010ADAStandards/2010ADAStandards.pdf

Design, U.-C. Inc. (n.d.). *User-Centered Design, Inc - Home*. Retrieved March 11, 2014, from http://www.user-centereddesign.com/index.php

DisAbled Women's Network Ontario. (2006, February 6). *Women with DisAbilities Online community - DisAbled Women's Network Ontario*. Retrieved March 11, 2014, from http://dawn.thot.net/list.html

eBay. (2014). *Electronics, Cars, Fashion, Collectibles, Coupons and More Online Shopping | eBay*. Retrieved March 11, 2014, from http://www.ebay.com/

Facebook. (2014). Share Where You Are. *Facebook*. Retrieved March 11, 2014, from https://www.facebook.com/about/location

Fougner, J. (2011, January 31). *Introducing Deals*. Retrieved March 11, 2014, from https://www.facebook.com/notes/facebook/introducing-deals/446183422130

Foursquare. (2014). *Foursquare*. Retrieved March 11, 2014, from https://foursquare.com/

Gallotti, P., Raposo, A., & Soares, L. (2011). v-Glove: A 3D Virtual Touch Interface. In *2011 XIII Symposium on Virtual Reality (SVR)* (pp. 242–251). doi:10.1109/SVR.2011.21

Garage, W. (2010, May 4). *The Results Are In PR2 Beta Program Recipients! | Willow Garage*. Retrieved March 11, 2014, from http://www.willowgarage.com/blog/2010/05/04/pr2-beta-program-recipients

Garage, W. (2014a). *Overview | Willow Garage*. Retrieved March 11, 2014, from http://www.willowgarage.com/pages/pr2/overview

Garage, W. (2014b). *Willow Garage*. Retrieved March 11, 2014, from http://www.willowgarage.com/

GoGet CarShare. (2014). Home. *GoGet Carshare*. Retrieved March 11, 2014, from http://www.goget.com.au/

Google. (2014a). *A smart, virtual wallet for in-store and online shopping – Google Wallet*. Retrieved March 11, 2014, from http://www.google.com/wallet/

Google. (2014b). *Google Offers*. Retrieved March 11, 2014, from https://www.google.com/offers/?gl=US

Google. (2014c). *Places for businesses – Google*. Retrieved March 11, 2014, from http://www.google.com/business/placesforbusiness/

Groupon. (n.d.). *Groupon*. Retrieved March 11, 2014, from http://www.groupon.com/app/subscriptions/new_zip?

Hanlon, M. (n.d.). *Intelligent Vending Machines point towards a cashless future*. Retrieved March 11, 2014, from http://www.gizmag.com/go/3308/

Hollister, S. (2011, November 30). Sony HMZ-T1 Personal 3D Viewer review. *The Verge*. Retrieved March 11, 2014, from http://www.theverge.com/2011/11/10/2552518/sony-hmz-t1-personal-3d-viewer-review

IBM. (2013, February 20). IBM Design. *CTZZZ*. Retrieved March 11, 2014, from http://www.ibm.com/design/

IDEO. (2010). *futureselfservicebanking.com*. Retrieved March 11, 2014, from http://futureselfservicebanking.com/

IDEO. (2014). *IDEO | A Design and Innovation Consulting Firm*. Retrieved March 11, 2014, from http://www.ideo.com/

Indeed. (2014). *User-experience Job Trends | Indeed.com.* Retrieved March 11, 2014, from http://www.indeed.com/jobanalytics/jobtrends?q=User-experience&l=

Industrias Tomás Morcillo, S. L. (2014). *ITM Polycart - Plastic Shopping Carts and Baskets.* Retrieved March 11, 2014, from http://www.polycartgroup.com/english/index.html

Khronos Group. (2014). *OpenGL - The Industry Standard for High Performance Graphics.* Retrieved March 11, 2014, from http://www.opengl.org/

KIST. (n.d.). *KIST Korea Institiue of Science and Technologhy.* Retrieved March 11, 2014, from http://eng.kist.re.kr/kist_eng/main/

Landshare. (n.d.). Landshare - connecting growers to people with land to share. *Landshare.* Retrieved March 11, 2014, from http://www.landshare.net/

Living Social Inc. (2014). *LivingSocial - Save money while discovering amazing things to do.* Retrieved March 11, 2014, from https://www.livingsocial.com/

Mangu-Ward, K. (2011, August 10). *Robot Teachers Invade South Korea, Ruin Workers' Dance Party in Taiwan - Hit & Run : Reason.com.* Retrieved March 11, 2014, from http://reason.com/blog/2011/08/10/robot-teachers-invade-south-ko

Marcus, S. (2010, August 30). HOW TO: Respond when Social Media Attacks Your Brand. *Mashable.* Retrieved March 11, 2014, from http://mashable.com/2010/08/30/social-media-attacks-brand/

Marketwire. (2011, September 13). Select2gether Launches First Mobile Interactive Social Commerce Experience at DEMO Fall 2011. *Marketwire.* Retrieved March 11, 2014, from http://www.marketwired.com/press-release/-1560402.htm

Microso. (2014). *Xbox | Games and Entertainment on All Your Devices - Xbox.com.* Retrieved March 11, 2014, from http://www.xbox.com/en-US/#fbid=fQIXuPAgqou

Microsoft. (2006, October 11). DirectX SDK - (October 2006). *Microsoft Download Center.* Retrieved March 11, 2014, from http://www.microsoft.com/en-us/download/details.aspx?id=9977

Microsoft. (2014). *Xbox Kinect | Full Body Gaming and Voice Control - Xbox.com.* Retrieved March 11, 2014, from http://www.xbox.com/en-US/kinect

Murray, J. (2011, September 8). Square vs. Google Wallet: Who will win the mobile payment war? *Anthill Online.* Retrieved from http://anthillonline.com/square-vs-google-wallet-who-will-win-the-mobile-payment-war/

NamingForce.com. (2014). Naming Force - business name contests. *Naming Force.* Retrieved March 11, 2014, from http://www.namingforce.com/

Neigborrow. (n.d.). *Need to use something short term.* Retrieved March 11, 2014, from http://beta.neighborrow.com/

Networld Media Group. (2014). *ATM / Automated Teller Machine business news, research, more | ATM Marketplace.* Retrieved March 11, 2014, from http://www.atmmarketplace.com/

Newswire, P. R. (2011, March 3). *The Dealmap and Microsoft Collaborate to Bring Local and Daily Deals. -- MENLO PARK, Calif., March 3, 2011 /PRNewswire/.* Retrieved March 11, 2014, from http://www.prnewswire.com/news-releases/the-dealmap-and-microsoft-collaborate-to-bring-local-and-daily-deals-to-bing-117323418.html

Online Directory. (n.d.). *Information on Disabilities - Online Directory.* Retrieved March 11, 2014, from http://www.disabilities-online.com/index.php?viewCat=7

Oracle. (2013). *Java 3D Parent Project — Project Kenai*. Retrieved March 11, 2014, from https://java3d.java.net/

Pachal, P. (2011, December 9). Will Apple iTV Trade the Remote for Kinect-Like Control? *Mashable*. Retrieved March 11, 2014, from http://mashable.com/2011/12/09/apple-itv-gestures/

Patel, N. (2011, November 3). Google Offers Android app. now in Market. *The Verge*. Retrieved March 11, 2014, from http://www.theverge.com/2011/11/3/2535367/google-offers-android-app

Perry, J. (2009, November 20). *Social media: Why M&S is listening to the word on the web*. Retrieved March 11, 2014, from http://www.retail-week.com/social-media-why-ms-is-listening-to-the-word-on-the-web/5008089.article

Plasticpals. (2010, February 22). *South Korea: Robot Teachers Rolling Out in 2012*. Retrieved from http://www.plasticpals.com/?p=21283

Plus, H. (n.d.). 홈플러스 인터넷 쇼핑몰 : *e*-생활에 플러스가 됩니다. Retrieved March 11, 2014, from http://www.homeplus.co.kr/app.exhibition.main.Main.ghs?paper_no=category

Rao, L. (2011a, May 23). Square's Disruptive New iPad Payments Service Will Replace Cash Registers. *TechCrunch*. Retrieved from http://techcrunch.com/2011/05/23/squares-disruptive-new-ipad-payments-service-will-replace-cash-registers/

Rao, L. (2011b, July 31). Square Now Processing $4 Million In Mobile Payments Per Day. *TechCrunch*. Retrieved from http://techcrunch.com/2011/07/31/square-now-processing-4-million-in-mobile-payments-per-day/

Rathore, A., & Valverde, R. (2011). An RFID based E-commerce solution for the implementation of secure unattended stores. *Journal of Emerging Trends in Computing and Information Sciences*, 2(8), 376–389.

Retail, I. (2011). *Imagine Retail Management System - Software for Footwear and Apparel Stores*. Retrieved March 11, 2014, from http://imagineretail.com/index.asp

Samsung. (2014). *Samsung US | TVs - Tablets - Smartphones - Cameras - Laptops - Refrigerators*. Retrieved March 11, 2014, from http://www.samsung.com/us/

Schwartz, A. (2010, December 15). Samsung Snags Willow Garage's PR2 Robot. *Fast Company*. Retrieved March 11, 2014, from http://www.fastcompany.com/1710096/samsung-snags-willow-garages-pr2-robot

Shapiro, L. (2011, November 16). *Sony's 3D Headset: Virtual Reality Goes Mainstream | Sound & Vision*. Retrieved March 11, 2014, from http://www.soundandvision.com/content/sonys-3d-headset-virtual-reality-goes-mainstream

Shelf, X. (2013). www.shelfx.com. Retrieved from http://www.shelfx.com/

Silicon Micro Display. (2012). ST1080 features, 1080p hmd features, hmd specs | SiliconMicroDisplay, Silicon Micro Display, SMD. *Silicon Micro Display*. Retrieved March 11, 2014, from http://www.siliconmicrodisplay.com/st1080-features.html

Square. (2014a). Square - Accept credit cards with your iPhone, Android or iPad. *Square*. Retrieved March 11, 2014, from https://squareup.com/#!home

Square. (2014b). Square Wallet - Pay with your name at your favorite Square merchants. *Square*. Retrieved March 11, 2014, from https://squareup.com/wallet

Swallow, E. (2011, August 31). The Anatomy of a Social Media Crisis. *Mashable*. Retrieved March 11, 2014, from http://mashable.com/2011/08/31/social-media-crisis/

Swapstyle. (n.d.). *Swapstyle.com*. Retrieved March 11, 2014, from http://www.swapstyle.com/

Swedberg, C. (2011, September 21). *French Supermarket Tests NFC Tool for Visually Disabled Shoppers - RFID Journal*. Retrieved March 11, 2014, from http://www.rfidjournal.com/articles/view?8793

SWYF. (2014). *SWYF: alle vrouwenkleding en accessoires in een shop*. Retrieved March 11, 2014, from http://www.swyf.nl/

Tesco. (2014). *Tesco.com - online shopping, bringing the supermarket to you - Every little helps*. Retrieved March 11, 2014, from http://www.tesco.com/

Torena, R., Usero, J. Á. M., Van Isacker, K., Goranova-Valkova, M., Chalkia, E., & Bekiaris, E. ... Lange, R. (2010). Present and future of eAccessibility in public digital terminals. *European Journal of ePractice*, (10). Retrieved from http://www.epractice.eu/files/European%20Journal%20epractice%20Volume%2010.1.pdf

Trillenium, o. (2012). *Trillenium*. Retrieved March 11, 2014, from http://www.trillenium.com/home

Tripping International. (2014). *Tripping: Couches to Castles*. Retrieved March 11, 2014, from https://www.tripping.com

Wasserman, T. (2011, September 1). How Toyota Used Social Media To Digg Itself Out of a PR Nightmare. *Mashable*. Retrieved March 11, 2014, from http://mashable.com/2011/09/01/toyota-digg-recalls/

World, D. (n.d.). *Disability Community*. Retrieved March 11, 2014, from http://community.disabled-world.com/

Zipcar, Inc. (2014). *Car Sharing, an alternative to car rental and car ownership – Zipcar*. Retrieved March 11, 2014, from http://www.zipcar.com/

Zopa Ltd. (2014). *Zopa - Peer-to-peer Lending, Loans & High Interest on Savings*. Retrieved March 11, 2014, from http://www.zopa.com/

KEY TERMS AND DEFINITIONS

ATM: Automated Teller Machine. An electronic banking outlet, which allows customers to complete basic transactions without the aid of a branch representative or teller.

Collaborative Consumption: Collaborative consumption is a class of economic arrangements in which participants share access to products or services, rather than having individual ownership.

Internet of Things: The Internet of Things (IoT) is a computing concept that describes a future where everyday physical objects will be connected to the Internet and be able to identify themselves to other devices.

Product Design: Product design is the process of creating a new product to be sold by a business to its customers.

Service Design: Service design is the activity of planning and organizing people, infrastructure, communication and material components of a service in order to improve its quality and the interaction between service provider and customers.

Shopping: Shopping is an activity in which a customer browses the available goods or services presented by one or more retailers with the intent to purchase a suitable selection of them.

Social Shopping: The trend of shopping using social media.

Ticket Machine: A vending machine for tickets.

User Experience: User experience is any aspect of a user's experience with a given system, including the interface, graphics, industrial design, physical interaction, and the manual.

Vending Machine: A vending machine is a machine which dispenses items such as snacks, beverages, alcohol, cigarettes, lottery tickets, cologne, consumer products and even gold and gems to customers automatically, after the customer inserts currency or credit into the machine.

Chapter 11
Media and Entertainment

ABSTRACT

Media and entertainment is an area currently undergoing serious changes in its business models due to technology. Web TV channels, Smart TVs, new gaming consoles, new trends in gaming, and mobile computing are affecting the future of entertainment, which is becoming more interactive and engaging. People with disabilities and elderly were already facing a series of problems in using such devices and services. This chapter discusses current problems and future solutions and dangers that lie ahead in the area of media and entertainment looking at the Web as a platform for entertainment, the TV and changes in related technologies, the trends in publishing, and the effects for accessibility.

WEB ACCESSIBILITY ISSUES

Thanks to work lead by W3C the World Wide Web Consortium (W3C, 2014) guidelines already exist for web content accessibility since May 1999 with the publication of WCAG1.0 (EOWG & WCAG WG, 2006) which was upgraded with an improved version WCAG2.0 (Caldwell, Cooper, Reid, & Vanderheiden, 2008)in December 2008. These guidelines on web accessibility have been supplemented by Authoring Tool Accessibility Guidelines (EOWG & ATAG WG, 2013) to assist in the development of accessible ICT tools, User Agent Accessibility Guidelines (EOWG & UAWG, 2005)to assist in the development of media players and other devices not just web pages, as well as an Evaluation and Reporting Language called EARL (EOWG & ERT WG, 2011)to support the development of tools for the automated or semi-automated auditing of websites.

The guidelines are technical guidelines and do not deal with fuzzier concepts of good design. It is possible to create good and bad web-sites all the while conforming to these guidelines. There is scope for design research that goes beyond strict technical conformity with a view to providing excellent service to the specific user groups.

The W3C guidelines are strictly technical and address a basic set of needs of people with disabilities, the focus tends to be on areas such as users who have difficulties with sight, hearing or mobility and coordination. A design oriented research program could look at the specific needs of people in these categories especially with respect to daily tasks such as travel, banking, shopping, public administration, news and entertainment as

DOI: 10.4018/978-1-4666-6130-1.ch011

well as the many database, design, planning, collaboration and transaction management systems that are essential for professional life but which are usually available only through company intranets.

A design oriented approach could also explore the needs of people with temporary, progressive or situational disabilities, as well as the specific needs of people living with cognitive or developmental disabilities such as autism, dyslexia or early stage Alzheimer's.

The State of Web Accessibility

The UN Convention on the Rights of Persons with Disabilities (United Nations, 2007) addresses among other issues the rights of people with disabilities around the world to access information and services online.

In 2006 the UN engaged an independent consulting company to carry out an audit of 100 major websites (United Nations, 2007) across the world to determine to what extent these guidelines were being implemented. It chose five websites in each of 20 countries ranging from Argentina to Brazil, Morocco, China, India and the US. The list included France, Germany, Spain and the UK from Europe. In each country 5 major websites were chosen, one in each of 5 categories – airline travel, banking, newspapers, central government and retail.

Each site was evaluated according to the guidelines of WCAG1.0 and given a rating of A, AA or AAA according to WCAG convention which distinguishes 3 levels of priority for the 14 WCAG guidelines. The most basic guidelines for example are referred to as Priority 1 guidelines and a website that respects all of these is awarded an A rating. The website that respects all guidelines is awarded an AAA rating. Overall only 3 of the examined websites achieved single A rating. No site achieved double or triple A rating. Most did not achieve the most basic level of accessibility.

To understand in more detail what this means consider that 93% of the hundred sites for example contained images with no alternative text description, rendering these images incomprehensible for a blind person. 73% had content that relied on JavaScript to function. It is know that at least 10% of people on the internet are not able to access JavaScript on their browser so the use of JavaScript excludes this 10% whether they have a disability or not. 78% sites used colour and background combinations that did not provide good contrast, making them difficult for people with poor sight. 98% of the sites did not use valid code, in other words the code was old or out of date and risked not working as expected when the browser is upgraded. 97% of sites used units of measurement that limited the ability of users to view pages in browser of different sizes especially for smaller screen devices or with variable size text. 89% of sites did not use headings that convey the structure of the page and 86% used lists that were conveyed visually but not identified as such in the code. 87% of sites used pop-up windows without warning the user or providing options. 97% of pages did not provide clear alternative text for links. Just calling a link "more" or "button" does not inform someone what it is about. It forces them to read surrounding text which takes time and in any case may not be clear. 92% of sites did not provide skip-links enabling a user to skip through large blocks of text to find links they want. 74% did not define the natural language of the page so that readers and translators could be used. Those that did identify a natural language did not signal when this changed for example from Spanish to English.

Despite the existence of clear guidelines, the implementation of these guidelines is so far incomplete. Even in the case of countries such as the US and Australia where advocacy groups have successfully sued the government for inaccessible sites, the audited sites failed to achieve even the basic level of accessibility, a single A rating against the guidelines.

That was the situation in 2006. Although no global audit has since been carried out, it is clear that not much has changed since the UN audit of 2006. No laws exist in countries such as Greece and where laws do exist for example in countries such as France, they have essentially been ignored. The French law on accessibility loi n°2005-102 (*LOI n° 2005-102 du 11 février 2005 pour l'égalité des droits et des chances, la participation et la citoyenneté des personnes handicapées*, 2005) published in 2005 has not changed anything. In efforts to boost progress further legislation entitled décret n°2009-546 d'application (*Décret n° 2009-546 du 14 mai 2009 pris en application de l'article 47 de la loi n° 2005-102 du 11 février 2005 sur l'égalité des droits et des chances, la participation et la citoyenneté des personnes handicapées et créant un référentiel d'accessibilité des services de communication publique en ligne*, 2009) was published in May 2009, giving two more years for the websites of public administration to achieve conformity with WCAG2.0, but so far at least in the case of France little has changed. The story is more or less the same across Europe. There is a need therefore to look more closely at the reasons why. Organizations such as Braillenet in France have addressed the issue of web accessibility compliance at its 5th European eAccessibility Forum (BrailleNet, 2011) entitled "Benefits and costs of e-accessibility" held in Paris on 28 March 2011 and also recently on 26 March 2012 at its 6th convention entitled "Putting e-Accessibility at the core of information systems"(BrailleNet, 2012).

The European eAccessibility Forum of 2011 featured many experts working in the area of e-accessibility as well as people responsible for ICT in major French companies such as the SNCF. It is fair to say that the forum made a significant contribution to understanding the reasons for such slow progress.

Two major issues arose which are of immediate relevance to web accessibility. The first issue is a general perception that the cost of compliance is too high, or that the benefits provided are too low and too hard to justify either to a research and development department in a telecom pro-

vider or to the budget committee of a company with a major web presence. The second issue is that despite the availability of guidelines and the increasing availability of compliance tools, the goal of compliance is essentially impossible to reach due to ambiguities in what it means, and the impracticality of maintaining websites due to the rapid evolution of hardware platforms, screen formats, OS, web-technologies and content.

At least two other issues of major importance were highlighted at the 2011 Digital Access Forum, which may merit attention in the form of public support for research, development and innovation. One relates to the nature of digital publication, which as an industrial process has not really caught up with the digital age, and which does not reflect the growth of e-books, evolving business models or the possibility for re-use and re-purposing of content in different formats. The other has to do with the problem of annotating new and historic content so that it is accessible. These two issues apply not only to web content but also to text, audio, image, video and other formats destined for a wider range of devices such as e-readers, media players, game consoles and TVs.

Understanding the Complexity of Web-Compliance

Speaking at the Digital Access Forum (BrailleNet, 2011) in 2011, Brigitte Rigaud (SCNF, n.d.) of the SNCF spoke of the work done by the SNCF to address the issue of e-accessibility. In their case accessibility means helping all clients have easier access to the services and infrastructure of the SNCF group. That means not just their trains, but stations, offices, shops and websites selling SNCF products and services. Like any large public facing organisation the SNCF group has a great range of web-sites to support its own work as well as relations with customers and partners. Altogether the SNCF maintains 58 public internet sites and 458 intranet sites. The presentation however only dealt with the public sites. Accessibility of course is a much bigger issue than public web-site accessibility. It applies also to employees and therefore to internal sites or intranets. It could also apply also to extranets, sites oriented towards external providers, not just customer and employees. It applies to physical locations such as the stations, shops, ticket vending machines, food dispensers as well as to the trains themselves. There are opportunities for the application of ICT to all of these other areas of accessibility, but the discussion was limited to the issue of client facing public websites.

To maintain a corporate identity the SNCF applies across-the-board policies for the look and feel of the websites, consistent with their corporate identity and using standard logos and other forms of trade dress. The issue of accessibility did not really appear on their radar until about 2006 and they started to address it seriously in the period 2008-2009.

The issue is complex and the organisation has to learn as it goes so to get started they decided to implement keyboard navigation on all webpages. So far they employ 8 accessibility experts, 3 internal and one external auditor as well as one advisor. They try to make sure they are well rated by auditors so that they can wear the AccessiWeb label (AccesiWeb, n.d.). They were rated silver by AccessiWeb in 2010. They have two accessibility related sites. One is for the broad issue of accessibility (SCNF, n.d.) and the other deals more specifically with web accessibility.

SNCF is one of the most advanced large organisations in France in terms of its approach to web accessibility. It has adopted a phased approach and the first thing to recognise is the great number of web-sites involved, in this case 58 public sites, whereas ideally this could also extent one day to a further 458 intranet sites.

One of the challenges in web-accessibility stems from the fact that accessibility is for most sites an afterthought. It has not been built in from the start. It is much easier to start with a design that is accessible and easy to maintain than to start with one that needs to be repaired or patched.

Further challenges arise from the fact that most programmers know nothing about accessibility, and few web development tools make it easy or automatic for programmers to respect compliance guidelines. The programmers need to get trained, and since programming tends to be a team effort, as soon as a new member joins the team, there is the risk that non-compliant practices will creep in.

More challenges arise due to the fact that content is constantly changing. This is a general problem for retail sites which change their offer on a regular basis, knowing that dynamic sites which are often updated bring people back, create more traffic and more business.

Major retailers such as Tesco of the UK have 100s of websites. These are updated on average every week. The retailer has to react to the changing seasons, the holidays or the weekend shopping spree. They often make special offers. They try to entice people into the stores. They try to develop a dialogue with customers in different ways for example using competitions and prizes and soliciting feedback on new product ideas. The changes are not just to the text but to the layout and graphics. Every time changes are made there is a risk that navigation may become less compliant or graphic elements may not be qualified by helpful alternative text.

Change in itself is a challenge so is the pace of change. A website that changes every week means that compliance must become immediate or even automatic. The pace of change adds an extra layer of frustration and then there is the fact that the people who work in marketing, who supply any of the images and layout ideas, have no interest in compliance issues, and may request changes that create unnecessary work.

Temesis_(Temesis, n.d.), a French company specialised in web accessibility, pointed out that the challenge of multi-site systems is universal. One of their clients, a small biomedical research agency, already has 8 web sites, but larger organisations typically have about 100. They tend to be dynamic. Many integrate database technologies,

CRM systems, and systems for content management, transaction management, payment or collaboration. These sites integrate systems developed by third parties, and this too is another source of complexity.

Temesis explained how multi-site systems create possibilities for economies of scale in the development and maintenance of accessibility. There are also advantages in terms of training and image when the same approach to adding alternative text of captioning video is applied consistently across all sites and not in an independent ad-hoc fashion that differs from one site to the next.

Tools intended to help in the development, evaluation or maintenance of accessible websites need to take this into account. From the site owners point of view this can lead to considerable savings in the cost of compliance.

The Cost of Compliance

Aside from complexity there is the general issue of the cost of compliance. Speakers of the 5th Braillenet conference referred to the cost of the audit to gain the AccesiWeb label (AccesiWeb, n.d.), the label of the French web compliance body. The audit of a site is €3,420. For a company that has 100 sites, the price starts to become important. Awareness training costs €1,350 for a seminar. Reference was made to tools (such as "safeguard") intended to monitor the compliance of a site on a continuous basis costing almost €25,000 per year.

The general impression is that the existing business model is not workable. It may have been developed before a full understanding of the compliance challenge existed, but it now seems clear that it does not scale well and will not work. There seems to be a need to develop a new business model for tools and services as well as a whole new model for what compliance means and how to achieve it.

In France la Loi 758 imposes an obligation on telephone makers to make telephony accessible to everyone. Nevertheless French phone makers have great difficulties in developing accessible mobile telephony code. The industry is also very competitive and companies compete fiercely on the functionality of their models. This is where they put all of their effort in development and accessibility gets much less attention as a result.

It is useful to look at the numbers to understand why. A large phone maker might have 50 million users, using several different models, older models as well as new ones. Of the 50 million users, only 100,000 might use a given screen reader for mobile such as "mobile speak". Other groups will use other readers for example "voice over" or "talk back". These investments in accessibility are hard to justify for these small populations.

Bouygues of France has made "Mobile Speak" available to all of its disabled users. The cost seems high at €225. On the other hand the number of copies sold is small, and the price has to cover not only the cost of development, but royalties paid for technologies related to vocal synthesis as well as a margin for the distributor.

The impact of the "accessibility agenda" from the point of view of the phone companies is to lengthen time to market and increase costs. Furthermore the skills required are rare and cannot be obtained in the usual market for developer talent. These skills take a long time to develop in-house. They are not yet well understood or defined in terms of exact skill requirements and they are not supported by effective curriculum development.

The issue is not confined to France. Nokia experienced great difficulties in retaining the same level of performance of "mobile speak" in the transition from e71 to e72. Mobile Speak is only one of many screen readers. Despite their efforts, the upgrade destroyed many of the previous e-accessibility achievements.

The exception is Apple which retains $1 from every iPhone sold to reinvest in accessibility. Apple has optimal conditions in that it has very high margins, a very large market and a very small product range.

From the point of view of the screen readers there is a newly emerged problem related to the proliferation of various mobile phone operating systems, such as OS for Apple, Android and Windows Phone. This means that not only they are developed for a small market, but this market is itself fragmented in term of different mobile operating systems.

The Marketing and Communication Problem

According to the French IAN the organiser of the Digital Access Forum in Paris, there are more than 600 million people with disability in the world today. That means almost 100 million in Europe and about 12 million in France alone. This sounds like a large market but in reality it is a highly fragmented group. Fragmentation arises due to the fact that different people with disabilities are disabled in very different ways and to varying degrees.

Further fragmentation of these markets occurs due to the great number of different technology platforms, their ever-evolving nature and the need to keep them updated and maintained.

In reality organizations including technology companies, think of accessibility technologies as being relevant only for small markets of people with severe handicaps, such as blindness from birth. These markets are small, the cost of addressing them is high, and the return on investment very hard to justify.

In countries where appropriate legislation exists and where advocacy groups representing people with disabilities mange to get organised, it is possible to put pressure on organisations to imply using courts and due legal process. In these cases the threat of public sanction, adverse publicity and large financial penalties can be used to encourage compliance. However not all countries afford this possibility and as indicated in the 2006 UN audit, even in those countries where high profile court cases have succeeded and companies have been

fined, compliance is not very far in advance of those who have no legislation in place at all. There is a need to look for solutions that complement recourse to the law.

One approach is to address the issue of small markets and the burden of compliance. The cost of compliance has to be affordable and the affordable price point can only be determined with a clear understanding of the structure of the relevant markets and populations. There may be a need for greater clarity on how the cost of accessibility should be divided between society on the basis of social services, and private actors such as people with disability and their employers, and the providers of products and services from which they benefit.

The Travability (Travability Pty Ltd, 2013) website contains a very thought provoking discussion on the market for accessible holidays and travel. In the context of a new economic model of disability it provides a new way of thinking about the market for disabled travel. One that dispels common myths and misunderstandings about disabled travellers and the segmentation of markets they represent.

People having problems with vision, hearing or memory loss experience different levels of severity. Many who experience difficulty severe enough to cause discomfort or to have a tangible impact on their work productivity, are not formally considered to be "handicapped" because their condition is not acute enough. This means that current estimates of the size of the market for access technologies is much smaller than it seems at first sight. In the section on human productivity performance we will address issues raised by Microsoft at the Braillenet forum, showing for example how the productivity of someone with poor sight declines measurably and has an impact on their work long before they qualify as being legally blind or even before they may realise a need for reading glasses. Little is known however about the extent of this phenomenon and there is a need for further research that will enable us to know how and to what extent this increases the market for access technologies.

Other groups have access problems due to language, geography or transport infrastructure. They experience the same problems as people with disabilities even though the origin of the problem may be different. We know this in principle but so far we have no real estimates of how extensive are these needs of people with such situational disabilities, or by how much they could expand the market for accessibility products and services. The validity of the principle is illustrated by observing how the advent of smart phones such as Blackberries provided a sudden and unexpected boost to the adoption of screen readers. People either found the small format screens too small for reading long passages or they needed a way to read their email while driving. Drivers have also been lead adopters of another e-access technology - voice input.

It is already clear in an intuitive sense that organisations that consider the group of beneficiaries of accessible web-sites as being too small to justify the cost of compliance, may have succumbed to a series of myths about the market that now need to be dispelled. To be effective, a direct and rigorous approach will be required on both of these issues. Not necessarily ICT based research and innovation, but research and innovation is needed based on a realistic understanding of the long term burden of compliance, the economic cost of non-access, and the structure of markets for associated product and services.

While accessibility is necessary for those with disabilities, it is also highly desirable for many who are not; by not ignoring the fact that accessibility confers significant benefits to a much larger population of users than those officially recognised as "handicapped", it should be seen less through the lens of compliance and more from the perspective of worker productivity or excellence of the consumer experience.

Compatibility and Standards

From the discussion of the previous section there is a clear need for greater cooperation between mobile phone makers and makers of screen readers, with a view to reducing the cost of the reader for all concerned, phone makers and end-users as well as the developers of the screen readers themselves.

There is need for a mechanism that will enable all to evolve in a way that allows makers of screen readers to maintain a certain level of performance as one model makes way for another, as the number of models increase, as operating systems evolve and as applications are upgraded. This does not happen right now and an effort is required to enable the players to come together, to develop a common agenda and to coordinate their independent efforts and to develop open standards that will allow the industry to progressively lock in the benefits of previous e-accessibility R&D investments.

Every time there is an upgrade to the physical hardware such as the screen, the OS of the server or the client, the browser, a new version of html, an upgrade to an authoring tool, an upgrade to third party technologies for example to databases, e-commerce engines, CRM systems, unless everyone has played the game of compliance to perfection, there is there risk that a previously compliant site will change and no longer be compliant. Compliance does not involve a once-off fix to a system. It requires a constant on-going effort, as even perfectly static sites will drift away from the design specification as both the software and the hardware changes through successive cycles of upgrades and improvements.

In particular the recent proliferation of new platforms and the move away from the laptop or workstation as the access device of choice towards the smartphone, tablet or TV, has had a major impact on the technical challenge and cost of compliance.

Backwards compatibility is a problem. According to one participant at the Digital Access Provision forum, the transition from Windows CE7 to CE8 was particularly difficult and caused many who had invested in compliance have their investment wiped out when users upgraded from CE7 to CE8.

The issue of standardisation is not just a software issue. It also involves the hardware developers, in particular the makers of screens. For various reasons these have not been involved in talks about standards affecting screen readers for example. Industry experts at the 2011 Braillenet Forum (BrailleNet, 2014) were of the opinion that future efforts should include screen readers and take a truly global approach, not confining themselves to EU or the US but involving hardware component and product makers from Japan, China and Korea[1].

Compliance Tools and Standardisation

One of the strongest messages to emerge from the 2011 Braillenet forum was the need for a world wide effort on tools for testing.

It is felt that the current regulations create a large amount of work for developers. They are hard to understand and need to be made operational. Developers need operational guidelines that they can follow without having to read and interpret regulations and wonder how to implement them. They need practices and techniques that enable them to implement these guidelines. They need to be confident that in using these they will end up with systems that are compliant.

If compliance is to have any real legal meaning, it has to be possible to take any compliance tool, apply it to a single site and obtain the same verdict as to whether the site is compliant or not. Otherwise site owners and developers have no objective basis on which to base a judgment of whether a site is compliant or not.

They felt that WCAG was the way to go. One of the reasons is that recent legal cases in the US have referred to WCAG2.0 instead of their home grown Section 508 law.

Nevertheless they expressed great frustration at the current situation where testing the compliance of a site might require up to 15 different tools. One expert observed that 3 different tools intended to help test the compliance of a web site, often give three different verdicts for the same site. It is not unusual for one tool to declare the site compliant, another one declare the same site non-compliant, and a third declare that it simply does not know. Ideally the audit of a site should reduce more or less to the simple application of an audit tool and this should considerably reduce the cost of compliance.

They claim that ambiguities arise at the level of national standards for accessibility as well as at the level of WCAG2.0s which is intended to include and replace all of the national ones. Experts at the conference were of the opinion that WCAG mainly addressed desktop issues and were not yet broad enough to address accessibility issues for smart phones, tablets and readers, which host rich dynamic content, and subject to updates of frequent upgrades of a range of different underlying operating systems, client server and browser software as well as updates to a large range of specific integrated apps, not to mention browser- or user-side software such as screen-readers.

There is still work to be done and they expressed a desire for:

- Clear models,
- Reference code and
- Illustrative test examples.

There is a need for tools and practices or techniques to tame the complexity that regulation has created. Eventually there is a need for tools, techniques and practices that help developers not only to know what is wrong, but what to do about it and eventually to prioritise their work in view of limited time, human resources or budgets as well as non-compliance risks. Finally a good tool should create an audit trail so that in the event of a legal claim the position of the defendant can be defended.

The possibility of automated testing, where large sites and multi-site complexes belonging to the same owner can all be tested in a simple, actionable, low-cost and reliable way is also of interest.

One of the problems with current tools is that they are all proprietary black boxes. If something is wrong or inconsistent it is not possible to open it up and see where the problem lies. The other problem relates to the excessive specialisation of tools as exemplified in the case where 15 different tools are required to check a single site.

As one developer put it *"there is no need for 100 different tools that only do part of job"*, there is a need for one generic tool that everyone knows will work, that everyone can trust and that can be thought of as the de-facto benchmark for compliance.

The solution may be to support the development of an open source initiative to provide that tool. Such an approach would help to open up the "black box" so that people on the front line of compliance could look "under the hood" to understand inconsistencies or problems as they arise, recommend improvements and participate in communities of practice on how to use them in real life.

Furthermore, another approach for testing the validity, coverage and other factors of a testing tool could be a specific corpus of web-sites with already known problems injected in them used as a testing box where tools run their test and compare with what was expected and is considered wrong in the first place. This is an approach transferred from experiments and research in the information retrieval domain where libraries such as TREC libraries are being used for information retrieval algorithms to run tests and identify their strengths and weaknesses.

The Skills Challenge, Training and Expertise

Few developers are aware of accessibility as an issue or have acquired the relevant skills to run an accessibility project. One of the problems seems to be a lack of consensus on what these skills might be. Experts insisted on the need to define a set of programmer skills and practices necessary for e-accessible SW and system development.

While many suggested a need for a recognised form of certification that guarantees a minimum set of skills and knowledge and basic development practices, they also stressed that accessibility should be built into basic design practice and not treated as an afterthought. It is always more expensive to handle compliance as an afterthought to be managed by a series of patches, but it is much more desirable and ultimately cheaper to build it in from the outset. Without some system of certification it is hard to make a profession out of it and develop it in a systematic way.

They expressed a desire to see a systematic campaign to raise awareness among media intensive companies and ICT service providers. This should be aimed at the level of the CEO, the CIO and the developer. Often the CEO of a company is aware of the accessibility requirements, but the bottleneck occurs at the level of the developer. Since there are always other projects going on, this issue is never given the priority it deserves.

Other suggested future steps include the creation and support of communities of practice around this theme. The example of Ability Net (AbilityNet, 2013) in the UK was provided as an example of the kind of activity which would be beneficial all across Europe. Among the various services they provide is an online web-accessibility e-learning course.

An expert from a French consulting company called Micropol, observed that there is already demand for experts to work on accessibility projects for which they will be paid, and that they expect the demand for such expertise to increase rapidly in the coming years. Unfortunately he also observed that there is a high level of inertia among SW developers and service providers, and that for the time being the offer is much less than the level of demand. Even MS remarked on difficulties it had recruiting people with suitable training for their own accessibility efforts.

Micropol also emphasised that what is needed is a range of skills and expertise. The implementation of a system is not the same as the evaluation of its accessibility. There is also a need for people who can plan and lead projects, do the work, or simply intervene with advice and coaching. Overall he stressed the need to integrate accessibility into the design process from the start of an IT project. At the start of a web design project many basic choices must be made, usually of the order of 100 or more. Good choices reduce cost and ease the maintenance of accessibility. Poor choices lead to compliance related rework, delays in delivery, higher costs and lower margins, less client satisfaction.

WHEN PROBLEMS TURN INTO SOLUTIONS

The Problem with CAPTCHA

A "captcha" is a test used by a computer to verify that it is interacting with a person and not another machine or program. Typically it is used to check that someone accessing a website is a real customer or user and not a robot trying to enter without authorization for example to obtain information or execute tasks which would normally be denied.

Most regular users of the internet have come across them by now. When a user enters a website and is asked by the site to read a text hidden in a picture, manually type that text into a field and then hit return. The computer relies on its knowledge that few if any image recognition program are able to recognize the text and that a correct answer most likely implies the involvement of a

real human being. The image is usually written in a strange and distorted way. Many users may have difficulty even reading some images and so they may request a new image. This whole test where the user has to "capture" some meaning hidden in a text is called a "captcha".

This technique was invented by a group of researchers at Carnegie Mellon University in 2000. The name was chosen to sound like "capture" but it actually means "Completely Automated Public Turing test to tell Computers and Humans Apart". They are usually used to eliminate email spam and prevent automated posting to blogs and Wikis. The general idea is that the test is simple enough to be doable by all human beings, but complex enough to fool most automated form filling systems. Perhaps the simplest version of a captcha is a simple request to "please tick this box" but a captcha can be far more complex and interesting than this example suggests.

For most users captchas are merely a nuisance and a waste of time. It seems that already about 200 million people every day waste about 10 seconds or so reading and typing in a captcha. For people with a disability such as poor eyesight, they can be more than annoying, providing an effective barrier to access. Wikipedia ("CAPTCHA," 2014) gives a short but useful discussion on efforts to provide more accessible captchas, especially using audio captcha, and a dedicated captcha site (Carnegie Mellon University, 2010) allows programmers to avail of free captcha technology and stay abreast of developments using a system called reCAPTCHA provided by the Carnegie Mellon University.

The Solution of ReCAPTCHA and Massive Micro-Collaboration

Despite the problems that CAPTHA presents to persons with disabilities the efforts to solve them are on a good way. However the same system can also present great opportunities for persons with disabilities in a totally unexpected way. Luis Van Ahn, one of the original inventors of the captcha presented the most recent developments (von Ahn, 2011) of the captcha idea at TEDx CMU in December 2011.

The basic idea the Carnegie Mellon group tried to develop is the fact that the original captcha technology does a useful job for free, protecting websites and users from fraud and spam, while using a very small bit of their time and intellectual capacity each time they log on. 200 million times 10 seconds a day works out at about 10 man-years of effort mobilized every day or 3,500 people working full-time.

They then asked if were possible to develop tests that not only required intellectual capacity of users, but useful capacity that contributed to a large distributed task. Eventually they came up with a system called reCAPTCHA (Google, 2014) that would help to translate books, by basing the test on parts of a real scanned text that could not be recognized by an optical reader. It turns out that optical character recognition devices are far from infallible especially when they are used to scan older texts that employ old, unfamiliar or highly decorative fonts, or texts that have simply become blurred and hard to read over time. These fonts are still recognizable to a human and human intervention is required to recognize the text. The recaptcha system presents two images to the user, one where the response is known and one where the response is unknown or unsure. The user provides answers to both problems, but does not know for which problem is the answer known or which problem is the answer unknown. Only the computer knows that. It grants access based on the response to the known question, but uses the response to the unknown question to complete the work of the OCR device and recognize a greater range of fonts in future.

Using an OCR device that can scan up to 1,000 pages per hour, Google has already scanned 15 million books in 140 languages as part of its Google Books (Google, 2012) project. It estimates that there are about 130 million books in the world and that it can scan all of these by about 2020.

Large newspaper companies such as the New York Times also have book scanning projects. The recaptcha system has proven very effective in providing a solution to this problem. The recaptcha company was bought by Google in 2009. So far about 350,000 websites use recapture, and 750,000,000 different people, about 10% of the world's population, have helped digitize at least one word for a book using the recaptcha system.

It is tempting to apply this form of massive online micro-collaboration to other problems for which no complete and easy solution exists, for example to the problem of translating material on the web into other languages. The Spanish part of Wikipedia for example is about 20% of the size of the English part. According to Luis van Ahn, one of the original inventors of captcha, speaking at TEDx CMU in 2011 (von Ahn, 2011), if one were to pay translators to translate this, even using the lowest paid translators in the world, the total cost would come to at least $50M. His idea is based on the observation that by using great numbers of people online and some new variation on the captcha idea, it should be possible to mobilize 100,000 active users to translate this in 5 weeks or 1 million active users to translate this in about 80 hours. This is the thinking behind a new venture called Duolingo (Duolingo, n.d.), which attempts to translate the web on the basis of a new online language learning system.

About 1.2 billion people in the world are already involved in learning a foreign language. In the US alone, 5 million people have paid more than $500 for language learning software. The Duolingo language learning system is free, but in return users help to translate the web. The bits they have to translate are matched to their ability, knowledge and experience. The quality of individual translations can be rated or inspected by more experienced people. Everyone is therefore soon able to contribute regardless of their level of proficiency. The system is currently in beta but according to Luis van Ah, the quality of translation is consistently as good if not better than that of professional translators.

Language is the basis for at least one form of situational disability. Text recognition and translation are only two kinds of access technology that benefit from the organization of massive on-line collaboration or crowd-sourced solutions. Wikipedia is another example as is the Open Source code movement. These are example of what Dan Tapscott calls Wikinomics, the economics of large scale online collaboration.

People with disabilities require the textual captioning of audio, image and video. They also require the audio captioning of text, image and video. Books are not only made up of text, they contain images and diagrams, most of which are not provided with alternative text. The technologies that have been developed to do this automatically do so imperfectly and often need human intervention to work effectively.

It could be of great benefit to the broadest group of people with disabilities to use the dynamics of massive online collaboration, in conjunction with state of the art automated machine techniques to address the problems.

The Greater Picture of Crowdsourcing

The story of CAPTCHA and reCAPTCHA is an example of how web can is turning into an amazing platform for collaboration. People from all over the world can come together in groups and gather information, work on a specific problem, provide voluntary work etc. The trend has been identified as crowdsourcing and the idea is to use the power of a large crowd to solve a problem that would take years to be solved by a limited number of persons. Break the problem into really small pieces requiring a trivial amount of effort to be solved and give it to a large number of people to work on these small pieces. This makes the problem easier and faster to solve and it also reduces a lot the cost for such a solution.

The web provides an ideal platform for such solutions and there are already a large number of sites that deal especially with using this power of crowds. A typical example is the Mechanichal Turk by Amazon (Amazon.com, Inc, 2014) where people can either import a group of tasks to be completed by a large number of participants and participants volunteer to work on specific tasks and get rewards for their job. A list of similar examples is presented in Ranker (Ranker, 2014).

Given the power and potential that this crowd-sourcing trend is giving to complex tasks such as identifying and testing the accessibility of a web site, it could be seen as something quite easy if the appropriate platform is provided. If for example people are given pacific micro-tasks such as "does this link have a meaningful text?" they could easily contribute to large evaluations of web accessibility of sites. Furthermore, given that the platforms are themselves accessible in the first place this could work even better by giving web site developers feedback and evaluation right from the source.

This is something that already happens to some extend in sites that encourage users to send their feedback for accessibility problems but such a platform could easily lower down the cost of evaluations and act as an online community aiming to help web site developers with the accessibility evaluation task.

PUBLISHING FOR ALL

According to LIBREKA (Liberka, 2014) e-Books introduced to the market in about 1998 or 1999 were premature. In particular they only had about a 20 minute battery life. Things have changed especially with the introduction of Kindle by Amazon, in an attempt to create a market for books that no longer need to be delivered by post, but by download. Nook by Barnes and Noble has also had great success and the big explosion came with iPad. Now many companies are bringing out tablet and reader products. The turnover of

Random House from e-books will exceed 50% of revenue by 2013 and e-books seem to be on the verge of a breakthrough.

Today of the 1.2 million books available in print from bookshops in Germany, only about 34,000 titles are available for purchase in Braille format (3%). Only about 15,000 titles are available in DAISY audio compatible format (<1%). Only about 4,200 are available in large print format (<<1%). Blind people in Germany therefore have a hugely reduced choice of reading material or publications.

In 2-3 years almost any book you care to mention will be available in electronic format, for use either with a "reader" or a smart phone. This will have a huge impact on the availability of material for this group of people.

eBooks are an important aspect of e-access technology because they can easily be linked to screen reader technologies and replace the need for sight with hearing. Apart from that they are also very convenient. Growth of this medium is being driven by ordinary consumers and not by the needs of people with disabilities. Nevertheless those with disabilities clearly benefit, on a scale not possible (actually: not conceivable!) with traditional solutions such as Braille.

One of the current barriers to having all content available in a screen reader friendly format is for the traditional print sector to move to new methods of production that facilitate the distribution of content in digital format.

Most content today is produced with the goal of print distribution and not digital distribution. Most digital distribution is realised merely through the provision of a PDF version of the print version, with little or no extra functionalities. Page layout does pose a challenge for readers. Many modern books are non-linear in the sense that there are columns, colours, insets, pictures, diagrams, formulae, text included in pictures and reference to these texts in the content. All of this poses a challenge for the screen reader. In modern texts the layout and the content tends to be closely intertwined. There is

scope for research on how to make accessible to a non-sighted person the information that exists in graphs or tables. How to "represent" this for the non-sighted person? Or in the spirit of Universal Design (UD) how to represent it for busy people who cannot look down, people who want to read in the car for example or those who need to consult manuals using advanced displays (terminator style contact lenses, the visors and cockpit displays used by fighter pilots) while their hands are busy.

Current content-publication-distribution work-flows are not compatible with digital publication in the sense that content often has to be recaptured from the print, is often only manipulated as an image file, and has no metadata associated with/to it.

In any case there is a need to rethink how content is created, represented, published and distributed. Publishers need to acknowledge that content should be crated for a variety of different publication possibilities and distribution channels. This will allow them to develop different business models based on re-use or re-purposing of content.

An example of advanced thinking in this sense might be the Economist, also HBR. They create content that is made available online, in newsletters, in print as a magazine, self-contained reports that can be bought separately, and books that combine previously published content under a single theme.

The current standard format for creating e-Books is called "e-PUB". It is suited to text-only books and is not much good after that. This needs to evolve. There is a new version coming out called ePUB3.0. It is intended to handle rich media environments and to have full DAISY compatibility. A range of other barriers and challenges also need to be addressed:

- Digital workflows
- The technical capabilities of staff involved in the publishing industry
- DRM or Digital Rights management. The issue of copyright applied to print is already an urgent one as indicted by the con-

troversy around Kindle and the attempts by the writer's guild of America to block the spoken versions of their books distributed via Kindle.

TV ISSUES

The TV Remote Control in 2020

One of the worst things about the TV in general is the remote control. The person who holds the control has power! And the person who masters all its functions has the absolute power! To a more serious tone now, the remote also presents a problem for older and disabled users. The remote is hard to use, especially if it has fallen and broken or if the battery does not fit in very well. Then what about the confusion caused by having one remote that works with the TV, another that works with the Blue-Ray device and a third that works with the video recorder?

There has been considerable work and efforts to standardize and simplify operations and also for several years' research was undergoing in what was called "Universal remote control" i.e. a control that could be programmed to operate various brands of one or more types of TVs and other consumer electronics devices. The proliferation of smart phones and computer tablets gave also the opportunity that these devices would be used as universal remote controls too. The main advantages here are that smartphone and tablet universal remote software is usually highly customisable. However, looking to a horizon of 2020, these developments are already here and are not part of a forward-looking technology policy.

According to interviews and reports from technology magazines, Apple sees the future of the TV as a device that would respond to users' voices and movements as it is already explored in the European Guide project(GIUDE, 2014). This seems to be inspired by Siri and may draw upon Siri technology and it would address problems that

older people or people with disabilities generally experience with simply using the remote control. But what if there are several people in the room, whose voice does it obey? What happens if people don't agree or if 10 people who are watching together, all wanting something else?

Apple sees its iTV as something where the remote control can be replaced with the iPhone or the iPad. It sees it integrating smoothly with the iPhone, the iPad, iTunes, the iPod, the whole Apple product universe. That is great but what happens when 5 people are watching at the same time, all with their own iPad, iPod and iPhone?

Apple has been very successful with devices for individuals. However both Apple and its competitors may be entering into a whole new area that it does not understand with devices that are intended for use in groups.

There seems as though we are entering into unknown territory here and that the needs of people with disabilities should be integrated from the start, at least they should be involved in research at this stage as to how group dynamics will evolve and how people will want to use the TV to start with.

Main input modalities will be voice and gestures for controlling TV in the future. However, simplification of the remote control operations and use of smartphone and tablet as remotes with a simple and intuitive interface, customized to each user's preferences and capabilities will continue to attract interest from research and industry. These advances can promise better control for TV from persons with disabilities especially if they are all combined together and work complementary to each other.

Radio Trends and TV Personalization

All over the world the Media and Entertainment industry continues to grow at a healthy pace and there is a rising rate of investments by the private sector to improve entertainment infrastructures to a great extent. Furthermore, digitisation and technological improvements across the value chain have provided the required impetus for improving the quality of content and its ability to reach the masses of consumers. Growing broadband penetration has attracted more content online and at a pan-European scale the mobile telephony market provides a new platform for content delivery.

Media and entertainment may perhaps be the decisive factor that will act as a catalyst for the mainstreaming of accessibility for big parts of user population. Efforts that have been given for specific life aspects like enhancing access to learning and educational resources may seem comparably insignificant to those that will be given in the next years in the media and entertainment field.

TV remains the main source of entertainment, education and information about current events for most people. And though it becomes more and more integrated with other media, especially the Web, TV is becoming more interactive with phone-ins, SMS and email channels being used more frequently. So how will this mass medium, that fulfils many different needs, evolve in the coming years?

The fragmentation of audience will become a major problem for TV – the problem may start from advertising and result to the entirety of the content distributed over TV. Furthermore, there are major groups who will probably use both free and pay TV. Connected TV may become a totally new type of challenge for regulators. Should our programs be accessible to all types of user population? Last but not least another question that tantalises the key people in the TV industry sector is whether generation Y shall come back to TV.

Watching TV used to be a family experience - to some extent it is still a group experience so how can mixed groups use it, groups of non-disabled together with groups of people with a disability?

Independently on the changes to be faced in the TV front, perhaps the most promising breakthroughs should be expected to be seen from radio. In an interview of Jim Kerr vice president of strategy for Triton Digital Media, a global firm that provides digital tools to traditional media companies, he recognizes several trends for the future of radio (Kerr, 2011), all of which relate with the general media and entertainment industry trend for increasing personalization and addressing of the individual needs of consumers. Not all are relevant to our context so we focus on the ones we consider as more related to the accessibility field:

Gathering and organizing listener data becomes priority one: While radio has historically been about broadcast, at the centre of current digital development, from mobile to social media to streaming to advertising, is the unique user. Gathering, identifying, and communicating with radio listeners at a one-to-one level will be the centrepiece of radio's future.

User-level advertisements targeting will redefine the value chain: We will finally be seeing ads targeted to specific users based not only on demographics, but their actual interests and behaviour. This will be a huge leverage for the M&E industry Key drivers will be the continued growth of local digital initiatives based on improved user-level targeting.

Besides evolutionary aspects of the TV technologies, convergence between Internet and other broadcasting technologies and the probable proliferation of Web TV or some other TV standard, there are changes to be faced in the future as far as the underlying business models for development, production and distribution are concerned.

Media and entertainment was mainly in the past property of the few; now it seems that more and more power is given to the average individual, while this does not limit the power of the established media players.

The idea of convergence in TV and PCs has dramatically changed: though in the past it was mainly treated as a hardware compliance and standards problem, it was recognized that these two mediums, (broadcast) TV and (personal) Web, are sufficiently different (Social TV Forum, 2014), not in technical terms, but human ones: while TV is an audience-based 'thing' where many people can watch one movie together, the Web, on the other hand is highly personal and is inherently related with interactivity: one person may have very different responses compared to another, making it difficult for more than one person to surf the web together for extended periods, or participate in an interactive program, unless specifically designed for multiple players. However, the emergence of social networks that we currently experience is only but one of the attempts to change the structural character of Web: now it is mainly on how can email, Twitter, Facebook, advertising, localization of advertising all go together from within the TV.

Parallel Societies and the Social TV Experience

The term 'parallel societies' was coined as a sociological term in the 1990s to denote purportedly 'segregated' immigrant communities by William Hiscott (2005), a political publicist and professional editor based in Berlin.

Originally, the vision for people living in a multicultural Europe concentrated around the notion of integration: how can we achieve that people coming from different countries and with different backgrounds converge towards a future of sharing common values and principles. Rather unfortunately, this vision has now changed dramatically so that we now need to speak about segregated societies that, however, should recognise and respect each other. This means that TV programs or educational or entertainment content cannot fit all people's capacities, preferences, lifestyles and social or religious value systems. So why should we keep on the current suboptimal paradigm of one-TV-fits-all or, the equally suboptimal paradigm of supporting many different channels of thematic orientation and not try to homogenize media and entertainment content by adapting it to different settings? The following hypothetical example case may shed some light on what is possible to experience in the near future:

The Bhatti-Sorensen family lives in Brussels. They share a happy life of mutual respect though they have different capacities: the father who is a diplomat of an Asian country is deeply religious and prefers to not be exposed to content that may in any of the many ways harm his religious feelings or violate his principles about what is acceptable or not. Though not very common, besides his personal beliefs, Mr Bhatti is a follower of the Western civilisation and what we call the European Union's value system and is married to Mrs Sorensen who is not a religious person at all. Being deaf-mute, Mrs Sorensen wants to have access to TV programs that for religious reasons and because of their content or aesthetics should be considered as not accessible to Mr Bhatti. Living in the same home with their three children (and a dog), they have access to the same TV though the programs they watch need to be adapted content-wise for the husband and modality-related for the wife. Their smart TV needs to adjust to the viewer's profile dynamically, while also take care for the cases that both spouses decide to watch TV. Their smart TV instead of separating them helps them come closer after their busy working days (he as a diplomat, she as a translator for a publishing house).

Being in a hotel in Brussels, there are plenty of options for watching national channels all over the EU spectrum; being an elderly Portuguese citizen living with your child who is an academic and lives with her husband in U.K. does not give one as many options.

Though TV is still a collective shared social experience, new types of partnerships are emerging and there is a growing need for new business models (Private Television in Europe, n.d.) that are capable to explain the changing economics of content delivery, the bandwidth demands of exploding video consumption.

Research on behaviour is necessary as people tend to both under and over estimate how they spend their time - what people think they do and what they do is quite different.

New trends that may offer insight to new types of content and services are:

- The simultaneous use of television and internet so that we can safely predict that by 2020 all major manufacturers will offer internet-connected TV sets
- The produce local – distribute & broadcast global trend that with the proliferation of internet-connected TVs shall facilitate easier penetration into niche audiences and integrate communities across borders
- The produce local – distribute & broadcast local trend (also called local TV) that shall for first time in the history of TV prove and demonstrate economic viability though the local TV shall only address relatively smaller (both thematically and / or from a user profile highly fragmented) audiences
- The increased amount of time devoted to watching more TV by combining viewing with other activities that in total increases the daily media consumption

Language Options and Ethnicities

The Audiovisual Media Services Directive (Directive 2010/13/EU of the European Parliament and of the Council of 10 March 2010 on "the coordination of certain provisions laid down by law, regulation or administrative action in Member States concerning the provision of audiovisual media services") explicitly stresses the right of persons with a disability and of the elderly to participate and be integrated in the social and cultural life of the Union that is "*inextricably linked to the provision of accessible audiovisual media services. The means to achieve accessibility should include, but need not be limited to, sign language, subtitling, audio-description and easily understandable menu navigation*".

But do elderly Portuguese or Greeks constitute a critical mass for the TV sector to address their access-to-information needs? If there is a lesson that markets in all sectors of the economy have learned in the last ten years of the previous century, this is that one can turn profitable though

still addressing small or micro markets (Pine, 1999). It only needs the necessary skills to do so. So, find your customers and offer them a service may not be a trivial exercise but is always an option. Same way as for EU citizens who live in another EU member country, it is also an option to address infotainment needs of residents coming from countries outside EU: till today, their infotainment needs are satisfied with satellite dishes and access to their home countries TV programs. This situation further widens (and also deepens) the gap and drives to parallel societies that may have unwelcome results. Why not have a BBC that talks to all EU and some non-EU languages? So let's make it become affordable. And how can different ethnicities get what they need or want to have? And if done with ethnicities why not do it with minorities of any type? Thematic stratification worked well for several decades but one may seriously doubt whether this is the way to go for the future.

Recently in the Smarter Planet blog from IBM a new application for mobile devices was presented. Vorce (Osborne, 2012) can translate live what a person says in one language to another. Technologies like these are expected to expand in the near future and platforms of mobile, TV and desktop computers are already on the way of convergence. This means that in a few years such applications might be available widely through TV devices so that people can watch programs from whichever language they want. It is interesting to see that this application can also benefit persons with disabilities too. Especially if such a feature is combined with live translation in sign language it could totally break down communication barriers.

Unlike radio and print media that create meaning primarily through language, television engages in signification through the unity and conflict of verbal, visual and sound codes. The dynamics of this type of signification has not been studied adequately. Viewers and media professionals often claim that the visuality of television is a sufficient form of communication. Much like verbal languages, however, the visual and sound components of the television program are polysemic, i.e. they convey multiple meanings, and lend themselves to different, sometimes conflicting, and interpretations.

The Affective TV

Why should people get sleepy while watching TV? Why shouldn't a user friendly TV read our eye lids and take the courageous decision to either close or change program? Why shouldn't the user friendly TV take the liberty to freeze the running of a movie to let us go to the toilet or alert us to go to the toilet in case we need to but are unable to see the risk? Why shouldn't our user friendly TV adapt viewing settings so that we don't need our glasses – a self-calibration of the presented images would allow the user to watch his or her favourite program without changing the settings.

So, the TV is a device that enables access to content but may also have decision-making capabilities. Access to content does not take place the way we have been used at: a child is not enabled to follow an adult film, same way as a manic depressive person is not allowed to have access to certain broadcasts, while a deaf person is given the necessary support through captioning and / or subtitling so that he / she may follow the program.

Smart TVs shall not keep content only for themselves: quite the contrary, they will be able to send content to other devices if needed, so that a busy person will not miss a live concert and still have access through their mobile phone.

Furthermore, and in contrast to smart phones that have the capability to act as TV devices, an affective TV is capable to support groups of individuals that express their wish to watch a program: after identifying the individuals (a step not necessary – however, in that case of registering as guest and not as a registered user, nobody should blame the TV for broadcasting in English without captioning to a blind Croatian person who refused

to identify himself!), the affective TV takes the optimal decision to satisfy collectively the interaction needs and capabilities of the particular group.

In addition to recognizing the person, the affective TV can also recognize his/her state and needs and provide him/ her with appropriate content. For example an old lady who is tired from a day's activities and just wants to relax may have as a suggestion to watch an entertainment program, while on the other hand a blind young man who is about to prepare a meal for his girlfriend might get as a suggestion a program with recipe instructions properly subtitled and described through audio descriptions for him.

People (usually children and elderly) talk to the TV – either to the TV as a device hypothetically capable to listen to them, or to the program that is broadcasted. As with many other non-living objects, people feel comfortable to assign qualities and properties that are currently non-existing. This may facilitate the process of assigning more and more information processing and decision-taking capabilities to the TV, thus helping the latter become smarter, more intelligent and affective.

How much control will a person have on his/ her TV suggestions? How easy would it be to deviate from TV suggestions and how TV should respond to that kind of behaviour? What if the person decides to follow programs that are not accessible for him/her? How can an affective TV understand social roles in a group (i.e. the father) and interpret them to suggestions for the group? Questions like the previous ones may lead research on affective computing on new grounds combining it with social sciences and getting into a deeper level from understating the emotional state of a person. Research in the future should look into these issues too if we want to reach a level of devices that can really understand people not only as individuals but as parts of social groups and communities.

The Internet TV and Its Pace of Evolution

Two major players are Google TV (Google, n.d.) and Apple TV (Apple, 2014). The general idea is to combine the advantages of large screens offering shared high definition viewing with access to on-line content and interactivity.

Apple TV offers easy hi-definition, full-screen viewing of video from YouTube and vimeo as well as the possibility of viewing and sharing personal photos, videos, music collections as well as purchased movies and TV shows. If a user stores their videos and photos in the iCloud, then they can make it available to an Apple TV user, for example a family member of friend, for remote viewing. The next time they switch on their TV, this will be available for access via the iCloud. The Apple approach seems to be an extension of the Apple experience to the TV format, that leverages its investments in iTunes and relations with content vendors, rather than an extension of TV itself. Access to Apple TV is based on the purchase of a 'box' that is plugged into the internet and into the digital TV set. The idea is that Apple TV will provide a platform for App developers who will develop specifically with the habits and needs and possibilities of TV viewers in mind. Earlier attempts to launch Apple TV did not have the success that Apple intended, but this remains a very important project for the future.

The approach of Google is slightly different. There is a big focus on search and the ability to browse over the TV image. The idea is that you can search for programs or shows you want to watch in a more flexible and dynamic way. While watching you can browse the web and use search services. You can look up the history of a film or the biography of an actor without missing the program. You can rent movies and pay for access to sports events. You can interact with friends for example using tweet and watch.

In the case of Google you can access Google TV either using a separate box or a dedicated TV set. Currently the only provider of the dedicated Google TV set is Sony. This initiative with Sony and Logitech has not been very successful. Their product is generally considered over-priced and with an interface that is too complex to use. This does not bode well for access to smart TV by people with disabilities.

According to Samsung a smart TV has a *"built-in computer-style processors and a software platform that allows for custom-made applications"*. For the time being this is still an emerging technology and there is no dominant standard for smart TV software. One of the oft-cited difficulties of working in this area is collaboration with broadcasters and networks to get access to programs and listings.

Despite these difficulties, Google has been working with LG on a Google TV set and is close to a deal with Samsung (Lee, 2011), the largest supplier of high definition flat screen TV sets in the world. With Samsung it expects to launch a Google TV set in 2012. Samsung expects to sell 45 million TV sets this year, of which 12 million will be smart TV sets.

The development of technology for TV happens in a different way and is subject to a different rhythm than the development of web-technology or mobile telephony. People renew their mobile phone more or less once every year. Websites need maintenance every 3 months or so.

The opportunity for introducing new technologies for websites and browsers, or for smart phones and tablets is almost ever present. The opportunity for introducing new technologies for mass market TV applications requires more careful timing. This might have been a factor for the success of public funded research projects up to date. However, the convergence between TV and computing in general and the models followed in market that allow TVs to become platforms for applications that could be installed on TV sets anytime might change that pace. New TV sets will be able to get updates of their applications anytime making the pace of evolution in that direction even faster.

People might still change their TV sets after years, however the TV set bought today will not have the same functionalities in two years. The update and plethora of applications will make the TV another highly customized and constantly adapting device. R&D for accessibility should be prepared and ready to ride this new wave of evolution coming in TV sets.

Content and the Captioning Challenge

The United Nations Convention on the Rights of Disabled Persons, ratified by New Zealand, states that all persons with disabilities should enjoy equal access to television programmes, films, theatre and cultural activities in accessible formats. The main way for doing this is via captioning.

In its broadest sense captioning means alternative text descriptions for images, alternative audio or text descriptions for video as well as text descriptions for audio.

Many countries, Australia and the USA included, have mandatory captioning legislation. Such legislation indicates or example that a minimum of certain percentage of TV programs must be available with captioning. Captioning is time-consuming and expensive. National and private television stations are always under increasing pressure for budgets. For this reason the number of TV programmes that are captioned is a small percentage say 10% or 20% of those broadcasts, but always far below the ideal of 100% that is considered as practically not possible. Some countries do it very well and others not so well. There is an international market for film and TV. There is no guarantee that products created in one country are captioned in a way that is suitable for distribution in another.

Captioning is not just an issue for people with disabilities. An English, American or Chinese film or TV series distributed in France, Egypt or Germany will generally require dubbing or sub-titles before it is suitable for domestic consumption.

This is related to captioning, even if it is treated as a separate activity.

Another related issue is the tagging or annotation of film archives to make them searchable. Some progress has been made on the automation of captioning using advanced speech and search technologies, but a lot remains to be done.

Intelligent ICT systems are already used to generate sports articles for newspapers. This type of technology may one day generate narratives that reflect what has been happening onscreen. Technology for image recognition, speech recognition and automatic translation are already approaching a level of maturity that will make them useful for automated captioning of film and audio. Thus, one way forward to meet the captioning challenge is to develop this approach so that captioning no longer has to be done by hand but can be done in batch mode on a large scale with hand-checking only needed for spotting errors.

However there are other ways forward and this is not the only one. TV production companies have leveraged the internet for many years. Programmes have become more social in the sense that they involve audience ringing in, posting messages online, texting and voting. They can take part in forums online, post blogs commenting on actors, the characters they play, the writer or the presenter, as well as the evolution of the plot.

Nowadays there are communities providing within days of a programmes release subtitles for a variety of languages. Since the next step of TV will be tied with the web such online communities and their services could find a place for easier interaction, production and distribution of such material. Progress in interaction technologies already described such as speech recognition could allow persons to produce alternative content for captioning of programs almost in real time.

The latter show that the future might see applications based on crowdsourcing for providing captioning services. People watching a TV program could at the same time take notes on their tablet, annotate scenes, translate what is been told and produce alternative material almost on the fly. This could lead to communities of people producing annotation content of people with disabilities too. Persons being close to persons with disabilities (friends and family) could be one of the first contributors of such content to help their relatives. However the web and the internet connected TV could help in expanding the impact their content has by providing it easier to other persons with similar disabilities.

REFERENCES

AbilityNet. (2013). *Welcome to AbilityNet*. Retrieved March 12, 2014, from http://www.abilitynet.org.uk/

AccesiWeb. (n.d.). *AccessiWeb - Accueil*. Retrieved March 12, 2014, from http://www.accessiweb.org/

Amazon.com. Inc. (2014). *Amazon Mechanical Turk - Welcome*. Retrieved March 12, 2014, from https://www.mturk.com/mturk/welcome

Apple. (2014). *Apple - Apple TV - HD iTunes content and more on your TV*. Retrieved March 12, 2014, from http://www.apple.com/appletv/

ATIA. (n.d.). *Home - Assistive Technology Industry Association*. Retrieved March 13, 2014, from http://www.atia.org/i4a/pages/index.cfm?pageid=1

BrailleNet. (2011). *Proceedings - 5th European eAccessibility Forum Benefits and costs of e-accessibility*. Retrieved March 12, 2014, from http://inova.snv.jussieu.fr/evenements/colloques/colloques/70_actes_en.html#contenu

BrailleNet. (2012). *General description - 6th European eAccessibility Forum Putting eAccessibility at the core of information systems*. Retrieved March 12, 2014, from http://inova.snv.jussieu.fr/evenements/colloques/colloques/76_index_en.html#contenu

BrailleNet. (2014). *BrailleNet page d'accueil*. Retrieved March 12, 2014, from http://www.braillenet.org/

Caldwell, B., Cooper, M., Reid, L. G., & Vanderheiden, G. (2008, November 21). *Web Content Accessibility Guidelines (WCAG) 2.0*. Retrieved March 12, 2014, from http://www.w3.org/TR/WCAG20/

CAPTCHA. (2014, March 8). *Wikipedia, the free encyclopedia*. Retrieved from http://en.wikipedia.org/w/index.php?title=CAPTCHA&oldid=598761909

Carnegie Mellon University. (2010). *The Official CAPTCHA Site*. Retrieved March 12, 2014, from http://www.captcha.net/

Décret n° 2009-546 du 14 mai 2009 pris en application de l'article 47 de la loi n° 2005-102 du 11 février 2005 sur l'égalité des droits et des chances, la participation et la citoyenneté des personnes handicapées et créant un référentiel d'accessibilité des services de communication publique en ligne., 2009-546 (2009).

Duolingo. (n.d.). *Duolingo | Learn Spanish, French, German, Portuguese, Italian and English for free*. Retrieved March 12, 2014, from https://www.duolingo.com/

EOWG, & ATAG WG. (2013, October 5). *ATAG Overview*. Retrieved March 12, 2014, from http://www.w3.org/WAI/intro/atag.php

EOWG, & ERT WG. (2011, May 10). *EARL Overview*. Retrieved March 12, 2014, from http://www.w3.org/WAI/intro/earl.php

EOWG, & UAWG. (2005, July). *UAAG Overview*. Retrieved March 12, 2014, from http://www.w3.org/WAI/intro/uaag.php

EOWG, & WCAG WG. (2006, December 21). *WCAG 1.0 Documents*. Retrieved March 12, 2014, from http://www.w3.org/WAI/intro/wcag10docs.php

GIUDE. (2014). *European Project GUIDE - Gentle User Interfaces for Elderly People*. Retrieved March 12, 2014, from http://www. guide-project.eu/

Google. (2012). *Books Google*. Retrieved March 12, 2014, from http://books.google.com/

Google. (2014). *reCAPTCHA: Stop Spam, Read Books*. Retrieved March 12, 2014, from http:// www.google.com/recaptcha

Google. (n.d.). *Google TV*. Retrieved March 12, 2014, from http://www.google.com/tv/

Hiscott, W. (2005). Parallel societies, A neologism gone bad. *Focus Online*. Retrieved from http:// aa.ecn.cz/img_upload/f76c21488a048c95b-c0a5f12deece153/WHiscott_Parallel_Societies. pdf

Kerr, J. (2011, January 12). 5 Trends for Future of Radio. *Triton Digital*. Retrieved March 13, 2014, from http://www.tritondigital.com

Lee, J.-A. (2011, November 23). Samsung in Final Talks on Google TV. *Wall Street Journal*. Retrieved from http://online.wsj.com/news/ articles/ SB1000142405297020444434045770 53153432777594?mod=djemIndiaUpdate_h& mg=reno64-wsj&url=http%3A%2F%2Fonline. wsj.com%2Farticle% 2FSB1000142405 2970204444340457705315343 2777594. html%3Fmod%3DdjemIndiaUpdate_h

Liberka. (2014). *libreka! Bücher & E-Books*. Retrieved March 13, 2014, from http://www. libreka.de/

LOI n° 2005-102 du 11 février 2005 pour l'égalité des droits et des chances, la participation et la citoyenneté des personnes handicapées., 2005-102 (2005).

Osborne, C. (2012, March 7). Vocre&#039,s live translation video tool breaks language barriers. *SmartPlanet*. Retrieved March 13, 2014, from http://www.smartplanet.com/blog/smart-takes/ vocres-live-translation-video-tool-breaks-language-barriers/23887

Pine, B. J. (1999). *Mass Customization: The New Frontier in Business Competition*. Harvard Business Press.

Private Television in Europe. (n.d.). *Is there a future for private television?*. Author.

Ranker. (2014). Top 10 Lists & Much More - The Best Lists About Everything. *Ranker*. Retrieved March 12, 2014, from http://www.ranker.com/

SCNF. (n.d.). *Accessibilité SNCF - Site Internet de la délégation à l'accessibilité et aux voyageurs handicapés*. Retrieved March 12, 2014, from http:// www.accessibilite.sncf.com/

Social, T. V. Forum. (2014). *Social TV Forum - TV Apps Hackathon, Social TV Events*. Retrieved March 12, 2014, from http://www.social-tv.net/

Temesis, E. (n.d.). *Temesis : qualité et accessibilité web*. Retrieved March 12, 2014, from http:// temesis.com/

Travability Pty Ltd. (2013). *Travability - Making the World Accessible to All*. Retrieved March 12, 2014, from http://travability.travel/

United Nations. (2007). *UN Enable*. Retrieved March 12, 2014, from http://www.un.org/esa/ socdev/enable/gawanomensa.htm

Von Ahn, L. (2011). *Massive-scale online collaboration*. Retrieved from http://www.ted.com/ talks/luis_von_ahn_massive_scale_online_collaboration

W3C. (2014). *World Wide Web Consortium (W3C)*. Retrieved March 12, 2014, from http:// www.w3.org/

KEY TERMS AND DEFINITIONS

Crowdsourcing: Crowdsourcing is the practice of obtaining needed services, ideas, or content by soliciting contributions from a large group of people, and especially from an online community, rather than from traditional employees or suppliers.

E-PUB: E-PUB (short for electronic publication) is a free and open e-book standard by the International Digital Publishing Forum (IDPF).

Internet TV: A TV with connection to internet.

Publishing: Publishing is the process of production and dissemination of literature, music, or information—the activity of making information available to the general public.

Smart TV: A TV with computer features that may enable it to interact with computerized systems, send e-mails, and access the web.

TV: Television (TV) is a telecommunication medium for transmitting and receiving moving images that can be monochrome (black-and-white) or colored, with or without accompanying sound.

Web Accessibility: Web accessibility refers to the inclusive practice of removing barriers that prevent access to websites by people with disabilities.

World Wide Web: The World Wide Web is the universe of network-accessible information, an embodiment of human knowledge.

ENDNOTES

[1] This point was made in particular by David Dikter of the US based Assistive Technology Industry Association (ATIA, n.d.) who expressed an interest in being involved in being involved in any follow-up discussion on this.

Chapter 12
Democracy, Citizenship, and Activism

ABSTRACT

Issues of participation of people with disabilities in politics and public administration are the focus of this chapter. People with disabilities can have an effective impact on society and policies if they are allowed and encouraged to participate in democratic processes, public administration, and activism actions. Through these channels, their voice can be heard even louder and clearer and can have an increased impact. This chapter discusses how ICT can help in encouraging such participation and how it can also assist in activist actions for disability rights. Citizenship in the age of social media, social media as a tool for social innovation, issues of compliance, the politics of disability, and design issues are some of the aspects discussed in the chapter.

CITIZENSHIP IN THE AGE OF SOCIAL MEDIA

The perception of politics from a citizen's point of view has changed dramatically over the last decade, largely thanks to participatory technologies and, more recently, to social networking. This promises to have a much more profound impact on the experience of democracy and the nature of citizenship than all of the previous efforts at online democracy or e-voting or e-administration put together. Most of the efforts of the past have merely been literal and largely uninspired attempts to translate cumbersome 'analog' processes into IT enabled but equally cumbersome digital processes.

Experiments still go on to explore new ways for how people with disabilities to vote. In November 2011 the state of Oregon (Seelye, 2011) in the US became the first state to allow people with disabilities to vote using an iPad instead of a voting machine or ballot box. The article did not specify whether non-disabled people could vote in this way too, not to allow what would seem like discrimination against people without disabilities. It is expected that other states will follow soon. In actual fact the person selects their candidate and the computer prints out a completed ballot. The voters or assistants either mail the printed ballots or drop them in the ballot box. For the time being Internet voting is not common even

DOI: 10.4018/978-1-4666-6130-1.ch012

in the US and the example of the use of the iPad would seem to represent the current state of the art. There is some value in this to the voter however. A person with reduced vision can magnify the ballot on the screen or in principle understand the options using audio captions. Someone with arthritis, who cannot hold a pen, could touch the screen with his finger to mark the ballot. This kind of experimentation is almost inevitable in the US as a response to HAVA, the Help America Vote Act of 2002 which supports the financing of demonstration and pilot projects to ensure that people with disabilities are able to vote.

In this chapter we will not elaborate on these aspects of e-democracy for people with disabilities or even on the related issue of e-administration. Access to e-administration more or less comes down to interaction with web-site or portal and this issue has been covered in some detail in the chapter on media and entertainment under the heading of web-access.

Instead we look at the impact of social networking on the experience of democracy and on the nature of citizens participation in political life.

The real power of ICT in politics was shown during the campaign to elect Barack Obama in 2008. He refused to accept campaign donations from big industry and he refused to avail of public financing. He pioneered the use of social networking to break previous records for raising funds for both his presidential primary and general campaigns. Using Facebook, YouTube and instant messaging his campaign committee raised more than $650M to fund his campaigns. All of these were private donations each one consisting of small amounts typically of the order of $50 or $100. The story is told in more detail in a Wikipedia article ("Barack Obama presidential campaign, 2008," 2014) or in one of the many books about this achievement such as "Yes We Did: An inside view of how social media built the Obama brand" (Harfoush, 2009) by his online campaign manager. The campaign was triumph of the use of social media in targeted marketing and

it is highly likely that by 2020 these techniques will be commonplace in Europe as well.

Projects to exploring the use of social media in politics have been funded by FP7. The FUPOL (FUPOL, n.d.) project looks at how this will affect future policy making in the EU.

It is interesting to note that a World Report on Disability (WHO, 2011) published for the first time by the WHO and The World bank in 2011 notes that "*responses to disability have changed since the 1970s, prompted largely by the self-organization of people with disabilities…*" It turns about that self-organization has been an important element in the evolution of rights for disabled people.

In many ways this chapter is about how the use of ICT as a tool for self-organization could help communities of disabled people ensure that legislation intended for their benefit is actually enforced. There are many example of legislation that has been created but is in fact ignored. The reasons for this are many and it is not always done in bad faith. But someone has to raise the issue, bring it to the attention of politicians, researchers and industrialists so that they are first of all aware of the issue, and know who they can turn to for help to address it.

The Case of Maptivism

What is perhaps more interesting however is the rise of activism supported by an increasing rich array of smart-phone tools, in particular for phones and tablets that incorporate GPS and feature screens, even built-in compasses. Already this is referred to as "maptivism" and there is a substantial movement of people actively experimenting with the use of mobile technology to achieve specific goals for the public good. This has also been embraced by forward looking agencies and actors in public administration. One of the reasons for embracing this trend is to find ways to engage in political dialogue with specific groups, in particular younger groups who readily absorb new technologies and which can most easily be reached using these non-traditional channels of communication. In particular these technologies enable communities to find each other, develop assets that they can share as a community and use, while engaging in a sociable past-time that often amounts to a form of self-help on the basis of self-organization using a combination of social networking, easy to use smart phones and tablets with built in capabilities for taking photos and videos, recording sound, sensing position and orientation, displaying maps, aggregating and visualizing complex but useful information. An increasing number of simple, low-cost sensors are now being made available as accessories for these phones that turn them into microscopes and scanners or tools for chemical or environmental analysis.

No wonder that in a recent speech (European Commission, 2011) Neelie Kroes said:

I want out-of-the box thinking. I want to know what the Commission can do to facilitate media's contribution to our democracy and economic growth. The digital revolution is turning media upside down: how can we use the digital Single Market and other tools to capture the potential of this new dynamic?

The phenomenon of using maps for social activism is called maptivism (Kreutz, 2009). It relies on a whole new vocabulary of social dynamics, the idea of using the natural movement of people and their gregarious nature, their need to "check-in" ("Maps, Activism and Technology," n.d.) with friends and like-minded people to share the moment. The use of maptivism to help people with a disability is seen as a form of social justice.

A typical example of a maptivism application is Fix My Street (FixMyStreet, n.d.). It is the name of a UK service provided to citizens by an NGO called My Society (MySociety Limited, n.d.). This enables citizens to alert councils to problems with public infrastructure, problems such as potholes, damage to the sidewalk, graffiti, rubbish, blocked drains or faulty street lighting.

Each council in the UK is listed. You can list all the councils, to see how many problems have been reported, and how any have been solved. By clicking on the link to individual councils you can see a detailed breakdown of the problems by type as well as their current status.

Ease of Use Is Important

Another example of a similar application is Toilet-radar ("NYC Toilet Map | Toilet Radar," n.d.). It only seems to apply to a part of New York City. It helps people find public toilets. The system is not necessarily intended for someone with a disability, so it lacks information about access for people with disability. The website can be accessed by anyone with an iPhone. Users of the app can tag the existence of toilets. They can also look-up nearby toilets. Those who don't have an iPhone can find the nearest toilet by sending an texting the world toilet followed by the location address or cross street to a special number, in this case 41411. After about 20 or 30 seconds they should receive reply indicating the three nearest toilets.

At least for now the system does not seem to get a lot of use. It would be interesting to understand why. The texting feature though clever does not seem ideal for someone who is a visitor or unfamiliar with New York streets. It is probably possible to re-design such as system to do better.

The use of maps and augmented reality technologies which provide more intuitive interfaces than texting can be exploited in applications for more engagement and it would be interesting to see the effects these technologies can have.

The Issue of Valid and Important Information

One of the problems with toilets is that they are often vandalized. Many public toilets are therefore closed and only accessible by those who possess an appropriate key. There are over 7,000 disabled toilets in the UK that are only accessible by key. A UK program called toilet radar provides a single key, providing access to all of these locked toilets that can be purchased for about €5, but it is hard to expect visitors to know about the scheme.

People posting to UK government websites have in the past petitioned that all public toilets should use the same key system, so that access is provided whether they are intended for the disabled or not. Others have suggested that temporary toilets provided at public events should be accessible suing the radar key scheme.

There is scope to improve on such as system, making the toilets more easily locatable and perhaps using access based on electronic keys downloaded to mobile phones or other ICT based methods. The problem presented also shows that sometimes the information provided by a maptivism application might not be enough and especially in the case of accessibility problems might rise from situations totally irrelevant to typical accessibility information such as wheelchair access. This is an interesting lesson for such applications for the way they gather and organize information.

The Problem of Awareness and Interest

Wheelmap (Wheelmap.org, n.d.) is an Open Street Map (OpenStreetMap, n.d.) based initiative of a German NGO called Sozialhelden (SOZIALHELDEN.e.V, n.d.) to list all wheelchair accessible places in a city. It can be easily used by people on the move who have downloaded their iPhone or iPad app. It also compiles a black-list of non-accessible places. This is intended as a means for putting pressure to comply on places that are required by law to provide access to people with disabilities.

Places identified on street maps can be tagged by users as having good access, limited access, no access or unknown access. Each place is categorized by type, as a station, a toilet, a restaurant,

a bank or a bar for example, a sports facility a shop or a hotel.

Although the map for Brussels indicates many places, but only one bar has been tagged as providing limited access, whereas two public toilets and one train station have no wheelchair access.

There is clearly an issue of how to mobilize large numbers of people through "mapping parties" or other events to populate the map with relevant data. A big effort is needed to raise awareness of such facilities, complete the mapping projects and then, where there are substantial blacklist of non-accessible places, to organize campaigns to raise awareness of the problem and determine a time-table for compliance.

The focus of Wheelmap is specifically on wheelchair access. The authors believe that for those with other disabilities such as blindness or deafness, there is a need for another approaches. This could be work for the future.

In this direction the uptake of sign-in applications that are combined with gaming features is a good example to exploit. Users of Foursquare are awarded with points each time they check in a place. They earn badges, can follow quests and generally there is a gaming feeling behind the application idea. The uptake of the application indicates that it could be possible to exploit such techniques to engage people in tagging places for accessibility. For example award points to them, organize championships of tagging places in a city, provide special offers to persons that tag places with valid information etc.

SOCIAL MEDIA FOR SOCIAL JUSTICE

An initiative to develop a Global Disability Rights Library (Global Disabiliy Rights Library, n.d.) is supported by the US International Council for Disabilities (United States International Council on Disabilities, 2014). It naturally has a strong US orientation. As well as linking to key documents on disability rights it includes resources on advocacy and lobbying. Almost in itself a statement that often the best help is self-help.

Nevertheless the initiative is international and aims in particular to advance disability rights in the developing world. As we will see later, there may be a real need for resources such as these in the developed world as well.

Tools for Social Change and Their Accessibility

Socialbrite (Socialbrite, n.d.) is a website dedicated to the use of social media for local politics, by non-profits and people trying to defend a cause. Its motto is "social tools for social change". The site contains information and other resources relating to online petition tools (Katz, 2010). It has a section dedicated to how geolocation (Reed, 2010) is changing the world. It hosts lists of platforms for social good (Heppler, 2010) or tools for social change (Lasica, 2010a) or social action hubs by think tanks and NGOs such as Changemakers (Ashoka Changemakers, 2014). Typical themes relate to travel or getting about more efficiently, also networking using concepts such as checking in for good and local political activism related to the concept of networked neighbourhoods.

Some other interesting and innovative initiatives include:

- **Idealist:** (Action Without Borders, 2014) intended to help turn intentions into action
- **SeeClickFix:** (SeeClickFix, Inc., 2013) intended to expedite the solving of local problems by local government
- **OpenIDEO:** (OpenIDEO, n.d.) an open innovation platform sponsored by the design company intended to support co-design projects for social good
- **OpenStreetMap:** (OpenStreetMap, n.d.) is a technology alternative used by those who don't like Google Maps

- **BlogTalkRadio:** (BlogTalkRadio.com, 2014) is intended to extend the reach of your non-profit organization
- **Spot.us:** (American Public Media, 2014) & DocumentCloud (DocumentCloud, n.d.) are both dedicated to collaborative journalism.

The action is not limited to activists and NGOs; in some cases public administration has embraced this approach as well. A list of 20 good reference sites belonging to local government (Lasica, 2010b) is provided by Social Brite. This list includes a site called Open 311 (Open311, n.d.) dedicated to open standards for local government services.

Organizing activism for social good is not only about occupying public space and protesting. IT is often about mobilizing ordinary citizens to care to contribute to works for the benefit of the public good. But it is not easy (Social Innovation Camp, n.d.). If you take a banal example, the first idea that might occur to any social activist in London, namely the issue of wheelchair access across London, it is clear from some experiences that sustained effort, a clear strategy and an understanding of the dynamics of social media is a prerequisite as well as mastery of the appropriate tools and the tenacity to see a project through to the end.

An article at Londonist (Osburn, 2008) indicates that information about wheelchair accessible places in London is pretty scant. Efforts have been made to make London Underground ("London Underground weblog Blog," 2008) Tube maps more readable for disabled people. A lot could be done in this information age to make them more readable to non-disabled peopled as well. The new maps are meant to help people who are disabled, pregnant or elderly ("Tube maps made for the disabled," 2009) These are public efforts, but they are often incomplete.

Creating systems based on self-help that tap the motivation of real stakeholders allowing them to add value on a cumulative basis over time or punctuated with massive public efforts based on awareness days and mapping parties complete with DJs and music, may be a better way forward. Two alternative approaches that are worth to explore their potential are:

- To train groups of activists with disability who are interested in learning more about the use of social network for social good;
- Instead of investing money in new maps, it would be more productive for companies such as the London Underground to seed fund social activism. This *might possibly* yield a better and more sustainable result in shorter time and lower cost.

Communities create their own heroes. Someone confined to a wheelchair still needs to experience freedom of movement. Some have a strong competitive spirit and need space in which to play. There was a time before the invention of skateboards where cities did not like skateboards. There were no places to use them. Young people just occupied public spaces, used their skateboards and established the need for space and asserted their right to play the way they wanted to in a public space. Nowadays most cities have set aside areas where people can come and bring their skateboards and hang out with friends unbothered and in safety. Anyone who has seen the film Murder Ball, a tale about people who play wheelchair rugby, will have no doubt about similar needs among people using wheelchairs. There is a movement called the freedom of movement campaign (ENIL, 2013b) run by ENIL - the European Network on Independent Living (ENIL, 2013a) that fights for the rights of people with disabilities. It features performance artists like Bill Shannon (*Visa TV Ad starring Bill Shannon*, 2009) whose dance work relies on the use of crutches in something that resembles a cross between dance and parkour ("Parkour," 2014).

Occupying space would appear to be an important activity in any movement. It requires coordination and planning and maps. One of the most important tools in this respect is Sukey. This has played an important role in the Arab Spring, places like Tunisia and Egypt. It effectively allows groups of people to assemble spontaneously and maintain an awareness of escape route based on what it calls its safety compass, a picture or a compass that points the way to safety helping to move quickly in the right direction when tensions run high, such as when the police start shooting live rounds into the crowd.

At least one project is tracking civil rights and humanitarian activism (Pauli Murray Project, n.d.), while a US initiative called Sound Out (SoundOut, 2012) tracks student activism in the US.

It would be interesting to track activism in relation to the rights and needs of people with disabilities in social media. It would also be interesting to see the impact that social media activism has on businesses, politics and generally the society. However in order for that to happen, social media have to be accessible for persons with disabilities in the first place.

Social Media Activism and a New Social Status Currency

Google maintains a blistering pace of innovation and experimentation with new ways for collaborating around data. The key elements in its arsenal are search, not only text but video and image search as well, maps and collaboration around the use of maps using mash-ups, as well as a high quality email editor based on Gmail. It relentlessly pursues research and experimentation in a wide range of areas making not only the gathering, sharing and processing of data easy, but also collaboration and social activities around the use of this information.

Google Currents (*Introducing Google Currents*, 2011) pulls together in an intelligent way all of the websites a user wants to monitor in one place for browsing or use on their mobile device. An interesting point is that material is automatically synched and remains available when you are offline. This is one of many apps which effectively redesign or re-render the user interface so that material primarily intended for a laptop or PC is more accessible and usable on a mobile, smart-phone or tablet device.

It is possible to imagine applications such as this acting as an aggregator of all the various fragmented initiatives necessary to help a person with disability to get around and achieve as much as possible in the course of a day.

Major social media sites are showing some interest on accessibility. Facebook was recently hiring accessibility experts and according to a brief history of Facebook's communication with AFB and according to AFB's blog (American Foundation for the Blind., 2010) they were open to discuss accessibility problems and committed to work on finding solutions. Google also stated that Google+ was built from scratch with accessibility in mind and calls for users to bring up accessibility issues in order to deal with them. A recent survey by WebAIM (WebAIM, 2009) also shows trends and habits among screen reader users who also report their perception of accessibility of various social media. In general the most accessible social media site seems to be Twitter, possibly because of the simplicity of its interface and structure but there is no official statement for accessibility compliance from any of them.

One of the challenges for a future e-Access program in ICT may be to make sure that communities of people with disabilities are able to participate in and contribute to the development of these new technologies at the earliest stage possible, for example to make sure that basic principles of compliance with accessibility laws, or universal design are built into the design process from the start.

One of the most recent developments however is the Google + project (Google, n.d.). It has recently elicited a lot of comments (*The New Google*

Social Network-- Google+ Project -- Why It will be a Success?, 2011) on the internet. It brings a new approach to social networking that seems to go beyond merely sharing photos on your wall and signalling to 'friends' what you 'like'. It employs a new vocabulary and a set of basic social networking functions such as circles, hangouts, huddles and sparks that could provide the atoms from which dynamic new communities can be built.

In another attempt a Facebook app called Causes (Heppler, 2010) aims to bring the social activism closer to social gaming. People can start campaigns or support campaigns and gain point from recruiting friends in a cause. However, it is important to investigate how these campaigns can actually be transferred in reality. People start to believe that pressing a support button is enough to contribute to a campaign but how much of activism is that? How much of an impact can this simple move have?

It would be interesting to see the effects of more complex social gaming systems where other users reward you for your activism in a topic such as accessibility. For example, people that read your blog where you point out web accessibility problems in web sites could reward the user with activism points. So building up our social profiles will be based on other people's opinions for our actions. This way a new kind of social status currency could emerge and having a high social status will not depend on what you possess but on what you act on.

The Emerging Picture

The picture that has emerged with the use of social media and the web in general is one of citizenship and democratic participation of people with disabilities that features activism of various kinds – advocacy, lobbying, or campaigning by more radical means. In general we can see the following 4 models of actions taken from people with disabilities to have the biggest impact:

- Action by *disabled people as citizens* using e-democracy, by integrating the voices of people with disability into local e-government and public procurement. In particular in areas of importance to people with a disability.
- Action by *disabled citizens as consumers* where using their power as consumer based on the "market model" of accessibility they could force businesses to think and take into account accessibility.
- Action by *disabled citizens as employees* where by demanding reasonable accommodations they can access and enjoy their right to work.
- Action by *disabled citizens as entrepreneurs* who might be end-users, inventors and investors who focus their energy, resources and lobbying skills on enabling well designed assistive, inclusive and e-access technologies.

THE PROBLEM OF COMPLIANCE

As already referred one of the key points for the future of social activism to support accessibility issues is how accessible are the tools for that activism. The current status of accessibility of social media is already presented in brief and the point was made in the previous section. However, accessibility compliance is not something that refers to social media only. The case of web accessibility is analysed in the media and entertainment chapter and we also dealt in detail with the case of access to ATM technology in the chapter entitled Consumer and Lifestyle. Despite the existence for a long time of disability legislation at EU level aimed at the use of ATMs, this legislation never seems to have been implemented. There may be many reasons for this, but the fact remains that it was not implemented and people with disabilities did not enjoy the level of access that the legislation was intended to provide.

To reinforce this point and provide evidence for the possible need for such legislation we look at a number of cases in point. It often happens that legislation is ignored. Usually this is because the legislation itself is poorly designed. Sometimes it is simply not realizable because the cost it would impose is too high. Whatever the reason, the intended beneficiary is left with the problem of what to do and how to improve their situation. This is the problem of compliance, the fact that the law is not enough. When the law does not work, what can one do?

To make the point we look in more detail at what has happened in the past in the case of two industries, media and entertainment as well as travel and tourism.

Media, Entertainment and Law Enforcement

In spite of a great number of laws governing access to communications and media in Europe, in particular in the area of access to websites and their content, there have been considerable delays even by major public companies to comply with available legislation. As far as we know there has been no real stakeholder movement to drive or enforce compliance.

The situation in the US is very different. At the Braillenet Meeting (BrailleNet, 2011) held in Paris on 28 March 2011, Cynthia D. Waddell of the ICDRI (International Center for Disability Resources on the Internet, 2012) or International Centre for Disability Resources on the Internet, spoke about the role of litigation in the US and how it has created an urgent need for compliance to avoid heavy fines and sanctions.

The modern history of disability legislation goes back to Sections 504 and 508 of the Rehabilitation Act of 1973. The act basically said that any organisation that receives federal funds had to comply with disability law and provide access for the disabled in accordance with that law. There was a lot of resistance however as the act was seen as too expensive. It languished until 1977 when Cynthia led a group of activists to occupy federal buildings. Eventually after 25 days of protest, she succeeded in having the act passed.

Nowadays US media and communications related disability law is nowadays governed by the 21st Century Communication Act (International Center for Disability Resources on the Internet, 2010). This came into force early on in the Obama government. It refers to the principle that all people of all disabilities can access broadband and other 21st century communication and video technologies. As a result all legislation that applied to TV and film automatically extends to any new 21st century technology. One of the consequences in law was that the iPhone has to be compatible with the hearing aid.

Despite such progress, compliance nevertheless remains a problem and many large companies have already fallen foul of the law, being subject to often quite large fines and demands to take measures to ensure compliance.

The risk is that if they don't they will have to pay attorney fees plus damages via a department of justice enforcement. To understand how it works note that every website element which is not accessible incurs damages of $4000 per day until it is put right. This adds up quickly, for example 20 errors over 30 days becomes $2.4M!

Although communications and media related litigation in the US has tended to focus on the needs of the blind, strong advocacy groups to defend the interests of professionals with all kinds of disabilities.

The "Walt Disney company websites online parks and resorts" complaint of 2010 (PRWeb, n.d.) pointed out that their sites were not accessible to screen reading technologies. In particular it is not possible for someone who cannot use a mouse to remove advertising which otherwise drowns out the site and renders it unusable.

Even bricks and mortar businesses such as Target which have websites have to be accessible under the so called "nexus theory". The NFB

versus Target case of 2006 was settled in 2008. Under this settlement:

- Target had to pay NFB $90,000 for the certification and first year of monitoring and then $40,000 per year thereafter.
- Target's web developers would receive at least one day of accessibility training, to be provided by NFB at a cost of up to $15,000 per session.
- Target would need to respond to accessibility complaints from web site users.
- Target had to pay damages of $6,000,000 to the class action claimants, or at most $7000 per claimant, and had to pay $20,000 to the California Center for the Blind.

This was a landmark case in the US as it affirmed that all businesses for California residents must be accessible regardless of whether or not they have a bricks and mortar businesses.

Things can get complicated in unexpected ways. When Amazon created Kindle and added a text-to-speech facility to their e-reader with a view to enabling access for un-sighted or poor-sighted people, authors objected saying that this violated copyright and moved to stop Amazon providing access via screen readers.

This is not the only way in which the situation can get more complicated. In 2010 the Campus Technology (1105 Media Inc, Ed-Tech Group, 2014) website published news of a court case (Schaffhauser, 2010) brought by the federal government of the US against educational institutions carrying out technology pilot projects using Amazon kindle e-readers. The United States Department of Education (U.S. Department of Education, n.d.) and Department of Justice ((DOJ), n.d.) had just issued a reminder calling for colleges, universities and K-12 school districts, to make sure devices such as e-readers that are required in the classroom comply with accessibility laws. This action came in the wake of a settlement between the Department of Justice and five educational institutions that were using Amazon Kindle e-book readers in their educational technology pilot projects. The warning was based on the observation that "*Kindle devices aren't accessible to students who are blind or have low vision.*"

According to Cynthia Waddell, it is generally considered that the authors are wrong in their demands and that they are effectively blocking the efforts of Amazon to comply with the Disabilities Act. She explained that there is a move against the authors' guild to clarify the situation. Until this issue is resolved however it is hard for Amazon Kindle to demonstrate compliance with the law.

The 21st Century communications act protects not only consumers but employees as well. Cynthia Waddell was directly involved in the case of Darla Rogers versus the state of Florida. Rogers lost her job and sued on the basis that the state provided no accessibility technology. She won and regained her post. Cynthia was able to prove that the state had ignored accessibility guidelines and that no access technology would work with their system.

This is a shot across the bow of public administration in the sense that public internal IT systems must also be compliant with the disabilities act, and public employers must not only provide accessibility technology but make sure it will work with the IT systems on which work depends.

The examples presented show that compliance is not just a matter of law but also a matter of enforcement too. And for this enforcement to be effective people and public services should devote significant effort and time. However, the existence of a law such as section 508 seems to have helped in raising web-site accessibility cases in courts and promote its awareness especially to major site owners and companies. Europe has to catch up in legislation and provide a solid legislative framework in order to help in that direction. For the time being web accessibility is dealt in a member-state level legislation.

Travel, Tourism, and the Economic Benefits

Travability (Travability Pty Ltd, 2013b), the innovative travel and tourism business that provides services aimed at people with disabilities, maintains a blog (Travability Pty Ltd, 2013a) about violations or compliance failures by airlines and other travel related companies and tour operators. It has recently written about a blind couple stranded by Jetstar (Travability Pty Ltd, 2009), an incident with Jetstar involving Kurt Fearnley a 4 time New York marathon winner and 2 time Paralympic gold medallist who 'crawled' a 60 mile trail through mountains in Papua New Guinea (Travability Pty Ltd, n.d.-a), only to be refused help by Jetstar getting around the airport and onto the plane. This article also refers to a Ryanair incident where staff refused to help a passenger carry his wheelchair bound passenger on board the aircraft due to 'health and safety rules'. The blog features an incident involving two airlines Qantas and Tiger Airways that refused to carry a passenger's seeing–eye dog (Heasley, 2009). She was told by one airline that dogs were not allowed on board and by the other that she would have to buy an extra ticket. When she complained the airport authorities became involved and they told her she would have to leave as dogs were not allowed at the airport. Other articles describe the lack of access on European river cruises (Travability Pty Ltd, n.d.-c) one of the fastest growing tourism sectors, as well as fines for violations by ships of Norwegian Cruise Line operating in the Pacific.

An underlying theme of the blogs is the idea that compliance is usually treated as a box ticking affair, and that travellers with disabilities are treated as problems or risks and not as clients who deserve value for money and a high level of service. One of the risks identified by the blogs is that the large tour operators or retail travel companies, which so far have eschewed the traveller with disability market, are becoming more concentrated due to merger and acquisition activity, and there is perceived difficulty for smaller players (Travability Pty Ltd, n.d.-b) that do cater to this market entering the game.

People with poor sight, hearing difficulties or limited mobility are not the only ones who have difficulty traveling. People who are exceptionally tall or exceptionally large perhaps having to cope with obesity, also experience difficulties traveling. Airlines vary in their ability to cater to these needs which can be considered a situational disability even if they do not correspond to a legal definition of disability.

Most people who travel buy their tickets online. We do not know how well these websites work for people with disability. There may be issues worthy of further investigation, both in term of actual services available, and what can be done automatically and efficiently via the retail site of the airline or travel company.

Travability (Travability Pty Ltd, 2013b) emphasizes the economic interest for companies to take account of these travel segments. The approach is to make change as broadly appealing as possible. If an operator is not impressed by arguments based on individual needs or social justice, then perhaps it can be moved by economic arguments which will help bring about sought after changes.

The Role of Public Procurement

One of the consequences of accessibility legislation is the need to incorporate accessibility as a criterion in relevant public procurement contracts. At EU level there is an initiative underway known as mandate 376 (CEN/CENELEC/ETSI Joint Working Group, 2013) to develop "European Accessibility Requirements for Public Procurement of Products and Services in the ICT Domain".

Given the fast pace of evolution of e-access technologies for disabilities as well as the fast pace of evolution of ICT in general, it will not be easy for the public sector in Europe to support innovation on the basis of its ICT buying programs.

There may be a need for research or innovation related research to help the public sector meet this obligation.

The website of GAATES – the Global Alliance on Accessible Technologies and Environments (GAATES.ORG, 2007), explains what measures are already being used to implement accessibility (GAATES.ORG, 2011) legislation in public procurement process for ICT goods and services in 20 countries.

One of the issues raised refers to the fact that not all available products responding to a request for tender may fully comply with existing standards for accessibility. In this case it will be necessary to choose "the most compatible product". This could be ambiguous, especially in the context of a supposedly single market where many countries such as Greece have no compliance legislation, but others have independent legislation possible differing from country to country. This could lead to controversy if a company who loses a bid decides to challenge the award on the basis of the criteria applied. It is therefore worthy to finance work on accessibility compliance with a view to providing guidelines of use in EU procurement.

The discussion on web accessibility in the chapter on media and entertainment, suggests that the compliance of a website is not a simple matter, even the designation A, AA or AAA based on WCAG is subject to considerable ambiguity. It is not easy to define an appropriate level of compliance or to ensure that a required promised level of compliance has been provided. It is another issue to ensure that this level of compliance can be maintained over a reasonable period of time.

One of the measures referred to in the GAATES presentation (GAATES.ORG, 2011) is called VPAT or Voluntary Product Accessibility Template. This is a tool provided by the Information Technology Industry Council of the US to help a company document the conformity of a product with the accessibility standards provide under the Rehabilitation Act of the US.

According to the September 2011 presentation at GAATES 420 companies have provided VPATs. MicroSoft and IBM have provided them for 400 products each, whereas Xerox, Canon and Apple have provided 184, 183 and 53 respectively.

The VPAT example is just a case to show that in order for public procurement to help promote accessibility there is also a need for appropriate tools and guidelines. Europe could learn from that example and produce its own process and template for validation. However, an internationally harmonized approach could benefit in that direction even more and solve potential differences in between businesses in countries with different processes and guidelines.

The VPAT refers to products. It is useful to see how this can be extended to cover services such as web-site development or other cases of public services, especially those provided to the public by private companies on contract. This issue could be used to accelerate compliance in Europe, market readiness of EU companies and innovation by companies attempting to serve these markets?

The final remark made by the GAATES presentation is the need for the procurement process itself to be accessible. On this topic it refers to steps taken in Canada and the US to develop an Accessibility Procurement Toolkit and an Accessible Buying Wizard by the GSA or General Services Administration.

From Compliance to Competitive Advantage

Another approach to encourage compliance is to encourage market oriented research on a whole new set of consumer needs and business opportunities. The economic advantages gained by reducing resource consumption, energy dependence and energy intensity of industrial production and business operation, have been extremely significant and have driven success for a whole range of industries. This has lifted the green agenda out of the philanthropy basket of being good for the soul, into the economic basket of being good for the bottom line. Is it possible that an e-Access movement could benefit from the same dynamic that has helped the green movement?

The Rick Hansen Foundation (Rick Hansen Foundation, 2014) based in Canada, is an important translational research actor in the area of spinal cord injury, and runs a map-based site called the global accessibility map_, advocates an approach to compliance based on the idea of "going beyond compliance to achieve competitive advantage", one of the themes being discussed at Interdependence 2012.

This concept applies not only to individuals, or companies, but to public administration and cities as well. It also ties up with the idea of the social currency being described earlier for social activism. Encouraging a business ecosystem where complying with accessibility requirements leads companies to improving their competitive advantages against competitors in the market can also provide an additional incentive for promoting, raising awareness and expand accessibility compliance.

THE POLITICS OF DISABILITY

Interesting and informative books on the history of disability and disability rights include

- Understanding Disability by Michel Oliver in 1996 (Oliver, 1996)
- Disability politics: understanding our past, changing our future by Oliver Campbell in 1996 (Campbell & Oliver, 1996)
- Nothing about us without us: disability, oppression and empowerment written by J Charlton in 1998 (Charlton, 2000)

Charlton wrote about the history of disability as a political movement. The author explains how he first came across the phrase in the title "nothing about us without us" in South Africa and draws parallels with the other political rallying cries such as "our bodies ourselves" and "power to the people". Campbell described how in the first half of the 20th century, the response to disability was a charitable one. People with disabilities were seen as unable to help themselves and well-meaning, often well-off people, including members of the church took it upon themselves to look after those with disabilities as an act of charity.

According to Campbell it was only in the 1970s in the UK that the 'charitable view' of people with disabilities started to change. This was due to people with disabilities getting organized themselves and speaking as a group about their own needs. It was only at this late stage, starting with communities of people who were blind that people with disabilities started to be seen as people with rights just as anyone else and as a group to be consulted ion issues that would affect them. Eventually they felt the need to join up with other groups of people with other disabilities, top make their case more forcefully. The political elite at the time resented this and fought them on their right to self-representation.

The view today is that the concept of disability itself is inappropriate, that society is diverse, made up of people with a great range of capabilities and that the onus is on everybody to accommodate differences where they arise. In many ways this is the basis for modern thinking about individual rights. It highlights the difference between the old school of thinking, dominated by charitable elites and a new way of thinking based on independence and self-determination.

European Policy and the Member States Fragmented Landscape

Recent reports (like the Measuring eAccessibility 2010) provide all the necessary information and go into almost every detail of EU and international policies and benchmarks of eAccessibility implementation in different sectors (telephony, TV, web, etc.) in different countries so it would not want

make much sense to include here information that has been reported elsewhere.

The core of EU policy on eAccessibility is described essentially in the 2008 Communication by the Commission, eventually adopted by the Council in 2009 entitled "Towards an accessible Information Society". Its preamble stated that "E-accessibility is a necessary prerequisite for a widespread use of ICT, and its cost can be greatly reduced through design for all approaches and better interoperability between services and devices. The Council concluded also that despite efforts and progress made in Member States through national initiatives, "e-accessibility remains overall poor in Europe".

The 2008 Communication came about as a conclusive step of a process started long before and as a policy response to the acknowledgement of substantial gaps in national policies and legislations, a good summary of which is contained in the 2010 MeAC report, on "Measuring Progress of eAccessibility in Europe".

Most Member States had also committed to achieve significant progress by 2010 by signing the Riga Declaration in 2006 at the conclusion of the ICT for an inclusive society conference organised under the Austrian presidency. The focus of the ministerial declaration was on addressing the needs of older works on one side and enhancing accessibility of disabled people on the other. Among the desired measures to bring change about were the stimulus to national governments to adopt own strategies as a contribution to the 2008 European eInclusion Initiative and the usage of funding instruments especially for deployment projects.

Despite of continuous attention to eAccessibility issues at policy level, the situation on the field (in Member States) in terms of legislation and concrete access and inclusiveness of society for people with disabilities or for the older people has not changed dramatically. The 2010 final MeAC report still points to a substantial fragmentation of eAccessibility policies and legislation in Member States. Many countries look at what is happening elsewhere in order to learn from others' experience and there is heated debate on how binding regulations should be both in the public and private domain. Progress has been achieved in single sectors, but we are still far away from systemic improvements.

The implementation of those obligations in Member States suffers from widespread reluctance among national policy makers. If legal provisions are not followed by some form of control on public and private actors compliance when issuing products or delivering services, it is unlikely that those service providers (especially from the business sector) will enforce higher levels of compliance than what they feel necessary to respond to the needs of the market. The 2010 MeAC report points to businesses and individual employers' fear of rising accessibility costs as one of the main challenges that Member States have to tackle. Concerns of putting a burden on economy are among the main bottlenecks at national policymaking level.

Whereas the EU has promoted policies addressing disability issues (some if this translated into legislation like the Employment Equality Directive of 2006, the Public Procurement directives of 2004 and accessibility aspects contained in the Directive for a common regulatory framework for electronic communications networks and services of 2008), uptake and accompanying by binding measures in Member States has been very limited. When policies touch upon issues related to redistributive instruments, (social services, social or medical care), these are systematically interpreted in the light of national competences.

Right now roughly half of Member States (including the five largest countries) have adopted legislation that at least partially recalls provisions foreseen by the WACG 1.0, whereas some of them still refer to national standards or norms. This applies essentially to public websites (yet not equally in all countries, since some obligations apply only to central government websites and not to the entire administration). Germany, Italy and Portugal have adopted legislation that covers

also commercial websites, though in most cases without binding character.

Monitoring policies do not help to tackle the fragmentation issues, as benchmarking and reporting are irregular and not standardised.

Technologies and Systemic Innovation Enabling Factors

Despite progress made in policy at EU level and in the regulatory framework of a growing number of countries, two interrelated issues deserve immediate action: a) production and/or deployment of adapted technologies; b) acting on the pre-conditions that can determine policies impact, especially when addressing areas of great complexity such as innovation in social or healthcare systems.

No precise figures are available today as for the number of assistive devices of any sort available on the market. To make an example of how varied the offer can be, the Assistive Devices Program (Government of Ontario, 2008) run by the Ministry of Health and Long Term Care of Ontario, in Canada, covers as many as 8,000 separate pieces of equipment ranging from hearing aids to wheelchairs and seating systems.

Depending on the type of disabilities devices are made for, and depending on the price and reimbursement systems in place, technology providers might face different types of bottlenecks. The most feared appears to be the "small market syndrome", where developers might see specific or adapted products as a niche market, often squeezed between complex functional and legal compliance requirements and obstacles to a free pricing policy.

This is true of many assistive devices, the provision of which to the final user (the person with disability) is channelled through a public entity (healthcare authority or social services). As well as putting pressure on prices, this can create a "one client only" dynamic, where businesses are faced with one buying counterpart rather than with a portfolio of clients, which is often perceived as a risky situation. Additionally, disabilities or reduced abilities accompanying ageing are often coupled with low or even non-existing income, which hinder the possibilities of personalised solutions and direct sales to the final users.

The transition from the social to the economic model of disability may act as a catalyst to help overcome the small market syndrome.

Frequently Encountered Problems in EU Funded Projects

In the current funding cycle (2007-2013) several projects have been funded in research and innovation programmes that deal with eAccessibility, from different angles. Interestingly, the ICT PSP (under the CIP, Competitiveness and Innovation Programme) has financed deployment actions across domains such as eHealth or services for the older people in an increasingly self-serve society.

Pilot A projects (comparable for consortia and budget size to the Integrated Projects funded in FP7) have special requirements in terms of partnership, as they demand the direct involvement or express mandate of national (or regional depending on distribution of competences at state level) authorities responsible for the deployment of IT in a given sector.

The rationale for this is obviously the need to accompany the deployment of technology with the appropriate enabling factors determined by policymakers or national schemes owners. While this is a sound principle, the key question is whether those projects are the right instrument to enhance change in very complex environments such healthcare or social services. One of the key questions is: what are the preconditions for new technologies to bear an impact on society?

Design is for sure one of the elements. Some of the problems yet to be solved in exoskeleton technologies today touch for instance upon usability rather than on technical performance or degrees of freedom. Would the person wearing the armour be able to do it without incurring in bruises or abrasions? Or will smart wheelchairs be affordable to users or the ones paying for them? Will healthcare systems provide the conditions for patients' single devices to exchange information with their infrastructure so as to provide smarter services?

Is a 3 years project like a typical ICT PSP pilot A projects with at least 6 countries participating and where policymakers need to be involved, enough to bring systemic innovation about?

From The Social to the Economic Model of Disability

Companies in robotics, prosthetics, e-assistance and other domains are making efforts to lower the prices of their products. Yet, even substantial decreases in costs might not be enough for large portions of customers whose purchase power is reduced also (if not essentially) as an effect of disability. Prices, affordability and payment schemes constitute preconditions likely to substantially influence the spreading and impact of new technologies and therefore the success of eAccessibility policies. From this perspective, the type of "disability model" European societies will choose is not a trivial issue. The last decades have marked in most industrialised countries a shift from the medical to the social model of disability, thus stressing the importance of public policies in changing both social attitudes and the overall environment (including physical environment) towards disabled people.

Beyond the social model, a new paradigm is gaining consensus especially in industrialised (and ageing countries), under the name of economic model of disability. Here, stress is put on individual needs and abilities as drivers for market demand within a customer driven dynamic. The economic model focuses less on compliance and rights than on markets. A market based approach to abilities and needs might actually blur the boundaries between different types of disabilities and ageing, or with the needs of non impaired people to perform beyond their current limits (issues of augmented performance). Yet, the detection of those needs and the identification of increasingly dynamic market segments does not seem to be embedded in customary business practice and routine design processes. Examples of shortcomings in design come from the experience of advocacy organisations like EDF (European Disability Forum) and the AGE Platform within EU funded projects either in research or innovation programmes. User driven design is often absent in project's workflow, or comes at a late stage, when requirements, technical specifications and architecture phases have already been completed without a sufficient involvement of users. The same goes for validation phases, often run on insufficient number of users. The funding mechanisms currently in place in European programmes do not help either. Demonstration activities in research programmes are funded at 50% under the FP7. Participation in the ICT PSP is funded for pilot projects (the ones that deploy services at large scale, where involvement of users is fundamental) at 50% + overheads, a rate that businesses with exploitation perspectives can find attractive, whereas it can be discouraging for non-governmental or advocacy organisations. Moreover, reimbursement applies essentially to participating organisations' personnel and not to external individuals such as users, whose involvement proves at times difficult as an effect of such administrative barriers.

Obligations on the one hand and incentives on the other might result in enabling factors for an economic model of disability, but action in this sense should be taken essentially by Member States, which is unlikely to happen in a sufficiently coordinated manner within a short time.

Our understanding is that an economic model of disability changes the basic driver from a rights and compliance issue to a market demand driver. A sound argumentation for the issues of inclusiveness in travel related matters can be found in Travability (Travability Pty Ltd, n.d.-d) (see also Sections 12.4.6 and 12.4.7). Also, a previous study (Internal market for inclusive and assistive ICT, SMART 2008/0067, Final report, June 2011, conducted by Deloitte & AbilityNet) identifies the consumer model which it relates to the end-user capability to decide on the best assistive ICT product. According to it, "the difference with the medical / social model is that the service provider takes on the role of advisor and funding provider but does not make the final selection".

We deliberately speak of an *economic model* that is a broader term that *includes consumer-related aspects*, but does not only limit to them. When considering products that are ready-for-use and purchase by customers, the term consumer model reflects pretty well the reality faced in the market. However, and as our study encompasses issues related to the identification of needs and the recognition of areas of future research and development, there it is not about stable or defined consumer populations; needs may create new types of consumers, while innovation in the use of existing technologies or ones that will appear in the years to come will give shape to new types of products that will, again, find new target audiences.

In strict sense, the term of the Economic Model is primarily used to assess distribution of benefits to those who are unable to have access to them in other ways. As recognised by the Michigan Disability Rights Coalition (Michigan Disability Rights Coalition, n.d.), a disability justice movement working to transform communities, "[t]he true value of the Economic Model is maintaining this balance in the macroeconomic context of trade cycles, inflation, globalization and extraordinary events such as wars". And using the words of Michael Janger_(DrumBeat Consulting, 2012), "[i]t's not just a better wheelchair, or an iPhone that doubles as a virtual cane for a blind person. Of course, product innovation for the disability market is essential to increased productivity and participation for these consumers in society. Yet, *it's more than that: when more products and services are made accessible, consumers with disabilities are not the only ones that benefit. Everyone else benefits. Everyone just wants an easier way of using these products."*

The Absence of Benefit Metrics

Another missing piece of the puzzle is evidence of benefit from eAccessibility implementation measures for technologies or service providers.

While it can be argued that complying with eAccessibility standards and good practices clearly benefits the ones for which those standards and practices are conceived, no universal metrics are in place to assess the impact that eAccessibility provisions have on services and products. In the absence of appropriate measurement methodologies, business fears of putting extra efforts and resources to comply with legal obligations without a positive return cannot be dispelled.

More in general, progress monitoring is so far carried out through annual reviews focussing essentially on policy, legislation and surveys detecting the percentage of eAccessibility compliant (totally or partially) websites and other IT services.

The WCAG 2.0 checklist on accessibility provides an extensive list of parameters against which accessibility features of websites are benchmarked, but information on the impact on markets and/or effects on companies expansion or acquisition of new market shares is generally not available and most probably has not been the object of structured investigation until now.

There is a serious lack of metrics to measure the economic impact (especially on business) deriving from making services and products more accessible. Without data of this kind it is difficult to convince businesses that investment on eAccessibility will pay off (also: *how much* and *how soon* it will pay off).

Three Models of Accessibility

The story about the history of the politics of disability can be related to what are known as the two schools of thinking about accessibility.

The earliest thinking is known as the medical model of disability, in which disability is more or less seen as a medical condition to be cured with the help of experts such as doctors and engineers, but otherwise a private issue for each individual to address on their own. This is the view that leads to the exclusion of people from school or their confinement to an institution or home to the point of missing out on schooling or job opportunities. Accessibility is essentially a private affair.

The next wave of thinking is often referred to as the social model. It emphasizes that disability is a question of degree, that people have many capabilities, some in which they exceed the average and others in which they don't. According to this thinking it is the job of society to accommodate differences. Accessibility is no longer a private affair but a shared responsibility, and can come about as the result of a collaborative effort between individuals and their peers, not just immediate members of their family but their friends, their colleagues and those who are unknown but who they meet in the course of a day.

This model is more compassionate but imposes obligations on society. Not everyone is happy about that. Laws are needed just in case there is doubt as to where the boundaries of giving, taking and accommodating should reasonably lie. The second model has led to the passage of legislation that guarantees rights and protects against discrimination. Its application is imperfect but the law is there and groups that want to defend their rights have a strong basis from which to assert them. Social networking and the technologies of modern participative democracy can help achieve this where necessary.

There is a third model however, the so called economic model. It confers on those with a disability another form of power, their power as a member of a consumer group with specific needs, also their power as employees or even as employers with a different sets of rights, obligations and needs.

This is explained very eloquently by Travability (Travability Pty Ltd, 2013a)and illustrated for the case of travel and tourism. Travability is a company founded in 2007 to provide accessible travel for all. It operates in Australia and the US and is a member of ENAT, the European Network of Accessible Tourism (ENAT, 2013). In a series of articles available on its website, it introduces what it refers to as an economic model of disability (Travability Pty Ltd, n.d.-d). It explains this and compares it with the medical model and the social model.

- The *medical model* of disability was defined as an individual problem and it was that individual's problem to adapt to their circumstance. The response was very much based on medical care, individual treatment, professional help and individual adjustment and adaptation.
- The *social model* emphasizes the fact that it is also up to a just society to make changes to include the disabled person, and not simply leave it up to them alone. This view imposes norms on society in the name of social justice. Non-adherence to such norms will bring the risk of fines or sanctions of some kind.
- The *economic model* points out that people with disabilities have a different set of needs and tastes and preferences and that they are both willing and able to pay for the products and services that cater to these needs.

All three approaches have certain validity. However the economic model has not been fully explored at least not until recently. The case of tourism is a good place to start.

The Economics of Accessible Tourism

According to Travability, it is a myth that people with a disability travel far less than the general population. It is also a myth that that people with disabilities do not spend as much when they do travel because of economic circumstance. There tends to be an implicit assumption made by the industry and its designers that the disabled traveller, is of a lower social economic group. Where accessible rooms are provided, they were invariably of the lowest room type.

In reality people with disabilities travel on a level comparable with the general population for domestic overnight and day trips, and they are equally represented in all segments of each travel market.

Inclusive Tourism is already a major tourism sector with Australian research putting its value at 11% of the total industry market share. Over 40% of those retiring from the baby boomer generation, will retire with some form of disability. This will bring the Inclusive Tourism sector to over 25% of the market by 2020.

In 2008, the Australian National Visitor Survey (Tourism Australia, 2013) estimated that 88% of people with disabilities in Australia take a holiday each year accounting for some 8.2 million overnight trips. According to their statistics the average travel group size for people with a disability is 2.8 people for a domestic overnight trip and 3.4 for a day trip. The total tourism expenditure attributable to this group is $8B per year or 11% of overall tourism expenditure.

This is not just an Australian phenomenon. Mc Kinsey (McKinsey & Company, n.d.) predicts that in the US alone, the baby boomer generation will command almost 60% of net personal wealth and 40% of consumer spending by 2015. In categories such as travel, the baby boomers are expected to account for over 50% of tourism expenditure.

The latter demonstrate the significant economic benefit for industries that accessibility can have.

Moreover they point out that this benefit is not going to be reduced in the future. On the contrary it is going to increase even more. Promoting this kind of economic opportunities that business can exploit by investing in accessibility is critical to convince them invest on it. Similar cases, surveys and research is also needed in the area of ICT products to attract more businesses interest on accessibility

DESIGN ISSUES

Information Matters

Travability points out that in the case of tourism at least, the availability of accessible venues is not an issue. What is an issue though is the lack of information provided to enable consumers to make informed decisions about where to go. As a rule, either such information is entirely lacking or it lacks critical detail.

For most companies accessibility is merely a compliance issue for facility management or risk management to handle. The approach tends to be to simply tick the box on accessible car parks, rooms and floors. This is done so as to avoid a fine, or a sanction rather than as part of the service or product offering.

Service providers such as tour operators or hotels generally only recognize a generic set of accessibility requirements imposed by law and with which they must comply. Compliance allows them to claim that the hotel has "disabled facilities". These may only amount to car parking, accessible rooms, and toilet facilities. At a push the facilities may have Braille and or audio announcements in the lifts. But most facilities will not distinguish between the needs of groups of people with different disabilities. They do not see the need to accommodate a client in a way that makes their stay useful, productive and enjoyable.

Accessible rooms are often defined as rooms with roll-in showers. However if these rooms are to be comfortable they also need to have space under the bed, knee clearance under the writing desk and balconies need a sill. Even where facilities are fully compliant, there is little understanding of the practical needs of the traveller with disability and compliance is not fully communicated.

The codes of compliance are partly to blame. The standards do not encourage resort owners or suppliers to think about the disabled traveller as a consumer with varying tastes, demands and spending power. Of course the business owners are also to blame in that they have not understood the economic opportunity that serving this sector actually represents. The sector is not limited to those with disabilities. The services and facilities offered to those are also of interest to people who are older and more fragile, who have less energy or stamina or who are receiving from illness.

The evidence show that accessibility related information over a product, facility or service is not something that can be suggested and decided light-hearted. There are a number of factors in accessibility that have to be taken under account when providing relevant information and there is a need for better clarification and definition through legislation.

Design Marketing and Communication

Another approach that could also be followed to harness the economic power of people with disabilities is to introduce an awareness of disability into professions such as:

- Industrial design
- Product design
- Interaction design
- Consumer or User Experience Design
- Architecture
- Marketing
- Communication

This could be done either by supporting curricular reform or entrepreneurial and business leadership by people who are active in these sectors. The introduction of design principles such as universal design is one way forward.

The issue of access is also a global design concept. It is not enough for a hotel to be accessible the other facilities around it must be accessible too. The transport network used to get as well. In general when talking for example about tourism experience, the experience is made up of a number of major components:

- The transport network
- The hotel or accommodation, its toilets, showers, hallways and lifts
- The restaurants, bars and cafés
- The culture, leisure and sports facilities, as well as all
- Surrounding paths and routes linking them

This shows that a number of professions have to be aware of the problems, the potential solutions, the applications and the principles such as universal design in order to achieve an overall accessible life experience. The point is that the introduction of awareness of disability problems in the training and education level of certain design related professions can lead to a new generation of designers in all fields able to think about accessibility proactively and produce appropriate accessible products. However this introduction is not enough if made only in people in the interaction design domain. It needs to cross all levels and fields of design related professions.

Universal Design

Meetings on the general topic of accessibility almost always refer to the concept of Universal Design or UD. The idea has been around for a long time. Twenty years ago in Japan the concept was referred to as "Kyou Sei" which roughly translates to collaborative living or co-living. The general idea was "*why have two ways of doing something, one for disabled people and one for non-disabled people, when one will do for both and cost less*".

The problem is that few designers seem to know about it and few studies have been carried out to clearly demonstrate the value it can create. The current situation in many ways resembles the green movement a decade ago. Companies resisted at first, but then they discovered that when they put their minds to it, they found that saving energy or being good to the environment provide many tangible economic benefits.

At Braillenet 2011 James Odeck (BrailleNet, 2011)from the Norwegian Public Roads Administration provided very convincing arguments as to the value of UD, based on studies conducted on the implementation of UD principles in their public transport system. His study revealed the variety and extent of savings created by the provision of ramps or low loading buses. These features, originally intended for people in wheelchairs, were also of benefit to older people, injured people, pregnant women, people with children or laden with shopping bags not to mention luggage being carried to the airport. This led to savings far beyond expectations due to quicker loading times, more punctual services, lower overall rote times and more routes per driver.

The principles of UD are fairly simple. As laid out in the Strategic Plan (Travability Pty Ltd, 2013c) of Travability.

- **Equitable Use:** accessible to all users, provide the same means for all users, identical where possible, equivalent when not, does not disadvantage, stigmatize or privilege any group of users
- **Flexibility in Use:** accommodate a wide range of individual preferences and abilities, provide choice for all
- **Simple and Intuitive:** understanding and context should be easy, regardless of the user's experience, knowledge, language or skill

- **Perceptible Information:** information is communicated effectively to the user regardless of ambient conditions or the user's sensory abilities.
- **Tolerance for Error:** hazards and the adverse consequences of accidents are minimized (most used elements are the most accessible, hazardous elements are isolated or eliminated, provide warnings)
- **Low Physical Effort:** the design can be used efficiently and comfortably with a minimum of fatigue.
- **Size and Space for Approach and Use:** appropriate size and space is provided for approach, reach, manipulation, regardless of user's body size, posture or mobility.

Of course ingenuity is required when applying them in any real life situation. The concept of UD applies to non-IT issues such as transport infrastructure. Companies such as KAO of Japan (Scott Rains, 2011) for example systematically apply UD principles to all of their product development. The concept also applies to IT products such as ATMs, mobile phones, apps, laptops and websites. In principle it applies to service as well.

There seems to be a need to carry out research on the economic impact of the application of UD principles in general, but to accessible ICT in particular. In principle the UD concept can apply to services as well, especially as most services nowadays are implemented on the basis of ICT systems.

The UD concept could apply to processes too, for example to the processes of public administration and to work in general. It is worthwhile developing the concept of accessible processes with a view to extending the UD concept as deeply as possible into the heart of the knowledge economy.

REFERENCES

Action Without Borders. (2014). *Volunteer, work, intern, organize, hire and connect.* Change the world - idealist.org. Retrieved March 13, 2014, from http://www.idealist.org/

American Foundation for the Blind. (2010). *AccessWorld? - March 2010.* Retrieved March 13, 2014, from http://www.afb.org/afbpress/pub.asp?DocID=aw1101toc&All#aw110108

American Public Media. (2014). *Spot.us - Home.* Retrieved March 13, 2014, from http://spot.us/

Ashoka Changemakers. (2014). *Changemakers | Changemakers.* Retrieved March 13, 2014, from http://www.changemakers.com/

Barack Obama presidential campaign, 2008. (2014, March 11). *Wikipedia, the free encyclopedia.* Retrieved from http://en.wikipedia.org/w/index.php?title=Barack_Obama_presidential_campaign,_2008&oldid=598033438

BlogTalkRadio.com. (2014). BlogTalkRadio. *BlogTalkRadio.* Retrieved March 13, 2014, from http://www.blogtalkradio.com

BrailleNet. (2011, March 28). *Proceedings - 5th European eAccessibility Forum Benefits and costs of e-accessibility.* Retrieved March 13, 2014, from http://inova.snv.jussieu.fr/evenements/colloques/colloques/70_actes_en.html#contenu

Campbell, J., & Oliver, M. (1996). *Disability Politics: Understanding Our Past, Changing Our Future.* Psychology Press.

CEN/CENELEC/ETSI Joint Working Group. (2013, May 25). *European Accessibility Requirements for Public Procurement of Products and Services in the ICT Domain.* Retrieved March 13, 2014, from http://www.mandate376.eu/

Charlton, J. I. (2000). *Nothing about Us Without Us: Disability Oppression and Empowerment.* University of California Press.

DocumentCloud. (n.d.). *DocumentCloud*. Retrieved March 13, 2014, from http://www.documentcloud.org/home

(DOJ), U. S. D. of J. (n.d.). *United States Department of Justice Home Page*. Retrieved March 13, 2014, from http://www.justice.gov/

DrumBeat Consulting. (2012, June 5). DrumBeat's Value Proposition. *DrumBeat Consulting*. Retrieved March 13, 2014, from http://drumbeatconsulting.com/blog/2012/06/05/drumbeats-value-proposition/

ENAT. (2013). *ENAT | European Network for Accessible Tourism*. Retrieved March 13, 2014, from http://www.accessibletourism.org/

ENIL. (2013a). *ENIL – European Network on Independent Living*. Retrieved from http://www.enil.eu/

ENIL. (2013b). *Freedom of movement » ENIL – European Network on Independent Living*. Retrieved from http://www.enil.eu/tag/freedom-of-movement/

European Commission. (2011). *Europa - Press Releases - Press release - Digital Agenda: First meeting of EU Media Futures Forum*. Retrieved March 13, 2014, from http://europa.eu/rapid/press-release_IP-11-1506_en.htm?locale=en

FixMyStreet. (n.d.). FixMyStreet. *FixMyStreet*. Retrieved March 13, 2014, from http://www.fixmystreet.com/

FUPOL. (n.d.). *FUPOL Project*. Retrieved March 13, 2014, from http://www.fupol.eu/

GAATES.ORG. (2007, May 25). GAATES Home Page. *Collection*. Retrieved March 13, 2014, from http://www.gaates.org/

GAATES.ORG. (2011, September 8). *Procurement of Accessible ICTs*. Retrieved from http://www.gaates.org

Global Disabiliy Rights Library. (n.d.). *The Global Disability Rights Library | www.widernet.org*. Retrieved March 13, 2014, from http://www.widernet.org/egranary/gdrl

Google. (n.d.). *Google+*. Retrieved March 13, 2014, from https://plus.google.com/

Government of Ontario. M. of H., & L.-T. C. (2008). *Assistive Devices Program- About the Program - Public Information - MOHLTC*. Retrieved March 13, 2014, from http://www.health.gov.on.ca/en/public/programs/adp/about.aspx

Harfoush, R. (2009). *Yes we did: an inside look at how social media built the Obama brand*. Berkeley, CA: New Riders.

Heasley, A. (2009, December 8). *Qantas now leaves a Blind Passenger Stranded*. Retrieved March 13, 2014, from http://travability.travel/blogs/qantas.html

Heppler, K. (2010, August 5). 12 awesome platforms for social good. *Socialbrite*. Retrieved March 13, 2014, from http://www.socialbrite.org/2010/08/05/top-12-platforms-for-social-good/

International Center for Disability Resources on the Internet. (2010, September 30). *Passage of the 21st Century Communications & Video Accessibility Act of 2010*. Retrieved March 13, 2014, from http://www.icdri.org/News/21CentCommACT.htm

International Center for Disability Resources on the Internet. (2012). *ICDRI Home*. Retrieved March 13, 2014, from http://www.icdri.org/

Introducing Google Currents. (2011). Retrieved from http://www.youtube.com/watch?v=5LOcUkm8m9w&feature=youtube_gdata_player

Katz, J. (2010, July 20). 9 online petition tools: How to make a difference. *Socialbrite*. Retrieved March 13, 2014, from http://www.socialbrite.org/2010/07/20/9-online-petition-tools-how-to-make-a-difference/

Kreutz, C. (2009, September 14). *Maptivism: Maps for activism, transparency and engagement.* Retrieved March 13, 2014, from http://www. crisscrossed.net/2009/09/14/maptivism-maps-for-activism-transparency-and-engagement/

Lasica, J. (2010a, July 6). Change-makers share 10 of their favorite tools. *Socialbrite.* Retrieved March 13, 2014, from http://www.socialbrite. org/2010/07/06/social-change-experts-share-10-favorite-tools/

Lasica, J. (2010b, August 10). Cool Gov 2.0 sites you don't know about. *Socialbrite.* Retrieved March 13, 2014, from http://www.socialbrite. org/2010/08/10/cool-gov-2-0-sites-you-dont-know-about/

London Underground Weblog Blog. (2008, July 9). Retrieved March 13, 2014, from http://london-underground.blogspot.gr/2008/07/tube-map-for-disabled-developed-by.html

Maps, Activism and Technology: Check-In's with a Purpose. (n.d.). *iRevolution.* Retrieved from http://irevolution.net/2011/02/05/check-ins-with-a-purpose/

McKinsey & Company. (n.d.). *McKinsey & Company | Home Page.* Retrieved March 13, 2014, from http://www.mckinsey.com/

1105. Media Inc. Ed-Tech Group. (2014). *Campus Enterprise Networking & Infrastructure -- Campus Technology.* Retrieved March 13, 2014, from http://campustechnology.com/Home.aspx

Michigan Disability Rights Coalition. (n.d.). *Economic Model of Disability | Michigan Disability Rights Coalition.* Retrieved March 13, 2014, from http://www.copower.org/models-of-disability/176-economic-model-of-disability.html

MySociety Limited. (n.d.). *mySociety.* Retrieved March 13, 2014, from http://www.mysociety.org/

NYC Toilet Map | Toilet Radar. (n.d.). Retrieved March 13, 2014, from http://www.toiletradar. com/map

Oliver, M. (1996). *Understanding Disability: From Theory to Practice.* Palgrave Macmillan.

Open311. (n.d.). *Open311.* Retrieved from http:// open311.org/

OpenIDEO. (n.d.). OpenIDEO - Home. *OpenIDEO.* Retrieved March 13, 2014, from http://www.openideo.com/

OpenStreetMap. (n.d.). *OpenStreetMap.* Retrieved March 13, 2014, from http://www.openstreetmap. org/#map=5/51.500/-0.100

Osburn, C. (2008, March 6). Accessing Wheelchair Accessible London? *Londonist.* Retrieved March 13, 2014, from http://londonist.com/2008/03/accessing_wheel.php

Parkour. (2014, March 9). *Wikipedia, the free encyclopedia.* Retrieved from http.// en.wikipedia.org/w/index.php?title=Parkour&oldid=598815016

Pauli Murray Project. (n.d.). *Mapping Civil & Human Activism – Live Now | Pauli Murray Project.* Retrieved March 13, 2014, from http:// paulimurrayproject.org/mapping-civil-human-activism-live-now/

PRWeb. (n.d.). Class Action Lawsuit Against Disney Alleges Inaccessible Websites and Failure to Accommodate Blind Persons in Violation of ADA, Case No. 10-cv-5810. *PRWeb.* Retrieved March 13, 2014, from http://www.prweb.com/ releases/2011/02/prweb5073794.htm

Reed, R. (2010, July 29). 10 ways geolocation is changing the world. *Socialbrite.* Retrieved March 13, 2014, from http://www.socialbrite. org/2010/07/29/10-ways-geolocation-is-changing-the-world/

Rick Hansen Foundation. (2014). *Rick Hansen Foundation > Home.* Retrieved March 13, 2014, from http://www.rickhansen.com/

Schaffhauser, D. (2010, June 29). *Department of Ed Lays Down Law on Kindle E-Reader Usage -- Campus Technology*. Retrieved March 13, 2014, from http://campustechnology.com/articles/2010/06/29/department-of-ed-lays-down-law-on-kindle-e-reader-usage.aspx

Scott Rains. (2011, September 17). *KAO on Universal Design*. Technology. Retrieved from http://www.slideshare.net/srains/kao-on-universal-design

SeeClickFix, Inc. (2013). Report non-emergency issues, receive alerts in your neighborhood. *SeeClickFix*. Retrieved March 13, 2014, from http://seeclickfix.com/introductions/home

Seelye, K. Q. (2011, November 16). Oregon Tries Out Voting by iPad for Disabled. *The New York Times*. Retrieved from http://www.nytimes.com/2011/11/17/us/oregon-tries-out-voting-by-ipad-for-disabled.html

Social Innovation Camp. (n.d.). Map of disabled access for the UK. *Social Innovation Camp*. Retrieved from http://sicamp.org/si-camp-uk/previous-camps/submitted-ideas/map-of-disabled-access-for-the-uk/

Socialbrite. (n.d.). Socialbrite. *Socialbrite*. Retrieved March 13, 2014, from http://www.socialbrite.org

SoundOut. (2012). *Student Activism Map*. Retrieved March 13, 2014, from http://www.soundout.org/activism.html

SOZIALHELDEN.e.V. (n.d.). *Einfach mal machen! - SOZIALHELDEN e.V.* Retrieved March 13, 2014, from http://www.sozialhelden.de/

The New Google Social Network-- Google+ Project -- Why It will be a Success?? (2011). Retrieved from http://www.youtube.com/watch?v=3Onri3iHbL4&feature=youtube_gdata_player

Tourism Australia. (2013). *Home - Tourism Australia*. Retrieved March 13, 2014, from http://www.tourism.australia.com/home.aspx?redir=en-au/

Travability Pty Ltd. (2009). *Jetstar refuses to carry blind passengers guide dog*. Retrieved March 13, 2014, from http://travability.travel/blogs/jetstar3.html

Travability Pty Ltd. (2013a). *Travability - About Us*. Retrieved March 13, 2014, from http://travability.travel/about%20us.html

Travability Pty Ltd. (2013b). *Travability - Making the World Accessible to All*. Retrieved March 13, 2014, from http://travability.travel/

Travability Pty Ltd. (2013c). *Untitled Document*. Retrieved March 13, 2014, from http://travability.travel/blogs.html

Travability Pty Ltd. (n.d.a). *Kurt Fearnley*. Retrieved March 13, 2014, from http://travability.travel/blogs/fearnley.html

Travability Pty Ltd. (n.d.b). *Retail Travel Chains and Inclusive Travel - When?* Retrieved March 13, 2014, from http://travability.travel/blogs/retail_travel.html

Travability Pty Ltd. (n.d.c). *River Cruising*. Retrieved March 13, 2014, from http://travability.travel/blogs/river_cruising.html

Travability Pty Ltd. (n.d.d). *The Economic Model of Disability*. Retrieved March 13, 2014, from http://travability.travel/blogs/economic_model.html

Tube maps made for the disabled. (2009, January 26). *BBC*. Retrieved from http://news.bbc.co.uk/2/hi/uk_news/england/london/7850675.stm

United States International Council on Disabilities. (2014). *United States International Council on Disabilities - Global Disability Rights Library>>*. Retrieved March 13, 2014, from http://www.usicd.org/index.cfm/global-disability-rights-library

U.S. Department of Education. (n.d.). *U.S. Department of Education*. Retrieved March 13, 2014, from http://www.ed.gov/

Visa TV Ad starring Bill Shannon. (2009). Retrieved from http://www.youtube.com/watch?v=I6RGyJirL3g&feature=youtube_gdata_player

WebAIM. (2009). *WebAIM: Screen Reader User Survey #2 Results*. Retrieved March 13, 2014, from http://webaim.org/projects/screenreadersurvey2/

Wheelmap.org. (n.d.). Wheelmap.org - Rollstuhl-gerechte Orte suchen und finden. *Wheelmap.org*. Retrieved March 13, 2014, from http://wheelmap.org/

WHO. (2011). *World Report on Disability*. Retrieved from http://whqlibdoc.who.int/publications/2011/9789240685215_eng.pdf?ua=1

KEY TERMS AND DEFINITIONS

Activism: Activism consists of efforts to promote, impede, or direct social, political, economic, or environmental change, or stasis.

Citizenship: Citizenship is the status of a person recognized under the custom or law of a state that bestows on that person (called a citizen) the rights and the duties of citizenship.

Compliance: Adherence to standards, regulations, and other requirements.

Maptivism: Mapping Information for Advocacy and Activism.

Policy: A policy is a principle or protocol to guide decisions and achieve rational outcomes.

Social Change: Social change refers to an alteration in the social order of a society.

Social Media: Social media is the interaction among people in which they create, share or exchange information and ideas in virtual communities and networks.

Section 3
Common Issues

Chapter 13
Human Performance

ABSTRACT

This chapter looks into horizontal issues in ICT advances and discusses how the factor of human performance could help in increasing the impact of eAccessibility and assistive technologies in the future. More specifically, it revisits some of the ideas presented in earlier chapters looking at them from a different angle. The one of maximizing the audience and target group for assistive technologies through the increase in human performance, issues related with exoskeletons for working environments and dual use of assistive technology, sports as a motivator, aesthetics and fashion of prosthetics are discussed from this same perspective. Human performance could be a critical factor for the future of assistive technologies, and today's people with disabilities could become tomorrow's people with super-abilities and leaders in human performance issues.

INTRODUCTION

According to the French Institut de l'Accessibilité Numérique (IAN) there are more than 600 million handicapped people in the world today. That means almost 100 million in Europe and about 12 million in France alone. This is the number of people excluded at least partially from many of the benefits of ICT as an enabler of communication, content, commerce, entertainment, health, social networking and work productivity tools and services.

It sounds like a large market but in reality is a highly fragmented group. Fragmentation arises due to the fact that different people are handicapped in different ways. People have problems with vision, hearing and memory loss with different levels of severity. Many who experience difficulty severe enough to cause discomfort or to have a tangible impact on work their productivity, are not formally considered to have a disability because their condition is not acute enough.

Others have "access" problems due to language, geography or mobility infrastructure, experience the same problems, though the origin of the problem may be different. Further fragmentation of these markets occurs due to the great number of different technology platforms, their ever-evolving nature and the need to keep them updated and maintained.

In reality companies, and that includes technology companies, think of "accessibility" technologies as being only for small markets of people with severe handicaps, such as blindness from birth.

DOI: 10.4018/978-1-4666-6130-1.ch013

The market is small, the cost of addressing it is low, and the return on investment in accessibility solutions, very hard to justify.

While meaning well, the identification of this technology sector with relatively small populations of users, ignores the fact that significant benefits are available for a much larger population of users, and now seems to pose a barrier to the widespread adoption of what could in many cases be considered a much larger family of general productivity tools.

Bonnie Kearney (Microsoft, 2013), Director of Accessibility Marketing at Microsoft pointed out that 57% of adults can benefit from accessibility technologies. She claims that there are 74.2 million computer users in the US with some kind of impairment. She also claims that by 2050 in the US, 45% of the working population will be over 65.

With age the incidence and severity of a disability goes up. It starts as a low level of difficulty in seeing, hearing or moving. It gradually becomes more severe over time until it is eventually classified as a handicap or impairment. At all stages of this process, people can benefit from accessibility technologies. These have a positive effect on their comfort, quality of life and professional productivity.

Very little research has been done on the productivity gains afforded by accessibility technologies. Microsoft (MS) has done some studies where they compare the performance of normal users with that of users having some kind of disability. Using small samples and comparing the performance of both groups on basic tasks such as composing a document, saving a document or sending an email, MS found that those with a severe form of disability can take up to 6 times longer to complete these tasks. MS is quick to point out that these were not very scientific studies. They were exploratory first attempts, can be improved, and need follow-up. Their initial results however indicate that 1 in 4 people have trouble with vision and 1 in 5 people have trouble hearing.

There seems to be a need for further research on personal productivity issues. At what point does a productivity start to decline and how much. How much productivity is lost before one realizes that a decline has set in or before one employs an aid? What impact does this have on work, on the employer and on the future employability of the employee?

The tentative results reported above by Microsoft indicate that this could be a fruitful direction for future research. We could expect that this kind of research could have an important impact on:

- Attitudes towards disability,
- The employment of people with disabilities,
- The careers of older workers
- The adoption of e-assistive technologies and ultimately
- The employer's bottom line.

HULC, E-LEGS, REWALK, AND HAL HUMAN EXOSKELETONS

A March 2011 TED talk (Bender, 2011) by Eythor Bender of Berkley Bionics presented the state of the art of personal bionics and demonstrated HULC, the Human Universal Load Carrier intended to assist soldiers in action, and eLEGS intended to help people confined to a wheelchair to walk again.

These have been developed Lockheed Martin. HULC has been in field trials since 2010 (Stevens, 2010). It weighs about 20kg and can help a soldier carry loads of up to 100kg across rough terrain for long periods of time without getting tired.

Amanda Boxtel a downhill skier who was paralyzed from the hips down due to a skiing accident 19 year ago, demonstrated the use of eLEGS to help her get out of her wheelchair and walk for the first time since her accident.

Today about 68 million people worldwide are confined to a wheelchair for personal mobility, and this corresponds to about 1% of the world population. The reasons range from injury to weakness from old age. Many more people use wheelchairs on an occasional basis as they recovered from an injury or accident. The use of wheelchairs goes back about 500 years and will likely increase as the world population ages.

Other systems like this already exist such as ReWalk (Bionics Research, n.d.) from New Zealand, a wearable quasi robotic exoskeleton suit that is intended to provide mobility to individuals with spinal cord injury.

HULC was developed with the military market in mind, but it clearly also has applications in medicine and civilian life.

HAL, the Hybrid Assistive Limb (Cyberdyne Inc., 2014) was developed in Japan. It was originally intended for use in hospital or clinical environments, especially as a device to help in physical therapy of people recovering from operations or injury, as well as for helping people in old age recover the strength of their limbs. It is interesting to see how the business model for HAL has evolved over a few years. It used to be for outright purchase by users at a cost of about €100,000 per unit. Since then a rental model has evolved and it rents out at about €1,000 a month including maintenance. Maintenance and service are important issues in general with robots. There are very few local garages that know what to do with them if there is a problem. One of the interesting discoveries with HAL is the potential for a market to develop among people interested in extreme sports.

The examples of human exoskeletons presented all have a common denominator. They were developed to increase human capabilities under specific circumstances. It might be that a person is disabled but it might also be that a person is in need of this specific capability in his job such as the HULC case. The interesting point is how the transfer of technologies such as exoskeletons which were developed to augment a person's capabilities under specific circumstances can be transferred and used by persons with disabilities. Future eAccessibility research should definitely try to exploit this path of innovation.

THE ROLE OF SPORTS AS A MOTIVATOR

Much of the motivation for high-end e-assistive and e-access devices such as autonomous vehicles, humanoid or animal-like robots, exoskeletons and devices controlled directly by the brain has come from the military. Many of the most advanced technologies have been developed by military application oriented research organisations such as DARPA of the US.

Most EU countries have 'soldier of the future' type research programs, but there are few common projects and none of them have the scope or scale of those of the US. The EU has a number of grand challenge projects such as the euro-fighter and airbus, the ISS and ITER. These have needs to support for people working in extreme environments. Such people can be considered to have situational disabilities, for example difficulty moving due to high G-forces for example, or lack of fine motor control due to the need to wear a space suit. It has even been said that the next generation of fighter planes will not be flown by humans. The G-forces would be too great and almost humanly impossible to withstand. At EU level there may be motivation for advanced systems that augment, extend or compliment human capabilities, for example using advanced robotics and autonomous systems.

Europe buys its drone technology from Israel and the US. Setting up challenges in parallel with those of the US military would have the advantage of developing an independent capability, as has been done in the case of Galileo.

It is worth to explore the possibilities for launching a number of grand challenge projects in "future assistive technologies" in conjunction with EU military, marine, and aero-spatial or nuclear energy research complexes.

An alternative or complementary source of inspiration for grand challenge ideas is sports. The analogy is not so much with the Olympic Games as with F1 racing. The spirit of the Olympic Games is all about what a human can do un-assisted by technology, whereas F1 racing tests what can be achieved by the combination of man and machine. It is a competition at once between car-makers and between car-drivers that pushes both to great levels of performance. It provides pleasure and entertainment to those who watch a sense of purpose and achievement to those who take part, and inspiration to all. It is also a hugely profitable business with opportunities for entertainment, advertising and sponsorship.

The Paralympics has already created controversy over the use of advanced prosthetic devices and questions exist as to how advanced they can be before being considered inappropriate for the games. The Paralympic Games have steadily grown in popularity over the years. In some areas Paralympic records exceed those set in the Olympics. Oscar Pistorius, the so-called blade-runner from South Africa is a case in point. He is one of an increasing number of Paralympic athletes that have achieved status as sex-symbols and models associated with fashion and consumer goods. He already has the confidence and the ability to compete with non-disabled athletes. He wants to qualify for and compete in the original Olympic Games.

Maybe it is time to establish an open or assisted Paralympics, where both disabled and non-disabled athletes compete using assistive technologies, and which can be considered as much a display of the technology as of the athlete. Such games could feature competitions involving blind people playing tennis or basketball as well as high speed electric wheelchair racing.

THE ROLE OF AESTHETICS AND DESIGN

Progress has been impressive in the area of prosthetics. Thanks to advances in materials, better design tools, the use of electronics, compact motors and battery packs, missing a limb is much less debilitating than it was even 20 years ago. Nevertheless there is still scope for fundamental low cost innovation in how to provide amputees and others with disabilities with more independence and freedom than they had before.

In the area of sports, specially adapted skis exist for people with missing limbs, but until recently very little was available to enable people who wanted to swim. Most available prosthetics resemble clip-on canoe paddles for hands or flippers for feet. A recent article describes how a Swedish design student called Richard Stark (Aguilar, 2010) developed an innovative water-friendly prosthetic called Neptune (Yanko Design, 2010). He was inspired by Paralympic sprinters such as Aimee Mullins, and by the observation that she not only has an extensive collection of prosthetic legs, but that some of them were designed by high end celebrity designers like Alexander McQueen. Stark's vision was not only to enable amputees to swim and enjoy the water, but to be able to choose from a variety of different colours and styles. He worked with a pair of competitive amputee swimmers and their coaches to understand the problems encountered in the pool and come up with a new fin design where the fin is divided into three "fingers" that allow the wearers to emulate the vaguely circular motion of treading water. A slider allows them to adjust the flexibility of the fin to match their strength. A further modification allows the fin to rotate 90 degrees to switch from the sideways kick of the breaststroke to the up-and-down motion of the crawl. The response has been very positive and he claims that *"Amputees all around the world were asking me if they could order it,"* He is now working on bringing the cost down so that rather than relying on medical or health insurance, people will be able to pay for it out of their own pocket, at a price of about $350.

The story of Richard Stark is just an example of how assistive technology in general should take under account aesthetics apart from functionality. Assistive devices will certainly need to be designed with functionality and user-friendliness in mind however the role of aesthetics in them can be crucial when getting to the market. A prosthetic leg or white cane or an exoskeleton that doesn't stigmatize the person using it and in some cases attracts attention with its aesthetics can play significant role in spreading the market and lowering the cost.

FASHION AND THE PROSTHETIC ENVY PHENOMENON

It is interesting to draw an analogy between the evolution of assistive technologies such as advanced prosthetics and so called "plastic surgery". Although plastic surgery has a very long history, it used to be mainly applied in the case of dire medical need, for example to those who had been severely mutilated or burned. Nowadays it has developed in a wide range of different medical and commercial fields. The various areas of cosmetic surgery including cosmetic areas of dentistry have become huge multi-billion global business sectors and are seen by many young professionals as interesting and lucrative ways to earn a living. Clients used to be mainly women, especially those involved in film or media, but nowadays otherwise ordinary young teenagers and men make up the bulk of clients and they see a need to correct or improve aspects of their appearance to make themselves more appealing either from a professional or a personal point of view.

A recent NYT article (Ellin, 2011) covering the phenomenon of plastic or aesthetic surgery for the elderly revealed that already in 2010 more than 84,645 procedures were carried out on people over 65. They are willing to pay of the order of $8,000 for procedures to help them 'freshen up'. Many express a need to align their physique with their psyche, saying that they are already very healthy, they expect to live a long time and want to continue to do the things they enjoy. Research indicates that the hazards are no greater for those over 65 than for younger people.

Given such trends, it is natural to ask at what point perfectly healthy able-bodied people will start to remove limbs so as to replace them with better prosthetic limbs. This question was put to David Lam from the European office of the Telemedicine & Advanced Technology Research Center (TATRC, n.d.), while attending the 8 March 2011 meeting of the AAL on social robotics. The TATRC is a part of the US Army Medical Research and Material Command (MRMC). David pointed out that this phenomenon of people wanting to replace healthy limbs with advanced prosthetic devices is already happening. David explained that nowadays some of the guys with limbs are less well off than those with missing limbs using modern prosthetics. Many soldiers, after a few years or pain and discomfort, look at those who had lost limbs and see that they are better able to get around despite the fact that their own injuries were less severe. They experience less mobility and freedom than their more traumatized colleagues, who benefit from advanced prosthetic technologies. They want to have their salvaged limb removed and get fitted with the bionic gadget. This is already the reality. People are asking to have their limbs removed so as to be fitted with the latest prosthetic. They want this so as to enjoy improved physical performance, greater freedom, quality of life and comfort. It enables a fuller integration into society.

A person who lost two fingers in an accident and now uses robotic fingers says that he would cut off the rest of the hand if he could make all five fingers robotic. He expresses surprise at his own reaction and says that "When I'm wearing it, I do feel different: I feel stronger. As weird as that sounds, having a piece of machinery incorporated into your body, as a part of you, well, it makes you feel above human. It's a very powerful thing." (Hochman, 2010)

A representative of Otto Bock HealthCare (Ottobock, 2014) says that amputees are now regularly removing healthy tissue to make room for more powerful technology, that is to say getting a second amputation or moving the amputation up their leg. This has been described as the prosthetic equivalent of a hotter car. The costs are not covered by insurance and patients pay for it out of their own pocket. In many cases when the injured part of the body is removed, there is little room for machinery. So you need to remove the whole limb to benefit from the best prosthetic device. People often come back for what are called "revisions".

People with prosthetics can get upgrades, people without prosthetics cannot. A double amputee can chose what height they want to be. They can go from being 5-feet-8 to 6 feet tall if they want. Eyeglasses are prosthetic. And while they were once purely medical devices, they're now expensive fashion items. People put glasses on to make themselves look more intelligent, to augment their appearance, not just their performance. Even when they can wear contact lenses they sometime wear glasses in certain social situations. They are an accessory, a fashion item, not a medical device.

According to one expert, the better prostheses make us perform, and the more glamorous they look, the more beautiful they will make amputees seem, even though their sheen, contour, texture, and colour have ceased to look human. People are already saying "What is the obsession with looking human?" If cars can be beautiful, then why not prosthetic limbs? Why can't they become fashion items, make social statements, be sculptures?

In this section we have mainly been talking about prosthetic limbs, but we may expect a similar phenomenology to occur in the case of eyes and brain implants. Already there has been marked increase in the number of seniors resorting to plastic surgery to make them feel younger, or provide them with an advantage in the marketplace for jobs or mates. It is easy to imagine this trend spreading over to all kinds of other medical interventions, the use of advanced prosthetics, companion robots and other helpers. Apart from technology as an enabler, the trigger will be fashion and the enabler will be design. William Gibson-like references to "the girl with the Nikon eyes" may not be so far away from reality.

REFERENCES

Aguilar, M. (2010, November 29). Design: Prosthetic Flippers Could Help Amputees Swim Again | Wired Magazine | Wired.com. *Wired Magazine*. Retrieved March 13, 2014, from http://www.wired.com/magazine/2010/11/pl_designlimbs/

Bender, E. (2011). *Human exoskeletons -- for war and healing*. Retrieved from http://www.ted.com/talks/eythor_bender_demos_human_exoskeletons

Bionics Research. (n.d.). *Bionics Research ReWalk™ U.S. - the wearable bionic suit*. Retrieved from http://rewalk.us/

Cyberdyne Inc. (2014). *CYBERDYNE*. Retrieved March 13, 2014, from http://www.cyberdyne.jp/

Ellin, A. (2011, August 8). A Boom in Plastic Surgery for Those in the Golden Years. *The New York Times*. Retrieved from http://www.nytimes.com/2011/08/09/health/09plastic.html

Hochman, P. (2010, February 1). Bionic Legs, i-Limbs, and Other Super Human Prostheses You'll Envy. *Co.Design*. Retrieved March 13, 2014, from //www.fastcodesign.com//www.fastcodesign.com/1514543/bionic-legs-i-limbs-and-other-super-human-prostheses-youll-envy

Microsoft. (2013). *Author: Archives*. Retrieved March 13, 2014, from http://www.microsoft.com/eu/author/bonniekearney.aspx

Ottobock. (2014). *Ottobock - Home*. Retrieved March 13, 2014, from http://professionals.ottobockus.com/cps/rde/xchg/ob_us_en/hs.xsl/index.html

Stevens, T. (2010, July 21). HULC exo-skeleton ready for testing, set to hit the ground running next year (video). *Engadget*. Retrieved March 13, 2014, from http://www.engadget.com/2010/07/21/hulc-exo-skeleton-ready-for-testing-set-to-hit-the-ground-runni/

TATRC. (n.d.). *Telemedicine & Advanced Technology Research Center*. Retrieved March 13, 2014, from http://www.tatrc.org/

Yanko Design. (2010, June 22). *Neptune orthopaedic swimming aid for lower limb amputees by Richard Stark » Yanko Design*. Retrieved from http://www.yankodesign.com/2010/06/22/clip-on-fin-to-turn-to-aquaman/

KEY TERMS AND DEFINITIONS

Aesthetics: Aesthetics (also spelled æsthetics and esthetics) is a branch of philosophy dealing with the nature of art, beauty, and taste, with the creation and appreciation of beauty.

Design: Design is the creation of a plan or convention for the construction of an object or a system.

Dual Use: In politics and diplomacy, dual-use is technology that can be used for both peaceful and military aims.

Exoskeletons: An exoskeleton is the external skeleton that supports and protects an animal's body, in contrast to the internal skeleton (endoskeleton) of, for example, a human.

Fashion: Fashion is a popular style or practice, especially in clothing, footwear, accessories, makeup, body piercing, or furniture.

Prosthetics Envy: A trend of desire to change prosthetic limbs for better ones because of envy.

Prosthetics: In medicine, a prosthesis, is an artificial device that replaces a missing body part lost through trauma, disease, or congenital conditions.

Sports: Sport (or sports) is all forms of usually competitive physical activity which through casual or organised participation, aim to use, maintain or improve physical ability and skills while providing entertainment to participants, and in some cases, spectators.

Chapter 14
Systems and Complexity

ABSTRACT

Past efforts in e-Access, e-assistive, and e-inclusive technologies have largely focused on "parts of a problem." That is to say, they have identified key tasks in day-to-day living and working or key elements in the experience of those with disability care and focused on the development of independent solutions for these specific tasks. Although this approach has yielded many successes, it may be time to stand back and take a look at the bigger picture. To the extent that systems have been discussed, the focus has been on technological systems. Typically, these systems are engineered systems that link otherwise weakly linked groups, such as doctors and carers with those cared for and their families or friends. In this chapter, the authors would like the reader to stand back and explore systems from a broader perspective, in particular from the human systems point of view.

COMPLETE SOLUTIONS FOR HUMAN SYSTEMS AND REDUNDANCY

The concept of the complete solutions comes from modern theories of quality management that apply a systems approach. When the solution to a problem requires many steps or many processes or effective action on the part of many different people, and if only one of these is missing, then there is as yet no solution. It is only when all of the necessary events happen in the right way that things can move forward. Though seemingly obvious this idea assumes great significance when most or even all but one of the necessary parts of a system are in place, but everything stands still, and no-one is responsible. Almost everyone has done their job to contribute to the solution. For whatever reason all but one, absence, inattention, lack of training or proper resources, has not done what was required and the whole thing fails. Who is responsible to remedy the situation? All who know have done their job and the one who did not remains blissfully unaware. The problem is extremely common. It is only resolved when some dedicated soul, often standing over or outside the system takes responsibility for the final outcome. Typically this is a manager and in modern systems approaches to management, one of the key roles of the manager is to assume responsibility for the systemic dimension of the problem to ensure that a complete solution is present and so that things can move on as intended.

DOI: 10.4018/978-1-4666-6130-1.ch014

In previous and on-going programs to address e-Access challenges, a lot of attention has been paid to the issue of travel and mobility. In the Braillenet meeting held in Paris in early 2011, experts from companies such as the French SNCF spoke about the challenge of e-accessibility of web-sites. The discussion was rich and raised many issues related to the compliance of websites with appropriate e-Access legislation. There is a lot of work to be done and the challenge is being addressed with a good will, in a serious and systematic way. However there is a bigger issue. If someone who is blind has difficulty reading or as a foreign visitor has difficulty understanding the language, the availability of a well-designed highly accessible website will enable that person to find out routes and timetables and plan their travel, but many more obstacles remain to be overcome before they can complete a journey.

In particular they may have to find their way to the station or airport. Once there, they may have to find the right platform. How difficult it is even for non-disabled people to read the big screens at airports and major rain-stations. How much harder it must be when someone does not even know if and where they are. Once one has found the platform, there are further challenges. Knowing which of the two trains on the same platform is the correct one. Easy if you can read the sign on the side, or ask a conductor having a coffee over 50 meters away. Finding the right carriage and then the right seat also remain challenges. Of course other people are often willing to help, but less so during rush hour, or when a train changes track to arrive on a totally different platform. Much of the effort spent providing good e-access compliant websites will be for nothing if the rest of the system has not also been put in place.

Those responsible for fixing the website to ensure its compliance will not normally see the larger e-access picture. Even if they do, it will most likely lie beyond their ability to address it. This is a typical system level problem and though everyone may do what is required of them, it will

never be enough and the original problem will remain.

In the case of mobility and transport, the issue is not just what happens at the train station. It starts at home. There is a mobility and transport challenge at home, in the building, in the neighbourhood as far as the metro, in the metro, on the side walk from the metro through car-parks and tunnels to the station itself, and more of the same on the other side. Until all of this is navigable by someone with a disability, society cannot consider that it enables all citizens to enjoy independent living. The example demonstrates that systems, solutions, applications and services should see the bigger picture when developed in order to allow integration, cooperation and interoperability. This way the road to a complete solution such as in the example described could be easier to achieve.

There is a need to address system level issues that start by supporting projects whose aim is to raise awareness of the importance of providing complete solutions, what they might look like and what kind of partnerships would be needed to provide them.

One way to deal witth this is by targetting large institutions as environments in which locally complete solutions can be reasonable envisaged and developed as living laboratories that integrate all parts of an intended complete solution. An approach to this is to focus on large-scale demonstration of concept projects or, alternatively, clusters of projects around sponsoring partners.

Another principle that arises in systems thinking is the principle of redundancy. Components of a system occasionally break-down. In any system of reasonable complexity it is certain that at any time one or more of those components will fail. Redundancy ensures that everything works despite a failure. In the case of transport and mobility this means options so that no one gets stranded or finds that they are unable either to move forward to their destination or get back to where they came from. Redundancy is a good idea. It exists already in the sense that when the train or the metro fails there is usually a bus. Some modern smart-phone base taxi services no longer require the client to call from their home address or a known landmark such as a restaurant or a taxi-rank, but can pick them up in the street.

LIFE-LONG SOLUTION SYSTEMS

Another non-technology systems dimension can be thought of as a life-cycle dimension. This addresses the prospect of independent living for people of any age, whether they are infant, child, youth, young adult, active retiree or elderly person in care. It also applies whether they have disability which is chronic or mild, permanent, progressive or situational.

The physical needs of someone with a disability such as a missing limb or limited functioning due to a disease such as polio or trauma from accident, changes with age. The change occurs in several different ways. The first and most obvious change is physical, the change in size of the person, the need for training or re-habituation when an old limb is replaced with a new one. Secondly, there is the associated cost, some of which may be borne by healthcare systems, but much of which may have to be borne by the individual, their family or care institution.

The third main area of change relates to the differing needs of the person as they get older. These needs may vary depending on gender and on other parameters such as ethnic group and religious belief. The needs of an infant who would normally learn to walk are different from that of a child who wants to run around, burn-off energy and grow physically with increased fitness and strength and coordination. Those of a teenager who needs to learn to build personal confidence and learn to socialise are different from those of a young adult who wants to perform and prove themselves at work and in society. The needs of someone who wants to work in a job, get married and raise children are different from those of

someone who wants an active retirement while keeping in touch with their family, are different also from someone who is older and wants to play the role of a grandparent, providing advice and support their children in their times of trouble. The concept of independent living is in principle different for people of all ages and this should be reflected in the design of e-assistive technologies and services.

A 2004 article on adolescent disability published by Nora Groce of the Yale School of Public Health, delves into the specificity of youth populations with disability, and the problem of their unrealized potential. According to this work, in 2004 there were more than 180 million young people and adolescents with some kind of physical, sensory, intellectual or mental disability in the world, significant enough to affect their quality of life. Although the article takes a global view, it has lessons for advanced economies such as Europe, and is of significance for industrial actors who want to tap into global markets for e-access and e-assistive technologies and services.

The needs of people with disabilities vary significantly with age. The way in which a disability prevents them from meeting these needs, varies of course according to the nature of the disability, as well as the infrastructure and programmes in place to address them. The physical, intellectual and emotional needs of children, adolescents, young adults, mature adults and the elderly are very different. Even in the case of adolescents, the needs of a 12 year old and a 17 year old are very different. Wheelchairs quickly grow small, glasses need changing and prostheses need to be adapted in size, weight and overall design to the growing adolescent body. As they grow, their relationship to technology changes too. The author points out that "*in transition between childhood and adulthood, these are the years when young people are expected to acquire skills, go through physical and psychological maturation and assume a social identify that will enable them to fully participate in their communities.*"

The article points out that the "*call made by UNICEF in 1999 in its global survey on adolescents, for more research on the wide array of issues that influence the lives of disabled young people, remains largely unanswered*". It points out that apart from issues such as access to education, very little is generally understood about the specific needs of adolescents with disabilities even in developed countries.

According to Article 23 of the United Nations' Convention on the Rights of the Child, young people with disabilities have needs very similar to the needs of all other young people. They need a safe and supportive environment, education, health services and access to sport and recreation. They also need to develop skills that will serve them well in the community and the work place. Even in an advanced country like Iceland the transition to adulthood of young people with disability describes this as an "eternal youth", a limbo in which these young people are not expected to reach adulthood, but remain enmeshed in segregated services.

Personal assistance, if needed, tends to be provided by immediate family members. This means that young people often have little or no say over even most basic aspects of their lives. It limits their ability to establish a sense of autonomy or gain experience in making independent decisions.

In society in general there is an expectation that young adults will eventually live independently of their parents. The tacit assumption seems to be that young disabled adults will continue living at home, cared for by parents or siblings, making their lives increasingly different from that of non-disabled peers. This has very important consequences for the development of the young adults, their ability to get and keep a job, their prospects of getting married and having a family, indeed the overall sustainability of a good quality of life beyond childhood.

The report stresses that young men and women with disability are often involved in relationships and that they do engage in sexual activity. This however is often not socially acknowledged and all of the usual risks of sexually transmitted disease or unwanted pregnancy are poorly handled, with important consequences for the individual. According to the report, there is a growing number of accounts of disabled young people being targeted by sexual predators in developing and industrialized countries. The reason seems to be because they either cannot report the abuse or will not be believed when such abuse is reported. The threat of violence or sexual abuse is also of concern for the significant number of young people who are institutionalized in schools, hospitals and asylums.

These concerns will not be immediately obvious to someone without detailed and even intimate knowledge of the lives of people living with disabilities. It is clear that needs and uses of e-assistive and e-access technologies will vary not just as a function of the nature of the disability, but also as a function of age and living condition. Future research in this domain might benefit from a more explicit focus on specific segments. In other words rather than treating the domain in general as a monolithic whole, to treat more specific issues like e-access and e-assistive technologies aimed at adolescents and their specific life-style and developmental needs, so that they can converge with their peers in terms of real-life goals and aspirations.

E-ACCESS TECHNOLOGIES FOR NON-DISABLED PEOPLE

Much of the focus in the past of research on technologies for e-Access, e-Assistance and e-Inclusion, has been on the needs of "people with disabilities". Most countries have definition of disabilities. Some of these are rigorously defined in legislation, and this legislation may differ from one country to another. Many conditions for example related to back-pain and whip-lash injuries are more difficult to pin down. These are often the subject of fraud allegations and insurance companies go to great lengths to detect the minority of people who exaggerate their claims or misrepresent their case.

This indicates that even in dealing with official concepts of disability, there are grey zones between what is officially recognized as a disability by the state, and therefore the subject of dedicated legislation on the one hand, and the reality that people may have to live on the other hand.

Many conditions may not be recognised at all, Chronic Fatigue Syndrome being one example, Burnout from overwork being another. Alcohol abuse and substance dependence in general are debilitating conditions that could in many ways be considered a disability. Depression is another case. These are all progressive situations where the effects accumulate over time. The condition may be present, but go unnoticed for a long time. The same could be said for poor eye-sight or hearing difficulties, tinnitus for example, loss of sense of smell or loss of taste all of which are conditions which may be temporary or permanent, progressive or stable and all of which affect quality of life, personal independence, ability to work and relations with those around us. Snoring and sleeping disorders, being over- or under-weight and obesity, all affect us in ways that reduce our ability to function and can be considered as a source of disability. People who are only slightly overweight may already experience problems bending over to pick something up, tying shoelaces or getting in or out of the bath. These conditions start and progress and have a cumulative effect on lives, until they reach a stage where they become debilitating.

The concept of disability prevention or disability avoidance could include devices or systems and services for early diagnosis of conditions that may lead to or can be associated with disabilities and the slowing or progression or the prevention of chronic cases.

One of the important topics in elderly care is the care of people with various forms of dementia for example due to Parkinson's disease or Alzheimer's. Early identification and treatment can have a major impact on the quality of life of the person by slowing the progression of the disease. The difficulty with diagnosis is that the onset can start very early and the symptoms may not be visible for a long time. One of the symptoms is memory loss. Anyone can experience periods of forgetfulness. This can happen for a variety of reasons including tiredness, stress, depression or the effects of medication. And as a result the person and even their close family members are not very good at spotting the symptoms even when well informed. Elderly care is one of the mainstream areas of e-Access applications. The focus seems to have been on the care of people with advanced or chronic conditions. A more systemic approach is one that looks at the much broader care program who ultimate goal is to eliminate the need for care at all.

Aside from medical conditions one can also associate social conditions with the need for e-Access, e-Assistive and e-inclusive technologies. In popular parlance, people who cannot drive are often referred to as being "socially handicapped". There is no doubt that poorer people living in the suburbs of major Metropolitan areas, designed for an era when everyone would own their own car, can be severely handicapped by lack of access to a wide variety of low cost and convenient transport options. Given the employment difficulties faced by many people with a disability, they can easily find themselves in such a situation along with their almost equally afflicted non-disabled co-citizens.

People who cannot read or have poor writing skills exist. The reason is not necessarily learning difficulties or lower cognitive ability; it may be due to the family situation. Many people in their sixties today were eldest children when they were young and started work at age 10 or 11 so as to put their younger siblings through school. Many of these do not read or write with facility today and would benefit greatly from e-Access technologies.

The same could be said for people visiting from foreign countries, the children of diplomats, exchange students, etc. The traffic goes both ways.

It could apply equally to a European visiting North Korea for the first time or trying to understand what is being said in any one of Nigeria's 500 or so local languages.

Nowadays we rarely hear the old joke about people who don't use the internet as being "people of no account" but they exist and internet usage is far lower even in developed economies than we would like to believe. This is a serious e-Access issue that falls far outside the traditional focus of disability oriented e-Access programs. But success in e-Access for non-disabled people may condition success in e-Access for disabled one too. It may be the case that to succeed in one of these goals we may also need to succeed with the other.

A November 2007 memo (European Commission, 2007) published by the European Commission, observed that 30 to 40% of the EU population did not fully benefit from the digital society and that this resulted in *"fewer jobs, higher costs, especially faced with an ageing population, less social cohesion, and ultimately a less competitive Europe."*

The reasons given were many and ranged across challenge of geography, culture and language, a lack of skills or information, low levels of economic well-being, as well as gender, age and disability.

The memo noted that roughly 200 million Europeans did not use the Internet at that time. It noted that 15% of European citizens have some form of disability, making it harder for many of them to enjoy the social, economic and life-style benefits of ICT. It pointed out that only 10% of those over 64 used the internet compared with 73% of those aged 16 to 24.

In one way or another access to ICT is a therefore significant issue for 30% to 40% of the population of Europe. It is especially a significant issue for groups that already face challenges, in particular those dealing with disabilities or the problems of ageing. Better access benefits everyone, but it is a challenge with many distinct parts.

E-Access concerns the design of products and services based on ICT, which need to be usable by everyone, including older people and those with disabilities. For people with visual impairments, hearing impairments or other difficulties to communicate, e-Accessibility is indispensable, since products and services based on ICTs are essential for everyday social and economic life. Twenty years ago, this mainly meant the ability to use a keyboard or interact with a system using a mouse and screen. Nowadays it means much more. It means the ability to benefit from use and interaction with smart-phones, and other evolving platforms, readers and other handheld devices, games consoles, TVs, ATMs, kiosks and consumer electronics, the tools and appliances of everyday life in the home, the street, the place of work, air-ports, bus-stops, hospitals and other infrastructure of our lives. In future it will mean interaction with advanced tools such as humanoid and social robots used in therapy, in the home as assistants or companions, not to mention mobile telepresence tools or driverless cars.

EVOLUTIONARY APPROACHES TO THE DEVELOPMENT OF E-ACCESS MARKETS

The potential and even explicit intention of e-Access technologies to be of dual-use is a possible source of confusion in thinking about future research and innovation program design. By dual-use we refer not only to the possibility of technologies primarily intended for military use to be one day declassified and adapted for civilian use, we also refer to technologies that are of possible benefit as e-Access, e-Assistive or e-inclusion applications, that re primarily intended for use in other areas.

The original concept of dual-use was a strategy to redirect military research complexes of Eastern Europe and the former Soviet Union towards civilian objectives. Nowadays it also refers to strategies to justify military investment in research in areas that yield returns on investment from civilian applications. The difference is that dual-use has migrated from being an after-thought to being a fore-thought or an explicit intention.

The development of advanced humanoid and other service robots as well as robotic exoskeletons and systems for manipulation by remote telepresence can be seen as being of use to the military or to a wide range of other markets. There is a choice as to whether we wait for the benefits of military research or embark immediately on complementary and even parallel work to realise benefits for civilian life much sooner. There are benefits for industry and society in moving ahead with agenda for civilian projects without delay. The example of advanced military projects may demonstrate the feasibility of an advanced concept and set the bar for acceptable goals of performance.

Other examples of dual use exist in the area of e-Access. One is the possibility of using advanced prosthetics in sports, especially in the context of the Paralympics. e might try to use elite disabled sports-persons as lead users in new developments. The answer to "how far we should go" might be "until EU countries consistently win all the medals in the Paralympics games!" We could also answer "until someone with no-sight wins prizes for the quality of their photography."

There is no doubt that BMI (brain-machine interface) and BCI (brain-computer interface) technologies may one day be general purpose, general use devices of utility to almost anyone. Important investments are being made by organisations such as DARPA and commercial proof of concept projects have been awarded to large companies such as Northup–Grumman to develop brain in the loop systems to improve the perception and reaction time of soldiers beyond what is normally possible for human beings.

Low end BMI/BCI systems such as EEG headsets are now easily available for as little €50. These can be integrated in games, used in modern neuromarketing research and as general think-to-do direct access technologies for general users. It is therefore not beyond reason to consider thee as gaming technologies, or productivity technologies?

ACCELERATING THE EMERGENCE OF NEW INDUSTRIAL ECOSYSTEMS

Ford did not invent the motor car, but championed the early market development and pioneered its production at a time when people felt that roads were for horses, cars were noisy and too reliable to ever be used for anything other than sports and gambling.

Ford was a friend of Thomas Edison and they used to speculate as to whether electric or petrol would prevail. Very little infrastructure was in place and cars often had to be towed home by hors when they either broke down or simply ran out of fuel. In the early days there was no second hand market, garages with spare parts were far and few between, as were small companies to specialise in making the many components required building one.

Ford had to make the glass that went into his car windows, harvest and process the rubber that went into his tyres and build railway lines to distribute the finished products to markets far away. As time went by and competition grew specialisation became a necessity. Modern car-makers are best described as designers, brand developers and orchestrators of subs-system assembly and distribution. This is how many industries evolve. At first they are generalists out of necessity. Then they specialise and finally their skill lies in the ability to organise vast networks of suppliers and distributors as well as retailers and after-sales service providers.

Many e-access related industries are in this first phase moving towards the second one. We already observe specialisation in the sense that some companies focus on face for affective computing, others on visions systems, others on hardware, within that group some focus on hands. Start-ups are popping up with ambitions in sensors, new methods for controlling movement for example using some form of artificial muscles, others on skin replete with sensors. Services are available for 3-D design, 3-D printing and fast proto-typing, new material, body area or near area networks, flexible implantable electrodes, and wireless power systems, energy harvesting and thought-processing neural connectors. A complex network of specialisations has arisen around fields such as BMI/BCI, advanced prosthetics and humanoid robotics.

That is on the side of providers of technologies. Vast complexes also exist in terms of users. The users are not just individuals but healthcare systems, service providers and insurance companies.

Therefore there is a need to identify what can be done to support and accelerate the emergence of these industrial eco-systems. Europe needs to find out what needs to be done to create the conditions for them to exploit early markets position themselves for investment and make it in the wake of the financial crisis in Europe and the difficult years ahead.

We think that some of the answers lie ahead under the general heading of 'tools for managing change in complex systems".

TOOLS FOR MANAGING CHANGE IN COMPLEX SYSTEMS

In this section we are looking at the role of open standards for SW and HW as well as open architectures and platforms as tools that accelerate progress in technology domains. Essentially these are tools for managing change in the face of complexity. Early players lock-in progress on the technology at a certain level, so as to shift the focus of research and development to a higher level of abstraction.

This creates a space for late-comers to get into the game. It permits many companies to collaborate on the development of large complex technological systems.

There are turning points in the evolution of a field. In the case of medical devices, a major turning point is when a technique, device or treatment moves out of the laboratory phase and moves into the mainstream phase. Once this happens the number of people involved in the development of the field can explode. The actors are no longer confined to pioneering doctors and chronic or terminally ill patients, but ordinary clinics, doctors and paramedics, as well as a much greater population of users. This totally changes the innovation dynamic. In the case of e-assistive or e-access technologies, major changes have occurred or are occurring right now in the area of EEG, implantable neural prostheses such as retinal implants, as well as in the area of social robotics.

In this sense important accelerators of innovation are the availability of approved standard retinal implants, patient ready neural processing chips that can be implanted in the brain and provide a platform for brain-machine interfaces and thought controlled machines, as well as commercially available models of mobile telepresence robots and highly affective social robots and exoskeletons intended for mass markets such as teaching assistants, nursing assistants and adventure sports enthusiasts.

In research, events or initiatives that accelerate development and provide inflection points in the development of a domain include the adoption of norms, standards, libraries and repositories, tools and test-beds as well as reference models for evaluation. These allow researchers to build upon the work of others, taking short cuts, focusing on elements or subsystems of the whole, and avoiding the expense of developing whole systems from scratch.

Building a whole robot requires great investment. The same can be said of brain machine interfaces. It is hard to say what industrial models will prevail in the future.

One question is whether future development in these industrial eco-systems will be organised more like the car industry, or more like the internet. However, even the car industry is changing. A UK based electrical vehicle (EV) start-up called River Simple (Riversimple LLP, 2014) wants to transform the automobile industry based on a mobility-as-a-service model. Their goal is not to sell the greatest number of EV cars but to provide mobility services to the greatest number of people using a car sharing model. To leverage their idea they are open-sourcing many aspects of the design of the car. They feel this is possible because many aspects of the EV are very different from the conventional fossil fuel vehicle. The engine is lighter, so is the transmission, steering, braking, suspension. The tyres can also be much lighter and smaller. This makes it easier to work with parts suppliers avoiding conflicts of interest and reduces the prospect of costly litigation due to the aggressive IP strategies of competitors. They see the cars being gradually improved over time in the same manner as software. They even intend to versions number models just as is done in SW. Their ides is that entrepreneurs will compete using their technology based on branding, other maybe more local design adaptations and service. To facilitate all of this the collaboration with suppliers and open design and intellectual property management has been assigned to a foundation called 40 Fires (The 40 Fires Foundation, 2010).

THE ROLE OF OPEN STANDARDS IN SOFTWARE

The secret of the development of the WWW was the work of the W3C consortium, based on a model for developing and maintaining an open architecture that recognised the interest of large established players and provided opportunities for smaller ones to also play a part. Similar models worked in the base of the GSM and Bluetooth. All resulted in industrial eco-systems, bound together by standards that gave them freedom for independent invention while providing a basis for integration at system level and guaranteeing a measure of interoperability.

The closest to this example in the realm of accessibility is arguably the DAISY (DAISY Consortium, 2014) standard for publishing and reading electronic content (Digital Accessible Information

SYstem). This enables publishers of digital content to make it available to screen readers, so that texts can be heard by those with limited sight. It has also been very useful for those who are simply too busy to read, for example people who want to check emails while driving or merely rest their eyes while using a mobile phone. It enables developers of screen readers and other e-access technologies to access such content. The overall philosophy is mindful of the fact that as the standard evolves, older content will maintain compatibility moving forward and digital collections will not need to be re-edited every time changes are made.

These processes are managed by a mixture of industrial secret and open source licensing model. This is well known in the case of Software. The existence of Open Source software not only leads to potentially better complex code, but it lowers the barrier to entry by new players into fast evolving domains.

It is possible to imagine a future in which small players, perhaps originally focused on the prosthetic limb market, will become powerful forces specialised in robotic limbs. Some may focus on legs and hands, one day surpassing in speed and dexterity exceeding even that of humans. Some may specialise in subsystems for sight and hearing. Others may specialise in artificial skin, dense in sensors and actuators, capable of being designed for arbitrary human or robotic frames. Others will focus on neural interfaces, and other implantable devices. More will focus on energy-harvesting, networking, flexible electronics, skeletons, motors and other actuators. The ideal assistant or domestic, public or private use will be one where components can be swapped out and replaced, or upgraded using software.

The large scale adoption of robotics will reply on such a healthy competitive eco-system. The same argument holds for other areas which require the interaction of many complex systems, in constant need of further development and improvement.

Since 2008 a US based robotics research institute and incubator called Willow Garage (Willow Garage, 2014c)has been promoting systems based on a Robot Operating System (ROS) originally developed at Stanford University. The initial work was based on an AI Robot project called STAIR(Artificial Intelligence Laboratory, Computer Science Department, Stanford University, n.d.). This ROS provides a basis for collaboration among at least 20 research institutes. The Willow-Garage site now hosts a repository of open source code based on its ROS (Willow Garage, 2014b) and as well as a project entitled OpenCV (Willow Garage, 2014a) which develops open source computer vision code for real time robotic perception.

Aldebaran Robotics of France has based the development of its Nao on the Willow garage ROS. There are reports ("NAO Humanoid Robot is Going to Open Source," 2011) that it will open-source much of its code. It already provides the hardware and basic platform at a very good price for developers, apparently at about €3,600 per unit. Members of the development network have access to its code to facilitate their work of development.

The Fraunhofer Institute for Manufacturing Engineering and Automation (IPA) in Stuttgart has developed its Care-O-bot (Fraunhofer IPA, n.d.) platform based on the Willow-garage ROS. This supports the work of a greater community of researchers. From 2010 they have been giving away their platform to other researchers to use, play with and carry out research on. The robot will also be available for remote use via the internet. This can be used for teaching and demonstration as well as for the evaluation of algorithms. The approach seems to have met with some success in the sense that the Care-O-Bot platform has been used by a variety of other projects and research teams such as the WIMI-Care (Universität Duisburg-Essen, 2014) initiative funded by the BMBF (Federal Ministry of Education and Research) for the purpose of fostering the transfer of robotics

technologies into the elderly care sector, as well as the EU funded SRS – Multi-Role Shadow Robotic System for Independent Living (SRS project, 2014) project which aims to develop and prototype remotely-controlled, semi-autonomous robotic solutions for domestic environments to support elderly people.

iGesture (Global Information Systems Group,, 2012) is an attempt to create a standard for gesture recognition. This will simplify and speed up the work of researchers working in this domain. It will provide developers with the possibility of future-proofing projects, by anticipating how to integrate eventual gesture based features. It is a Java-based framework for on extensibility and cross-application reusability. It comprises a gesture recognition framework as well as a tool for the creation of specific gesture sets. It enables the evaluation and optimization of new or existing gesture recognition algorithms. It is not limited to specific input devices. It can be used for traditional screen and mouse-based interaction. It works with digital pen and paper input. It supports interaction via Wii Remote and TUIO devices.

OPEN STANDARDS IN HARDWARE: THE CERN OHL

CERN has for a long time been at the centre, not only of scientific developments in high energy physics, but of advances in computing, networking and sensor technology. Its most famous spin-off is arguably the WWW. CERN is where the first user friendly web browser was developed by a British graduate student working under his Belgian PhD supervisor. It was initially intended to support collaboration among scientists scattered around the globe. This is where essential elements of the internet such as URL, http, and html were originally developed. It is where the most advanced applications of GRID computing are currently being developed. It is where many of the technologies of NMR and other medical imaging techniques were developed. It earns millions of euros each year selling technology transfer services in many of these domains. One of its most recent innovations is an open hardware license (Katz, 2012).

The CERN OHL was originally written to protect designs hosted in CERN's Open Hardware Repository, but it is now being promoted as a general model for open hardware available for use by anyone around the world, with a view to making research more efficient and less costly, and as a response to a perceived global increase in costly patent litigation. It is the hardware equivalent of the well-known GPL or General Public License used by the open source software community. It governs the use, copying, modification and distribution of hardware design documentation, and the manufacture and distribution of products. The philosophy is that anyone should be able to see the source (the design documentation in case of hardware), study it, modify it and share it. As in the case of the GPL for software, modifications can be made and distributed, but only under the same license conditions.

It is easy to see the potential need for new standards that facilitate the future development and market adoption of e-access and e-assistive technologies, especially as they move out of the proof-of-concept phase, and as invasive procedures or implantable devices stabilize enough to be considered platforms for further development.

TRANSFORMING PIONEERING PRODUCTS INTO PLATFORMS

In the chapter on humanoid assistant and companion robots we mentioned the Big Dog project of the US military, a man-sized autonomous robot that can carry heavy loads and navigate difficult terrain. More recently Big Dog has been joined by Little Dog a platform for the development of Big Dog capabilities and possible non-military spin-off technologies and applications.

Developed with funding from DARPA Big Dog is a quadruped robot designed to carry loads over rough terrain in combat zones, working with ground troops. Impressive YouTube videos (*BigDog Overview (Updated March 2010)*, 2010) show it fully laden climbing snow-covered hills, walking through brushwood, walking on the beach (*BigDog Beach'n*, 2009), walking on ice and successfully avoiding being pushed over by a man in combat gear. The hardware alone relies on a great range of breakthrough technologies, but it is expected that the performance will be improved and extended on the basis of software.

DARPA, who funded the original Big Dog project, also funded a scaled down version called Little Dog. It is produced by Boston Dynamics the same company that developed Big Dog. It is now being used by leading research institutes as a platform for research on motor learning, dynamic control, perception of the environment, and rough terrain locomotion. A recent video published on YouTube by the University of Southern California (Computational Learning and Motor Control Lab, 2013) demonstrates the state of the art of Little Dog capability over rough terrain (*The latest version of the LittleDog Robot*, 2010).

An important area of research for military systems is autonomy and survivability. One aspect of autonomy is the ability to operate for long periods without battery changes or recharges. This is one of the major factors limiting the deployability of such technologies today. Unless the system can operate at least for days at a time, they are of little practical value, regardless of their other capabilities. Rapid advances in battery technology and eventual breakthroughs in areas such as fuel cell technology will eventually help us overcome that obstacle. This limitation does not really apply in a domestic, institutional or modern urban environment. Homes and institutions have power outlets that enable service robots such as the Roomba and early companion robots such as Nao to recharge. The ability to anticipate the need for a recharge and then to autonomously locate and avail of power outlets are taken as given in robots intended for use in a domestic or institutional environment. In any EU countries urban areas are being fitted with EV or electric vehicle charging infrastructure. In principle this could allow domestic robots to extend their field of operation beyond the home or hospital and across urban spaces. This could be a future area for research where the capability of the robot to plan journeys and pay for energy as it goes may need to be developed. Complex system level issues also need to be explored so that we can in future avoid violent confrontation between radical environmentalists and groups of humanoid robots loitering around charging stations in car-parks, as one group tries to assert superior right of access over the other.

Someone involved in the development of the artificial retina, is primarily concerned with the patient and the performance of the system. The first models allowed a patient to see a simple 6 pixel image. Currently approved devices allow a patient to see a monochrome 60 pixel image and restore up to 10% of normal sight. Other epi-retinal and sub-retinal approaches are being used. Future generations of devices will have larger resolutions, may introduce colour, or may entirely bypass the retina and provide input directly to the visual cortex. This is the kind of trajectory that immediately occupies the development of a typical team working on such subjects, as well as issues related to learning the use of the system, and the length of time it can stay in the body, as well as changes in performance of the system over time.

An e-access approach might use the implant as a platform to develop a further level of functionality exploiting other degrees of freedom in the space of researchable possibilities. For example research could focus on the camera and image processing treating the implant as a platform:

- The camera does not have to use normal light. It could use radar, IR or sonar.
- They need not be direct images, they could be processed images, a form of game-like

or augmented reality that has been simplified by AI before being passed to the eye, so as to enable navigation or tasks or easier recognition by the user.

- Images passed to the retina need not be images in the vicinity of the user but images from another person, from the internet, a film or music archive, the screen of a controller, a computer or mobile phone.
- The camera could try to mimic the human eye by changing resolution, zooming in and out. It could compensate for low angular resolution by scanning scenes, or by switching from one feature to another as the human eye does. When one looks at the face of a person, the eye rapidly switches from one eye to another t the nose, to the mouth and back again, in a rapid almost arbitrary manner. In principle the external (camera and image processing) part of the artificial eye can be developed in this way.
- The sensation of colour could be provided by connecting the implant to colour specific structures in the retina or from the user's brain learning to combine images from 3 colour filtered cameras.
- There is scope for understanding the limits of neuronal plasticity. To what extent can the brain adapt to the implant and to what extent does the implant have to be adapted to the brain at the level of detailed connections to neurons?

In principle there is great scope for the development of new e-assistive or e-access technologies built upon state of the art pioneering products, creating knowledge and technology that is reusable for every new generation of products, applications and services. Especially in cases where the number of people using the product is still quite small, there may be a need to look at news ways for organizing research in this domain.

REFERENCES

Artificial Intelligence Laboratory, Computer Science Department, Stanford University. (n.d.). *STAIR*. Retrieved March 13, 2014, from http://stair.stanford.edu/

BigDog Beach'n. (2009). Retrieved from http://www.youtube.com/watch?v=P0s7aRUIoTw&feature=youtube_gdata_player

BigDog Overview (Updated March 2010). (2010). Retrieved from http://www.youtube.com/watch?v=cNZPRsrwumQ&feature=youtube_gdata_player

Computational Learning and Motor Control Lab. (2013, November 20). *Computational Learning and Motor Control Lab | Main / Home Page browse.* Retrieved March 13, 2014, from http://www-clmc.usc.edu/

DAISY Consortium. (2014). *Home | DAISY Consortium.* Retrieved March 13, 2014, from http://www.daisy.org/

European Commission. (2007, November 29). *Europa - Press Releases - Press release - European initiative on an all-inclusive digital society: Frequently Asked Questions.* Retrieved March 13, 2014, from http://europa.eu/rapid/press-release_MEMO-07-527_en.htm?locale=en

Fraunhofer, I. P. A. (n.d.). Research. *Fraunhofer Institute for Manufacturing Engineering and Automation.* Retrieved March 13, 2014, from http://www.care-o-bot.de/en/research.html

Global Information Systems Group. (2012). *iGesture - About.* Retrieved March 13, 2014, from http://www.igesture.org/

Katz, A. (2012). Towards a Functional Licence for Open Hardware. *International Free and Open Source Software Law Review*, 41–62. doi:10.5033/ifosslr.v4i1.69

NAO Humanoid Robot is Going to Open Source. (2011, May). Retrieved from http://www.ubuntubuzz.com/2011/05/nao-humanoid-robot-is-going-to-open.html

Riversimple, L. L. P. (2014). *Riversimple - home.* Retrieved March 13, 2014, from http://www.riversimple.com/

SRS project. (2014). *srs-project.eu | Multi-Role Shadow Robotic System for Independent Living.* Retrieved March 13, 2014, from http://srs-project.eu/

The 40 Fires Foundation. (2010). *40Fires: Main.* Retrieved March 13, 2014, from http://www.40fires.org/

The latest version of the LittleDog Robot. (2010). Retrieved from http://www.youtube.com/watch?v=nUQsRPJ1dYw&feature=youtube_gdata_player

Universität Duisburg-Essen. (2014, February 7). *Projektbeschreibung.* Retrieved March 13, 2014, from https://www.uni-due.de/wimi-care/

Willow Garage. (2014a). *OpenCV | Willow Garage.* Retrieved March 13, 2014, from http://www.willowgarage.com/pages/software/opencv

Willow Garage. (2014b). *ROS | Willow Garage.* Retrieved March 13, 2014, from http://www.willowgarage.com/pages/software/ros-platform

Willow Garage. (2014c). *Willow Garage.* Retrieved March 13, 2014, from http://www.willowgarage.com/

KEY TERMS AND DEFINITIONS

Complete Solutions: Solutions that tackle a problem in its entirety and not partially.

Complex Systems: Systems of high complexity.

Industrial Ecosystems: A set of specific businesses in industry that cooperate in a form of an ecosystem.

Life-Long Systems: Systems that tackle a problem throughout different stages of a person's lifetime.

Open Hardware: Open source hardware consists of physical artifacts of technology designed and offered by the open design movement.

Open Standards: An open standard is a standard that is publicly available and has various rights to use associated with it, and may also have various properties of how it was designed (e.g. open process).

Platform: A computing platform is, in the most general sense, whatever pre-existing environment a piece of software is designed to run within, obeying its constraints, and making use of its facilities.

Redundancy: The same task executed by several different methods.

Chapter 15
Innovation

ABSTRACT

This is the third chapter looking at the bigger picture of eAccessibility and inclusion technologies. In this chapter, issues dealing with innovation and how this can be boosted in the next years are discussed. More specifically, this chapter discusses how the organization of research and innovation can affect future innovation, how open innovation-led users, living labs, and DIY can have an impact on how innovative solutions are achieved in the future. It also discussed the effect of platforms in boosting innovation in specific areas give the recent lessons from mobile and how prizes and competitions can help even more in that direction. Finally, it looks into issues of business model innovation and emerging market models of innovation while also looking at how design plays a role and how new financing techniques such as crowdfunding can have an impact on future developments.

INNOVATIONS IN THE ORGANIZATION OF RESEARCH AND INNOVATION

The organization of research has come a long way from the weird but wonderful inventors' model based on Edison's workshop or Alfred Nobel's shed at the end of the garden. Modern scientific research is too vast, too expensive and too collaborative to make further progress in this way.

It is no longer appropriate to simple fund research and hope for some trickle-down effect. The link with innovation, commercial development and final use of a new technology must be built into research from the start. The whole chain of activities from needs discovery, scientific discovery, technology development, demonstra- tion and validation as well as business model development, the financing of entrepreneurs and the creation of appropriate framework conditions for adoption must all be given due consideration if public investments in research are to benefit the intended user groups.

As a result the way we 'do' research constantly evolves in form as well as in substance. It will continue to evolve as research becomes a mainstream part of all forms of work, as the idea of selling a 'finished product' in a 'final form' yields completely to that of the never ending work in progress, where learning about needs, that informs the design of the next version, is based on the real-life use of versions that are already in the market.

DOI: 10.4018/978-1-4666-6130-1.ch015

In future, even more so than is the case today, all products, services and systems will continuously evolve and the boundary between the laboratory and the real world will cease to have any real meaning.

OPEN INNOVATION, LEAD USERS, AND LIVING LABS

Professor Eric Von Hippel of MIT is generally credited with being the first to observe that innovation is often driven by users who take what is already available and adapt it to their special more demanding needs, sometimes in radical and unexpected ways, to create innovative products that respond to the needs of new and unanticipated markets. He came up with key concepts such as the locus of innovation and the lead-user of an innovative new product or service. These insights have spurred efforts by both the public and private sector to systematically organize innovation and research activities around the activities of diverse sets of people, not all of whom are engineers or scientists in the traditional sense of the word, many of whom are basically users, and all of whose involvement in the innovation process is important for rapid progress.

An important new aspect of this approach is that most new products and services are available as parts of complex constantly changing systems, their use must smoothly integrate into living and working, and aspects of use such as access, price, payment and ease of adoption are not easily studied in the laboratory, but must be systematically observed in situ in the laboratory of life, in the real world with all its attendant complexity and frustrating imperfection.

Many scientists work on the development of systems for use in hospitals or clinical environments, for example giving access to patient records. A lot of research takes place in the confines of a traditional research lab, designed to protect secrets in industry or for teaching purposes in a university setting. It is very difficult from such a stand-point to appreciate the conditions under which technology must be used. The fact that there are in reality many different users, often not just individuals but groups, all with different needs and many different venues where the application must be available under a variety of conditions. It is only really through the intelligent observation of users in their place of work that a real understanding of the design challenge can emerge.

In the case of smart clothing, an area potentially close to that of e-access and-assistive technology, the traditional laboratory environment provides few opportunities to understand and explore how to reconcile the benefit of electronics embedded in clothing, potentially involving elements for power, sensing, networking and processing with the fact that clothes get changed, the mechanical stress on clothing is different for sleeping, working, walking, swimming, jogging, or relaxing in the evening, that these are different in summer and winter, that clothes need to be changed, washed and may be shared by colleagues, friends of members of the same family. The living laboratory is the venue for discovering all of these issues and understanding the impact on technologies and its design as well as likely modes of adoption.

This is the kind of thinking that led various groups starting at MIT in the 1980s to develop the concept, vocabulary and preliminary methodologies for open-living labs where people from diverse backgrounds systematically co-create, explore, experiment and evaluate results in pursuit of a shared research agenda. The idea of an open living lab applied initially at MIT in the fields of ambient intelligence and human-dynamics. It migrated from MIT to Europe along with Finnish post-docs and PhD students. The philosophy has been adopted not only in Finland but in Europe at the level of the European Commission where it is now integrated in the Framework Programme for ICT. Dedicated programmes now exist to support the work of living labs in areas such as agriculture, GIS, e-government and healthcare.

There is a network called the ENoLL – the European network of Living Labs and the model has been exported outside of Europe to support EU research collaboration in ICT in the US, Asia, Latin America and Africa.

MIT still has a dedicated Living Labs website. One of the original living labs called PlaceLab is still in existence and European companies such as Philips have adapted the concept in their own way to create what is known as the ExperienceLab. In addition to Philips, other giants of EU ICT research, Nokia and SAP have embraced the Living Labs approach and have integrated this philosophy into their corporate approach to R+D. Although Steve Jobs always put the customer first, it is said that he never asked people what they wanted. Instead he observed them and studied them to creatively imagine what would appeal or make a difference to their lives. Intel has a similar philosophy. It employs anthropologists to observe people living and working in an attempt to understand what is important for them and what role their technologies could play in their lives in future.

Research work organized in this way, is very much in line with a set of industry behaviours identified by Henry Chesbrough, who tends to be associated with the term open innovation. It might be useful to exploit with research areas related with e-Access and e-Assistive technologies can benefit the most form such a research organisation and what are the benefits for volunteers participating in it.

THE R+DIY: RESEARCH AND 'DO IT YOURSELF' MODEL

Britta Riley wanted to grow her own food in her tiny New York apartment. She became interested in the use of hydroponics and developed a primitive system allowing her to grow food in this way in her small New York apartment. She told her story at a TEDx talk (Riley, 2011) given in Manhattan in February 2011 explains her mass collaboration system on given in

Her first effort at making a hydroponic urban window garden was successful in that it allowed her to produce about 1 lettuce a week, along with some cherry tomatoes, cucumbers. But the overall system made a lot of noise, used a lot of energy and was not very aesthetic. She set up a website hoping to solicit help from other people and develop the idea further using massive open collaboration. She published the design of her system at her website R+DIY (Crux Strategies, LLC, 2011), explained the many problems she had found with it, invited people to work with her to solve them and spread the word using social media. By early 2011 the community had grown to more than 18,000 members all over the world. The development model called R+DIY instead of R+D is a reaction against the use of experts with an emphasis on purposeful research linked directly to implementation. There is more cachet associated with testing other people's ideas than in creating the ideas in the first place. The ongoing development work emphasizes two kinds of problem - universal problems that are of interest to everyone and local ones that are of interest mainly to sub-groups.

One of the New York community members found out how to produce strawberries for 9 months of the year in low light conditions by experimenting with the organic nutrient mix. Another in Finland developed a system based on grow LEDs to continue growing during the long dark winter months. The area of hydroponics is one of the fastest growing areas for patent creation in the US right now. The group has at least one patent submitted and ownership is shared by the whole community. They expect to produce new ones in areas such as aquaponics and LED grow lighting systems.

This is an example also of citizen science. It touches upon the methodologies used in professions such as management and teaching and may have a role in extending the work done by people in the Quantified Self movement addressed in the section on healthcare.

The expansion of online communities and the sharing of knowledge between people participating in them is an important driver for this kind of innovation. As social networks, online communities and exchange of information extend we expect innovation coming from DIY to become even more evident and one of the major contributors. Therefore there is a need for policies facilitating DIY innovation.

OTHER ORGANIZATIONAL PARADIGMS

Through the work of ENoLL the concept of the Living Laboratory continues to evolve, in addition to our understanding of the management challenge they represent as well as the tools and techniques that can be applied to address them.

The Living laboratory however is one of the new and emerging organizational paradigms for research and innovation. It has evolved to address specific innovation challenges. Other organizational models are emerging to address other challenges.

One such model developed by the NSF of the United States is referred to as the Synthesis Centre. These are research centres intended to accelerate progress in domains where a multidisciplinary approach is required. This mechanism focuses the efforts of scientists working in board well established domains, to focus their efforts on the application of their work to specific fields or problem sets, ones that might otherwise be overlooked or which require a critical mass of attention, for progress to be made. Until now there seem to be only six of these mainly focused on domains of the social and environmental sciences.

A related organisational model, again from the US is that of the "Third Generation Engineering Research Centre". There are 17 of these in the US. They are intended to accelerated progress

by industry in themes that require considerable combined effort in engineering and research. These centres are financed for a limited period of time, typically for 5 years. Their goal is to create knowledge and innovations that address significant societal issues in areas such as health and sustainability while advancing the competitiveness of industry. They have a strong educational element as well to prepare the work force with technical and entrepreneurial skills needed for the future. One of the newest centres (Advantage Business Media, 2011) is the NSF ERC for Sensorimotor Neural Engineering,(Gonzalez, 2011) whose task is to pursue mind-machine interfaces and other devices to restore and augment health.

Europe should also try to identify new organisational paradigms such as the Synthesis Centre and the Third Generation Research Centre to accelerate progress in complex inter-disciplinary areas of e-access technologies. Areas that could benefit eAccessibility could be new neuro-sensory implant technologies, brain-computer interfaces, advanced prosthetics or social and companion robotics, technologies for independent living etc.

TECHNOLOGY INNOVATION PLATFORMS AND THE 'APP' MODEL

An important trend of the last 5 years in the organisation of innovation is most easily illustrated in terms of mobile phone apps, but has much broader implications

Nokia claims that it links more than 5 million software developers from round the world, via its Nokia Forum. They claim it is the largest research community in the world. Apple has done the same for its developers. Their open platform has quickly led to the availability of more than 250,000 apps for mobile phone users around the world. The members of networks supported by these development platforms have easy access to resources that allow them to develop, test and market smart-phone applications. This considerably reduces the time and cost associated with the development of new products and services. In the case of Nokia, Apple or indeed almost any mobile technology company, an investment of as little as 10 days and several thousand of euros, is sufficient to produces an app of sufficient quality that it can be offered to a global market. If it is popular the distribution system is already in place for it to reach millions of customers in just a few days. This requires no further investment on the part of the entrepreneur. Everything has been taken care of, IP, marketing, distribution and payment. The business model for the mobile technology company is based on revenue sharing. In the case of Apple, Apple retains 30% of all transactions as a fee. If there is no payment, there is no transaction fee. Although many complain about this, it is a small price to pay for access to a world class infrastructure that would have taken years to develop, at considerable cost and risk that provides immediate access to a global market as well as the benefit of association with one of the most powerful global brands.

This has transformed the economics of innovation first in mobile telephony and more recently for tablet computing. The platform makes everything in the innovation process, apart from the act of invention itself, the normally expensive risky and time consuming work of market testing and tweaking, as simple, seamless and cheap as possible. It totally changes the economics of the process, not only in terms of cost, but in terms of the time and resources needed to complete an initiative intended to complete the entire cycle from discovery and invention to prototyping, production, marketing, revenue creation and scale-up.

These are not just 'technology platforms', but 'total innovation platforms'. They exist also in other domains. Intel has many developer forums, for example to help development SW to exploit the power of its next generation low-energy, high-performance multi-core chips. They also run a business exchange to help businesses in their industrial eco-systems, who try to develop products and services based on their technology, to get in touch with each other and do business. E-Bay, Google, Facebook all run similar systems too.

INNOVATION PRIZES, COMPETITIONS, AND TOURNAMENTS

John Harrison an English clock-maker invented the chronometer in the 1700s in response to a prize offered by the English Parliament of the time. The story is told in detail in a best-selling book entitled 'Longitude' and this is often considered to be an early example of government intervention in strategic research.

Much later, in 1919 a New York hotel owner called Raymond Orteig was inspired by the idea that people might one day fly from Paris to New York and spend the weekend at his hotel. He thought it would be a boon for hoteliers like him and offered a grand prize of $25,000 to the first aviator to fly from New York to Paris, proving the concept and demonstrating the feasibility of this vision. The prize was not won until 1927, by Charles Lindberg when he became the first to fly non-stop from New York to Paris. This along with the many other aviation incentive prizes offered in the early 20th century paved the way for the development of the commercial airline industry, an industry that is worth many billions of Euros a year today.

More recently the US based X-prize captured the imagination of the public when $10M was awarded by the Ansari family to the company that created and launched and returned to earth with Spaceship One in October 2004 by a private company called Scaled Composites. The prize mobilized 26 teams in 7 different nations that collectively spent more than $100M in pursuit of the prize. Since then Richard Branson, founder and President of the Virgin Group has established Virgin Galactic ("Virgin Galactic," 2014)in partnership with Scaled Composites. The ambition of Virgin Galactic is to provide sub-orbital space-flights to the paying public, along with sub-orbital space science missions and orbital launches of small satellites and eventually orbital human space-flights as well.

Since then the idea of an innovation prize as a path to achieving highly ambitions technological goals has proven very effective in mobilising corporate investments and launching whole new industries. The Ansari X-prize has since been replaced by the Google Lunar X PRIZE (XPRIZE Foundation, 2014), a $30 million competition for the first privately funded team to send a robot to the moon, travel 500 meters and transmit video, images and data back to the Earth. Already more than 20 consortia are competing for the prize. The X-prize foundation actively searches for ideas and sponsors for new X-prizes and several already exist in areas such as genomics, energy and the environment. The philosophy is simple. Rather than reward people for past achievements, the goal is to incentivize them for future achievements that will benefit the whole of humanity.

In January 2010 the X-Prize foundation held a meeting on brain computer interfaces at MIT co-sponsored by the Singularity University (Furlan, 2010). Among those present was Ray Kurzweil (*Ray Kuzweil at the MIT/XPrize BCI workshop*, 2010) who provided his views on the future of Brain-Computer Interfaces. This conference helped move thinking on the subject of BCI away from research and towards high impact real world applications.

The Foundation is now planning to launch an X-Prize for "Vision Restoration X PRIZE" (XPrize Foundation, 2014) pointing out that over 160 million Americans today suffer from poor or no vision. The winner of the Vision Restoration competition will be the first team to restore vision in a person once blinded by retinal degenerative disease. Teams may select their own participant, who must be medically certified as blind from a retinal degenerative disease, and may work to impart their solution and train them by any means available.

The X-Prize Foundation is currently investigating a range of other related prize concepts

- **Bionics X Legs:** According to a study by the Christopher & Dana Reeve Foundation, nearly one in fifty people live with paralysis, approximately six million people in the US alone. This prize is for a set of bipedal bionic legs that give a paraplegic full mobility and remove the limitations of wheelchairs, thereby improving the quality of life and physical capabilities of paraplegic patients.

- **Blind Tennis:** Over 160 million Americans suffer from poor or no vision yet overall progress in the restoration of vision lags behind restoration of any other sense. The winner of the Blind Tennis competition will be the first team to develop a wearable, transportable, non-tethered solution that can enable a blind person to play tennis. Teams may train their subject in any means available to them, and the subject must be able to complete all aspects of the game of tennis within a 60 minute time period.

- **Brain Computer Interface:** Technologies that can directly read information from the brain or write information to the brain have the potential to revolutionize a number of industries including healthcare, disease, communications and computer-related technologies. There could also be multiple opportunities for creating better diagnostic, management and assistive technologies that can be used in biomedical and industrial applications. The winner of the Brain Computer Interface competition will be the team that successfully demonstrates a bi-directional non-verbal brain-computer communication. Teams may use an invasive or non-invasive brain transmission device, and may train the human participant in any way they desire.

- **Enduring Brain Computer Communication:** With advances in this field, technologies such as those that are implanted for long periods of time into the human brain can provide us with more robust and longer-term data that can be applied to a number of industries: healthcare, disease, communications and computer-related technologies. The winning team of the Enduring Brain Computer Communication competition will be the first to develop a functional brain implanted electrode that can last for three years.

- **Vision Surrogate:** This competition will award a prize purse to the team that is able to design a portable hand-held device that provides the blind the freedom, comfort, and awareness to explore the world and to safely navigate their surroundings. The goal of this competition is to enable blind individuals to perform basic daily-life functions that a white cane or guide dog cannot.

- **Robotic Home Helper:** In the US, the elderly increased by a factor of 11 in the past century, while the population under 65 years old only tripled. As a result there are more and more elderly, but fewer younger adults available to care for them. Assistive technology is crucial for baby boomers that are searching for solutions to help them care for aging parents. The Robotic Home Helper competition will result in a robot capable of improving the quality of life of elderly and disabled persons. The goal of the competition will be to develop a robot that can (1) demonstrate the ability to evaluate and learn the layout of a test space and (2) restore that test space to its original condition after the contents have been rearranged.

Progress in some of these domains is already so fast that some of these goals may already have become redundant. Many however will remain hard for years to come. If an X-Prize can have an impact on the industry even approaching the impact of the Ansari prize on the space industry, it could transform the field of e-assistive technology and e-access technologies in a relatively short amount of time.

There are other prizes of relevance. These are more in the line of open innovation tournaments. One of the most important initiatives, touching upon the area of assistive technology, access technology or inclusive innovation is the Microsoft Imagine Cup (Micosoft, 2014a).

MS claims that there is a *"tremendous need for assistive technology (AT) to meet the needs of those with disabilities"*. Typical systems are screen readers and magnifiers. Less obvious examples are the use of learning software such as talking dictionaries to help people with conditions such as dyslexia. MS has made a strong commitment to promoting access technologies and has recently opened an Inclusive Innovation Showroom (Micosoft, 2014b). It has developed a network of Accessibility Resource Centres (Microsoft, 2014a) across the US. MS accessibility (Microsoft, 2014b) says that *"accessibility is what enables people of all abilities to realize their full potential."* It states that its mission is to create *"technology that is accessible to people around the world, of all ages and abilities."* This mission is strongly reflected in the themes of the Imagine Cup.

The Imagine Cup started in 2001 and the first competition was held in 2003 attracting about 1000 students, mainly from universities and technical colleges at post-secondary school level, though some secondary or high school teams have been involved. MS claims with some justification that the competition has grown into "the world's premier student technology competition". A total of 358,000 students from 183 countries and regions registered for the 2011 competition.

A product called *Note Taker* (*Blind Ambition (FULL VERSION)*, 2011)developed by a team from Arizona State University developed is intended to help low-vision and legally blind students take notes in their secondary and post-secondary classrooms as quickly (and with the same ease) as their fully-sighted peers. Though they did not win the international competition, it seems to have attracted great interest from MS accessibility (Microsoft, 2014b).

The first competition was held in 2003. There was only one category in the competition "SW design". Now there are 10 categories but the cup is still awarded to the winner in SW design. In 2012 the teams are asked to focus on ideas that will help realize the UN Millennium Development Goals. MS has recently committed $3M over a 3 year period to help winning teams.

The Imagine Cup is not the only competition run by Microsoft of potential relevance to the theme of e-Access. MS also runs a robotics competition called *Robotics at Home* (Microsoft, 2012). It may be of interest to support activities intended to feed in to innovation support mechanisms like these if they can accelerate path to market and link the creator or inventor with partner capable of supporting all steps of the innovation process.

Many private companies now use this approach in pursuit of specific R+D or innovation challenges. One high profile example of recent years was the $1M *Netflix Prize* for the best algorithm for recommending videos based on a buyers profile data. Another example was the US government *Cryptolympics* competition launched in 1997. This was won by a Belgian team in 2002. The selected algorithm, now known as the Rijndael algorithm, became the new Advanced Encryption Standard which is used by U.S. Government agencies, replacing the Data Encryption Standard which had been in use for more than 30 years. Other examples include the $200m *Ecomagination programme* of GE, the *Shell Springboard programme* and the *Rushlight prize fund*. These programmes are interesting in that they are set up with the intention of focusing research and innovation efforts on specific sets of problems of considerable importance for industry and society, with a view to creating industrial eco-systems in these new and emerging domains. They are often run in partnership with commercial venture capital firms so that the money to commercialise promising new ideas is already available.

At least one small bio-medical firm in Germany, working in the area of EEG systems, has launched its own prize worth several thousand euros per year. It uses this prize to encourage researchers involved in related domains to orient their research towards problems of immediate relevance for the company and the markets it serves.

In the area of mobile telephony Vodafone has launched its Vodafone Foundation Smart Accessibility Awards (Vodafone Group, 2012). It offers €200,000 or 4 prizes of €50,000 each to smart phone application developers who develop applications under 4 major headings:

- Social participation
- Independent living
- Mobility
- Wellbeing

The program held workshops in Belfast and London and was launched in Brussels. It is supported and co-organized by AGE Platform Europe (AGE Platform Europe, 2014), the European network of around 160 organizations of and for people aged 50+, as well as the European Disability Forum (EDF, n.d.), an NGO that represents the interests of 80 million Europeans with disabilities. Twelve entries will be selected and will compete for the prizes in a final competition in Brussels in December 2011.

To support people in their endeavours, Vodafone provides online material to help developers understand the needs of people with disabilities using mobile phones as well as guidelines on how to design for accessibility.

A recent theme in the research and innovation literature from the US is the idea of involving more undergraduates and even secondary schools students in research projects. In principle it is not necessary for people to complete a graduate degree or even a PhD before being able to do research. In practise everyone, whether they work in formal research positions or not, must acquire advanced problem solving and research capabilities to be able to perform in modern knowledge-intensive work. Stanford University organises an annual summer school with the Army High-Performance Computing Research Center. This two-month immersion in advanced computing is organized around team work and American Idol type competitions to complete ambitious innovative projects. In one case a group was asked to create a character-recognition application that would use the camera on a mobile device – a phone or tablet, to transform pages of Braille into readable text. Working with the Stanford University Office for Accessible Education, they found that the problem they imagined was not the most important one. For example there were basic problems with a blind person using a tablet. How could they orient it for example? They also found that a *touch-screen Braille Writer* (Stanford Engineering, 2011) would be more useful than a Braille reader. Eventually they came up with innovative strategies for a blind person to use a tablet, write into it and communicate with it using Braille. They were able to overcome basic problem such as orientation and finding the keys by programming it so that instead of the person having to find the keys, the person could put their hands on the touch screen and instead the keys would find their fingers, enabling them to start typing. The lesson in this is that good results can come from short sessions, in this case two months by two people in the right environment. It is not necessary to spend two years and millions of euros to have good results, but it is necessary to organize the work and provide the right environment.

The US has taken aggressive steps to boost the interest of young people in the STEM areas of Science Technology, Engineering and Mathematics. One element of this is a high profile youth robot competition called FIRST (USFirst, 2014)- For Inspiration and Recognition of Science and Technology.

This is led by Dean Kamen one of the most publicly recognizable high profile entrepreneurs in the US. It is supported by a large number of rock stars and media celebrities including rappers and musicians such as Snoop Dog and Will.I.Am of the Black Eyed peas, Bono of U2, the comedy actor Joe Black, Morgan Freeman who played Nelson Mandela in the film Invictus, Justin Timberlake and child stars such as Justin Bieber and Miley Cyrus, proclaiming things like "geeks and nerds are the coolest people in the planet" (*My Robot is Better Than Your Robot*, 2011) to the strains of a song entitled "my robot is better than your robot".

Dean Kamen creator the Luke Arm, currently the most advanced prosthetic arm in the world, considers that his greatest invention was the creation of the FIRST (USFirst, 2014) series of international robotic competitions in the US. This is a series of international robotics competitions for kids aged between 6 and 18 years of age. Already more than 1 million kids have taken part in this. Kamen claims that many of the next great entrepreneurs will have found their inspiration and cut their teeth as entrepreneurs through participation in these events. The focus is not just on the technology but on working in teams. Eligible teams compete to build robots to address specific challenges, under time –pressure for example over a two week period. Teams are often sponsored by large corporations. For example NASA (NASA, 2011) has sponsored FIRST events.

One vision for the future entitled NIBEye (NIBEye, n.d.) or Neural Interface Bionic Eye was created by the winners of the 2010 ExploraVision ("WGES ExploraVision," n.d.) student science competition. This competition is sponsored by Toshiba and the National Science Teachers Association of America and is intended to encourage a love of science, technology, engineering and mathematics in children of up to 12 years of age. The approach of the competition is to encourage teams to choose a technology or technical challenge of interest, study the state of the art, imagine what it could be like in 20 years and describe what needs to be done to make it all happen. This vision developed b children aged 10 to 12 years of age combined 7 different technologies including an artificial retain, a brain machine interface to control the movement of the eye, a cortical stimulator to transmit vision data to the brain and a battery that transforms glucose in the users blood into the energy required to make it all work.

According to a fact sheet (EyeCare America, 2007) of Eye Care America, a foundation of the American Academy of Ophthalmology, 3.4 million people over the age of 40 in the US, almost 3% of the total, have some form of vision disability. 81% of these are unemployed. The total annual cost in terms of benefits and lost income is about $4B. By the time a person reaches 60 years of age about 1 in 3 have some form of visual impairment. The risk is 25 times higher for those who also suffer from diabetes. On a global scale about 180 million people are believed to have some form of visual disability. About 90% of these live in developing economies. The chances of someone having a visual impairment are 10 time higher than in the developed world. The overall number of people affected is expected to double by 2020.

There are two salient points about this kind of competition. The first is that it focuses not so much on building a prototype, but on developing a vision for what that prototype should be. The second is that it focuses on people in the K-12 age-group, kids of up to and not over 12 years of age.

It is also interesting to see to what extent they are interested in what are essentially assistive technologies. Another one of the innovation vision developed by the most recent competitor includes a Sign Language Interpreter converts hand-created signing into verbal words to help deaf people better communicate with people who do not understand sign language. Electrodes on the signers' fingertips sense movement and send signals to a tiny computer inside a finger ring that translates the signals into recognizable sounds.

Competitions such as the BCI X-Prize, the Imagine Cup and the Vodafone challenge are clearly drivers of progress, perhaps even stronger drivers of progress on real life problems than traditional research programmes. They do not replace traditional research programmes, they complement them. When used in a timely fashion they focus critical resources on a subject at the right time. Therefore it might be useful for EC to exploit this direction by establishing tournaments and prizes for specific e-Access challenges.

Each year Japan hosts and annual national robot awards competition. This started in 2006 as an initiative of METI - the Japanese Ministry for the Economy, Trade and Industry ("Ministry of Economy, Trade and Industry," 2014). Each year awards are made in three main application domains in addition to parts and software used in robot manufacture.

- Service Robots for offices, homes and public facilities
- Industrial Robots for manufacturing and shop floor tasks
- Public and Frontier Robot for special purposes, such as search and rescue, as well as space and deep-sea exploration.

The 2007 annual robot award (*Japanese Robot Of The Year*, 2009) was won by an extraordinary robotic arm called the M430-117 able to carry out small precise operations on delicate materials at high speed, for example identifying, picking up and placing delicate food items in boxes. This meeting also introduced the Miuro (*Miuro, the new music robot*, 2006) a small dancing robot that plays music, acts as an iPod dock and follows its owner around the house, a bit like a dog or a child. It also introduced a robot scorpion (*Lego mindstorm NXT Scorpion robot*, 2007) based on Lego Mindstorms (LEGO Group, 2014)technology from Denmark that seemed to suggest interesting forms of robot-mediated play.

MARKET INNOVATION PLATFORMS

Peter Druker, considered by many to be the father of modern management, held that social challenges provided an important source of business opportunity. This is certainly the case for e-Access technologies. But we can go further and ask where? An interesting art of the answer was provided by the late C. K. Prahalad who coined the term "Bottom of the Pyramid" referring to the huge under-served markets involving less well-off people. He advised businesses seeking growth to consider that these markets consist of people, who though poor, have pressing needs and the means to pay for appropriate goods and services. He counselled that a different approach was needed to serve such market, but that they offered important possibilities for growth, especially when growth has slowed in advanced economies. Nowadays most large retail and consumer goods companies have strategies that target markets at the 'Bottom of the Pyramid'. High profile case such as Vestas of Denmark have moved almost all research and production to places such as China, and even GE of the US has opening up major new technology and market research centers in the developing world to position them close to their customers, helping them to design, develop and test the goods and services they require. Although Prahalad originally referred to 'Bottom of the Pyramid' markets as those living in emerging markets in China, India, Africa and Latin America, the concept applies equally to many living at the 'Bottom of the Pyramid' in Europe and the US.

In announcing her desire to develop a European disabilities act, Viviane Redding has expressed a wish that Europe become a global exporter of e-access products and services. If this ambition is to be taken seriously we should distinguish at least between 4 broad categories of market, each presenting its own specific challenges which have a potential impact on future research and innovation policies:

- European markets subject to shared legislation and where the main challenges beyond invention might be seen as accelerated adoption of new products and services as a spur to entrepreneurship, employment and quality of life for a caring, ageing society.

- The markets of other industrialized or advanced economies, in countries such as Canada, the US, Japan, South Korea, Australia and New Zealand. These are also competitors especially in areas such as social and assistant robotics. Korea and Japan in particular have started long ago and have accelerated adoption of social and assistant robotics in domains such as child education and care of the elderly.

- The markets of the so called emerging economies, countries such as Brazil, Russia, India and China. Many of these owe their spectacular growth through becoming the 'workshop of the world' or the service centre of the world. They have their own global ambitions, their own specific needs, huge numbers of home-grown entrepreneurs and engineers and vast reserves of cash with which to finance their own development.

- The markets of the poorest countries. For example most countries of Africa fall into this category, as well as some countries of South East Asia, any country that has suffered the horrors of war, vast campaigns of land mines, cluster bombing, systematic torture and maiming. Countries with high incidents of disease such as AIDS or river-blindness lose a large part of their work force due to temporary and permanent disability. All of these have a great need for assistive technologies, but these have to operate under very different conditions than those available in Europe, provided at very different price points, enabled by different business models for manufacture, distribution and maintenance. Although the ability to pay of either governments or individuals is always an issue, many NGOs try to address these gaps. Opportunities exist in terms of low cost, adequate, resource light solutions adapted to local conditions. Venture capital fund such as Acumen fund run by Jacqueline Novogradz, have proven effective in funding developing ventures based on scalable solutions.

If the ambition of Viviane Redding is to be realized, these factors should all be addressed. Success in many of these markets will rely more on capability in terms of design, marketing and entrepreneurial development, than in research and engineering. There is as much need for new market and techno-social system insight as there is for new technology ideas. Future research programmes might build these factors into their design.

BUSINESS MODEL INNOVATION

A report on assisted living technologies for older and disabled people in 2030 (Lewin et al., 2010) the organizers claim that there is a need for innovative approaches to financing and delivering solution as current care models are unsustainable in terms of efficiency, and effectiveness.

A key element in the successful introduction of new e-Access technologies will be the business model. Entrepreneurs will need to build market and financial thinking into the development of their systems from the earliest stage. This is an issue that goes beyond traditional science, technology and engineering, in ways that have also been explained in the section on living labs.

The issue of 'business model innovation' though an essential component of innovation in itself, will become all the more important due to

an austerity drive that affects most countries in Europe, as part of the fall-out from the current financial crisis. The European Healthcare Fraud and Corruption Network (EHFCN, n.d.) recently published an article entitled "Disabled people live in terror of the future". They refer to findings of a report by the European Disability Forum which claim that this includes "*cuts in disability allowances, a reassessment of disability status and a reduction in services for disabled people.*" They indicate that in the UK alone "*over 400,000 disabled people will be affected by a decision to limit employment and support allowance to one year.*" In the Netherlands they claim that "*the number of people eligible for a personal budget scheme, used for things such as home nursing, has been cut by 90%.*" Whereas for Spain they claim that "*a decision to reduce supported employment for those with intellectual disabilities in Spain could see up to 12,000 such jobs being lost.*"

One initiative entitled ALIP for Assisted Living Innovation Platform (Technology Strategy Board, 2013) provides a new approach to making technology better, cheaper and more desirable. ALIP is not a platform in the previous more technology oriented sense. Instead it focuses on making the products, systems and services for independent living are relevant, acceptable, scalable and marketable. The potential market for many goods and services is already quite considerable, but they have to be provided at the right price or with the right financing model.

The need for new business models is more general that this. A good case in point is that for exoskeletons. Some exoskeleton makers try to sell their product for $150,000. Most are developed for military use or for use by hospitals and clinics are tools for rehabilitation. This is not a price affordable by ordinary citizens and priced this way it is unlikely that there will ever be a big market even among institutional users. It is likely that they will buy a limited number for use with multiple patients at limited times of the day.

Cyberdyne of Japan has made efforts to break out of this mould. According to one report it started producing its HAL exoskeleton in October 2008. Initial plans for production were for 400 to 500 units per year. HAL stands for Hybrid Assistive Limb and Cyberdyne claims that this can multiply the strength of an average user by a factor of 10 and that when fully charged it can operate for up to 2 hours and 40 minutes. As well as the intended markets in hospitals and clinics, it has attracted considerable interest from extreme sports fans, who want to test it to the limit, outdoors, to see if it can help them run, jump and fight and play faster or better than they could before. Although originally developed with healthcare applications in mind, maybe the early market development will depend more on the kind of entrepreneurship associated with paint-ball and venture sports.

This market, if it takes off it could transform the economics of the industry considerably. Bear in mind that the very first cars often had to be towed back to the garage by horse. Their main domain of application was not to help with work on farms as envisaged by Henry Ford, making up for the inconvenience and inefficiencies of using horses. Sports racing and all the spectacle it involved was a great marketing tool and provided an essential stepping stone to the economic viability of the early automobile industry. For this reason, in the early stage of the development of the auto industry, banks refused to invest in the car because they thought of riving as a trivial and immoral being associated with gambling and other vices.

It is possible that in the case of the exoskeleton, further development of the device in response to the demands from lead users in areas such as extreme sports and entertainment could drive improvements that will have spin-offs for the healthcare industry.

One of the pricing options being considered by Cyberdyne is the leasing option where an organisation such as a hospital might lease it for about €1,000 a month, for use with many patients. Leasing may be attractive for people running theme parks or in the entertainment business, where end-users may only want to use the device for one hour.

Understanding the right price or financing model for each segment will require a detailed cost-benefit analysis, for example comparing it to paint-ball, scuba-diving or parachuting in the case of adventures sports. In institutional or healthcare settings, this may require and realistic analysis of the total cost of care that includes the attention of professional caretakers and other care options. Early establishment of competitive cost points for such devices could provide a valuable input to the innovation process, enabling researchers and entrepreneurs to make better more commercially oriented decisions earlier in the innovation process.

Everything Robotic recently published a survey (Tobe, 2011) on breakthroughs in robotics that promise to dramatically reduce the cost of robots and open up the domain to entirely new markets. According to their analysis the breakthrough will occur when the cost of a general purpose robot comes down to the €5,000 to €15,000 price range.

The INNOROBO Summit held in Lyon in March 2011 featured representatives from Aldebaran Robotics (Aldebaran Robotics, 2014), a five year old French maker of humanoid domestic service and companion robots. Their 'Nao' model, comparable in many ways to the better known 'Asimo' by Honda, has already sold over a 1,000 units in France at a cost of about €16,000 each. The CEO of Aldeberan says he wants to see the cost of the robot come down to the €1,000 to €2,000 range, over the next 5 years. He thinks it can be a major consumer item and is of the opinion that sales are already growing in the way that laptops grew in the early market phase. In an interview broadcast on YouTube, he claims that there are significant opportunities for humanoid robots in both domestic and institutional settings either to provide services or companionship and general assistance.

This will require efforts to expand the market and range of applications as much as possible, coupled with process engineering and value engineering and a range of innovations intended not so much to prove the concept, but to drive down the cost to make it attractive to the largest market possible.

It is interesting to draw analogies between the possible future evolution of areas such as service and companion robots, and the evolution of the car industry in recent years. The business model for cars has evolved over the years from a business based on selling new cars in 'any colour as long as it is black', to a larger more diverse business with differentiation based on budget and personal preferences for colour and style as well as functionality. Then a second hand market was created. This allowed experienced users to trade-up using the revenue from the sale of an old car to partly finance the purchase of a new one. Then purchasing plans came along allowing someone to acquire and use a car before they have actually paid the full price. Now there is also leasing market. People no longer need to own the car because they can simply pay for the use of the car. The old model of leasing is to pay by the day. A newer model, that applied by car-sharing companies such as ZipCar of London, is to pay by the distance travelled, perhaps even with a price varying on the time of the day.

This type of 'service model' has already been introduced in other areas such as aviation and trucking. An airline does not need to own its planes, it can lease them. Many of the parts of a plane are not even owned by the leasing company. The engines are paid for as they are used and in terms of the energy they produce. The breaks on a large jetliner are invoiced every time the pilot touches them. The tyres of a truck in many cases are paid for according to the distance driven. Decisions about when to change and what type of tyre to use are made by the tyre company based on their database of driving conditions associated to routes and driving behaviours associated to drivers. Trucking companies no longer have to buy their tyres, they pay as they go.

As described earlier in the references to River Simple, in relatively short time the Electric Vehicle or EV has transformed the design of cars and thinking about transport and mobility. Many governments have invested heavily in this sector, not only as a way to reduce their energy dependency or carbon footprint, but also as a way to create jobs. They believe that the EV is a whole new industry, quite apart from the traditional car industry and that it provides opportunities to generate jobs on a large scale. For this reason they have been pro-active facilitating the introduction of EV infrastructure in city areas and the adoption of EV transport solutions by business, taxi and public owned fleets.

A future where large numbers of companion robots, EV wheelchairs or advanced 'walkers' such as exoskeletons and other assistive devices, that allow mobility for disabled people, not only in the home or in an institutional environment, but in the neighbourhood and eventually throughout Europe, will require infrastructure for charging and navigation. One that allows whatever services they require to follow them in their travels.

Many people are less interested in owning a car today that those of a previous generation. They are in having a mobility solution or a transport option. They are happy to rent bikes when they visit other cities, using bike-sharing schemes. They are happy to rent time in a car using car-sharing schemes. Many cities in Europe and around the world actively collaborate with providers and advertising agencies, to encourage the development of bike sharing and car-sharing solutions that complement and extent what is offered by the classical modes of public transport such as bus, tram and metro.

THE ROLE OF DESIGN IN INNOVATION

The role of design is often neglected in science and technology oriented research. However it may play a much more important role in the successful development of e-Access technologies for the future.

The traditional intersection of e-Access and design occurs in areas such as ergonomics or in the principle of Universal Design. This is the idea that systems should be designed from the beginning in a way that anyone can use them. Rather than having a generic solution that can be used by non-disabled people, and a range of customized solutions catering to the specific needs of people with disabilities, a single solution should suffice. Although there are many examples of successful UD solutions, they are often not so easy either to create or to implement. The spirit of UD is often lost when upgrades or modification are made by people who are not the original designers.

The most promising UD technologies of recent years may be direct brain machine interfaces or service and companion robotics. The advantage of these is that once the hardware is in place, the system can be improved and adapted on almost a continuous basis using SW upgrades. Eventually it is hoped that even this will become automatic as machines acquire the ability to learn by themselves either through observation, experimentation or machine-to-machine knowledge exchange.

A first step in this direction is affective computing. This means computing that is sensitive to the emotional state and level of attention of the human involved in the interaction. It also refers to the ability of systems to simulate emotion, communicating not only with word, but with tone of voice, facial expressions, more generally with a sense of timing and the use of body language.

In its most primitive form for a companion robot this means moving the head and eyebrows, establishing eye-contact or shifting the gaze. It means changing posture and the tone of voice. It means having an appearance that is friendly, human-like and affective.

All of this requires an approach that goes way beyond the traditional approaches to machine-communication. It requires inputs from linguists, specialists in theatre or psychology, designers from fashion, sculpture and visual media, as well as the people who are strong in craftsmanship, able to create the objects designed and connect them up with motors and actuators and sensors, in the way that works best with human and maybe even animal subjects.

People of all ages can respond well to robots. They tend to personalise them giving them names and forming attachments or emotional bonds. In this sense the design of the system is an important aspect of its adoption by a user community.

A number of groups have started to specialise in this aspect of computing. A Spanish group from Universidad Carlos III de Madrid have made great strides developing speech and dialogue systems that respond to the emotional state (Universidad Carlos III de Madrid, 2011) of the speaker.

A group at the Technical University of Munich in collaboration with the AIST or National Institute of Advanced Industrial Science and Technology in Japan has developed a system called Mask-Bot (Kuratate, 2011). It displays 3-D images on a transparent model of the human face. The images are animated giving the impression of a face with moving eyes and eye-brows, able to change expression and convey emotion. They have tested it in conjunction with systems that also enable the voice or rather synthetic speech to express emotion. They think that one of the first areas of application will be the area of companion robotics for use in elderly care. The prototype cost only €3,000 to build and they intend to retail the system for about €400.

Another related dynamic can be observed in the case of advanced prosthetics and wearable devices. Assistive devices such as prosthetic limbs used to be nothing more than costly lumps of funny pink plastic. They were ugly and inconvenient. They were engineered but not designed and arguably did as much to stigmatise someone with a disability as the disability itself. Fashion and design are ways for individuals to project an image of themselves and their self-worth. It is important to respect the right of people with disabilities to feel good about themselves by allowing them to be fashionable or to express their individualism via the devices they use.

In an earlier section we referred to HAL (Hybrid Assistive Limb) by Cyberdyne of Japan. Aesthetic design has played an important role in attracting the attention of users and the general public. In particular its blue lights have excited Sci-Fi fans by evoking images from the film TRON.

Much of the progress in this domain in the US is based on the needs of military veterans and funding from military oriented research centres such as DARPA. One example the so called Luke Arm(DEKA Research and Development Corporation, 2009), is the subject of a TEDMED talk by Dean Kamen (Saenz, 2010) the developer of the Luke Arm, featured on the website of the Singularity University. In this talk he explains why he thinks that research on these subjects should continue until prosthetic arms are so good that non-disabled people will envy them, and even want one for themselves.

A 2010 Fast Company article (Hochman, 2010) on new generation prosthetics entitled "Bionic Legs iLimbs (Touch Bionics Inc., 2014b)and Other Super Human Prostheses You'll Envy" explained how a recent boom in sophisticated prostheses has created envy as a by-product that is envy among non-disabled peers. The article interviewed a user of iWalk ankles (Saenz, 2010) that integrate batteries and controllers to provide a 400-watt power-assist to the user as they walk, so as to provide natural gait. The interviewee remarked "I don't walk my legs. My legs walk me."

A woman who wears a prosthetic arm by Touch Bionics (Touch Bionics Inc., 2014a) explained that the reaction of strangers to what she can do with her arm is often 'I want one like that.'. She claimed that she gets a lot of attention when she walks into a room, commenting "*I love it … its bad-ass looking.*" Another wearer of a high-end prosthetic claimed he felt that it gave him "*power*

and allure" and the "*strange animal magnetism of a very bad boy*". He claims that "*when the technology works, when it can make you stronger or faster than you were, it overnight becomes sexy and powerful and threatening.*"

Another is quoted as saying "*I find there are a lot of envious people. They say, 'Hey! I want a robot hand.'* "

EMERGING MARKET MODELS OF INNOVATION

Major European Companies like Ericsson and Nokia are already focusing on emerging markets of Africa. It is worth making some remarks about creativity and innovation at the Bottom of the Pyramid and speculating as to how this will affect research and innovation in Europe.

The importance of these markets and their potential was first written about and extensively explored by the late C. K. Prahalad who first made his name by pointing out the importance of "core-competencies" for realizing future growth of the firm. His seminal book entitled "Opportunities at the Bottom of the Pyramid" was based on work with Indian business students who studied in the US and carried out business research projects on interesting companies in India. They noted that many companies in India were focusing not on exports to wealthy countries like the EU or the US and Japan, but on local market opportunities. For them it was clear that growth in the advanced markets was stalled, that competition would intensify in a race to the bottom, and they saw important opportunities in meeting the needs of the very large and increasingly prosperous markets that we now refer to as markets at 'the bottom of the pyramid'. Others have written in detail about these markets. Bill Gates has written about the "the next billion" and developmental economists such as Paul Collier refers to "the bottom billion". In any case C. K. Prahalad and his students uncovered many examples of highly innovative companies that were providing value, serving markets and creating wealth in areas such as finance, insurance, logistics, healthcare, construction and mobile telephony. In the last ten years we have seen the emergence of major initiatives to develop the $100 laptop, the $10 mobile phone the $1000 car, the $3000 heart bypass operation and the $300 house. The ultimate ambition of these companies is to go global and they are already starting to compete with the best in Europe.

One of the most celebrated examples of innovative "bottom of the pyramid" business models is the Aravind Eye Clinic (Krishna, 2011) in India, discovered by the late C. K. Prahalad and his students. The Aravind eye clinic provides services to all people regardless of their income. That means it provides services for free to the poor and those who are wealthy pay. It does so in a profitable sustainable way, paying good salaries to its entire staff, investing in research and continuously improving its service and its scope of operation.

A number of terms are currently used to describe this kind of innovation, often racial innovation that is driven by the need for a drastic reduction in the cost of the product, a very different approach to distribution, financing or the conditions of use such as available infrastructure or even a steady supply of electricity. These terms include *frugal innovation, reverse innovation* and *inside-out* or *outside-in* innovation.

The term *frugal innovation* was probably coined by Santosh Ostwal It refers to innovation that strips away features rather than adding them. Innovation that is aimed at those with a modest income, rather than lead consumers or adventuresome consumers prepared to pay a premium to have the latest and most advanced thing. It means innovation for a frugal environment, for example one with a steady supply of electricity, one without roads and pavements, where streets become impassable after rain.

The term reverse innovation was coined by Jeffrey Immelt of GE. He wanted to describe how innovative products developed for markets such as China will eventually replace the over-engineered, high-cost products that are currently used in the US. This has already been the experience of GE for example in China. US based GE electric used to sell its ultrasound machines at about $100,000 per unit. It developed a simplified model for the Chinese market that sold at $15,000 per unit. In future they will sell these models in the US and Europe too. His kind of innovation has enabled revenues from such devices to grow from $2M in 2002 to over $278M in 2008. This experience has transformed their view of how to innovate and how to respond to the fierce competition coming from emerging economies such as China. It has since moved its unit for medical equipment innovation to China.

According to S.D. Shibulal of Infosys, the terms "Outside-In" and "Inside-Out Innovation" are used internally to distinguish between classical or traditional innovation and the 'frugal' and 'reverse' modes of innovation

The traditional approach tends to rely on adding features to existing products and services. The corporate goal is to maintain current prices or increase them, even if only for a while. This has been the pattern in IT, where hardware such as laptops and PCs for many years stagnated around the €1000 price range, despite the additional of 'improvements' over the years in terms of upgrades to the OS and basic productivity software. New versions are often brought out as premium products sold at a higher price to lead users and enthusiasts or to buyers with specific needs. But the €100 laptop project championed by Nicolas Negro Ponte changed that pattern.

Since then groups in Europe have also started to engage explicitly with markets at the bottom of the pyramid, often in collaboration with local entrepreneurs and research institutes.

In 2008 the Indian Institutes of Technology working with DataWind (Datawind, 2013) of the UK and the Indian Institute of Science developed a tablet PC intended for retail at between $35 and $60. This product is called the Aakash (Hindi for 'sky'). It is intended for use in schools and a more expensive version called the UbiSlate may be sold to other users. Since then at a time when Apple sells its iPAD at between $499 and $829, many competitors have emerged in countries like India and China. An Indian company called Reliance Communications sells a tablet PC for $280, another company called Beetel Teletech has brought one out for $220. More recently Lakshmi Access Communications (Krishna, 2011) has released a model for $99. They hope it will achieve mass market adoption and plan an IPO.

A recent related innovation is the Raspberry Pi (Raspberry Pi, n.d.). This is the name given to a new venture by a Cambridge University UK based group of scientists that has developed a small high performance PC. It will sell for only $25. It can run video even 3D video, Open Office, and supports web browsing. The first 10,000 units are expected to start shipping in December 2011. The raspberry Pi is initially aimed at schools and developing economies, but it is also suitable for use in robotics and home appliances. It is based on ARM Holdings (ARM Ltd., 2014) technology and runs GNU/Linux. It is the size of a credit card. A user need only plug in a key-board and a screen and they are ready to go. The developers will encourage the creation of a community of open source developers based on this platform.

Given the dynamics of these emerging market models of innovation and the phase of economic turbulence and uncertainty the Europe is undergoing it might be useful to exploit such market models. For example EC programs in the future could favour projects which set out to develop low cost solutions using available platforms and low cost systems such as the Raspberry Pi computer from Cambridge University or the Aakash tablet from India.

TRENDS IN ENTREPRENEURSHIP AND INNOVATION FINANCING

Most nations are struggling with the problem of how best to support for innovation and entrepreneurship. Some of interesting policy and program innovations of recent years include the many EU *Innovation Voucher Schemes* an NSF initiative called *I-Corps* and the *Lean Launch Pad* of Stanford University. All of these provide lessons for those designing programmes for research and innovation in the domain of e-access or e-assistive technologies.

Since 2006 many innovation voucher schemes have been launched across the European Union. These are especially well adapted to the needs of companies in the sense that they support small, short term projects, initiated and managed by the companies who select and engage the service provider and has total autonomy in managing their contract. The schemes tend to be highly simplified. Completing an application typically amounts to 30 minutes work and the decision to finance is given in days or weeks instead of months of years. Eligible services vary across the whole, range of inputs to an innovation project. They include scientific research or problem solving, technology development, market research, engineering and design. Although the amount is relatively small, ranging from about €5,000 to €25,000, and using both full and partial funding models, they have a large almost immediate impact on the innovation capabilities of the beneficiary.

So far the EC has not tried to launch its own voucher program. There is a general belief that the administrative culture of EC institution is far too slow and cumbersome to run one effectively. It has been suggested that the EC could however co-finance programmes run by EU intermediaries in areas that correspond to EC policy priorities.

One innovative model allowing universities to efficiently support new companies is the Lean Launch Pad model recently launched by Stanford University. This is based on an innovative course on entrepreneurship given by Steve Blank ("Steve Blank," n.d.) at Stanford University from December 2011 to May 2011. The course of aimed at students who want to test real business ideas. It helps them formulate the business as a series of hypotheses about their business model, value proposition, customer, customer relationship, distribution and revenue. The course leads through a series of steps through which they formulate and then test these hypotheses in the field. The idea is not to waste time on useless theorising but to find out what works and what does not work in as short a time as possible. The general aim is to get the students out of the laboratory and into the world to create a company ad get orders in a period of only 10 weeks.

A related initiative is the I-Corp programme (Tice, 2011) launched in the US by the NSF in 2011. The approach is modelled on the experience of the Lean Launch Pad course pioneered at Stanford in late 2010. It is based on the belief that "a lot of great business ideas lurk in the halls and research labs of science and engineering schools at America's colleges and universities". It takes the form of a public-private partnership that will invest $5M in the launch of successful business start-ups from their research base. The first I-Corps training class will take place at Stanford and is scheduled for October to December 2011.

Given the previous examples and their stories it could be useful for EC to consider innovative start-up and new business funding models in relation to e-Access technologies. This presupposes that EC will also need to identify the areas that would seem most attractive for investment or most likely to generate growth and jobs. This book has already suggested a number of areas that could help e-Access technologies.

REFERENCES

Advantage Business Media. (2011, August 17). NSF launches four new engineering research centers. *Research & Development*. Retrieved March 13, 2014, from http://www.rdmag.com/news/2011/08/ nsf-launches-four-new-engineering-research-centers

Aldebaran Robotics. (2014). Aldebaran Robotics. *Aldebaran Robotics*. Retrieved March 13, 2014, from http://www.aldebaran.com/en

Blind Ambition (FULL VERSION). (2011). Retrieved from http://www.youtube.com/watch?v=EvhYZKnEk5Y& feature=youtube_gdata_player

Crux Strategies, L. L. C. (2011). *R&D-I-Y | Research and Develop It Yourself*. Retrieved March 13, 2014, from http://www.rndiy.org/

Datawind. (2013). *DATAWIND Makers of - Cheap Tablet phone| Cheapest Android Smartphone| Order tablet Online| Android Calling Tablet|Book Tablet online*. Retrieved March 13, 2014, from http://www.datawind.com/

DEKA Research and Development Corporation. (2009). *DEKA Research and Development - Technologies and Applications - DEKA prosthetic arm*. Retrieved March 13, 2014, from http://www.dekaresearch.com/deka_arm.shtml

EDF. (n.d.). *The representative organisation of persons with disabilities in Europe*. Retrieved March 13, 2014, from http://www.edf-feph.org/

EHFCN. (n.d.). *EHFCN*. Retrieved March 13, 2014, from http://www.ehfcn.org/

EyeCare America. (2007). *Facts About Blindness and Eye Health*. Retrieved from http://www.aao.org/eyecare/ news/upload/Eye-Health-Fact-Sheet.pdf

Furlan, R. (2010, January 21). Igniting a Brain-Computer Interface Revolution - BCI X PRIZE. *Singularity Hub*. Retrieved March 13, 2014, from http://singularityhub.com/2010/01/21/igniting-a-brain-computer-interface-revolution-bci-x-prize/

Gonzalez, C. (2011, August 9). *nsf.gov - Engineering (ENG) News - New NSF Engineering Research Center to Pursue Ideal Mind–Machine Interface - US National Science Foundation (NSF)*. Retrieved March 13, 2014, from http://www.nsf.gov/ news/news_summ.jsp?cntn_id=119842&org=ENG&from=news

Hochman, P. (2010, February 1). Bionic Legs, i-Limbs, and Other Super Human Prostheses You'll Envy. *Fast Company*. Retrieved March 13, 2014, from //www.fastcompany.com/1514543/ bionic-legs-i-limbs-and-other-super-human-prostheses-youll-envy

Japanese Robot Of The Year. (2009). Retrieved from http://www.youtube.com/ watch?v=W3f6 BOrD9Ek&feature=youtube_gdata_player

Krishna, R. J. (2011, August 19). Indian Firm Launches $99 Android-Based Tablet. *Wall Street Journal*. Retrieved from http://online.wsj.com/news/articles/ SB100014240 531119036394 04576518122965650898?mg= reno64-wsj&url= http%3A%2F% 2Fonline. wsj.com%2 Farticle%2FSB 10001424053 111903639404 576518122965 650898.html# mod=djemWMPIndia_t

Kuratate, T. (2011, July 11). Mask-bot: A robot with a human face. *Research & Development*. Retrieved March 13, 2014, from http://www.rdmag. com/news/2011/11/ mask-bot-robot-human-face

LEGO Group. (2014). *LEGO.com Mindstorms*. Retrieved March 13, 2014, from http://www.lego.com/ en-us/mindstorms/ ?domainredir=mindstorms.lego.com

Lego mindstorm NXT Scorpion robot. (2007). Retrieved from http://www.youtube.com/ watch?v=aec-YxOw-28&feature=youtube_gdata_player

Lewin, D., Adshead, S., Glennon, B., Williamson, B., Moore, T., Damodaran, L., & Hansell, P. (2010). *Assisted living technologies for older and disabled people in 2030*. Plum Consulting. Retrieved from http://www.plumconsulting.co.uk/ pdfs/Plum_June2010_Assisted_living_technologies_for_older_and_disabled_people_in_2030. pdf

Ltd, A. R. M. (2014). *ARM - The Architecture For The Digital World*. Retrieved March 13, 2014, from http://www.arm.com/

Microsoft. (2014a). *Home Page*. Retrieved March 13, 2014, from http://www.imaginecup. com/#?fbid=5XMH9y_J6bw

Micosoft. (2014b). *Inclusive Innovation Showroom Demonstrates Accessibility*. Retrieved March 13, 2014, from http://www.microsoft.com/ enable/ news/showroom.aspx

Microsoft. (2012, June 3). RDS 4. *Microsoft Download Center*. Retrieved March 13, 2014, from http://www.microsoft.com/ en-us/download/ details.aspx?id=29081

Microsoft. (2014a). *Microsoft Accessibility Resource Centers*. Retrieved March 13, 2014, from http://www.microsoft.com/ enable/centers/ marc.aspx

Microsoft. (2014b). *Microsoft Accessibility: Technology for Everyone, Home*. Retrieved March 13, 2014, from http://www.microsoft.com/enable/

Ministry of Economy. Trade and Industry. (2014, February 27). *Wikipedia, the free encyclopedia*. Retrieved from http://en.wikipedia.org/w/ index. php?title= Ministry_of_Economy,_Trade_and_ Industry&oldid=589936000

Miuro, the new music robot. (2006). Retrieved from http://www.youtube.com/ watch?v=gFxpuUMil 5U&feature=youtube_gdata_player

My Robot is Better Than Your Robot. (2011). Retrieved from http://www.youtube.com/ watch?v=vYuOK b3gO7E&feature= youtube_gdata_player

NASA. (2011, August 1). *Robotics Alliance Project.* Retrieved March 13, 2014, from http:// frc-grants.arc.nasa.gov /rcs/directions.php

NIBEye. (n.d.). *NIBEye: Home.* Retrieved March 13, 2014, from http://dev.nsta.org/evwebs/ 4150A/ index.html

Platform Europe, A. G. E. (2014). *Home | AGE Platform Europe.* Retrieved March 13, 2014, from http://www.age-platform.org/

Raspberry Pi. (n.d.). *Raspberry Pi | An ARM GNU/Linux box for $25. Take a byte!* Retrieved March 13, 2014, from http://www.raspberrypi.org/

Ray Kuzweil at the MIT/XPrize BCI workshop. (2010). Retrieved from http://www.youtube. com/ watch?v=15sh05 wrQ6Y&feature= youtube_gdata_player

Riley, B. (2011). *A garden in my apartment.* Retrieved from http://www.ted.com/talks/ britta_riley_a_garden_in_my_apartment

Saenz, A. (2010, January 20). iWalk Presents World's First Actively Powered Foot and Ankle. *Singularity Hub.* Retrieved March 13, 2014, from http://singularityhub.com/ 2010/01/20/ iwalk-presents-worlds-first-actively-powered-foot-and-ankle/

Stanford Engineering. (2011, October 17). *Stanford Summer Course Yields Touchscreen Braille Writer.* Retrieved March 13, 2014, from http://www.pddnet.com/news/ 2011/10/stanford-summer-course-yields-touchscreen-braille-writer

Steve Blank. (n.d.). *Steve Blank.* Retrieved March 13, 2014, from http://steveblank.com/

Technology Strategy Board. (2013). *Healthcare Technolgy Development Innovation, Stem Cell Research - innovateuk.* Retrieved March 13, 2014, from https://www.innovateuk.org/healthcare

Tice, C. (2011, August 5). Uncle Sam's New, $5M Incubator for Student Entrepreneurs. *Entrepreneur.* Retrieved March 13, 2014, from http:// www.entrepreneur.com/blog/220110

Tobe, F. (2011, July 30). *Everything-Robotic by The Robot Report - tracking the business of robotics.* Retrieved from http://www.everything-robotic.com/ 2011/07/recent-breakthroughs-are-enabling.html

Touch Bionics Inc. (2014a). *Home Touch Bionics.* Retrieved March 13, 2014, from http://www. touchbionics.com/

Touch Bionics Inc. (2014b). *The world's leading prosthetic hand Touch Bionics.* Retrieved March 13, 2014, from http://www.touchbionics.com/ products/active-prostheses/i-limb-ultra/

Universidad Carlos III de Madrid. (2011, November 21). Machines Able to Recognize a Person's Emotional State. *Product Design & Development.* Retrieved March 13, 2014, from http:// www.pddnet.com/news/ 2011/11/machines-able-recognize-persons-emotional-state

USFirst. (2014). *USFIRST.org.* Retrieved March 13, 2014, from http://www.usfirst.org/

Virgin Galactic. (2014, March 9). *Wikipedia, the free encyclopedia.* Retrieved from http:// en.wikipedia.org/w/ index.php?title= Virgin_ Galactic&oldid=598899679

Vodafone Group. (2012). *Home | Mobile Apps Developer | Vodafone.* Retrieved March 13, 2014, from http://developer.vodafone.com/ smartaccess2012/home/

WGES ExploraVision. (n.d.). Retrieved March 13, 2014, from http://dev.nsta.org/evwebs/2237Q/

XPrize Foundation. (2014). *Life Sciences Prize Group | XPRIZE*. Retrieved March 13, 2014, from http://www.xprize.org/prize-development/life-sciences

XPRIZE Foundation. (2014). Google Lunar XPRIZE. *Google Lunar XPRIZE*. Retrieved March 13, 2014, from http://www.googlelunarxprize.org/

KEY TERMS AND DEFINITIONS

Business Model Innovation: Business model innovation (BMI) refers to a business's attempt to reinvent itself in order to obtain a competitive edge and stimulate company growth.

Crowdfunding: Crowdfunding is the collection of finance to sustain an initiative from a large pool of backers—the "crowd"—usually made online by means of a web platform.

Competitions: Competition in biology, ecology, and sociology, is a contest between organisms, animals, individuals, groups, etc., for territory, a niche, or a location of resources, for resources and goods, mates, for prestige, recognition, awards, or group or social status, for leadership. Competition is the opposite of cooperation.

Design: Design is the creation of a plan or convention for the construction of an object or a system.

DIY: Do it yourself (DIY) is the method of building, modifying, or repairing something without the aid of experts or professionals.

Lead Users: In other words, lead users are users of a product or service that currently experience needs still unknown to the public and who also benefit greatly if they obtain a solution to these needs.

Living Labs: A living lab is a research concept. A living lab is a user-centred, open-innovation ecosystem, often operating in a territorial context (e.g. city, agglomeration, region), integrating concurrent research and innovation processes within a public-private-people partnership.

Open Innovation: Open innovation is a paradigm that assumes that firms can and should use external ideas as well as internal ideas, and internal and external paths to market, as the firms look to advance their technology.

Platforms: A computing platform is, in the most general sense, whatever pre-existing environment a piece of software is designed to run within, obeying its constraints, and making use of its facilities.

Research Organisation: The organizing of research activities.

Compilation of References

(DOJ), U. S. D. of J. (n.d.). *United States Department of Justice Home Page*. Retrieved March 13, 2014, from http://www.justice.gov/

10 TV. (2011, July 27). *FBI: Cyber Crime Will Soon Be Agency's Biggest Threat | WBNS-10TV Columbus, Ohio*. Retrieved March 8, 2014, from http://www.10tv.com/content/stories/2011/07/27/stories-columbus-FBI-cyber-crime.html

1105 Media Inc. Ed-Tech Group. (2014). *Campus Enterprise Networking & Infrastructure -- Campus Technology*. Retrieved March 13, 2014, from http://campustechnology.com/Home.aspx

1800 wheelchair.ca Inc. (2014). *Modern Wheelchair Inventions*. Retrieved March 9, 2014, from http://www.1800wheelchair.ca/news/post/modern-wheelchair-inventions.aspx

2 getthere. (2012). *2getthere*. Retrieved March 9, 2014, from http://www.2getthere.eu/

A Force More Powerful. (n.d.). *A Force More Powerful*. Retrieved March 10, 2014, from http://www.aforcemore-powerful.org/game/index.php

AbilityNet. (2009a). *Factsheets - Play AT IT*. Retrieved March 9, 2014, from http://www.abilitynet.org.uk/play/factsheets.htm

AbilityNet. (2009b). *Factsheets and Skillsheets - Play AT ICT Northern Ireland*. Retrieved March 9, 2014, from http://www.abilitynet.org.uk/playni/factsheets.htm

AbilityNet. (2009c). *Play AT ICT Northern Ireland*. Retrieved March 9, 2014, from http://www.abilitynet.org.uk/playni/

AbilityNet. (2009d). *Play AT IT*. Retrieved March 9, 2014, from http://www.abilitynet.org.uk/play/

AbilityNet. (2013). *Welcome to AbilityNet | AbilityNet*. Retrieved March 9, 2014, from http://www.abilitynet.org.uk/index.php

AbilityPath.org. (2011, February 15). *Silent Epidemic of Bullying Against Children With Special Needs*. Retrieved March 10, 2014, from http://www.disabled-world.com/disability/education/special/bullying-special-needs.php

AbleData. (n.d.a). *AbleData: Assistive Technology Products, News, Resources*. Retrieved March 10, 2014, from http://www.abledata.com/abledata.cfm

AbleData. (n.d.b). *AbleData: Products*. Retrieved March 10, 2014, from http://www.abledata.com/abledata.cfm?pageid=19327&ksectionid=19327

Abrams, H., Edwards, B., Valentine, S., & Fitz, A. (2011, March 2). *A Patient-adjusted Fine-tuning Approach for Optimizing the Hearing Aid Response | Hearing Review*. Retrieved March 8, 2014, from http://www.hearingreview.com/2011/03/a-patient-adjusted-fine-tuning-approach-for-optimizing-the-hearing-aid-response/

AccesiWeb. (n.d.). *AccessiWeb - Accueil*. Retrieved March 12, 2014, from http://www.accessiweb.org/

Aceves, M., Grimalt, J., Sunyer, J., Anto, J., & Reed, C. (1991). Identification of soybean dust as an epidemic asthma agent in urban areas by molecular marker and RAST analysis of aerosols. *The Journal of Allergy and Clinical Immunology, 88*(1), 124–134. doi:10.1016/0091-6749(91)90309-C PMID:2071776

Action on Hearing Loss. (n.d.). *Deafness Research UK (DRUK) - Action On Hearing Loss: RNID*. Retrieved March 15, 2014, from http://www.actiononhearingloss.org.uk/about-us/druk.aspx

Action research. (n.d.). *Wikipedia, the free encyclopedia*. Retrieved March 10, 2014, from http://en.wikipedia.org/wiki/Action_research

Action Without Borders. (2014). *Volunteer, work, intern, organize, hire and connect*. Change the world - idealist.org. Retrieved March 13, 2014, from http://www.idealist.org/

Adams, K., & Rice, S. (2011, September 19). *Brief Information Resource on Assistance Animals for the Disabled*. Retrieved March 9, 2014, from http://www.nal.usda.gov/awic/companimals/assist.htm

Adams-Spink, G. (2010, February 15). *BBC News - EU smart-home concept shown off*. Retrieved March 10, 2014, from http://news.bbc.co.uk/2/hi/8495479.stm

Adept Mobilerobots, L. L. C. (2013). *Intelligent Mobile Robotic Platforms for Research, Development, Rapid Prototyping*. Retrieved March 9, 2014, from http://www.mobilerobots.com/Mobile_Robots.aspx

Adept Technology Inc. (2014). *Adept Technology, Inc.* Retrieved March 9, 2014, from http://www.adept.com/

Adobe Systems Inc. (2014a). *Adobe*. Retrieved March 9, 2014, from http://www.adobe.com/

Adobe Systems Inc. (2014b). *Web conferencing software - video conferencing - webinars | Adobe Connect 9*. Retrieved March 9, 2014, from http://www.adobe.com/products/adobeconnect.html

Advanced Bionics, A. G. (2013). *The Cochlear Implant Technology Innovation Leader | Advanced Bionics*. Retrieved March 8, 2014, from http://www.advanced-bionics.com/

Advanced Telecommunications Research Institute International (ATR). (2012). *ATR? Advanced Telecommunications Research Institute International*. Retrieved March 9, 2014, from http://www.atr.jp/index_e.html

Advantage Business Media. (2011, August 17). NSF launches four new engineering research centers. *Research & Development*. Retrieved March 13, 2014, from http://www.rdmag.com/news/2011/08/nsf-launches-four-new-engineering-research-centers

Aguilar, M. (2010, November 29). Design: Prosthetic Flippers Could Help Amputees Swim Again | Wired Magazine | Wired.com. *Wired Magazine*. Retrieved March 13, 2014, from http://www.wired.com/magazine/2010/11/pl_designlimbs/

AIBO-Life.org. (2012). *AIBO-Life Bot House: Forums Chat Shindig: Happy AIBOing*. Retrieved February 22, 2014, from http://www.aibo-life.org/

Aigner, F. (2011, May 17). *Technische Universität Wien: The World's Smallest 3D Printer*. Retrieved March 8, 2014, from http://www.tuwien.ac.at/news/news_detail/article/7009/EN/

Aldebaran Robotics. (2014). *Aldebaran Robotics Aldebaran Community*. Retrieved February 22, 2014, from https://community.aldebaran-robotics.com/

Alliance, E. (2011). *Equity in Inclusive Education Global Initiative | The Equity Alliance at ASU*. Retrieved March 10, 2014, from http://www.equityallianceatasu.org/ii

Amazon.com. Inc. (2014). *Amazon Mechanical Turk - Welcome*. Retrieved March 12, 2014, from https://www.mturk.com/mturk/welcome

American Chemical Society. (2011). *Chem. with Disabilities - Division of Professional Relations*. Retrieved March 10, 2014, from http://prof.sites.acs.org/chemwithdisabilities.htm

American Foundation for the Blind. (2010). *AccessWorld? - March 2010*. Retrieved March 13, 2014, from http://www.afb.org/afbpress/pub.asp?DocID=aw1101toc&All#aw110108

American Foundation for the Blind. (2013). *Careers for Blind and Visually Impaired Individuals - American Foundation for the Blind*. Retrieved March 10, 2014, from http://www.afb.org/info/living-with-vision-loss/for-job-seekers/for-family-and-friends/careers-for-blind-and-visually-impaired-individuals/1235

American Public Media. (2014). *Spot.us - Home*. Retrieved March 13, 2014, from http://spot.us/

Analytica. (n.d.). *Analytica | Data Integration*. Retrieved March 11, 2014, from http://www2.analytica-usa.com/

Analytics, B. (2013). *PowerPoint Twitter Tools | Business Analytics*. Retrieved March 10, 2014, from http://timoel-liott.com/blog/powerpoint-twitter-tools/

Annual, B. C. I. Award. (2009). *bci-award.com*. Retrieved March 8, 2014, from http://www.bci-award.com/

Ansberry, C. (2009, February 23). *Elderly Emerge as a New Class of Workers -- and the Jobless - WSJ.com*. Retrieved March 10, 2014, from http://online.wsj.com/news/articles/SB123535088586444925?mg=reno64-wsj&url=http%3A%2F%2Fonline.wsj.com%2Farticle%2FSB123535088586444925.html

Anybots Inc. (2014). *Anybots | ANYBOTS® Virtual Presence Systems. It's You, Anywhere?* Retrieved March 9, 2014, from https://www.anybots.com/

Anybots. (2014). *Anybots | ANYBOTS® Virtual Presence Systems. It's You, Anywhere?* Retrieved March 10, 2014, from https://www.anybots.com/#front

Aphasia. (n.d.). *Wikipedia, the free encyclopedia*. Retrieved March 8, 2014, from http://en.wikipedia.org/wiki/Aphasia

Apostolopoulos, I., Fallah, N., Folmer, E., & Bekris, K. E. (2012). *Integrated online localization and navigation for people with visual impairments using smart phones*. doi:10.1109/ICRA.2012.6225093

Apple. (2013a, March 20). *Explorer: The American Museum of Natural History on the App. Store on iTunes*. Retrieved March 9, 2014, from https://itunes.apple.com/us/app/explorer-american-museum-natural/id381227123?mt=8

Apple. (2013b, November 14). *FastMall - Shopping Malls, Community & Interactive Maps on the App. Store on iTunes*. Retrieved March 9, 2014, from https://itunes.apple.com/us/app/fastmall-shopping-malls-community/id340656157?mt=8

Apple. (2014). *Apple - Accessibility - iOS*. Retrieved March 10, 2014, from http://www.apple.com/accessibility/ios/

Apple. (2014). *Apple - Apple TV - HD iTunes content and more on your TV*. Retrieved March 12, 2014, from http://www.apple.com/appletv/

Apple. (2014a). *Apple - iOS 7 - Siri*. Retrieved March 8, 2014, from http://www.apple.com/ios/siri/

Apple. (2014b). *Apple - iPhone*. Retrieved March 8, 2014, from http://www.apple.com/iphone/

Apple. (n.d.). *Apple - iOS 7 - Siri*. Retrieved February 7, 2014, from http://www.apple.com/ios/siri/

Apple. (n.d.a). *Apple - Accessibility - iOS*. Retrieved February 10, 2014, from http://www.apple.com/accessibility/ios/

Artificial Intelligence Laboratory, Computer Science Department, Stanford University. (n.d.). *STAIR*. Retrieved March 13, 2014, from http://stair.stanford.edu/

Ashoka Changemakers. (2014). *Changemakers | Changemakers*. Retrieved March 13, 2014, from http://www.changemakers.com/

Asperger Syndrome. (n.d.). *Wikipedia, the free encyclopedia*. Retrieved March 8, 2014, from http://en.wikipedia.org/wiki/Asperger_syndrome

Assistivetech.net. (2010, August 26). *AutoSyringe - ATWiki*. Retrieved March 8, 2014, from http://atwiki.assistivetech.net/index.php/AutoSyringe

Association for the Advancement of Assistive Technology in Europe. (2014). *Welcome to AAATE! | Association for the Advancement of Assistive Technology in Europe*. Retrieved March 10, 2014, from http://www.aaate.net/

ASTALAVISTA. (2013). *ASTALAVISTA - Cloud-Based Security Scans*. Retrieved March 8, 2014, from http://www.astalavista.com/

ASTERICS. (2007). *AsTeRICS: Homepage*. Retrieved from http://www.asterics.eu/index.php?id=2

Atherton, M. (2008, February 1). *Deaf studies - A-Z Careers - Career Planning - The Independent*. Retrieved March 10, 2014, from http://www.independent.co.uk/student/career-planning/az-careers/deaf-studies-671539.html

ATIA. (n.d.). *Home - Assistive Technology Industry Association*. Retrieved March 13, 2014, from http://www.atia.org/i4a/pages/index.cfm?pageid=1

ATIS4All. (n.d.). *Home page - ATIS4all*. Retrieved March 10, 2014, from http://www.atis4all.eu/

ATM Industry Association. (2014). *ATM Industry Association*. Retrieved March 11, 2014, from https://www.atmia.com/

Attention deficit hyperactivity disorder predominantly inattentive. (n.d.). *Wikipedia, the free encyclopedia*. Retrieved March 8, 2014, from http://en.wikipedia.org/wiki/Attention_deficit_disorder

Auditory Brainstem Implant. (n.d.). *Wikipedia, the free encyclopedia*. Retrieved March 8, 2014, from http://en.wikipedia.org/wiki/Auditory_brainstem_implant

Autism rights movement. (n.d.). *Wikipedia, the free encyclopedia*. Retrieved March 8, 2014, from http://en.wikipedia.org/wiki/Autism_rights_movement

Autism spectrum. (n.d.). *Wikipedia, the free encyclopedia*. Retrieved March 8, 2014, from http://en.wikipedia.org/wiki/Autism_spectrum_disorder

Autisme Centraal. (n.d.). *Autisme Centraal | Welkom*. Retrieved March 8, 2014, from http://www.autismecentraal.com/index.html

Autistic Self Advocacy Network. (2014). *Autistic Self Advocacy Network | Nothing About Us Without Us*. Retrieved March 8, 2014, from autisticadvocacy.org/

Auto Express. (2011, November 14). *New Mercedes S-Class to drive itself | News | Auto Express*. Retrieved March 9, 2014, from http://www.autoexpress.co.uk/mercedes/s-class/35181/new-s-class-drive-itself

Avax News. (2011, December 19). *Computer Fashion Show*. Retrieved March 8, 2014, from http://avaxnews.net/disgusting/Computer_Fashion_Show.html

Bacigalupo, M., & Cachia, R. (2011). *Teacher collaboration networks in 2025: What is the role of teacher networks for professional development in Europe? notes from the workshops held on the 6th and 7th June 2011 at the Institute for Prospective Technological Studies of the European Commission Joint Research Centre*. Retrieved from http://ftp.jrc.es/EURdoc/JRC67530_TN.pdf

BackHome. (n.d.). *BackHome | BackHome*. Retrieved March 8, 2014, from http://www.backhome-fp7.eu/

Baltimore Sun. (2011, October 24). *Medicare and Medicaid cuts: Nursing and rehabilitation centers are at risk again - Baltimore Sun*. Retrieved March 10, 2014, from http://articles.baltimoresun.com/2011-10-24/news/bs-ed-long-term-care-20111023_1_state-cuts-nursing-and-rehabilitation-health-facilities-association

Banco Bilbao Vizcaya Argentaria, S. A. (2014). *BBVA*. Retrieved March 11, 2014, from http://www.bbva.com/TLBB/tlbb/esp/index.jsp

Barack Obama presidential campaign, 2008. (2014, March 11). *Wikipedia, the free encyclopedia*. Retrieved from http://en.wikipedia.org/w/index.php?title=Barack_Obama_presidential_campaign,_2008&oldid=598033438

Barazandeh, G. (2005). Attitudes Toward Disabilities and Reasonable Accommodations at the University. *The UCI Undergraduate Research Journal*, 1-11. Retrieved from http://www.urop.uci.edu/journal/journal05/01_barazandeh.pdf

Barrett, L. L. (2008). *Healthy @ Home*. Retrieved from http://assets.aarp.org/rgcenter/il/healthy_home.pdf

Beckert, B., Blumel, C., & Friedewald, M. (2007). Exploring the technology base for convergence. *Visions and Realities in Converging Technologies*, *20*(4), 375–394.

Belkin, L. (2010, April 20). *Parenting an Autistic Adult - NYTimes.com*. Retrieved March 8, 2014, from parenting.blogs.nytimes.com/2010/04/20/parenting-an-autistic-adult/

Bell, G., Parisi, A., & Pesce, M. (1995, November 9). *VRML 1.0C Specification*. Retrieved March 9, 2014, from http://www.web3d.org/x3d/specifications/vrml/VRML1.0/index.html

Bell, G., Parisi, A., & Pesce, M. (1996, January 25). *VRML 1.0C Specification*. Retrieved March 11, 2014, from http://www.web3d.org/x3d/specifications/vrml/VRML1.0/index.html

Bell, C. G., & Gemmell, J. (2009). *Total recall: How the E-memory revolution will change everything*. New York: Dutton.

Bell, C. G., & Gemmell, J. (2010). *Your life, uploaded: The digital way to better memory, health, and productivity.* New York: Plume.

Bender, E. (2011). *Human exoskeletons -- for war and healing.* Retrieved from http://www.ted.com/talks/eythor_bender_demos_human_exoskeletons

Bennett, S., Maton, K., & Kervin, L. (2008). The digital natives debate: A critical review of the evidence. *British Journal of Educational Technology, 39*(5), 775–786. doi:10.1111/j.1467-8535.2007.00793.x

Berger, C. Gerhardt, McFarland, Principe, Soussou, … Tresco. (2007). *International Assessment of Research and Development in Brain-Computer Interfaces. WTEC Panel Report.* Retrieved from http://www.wtec.org/bci/BCI-finalreport-10Oct2007-lowres.pdf

Berkeley Robotics & Human Engineering Laboratory. (n.d.a). *Austin | Berkeley Robotics & Human Engineering Laboratory.* Retrieved February 22, 2014, from http://bleex.me.berkeley.edu/research/exoskeleton/medical-exoskeleton/

Berkeley Robotics & Human Engineering Laboratory. (n.d.b). *BLEEX | Berkeley Robotics & Human Engineering Laboratory.* Retrieved February 22, 2014, from http://bleex.me.berkeley.edu/research/exoskeleton/bleex/

Berkeley Robotics & Human Engineering Laboratory. (n.d.d). *ExoClimber™ | Berkeley Robotics & Human Engineering Laboratory.* Retrieved February 22, 2014, from http://bleex.me.berkeley.edu/research/exoskeleton/exoclimber/

Berkeley Robotics & Human Engineering Laboratory. (n.d.e). *ExoHiker™ | Berkeley Robotics & Human Engineering Laboratory.* Retrieved February 22, 2014, from http://bleex.me.berkeley.edu/research/exoskeleton/exohiker/

Berkeley Robotics & Human Engineering Laboratory. (n.d.f). *HULC™ | Berkeley Robotics & Human Engineering Laboratory.* Retrieved February 22, 2014, from http://bleex.me.berkeley.edu/research/exoskeleton/hulc/

Bernard, S. (2010, December 10). *5 Apps That Could Help to Stop Cyberbullying | MindShift.* Retrieved March 10, 2014, from http://blogs.kqed.org/mindshift/2010/12/5-apps-that-could-help-to-stop-cyberbullying/

BigDog Beach'n. (2009). Retrieved from http://www.youtube.com/watch?v=P0s7aRUIoTw&feature=youtube_gdata_player

BigDog Overview (Updated March 2010). (2010). Retrieved from http://www.youtube.com/watch?v=cNZPRsrwumQ&feature=youtube_gdata_player

BigKeys Keyboards. (2014). *BigKeys Company - BigKeys LX.* Retrieved March 10, 2014, from http://www.bigkeys.com/productcart/pc/viewCategories.asp?idCategory=2

BIK project. (2014). *BIK BITV-Test | Articles | Tests - The accessibility of Facebook.* Retrieved March 10, 2014, from http://www.bitvtest.eu/articles/article/lesen/fb-accessibility.html

Bionics Institute. (n.d.). *Home.* Retrieved March 8, 2014, from http://www.bionicsinstitute.org/Pages/default.aspx

Bionics Research. (2013a). *Bionics Research ReWalk™ U.S. - the wearable bionic suit.* Retrieved February 22, 2014, from http://rewalk.us/

Bipolar disorder. (n.d.). *Wikipedia, the free encyclopedia.* Retrieved March 8, 2014, from http://en.wikipedia.org/wiki/Bipolar_disorder

BlackBoard. (2013a). *Blackboard Engaging Online Collaborative Learning | Blackboard Collaborate.* Retrieved March 9, 2014, from http://www.blackboard.com/Platforms/Collaborate/Products/Blackboard-Collaborate.aspx

BlackBoard. (2013b). *Blackboard.* Retrieved March 9, 2014, from http://uki.blackboard.com/sites/international/globalmaster/

Blamey & Saunders Hearing. (2014). *Hearing Aids | Blamey Saunders Buy Hearing Aids Online with IHearYou.* Retrieved March 8, 2014, from http://www.blameysaunders.com.au/

Blankertz, B., Losch, F., Krauledat, M., Dornhege, G., Curio, G., & Muller, K. (2008). The Berlin Brain--Computer Interface: Accurate Performance From First-Session in BCI-Naïve Subjects. *IEEE Transactions on Biomedical Engineering.* doi:10.1109/TBME.2008.923152

Blind Ambition (FULL VERSION). (2011). Retrieved from http://www.youtube.com/watch?v=EvhYZKnEk5Y&feature=youtube_gdata_player

Bliton, N. (2011, December 18). *Disruptions: Wearing Your Computer on Your Sleeve*. Retrieved March 8, 2014, from bits.blogs.nytimes.com/2011/12/18/wearing-your-computer-on-your-sleeve/?_php=true&_type=blogs&_php=true&_type=blogs&_r=1

BlogTalkRadio.com. (2014). BlogTalkRadio. *Blog-TalkRadio*. Retrieved March 13, 2014, from http://www.blogtalkradio.com

Blue Brain Project (EFPL). (2014, February 27). *Blue-brain | EPFL*. Retrieved March 8, 2014, from http://bluebrain.epfl.ch/

Blue Brain Project (EPFL). (2013, February 6). *The Human Brain Project | EPFL*. Retrieved March 8, 2014, from http://jahia-prod.epfl.ch/site/bluebrain/op/edit/page-52741.html

Boisseau, S., & Despesse, G. (2012, February 27). Energy harvesting, wireless sensor networks & opportunities for industrial applications. *Embedded*. Retrieved from http://www.embedded.com/design/smart-energy-design/4237022/Energy-harvesting--wireless-sensor-networks---opportunities-for-industrial-applications

BookMooch. (n.d.). *BookMooch: trade your books with other people*. Retrieved March 11, 2014, from http://bookmooch.com/

Bosch. (2010, June). *Robert Bosch LLC. - Media Center*. Retrieved March 11, 2014, from http://www.bosch-press.com/tbwebdb/bosch-usa/en-US/PressText.cfm?id=418

Bosch. (n.d.). *Bosch - Bosch Research and Technology Center*. Retrieved March 11, 2014, from http://www.bosch.us/content/language1/html/rtc.htm

Boston Dynamics Big Dog. (2008, March 17). Retrieved from http://youtu.be/W1czBcnX1Ww

Boston Dynamics. (2013b). *Boston Dynamics: Dedicated to the Science and Art of How Things Move*. Retrieved February 21, 2014, from http://www.bostondynamics.com/

Botsman, R. (2010). *The case for collaborative consumption*. Retrieved from http://www.ted.com/talks/rachel_botsman_the_case_for_collaborative_consumption

Boulder Valley School District. (n.d.). *Boulder Valley School District*. Retrieved February 10, 2014, from http://www.bvsd.org/Pages/default.aspx

Bourke, P. D. (2008). Evaluating Second Life as a tool for collaborative scientific visualisation. *Computer Games and Allied Technology*. Retrieved from http://paulbourke.net/papers/cgat08/

Bowman, P., Ng, J., Harrison, M., Lopez, T. S., & Illic, A. (2009). *Sensor based condition monitoring*. Retrieved from http://www.bridge-project.eu/data/File/BRIDGE_WP03_sensor_based_condition_monitoring.pdf

BrailleNet. (2011, March 28). *Proceedings - 5th European eAccessibility Forum Benefits and costs of e-accessibility*. Retrieved March 13, 2014, from http://inova.snv.jussieu.fr/evenements/colloques/colloques/70_actes_en.html#contenu

BrailleNet. (2012). *General description - 6th European eAccessibility Forum Putting eAccessibility at the core of information systems*. Retrieved March 12, 2014, from http://inova.snv.jussieu.fr/evenements/colloques/colloques/76_index_en.html#contenu

BrailleNet. (2014). *BrailleNet page d'accueil*. Retrieved March 12, 2014, from http://www.braillenet.org/

BRAIN. (2008, September 1). *EU project BRAIN - Brain-project.org*. Retrieved March 8, 2014, from http://www.brain-project.org/

Brainable. (2009). *Home*. Retrieved March 8, 2014, from http://www.brainable.org/

BrainGate. (2013). *BrainGate - Home*. Retrieved March 8, 2014, from http://www.braingate2.org/

Brockman, J. (1999, December 31). *THE SECOND COMING — A MANIFESTO | Edge.org*. Retrieved March 8, 2014, from http://www.edge.org/conversation/the-second-coming-a-manifesto

Brunner, P., Bianchi, L., Guger, C., Cincotti, F., & Schalk, G. (2011). Current trends in hardware and software for brain–computer interfaces (BCIs). *Journal of Neural Engineering*, *8*(2), 025001. doi:10.1088/1741-2560/8/2/025001 PMID:21436536

Bryne, C. (2011, March 9). ShopWithYourFriends brings you real-time, social shopping. *VentureBeat*. Retrieved from http://venturebeat.com/2011/03/09/shopwithyourfriends-real-time-social-shopping/

Bulkin, D. A., & Groh, J. M. (2011). Systematic mapping of the monkey inferior colliculus reveals enhanced low frequency sound representation. *Journal of Neurophysiology*, *105*, 1785–1797. doi:10.1152/jn.00857.2010 PMID:21307328

Business Disability Forum. (2014). *Welcome to Business Disability Forum*. Retrieved March 10, 2014, from http://businessdisabilityforum.org.uk/

Business Respect. (2002, July 14). *CSR News - UK: Top companies acclaimed for Attention to Disability*. Retrieved March 10, 2014, from http://www.businessrespect.net/page.php?Story_ID=484

Busy Mom Boutique. (2014). *The Busy Mom Boutique: Mom-Invented Products for Maternity, Baby & Beyond*. Retrieved March 10, 2014, from http://www.busymomboutique.com/

Caixa, L. (n.d.). Prehome. *la Caixa*. Retrieved March 11, 2014, from http://www.laCaixa.com/index.html?Origen=Facebook-Like-Prehome-es

Caldwell, B., Cooper, M., Reid, L. G., & Vanderheiden, G. (2008, November 21). *Web Content Accessibility Guidelines (WCAG) 2.0*. Retrieved March 12, 2014, from http://www.w3.org/TR/WCAG20/

Callejas, Z., Griol, D., & López-Cózar, R. (2011). Predicting user mental states in spoken dialogue systems. *EURASIP Journal on Advances in Signal Processing*. doi:10.1186/1687-6180-2011-6 PMID:24348546

CALO. (n.d.). *Wikipedia, the free encyclopedia*. Retrieved February 8, 2014, from http://en.wikipedia.org/wiki/CALO

Campbell, J., & Oliver, M. (1996). *Disability Politics: Understanding Our Past, Changing Our Future*. Psychology Press.

CamStudio.org. (2013). *CamStudio - Free Screen Recording Software*. Retrieved March 10, 2014, from http://camstudio.org/

CapAbility Games Research Group. (n.d.). *CapAbility Games Research Group*. Retrieved March 10, 2014, from http://www.arts.rpi.edu/~ruiz/capAbilityGamesOverview_files/capAbilityGamesOverview.htm

CAPTCHA. (2014, March 8). *Wikipedia, the free encyclopedia*. Retrieved from http://en.wikipedia.org/w/index.php?title=CAPTCHA&oldid=598761909

Carnegie Mellon University. (2010). *The Official CAPTCHA Site*. Retrieved March 12, 2014, from http://www.captcha.net/

CASAGRAS2. (n.d.). *CSA for Global RFID-related Activities and Standardisation (CASAGRAS2) | CASAGRAS2 - Internet of Things*. Retrieved February 7, 2014, from http://www.iot-casagras.org/

Casino, G. (n.d.). *Groupe Casino*. Retrieved March 11, 2014, from http://www.groupe-casino.fr/en

CCC-TV. (2014, January 13). *CCC-TV*. Retrieved March 8, 2014, from http://media.ccc.de/index.html

CEN/CENELEC/ETSI Joint Working Group. (2013, May 25). *European Accessibility Requirements for Public Procurement of Products and Services in the ICT Domain*. Retrieved March 13, 2014, from http://www.mandate376.eu/

Centers for Disease Control and Prevention. (2010, May 6). *CDC - Traumatic Brain Injury - Injury Center*. Retrieved March 15, 2014, from http://www.cdc.gov/TraumaticBrainInjury/index.html

Centro de Investigación en Tecnologías Gráficas. (n.d.). *Centro de Investigacion en Technologias Graficas - UPV*. Retrieved March 8, 2014, from http://www.citg.es/

Chai, W., Zhou, J., Chen, C., Nies, H., & Loffeld, O. (2011). Continuous Indoor Localization and Navigation Based on Low-cost INS/Wi-Fi Integration. *International Conference on Indoor Positioning and Indoor Navigation*. Retrieved from http://ipin2011.dsi.uminho.pt/PDFs/Shortpaper/11_Short_Paper.pdf

Chappell, B. (2011, April 11). *New Electronic Sensors Stick To Skin As Temporary Tattoos: The Two-Way: NPR*. Retrieved January 7, 2014, from http://www.npr.org/blogs/thetwo-way/2011/08/11/139554014/new-electronic-sensors-stick-to-skin-as-temporary-tattoos

Charlton, J. I. (2000). *Nothing about Us Without Us: Disability Oppression and Empowerment*. University of California Press.

Chat About News. (2011, January 4). Retrieved from http://youtu.be/PbtaFPpiF08

Chessware, S. A. (2013). *Touch-It - Home*. Retrieved February 10, 2014, from http://www.chessware.ch/virtual-keyboard/

Children's Vision Coalition. (2013). *Children's Vision Coalition*. Retrieved February 10, 2014, from http://cvcny.org/

Cisco. (n.d.). *Cisco Mobility Services Engine - Products & Services - Cisco*. Retrieved March 9, 2014, from http://www.cisco.com/ c/en/us/products/wireless/ mobility-services-engine/index.html

Citizen science. (n.d.). *Wikipedia, the free encyclopedia*. Retrieved March 8, 2014, from http://en.wikipedia.org/wiki/Citizen_science

Civication, Inc. (2012). *Deaf Justice | Civication, Inc. | Promoting Civic Learning and Civil Responsibility*. Retrieved March 10, 2014, from http://www.civication.org/blog

Clark, S. (2011, June 23). Tesco Korea points to the future of mobile grocery shopping. *NFC World*. Retrieved from http://www.nfcworld.com/2011/06/23/38280/tesco-korea-points-to-the-future-of-mobile-grocery-shopping/

CNN. (2003, March 24). *CNN.com - Dog translation device coming to U.S. - Mar. 24, 2003*. Retrieved March 9, 2014, from http://Ed.cnn.com/2003/TECH/biztech/03/24/tech.dogs.language.reut/

Cochlear Ltd. (2014). *Home*. Retrieved March 8, 2014, from http://www.cochlear.com/wps/wcm/connect/intl/home

COGAIN. (n.d.). *Communication by Gaze Interaction | The COGAIN Association, evolved from the COGAIN Network of Excellence*. Retrieved February 10, 2014, from http://www.cogain.org/

Collaborative Consumption. (n.d.). Collaborative Consumption - Sharing reinvented through technology. Watch Rachel's TED Talk. *Collaborative Consumption*. Retrieved March 11, 2014, from http://www.collaborativeconsumption.com/

Commission for Communications Regulation. (2007). *The Internet and Broadband Experience for Residential users: A Communications Survey Report based on the Trends Survey Series* (07/12). Retrieved from http://www.comreg.ie/_fileupload/publications/ComReg0712.pdf

Commission for Communications Regulation. (2014). *Commission for Communications Regulation - ComReg*. Retrieved March 10, 2014, from http://www.comreg.ie/

Computational Learning and Motor Control Lab. (2013, November 20). *Computational Learning and Motor Control Lab | Main / Home Page browse*. Retrieved March 13, 2014, from http://www-clmc.usc.edu/

Cool Hunting. (n.d.). *Cool Hunting: Tech*. Retrieved March 8, 2014, from http://www.coolhunting.com/tech

Cooney, T. (2008). Entrepreneurs with Disabilities: Profile of a Forgotten Minority. Dublin Institute of Technology: ARROW@DIT, 4(1), 119-129.

Cornell University. (2013). *Disability Statistics*. Retrieved March 10, 2014, from http://www.disabilitystatistics.org/reports/acs.cfm?statistic=2

Cornell University. (2014). *Employment & Disability Institute (EDI), Advancing knowledge on disability & employment issues*. Retrieved March 10, 2014, from http://www.ilr.cornell.edu/edi/

Coronado, V. G. (2011). *Surveillance for traumatic brain injury-related deaths: United States, 1997-2007*. Atlanta, GA: U.S. Department of Health and Human Services, Centers for Disease Control and Prevention.

COST | COST Foresight 2030 - Living the Digital Revolution. (2009, October 9). Retrieved from http://www.cost.eu/events/foresight_2030_society

Couchsurfing International, Inc. (2014). *Welcome to Couchsurfing! - Couchsurfing*. Retrieved March 11, 2014, from https://www.couchsurfing.org/

Coxworth, B. (2010, October 4). *Developing a 'smart cane' for the blind*. Retrieved March 9, 2014, from http://www.gizmag.com/ smart-cane-uses-laser-range-finder/16562/

Coxworth, B. (2011, March 7). *What humans really want - creating computers that understand users*. Retrieved March 8, 2014, from http://www.gizmag.com/designing-computer-software-to-recognize-users-emotions/18078/

Crux Strategies, L. L. C. (2011). *R&D-I-Y | Research and Develop It Yourself*. Retrieved March 13, 2014, from http://www.rndiy.org/

CSR. (2012, February 27). *CSR Demonstrates Breakthrough Indoor Navigation Accuracy at Mobile World Congress 2012*. Retrieved March 9, 2014, from http://www.csr.com/news/pr/release/706/en

CureTogether. (2014). *Treatment Ratings and Reviews for 637 Conditions. Self Tracking. Free Tools to Help You Manage Your Health. | CureTogether.com*. Retrieved March 8, 2014, from http://curetogether.com/

Cyberdyne Inc. (2014). *CYBERDYNE*. Retrieved March 13, 2014, from http://www.cyberdyne.jp/

D'Mello, S. K., Lehman, B., & Graesser, A. (2011). *A Motivationally Supportive Affect-Sensitive AutoTutor*. doi:10.1007/978-1-4419-9625-1_9

DailyStrength, Inc. (2012). *Online Support Groups For Seniors - DailyStrength*. Retrieved March 11, 2014, from http://www.dailystrength.org/support-groups/Seniors Department of Justice. (2010). *2010 ADA Standards for Accessible Design*. Department of Justice. Retrieved from http://www.ada.gov/regs2010/2010ADAStandards/2010 ADAStandards.pdf

DAISY Consortium. (2014). *Home | DAISY Consortium*. Retrieved March 13, 2014, from http://www.daisy.org/

DARPA LifeLog. (n.d.). *Wikipedia, the free encyclopedia*. Retrieved March 8, 2014, from http://en.wikipedia.org/wiki/LifeLog_%28DARPA%29

DARPA. (n.d.). *Maximum Mobility and Manipulation (M3)*. Retrieved February 22, 2014, from http://www.darpa.mil/Our_Work/DSO/Programs/Maximum_Mobility_and_Manipulation_%28M3%29.aspx

DARPA. (n.d.). *Revolutionizing Prosthetics*. Retrieved March 8, 2014, from http://www.darpa.mil/Our_Work/DSO/Programs/Revolutionizing_Prosthetics.aspx

Dasher Project. (2011, February 16). *Inference Group: Dasher Project: Home*. Retrieved February 10, 2014, from http://www.inference.phy.cam.ac.uk/dasher/

Datawind. (2013). *DATAWIND Makers of - Cheap Tablet phone| Cheapest Android Smartphone| Order tablet Online| Android Calling Tablet|Book Tablet online*. Retrieved March 13, 2014, from http://www.datawind.com/

D'Costa, K. (2011, September 19). *A Robot in Every Home? We're Getting Close | Anthropology in Practice, Scientific American Blog Network*. Retrieved February 22, 2014, from http://blogs.scientificamerican.com/anthropology-in-practice/2011/09/19/a-robot-in-every-home-were-getting-close/

Debating Europe. (2012, March 21). *EU 2050: Europe's Tech Revolution? Debating Europe*. Retrieved March 10, 2014, from http://www.debatingeurope.eu/2012/03/21/eu-2050-europes-tech-revolution/#.Ux3-oPmSyQI

deCharms, C. (2008, February). *Christopher deCharms: A look inside the brain in real time | Talk Video | TED*. [Video file]. Retrieved from http://www.ted.com/talks/christopher_decharms_scans_the_brain_in_real_time

DECODER. (2013). *DECODER*. Retrieved March 8, 2014, from http://www.decoderproject.eu/

Décret n° 2009-546 du 14 mai 2009 pris en application de l'article 47 de la loi n° 2005-102 du 11 février 2005 sur l'égalité des droits et des chances, la participation et la citoyenneté des personnes handicapées et créant un référentiel d'accessibilité des services de communication publique en ligne., 2009-546 (2009).

Deep Blue (Chess Computer). (n.d.). *Wikipedia, the free encyclopedia*. Retrieved February 8, 2014, from http://en.wikipedia.org/wiki/Deep_Blue_%28chess_computer%29

DEKA Research and Development Corporation. (2009). *DEKA Research and Development - Technologies and Applications - DEKA prosthetic arm*. Retrieved March 13, 2014, from http://www.dekaresearch.com/deka_arm.shtml

DEKA. (2009). *Welcome to DEKA Research and Development*. Retrieved March 8, 2014, from http://www.dekaresearch.com/index.shtml

Deloitte. (2012). *Technology, Media & Telecommunications Predictions*. Retrieved from Deloitte website: https://www.deloitte.com/assets/Dcom-Global/Local%20Content/Articles/TMT/TMT%20Predictions%202012/16264A_TMT_Predict_sg6.pdf

Dept, U. S. of Justice. (2012). *Text of the Revised Title II Regulation*. Retrieved March 9, 2014, from http://www.ada.gov/regs2010/ titleII_2010/titleII_2010_withbold.htm

Design, U.-C. Inc. (n.d.). *User-Centered Design, Inc - Home*. Retrieved March 11, 2014, from http://www.user-centereddesign.com/index.php

Deyle, T. (2009, February 11). *iBOT Discontinued -- Unfortunate for the Disabled but Perhaps a Budding Robotics Opportunity? | Hizook*. Retrieved March 9, 2014, from http://www.hizook.com/blog/2009/02/11/ ibot-discontinued-unfortunate-disabled-perhaps-budding-robotics-opportunity

Diagonal View. (2009, July 7). *Amazing Robot Chef*. [Video file]. Retrieved from http://youtu.be/CNSKMGurrPI

Dickens, C. (1859). *A tale of two cities*. London: Chapman & Hall.

Didden, R., Scholte, R. H., Korzilius, H., Moor, J. M., Vermeulen, A., O'Reilly, M., & Lancioni, G. E. (2009). Cyberbullying among students with intellectual and developmental disability in special education settings. *Developmental Neurorehabilitation*. doi:10.1080/17518420902971356 PMID:19466622

Dillow, C. (2010, January 12). Microsoft Building Shape-Shifting Touchscreen For True Tactile Touch Tech. *Popular Sicence*. Retrieved from http://www.popsci.com/technology/article/2010-12/patent-filing-reveals-microsofts-novel-attempt-true-tactile-touchscreen-tech

Ding, D., Cooper, R. A., Pasquina, P. F., & Fici-Pasquina, L. (2011). Sensor technology for smart homes. *Maturitas*, *69*(2), 131–136. doi:10.1016/j.maturitas.2011.03.016 PMID:21531517

Disabled Businesspersons Association. (n.d.). *About The DBA - Disabled Businesspersons Association Disabled Businesspersons Association | Serving the needs of America's enterprising disabled, and professionals in rehabilitation. Since1985*. Retrieved March 10, 2014, from http://disabledbusiness.org/

Disabled Entrepreneurs. (2012). *Home | Disabled Entrepreneurs - Inspiring Potential*. Retrieved March 10, 2014, from http://www.disabledentrepreneurs.co.uk/

Disabled Person, Inc. (2014). *Disabled Person: Home*. Retrieved March 10, 2014, from https://www.disabled-person.com/

DisAbled Women's Network Ontario. (2006, February 6). *Women with DisAbilities Online community - DisAbled Women's Network Ontario*. Retrieved March 11, 2014, from http://dawn.thot.net/list.html

Disabled Workers Co-operative Ltd. (2004). *Jobs for Disabled People - Employment - Disabled Workers Co-operative*. Retrieved March 10, 2014, from http://www.disabledworkers.org.uk/careers/

Disabled World. (2008, January 20). *Famous Blind and Vision Impaired Persons*. Retrieved March 10, 2014, from http://www.disabled-world.com/artman/publish/famous-blind.shtml

Disney Canada Inc. (2014). *Club Penguin | Waddle around and meet new friends*. Retrieved March 9, 2014, from http://www.clubpenguin.com/

Diversity World. (2014). *Self-Employment for People with Disabilities*. Retrieved March 10, 2014, from http://www.diversityworld.com/Disability/selfempl.htm

DocumentCloud. (n.d.). *DocumentCloud*. Retrieved March 13, 2014, from http://www.documentcloud.org/home

Dodds, P. S., Harris, K. D., Kloumann, I. M., Bliss, C. A., & Danforth, C. M. (2011). Temporal patterns of happiness and information in a global social network: Hedonometrics and Twitter. *PLoS ONE*. doi:10.1371/journal.pone.0026752 PMID:22163266

Donald, B. (2011, December 13). *Facebook Aims to Help Prevent Suicide*. Retrieved March 14, 2014, from http://www.pddnet.com/news/2011/12/facebook-aims-help-prevent-suicide

Dority, K. (2009, May 21). *FreePint: Disability Statistics: Challenges and Sources [ABSTRACT]*. Retrieved March 10, 2014, from http://web.freepint.com/go/blog/3933

Dorwick, P. W., Anderson, J., Heyer, K., & Acosta, J. (2005). Postsecondary education across the USA: Experiences of adults with disabilities. *Journal of Vocational Rehabilitation*, 22(1), 41–47.

DotComGuy. (n.d.). *Wikipedia, the free encyclopedia*. Retrieved March 8, 2014, from http://en.wikipedia.org/wiki/DotComGuy

Dow Jones & Company, Inc. (n.d.). *WSJ.D Conference2014*. Retrieved March 8, 2014, from http://wsjd-conference.wsj.com/

Drinkwater, D. (2010, November 14). *Kazakhstan to bring tablets to all school children by 2020 | TabTimes*. Retrieved March 10, 2014, from http://tabtimes.com/news/education/2011/11/14/kazakhstan-bring-tablets-all-school-children-2020

DrumBeat Consulting. (2012, June 5). DrumBeat's Value Proposition. *DrumBeat Consulting*. Retrieved March 13, 2014, from http://drumbeatconsulting.com/blog/2012/06/05/drumbeats-value-proposition/

Duke University. (2011, July 10). *Monkeys 'Move and Feel' Virtual Objects Using Only Their Brains*. Retrieved March 8, 2014, from http://www.pddnet.com/news/2011/10/monkeys-move-and-feel-virtual-objects-using-only-their-brains

Duolingo. (n.d.). *Duolingo | Learn Spanish, French, German, Portuguese, Italian and English for free*. Retrieved March 12, 2014, from https://www.duolingo.com/

Eaton, K. (2008, February 21). *Cellphone Display Concept Designed for Dracula Is Bloody, Ridiculous*. Retrieved February 7, 2014, from http://gizmodo.com/359018/cellphone-display-concept-designed-for-dracula-is-bloody-ridiculous

eBay. (2014). *Electronics, Cars, Fashion, Collectibles, Coupons and More Online Shopping | eBay*. Retrieved March 11, 2014, from http://www.ebay.com/

Ebersold, S., Schmitt, M. J., & Priestley, M. (2011). *Inclusive Education For Young Disabled People In Europe: Trends, Issues And Challenges*. Retrieved from Academic Network of European Disability website: http://www.disability-europe.net/content/aned/media/ANED%20 2010%20Task%205%20Education%20final%20report%20-%20FINAL%20(2)_0.pdf

EBU. (n.d.a). *Categories of jobs undertaken by blind and partially sighted people | EBU Job Website | Employment, rehabilitation and vocational training | Working Areas | European Blind Union*. Retrieved March 10, 2014, from http://www.euroblind.org/about-ebu/ebu-employment-website/blind-and-partially-sighted-people/

EBU. (n.d.b). *European Blind Union*. Retrieved March 10, 2014, from http://www.euroblind.org/

EBU. (n.d.c). *Useful links | Resources | European Blind Union*. Retrieved March 10, 2014, from http://www.euroblind.org/resources/useful-links/#Employment

ECAALYX. (2009). *Welcome to eCAALYX!* Retrieved February 7, 2014, from http://ecaalyx.org/

Economist Group. (2011, November 16). *The Economist Insights? Expert Analysis and Events | Frontiers of disruption*. Retrieved March 10, 2014, from http://www.economistinsights.com/technology-innovation/analysis/frontiers-disruption

Economist Group. (2014). *Country, industry and risk analysis from The Economist Intelligence Unit*. Retrieved March 10, 2014, from http://www.eiu.com/Default.aspx

EDF. (n.d.). *The representative organisation of persons with disabilities in Europe*. Retrieved March 13, 2014, from http://www.edf-feph.org/

EG. (n.d.). *Welcome | e.g. Conference*. Retrieved February 7, 2014, from http://www.the-eg.com/

EHFCN. (n.d.). *EHFCN*. Retrieved March 13, 2014, from http://www.ehfcn.org/

Eichhorst, Kendzia, Knudsen, Hansen, & Vandeweghe. (2010). *The mobility and integration of people with disabilities into the labour market: Based on a study conducted for the European Parliament under contract IP/A/EMPL/FWC/2008-002/C1/SC4.* Retrieved from http://www.iza.org/en/webcontent/publications/reports/report_pdfs/iza_report_29.pdf

Ellin, A. (2011, August 8). A Boom in Plastic Surgery for Those in the Golden Years. *The New York Times.* Retrieved from http://www.nytimes.com/2011/08/09/health/09plastic.html

Emotiv. (2014). *Emotiv | EEG System | Electroencephalography.* Retrieved March 8, 2014, from http://www.emotiv.com/index.php

Enable, U. N. (2008). *UN Enable - Work of the United Nations for Persons with Disabilities.* Retrieved March 10, 2014, from http://www.un.org/disabilities/

Enabling Devices. (2014). *Enabling Devices - Assistive Technology - Products for People with Disabilities.* Retrieved March 10, 2014, from http://enablingdevices.com/catalog

ENAT. (2013). *ENAT | European Network for Accessible Tourism.* Retrieved March 13, 2014, from http://www.accessibletourism.org/

ENIL. (2013a). *ENIL – European Network on Independent Living.* Retrieved from http://www.enil.eu/

ENIL. (2013b). *Freedom of movement » ENIL – European Network on Independent Living.* Retrieved from http://www.enil.eu/tag/freedom-of-movement/

EOP, Inc. (2012). *Equal Opportunity Publications - Magazines Page - Careers & the Disabled.* Retrieved March 10, 2014, from http://www.eop.com/mags-CD.php

EOWG, & ATAG WG. (2013, October 5). *ATAG Overview.* Retrieved March 12, 2014, from http://www.w3.org/WAI/intro/atag.php

EOWG, & ERT WG. (2011, May 10). *EARL Overview.* Retrieved March 12, 2014, from http://www.w3.org/WAI/intro/earl.php

EOWG, & UAWG. (2005, July). *UAAG Overview.* Retrieved March 12, 2014, from http://www.w3.org/WAI/intro/uaag.php

EOWG, & WCAG WG. (2006, December 21). *WCAG 1.0 Documents.* Retrieved March 12, 2014, from http://www.w3.org/WAI/intro/wcag10docs.php

Ergonurse. (n.d.). *Compression Force on the Back.* Retrieved from http://www.ergonurse.com/BackCompressionFlyer.pdf

ETwinning. (n.d.). *eTwinning - Homepage.* Retrieved March 9, 2014, from www.etwinning.net/en/pub/index.htm

European Agency for Development in Special Needs Education. (2009). *Key principles for promoting quality in inclusive education: Recommendations for policy makers.* Retrieved from http://www.european-agency.org/sites/default/files/key-principles-EN.pdf

European Commission, Joint Research Centre, Institute for Prospective Technological Studies. (2009). *IS UNIT WEB SITE - IPTS - JRC - EC.* Retrieved March 9, 2014, from http://is.jrc.ec.europa.eu/pages/EAP/eLearning.html

European Commission. (2007, November 29). *Europa - Press Releases - Press release - European initiative on an all-inclusive digital society: Frequently Asked Questions.* Retrieved March 13, 2014, from http://europa.eu/rapid/press-release_MEMO-07-527_en.htm?locale=en

European Commission. (2010). *People with disabilities have equal rights: The European Disability Strategy 2010-2020.* Retrieved from http://eur-lex.europa.eu/LexUriServ/LexUriServ.do?uri=COM:2010:0636:FIN:EN:PDF

European Commission. (2010, January 8). *European Commission: CORDIS: Projects: Search.* Retrieved March 8, 2014, from http://cordis.europa.eu/projects/rcn/71108_en.html

European Commission. (2011). *Europa - Press Releases - Press release - Digital Agenda: First meeting of EU Media Futures Forum.* Retrieved March 13, 2014, from http://europa.eu/rapid/press-release_IP-11-1506_en.htm?locale=en

European Commission. (2012a). *European Commission : CORDIS : Projects : FUTURE BNCI.* Retrieved March 16, 2014, from http://cordis.europa.eu/projects/rcn/93832_en.html

European Commission. (2012b). *European Commission : CORDIS : Projects : TREMOR*. Retrieved March 16, 2014, from http://cordis.europa.eu/projects/rcn/87753_en.html

European Commission. (2013, March 27). *Home page - Innovation Union*. Retrieved March 8, 2014, from ec.europa.eu/research/innovation-union/ic2011/index_en.cfm

European Commission. (2014). *Digital Agenda for Europe - European Commission*. Retrieved March 16, 2014, from http://ec.europa.eu/digital-agenda/life-and-work

European Commission. Enterprise and Industry. (2013, April 15). *Encouraging women entrepreneurs - Small and medium sized enterprises - Enterprise and Industry*. Retrieved March 10, 2014, from ec.europa.eu/enterprise/policies/sme/promoting-entrepreneurship/women/index_en.htm

European Thematic Network on Assistive Information Technologies. (2013). *Homepage - ETNA*. Retrieved March 10, 2014, from http://www.etna-project.eu/

Eurostat. (2013, December). *Information society statistics at regional level - Statistics Explained*. Retrieved February 7, 2014, from http://epp.eurostat.ec.europa.eu/statistics_explained/index.php/Information_society_statistics_at_regional_level

Eurostat. (2013a, October 17). *Individuals never having used the Internet*. Retrieved March 8, 2014, from http://epp.eurostat.ec.europa.eu/tgm/refreshTableAction.do?tab=table&plugin=1&pcode=tin00011&language=en

Eurostat. (2013b). *Individuals using the Internet for seeking health-related information*. Retrieved March 14, 2014, from http://epp.eurostat.ec.europa.eu/tgm/table.do?tab=table&init=1&language=en&pcode=tin00101&plugin=1

Eurostat. (2013c, October 17). *Mobile phone subscriptions*. Retrieved March 8, 2014, from http://epp.eurostat.ec.europa.eu/tgm/table.do?tab=table&plugin=1&language=en&pcode=tin00060

EYE 2021. (2013). *EYE21 is the first and only system in the world of mobility aids for the blind people which allows its use in any environment*. Retrieved March 8, 2014, from http://www.eye2021.com/

EyeCare America. (2007). *Facts About Blindness and Eye Health*. Retrieved from http://www.aao.org/eyecare/news/upload/Eye-Health-Fact-Sheet.pdf

Facebook. (2014). Share Where You Are. *Facebook*. Retrieved March 11, 2014, from https://www.facebook.com/about/location

Fair trade. (n.d.). *Wikipedia, the free encyclopedia*. Retrieved March 10, 2014, from http://en.wikipedia.org/wiki/Fair_trade

Fallah, N., Apostolopoulos, I., Bekris, K., & Folmer, E. (2012). *The user as a sensor: navigating users with visual impairments in indoor spaces using tactile landmarks*. doi:10.1145/2207676.2207735

Farina, N. (2011, October 11). *Why indoor navigation is so hard - O'Reilly Radar*. Retrieved March 9, 2014, from http://radar.oreilly.com/2011/10/indoor-navigation.html

FAST. (2014). *FAST - Foundation For Assistive Technology*. Retrieved March 10, 2014, from http://www.fastuk.org/home.php

Ferenstein, G. (2010, March 1). *How Twitter in the Classroom is Boosting Student Engagement*. Retrieved March 10, 2014, from http://mashable.com/2010/03/01/twitter-classroom/

Fernández-Ardèvo, M. (2010). Interactions with and through mobile phones: what about the elderly population? In *Proceedings of ECREA Conference 2010*. ECREA. Retrieved from http://www.academia.edu/782946/Interactions_with_and_through_mobile_phones_what_about_the_elderly_population

Fish, E. (2011, June 27). *Home Automation: Inside a DIY Smart House | TechHive*. Retrieved March 8, 2014, from http://www.techhive.com/article/231260/home_automation_inside_a_diy_smart_house.html

FixMyStreet. (n.d.). FixMyStreet. *FixMyStreet*. Retrieved March 13, 2014, from http://www.fixmystreet.com/

Fleming, N. (2007, February 2). *Woman with bionic arm regains sense of touch - Telegraph*. Retrieved March 8, 2014, from http://www.telegraph.co.uk/news/worldnews/1541406/Woman-with-bionic-arm-regains-sense-of-touch.html

Foley, M. J. (2012, March 6). Microsoft showcases new Kinect-centric projects at its TechFest research fair. *ZDNet*. Retrieved from http://www.zdnet.com/blog/microsoft/microsoft-showcases-new-kinect-centric-projects-at-its-techfest-research-fair/12131

Fougner, J. (2011, January 31). *Introducing Deals*. Retrieved March 11, 2014, from https://www.facebook.com/notes/facebook/introducing-deals/446183422130

Foursquare. (2014). *Foursquare*. Retrieved March 11, 2014, from https://foursquare.com/

Fox, S. (2006, April 11). *Are Wired Seniors Sitting Ducks? | Pew Research Center's Internet & American Life Project*. Retrieved March 16, 2014, from http://www.pewinternet.org/2006/04/11/are-wired-seniors-sitting-ducks/#fn-836-1

Framework, P. A. L. (n.d.). *Overview — PAL*. Retrieved February 7, 2014, from https://pal.sri.com/Plone/framework

Fraunhofer, I. P. A. (n.d.). Research. *Fraunhofer Institute for Manufacturing Engineering and Automation*. Retrieved March 13, 2014, from http://www.care-o-bot.de/en/research.html

Freedman, D. (2008, December 1). *Reality Bites -- Emotiv -- Mind Reading Device | Inc.com*. Retrieved March 8, 2014, from http://www.inc.com/magazine/20081201/reality-bites.html

Freedom Scientific Inc. (2014a). *Products for low vision, blindness, and learning disabilities from Freedom Scientific*. Retrieved March 10, 2014, from http://www.freedomscientific.com/default.asp

Freedom Scientific, Inc. (2014b). *JAWS Screen Reading Software by Freedom Scientific*. Retrieved March 10, 2014, from http://www.freedomscientific.com/products/fs/jaws-product-page.asp

Friends of Europe. (n.d.). *Friends of Europe | Home*. Retrieved March 10, 2014, from http://www.friendsofeurope.org/Home/tabid/1124/Default.aspx

Fundacion, O. N. C. E. (n.d.a). *Miguel Carballeda Piñeiro - Prologues - CSR-D Guie corporate social responsibility and disability of Fundación ONCE*. Retrieved March 10, 2014, from http://rsed.fundaciononce.es/en/prologos.html

Fundacion, O. N. C. E. (n.d.b). *Portada - Fundación Once*. Retrieved March 10, 2014, from http://www.fundaciononce.es/EN/Pages/Portada.aspx

FUPOL. (n.d.). *FUPOL Project*. Retrieved March 13, 2014, from http://www.fupol.eu/

Furlan, R. (2010, January 21). Igniting a Brain-Computer Interface Revolution - BCI X PRIZE. *Singularity Hub*. Retrieved March 13, 2014, from http://singularityhub.com/ 2010/01/21/igniting-a-brain-computer-interface-revolution-bci-x-prize/

Future, B. C. N. I. (2012). *Future BCNI: A roadmanp for future directions in Brain / Neuronal Computer Interaction Research*. Retrieved from http://future-bnci.org/images/stories/Future_BNCI_Roadmap.pdf

GAATES.ORG. (2007, May 25). GAATES Home Page. *Collection*. Retrieved March 13, 2014, from http://www.gaates.org/

GAATES.ORG. (2011, September 8). *Procurement of Accessible ICTs*. Retrieved from http://www.gaates.org

Gadget Lab Staff. (2010, December 29). *The 10 Most Significant Gadgets of 2010 | Gadget Lab | Wired.com*. Retrieved March 14, 2014, from http://www.wired.com/gadgetlab/2010/12/top-tech-2010/?pid=928#slideid-928

Gallaudet University. (1998). *Jobs and Careers of Deaf and Hard of Hearing People*. Retrieved March 10, 2014, from http://www.gallaudet.edu/clerc_center/information_and_resources/info_to_go/transition_to_adulthood/working_and_careers/jobs_and_careers_of_dhoh_ppl.html

Gallotti, P., Raposo, A., & Soares, L. (2011). v-Glove: A 3D Virtual Touch Interface. *Virtual Reality (SVR), 2011 XIII Symposium on Virtual Reality*, (pp. 242-251). doi:10.1109/SVR.2011.21

Game On Extra Time. (n.d.). *Game On Extra Time*. Retrieved March 10, 2014, from http://goet-project.eu/

Garage, W. (2010, May 4). *The Results Are In PR2 Beta Program Recipients! | Willow Garage*. Retrieved March 11, 2014, from http://www.willowgarage.com/blog/2010/05/04/pr2-beta-program-recipients

Garage, W. (2014a). *Overview | Willow Garage*. Retrieved March 11, 2014, from http://www.willowgarage.com/pages/pr2/overview

Garage, W. (2014b). *Willow Garage.* Retrieved March 11, 2014, from http://www.willowgarage.com/

Gartner. (2010, November 10). *Gartner Says Worldwide Mobile Phone Sales Grew 35 Percent in Third Quarter 2010, Smartphone Sales Increased 96 Percent.* Retrieved from http://www.gartner.com/newsroom/id/1466313

Gates, B. (2007). A Robot in Every Home. *Scientific American.* doi:10.1038/scientificamerican0107-58 PMID:17186834

Gelernter, D. (1992). *Mirror Worlds: Or the Day Software Puts the Universe in a Shoebox. How It Will Happen and What It Will Mean.* New York: Oxford University Press.

Gesture Recognition. (n.d.). *Wikipedia, the free encyclopedia.* Retrieved February 10, 2014, from http://en.wikipedia.org/wiki/Gesture_recognition

GIUDE. (2014). *European Project GUIDE - Gentle User Interfaces for Elderly People.* Retrieved March 12, 2014, from http://www.guide-project.eu/

Glazer, E. (2012, March 9). *What Does It Say When a Robot Is the Life of a Party? - WSJ.com.* Retrieved March 9, 2014, from http://online.wsj.com/news/articles/SB10001424052 9702034586045 7726532159588 2542?KEYWORDS= vgo&mg=reno64-wsj&url= http%3A%2F%2Fonline.wsj.com%2 Farticle%2FSB 1000142405297 0203458604577 2653215958825 42.html%3FKEYWORDS%3Dvgo

Global Disabiliy Rights Library. (n.d.). *The Global Disability Rights Library* |www.widernet.org. Retrieved March 13, 2014, from http://www.widernet.org/egranary/gdrl

Global Industry Analysts, Inc. (2012, February). *Smart Sensors (MCP-1234) - Global Industry Analysts, Inc.* Retrieved February 7, 2014, from http://www.strategyr.com/Smart_Sensors_Market_Report.asp

Global Information Systems Group. (2012). *iGesture - About.* Retrieved March 13, 2014, from http://www.igesture.org/

Global Initiative for Inclusive ICTs. (2014). *G3ict: The Global Initiative for Inclusive ICTs.* Retrieved March 10, 2014, from http://g3ict.com/

GloPos Technologies. (2009). *Glopos - Glopos.* Retrieved March 9, 2014, from http://www.glopos.com/

GoGet CarShare. (2014). Home. *GoGet Carshare.* Retrieved March 11, 2014, from http://www.goget.com.au/

Gonzalez, C. (2011, August 9). *nsf.gov - Engineering (ENG) News - New NSF Engineering Research Center to Pursue Ideal Mind–Machine Interface - US National Science Foundation (NSF).* Retrieved March 13, 2014, from http://www.nsf.gov/ news/news_summ.jsp?cntn_id=119842&org=ENG&from=news

Google. (2011, November 29). *Official Google Blog: A new frontier for Google Maps: mapping the indoors.* Retrieved March 9, 2014, from http://googleblog.blogspot.gr/2011/11/new-frontier-for-google-maps-mapping.html

Google. (2012). *Books Google.* Retrieved March 12, 2014, from http://books.google.com/

Google. (2014). *Goggles overview and requirements - Search Help.* Retrieved March 8, 2014, from https://support.google.com/websearch/answer/166331

Google. (2014). *reCAPTCHA: Stop Spam, Read Books.* Retrieved March 12, 2014, from http://www.google.com/recaptcha

Google. (2014a). *A smart, virtual wallet for in-store and online shopping – Google Wallet.* Retrieved March 11, 2014, from http://www.google.com/wallet/

Google. (2014a). *Google Analytics Official Website? Web Analytics & Reporting.* Retrieved March 10, 2014, from http://www.google.com/analytics/

Google. (2014b). *Google Offers.* Retrieved March 11, 2014, from https://www.google.com/offers/?gl=US

Google. (2014b). *Google+.* Retrieved March 10, 2014, from https://plus.google.com/?

Google. (2014c). *Places for businesses – Google.* Retrieved March 11, 2014, from http://www.google.com/business/placesforbusiness/

Google. (2014c). *YouTube.* Retrieved March 10, 2014, from https://www.youtube.com/

Google. (n.d.). *Google+.* Retrieved March 13, 2014, from https://plus.google.com/

Gorilla Foundation. (2010). *Gorilla Foundation - Koko the Gorilla*. Retrieved March 9, 2014, from http://www.koko.org/friends/index.html

Gostai. (n.d.). *Gostai*. Retrieved March 9, 2014, from http://www.gostai.com/

Government of Ontario. M. of H., & L.-T. C. (2008). *Assistive Devices Program- About the Program - Public Information - MOHLTC*. Retrieved March 13, 2014, from http://www.health.gov.on.ca/en/public/programs/adp/about.aspx

Grabianowski, E. (2007, November 16). *HowStuffWorks How Thought-Controlled Wheelchairs Work*. Retrieved March 9, 2014, from http://computer.howstuffworks.com/audeo.htm

Grant, C. (2010, December 20). Kinect Hacks: American Sign Language recognition. *Joystiq*. Retrieved from http://www.joystiq.com/2010/12/20/kinect-hacks-american-sign-language-recognition/

Great Britain Equality and Human Rights Commission. (2011). *Equality Act 2010: Summary guidance on employment*. Retrieved from http://www.equalityhumanrights.com/uploaded_files/EqualityAct/ea_employment_summary_guidance.pdf

Great Britain National Audit Office. (2007). *Government on the internet: Progress in delivering information and services online*. Retrieved from http://www.nao.org.uk/report/government-on-the-internet-progress-in-delivering-information-and-services-online/

Greenemeier, L. (2009, December 14). *On a Roll: Autonomous Navigation Lasers and Robotics Push Smart Wheelchair Technology to the Cutting Edge [Slide Show] - Scientific American*. Retrieved March 9, 2014, from http://www.scientificamerican.com/article/smart-wheelchair/

Greve, B. (2009). *The labour market situation of disabled people in European countries and implementation of employment policies: a summary of evidence from country reports and research studies*. Retrieved from http://www.disability-europe.net/content/aned/media/ANED%20Task%206%20final%20report%20-%20final%20version%2017-04-09.pdf

GRIFS. (2008). *Home*. Retrieved February 7, 2014, from http://www.grifs-project.eu/

Groce, N. E. (2004). *Adolescents and youth with disability: issues and challenges*. Asia Pacific Disability Rehabilitation Journal.

Groupon. (n.d.). *Groupon*. Retrieved March 11, 2014, from http://www.groupon.com/app/subscriptions/new_zip?

GS1. (n.d.). *EPCglobal | Products & Solutions | GS1 - The global language of business*. Retrieved from http://www.gs1.org/epcglobal

Gunther, E. W. (2008, January 30). *Smart Grid: Wireless home sensor network finally possible*. Retrieved March 8, 2014, from http://www.smartgridnews.com/artman/publish/article_399.html

Gus Communication Devices Inc. (2012). *Gus Communications Devices-Name brand speech aids at discounted prices*. Retrieved March 10, 2014, from http://www.gusinc.com/2012/Home.html

Gus Communication Devices, Inc. (n.d.). *Computer Access*. Retrieved March 10, 2014, from http://www.gusinc.com/2012/Computer_Access.html

Hack and Hear. (2012). *hack and hear*. Retrieved March 8, 2014, from http://blog.hackandhear.com/

Hanlon, M. (n.d.). *Intelligent Vending Machines point towards a cashless future*. Retrieved March 11, 2014, from http://www.gizmag.com/go/3308/

Harbor, B. (2008, September 18). *Whirlpool Brand Business Grant Recognizes Innovative Moms | FinancialContent Business Page*. Retrieved March 10, 2014, from http://markets.financialcontent.com/stocks/news/read?GUID=6604909&ChannelID=3197

Harfoush, R. (2009). *Yes we did: an inside look at how social media built the Obama brand*. Berkeley, CA: New Riders.

Harmon, A. (2004, May 9). *Neurodiversity Forever, The Disability Movement Turns to Brains - New York Times*. Retrieved March 14, 2014, from http://www.nytimes.com/2004/05/09/weekinreview/neurodiversity-forever-the-disability-movement-turns-to-brains.html?pagewanted=all&src=pm

Harmon, A. (2011a, September 17). *Autistic and Seeking a Place in an Adult World - NYTimes.com*. Retrieved March 8, 2014, from http://www.nytimes.com/2011/09/18/us/autistic-and-seeking-a-place-in-an-adult-world.html?ref=us&pagewanted=all

Harmon, A. (2011b, December 26). *Navigating Love and Autism - NYTimes.com*. Retrieved March 8, 2014, from http://www.nytimes.com/2011/12/26/us/navigating-love-and-autism.html?_r=1&nl=todaysheadlines&emc=tha2&pagewanted=all

Harrell, E. (2010, April 20). *Study: Brain Games Don't Boost Overall Mental Function - TIME*. Retrieved March 10, 2014, from http://content.time.com/time/health/article/0,8599,1983306,00.html

Hartien, R. (2013, July 10). *Sony HMZ-T3W Headmount Gets In, and On, Your Face | Sony*. Retrieved March 10, 2014, from http://blog.sony.com/2013/10/sony-headmount/

Hartstein, D. (2011, April 26). *How Schools Can Use Facebook to Build an Online Community*. Retrieved March 10, 2014, from http://mashable.com/2011/04/26/facebook-for-schools/

HAVEit - Highly Automated Vehicles for Intelligent Transport. (n.d.). *HAVE IT Website*. Retrieved March 9, 2014, from http://www.haveit-eu.org/displayITM1.asp?ITMID=6&LANG=EN

Hawkins. (2008, February). *Jeff Hawkins: How brain science will change computing | Talk Video | TED*. [Video file]. Retrieved from http://www.ted.com/talks/jeff_hawkins_on_how_brain_science_will_change_computing

Hawthorne effect. (n.d.). *Wikipedia, the free encyclopedia*. Retrieved March 10, 2014, from http://en.wikipedia.org/wiki/Hawthorne_effect

Heasley, A. (2009, December 8). *Qantas now leaves a Blind Passenger Stranded*. Retrieved March 13, 2014, from http://travability.travel/blogs/qantas.html

Heitin, L. (2011, October 12). *Education Week Teacher Professional Development Sourcebook: Pairing Up*. Retrieved March 9, 2014, from http://www.edweek.org/tsb/articles/2011/10/13/01coteach.h05.html

Heppler, K. (2010, August 5). 12 awesome platforms for social good. *Socialbrite*. Retrieved March 13, 2014, from http://www.socialbrite.org/2010/08/05/top-12-platforms-for-social-good/

Herman, J. (2011, March 4). *Google's self-driving car. In action - SmartPlanet*. Retrieved March 9, 2014, from http://www.smartplanet.com/blog/thinking-tech/googles-self-driving-car-in-action/6422

Hess, R. (2011, December 5). *Why Education Innovation Tends to Crash and Burn - Rick Hess Straight Up - Education Week*. Retrieved March 10, 2014, from http://blogs.edweek.org/edweek/rick_hess_straight_up/2011/12/why_education_innovation_tends_to_crash_and_burn.html

Heydarian, H. (2012, May 22). *Announcing the Winners of the Microsoft Robotics @ Home Competition - Microsoft Robotics Blog - Site Home - MSDN Blogs*. Retrieved March 14, 2014, from http://blogs.msdn.com/b/msroboticsstudio/archive/2012/05/22/announcing-the-winners-of-the-microsoft-robotics-home-competition.aspx

High power militar robotic exoskeleton. (2007, November 26). Retrieved from http://youtu.be/0hkCcoenLW4

High Tech High. (2000). *High Tech High*. Retrieved March 10, 2014, from http://www.hightechhigh.org/

Hiscott, W. (2005). Parallel societies, A neologism gone bad. *Focus Online*. Retrieved from http://aa.ecn.cz/img_upload/f76c21488a048c95bc0a5f12deece153/WHiscott_Parallel_Societies.pdf

Hochman, P. (2010, February 1). Bionic Legs, i-Limbs, and Other Super Human Prostheses You'll Envy. *Fast Company*. Retrieved March 13, 2014, from //www.fastcompany.com/1514543/ bionic-legs-i-limbs-and-other-super-human-prostheses-youll-envy

Hollister, S. (2011, November 30). Sony HMZ-T1 Personal 3D Viewer review. *The Verge*. Retrieved March 11, 2014, from http://www.theverge.com/2011/11/10/2552518/sony-hmz-t1-personal-3d-viewer-review

HomeToys. (2013). *AV and Automation Industry eMagazine - Hometoys Interview - Guy Dewsbury Smart Homes for Disabled People in the UK | HomeToys*. Retrieved March 10, 2014, from http://hometoys.com/emagazine.php?url=/ezine/09.05/dewsbury/index.htm

Honda. (2014). *ASIMO by Honda | The World's Most Advanced Humanoid Robot*. Retrieved February 22, 2014, from http://asimo.honda.com/

Human Connectome Project. (n.d.). *Human Connectome Project | Mapping the human brain connectivity*. Retrieved March 8, 2014, from http://www.humanconnectomeproject.org/

Hurst, A., & Tobias, J. (2011). *Empowering individuals with do-it-yourself assistive technology*. doi:10.1145/2049536.2049541

I2Home. (n.d.). *i2home > Home*. Retrieved March 10, 2014, from http://www.i2home.org/

I2osig.org. (2004). *Speech Recognition*. Retrieved February 10, 2014, from http://www.i2osig.org/speech.html

IBM. (2013, February 20). IBM Design. *CTZZZ*. Retrieved March 11, 2014, from http://www.ibm.com/design/

IBM. (n.d.). *IBM INNOV8: CityOne*. Retrieved March 10, 2014, from http://www-01.ibm.com/software/solutions/soa/innov8/cityone/index.html

IBM. (n.d.). *IBM Watson*. Retrieved February 7, 2014, from http://www-03.ibm.com/innovation/us/watson/index.html

ICT SHOCK Future Internet. (2007). *Research agenda*. Retrieved from http://www.futureinternet.fi/publications/ICT_SHOK_FI_SRA_Research_Agenda.pdf

IDC. (n.d.). *IDC Home: The premier global market intelligence firm*. Retrieved February 7, 2014, from http://www.idc.com/

IDEO. (2010). *futureselfservicebanking.com*. Retrieved March 11, 2014, from http://futureselfservicebanking.com/

IDEO. (2014). *IDEO | A Design and Innovation Consulting Firm*. Retrieved March 11, 2014, from http://www.ideo.com/

IDF. (n.d.). *International Diabetes Federation*. Retrieved February 7, 2014, from http://www.idf.org/

IERC. (2010). *IERC-European Research Cluster on the Internet of Things*. Retrieved February 7, 2014, from http://www.internet-of-things-research.eu/

IFR. (2013). *Statistics - IFR International Federation of Robotics*. Retrieved February 22, 2014, from http://www.ifr.org/service-robots/statistics/

Immersion Corporation. (2013). *TouchSense Tactile Feedback Systems*. Retrieved March 10, 2014, from http://www.immersion.com/products/touchsense-tactile-feedback/

Immersion. (2013). *TouchSense Tactile Feedback Systems*. Retrieved February 10, 2014, from http://www.immersion.com/products/touchsense-tactile-feedback/

ImpactGames LLC. (2010). *PeaceMaker Home: PeaceMaker - Play the News. Solve the Puzzle*. Retrieved March 10, 2014, from http://www.peacemakergame.com/

Inclusive Education Canada. (n.d.). *Inclusive Education Canada*. Retrieved March 10, 2014, from http://inclusiveeducation.ca/

Indeed. (2014). *User-experience Job Trends | Indeed.com*. Retrieved March 11, 2014, from http://www.indeed.com/jobanalytics/jobtrends?q=User-experience&l=

Independence Technology, L. L. C. (2001). *Independence Technology, L.L.C*. Retrieved March 9, 2014, from http://www.ibotnow.com/

Industrias Tomás Morcillo, S. L. (2014). *ITM Polycart - Plastic Shopping Carts and Baskets*. Retrieved March 11, 2014, from http://www.polycartgroup.com/english/index.html

INNOROBO 2011 - Video by TLM. (2011, October 26). Retrieved from http://youtu.be/no2nUSkuqjw

Inspiration Software, Inc. (2014a). *WebspirationPRO | inspiration.com*. Retrieved March 10, 2014, from http://www.inspiration.com/WebspirationPRO

Inspiration Software, Inc. (2014b). *Inspiration Software, Inc. - The Leader in Visual Thinking and Learning | inspiration.com*. Retrieved March 10, 2014, from http://www.inspiration.com/

Instituto de Biomecánica. (n.d.). *Instituto de Biomecánica*. Retrieved March 8, 2014, from http://abcproject.ibv.org/

Instituto TeCIP. (2014). *Scuola Superiore Sant' Anna - Instituto TeCIP*. Retrieved March 9, 2014, from www.sssup.it/ist_home. jsp?ID_LINK=10509&area=199

Intendix. (2009). *intendix.com*. Retrieved March 8, 2014, from http://www.intendix.com/

International Center for Disability Resources on the Internet. (2010, September 30). *Passage of the 21st Century Communications & Video Accessibility Act of 2010*. Retrieved March 13, 2014, from http://www.icdri.org/News/21CentCommACT.htm

International Center for Disability Resources on the Internet. (2012). *ICDRI Home*. Retrieved March 13, 2014, from http://www.icdri.org/

Internet World Stats. (2012). *World Internet Users Statistics Usage and World PopulationStats*. Retrieved February 7, 2014, from http://www.internetworldstats.com/stats.htm

InTouch Technologies, Inc. (2014). *InTouch Health*. Retrieved March 9, 2014, from http://www.intouchhealth.com/

Introducing Google Currents. (2011). Retrieved from http://www.youtube.com/watch?v=5LOcUkm8m9w&feature=youtube_gdata_player

IRobot Corporation. (2013). *iRobot Corporation: Robots that Make a Difference*. Retrieved March 9, 2014, from http://www.irobot.com/us

iRobot. (n.d.). *Wikipedia, the free encyclopedia*. Retrieved March 4, 2014, from http://en.wikipedia.org/wiki/IRobot

ISNT. (2002). *Institute for the Study of the Neurologically Typical*. Retrieved March 14, 2014, from http://isnt.autistics.org/

Japanese Robot Of The Year. (2009). Retrieved from http://www.youtube.com/ watch?v=W3f6BOrD9Ek&feature=youtube_gdata_player

Jawbone. (2014). *UP24 by Jawbone | Wristband + App. | Track how you sleep, move and eat*. Retrieved March 8, 2014, from https://jawbone.com/up

Jennifer Ringley. (n.d.). *Wikipedia, the free encyclopedia*. Retrieved March 8, 2014, from http://en.wikipedia.org/wiki/JenniCam

Jobaccess.co.za. (2012). *People With Disabilities, Disabled People, Disbility, People With Disabilities, Jobs, PWD, Search Hundreds Of Jobs Within The South Africa*. Retrieved March 10, 2014, from http://www.jobaccess.co.za/

Jones, M. K., Latreille, P. L., & Sloane, P. J. (2006). *Disability, gender, and the British labour market*. Oxford Economic Papers-new Series.

Joshi, P. (2011, November 29). *Finding Good Apps for Children With Autism - NYTimes.com*. Retrieved March 8, 2014, from gadgetwise.blogs.nytimes.com/2011/11/29/finding-good-apps-for-children-with-autism/

Justin.tv Inc. (2014). *Watch Live Video*. Retrieved March 8, 2014, from http://www.justin.tv/

K12 Inc. (2014). *K12 | Online Public School, Online High School, Online Private School, Homeschooling, and Online Courses options*. Retrieved March 10, 2014, from http://www.k12.com/

Katz, A. (2012). Towards a Functional Licence for Open Hardware. *International Free and Open Source Software Law Review*, 41–62. doi:10.5033/ifosslr.v4i1.69

Katz, J. (2010, July 20). 9 online petition tools: How to make a difference. *Socialbrite*. Retrieved March 13, 2014, from http://www.socialbrite.org/2010/07/20/9-online-petition-tools-how-to-make-a-difference/

Keese, M. (2006). *Live longer, work longer*. Retrieved from http://www.oecd.org/employment/livelongerwork-longer.htm

Kelly, G. (2011, September 21). *Vuzix Wrap 1200 Video Eyewear review - Peripheral - Trusted Reviews*. Retrieved February 10, 2014, from http://www.trustedreviews.com/vuzix-wrap-1200-video-eyewear_Peripheral_review

Kelly, K. (2008, July 29). *The first 5,000 days of the web, and the next 5,000: Kevin Kelly on TED.com | TED Blog*. Retrieved February 7, 2014, from http://blog.ted.com/2008/07/29/the_first_5000/

Kenguru. (n.d.). *Kenguru - The car you have all been waiting for*. Retrieved March 9, 2014, from http://www.kengurucars.com/

Kerr, J. (2011, January 12). 5 Trends for Future of Radio. *Triton Digital*. Retrieved March 13, 2014, from http://www.tritondigital.com

Kessler, S. (2011, November 1). *Robot Invasion: Toyota Unveils Four Healthcare Assistants [PICS]*. Retrieved February 22, 2014, from http://mashable.com/2011/11/01/toyota-healthcare-robots/

Khronos Group. (2014). *OpenGL - The Industry Standard for High Performance Graphics*. Retrieved March 9, 2014, from http://www.opengl.org/

KIST. (n.d.). *KIST Korea Institiute of Science and Technologhy*. Retrieved March 14, 2014, from http://eng.kist.re.kr/kist_eng/main/

Knovel. (2012, March 5). *Engineers unveil new framework to enhance efficiency of energy harvesting devices*. Retrieved February 7, 2014, from http://why.knovel.com/all-engineering-news/1316-engineers-unveil-new-framework-to-enhance-efficiency-of-energy-harvesting-devices.html

Knowledge Adventure, Inc. (2014). *Fun Games for Kids | Free 3D Games Online | JumpStart*. Retrieved March 9, 2014, from http://www.jumpstart.com/

Ko, E., Ju, J. S., & Kim, E. Y. (2011). *Situation-based indoor wayfinding system for the visually impaired*. doi:10.1145/2049536.2049545

KQED Inc. (2014). *Children and Media | MindShift*. Retrieved March 10, 2014, from http://blogs.kqed.org/mindshift/feature/children-and-social-media/

Kraska, M. (2003). Postsecondary Students with Disabilities and Perceptions of Faculty Members. *The Journal for Vocational Special Needs Education*, 25(2), 11–19.

Kreutz, C. (2009, September 14). *Maptivism: Maps for activism, transparency and engagement*. Retrieved March 13, 2014, from http://www.crisscrossed.net/2009/09/14/maptivism-maps-for-activism-transparency-and-engagement/

Krishna, R. J. (2011, August 19). Indian Firm Launches $99 Android-Based Tablet. *Wall Street Journal*. Retrieved from http://online.wsj.com/news/articles/ SB100014240 531119036394 04576518122965650898?mg= reno64-wsj&url= http%3A%2F% 2Fonline.wsj. com%2 Farticle%2FSB 10001424053 111903639404 576518122965 650898.html# mod=djemWMPIndia_t

Kuipers, B. J. (n.d.). *Intelligent Wheelchair Resources*. Retrieved March 9, 2014, from http://www.cs.utexas.edu/~kuipers/wheelchair.html

Kumaran, U. (2011, April 1). *India's first call centre for the disabled launched in Chembur | Latest News & Updates at DNAIndia.com*. Retrieved March 10, 2014, from http://www.dnaindia.com/mumbai/report-india-s-first-call-centre-for-the-disabled-launched-in-chembur-1526860

Kuratate, T. (2011, July 11). Mask-bot: A robot with a human face. *Research & Development*. Retrieved March 13, 2014, from http://www.rdmag.com/ news/2011/11/mask-bot-robot-human-face

Kurzweil. (n.d.a). *Kurzweil 1000 | Assistive Technology for Vision Impaired*. Retrieved March 10, 2014, from http://www.kurzweiledu.com/kurzweil-1000-v12-windows.html

Kurzweil. (n.d.b). *Kurzweil 3000: Kurzweil Educational Systems*. Retrieved March 10, 2014, from http://www.kurzweiledu.com/products/k3000-win.html

Kurzweil. (n.d.c). *Text to Speech, Literacy Software | Kurzweil Educational Systems*. Retrieved March 10, 2014, from http://www.kurzweiledu.com/default.html

L' express. (2011, March 26). *Ces robots qui vont devenir vos meilleurs amis - L'EXPRESS*. Retrieved February 22, 2014, from http://videos.lexpress.fr/economie/ces-robots-qui-vont-devenir-vos-meilleurs-amis_1240903.html

Landshare. (n.d.). Landshare - connecting growers to people with land to share. *Landshare*. Retrieved March 11, 2014, from http://www.landshare.net/

Lasica, J. (2010a, July 6). Change-makers share 10 of their favorite tools. *Socialbrite*. Retrieved March 13, 2014, from http://www.socialbrite.org/2010/07/06/social-change-experts-share-10-favorite-tools/

Lasica, J. (2010b, August 10). Cool Gov 2.0 sites you don't know about. *Socialbrite*. Retrieved March 13, 2014, from http://www.socialbrite.org/2010/08/10/cool-gov-2-0-sites-you-dont-know-about/

Latré, B., Braem, B., Moerman, I., Blondia, C., & Demeester, P. (2011). A survey on wireless body area networks. *Wireless Networks*. doi:10.1007/s11276-010-0252-4

Learning, L. (2010). *Liberated Learning Project - Speech Recognition Technology in the Classroom - Halifax, Nova Scotia*. Retrieved March 10, 2014, from http://transcribeyourclass.ca/index.html

Learning, L. (2014). *Partners | Liberated Learning*. Retrieved March 10, 2014, from http://liberatedlearning.com/?page_id=99

Lee, A. (2010, February 1). *Interview: David Brown & Penny Standen | Platform Online*. Retrieved March 10, 2014, from http://platform-online.net/2010/02/interview-david-brown-penny-standen/

Lee, J.-A. (2011, November 23). Samsung in Final Talks on Google TV. *Wall Street Journal*. Retrieved from http://online.wsj.com/news/articles/ SB10001424052970204443404577053153432777594?mod=djemIndiaUpdate_h&mg=reno64-wsj&url=http%3A%2F%2Fonline.wsj.com%2Farticle%2FSB10001424052970204443404577053153432777594.html%3Fmod%3DdjemIndiaUpdate_h

LEGO Group. (2014). *LEGO.com Mindstorms*. Retrieved March 13, 2014, from http://www.lego.com/ en-us/mindstorms/ ?domainredir=mindstorms.lego.com

Lego mindstorm NXT Scorpion robot. (2007). Retrieved from http://www.youtube.com/watch?v=aec-YxOw-28&feature=youtube_gdata_player

LEGO. (n.d.). *LEGO.com Mindstorms*. Retrieved February 22, 2014, from http://www.lego.com/en-us/mindstorms/?domainredir=mindstorms.lego.com

Let's Play! Projects. (2004). *Welcome to the Let's Play Projects!* Retrieved March 9, 2014, from http://letsplay.buffalo.edu/index.html

Lewin, D., Adshead, S., Glennon, B., Williamson, B., Moore, T., Damodaran, L., & Hansell, P. (2010). *Assisted living technologies for older and disabled people in 2030*. Plum Consulting. Retrieved from http://www.plumconsulting.co.uk/ pdfs/Plum_June2010_Assisted_living_technologies_for_older_and_disabled_people_in_2030.pdf

Li, H., Takizawa, K., Zheri, B., & Kohno, R. (2007). Body Area Network and Its Standardization at IEEE 802.15. MBAN. *Mobile and Wireless Communications Summit, 2007. 16th IST*, 1-5. doi:10.1109/ISTMWC.2007.4299334

Libelium. (2013, January). *Libelium - Redes Sensoriales Inalámbricas - ZigBee - Mesh Networks | Libelium*. Retrieved February 7, 2014, from http://www.libelium.com/130220224710

Liberka. (2014). *libreka! Bücher & E-Books*. Retrieved March 13, 2014, from http://www.libreka.de/

Lifelog. (n.d.). *Wikipedia, the free encyclopedia*. Retrieved March 8, 2014, from http://en.wikipedia.org/wiki/Lifelog

Lifestreaming. (n.d.). *Wikipedia, the free encyclopedia*. Retrieved March 8, 2014, from http://en.wikipedia.org/wiki/Lifestreaming

Limb, C. (2010). *Your brain on improv*. Retrieved from http://www.ted.com/talks/charles_limb_your_brain_on_improv.html

Lim, H. H., Lenarz, M., & Lenarz, T. (2009). Auditory Midbrain Implant: A Review. *Trends in Amplification*. doi:10.1177/1084713809348372 PMID:19762428

Lin, K. H., Chang, C. H., Dopfer, A., & Wang, C. C. (2012). Mapping and Localization in 3D Environments Using a 2D Laser Scanner and a Stereo Camera. *Journal of Informaiton Science and Engineering*, *28*, 131–144.

LinkedIn. (2014). *World's Largest Professional Network | LinkedIn*. Retrieved March 10, 2014, from https://www.linkedin.com/

Lin, Y. C., Shieh, C. S., Tu, K. M., & Pan, J. S. (2012). Implementation of Indoor Positioning Using Signal Strength from Infrastructures. *Intelligent Information and Database Systems*, *7198*, 206–215. doi:10.1007/978-3-642-28493-9_23

Littlewort, G. C., Bartlett, M. S., Salamanca, L. P., & Reilly, J. (2011). *Automated measurement of children's facial expressions during problem solving tasks.* doi:10.1109/FG.2011.5771418

Living Social Inc. (2014). *LivingSocial - Save money while discovering amazing things to do.* Retrieved March 11, 2014, from https://www.livingsocial.com/

LOCO-Analyst. (2014). *LOCO-Analyst.* Retrieved March 10, 2014, from http://jelenajovanovic.net/LOCO-Analyst/

LOI n° 2005-102 du 11 février 2005 pour l'égalité des droits et des chances, la participation et la citoyenneté des personnes handicapées., 2005-102 (2005).

London Underground Weblog Blog. (2008, July 9). Retrieved March 13, 2014, from http://london-underground.blogspot.gr/2008/07/tube-map-for-disabled-developed-by.html

Looxcie, Inc. (2014). *Looxcie: Wearable Streaming Cameras for Consumers & Business.* Retrieved March 14, 2014, from http://www.looxcie.com/

Ltd, A. R. M. (2014). *ARM - The Architecture For The Digital World.* Retrieved March 13, 2014, from http://www.arm.com/

Lumosity. (n.d.). *Brain Games & Brain Training - Lumosity.* Retrieved March 10, 2014, from http://www.lumosity.com/

Mackenzie, A. (2010, October 2). *BBC News - Japan develops robotic seals to comfort sick and elderly.* Retrieved February 22, 2014, from http://www.bbc.co.uk/news/health-11459745

Macrae, F. (2011, November 23). *Terminator-style contact lenses will keep you up to date with news | Mail Online.* Retrieved March 8, 2014, from http://www.dailymail.co.uk/sciencetech/article-2064543/Terminator-style-contact-lenses-date-news.html?ito=feeds-newsxml

Macsai, D. (2010, March 30). *The Most Influential Women in Technology 2010 - Tan Le | Fast Company | Business + Innovation.* Retrieved March 8, 2014, from http://www.fastcompany.com/3017230/women-in-tech-2010/the-most-influential-women-in-technology-2010-tan-le

Mad Pride. (n.d.). *Wikipedia, the free encyclopedia.* Retrieved March 8, 2014, from http://en.wikipedia.org/wiki/Mad_Pride

Madan, V. (2011, May 16). *6 Reasons Tablets Are Ready for the Classroom.* Retrieved March 10, 2014, from http://mashable.com/2011/05/16/tablets-education/

Mak, J. N., Arbel, Y., Minett, J. W., McCane, L. M., Yuksel, B., Ryan, D., & Erdogmus, D. (2011). Optimizing the P300-based brain-computer interface: current status, limitations and future directions. *Journal of Neural Engineering.* doi:10.1088/1741-2560/8/2/025003 PMID:21436525

Mangu-Ward, K. (2011, August 10). *Robot Teachers Invade South Korea, Ruin Workers' Dance Party in Taiwan - Hit & Run : Reason.com.* Retrieved March 11, 2014, from http://reason.com/blog/2011/08/10/robot-teachers-invade-south-ko

Maps, Activism and Technology: Check-In's with a Purpose. (n.d.). *iRevolution.* Retrieved from http://irevolution.net/2011/02/05/check-ins-with-a-purpose/

Marcus, S. (2010, August 30). HOW TO: Respond when Social Media Attacks Your Brand. *Mashable.* Retrieved March 11, 2014, from http://mashable.com/2010/08/30/social-media-attacks-brand/

Marketwire. (2011, September 13). Select2gether Launches First Mobile Interactive Social Commerce Experience at DEMO Fall 2011. *Marketwire.* Retrieved March 11, 2014, from http://www.marketwired.com/press-release/-1560402.htm

Markoff, J. (2008, November 29). *You're Leaving a Digital Trail. What About Privacy? - NYTimes.com.* Retrieved March 8, 2014, from http://www.nytimes.com/2008/11/30/business/30privacy.html?th=&emc=th&pagewanted=all

Markoff, J. (2010, September 4). *Smarter Than You Think - The Boss Is Robotic, and Rolling Up Behind You - NYTimes.com.* Retrieved March 9, 2014, from http://www.nytimes.com/2010/09/05/science/05robots.html?_r=0

Marquis, J. (2011, September 8). *Using Social Media in the Higher Education Classroom - OnlineUniversities.com.* Retrieved March 10, 2014, from http://www.onlineuniversities.com/blog/2011/09/using-social-media-in-the-higher-education-classroom/

Mason, C. Y. (2010). *Co-Teaching with Technology: The Power of? 3?* Retrieved March 9, 2014, from http://www.edimprovement.org/wp-content/uploads/2010/09/Co-Teaching-with-Technology.pdf

Mathers, C. Fat, D. M., & Boerma, J. T. (2008). The global burden of disease: 2004 update. Geneva, Switzerland: World Health Organization.

McConkey, R. (2003). *Understanding and responding to children's needs in inclusive classrooms: A guide for teachers.* Paris: UNESCO.

McKinsey & Company. (2010, March). *The Internet of Things | McKinsey & Company.* Retrieved February 7, 2014, from http://www.mckinsey.com/insights/high_tech_telecoms_internet/the_internet_of_things

McKinsey & Company. (n.d.). *McKinsey & Company | Home Page.* Retrieved March 13, 2014, from http://www.mckinsey.com/

McNamee, R. (2011, November). *Roger McNamee: 6 ways to save the internet | Video on TED.com.* Retrieved February 7, 2014, from http://www.ted.com/talks/roger_mcnamee_six_ways_to_save_the_internet.html

MED-EL. (2013). *Cochlear Implants for Hearing Loss | MED-EL.* Retrieved March 8, 2014, from http://www.medel.com/

Meebo. (n.d.). *Meebo: More of What You Love.* Retrieved March 9, 2014, from https://www.meebo.com/

Meeker, M., Devitt, S., & Wu, L. (2010). *Internet Trends.* Retrieved from http://comunicaciondecrisis.wikispaces.com/file/view/Internet_Trends_041210+Morgan+Stanley.pdf/289548087/Internet_Trends_041210%20Morgan%20Stanley.pdf

Meetup. (2011, March 8). *Brussels Quantified Self Show and Tell 2011 #1 - Quantified Self Show&Tell Brussels (Brussels)- Meetup.* Retrieved March 8, 2014, from http://www.meetup.com/Quantified-Self-Show-Tell-Brussels/events/15876800/

Mehta, P., Kant, P., Shah, P., & Roy, A. K. (2011). *VI-Navi: a novel indoor navigation system for visually impaired people.* doi:10.1145/2023607.2023669

Meijer, C. J. (2003). *Inclusive Education and Classroom Practice.* Retrieved from http://www.european-agency.org/sites/default/files/iecp-en.pdf

Meijer, C. J. (2005). *Inclusive Education and Classroom Practice in Secondary Education.* Retrieved from http://www.european-agency.org/sites/default/files/iecp_secondary_en.pdf

Meijer, C. J. (2010, February). *Special Needs Education in Europe: Inclusive Policies and Practices | Meijer | Zeitschrift für Inklusion.* Retrieved March 9, 2014, from http://www.inklusion-online.net/index.php/inklusion-online/article/view/136/136

Meijer, Inc. (2014). *download Meijer mobile apps - Meijer and Meijer Pharmacy.* Retrieved March 9, 2014, from www.meijer.com/content/ content.jsp?pageName=mobile_app

Mental Health Foundation. (n.d.). *Mental Health Statistics: UK & Worldwide.* Retrieved March 8, 2014, from http://www.mentalhealth.org.uk/help-information/mental-health-statistics/UK-worldwide/

Mentoring Network for Equal Employment Opportunities. (2009). *M-NET EOP - what is m-net-eop.* Retrieved March 10, 2014, from http://www.mneteop.eu/

MercuryApp. (2014). *MercuryApp. | Track your feelings and make better decisions!* Retrieved March 8, 2014, from https://www.mercuryapp.com/

Micello, Inc. (2010). *Micello.* Retrieved March 9, 2014, from http://www.micello.com/

Michigan Disability Rights Coalition. (n.d.). *Economic Model of Disability | Michigan Disability Rights Coalition.* Retrieved March 13, 2014, from http://www.copower.org/models-of-disability/176-economic-model-of-disability.html

Microsoft. (2014a). *Home Page.* Retrieved March 13, 2014, from http://www.imaginecup.com/#?fbid=5XMH9y_J6bw

Micosoft. (2014b). *Inclusive Innovation Showroom Demonstrates Accessibility.* Retrieved March 13, 2014, from http://www.microsoft.com/enable/news/showroom.aspx

Microso. (2014). *Xbox | Games and Entertainment on All Your Devices - Xbox.com.* Retrieved March 11, 2014, from http://www.xbox.com/en-US/#fbid=fQIXuPAgqou

Microsoft. (2006, November 10). *Download DirectX Software Development Kit from Official Microsoft Download Center.* Retrieved March 9, 2014, from http://www.microsoft.com/en-us/download/details.aspx?id=9977

Microsoft. (2006, October 11). DirectX SDK - (October 2006). *Microsoft Download Center.* Retrieved March 11, 2014, from http://www.microsoft.com/en-us/download/details.aspx?id=9977

Microsoft. (2008). *Happy Disabled Call Center by the Foundation for Disabled People.* Retrieved from http://download.microsoft.com/download/4/2/5/42519e83-2902-4041-bc5f-0bc7ca51b8e9/fiziksel_engelliler_vak-fi_-_turkey.pdf

Microsoft. (2012, June 3). *Download Microsoft Robotics Developer Studio 4 from Official Microsoft Download Center.* Retrieved February 22, 2014, from http://www.microsoft.com/en-us/download/details.aspx?id=29081

Microsoft. (2012, June 3). RDS 4. *Microsoft Download Center.* Retrieved March 13, 2014, from http://www.microsoft.com/ en-us/download/details.aspx?id=29081

Microsoft. (2013). *Author: Archives.* Retrieved March 13, 2014, from http://www.microsoft.com/eu/author/bonniekearney.aspx

Microsoft. (2013). *Microsoft Games.* Retrieved March 10, 2014, from http://www.microsoft.com/games/

Microsoft. (2014). *MyLifeBits - Microsoft Research.* Retrieved March 8, 2014, from http://research.microsoft.com/en-us/projects/mylifebits/default.aspx

Microsoft. (2014). *The Business Value of Accessible Technology.* Retrieved March 10, 2014, from http://www.microsoft.com/enable/business/value.aspx

Microsoft. (2014). *Xbox Kinect | Full Body Gaming and Voice Control - Xbox.com.* Retrieved March 11, 2014, from http://www.xbox.com/en-US/kinect

Microsoft. (2014a). *Microsoft Accessibility Resource Centers.* Retrieved March 13, 2014, from http://www.microsoft.com/ enable/centers/marc.aspx

Microsoft. (2014a). *Skype - Free internet calls and online cheap calls to phones and mobiles.* Retrieved March 9, 2014, from http://www.skype.com/

Microsoft. (2014b). *Microsoft Accessibility: Technology for Everyone, Home.* Retrieved March 13, 2014, from http://www.microsoft.com/enable/

Microsoft. (2014b). *Microsoft Surface Tablets - The Windows Tablet That Does More.* Retrieved March 10, 2014, from http://www.microsoft.com/surface/en-US

Microsoft. (2014c). *Xbox Kinect | Full Body Gaming and Voice Control - Xbox.com.* Retrieved March 10, 2014, from http://www.xbox.com/en-US/kinect

Microsoft. (2014d). *Xbox | Games and Entertainment on All Your Devices - Xbox.com.* Retrieved March 10, 2014, from http://www.xbox.com/en-US/

Microsoft. (n.d.a). *Download DirectX Software Development Kit from Official Microsoft Download Center.* Retrieved February 10, 2014, from http://www.microsoft.com/en-us/download/details.aspx?id=9977

Microsoft. (n.d.b). *Kinect - Xbox.com.* Retrieved February 10, 2014, from http://www.xbox.com/en-US/kinect

Microsoft. (n.d.c). *Kinect for Windows | Voice, Movement & Gesture Recognition Technology.* Retrieved February 10, 2014, from http://www.microsoft.com/en-us/kinect-forwindows/

Microsoft. (n.d.d). *Microsoft Surface Tablets - The Windows Tablet That Does More.* Retrieved February 10, 2014, from http://www.microsoft.com/surface/en-US

Microsoft. (n.d.e). *Xbox Home Page | Games and Entertainment | Microsoft - Xbox.com.* Retrieved February 10, 2014, from http://www.xbox.com/

Millan, J., Rupp, R., Muller-Putz, G. R., Murray-Smith, R., Giugliemma, C., Tengermann, M., & Vidaurre, C. (2010). Combining brain? computer interfaces and assistive technologies: state-of-the-art and challenges. *Frontiers in Neuroscience.* Retrieved from http://journal.frontiersin.org/Journal/10.3389/fnins.2010.00161/abstract

Milliken, N. (2011, August 14). *Inclusivity Requires A Paradigm Shift | atrophiedmind.* Retrieved February 10, 2014, from http://atrophiedmind.wordpress.com/2011/08/14/inclusivity-requires-a-paradigm-shift/

Mindwalker. (2009). *MINDWALKER Project Portal? mindwalker-project*. Retrieved March 8, 2014, from https://mindwalker-project.eu/

Ministry of Economy. Trade and Industry. (2014, February 27). *Wikipedia, the free encyclopedia*. Retrieved from http://en.wikipedia.org/w/ index.php?title= Ministry_of_Economy,_Trade_and_Industry&oldid=589936000

Mistry, P. (2009, November). *Pranav Mistry: The thrilling potential of SixthSense technology | Video on TED.com*. Retrieved February 10, 2014, from http://www.ted.com/talks/pranav_mistry_the_thrilling_potential_of_sixthsense_technology.html

MIT AgeLab. (2013). *AGNES (Age Gain Now Empathy System) | MIT AgeLab*. Retrieved February 22, 2014, from http://agelab.mit.edu/agnes-age-gain-now-empathy-system

MIT Intelligent Wheelchair Project. (n.d.). *Intelligent Wheelchair Project at MIT*. Retrieved March 9, 2014, from http://rvsn.csail.mit.edu/wheelchair/

MIT News Office. (2011, December 19). *MIT launches online learning initiative - MIT News Office*. Retrieved March 10, 2014, from http://web.mit.edu/newsoffice/2011/mitx-education-initiative-1219.html

Miuro, the new music robot. (2006). Retrieved from http://www.youtube.com/ watch?v=gFxpuUMil 5U&feature=youtube_gdata_player

Mixpanel. (n.d.). *Mixpanel | Mobile Analytics*. Retrieved March 10, 2014, from https://mixpanel.com/

MobiThinking. (2013, December). *Global mobile statistics 2013 Home: all the latest stats on mobile Web, apps, marketing, advertising, subscribers, and trends. | mobiThinking*. Retrieved February 10, 2014, from http://mobithinking.com/mobile-marketing-tools/latest-mobile-stats#subscribers

Mogul Mom. (2014). *The Mogul Mom | For moms running a business, raising a family and rocking both*. Retrieved March 10, 2014, from www.themogulmom.com/

Mom Invented. (2014). *Mom Invented: Business Advice & Inventing Help for Women Entrepreneurs*. Retrieved March 10, 2014, from http://www.mominventors.com/

Monitoring eAccessibility. (n.d.). *Monitoring eAccessibility*. Retrieved February 7, 2014, from http://www.eaccessibility-monitoring.eu/

Moodscope Ltd. (2014). *Moodscope - Lift your mood with a little help from your friends*. Retrieved March 8, 2014, from https://www.moodscope.com/

Moyer, C. S. (2010, November 15). *Cyberbullying a high-tech health risk for young patients - amednews.com*. Retrieved March 10, 2014, from http://www.amednews.com/article/20101115/profession/311159961/2/

Multiplemonitors.org. (n.d.). *Multiple Monitors dot Org | Multi Monitor Video Wall Collective & Blog*. Retrieved February 10, 2014, from http://www.multiplemonitors.org/

MUNDUS. (2010). *Home*. Retrieved March 8, 2014, from http://www.mundus-project.eu/

Murray, J. (2011, September 8). Square vs. Google Wallet: Who will win the mobile payment war? *Anthill Online*. Retrieved from http://anthillonline.com/square-vs-google-wallet-who-will-win-the-mobile-payment-war/

Murray, P. (2011, October 25). *South Korea Says Good-Bye To Print Textbooks, Plans To Digitize Entire Curriculum By 2015 (video) | Singularity Hub*. Retrieved March 10, 2014, from http://singularityhub.com/2011/10/25/south-korea-says-good-bye-to-print-textbooks-plans-to-digitize-entire-curriculum-by-2015-video/

My Robot is Better Than Your Robot. (2011). Retrieved from http://www.youtube.com/ watch?v=vYuOK b3gO7E&feature= youtube_gdata_player

MySociety Limited. (n.d.). *mySociety*. Retrieved March 13, 2014, from http://www.mysociety.org/

NamingForce.com. (2014). Naming Force - business name contests. *Naming Force*. Retrieved March 11, 2014, from http://www.namingforce.com/

Nao 1337 Audition on Vimeo. (2012). Retrieved from http://vimeo.com/24947744

NAO Charging Station Prototype. (2011, March 8). Retrieved from http://youtu.be/0xHaxTM7KH8

NAO Humanoid Robot is Going to Open Source. (2011, May). Retrieved from http://www.ubuntubuzz. com/2011/05/nao-humanoid-robot-is-going-to-open.html

NASA. (2011, August 1). *Robotics Alliance Project.* Retrieved March 13, 2014, from http://frc-grants.arc. nasa.gov /rcs/directions.php

National Geographic Society and Smart Bomb Interactive, Inc. (2013). *Animal Jam - Animal Jam - Meet friends, adopt pets, and play wild!* Retrieved March 9, 2014, from http://www.animaljam.com/

National Instruments. (2014). *NI LabVIEW - Improving the Productivity of Engineers and Scientists - National Instruments.* Retrieved February 22, 2014, from http:// www.ni.com/labview/

National Science Foundation. (n.d.a). *ROAR - Games.* Retrieved March 10, 2014, from http://gameslab.radford. edu/ROAR/games.html

Neigborrow. (n.d.). *Need to use something short term.* Retrieved March 11, 2014, from http://beta.neighbor-row.com/

Networld Media Group. (2014). *ATM / Automated Teller Machine business news, research, more | ATM Marketplace.* Retrieved March 11, 2014, from http://www. atmmarketplace.com/

Neurodiversity. (n.d.). *Wikipedia, the free encyclopedia.* Retrieved March 8, 2014, from http://en.wikipedia.org/ wiki/Neurodiversity

Neurogadget. (2011, April 22). *Video: Text Editor for Disabled People Using NeuroSky Mindset | Neurogadget. com.* Retrieved March 8, 2014, from http://neurogadget. com/2011/04/22/video-text-editor-for-disabled-people-using-neurosky-mindset/1939

Neurotycho. (n.d.). *Welcome to Neurotycho! | neurotycho. org.* Retrieved March 8, 2014, from http://neurotycho.org/

New Media Consortium EDUCAUSE (Association). (2011). *The horizon report: 2011 ed.* Retrieved from http:// www.nmc.org/pdf/2011-Horizon-Report.pdf

New Media Consortium. (2012). *NMC Horizon Report > 2012 Higher Education Ed.* Retrieved from http://www. nmc.org/pdf/2012-horizon-report-HE.pdf

New York Times. (2011, November 29). *Apps for Autistic Children - NYTimes.com.* Retrieved March 8, 2014, from parenting.blogs.nytimes.com/2011/11/29/apps-for-autistic-children/?_php=true&_type=blogs&_r=0

Newswire, P. R. (2011, March 3). *The Dealmap and Microsoft Collaborate to Bring Local and Daily Deals. -- MENLO PARK, Calif., March 3, 2011 /PRNewswire/.* Retrieved March 11, 2014, from http://www.prnewswire. com/news-releases/the-dealmap-and-microsoft-collaborate-to-bring-local-and-daily-deals-to-bing-117323418. html

Next Big Future. (2012, February 22). *Swimming through the blood stream: Stanford engineers create wireless, self-propelled medical device.* Retrieved February 7, 2014, from http://nextbigfuture.com/2012/02/swimming-through-blood-stream-stanford.html

NIBEye. (n.d.). *NIBEye: Home.* Retrieved March 13, 2014, from http://dev.nsta.org/evwebs/4150A/index.html

Nike Inc. (2014). *Nike+.* Retrieved March 8, 2014, from https://secure-nikeplus.nike.com/plus/#//dashboard/

Nirenberg, S. (2011). *A prosthetic eye to treat blindness.* Retrieved from http://www.ted.com/talks/sheila_ nirenberg_a_prosthetic_eye_to_treat_blindness.html

Nuance. (n.d.a). *Dragon - Dragon NaturallySpeaking - Nuance - Nuance.* Retrieved February 10, 2014, from http://www.nuance.com/dragon/index.htm

Nuance. (n.d.b). *Swype | Type Fast, Swype Faster.* Retrieved February 10, 2014, from http://www.swype.com/

Nurse Next Door Home Care Franchise. (2014). *Nurse Next Door Home Care Franchise? Home Health Care Franchising Opportunity.* Retrieved March 10, 2014, from http://www.nursenextdoorfranchise.com/

Nurse Next Door. (2011). *Growing Carepreneurs: 2011 Annual Conference.* Retrieved March 10, 2014, from https://www.facebook.com/media/set/?set=a.10150375 808544668.373474.92317029667&type=3

NYC Department of Education. (n.d.). *iZone NYC.* Retrieved March 10, 2014, from http://izonenyc.org/

NYC Toilet Map | Toilet Radar. (n.d.). Retrieved March 13, 2014, from http://www.toiletradar.com/map

O' Brien, D. (2011, February 10). *Brain Training Games for Seniors: Looking for the best brain training app. | SharpBrains*. Retrieved March 10, 2014, from http://sharpbrains.com/blog/2011/02/10/brain-training-games-for-seniors-looking-for-the-best-brain-training-app/

OGC. (n.d.). *Sensor Web Enablement DWG | OGC(R)*. Retrieved February 7, 2014, from http://www.opengeo-spatial.org/projects/groups/sensorwebdwg

Oliver, M. (1996). *Understanding Disability: From Theory to Practice*. Palgrave Macmillan.

Online Directory. (n.d.). *Information on Disabilities - Online Directory*. Retrieved March 11, 2014, from http://www.disabilities-online.com/index.php?viewCat=7

Open University. (2014a). *Distance Learning Courses and Adult Education - The Open University*. Retrieved March 10, 2014, from http://www.open.ac.uk/

Open University. (2014b, February 4). *Services for Disabled Students - Study Support - Open University*. Retrieved March 10, 2014, from http://www2.open.ac.uk/study/support/disability/orientation

Open, G. L. (n.d.). *OpenGL - The Industry Standard for High Performance Graphics*. Retrieved February 10, 2014, from http://www.opengl.org/

Open311. (n.d.). *Open311*. Retrieved from http://open311.org/

OpenIDEO. (n.d.). OpenIDEO - Home. *OpenIDEO*. Retrieved March 13, 2014, from http://www.openideo.com/

OpenStreetMap. (n.d.). *OpenStreetMap*. Retrieved March 13, 2014, from http://www.openstreetmap.org/#map=5/51.500/-0.100

Oracle. (2013). *Java 3D Parent Project — Project Kenai*. Retrieved February 10, 2014, from https://java3d.java.net/

Oracle. (2013). *Java 3D Parent Project — Project Kenai*. Retrieved March 11, 2014, from https://java3d.java.net/

Organisation for Economic Co-operation and Development. (2006). *Sickness, disability, and work: Breaking the barriers*. Retrieved from http://www.oecd-ilibrary.org/social-issues-migration-health/sickness-disability-and-work-breaking-the-barriers_9789264088856-en

Organisation for Economic Co-operation and Development. (2012). *Sick on the job? A myths and realities about mental health and work*. Retrieved from http://www.oecd-ilibrary.org/social-issues-migration-health/mental-health-and-work_9789264124523-en

Origin Instruments Corporation. (2011). *HeadMouse® Extreme [HM-0204-SP]: Shop at Origin Instruments*. Retrieved March 10, 2014, from http://shop.orin.com/shop/index.php?main_page=product_info&products_id=1

Origin Instruments Corporation. (2013). *Sip/Puff Switch*. Retrieved March 10, 2014, from http://www.orin.com/access/sip_puff/

Origin Instruments Corporation. (2014). *Origin Instruments Corporation*. Retrieved March 10, 2014, from http://www.orin.com/

Osborne, B. (2008, April 25). *Microsoft issues Robo-Champs challenge | Gadgets | Geek.com*. Retrieved March 14, 2014, from http://www.geek.com/gadgets/microsoft-issues-robochamps-challenge-574397/

Osborne, C. (2012, March 7). Vocre's live translation video tool breaks language barriers. *SmartPlanet*. Retrieved March 13, 2014, from http://www.smartplanet.com/blog/smart-takes/vocres-live-translation-video-tool-breaks-language-barriers/23887

Osburn, C. (2008, March 6). Accessing Wheelchair Accessible London? *Londonist*. Retrieved March 13, 2014, from http://londonist.com/2008/03/accessing_wheel.php

Ottobock. (2014). *Ottobock - Home*. Retrieved March 13, 2014, from http://professionals.ottobockus.com/cps/rde/xchg/ob_us_en/hs.xsl/index.html

Pachal, P. (2011, December 9). *Will Apple iTV Trade the Remote for Kinect-Like Control?* Retrieved March 10, 2014, from http://mashable.com/2011/12/09/apple-itv-gestures/

Pappas, S. (2011, May 10). *Machine that feels is key to 'Jedi' prosthetics - Technology & science - Science - LiveScience | NBC News*. Retrieved March 8, 2014, from http://www.nbcnews.com/id/44789955/ns/technology_and_science-science/t/machine-feels-called-key-jedi-prosthetics/#.UxtjcvmSzal

Parkour. (2014, March 9). *Wikipedia, the free encyclopedia*. Retrieved from http://en.wikipedia.org/w/index.php ?title=Parkour&oldid=598815016

PARO. (2014). *Paro Therapeutic Robot*. Retrieved February 22, 2014, from http://www.parorobots.com/

Participatory Action Research. (n.d.). *Wikipedia, the free encyclopedia*. Retrieved March 10, 2014, from http://en.wikipedia.org/wiki/Participatory_action_research

Patch clamp. (n.d.). *Wikipedia, the free encyclopedia*. Retrieved March 8, 2014, from http://en.wikipedia.org/wiki/Patch_clamp

Patel, N. (2011, November 3). Google Offers Android app. now in Market. *The Verge*. Retrieved March 11, 2014, from http://www.theverge.com/2011/11/3/2535367/google-offers-android-app

Pauli Murray Project. (n.d.). *Mapping Civil & Human Activism – Live Now | Pauli Murray Project*. Retrieved March 13, 2014, from http://paulimurrayproject.org/mapping-civil-human-activism-live-now/

Perera, N., Kennedy, G. E., & Pearce, J. M. (2008). *Are you bored? Maybe an interface agent can help*. doi:10.1145/1517744.1517760

Perry, J. (2009, November 20). *Social media: Why M&S is listening to the word on the web*. Retrieved March 11, 2014, from http://www.retail-week.com/social-media-why-ms-is-listening-to-the-word-on-the-web/5008089.article

Persyn, J. (2006, April 10). *jurriaanpersyn.com — Designing 'Autism-friendly' websites, principles and guidelines*. Retrieved March 8, 2014, from http://www.jurriaanpersyn.com/archives/2006/04/10/designing-autism-friendly-websites-principles-and-guidelines/

Philadelphia, D. (2008, September 15). *Business school retrains disabled Iraq veterans - Sep. 15, 2008*. Retrieved March 10, 2014, from http://money.cnn.com/2008/09/11/smallbusiness/bschool_to_iraq.fsb/index.htm

Phonak Hearing Systems. (n.d.). *Phonak Hearing Systems - life is on*. Retrieved March 8, 2014, from http://www.phonak.com/

Pine, B. J. (1999). *Mass Customization: The New Frontier in Business Competition*. Harvard Business Press.

Plasticpals. (2010, February 22). *South Korea: Robot Teachers Rolling Out in 2012*. Retrieved from http://www.plasticpals.com/?p=21283

Platform Europe, A. G. E. (2014). *Home | AGE Platform Europe*. Retrieved March 13, 2014, from http://www.age-platform.org/

Platform, A. G. E. (2008). *Older people and Information and Communication Technologies: An Ethical approach*. Retrieved from http://www.age-platform.eu/images/stories/EN/pdf_AGE-ethic_A4-final.pdf

Playgen.com. (2012). *FloodSim | PlayGen*. Retrieved March 10, 2014, from http://playgen.com/play/floodsim/

Plus, H. (n.d.). 홈플러스 인터넷 쇼핑몰 : *e-*생활에 플러스가 됩니다. Retrieved March 11, 2014, from http://www.homeplus.co.kr/app.exhibition.main.Main.ghs?paper_no=category

PRIME. (2008, September 29). *PRIME - Privacy and Identity Management for Europe — Portal for the PRIME Project*. Retrieved February 7, 2014, from https://www.prime-project.eu/

Private Television in Europe. (n.d.). *Is there a future for private television?*. Author.

Propeller Health. (2013). *Propeller Health - The leading mobile platform for respiratory health management*. Retrieved March 8, 2014, from http://propellerhealth.com/

Prosopagnosia. (n.d.). *Wikipedia, the free encyclopedia*. Retrieved March 8, 2014, from http://en.wikipedia.org/wiki/Prosopagnosia

PRWEB. (2012, March 5). *Global Smart Sensors Market to Reach US$6.7 Billion by 2017, According to New Report by Global Industry Analysts, Inc*. Retrieved February 7, 2014, from http://www.prweb.com/releases/smart_sensors/flow_pressure_sensors/prweb9251955.htm

PRWeb. (n.d.). Class Action Lawsuit Against Disney Alleges Inaccessible Websites and Failure to Accommodate Blind Persons in Violation of ADA, Case No. 10-cv-5810. *PRWeb*. Retrieved March 13, 2014, from http://www.prweb.com/releases/2011/02/prweb5073794.htm

Purewal, S. J. (2010, October 12). *Two Google Apps Help Blind Navigate | TechHive*. Retrieved March 9, 2014, from http://www.techhive.com/ article/207500/Two_Google_Apps_Helps_Blind_Navigate.html

Qing, L. Y. (2011, October 5). *India to debut $45 Android tablet for education | ZDNet*. Retrieved March 10, 2014, from http://www.zdnet.com/india-to-debut-45-android-tablet-for-education-2062302369/

Quantified Self Labs. (2011). *Quantified Self Guide*. Retrieved March 8, 2014, from http://quantifiedself.com/guide/

Quantified Self Labs. (2012). *Quantified Self | Self Knowledge Through NumbersQuantified Self | Self Knowledge Through Numbers*. Retrieved March 8, 2014, from http://quantifiedself.com/

Queen Elizabeth's Foundation for Disabled People. (2014). *Residential care for disabled people | Queen Elizabeth's Foundation for Disabled People*. Retrieved March 10, 2014, from http://qef.org.uk/our-services/

Quinn, K. (2010). Methodological Considerations in Surveys of Older Adults: Technology Matters. *International Journal of Emerging Technologies and Society*, *8*(2), 114–133.

Rains, S. (2011, April 26). *Notes from the First-ever International Blind Architects Conference - Part 1 - Rolling Rains Report*. Retrieved March 10, 2014, from http://www.rollingrains.com/2011/04/notes-from-the-first-ever-international-blind-architects-conference.html

Raising the Floor. (2011). *Components of the GPII | gpii.net*. Retrieved February 7, 2014, from http://gpii.net/components

Ranker. (2014). Top 10 Lists & Much More - The Best Lists About Everything. *Ranker*. Retrieved March 12, 2014, from http://www.ranker.com/

Rao, L. (2011a, May 23). Square's Disruptive New iPad Payments Service Will Replace Cash Registers. *TechCrunch*. Retrieved from http://techcrunch.com/2011/05/23/squares-disruptive-new-ipad-payments-service-will-replace-cash-registers/

Rao, L. (2011b, July 31). Square Now Processing $4 Million In Mobile Payments Per Day. *TechCrunch*. Retrieved from http://techcrunch.com/2011/07/31/square-now-processing-4-million-in-mobile-payments-per-day/

Raskind, M., & Stanberry, K. (n.d.). *Assistive technology for kids with learning disabilities: An overview - Assistive technology | GreatSchools*. Retrieved March 9, 2014, from http://www.greatschools.org/special-education/assistive-technology/702-assistive-technology-for-kids-with-learning-disabilities-an-overview.gs

Raspberry Pi. (n.d.). *Raspberry Pi | An ARM GNU/Linux box for $25. Take a byte!* Retrieved March 13, 2014, from http://www.raspberrypi.org/

Rathore, A., & Valverde, R. (2011). An RFID based E-commerce solution for the implementation of secure unattended stores. *Journal of Emerging Trends in Computing and Information Sciences*, *2*(8), 376–389.

Ray Kuzweil at the MIT/XPrize BCI workshop. (2010). Retrieved from http://www.youtube.com/ watch?v=15sh05wrQ6Y&feature= youtube_gdata_player

Raytheon. (2003). *Raytheon Company: Customer Success Is Our Mission*. Retrieved February 22, 2014, from http://www.raytheon.com/

Raytheon. (2014). *Raytheon Company: Businesses*. Retrieved February 22, 2014, from http://www.raytheon.com/ourcompany/businesses/

RB3D. (2011). *RB3D, solution mécatronique de prévention des TMS*. Retrieved February 22, 2014, from http://www.rb3d.com/

RB3D. (2011). *RB3D, solution mécatronique de prévention des TMS*. Retrieved March 9, 2014, from http://www.rb3d.com/

RECALL KA3 LLL Project. (2012). *RECALL - KA3 project*. Retrieved March 10, 2014, from http://recall-project.eu/

Redmond, W. (2011, August 3). *Dressing for the Future: Microsoft Duo Breaks Through with Wearable Technology Concept*. Retrieved March 8, 2014, from http://www.microsoft.com/en-us/news/features/2011/aug11/08-03printingdress.aspx

Reed, R. (2010, July 29). 10 ways geolocation is changing the world. *Socialbrite*. Retrieved March 13, 2014, from http://www.socialbrite.org/2010/07/29/10-ways-geolocation-is-changing-the-world/

Reemploy. (2014). *Remploy | Home*. Retrieved March 10, 2014, from http://www.remploy.co.uk/

Research, A. B. I. (2012). *Body Area Networks for Sports and Healthcare | ABI Research*. Retrieved from https://www.abiresearch.com/research/product/1005246-body-area-networks-for-sports-and-healthca/

Retail, I. (2011). *Imagine Retail Management System - Software for Footwear and Apparel Stores*. Retrieved March 11, 2014, from http://imagineretail.com/index.asp

Retina France. (n.d.). *Retina France - Accueil*. Retrieved March 8, 2014, from http://www.retina.fr/

Retina Implant. (n.d.). *Homepage -www.retina-implant. de. Retrieved March 8, 2014, from http://rctina-implant.de/default.aspx

Review, H. B. (2008, July). *A Field Is Born - Harvard Business Review*. Retrieved March 10, 2014, from http://hbr.org/2008/07/a-field-is-born/ar/1

Rick Hansen Foundation. (2014). *Rick Hansen Foundation > Home*. Retrieved March 13, 2014, from http://www.rickhansen.com/

Riken. (2011, August 2). *RIBA-II, the next generation care-giving robot | RIKEN*. Retrieved March 8, 2014, from http://www.riken.jp/en/pr/press/2011/20110802_2/

Riley, B. (2011). *A garden in my apartment*. Retrieved from http://www.ted.com/talks/ britta_riley_a_garden_in_my_apartment

Rio Tinto. (n.d.). *Home - Rio Tinto*. Retrieved March 9, 2014, from http://www.riotinto.com/

Riverdocs Bureau Service. (2011). *Corporate Intranets - web accessibility legal briefs - from Outlaw.com*. Retrieved March 10, 2014, from http://riverdocs.com/accessibility/legal/corporate_intranets.html

Riversimple, L. L. P. (2014). *Riversimple - home*. Retrieved March 13, 2014, from http://www.riversimple.com/

Robopec. (2010). *Robopec - Conception et réalisation de systèmes mécatroniques et de leur intelligence embarquée et développement logiciel*. Retrieved March 9, 2014, from http://www.robopec.com/

Robot Film Festival. (n.d.). Retrieved February 22, 2014, from http://robotfilmfestival.com/

Robots Dreams. (2011a, April 1). *GOSTAI JAZZ Telepresence Robot at InnoRobo 2011*. [Video file]. Retrieved from https://www.youtube.com/ watch?v=T7ya6JOAbp0

Robots Dreams. (2011b, March 29). *Le REETI - Expressive Robot from robopec*. [Video file]. Retrieved from https://www.youtube.com/ watch?v=3A8KRch-tR0

Robots Dreams. (2011c, March 30). *Robbixa Female Robot at InnoRobo 2011*. [Video file]. Retrieved from https://www.youtube.com/ watch?v=4PYxRnQnxow

Rock, M. (n.d.). *Half of U.S. Use Social Networks, Older Population Catching Up | Mobiledia*. Retrieved March 8, 2014, from http://www.mobiledia.com/news/105257.html

Rock, M. (n.d.). New Touch Screens Allow Blind to Read Braille. *Mobiledia*. Retrieved from http://www.mobiledia.com/news/97666.html

Rothwell, C. (2011, January 20). *About NCHS - Homepage*. Retrieved March 8, 2014, from http://www.cdc.gov/nchs/about.htm

Russel, C. (2013, March 25). *Selecting Assessment Technologies | UNSW Teaching Staff Gateway*. Retrieved March 10, 2014, from http://teaching.unsw.edu.au/assessment-technologies

Sachs, D., & Schreuer, N. (2011). Inclusion of Students with Disabilities in Higher Education: Performance and participation in student's experiences. *Disability Studies Quarterly, 31*(2). PMID:21966179

Saenz, A. (2009, January 12). *Deka's Luke Arm In Clinical Trials, Is it the Future of Prosthetics? (Video) | Singularity Hub*. Retrieved March 8, 2014, from http://singularityhub.com/2009/12/01/dekas-luke-arm-in-clinical-trials-is-it-the-future-of-prosthetics-video/

Saenz, A. (2010, January 20). iWalk Presents World's First Actively Powered Foot and Ankle. *Singularity Hub*. Retrieved March 13, 2014, from http://singularityhub.com/ 2010/01/20/iwalk-presents-worlds-first-actively-powered-foot-and-ankle/

Saenz, A. (2010, November 2). *A Robot in Every Korean Kindergarten by 2013? | Singularity Hub*. Retrieved March 9, 2014, from http://singularityhub.com/2010/11/02/a-robot-in-every-korean-kindergarten-by-2013/

Sam's West, Inc. (2010). *Sam's Club Mobile - Home*. Retrieved March 9, 2014, from www3.samsclub.com/mobile

Samsung. (2014). *Samsung US | TVs - Tablets - Smartphones - Cameras - Laptops - Refrigerators*. Retrieved March 11, 2014, from http://www.samsung.com/us/

Sanders, L. (2010, November 15). *Retinal Implant Restores Vision in Blind Mice - Wired Science*. Retrieved March 8, 2014, from http://www.wired.com/wiredscience/2010/11/blind-vision-implant/

SARTRE-Consortium. (n.d.). *The SARTRE project*. Retrieved March 9, 2014, from http://www.sartre-project.eu/ en/Sidor/default.aspx

Savitha. (2014, December 20). Disabled Can Use Computers With Gesture Recognition System. *MedIndia*. Retrieved from http://www.medindia.net/news/Disabled-Can-Use-Computers-With-Gesture-Recognition-System-45409-1.htm

Schaffhauser, D. (2010, June 29). *Department of Ed Lays Down Law on Kindle E-Reader Usage -- Campus Technology*. Retrieved March 13, 2014, from http://campustechnology.com/articles/2010/06/29/department-of-ed-lays-down-law-on-kindle-e-reader-usage.aspx

School of One. (n.d.). *Wikipedia, the free encyclopedia*. Retrieved March 10, 2014, from http://en.wikipedia.org/wiki/School_of_one

School of Piano Technology for the Blind. (2014). *Careers for the Blind and Visually Impaired*. Retrieved March 10, 2014, from http://pianotuningschool.org/

Schreuer, N., Rimmerman, A., & Sachs, D. (2006). Adjustment to severe disability: Constructing and examining a cognitive and occupational performance model. *International Journal of Rehabilitation Research. Internationale Zeitschrift fur Rehabilitationsforschung. Revue Internationale de Recherches de Readaptation*. doi:10.1097/01. mrr.0000210053.40162.13 PMID:16900040

Schwartz, A. (2009, August 3). *Smart Cane Makes it Easy for the Blind to Get Around | Fast Company | Business + Innovation*. Retrieved March 9, 2014, from http://www.fastcompany.com/ 1323616/smart-cane-makes-it-easy-blind-get-around

Schwartz, A. (2010, December 15). Samsung Snags Willow Garage's PR2 Robot. *Fast Company*. Retrieved March 11, 2014, from http://www.fastcompany.com/1710096/samsung-snags-willow-garages-pr2-robot

SCNF. (n.d.). *Accessibilité SNCF - Site Internet de la délégation à l'accessibilité et aux voyageurs handicapés*. Retrieved March 12, 2014, from http://www.accessibilite.sncf.com/

Scott Rains. (2011, September 17). *KAO on Universal Design*. Technology. Retrieved from http://www.slideshare.net/srains/kao-on-universal-design

Scuola Superiore Sant' Anna. (2014, January 28). *Scuola Superiore Sant' Anna - Istituto TeCIP*. Retrieved February 22, 2014, from www.sssup.it/ist_home.jsp?ID_LINK=10509&area=199

Second Life Wiki. (n.d.). *Second Life Education - Second Life Wiki*. Retrieved February 10, 2014, from http://wiki.secondlife.com/wiki/Second_Life_Education

Second Sight. (2013). *Mission*. Retrieved March 8, 2014, from http://2-sight.eu/en/home-en

SeeClickFix, Inc. (2013). Report non-emergency issues, receive alerts in your neighborhood. *SeeClickFix*. Retrieved March 13, 2014, from http://seeclickfix.com/introductions/home

Seelye, K. Q. (2011, November 16). Oregon Tries Out Voting by iPad for Disabled. *The New York Times*. Retrieved from http://www.nytimes.com/2011/11/17/us/oregon-tries-out-voting-by-ipad-for-disabled.html

Segway Inc. (2014). *Segway Personal Transporters for Individuals*. Retrieved March 9, 2014, from http://www.segway.com/individual

Segway. (2003). *The iBOT*. Retrieved March 9, 2014, from https://www.msu.edu/~luckie/segway/iBOT/iBOT.html

Senseg. (2011). *Senseg*. Retrieved March 10, 2014, from http://senseg.com/

Service Dog Central. (2013). *How was the definition of service animal changed July 23, 2010? | Service Dog Central*. Retrieved March 9, 2014, from http://www.servicedogcentral.org/ content/changes

Sharpio, L. (2011, November 16). Sony's 3D Headset: Virtual Reality Goes Mainstream. *Sound and Vision*. Retrieved from http://www.soundandvision.com/content/sonys-3d-headset-virtual-reality-goes-mainstream

Shelf, X. (2013). www.shelfx.com. Retrieved from http://www.shelfx.com/

Silicon Micro Display. (2012). ST1080 features, 1080p hmd features, hmd specs | SiliconMicroDisplay, Silicon Micro Display, SMD. *Silicon Micro Display*. Retrieved March 11, 2014, from http://www.siliconmicrodisplay.com/st1080-features.html

SimplyRaydeen. (2009, April 9). *Facebook - Accessibility*. Retrieved March 10, 2014, from http://www.simplyraydeen.com/faq/48-web-site-accessibility/71-facebook-works-with-the-blind-on-accessibility

Singularity Hub. (2010, July 20). *Your Entire Life Recorded – Lifelogging Goes Mainstream | Singularity Hub*. Retrieved March 8, 2014, from http://singularityhub.com/2010/07/20/your-entire-life-recorded-lifelogging-goes-mainstream/

Slavin, R. (2011, December 8). *How Education Innovation Can Thrive at Scale - Sputnik - Education Week*. Retrieved March 10, 2014, from http://blogs.edweek.org/edweek/sputnik/2011/12/how_education_innovation_can_thrive_at_scale.html?cmp=ENL-EU-VIEWS2

Sloan, K. (2010, October 11). *Wisconsin judge overcomes hearing impairment | National Law Journal*. Retrieved March 10, 2013, from http://www.nationallawjournal.com/id=1202473099157?slreturn=20140210140521

Smith, K. (2011, September 5). *Mental disorders affect more than a third of Europeans: Nature News*. Retrieved March 8, 2014, from http://www.nature.com/news/2011/110905/full/news.2011.514.html

Soares, C. (2007, November 23). *Move over Poirot: Belgium recruits blind detectives to help fight crime - Europe - World - The Independent*. Retrieved March 10, 2014, from http://www.independent.co.uk/news/world/europe/move-over-poirot-belgium-recruits-blind-detectives-to-help-fight-crime-760087.html

Sobocki, P., Jonsson, B., Angst, J., & Rehnberg, C. (2006). Cost of depression in Europe. *The Journal of Mental Health Policy and Economics*, 9(2), 87–98. PMID:17007486

Social Innovation Camp. (n.d.). Map of disabled access for the UK. *Social Innovation Camp*. Retrieved from http://sicamp.org/si-camp-uk/previous-camps/submitted-ideas/map-of-disabled-access-for-the-uk/

Social, T. V. Forum. (2014). *Social TV Forum - TV Apps Hackathon, Social TV Events*. Retrieved March 12, 2014, from http://www.social-tv.net/

Socialbrite. (n.d.). Socialbrite. *Socialbrite*. Retrieved March 13, 2014, from http://www.socialbrite.org

Socrato. (2013). *Learning Analytics and Test Scoring Software | Socrato*. Retrieved March 10, 2014, from http://www.socrato.com/

Sony Qrio. (2009, May 2). Retrieved from http://youtu.be/O8BFVLb-6IQ

SONY. (1998, June 10). *Sony Global - Press Release - Sony Develops OPEN-R Architecture for Entertainment Robots Demonstrates 4-legged robot prototypes based on the architecture*. Retrieved February 22, 2014, from http://www.sony.net/SonyInfo/News/Press_Archive/199806/98-052/

Sony. (n.d.). *Head Mounted Display - Personal 3D HDTV Viewer - HMZ-T3W Review - Sony US*. Retrieved February 10, 2014, from http://store.sony.com/wearable-hdtv-2d-3d-virtual-7.1-surround-sound-zid27-HMZT3W/cat-27-catid-3D-Personal-Viewer,pgid=rHRaIrP3UbxSRpRBmHdDPVWB0000bbXsVyFV?_t=pfm%3Dsearch%26SearchTerm%3DHMZ

SoundOut. (2012). *Student Activism Map*. Retrieved March 13, 2014, from http://www.soundout.org/activism.html

SOZIALHELDEN.e.V. (n.d.). *Einfach mal machen! - SOZIALHELDEN e.V.* Retrieved March 13, 2014, from http://www.sozialhelden.de/

Speech Synthesis. (n.d.). *Wikipedia, the free encyclopedia.* Retrieved February 10, 2014, from http://en.wikipedia.org/wiki/Text-To-Speech

Speech, F. X. Inc. (2013). *SpeechFX Inc Home Page.* Retrieved March 10, 2014, from http://www.speechfxinc.com/

Speedmatters.org. (n.d.). *Enabling People With Disabilities | Speed Matters - Internet Speed Test.* Retrieved February 7, 2014, from http://www.speedmatters.org/benefits/archive/enabling_people_with_disabilities/

Spletzer, J. R. (n.d.). *John R. Spletzer Home Page.* Retrieved March 9, 2014, from http://www.cse.lehigh.edu/~spletzer/

Square. (2014a). Square - Accept credit cards with your iPhone, Android or iPad. *Square.* Retrieved March 11, 2014, from https://squareup.com/#!home

Square. (2014b). Square Wallet - Pay with your name at your favorite Square merchants. *Square.* Retrieved March 11, 2014, from https://squareup.com/wallet

Srivastava, K. (n.d.). *Phone Makers Focus on Elderly | Mobiledia.* Retrieved March 8, 2014, from http://www.mobiledia.com/news/115093.html

SRS project. (2014). *srs-project.eu | Multi-Role Shadow Robotic System for Independent Living.* Retrieved March 13, 2014, from http://srs-project.eu/

Stadlmann, K. (2011, November 11). *TEDxVienna - Klaus Stadlmann - The world's smallest 3D Printer.* [Video file]. Retrieved from http://youtu.be/D2IQkKE7h9I

Stanford Engineering. (2011, October 17). *Stanford Summer Course Yields Touchscreen Braille Writer.* Retrieved March 13, 2014, from http://www.pddnet.com/news/2011/10/stanford-summer-course-yields-touchscreen-braille-writer

Stanford University. (2008). *Work, Technology & Organization.* Retrieved March 9, 2014, from http://www.stanford.edu/ group/WTO/cgi-bin/index.php

Starlab. (2011). *Starlab - Living Science.* Retrieved March 8, 2014, from http://starlab.es/products/enobio

Startup Week 2011. (n.d.). *Klaus Stadlmann (AUT) | Startup Week 2011 Vienna.* Retrieved March 8, 2014, from http://www.startupweek2011.com/speaker/klaus-stadlmann-aut/

Steph. (2010, April 5). *12 Ingenious Gadgets & Technologies Designed for the Blind | Urbanist.* Retrieved March 10, 2014, from http://weburbanist.com/2010/04/05/12-ingenious-gadgets-technologies-for-the-blind/

Steve Blank. (n.d.). *Steve Blank.* Retrieved March 13, 2014, from http://steveblank.com/

Stevens, T. (2010, July 21). HULC exo-skeleton ready for testing, set to hit the ground running next year (video). *Engadget.* Retrieved March 13, 2014, from http://www.engadget.com/2010/07/21/hulc-exo-skeleton-ready-for-testing-set-to-hit-the-ground-runni/

Stevens, T. (2011, May 10). *Google announces Android@ Home framework for home automation.* Retrieved March 8, 2014, from http://www.engadget.com/2011/05/10/google-announces-android-at-home-framework/

Stickam (n.d.). *Goodbye.* Retrieved March 14, 2014, from http://www.stickam.com/

Surprised Nao (Original). (2011, March 24). Retrieved from http://youtu.be/zJWFydDHJHw

Swallow, E. (2011, August 31). The Anatomy of a Social Media Crisis. *Mashable.* Retrieved March 11, 2014, from http://mashable.com/2011/08/31/social-media-crisis/

Swanson, G. (2011, December 17). *Apps in Education: Monster List of Apps for People with Autism.* Retrieved March 10, 2014, from http://appsineducation.blogspot.gr/2011/12/monster-list-of-apps-for-people-with.html

Swapstyle. (n.d.). *Swapstyle.com.* Retrieved March 11, 2014, from http://www.swapstyle.com/

Swedberg, C. (2011, September 21). *French Supermarket Tests NFC Tool for Visually Disabled Shoppers - RFID Journal.* Retrieved March 11, 2014, from http://www.rfidjournal.com/articles/view?8793

SWYF. (2014). *SWYF: alle vrouwenkleding en accessoires in een shop*. Retrieved March 11, 2014, from http://www.swyf.nl/

Tamagotchi. (n.d.). *Wikipedia, the free encyclopedia*. Retrieved March 14, 2014, from http://en.wikipedia.org/wiki/Tamagotchi

TATRC. (n.d.). *Telemedicine & Advanced Technology Research Center*. Retrieved March 13, 2014, from http://www.tatrc.org/

Taub, E. (2008, August 27). *Basics - For the Advanced in Age, Easy-to-Use Technology - NYTimes.com*. Retrieved March 8, 2014, from http://www.nytimes.com/2008/08/28/technology/personaltech/28basics.html?th&emc=th

Tec, G. (2014a). *Home - g.tec - Guger Technologies*. Retrieved March 8, 2014, from http://www.gtec.at/

Tec, G. (2014b). *g.SAHARA - active dry EEG electrode system: Perform recordings without gel*. Retrieved March 8, 2014, from http://www.gtec.at/Products/Electrodes-and-Sensors/g.SAHARA-Specs-Features

Technology Strategy Board. (2013). *Healthcare Technolgy Development Innovation, Stem Cell Research - innovateuk*. Retrieved March 13, 2014, from https://www.innovateuk.org/healthcare

TechSmith. (2014a). *Screen Capture Software for Windows, Mac and Chrome | Snagit*. Retrieved March 10, 2014, from http://www.techsmith.com/snagit.html

TechSmith. (2014b). *TechSmith | Camtasia, Screen Recorder and Video Editor*. Retrieved March 10, 2014, from http://www.techsmith.com/camtasia.html

Telcare Inc. (2014). *Telcare | Telcare Blood Glucose Monitoring System and myTelcare*. Retrieved March 8, 2014, from http://www.telcare.com/

Telegraph. (2010, January 3). *'Self-drive cars on roads within 10 years' - Telegraph*. Retrieved March 9, 2014, from http://www.telegraph.co.uk/ news/uknews/road-and-rail-transport/6926514/ Self-drive-cars-on-roads-within-10-years.html

Telesensory. (2008a). *Genie Pro: Description*. Retrieved March 10, 2014, from http://www.telesensory.com/product.aspx?category=desktop&id=11

Telesensory. (2008b). *Telesensory Video Magnifiers help people with Low Vision read again*. Retrieved March 10, 2014, from http://www.telesensory.com/

Tellnet. (n.d.). *TellNet - Welcome*. Retrieved March 9, 2014, from http://www.tellnet.eun.org/web/tellnet,jsessionid=0EAF6638D4D5B887A228FE6E263D3716

Temesis, E. (n.d.). *Temesis : qualité et accessibilité web*. Retrieved March 12, 2014, from http://temesis.com/

Tesco. (2014). *Tesco.com - online shopping, bringing the supermarket to you - Every little helps*. Retrieved March 11, 2014, from http://www.tesco.com/

Thayananthan, V., & Alzahrani, A. (2012). RFID-based Body Sensors for e-Health Systems and Communications. *eTELEMED 2012, The Fourth International Conference on eHealth, Telemedicine, and Social Medicine*, (pp. 237-242). Retrieved from http://www.thinkmind.org/index.php?view=article&articleid=etelemed_2012_10_30_40172

The 40 Fires Foundation. (2010). *40Fires: Main*. Retrieved March 13, 2014, from http://www.40fires.org/

The latest version of the LittleDog Robot. (2010). Retrieved from http://www.youtube.com/watch?v=nUQsRPJ1dYw&feature=youtube_gdata_player

The New Google Social Network-- Google+ Project -- Why It will be a Success ?? (2011). Retrieved from http://www.youtube.com/watch?v=3Onri3iHbL4&feature=youtube_gdata_player

The Seeing Eye, Inc. (2014). *Guide dogs for people who are blind or visually impaired | The Seeing Eye, Inc*. Retrieved March 9, 2014, from http://www.seeingeye.org/

The Best Five Anthropomorphic Robotic Hands/Arms. (n.d.). Retrieved March 8, 2014, from mindtrans.narod.ru/hands/hands.htm

Theogarajan, L., Wyatt, J., Rizzo, J., Drohan, B., Markova, M., Kelly, S., & Yomtov, B. (2006). Minimally Invasive Retinal Prosthesis. *Solid-State Circuits Conference, 2006. ISSCC 2006. Digest of Technical Papers. IEEE International*, 99-108. doi:10.1109/ISSCC.2006.1696038

Think Beyond the Label. (2012). *Think Beyond the Label | Evolve Your Workforce*. Retrieved March 10, 2014, from http://www.thinkbeyondthelabel.com/

Tice, C. (2011, August 5). Uncle Sam's New, $5M Incubator for Student Entrepreneurs. *Entrepreneur*. Retrieved March 13, 2014, from http://www.entrepreneur.com/blog/220110

Tinti-Kane, H., Seaman, J., & Levy, J. (2010, April 29). *Pearson Social Media Survey 2010*. Retrieved March 10, 2014, from http://www.slideshare.net/PearsonLearningSolutions/pearson-socialmediasurvey2010

Tiny Chick Robot. (2008, August 21). Retrieved from http://youtu.be/G5d3A-SV9Vo

Tobe, F. (2011, July 30). *Everything-Robotic by The Robot Report - tracking the business of robotics*. Retrieved from http://www.everything-robotic.com/ 2011/07/recent-breakthroughs-are-enabling.html

TOBI. Tools for Brain-Computer Interaction. (2008). *Welcome to TOBI | TOBI: Tools for Brain-Computer Interaction*. Retrieved March 8, 2014, from http://www.tobi-project.org/

Topchair. (n.d.). *TOPCHAIR a Powered Wheelchair. The only Stair Climbing Wheelchair capable of going up and down straight stairs and pavements / side walks without assistance*. Retrieved March 9, 2014, from http://www.topchair.fr/en/

Topolsky, J. (2007, November 25). *Sarcos' military exoskeleton becomes a frightening reality*. Retrieved February 22, 2014, from http://www.engadget.com/2007/11/25/sarcos-military-exoskeleton-becomes-a-frightening-reality/

Torena, R., Usero, J. Á. M., Van Isacker, K., Goranova-Valkova, M., Chalkia, E., & Bekiaris, E. … Lange, R. (2010). Present and future of eAccessibility in public digital terminals. *European Journal of ePractice*, (10). Retrieved from http://www.epractice.eu/files/European%20Journal%20epractice%20Volume%2010.1.pdf

Touch Bionics Inc. (2014a). *Home Touch Bionics*. Retrieved March 13, 2014, from http://www.touchbionics.com/

Touch Bionics Inc. (2014b). *The world's leading prosthetic hand Touch Bionics*. Retrieved March 13, 2014, from http://www.touchbionics.com/ products/active-prostheses/i-limb-ultra/

TouchType Ltd. (n.d.). *SwiftKey - smart prediction technology for easier mobile typing*. Retrieved February 10, 2014, from http://www.swiftkey.net/en/

Tourette syndrome. (n.d.). *Wikipedia, the free encyclopedia*. Retrieved March 8, 2014, from http://en.wikipedia.org/wiki/Tourette_syndrome

Tourism Australia. (2013). *Home - Tourism Australia*. Retrieved March 13, 2014, from http://www.tourism.australia.com/home.aspx?redir=en-au/

Toyota. (2011, November 1). *TMC Shows New Nursing and Healthcare Robots in Tokyo | Toyota Motor Corporation Global Website*. Retrieved February 22, 2014, from http://www2.toyota.co.jp/en/news/11/11/1101.html

Trading, I. S. L. (n.d.). *Celluon Virtual Keyboard - A laser projected full-sized virtual QWERTY keyboard*. Retrieved February 10, 2014, from http://www.virtual-laser-devices.com/?an=vlk-new

Travability Pty Ltd. (2009). *Jetstar refuses to carry blind passengers guide dog*. Retrieved March 13, 2014, from http://travability.travel/blogs/jetstar3.html

Travability Pty Ltd. (2013). *Changing the demand drivers for the provision of products and services in Inclusive Tourism: The Why and How*. Retrieved March 10, 2014, from http://travability.travel/papers/occasional_4.html

Travability Pty Ltd. (2013a). *Travability - About Us*. Retrieved March 13, 2014, from http://travability.travel/about%20us.html

Travability Pty Ltd. (2013b). *Travability - Making the World Accessible to All*. Retrieved March 13, 2014, from http://travability.travel/

Travability Pty Ltd. (2013c). *Untitled Document*. Retrieved March 13, 2014, from http://travability.travel/blogs.html

Travability Pty Ltd. (n.d.a). *Kurt Fearnley*. Retrieved March 13, 2014, from http://travability.travel/blogs/fearnley.html

Travability Pty Ltd. (n.d.b). *Retail Travel Chains and Inclusive Travel - When?* Retrieved March 13, 2014, from http://travability.travel/blogs/retail_travel.html

Travability Pty Ltd. (n.d.c). *River Cruising*. Retrieved March 13, 2014, from http://travability.travel/blogs/river_cruising.html

Travability Pty Ltd. (n.d.d). *The Economic Model of Disability*. Retrieved March 13, 2014, from http://travability.travel/blogs/economic_model.html

Trillenium. (2012). *Trillenium*. Retrieved February 10, 2014, from http://www.trillenium.com/home

Trimble Navigation Limited. (2013). *SketchUp | 3D for Everyone*. Retrieved March 9, 2014, from http://www.sketchup.com/

Tripping International. (2014). *Tripping: Couches to Castles*. Retrieved March 11, 2014, from https://www.tripping.com

Tube maps made for the disabled. (2009, January 26). *BBC*. Retrieved from http://news.bbc.co.uk/2/hi/uk_news/england/london/7850675.stm

Turner, L. (2012, March 13). Computer turns sign language into text, creating new world for deaf trainees. *The Sunday Morning Herald*. Retrieved from http://www.smh.com.au/technology/technology-news/computer-turns-sign-language-into-text-creating-new-world-for-deaf-trainees-20120312-1uwer.html

Twitter. (2014). *Twitter*. Retrieved March 10, 2014, from https://twitter.com/

U.S. Department of Education. (n.d.). *U.S. Department of Education*. Retrieved March 13, 2014, from http://www.ed.gov/

Uckelmann, D., Harrison, M., & Michahelles, F. (2011). *An Architectural Approach Towards the Future Internet of Things*. Architecting the Internet of Things. doi:10.1007/978-3-642-19157-2_1

UCorder. (2012). *uCorder | Record Your Life | Wearable Mini Pocket Camcorder*. Retrieved March 8, 2014, from http://www.ucorder.com/

UK Government Digital Service. (2013, November 8). *Disability rights - GOV.UK*. Retrieved March 10, 2014, from https://www.gov.uk/rights-disabled-person/education-rights

Ultimate Ears. (n.d.). *Home | Ultimate Ears*. Retrieved March 8, 2014, from http://www.ultimateears.com/en-us/

UNESCO. (n.d.a). *Advocacy | Education | United Nations Educational, Scientific and Cultural Organization*. Retrieved March 9, 2014, from http://www.unesco.org/new/en/education/themes/leading-the-international-agenda/education-for-all/advocacy/

UNESCO. (n.d.b). *Capacity Development | Education | United Nations Educational, Scientific and Cultural Organization*. Retrieved March 9, 2014, from http://www.unesco.org/new/en/education/themes/leading-the-international-agenda/education-for-all/capacity-development/

UNESCO. (n.d.c). *EFA Goals | Education | United Nations Educational, Scientific and Cultural Organization*. Retrieved March 9, 2014, from http://www.unesco.org/new/en/education/themes/leading-the-international-agenda/education-for-all/efa-goals/

UNESCO. (n.d.d). *Funding | Education | United Nations Educational, Scientific and Cultural Organization*. Retrieved March 9, 2014, from http://www.unesco.org/new/en/education/themes/leading-the-international-agenda/education-for-all/funding/

UNESCO. (n.d.e). *Monitoring | Education | United Nations Educational, Scientific and Cultural Organization*. Retrieved March 9, 2014, from http://www.unesco.org/new/en/education/themes/leading-the-international-agenda/education-for-all/monitoring/

UNESCO. (n.d.f). *Policy dialogue | Education | United Nations Educational, Scientific and Cultural Organization*. Retrieved March 9, 2014, from http://www.unesco.org/new/en/education/themes/leading-the-international-agenda/education-for-all/policy-dialogue/

United Nations Educational Scientific and Cultural Organisation. (2004). *Changing teaching practices: Using curriculum differentiation to respond to students' diversity*. Retrieved from http://unesdoc.unesco.org/images/0013/001365/136583e.pdf

United Nations. (2007). *UN Enable*. Retrieved March 12, 2014, from http://www.un.org/esa/socdev/enable/gawanomensa.htm

United States Bureau of Justice Statistics. (2007). *Crime against people with disabilities*. Retrieved from http://www.bjs.gov/content/pub/press/capd07pr.cfm

United States Department of Defense. (2007). *Unmanned systems roadmap: 2007-2032*. Retrieved from http://www.fas.org/irp/ program/collect/usroadmap2007.pdf

United States International Council on Disabilities. (2014). *United States International Council on Disabilities - Global Disability Rights Library>>*. Retrieved March 13, 2014, from http://www.usicd.org/index.cfm/global-disability-rights-library

Universal Studios Home Entertainment. (2010). *A Beautiful Mind on DVD | Trailers, bonus features, cast photos & more | Universal Studios Entertainment Portal*. Retrieved March 8, 2014, from http://www.universalstudiosentertainment.com/a-beautiful-mind/

Universidad Carlos III de Madrid. (2011, November 21). Machines Able to Recognize a Person's Emotional State. *Product Design & Development*. Retrieved March 13, 2014, from http://www.pddnet.com/news/ 2011/11/machines-able-recognize-persons-emotional-state

Universidad Carlos III de Madrid. (2011, November 21). *Machines Able to Recognize a Person's Emotional State*. Retrieved March 8, 2014, from http://www.pddnet.com/news/2011/11/machines-able-recognize-persons-emotional-state

Universität Duisburg-Essen. (2014, February 7). *Projektbeschreibung*. Retrieved March 13, 2014, from https://www.uni-due.de/wimi-care/

University of Buffalo. (2014). *School of Public Health and Health Professions*. Retrieved March 9, 2014, from http://sphhp.buffalo.edu/

University of Hertfordshire. (2011, February 12). *Robotic Companions for Older People*. Retrieved March 8, 2014, from http://www.pddnet.com/news/2011/12/robotic-companions-older-people

University of Pennsylvania. (2011, July 26). *Researchers Help Graft Olfactory Receptors onto Nanotubes*. Retrieved March 8, 2014, from http://www.pddnet.com/news/2011/07/researchers-help-graft-olfactory-receptors-nanotubes

University of Sheffield. (2008, December 21). *British Scientist Warns We Must Protect The Vulnerable From Robots -- ScienceDaily*. Retrieved March 8, 2014, from http://www.sciencedaily.com/releases/2008/12/081218141724.htm

University of Southampton. (2011). *Synote Home Page*. Retrieved March 10, 2014, from http://synote.org/synote/

University of Strathclyde. (2004). *Alternatives to what is assessed - Teachability: Creating accessible examinations and assessments for disabled students*. Retrieved March 10, 2014, from http://www.teachability.strath.ac.uk/chapter_8/reflectingonpractice8c.html

US Small Business Administration. (n.d.). *SBA.gov*. Retrieved March 10, 2014, from http://www.sba.gov/community/blogs/community-blogs/small-business-matters/disabled-entrepreneurs-resources-and-tips-highly-successful-business-grou

Use of social network websites in investigations. (n.d.). *Wikipedia, the free encyclopedia*. Retrieved March 8, 2014, from http://en.wikipedia.org/wiki/Use_of_social_network_websites_in_investigations

USFirst. (2014). *USFIRST.org*. Retrieved March 13, 2014, from http://www.usfirst.org/

Vecna Technologies, Inc. (2013). *Vecna | Better Technology, Better World*. Retrieved March 9, 2014, from http://www.vecna.com/

Velroyen, H. (2011, December 28). *Bionic Ears: Introduction into State-of-the-Art Hearing Aid Technology*. Retrieved March 8, 2014, from http://blog.hackandhear.com/wp-content/uploads/2011/12/2011_28c3_bionic_ears_v08_slides.pdf

Verdonschot, M. M., Witte, L. P., Reichrath, E., Buntinx, W. H., & Curfs, L. M. (2009). Community participation of people with an intellectual disability: a review of empirical findings. *Journal of Intellectual Disability Research*. doi: doi:10.1111/j.1365-2788.2008.01144.x PMID:19087215

Verwymeren, A. (2011, August 3). *The Home of the Future Is Almost Here | Fox News*. Retrieved March 14, 2014, from http://www.foxnews.com/leisure/2011/08/03/home-future-is-almost-here/

VGo Communications, Inc. (2013). *VGo robotic telepresence for healthcare, education and business.* Retrieved March 9, 2014, from http://www.vgocom.com/

Vicon Motion Systems Ltd. (n.d.). *Vicon | Homepage.* Retrieved March 14, 2014, from http://www.vicon.com/

Vidaurre, C., & Blankertz, B. (2010). Towards a Cure for BCI Illiteracy. *Brain Topography.* doi:10.1007/s10548-009-0121-6 PMID:19946737

Video game addiction. (n.d.). *Wikipedia, the free encyclopedia.* Retrieved March 8, 2014, from http://en.wikipedia.org/wiki/Video_game_addiction

ViPi Project. (2011, January 8). *ViPi.* Retrieved March 10, 2014, from http://www.vipi-project.eu/

Virgin Galactic. (2014, March 9). *Wikipedia, the free encyclopedia.* Retrieved from http://en.wikipedia.org/w/index.php?title= Virgin_Galactic&oldid=598899679

Virginia Commonwealth University. (2013, July 12). *VCU WorkSupport.* Retrieved March 10, 2014, from http://www.worksupport.com/resources/viewContent.cfm/295

Virtual World. (n.d.). *Wikipedia, the free encyclopedia.* Retrieved February 10, 2014, from http://en.wikipedia.org/wiki/Virtual_world

Visa TV Ad starring Bill Shannon. (2009). Retrieved from http://www.youtube.com/watch?v=I6RGyJirL3g&feature=youtube_gdata_player

Vislab. (2010). *Intercontinental Challenge.* Retrieved March 9, 2014, from http://viac.vislab.it/

Viswanathan, P., Little, J. J., Mackworth, A. K., & Mihailidis, A. (2011). *Navigation and obstacle avoidance help (NOAH) for older adults with cognitive impairment: a pilot study.* doi:10.1145/2049536.2049546

Vodafone Group. (2012). *Home | Mobile Apps Developer | Vodafone.* Retrieved March 13, 2014, from http://developer.vodafone.com/ smartaccess2012/home/

Von Ahn, L. (2011). *Massive-scale online collaboration.* Retrieved from http://www.ted.com/talks/luis_von_ahn_massive_scale_online_collaboration

Vrije Univeriteit Brussel. (2009). Retrieved February 22, 2014, from http://probo.vub.ac.be/

W3C. (2014). *World Wide Web Consortium (W3C).* Retrieved March 12, 2014, from http://www.w3.org/

Wall Street Journal Live. (2012, March 16). *Video - The DiVa Voice Synthesizer Translates Hand Gestures to Speech - WSJ.com.* Retrieved February 10, 2014, from http://live.wsj.com/video/new-voice-synthesizer-interprets-hand-gestures/316CC7FA-876C-4265-9913-0ABE4827191D.html#!316CC7FA-876C-4265-9913-0ABE4827191D

Walsh, K. (2010, February 7). *Over 100 ideas for using Twitter in the Classroom.* Retrieved March 15, 2014, from http://www.emergingedtech.com/2010/02/100-ways-to-teach-with-twitter/

Warrior, P. (2011, May 24). *TalkBack for Android (reviewed).* Retrieved March 10, 2014, from http://www.appszoom.com/android_applications/tools/talkback_eq.html

Wasserman, T. (2011, September 1). How Toyota Used Social Media To Digg Itself Out of a PR Nightmare. *Mashable.* Retrieved March 11, 2014, from http://mashable.com/2011/09/01/toyota-digg-recalls/

Watier, K. (2003, April 19). *Marketing Wearable Computers to Consumers.* Retrieved March 8, 2014, from http://www.scribd.com/doc/49892917/Marketing-Wearable-Computers-to-Consumers

Watkins, A. (2007). *Assessment in inclusive settings: Key issues for policy and practice.* Retrieved from http://www.european-agency.org/sites/default/files/Assessment-EN.pdf

Watkins, A. (2011a). *ICTs in Education for People with Disabilities: Review of innovative practice.* Retrieved from http://www.european-agency.org/sites/default/files/ICTs-in-Education-for-people-with-disabilities.pdf

Watkins, A. (2011b). *Special Needs Education, Country Data 2010.* Retrieved from http://www.european-agency.org/sites/default/files/SNE-Country-Data-2010.pdf

Watters, A. (2011, March 19). *How Well Are Schools Teaching Cyber Safety and Ethics? | MindShift.* Retrieved March 10, 2014, from http://blogs.kqed.org/mindshift/2011/05/how-well-are-schools-teaching-cyber-safety-and-ethics/

WebAIM. (2009). *WebAIM: Screen Reader User Survey #2 Results*. Retrieved March 13, 2014, from http://webaim.org/projects/screenreadersurvey2/

Webkinz. (n.d.). *Welcome to Webkinz? - a Ganz website*. Retrieved March 9, 2014, from http://www.webkinz.com/

West, D. M. (2011). *Using Technology to Personalize Learning and Assess Students in Real-Time*. Retrieved from http://www.brookings.edu/~/media/research/files/papers/2011/10/06%20personalize%20learning%20west/1006_personalize_learning_west.pdf

Westly, E. (2011, June 17). *Fixing the Brain-Computer Interface - IEEE Spectrum*. Retrieved March 8, 2014, from http://spectrum.ieee.org/biomedical/bionics/fixing-the-brain-computer-interface

WGES ExploraVision. (n.d.). Retrieved March 13, 2014, from http://dev.nsta.org/evwebs/2237Q/

Whalen, J. (2012, March 19). *Exoskeleton gets paralyzed man on his feet - News - Citizens' Voice*. Retrieved February 22, 2014, from http://citizensvoice.com/news/exoskeleton-gets-paralyzed-man-on-his-feet-1.1287452#axzz1qiQgrAVN

Wheelmap.org. (n.d.). Wheelmap.org - Rollstuhlgerechte Orte suchen und finden. *Wheelmap.org*. Retrieved March 13, 2014, from http://wheelmap.org/

WHO Global Observatory for eHealth, World Health Organization. (2011). *mHealth: New horizons for health through mobile technologies*. Retrieved from http://www.who.int/goe/publications/goe_mhealth_web.pdf

WHO. (2011). *World Report on Disability*. Retrieved from http://whqlibdoc.who.int/publications/2011/9789240685215_eng.pdf?ua=1

WHO. (2013, March). *WHO | Cardiovascular diseases (CVDs)*. Retrieved February 7, 2014, from http://www.who.int/mediacentre/factsheets/fs317/en/index.html

Williams, C. (2008, February 8). *Smartphone virus attacks soar - Telegraph*. Retrieved March 8, 2014, from http://www.telegraph.co.uk/technology/google/8310689/Smartphone-virus-attacks-soar.html

Willow Garage. (2008a). *Join the Community | Willow Garage*. Retrieved February 22, 2014, from http://www.willowgarage.com/pages/pr2/pr2-community

Willow Garage. (2008b). *Overview | Willow Garage*. Retrieved February 22, 2014, from http://www.willow-garage.com/pages/pr2/overview

Willow Garage. (2008c). *Willow Garage*. Retrieved February 22, 2014, from http://www.willowgarage.com/

Wired. (2008, June 23). *The Petabyte Age: Because More Isn't Just More? More Is Different*. Retrieved March 8, 2014, from http://www.wired.com/science/discoveries/magazine/16-07/pb_intro

Withings. (2014a). *Withings - Partner apps*. Retrieved March 8, 2014, from http://www.withings.com/en/app/partners

Withings. (2014b). *Withings - Smart products and apps - Homepage*. Retrieved March 8, 2014, from http://www.withings.com/

Wolf, G. (2010, September 27). *Gary Wolf: The quantified self*. [Video file]. Retrieved from https://www.youtube.com/watch?v=OrAo8oBBFIo&feature=youtu.be

Wong, G. (2011, June 4). *Apple granted patent for bumpy tactile touchscreens | Ubergizmo*. Retrieved February 10, 2014, from http://www.ubergizmo.com/2011/04/apple-patent-tactile-touchscreens/

Wood, D., Morris, C., & Ussery, J. (2009). Accessibility Solutions for 3D Virtual Learning Environments. In *Proceedings of IEEE Accessing the Future Conference*. IEEE.

World Education Forum. (2000). *WEF (The Conference)*. Retrieved March 9, 2014, from http://www.unesco.org/education/wef/en-conf/index.shtm

World Health Organization. (2011). *Mental health atlas 2011*. Retrieved from http://whqlibdoc.who.int/publications/2011/9799241564359_eng.pdf

World Health Organization. World Bank. (2011). *World report on disability*. Retrieved from World Health Organization website: http://whqlibdoc.who.int/publications/2011/9789240685215_eng.pdf

World, D. (2014). *Health and Disability Apps for iPhone Android and Mobile Devices - Disabled World*. Retrieved March 10, 2014, from http://www.disabled-world.com/assistivedevices/apps/

World, D. (n.d.). *Disability Community*. Retrieved March 11, 2014, from http://community.disabled-world.com/

Worldcarfans. (2008, February 25). *Nissan Engineers use Special Suit to Simulate the Elderly*. Retrieved February 22, 2014, from http://www.worldcarfans.com/10802252127/nissan-engineers-use-special-suit-to-simulate-the-elderly

XPRIZE Foundation. (2014). Google Lunar XPRIZE. *Google Lunar XPRIZE*. Retrieved March 13, 2014, from http://www.googlelunarxprize.org/

XPrize Foundation. (2014). *Life Sciences Prize Group | XPRIZE*. Retrieved March 13, 2014, from http://www.xprize.org/prize-development/life-sciences

Yachol call. (n.d.). Retrieved March 10, 2014, from http://www.callyachol.co.il/eng/

Yanko Design. (2010, June 22). *Neptune orthopaedic swimming aid for lower limb amputees by Richard Stark » Yanko Design*. Retrieved from http://www.yankodesign.com/2010/06/22/clip-on-fin-to-turn-to-aquaman/

Youtube. (2008, August 1). *Toyota's Winglet robotic transporter*. [Video file]. Retrieved from https://www.youtube.com/ watch?v=DSka-3uHcDw

Youtube. (2009a, August 17). *Electric Car-Amkar Wheelchair Access Version Get yours at Monmouth Vans-Wall, NJ (800) 221-0034*. [Video file]. Retrieved from https://www.youtube.com/ watch?v=l-J5Sc6zWKc

Youtube. (2009b, September 24). *Honda U3-X - a Japanese take on the Segway*. [Video file]. Retrieved from https://www.youtube.com/ watch?v=ghedatUdj3E

Youtube. (2009c, October 22). *The TOYOTA i-REAL personal mobility vehicle @ NAGOYA, Centrair International Airport*. [Video file]. Retrieved from https://www.youtube.com/ watch?v=fmoTLoJzluI

Youtube. (2011, March 18). *Robotic wheelchair takes elderly customers shopping*. [Video file]. Retrieved from http://youtu.be/1V78KPs8Y44

Zander, T. O., & Kothe, C. (2011). Towards passive brain-computer interfaces: applying brain-computer interface technology to human-machine systems in general. *Journal of Neural Engineering*. doi:10.1088/1741-2560/8/2/025005 PMID:21436512

Zervos, H. (2012). Positive Adoption Trends Expected to Double the Market Within 5 Years. *Energy Harvesting Journal*. Retrieved from http://www.energyharvestingjournal.com/articles/energy-harvesting-positive-adoption-trends-expected-to-double-00004265.asp?sessionid—1

Zipcar, Inc. (2014). *Car Sharing, an alternative to car rental and car ownership – Zipcar*. Retrieved March 11, 2014, from http://www.zipcar.com/

Zoomtext. (2014a). *Willkommen bei Zoomtext*. Retrieved March 10, 2014, from http://www.zoomtext.de/

Zoomtext. (2014b). *ZoomText Magnifier / Reader 10 Bildschirmvergrößerung*. Retrieved March 10, 2014, from http://www.zoomtext.de/produkte/zt/ztms/index.html

Zopa Ltd. (2014). *Zopa - Peer-to-peer Lending, Loans & High Interest on Savings*. Retrieved March 11, 2014, from http://www.zopa.com/

About the Author

Christos Kouroupetroglou was awarded his PhD in 2010 and his thesis subject was "Semantically Enhanced Web Browsing Interfaces." During his PhD research, he investigated the impact of Semantic Web-based assistive interfaces in Web browsing while he also worked for a number of research programs in the ATEI of Thessaloniki. The most important of them was the SeEBrowser project, which was funded by the Greek Ministry of Education and aimed to provide a set of tools to improve the Web browsing experience of visually impaired users. In parallel, he was also teaching as a scientific and laboratory associate at the ATEI of Thessaloniki and in Mediterranean College of Thessaloniki in modules related to Internet programming, databases and applications development, and administration. After his PhD research, he participated on a chair of experts team in the EC-funded "Study on Implications from Future ICT Trends on Assistive Technology and Accessibility," which aimed to explore and analyse the relationships between the emerging ICT landscape, within the societal and economic context. Currently, he is a research programmes manager for a start-up company titled Caretta-Net Technologies in Greece and is also working as a freelance lecturer for the University of Nicossia (Cyprus) teaching in the module of "Applications of Technology in Special Education." He is also a member of the Research and Development Working Group (RDWG) of the Web Accessibility Initiative (WAI) of W3C. Apart from Web accessibility, his research interests also include HCI, especially adaptive and intelligent interfaces, user modelling for accessibility, Semantic Web and Web 2.0 technologies, and mobile HCI.

Index

T

U

V

W